LAW RELATING TO ANIMALS

Cavendish
Publishing
Limited

London • Sydney

LAW RELATING TO ANIMALS

Simon Brooman, BA (Hons), PGCE,
Senior Lecturer in Law
Liverpool John Moores University

Dr Debbie Legge, LLB, MA, PhD
Lecturer in Law
Liverpool John Moores University

Cavendish
Publishing
Limited

London • Sydney

First published in 1997 by Cavendish Publishing Limited, The Glass House, Wharton Street, London, WC1X 9PX, United Kingdom

Telephone: +44 (0) 171 278 8000   Facsimile: +44 (0) 171 278 8080

E-mail: info@cavendishpublishing.com

Visit our Home Page on http://www.cavendishpublishing.com

Brooman, Simon
Law Relating to Animals
1. Domestic animals – Law and legislation – Great Britain
I. Title II. Legge, Debbie
344.1'0647

1-85941-238-6

Printed and bound in Great Britain

Dedicated to our families

for instilling in us an appreciation of the natural world.

PREFACE

The idea for a book containing a comprehensive analysis of the law relating to animals arose out of our creation of the Animal Law course for law students at Liverpool John Moores University. We had no idea how popular the course was to become with around 50 undergraduates choosing to study it every year. What became apparent as we developed our materials was the lack of an appropriate textbook which covered the many aspects of this area of law in the way we wished to approach it, touching as it does upon; philosophy, science, environmental politics, the origins of humankind and many entrenched historical, social and legal attitudes to animals.

The collection and sifting of materials and cases has been a mammoth task spanning four years from 1993 to the end of 1996. We decided early on that a simple regurgitation of statute or case law would not serve to enlighten the reader on the essential underpinning issues of animal law. This is a book about *issues*. We might very well have produced a textbook which goes to great lengths to dissect, for example, the appeals procedure for a refusal of a licence for a dog breeding establishment under the Breeding of Dogs Act 1973, or the powers of entry to agricultural premises under the Agriculture (Miscellaneous Provisions) Act 1968. Instead, we include what we consider to be the essential elements of statutory control and case law in each area but feel that to use *only* these sources would not highlight the essential issues in the various areas of animal law. In consequence, there are many contributions from outside the normal sources of English law. For example, we include: opinion from recognised environmental and 'animal rights' pressure groups who have specific expertise in some areas of animal law as they can contribute authoritatively on the future development of the law; and the experience and regulation of other countries as an essential component in order to compare our control with theirs. We also incorporate the role of philosophy throughout the text so as to challenge the philosophical basis of the law as it stands.

Chapters 1–5 and Chapter 10 were produced by Simon Brooman and Chapters 6–9 by Dr Debbie Legge. They all differ in the amount of case law, statute law or work from other sources which is included because of the nature of the subjects involved. Subjects such as animal experimentation, agriculture and the law relating to zoos are primarily statute based – there are very few cases on those subjects. In the case of others such as the law relating to domestic animals case law is a lot more prevalent. It is certainly the case that animal law crosses every boundary classifying law – from statute to case law, from the law of the European Union and international law to the work of respected animal welfare groups.

In Chapter 1 we begin with an essential journey through the philosophical and scientific contributions of some of the world's leading historical figures. This enables us to place our current legal attitudes to animals in the context of the development of humankind as thinkers – asking questions about the nature of humanity and comparing ourselves to the 'beasts'. The law of every country in the world is in some way connected to underlying philosophical attitudes to our fellow species. We also examine the crucial role of science after the revelations of the origin of the species by Charles Darwin in the 19th century. His was a contribution which challenged many of the preceding philosophical grounds which had almost entirely segregated humankind from animals for thousands of years. After Darwin, 'similarity' became the watchword rather than 'difference'.

In Chapter 2 we examine some of the most significant historical legal attitudes to animals which have, in part, guided us to where we stand today. We also examine some of the most curious legal attitudes to animals as viewed from the eyes of a 20th century observer. We recognise the criticism of historians who doubt whether it is wise to judge the past through the eyes of the present but some comment on practices which do appear strange by today's standards is inevitable. If we have broken any prominent historical convention then we apologise.

In Chapter 3 we examine the current status accorded to animals by contemporary philosophers and scientists. In light of the fact that an 'explosion' in the interest in 'animal rights' occurred in the 1970s, and since Darwin rewrote many of the conventions previously held by theologians and philosophers, we felt it wise to examine present attitudes to the status of animals based upon *current*, ever-expanding, scientific awareness of the actual attributes of animals and how this fits into the morality of how we should treat them. Obviously, this has significant potential to affect every law which relates to animals – scientific discovery influences morality which then influences law.

Each following chapter contains an outline of the current regulation of a specific area of law: the use of animals in farming; the keeping of animals in zoos, circuses and for hunting; the keeping of animals as pets; the use of animals in experimentation; and the protection of wildlife and endangered species. We then examine the issues which have been raised regarding the regulation of that area, constantly bearing in mind the philosophical challenges to the law and adding associated issues such as concern for the environment, species diversity, human health, economics, politics and the future of humankind. Law is treated, not as being an end in itself, but as being a record of the nature of human understanding of those issues. Without understanding the 'why?' of law there is little incentive to move on and to change what might be wrong.

The debate regarding the status of animals can, from time to time, become caught up in the use of terminology which serves only to exclude those who are unfamiliar with the terms. Our aim throughout the book has been to avoid over-complication of terms or language so as to make the book as accessible as possible. We use the terms 'animals', as opposed to 'humans' or 'people', throughout the book. We accept the obvious proposition that 'humans' or 'people' are, in fact, animals themselves but we regard the alternative term, 'non-human animals' as too clumsy.

We should also mention that we recognise that the term 'animal rights' is misleading and inadequate in itself even though an advocate of improved attitudes to animals is usually called an 'animal rights activist'. The diverse range of groups which represent claims for improved animal welfare from the moderate RSPCA to the more 'militant' Animal Liberation Front are constantly grouped together under the term 'animal rights'. In fact, the term 'right' is the subject of debate in relation to *humans* as well as animals. Philosophers are constantly arguing about what amounts to a 'human right' let alone an 'animal right' and many groups who are concerned with the *welfare* of animals would attack any suggestion that they are claiming 'rights' for animals. In light of this confusion, which is examined in further detail in Chapter 3, there has be philosophical hostility to the notion of 'rights' in relation to animals. However, the media use the term without thought and we have struggled, as have many, to find another term which encompasses the many diverse claims of those in the 'animal rights' movement. Therefore, we use the term 'animal rights' in the knowledge of its limitations in the absence of anything better and we use the term 'animal rights lobby' and 'animal welfare lobby' to mean the same thing – those representing the interests of animals.

In chapters 6–9 we have included some cases relating to cruelty. Names have been changed for legal reasons. Brooman and Legge footnotes appear without brackets in the text. Square brackets indicate that the footnote was included by the original author. The term 'EU' is used to refer to the whole European Union concept, whereas 'EC' refers to specific legislation or legislative powers.

As you read this book it might be worthwhile bearing in mind that although this is a law book it touches upon areas of study seldom examined by other areas of law. David Attenborough commented in the making of the highly respected BBC Television series *Life on Earth*:

> [I] may have given the impression that somehow man is the ultimate triumph of evolution, that all these millions of years of development have had no purpose other than to put him on earth. There is no scientific evidence whatever to support such a view and no reason to suppose that our stay here will be any more permanent than that of the dinosaur. The processes of evolution are still going on among plants and birds, insects and mammals. So it is more than likely that if men were to disappear from the face of the earth, for whatever reason, there is a modest, unobtrusive creature somewhere that would develop into a new form and take our place.

> But although denying that we have a special position in the natural world might seem becomingly modest in the eye of eternity, it might also be used as an excuse for evading our responsibilities. The fact is that no species has ever

had such wholesale control over everything on earth, living or dead, as we now have. That lays upon us, whether we like it or not, an awesome responsibility. In our hands now lies not only our own future, but that of all other living creatures with whom we share the earth.

Attenborough, David, *Life on Earth: A Natural History*, 1979, p 308, London: Collins.

We could not agree more.

The law is, as far as we are aware, correct until December 1996. We have tried to incorporate changes as the book went to press. Addresses for further information can be obtained on the Internet at www. ...catless.ncl.ac.uk/veg/Orgs/VeganSocUK/emblaa.html.

Simon Brooman
Dr Debbie Legge
April 1997

ACKNOWLEDGMENTS

The production of this book would not have been possible without the help of those working in the area of animal welfare who were kind enough to send materials. We would particularly like to thank Peter Stevenson of Compassion in World Farming, Andreas Steiger from the Swiss Federal Veterinary Office, the Human Farming Association in the United States, Karin Gabrielson of the Swedish Society Against Painful Experiments on Animals, Robert Baker of the Australian and New Zealand Council for the Care of Animals in Research and Teaching (ANZCCART), Peter Rudman of the National Farmer's Union, Reverend Professor Andrew Linzey of Mansfield College Oxford, Mark Simmonds of the Whale and Dolphin Conservation Society, Tim Jewell of the Humane Society International of Australia.

Organisations which have provided us with particularly useful information include ANZCCART, the Research Defence Society, the British Union for the Abolition of Vivisection, The British Association Promoting Science and Technology, the National Anti-Vivisection Society, the National Farmer's Union, English Nature, The Countryside Commission, Joint Nature Conservancy Council, the RSPCA and RSPB, the Hunt Saboteurs Association, The League Against Cruel Sports, the British Association of Shooting and Conservation, the British Field Sports Society, the Whale and Dolphin Conservation Society, the Marine Conservation Society, Sea Shepherd Society, Traffic International, The Environmental Investigation Agency, People for the Ethical treatment of Animals, Pieces, CITES Secretariat, Bonn Secretariat, Ramsar Secretariat, International Union for the Conservation of Nature, World Wildlife Fund, World Society for the Protection of Animals, Birdlife International, and the Department of the Environment Global Wildlife Division.

Thanks also go to all the publishers or writers who have allowed us to use materials: Oxford University Press, the Universities Federation for Animal Welfare, Centaur Press, Compassion in World Farming, Lennard Associates, the University of Georgia Press, Temple University Press, Philadelphia, the University of Michigan Press, Routledge, Hamish Hamilton, Hutchinson Radius, Faber and Faber, Elek, Gower Press, Little eco-Farms Publishing, Total Resources Centre, the International Society for Animal Rights in Pennsylvania, Blackwell Science, Random House UK Ltd, HMSO, ES Turner and Hans Ruesch, English Nature, The Countryside Commission, the Joint Nature Conservancy Council, the RSPCA and RSPB, the Hunt Saboteurs Association, The League Against Cruel Sports, the British Association of Shooting and Conservation, the British Field Sports Society, the Whale and Dolphin Conservation Society, the Marine Conservation Society, Traffic International, The Environmental Investigation Agency, CITES Secretariat, Bonn Secretariat, Ramsar Secretariat, the International Union for the Conservation of Nature, World Wildlife Fund, the World Society for the

Protection of Animals, Birdlife International, the Department of the Environment, the *London Evening Standard* and the *Guardian*.

Every effort has been made to trace all the copyright holders but if any have been inadvertently overlooked the publishers will be pleased to make the necessary arrangement at the first opportunity.

Closer to home we would like to thank Liverpool John Moores University for granting Simon Brooman a sabbatical in order to complete the work in the first semester of 1996–97. His teaching was mainly covered by Anthony Harvey, Lorie Charlesworth, John Cooke and Brian Kerrigan who deserve special thanks. Carolyn Stopforth of the LJMU Law Library also provided invaluable assistance. Elaine Tuffery at Cavendish Publishing also deserves a special mention for her enthusiasm, patience and hard work in the preparation of this manuscript.

Even closer to home we would like to thank Tracy and Nick for sacrificing some of their sanity to support the loss of ours.

CONTENTS

TABLE OF CASES

TABLE OF STATUTES

TABLE OF STATUTORY INSTRUMENTS

Regulations

European Union Legislation

Other treaties/conventions

CHAPTER ONE

PHILOSOPHY, SCIENCE AND ANIMALS

THE HISTORY OF PHILOSOPHICAL AND SCIENTIFIC ATTITUDES TO ANIMALS

As we approach a new millennium, the thought of a world with no consideration for animals and no laws to protect them seems irrational, uncivilised, cruel and somehow inhuman. But how did we arrive at this view? What has incited humankind to regard animals as significant and deserving of protection? Who were the prime movers in our change of attitudes from the hunter-gatherer of prehistory to the intellectual and philosophical legislator-protector of today? This chapter gives an overview of the main philosophical contributions which, since the Ancient Greeks, have provided the foundations upon which the legal treatment of animals has been built. It also examines the contribution made by science since the work of Charles Darwin, which has, increasingly, added more considerations for the legislators. It is not a chapter about law; rather it is a chapter about the essential philosophical and moral basis of how we should regard animals, which has developed across the centuries and which has sometimes, but not always, had an influence on the creation of specific laws. The contemporary philosophical and scientific status of animals is discussed in Chapter 3, but here we look at the main historical influences. Having examined the historical, philosophical and scientific contributions to the status of animals, the second part of this chapter will examine whether morality matters, and how it can exert its influence on the development of law. It is worth bearing in mind the effect philosophy or scientific discovery should have on the law relating to animals.

The subject of animal rights has been in and out of the news for almost two centuries in the UK. The movement, which can trace its origin to 19th century England[1] in the form of a small group of concerned individuals, has become a global movement represented by diverse interest groups and supported by a considerable body of philosophical contributions. There have been several instances of the animal rights issue hitting the headlines in the media across the globe. An example is the worldwide BSE scare of 1996 which led to a mass cull of cattle in the UK, bringing into question the moral implications of slaughtering apparently healthy animals in the pursuit of

---

1   Two abortive attempts to form animal welfare societies took place in 1809 in Liverpool, and in 1822 in London. Lasting success came with the formation of the 'society instituted for the purpose of preventing cruelty to animals' inaugurated on 16 June 1824. This society eventually became the RSPCA with the support of Queen Victoria in 1840.

1

consumer confidence. The British Veterinary Association described the cull as being 'on a par with the burning of witches'.[2]

The period 1994–95 also saw enhanced coverage of the animals issue resulting from the practice of transporting live animals from British airfields and ports to continental Europe. Much attention was given to the fact that the protestors included not only the traditional recognisable radicals who had previously been associated with the so-called 'animal rights movement', but also a new 'militant middle class'. The growth in the number of people involved on an active basis in the animal rights debate has been mirrored elsewhere in the world and the number of organisations concerned with animal welfare has swelled considerably. Why has there been such a growth in the number of concerned individuals? Has there been a sudden change in the collective consciousness of millions of individuals in the 20th century, or is there an identifiable historical source of the new militancy?

Perhaps the most compelling motivating force behind the comparatively recent surge in the numbers of people attaching themselves to the animal rights issue is the wealth of detailed and reasoned philosophical analysis which started to appear on a large scale from the mid-1970s onwards. Many writers have identified Peter Singer's *Animal Liberation* (1975) as representing a turning point in the credibility of the arguments of the animal rights activists.[3] Since 1975, the quantity of philosophical material produced on the subject of our treatment of animals has grown exponentially, as has the number of laws and treaties giving protection to animals.[4] The profound influence of moral discussion and its resulting growth in focused political pressure on the development of the law in this area cannot be doubted.

It would, however, be a mistake to assume that the discussion of the moral basis for the way in which we treat animals, and how that should be recognised in law, has been the preserve of the 20th century. The most notable philosophers in history have asked questions about the moral status of animals sometimes as a way of examining and contrasting the morality that underpins *human* interaction and development.

A good deal of the early writing on this subject is based upon Judaeo-Christian religious traditions, which saw humans beings as created in the image of God and having dominion over all other species. Humans were accorded the divine commission to exercise 'dominion over the fish of the sea, and over the birds of the air, and over the cattle, and over all the earth, and over every creeping thing which creeps upon the earth'; Noah was 'given' the

2   *The Sunday Telegraph*, 14 April 1996, p 5.

3   See, for example, Ryder, R, *Victims of Science*, 2nd edn, 1983, p 152, Fontwell, Sussex: Centaur Press; Singer, P, *Animal Liberation*, 1995, London: Pimlico.

4   If you require evidence of this, see Magel, C, *Keyguide to Information Sources in Animal Rights*, 1989, London: Mansell Publishing Ltd. It contains over 200 pages of references to books and articles (these have been added to considerably since 1989).

animals and plants.[5] Most of the early writing in those parts of the world dominated by European/Judaeo-Christian attitudes concentrates on distinguishing humans from the 'beasts' in order to justify our treatment of them, which is based on our 'dominion' over them. The literature also illustrates the wider search for the 'essence of mankind' as humans struggled to find reasons for their own existence including a blueprint of how they should treat each other, quite apart from how we should treat animals. When science was still in its embryonic stages there was a lack of detailed knowledge of human/non-human physiology and 'sentience'. It is, therefore, not at all surprising that historical analysis of the status of animals sought to find answers in religion.

The *Bible*, although widely interpreted as giving humans dominion over the animals, contains many references to how this dominion should be exercised in a compassionate and kind manner.[6] In the later texts of the *Old Testament*, humans are directed on several occasions to show kindness. For example: 'You shall not muzzle an ox when he treadeth out the corn',[7] and 'a righteous man has regard for the beast'.[8] In contrast, the ancient religious doctrines of the orient were reluctant to draw sharp distinctions between humans and animals. This, along with the belief that the immortal soul passed from one body to another, led to a different attitude to animals, as well as a predominantly vegetarian diet.

Theological analysis of the treatment of animals has continued down the centuries, although there are considerable differences in the status and treatment which different theologians have argued should be accorded to animals.[9] Theological approaches to the treatment of animals vary considerably depending on the scriptures of the various religions and how they have been interpreted. In the following passage, for example, Rabbi Immanuel Jakobovits reveals his clear view as to the status of animals which can be accorded by Judaism in his response to a request for his support from the International Association Against Painful Experiments on Animals. The Association had expressed its belief to him that *all* experiments on animals liable to cause pain are unacceptable, whatever the alleged purpose of the procedure, comparing human use of animals to the Nazi use of Jews for experimentation:[10]

> I appreciate the clarity with which you now inform me that your Association advocates a ban on all animal experiments liable to cause pain for whatever

5   *Genesis* 1:26–28 and *Genesis* 9:3.

6   *Deuteronomy* 25:4; *Proverbs* 12:10.

7   *Deuteronomy* 25:4.

8   *Proverbs* 10:10.

9   Compare the work of Rickaby, J, *Moral Philosophy*, 1905, London: Longmans with Linzey, A, *Animal Theology*, 1994, London: SCM Press.

10 Jakobvits, I, 'Some Letters on Jewish Medical Ethics' (1983) 8 *Journal of Medicine and Philosophy* 217–24.

purpose, including essential medical tests designed to relieve human suffering. For reasons fully explained in my previous letters, such a total ban would be incompatible with Judaism's commitment to the supreme value of human life and welfare.

I am rather taken aback by the comparison you make between such essential medical tests on animals and the diabolical Nazi experiments on Jews and other humans. It is precisely this equation of man and brute which prevents me from endorsing the objects of your Association. Your comparison, moreover, by condemning responsible medical researchers dedicated to the alleviation of human agony on the grounds that their work would justify the deliberate Nazi infliction of such agony on a terrifying scale, ignores the insistence of reputable scientists, and certainly of Jewish law, on protecting even animals from any avoidable pain contrasting with the callous brutality of the Nazis in denying even such consideration to their human victims. I therefore find such a comparison as fallacious as it is odious.

As noted above, interpretation of the Christian doctrines of the *Bible* in terms of animals being provided by God to be the tools of humankind has been the key source of attitudes towards animals for centuries. Despite the limited status accorded to animals by most theologians, there are others who have read the *Bible* in a different way to encompass a much wider duty placed on humans to take care of animals and to avoid cruelty towards them. In one of the many theological contributions to the animal rights debate over the centuries, and published around the same time as Jeremy Bentham was developing arguments which would shape the debate until the present day, Humphry Primatt presented a different interpretation of biblical teachings:[11]

Now, if amongst men, the differences of their powers of the mind, and their complexion, stature, and accidents of fortune, do not give any one man a right to abuse or insult any other man on account of these differences, for the same reason, a man can have no natural right to abuse and torment a beast, merely because a beast has not the mental powers of a man. For, such as the man is, he is but as God made him; and the very same is true of the beast. Neither of them can lay claim to any intrinsic merit, for being such as they are; for, before they were created, it was impossible that either of them could deserve; and at their creation, their shapes, perfections, or defects were invariably fixed, and their bounds set which they cannot pass. And being such, neither more nor less than God made them, there is no more merit in a man being a man; [and] there is neither merit nor demerit in either of them.

A brute is an animal no less sensible of pain than a man. He has similar nerves and organs of sensation; and his cries and groans, in case of violent impressions upon his body, though he cannot utter his complaints by speech, or human voice, are as strong indications to us of his sensibility of pain, as the cries of a human being, whose language we do not understand. Now, as pain is what we are all averse to, our own sensibility of pain should teach us to

---

11 Primatt, H, *The Duty of Mercy* (1776) 1992, pp 22–23, Fontwell, Sussex: Centaur Press.

commiserate it in others, to alleviate it if possible, but never wantonly or unmeritedly to inflict it.

Primatt's concern for animals and his recognition of pain as a significant interest to be protected against in animals as well as ourselves presaged many of the arguments used by the animal rights lobby today. Even though Jeremy Bentham has received much of the credit for being the 'grandfather' of the animal rights movement, Primatt can be credited with recognising the similarities between humans and animals which would later be confirmed and strengthened by Charles Darwin. He also recognised the significance of animal suffering and the philosophical links between what Richard Ryder and Peter Singer would later call 'speciesism', and racism. It was a book clearly ahead of its time.

One of the most notable contemporary theologians to re-examine the traditional notion which gave humans absolute dominion over the animals to use as they please is the Reverend Andrew Linzey:[12]

> Of all the claims emanating from within the Christian tradition, the claim that animals were made for human use or benefit appears singularly misplaced. Indeed, John Burnaby is surely right in seeing in this idea an early perversion of the Christian doctrine.[13] Latterly, a group of Anglican Theologians have argued that 'Although it cannot be denied that man is very much at the centre of biblical teachings on creation, this teaching does not hold that nature has been created simply for man's sake' and goes on to argue that to imagine so 'is a mark of folly'.[14]

> ... We have to ask what theological ground we have for denying the rights of animals, if we accept that such terminology is legitimate in relation to our fellow humans.[15] For, once we have accepted that animals have not only an instrumental value, but also an intrinsic one, then I believe we have to come to terms with – and ultimately embrace – the concept that on a theistic world view, creation has rights which can be derived from God-given autonomy and nature of each species ...

> Whatever we may assert about the moral superiority and intelligence of man, it appears to me most unacceptable that we should therefore claim for ourselves a relationship with animals which fails to do justice to our own moral senses. Victor Hugo recognised this discrepancy when he wrote of the

---

12 Extracts taken from Linzey, Rev A, 'Animals and Moral Theology', in Paterson, D and Ryder, R (eds), *Animal Rights – a Symposium*, 1979, pp 34–42, Fontwell, Sussex: Centaur Press.

[13] Burnaby, J, *The Belief of Christendom*, 1963, p 40, SPCK.

[14] Montefiore, H, *Man and Nature*, 1975, p 67, London: Collins.

[15] Some Christians maintain that we should never talk of moral rights, natural, assigned, relative or otherwise. I have sympathy for this view and I think it is certainly clear that Christians cannot accept that any being holds absolute rights. Nevertheless, if we are going to continue to hold that rights terminology, for all its difficulty and ambivalence, has a place in moral theology, then I see no reason why we should accept them in the case of fellow humans and then quibble about terminology in the cases of animals.

need for man to become 'civilised towards nature'.[16] But it is surely extraordinary that despite our present pre-occupation with man's misuse of the environment and the ethical issues involved in that sphere, we should have failed to give serious attention to the similar issues raised by man's treatment of other, often higher, similar, animals. And if we believe our capacity as moral beings is a gift from God freely bestowed upon us as an inherent part of our being made in the image of God, then we need to regard our moral responsibility towards animals with a degree of seriousness and urgency which hitherto has eluded us.

For 2000 years or more, a theological approach has remained as one of the starting points as philosophers have endeavoured to identify the key differences between humans and animals which would justify our treatment of them. Many other scholars have, however, contributed to the debate in different ways by emphasising the physiological, intellectual, self-awareness, reasoning and linguistic capacities of different species in order to present a blueprint for how we should treat them. Non-theological approaches have been notably prevalent since the 18th century and particularly since the work of Charles Darwin in the 19th century but are far from being a 'modern approach'.

Plato (427–347 BC) and Aristotle (384–322 BC) both examined the status of animals. Aristotle considered man to be the 'most excellent of all beings'. Whilst not directly addressing himself to what duties or rights should be extended to animals, he set the tone of the debate for centuries to come. He distinguished humans because of, for example, their government, society, 'gift of speech' and perceptions of good and evil.[17] However, the ancient Greeks, although paving the way for philosophical discussion in this area for centuries to come, never managed to agree on a coherent view of man's interaction with animals, as evidenced by their treatment of animals 'accused' of murder (see Chapter 2).

The fate of the animals during the Roman period of European history, the philosophy of which predominated until the sixth century AD, has been well documented through, for example, our knowledge of the uses of the great ampitheatres of the Roman Empire.[18] Animals were considered to be the playthings of entertainment and, at a time when *human* rights were accorded subject to status, it is easy to see why animals and humans alike suffered immeasurably. The opening of the Colosseum in Rome was celebrated by the killing of some 5,000 animals and a further 9,000 in the following three

---

[16] Hugo, V, 'The Relationship Between Men and the Animals', reprinted in *The Ark*, August 1967, p 116, Catholic Study Circle for Animal Welfare.

17 Aristotle, 'Politics' in Ellis, W (ed), *The Politics of Aristotle*, 1912, pp 1252–54, London: Dent.

18 For a good description of the inhumanity towards animals exhibited by the Romans, see Turner, ES, *All Heaven In A Rage*, 1964 (reprinted 1992), Chapter 1, Fontwell, Sussex: Centaur Press; and Carson, G, *Men Beasts and Gods*, 1972, Chapter 1, New York: Scribners.

months.[19] It has been noted that any concern which was shown by the more thoughtful philosophers would have been drowned out by the constant craving for excitement, despite the suffering inflicted on the participants, human and non-human.[20] Despite the public slaughter and apparent contempt for any notion of compassion for animals, the more humanitarian philosophers of the Roman Empire advocated a different attitude. Seneca, Plutarch and Porphyry preached the ideas of universal benevolence which incorporated a concern for the welfare of animals. Plutarch (AD 46–120) was a Greek tutor to the Emperor Hadrian and his teachings provide a stark contrast to the slaughter of the ampitheatres:[21]

> Law and justice we cannot in the nature of things employ on others than men; but we may extend our goodness and charity even to irrational creatures; and such acts flow from a gentle nature as water from an abundant stream. ...
>
> [An animal is entitled to cry] 'Kill me for thy feeding but do not take me for thy better feeding.' ... Yet for the sake of some little mouthful of flesh, we deprive a soul of the sun and light and of that proportion of life and time it had been born into the world to enjoy. ... Let us kill an animal; but let us do it with sorrow and pity and not abusing or tormenting it, as many nowadays are wont to do.

Porphyry (AD c.232–c.305) was born in Phoenicia and moved to Rome when he was 30. Being a vegetarian, he wrote at length on the moral case for avoiding animal flesh. He believed not only that this is an essential part of having a purified soul but that exploitation of the animal kingdom in general is a denial of justice to animals and is damaging to the treatment by people of each other. He dismissed arguments claiming that humans are the only beings with reason and language, which is deemed, therefore, to grant them entirely different moral treatment:[22]

> The difference, indeed, between our reason and theirs appears to consist, as Aristotle somewhere says, not in essence, but in the more and the less; just as many are of opinion, that the difference between the Gods and us is not essential, but consists in this, that in them there is a greater, and in us a less accuracy, of the reasoning power. And, indeed, so far as pertains to sense and the remaining organisation, according to the sensoria and the flesh, every one will grant that these are similarly disposed in us, as they are in brutes. For they not only similarly participate with us of natural passions, and the motions produced through these, but we may also survey in them such affections as are preternatural and morbid. No one, however, of sound mind, will say that brutes are unreceptive of the reasoning power, on account of the difference

19   Turner, above n 18, p 20.

20   See Brumbaugh, R, 'Of Man, Animals, and Morals: A Brief History', in Morris, K and Fox, M (eds), *On the Fifth Day*, 1978, Washington: Acropolis Books Ltd.

21   Turner, above n 18, pp 17–18.

22   Wynne-Tyson, E (ed), *Porphyry on Abstinence From Animal Food*, 1965, pp 116–17, Fontwell, Sussex: Centaur Press.

between their habit of body and ours, when he sees that there is a great variety of habit in men, according to their race, and the nations to which they belong and yet, at the same time, it is granted that all of them are rational.

These pleas for compassionate treatment were, however, lost in the blood-lust of the Empire. The only spectacles which the Roman public seemed to find exciting were those involving appalling barbarity and slaughter on a massive and bloody scale. The effects of this on the Roman public were far-reaching, as shown, for instance, by the link identified between the spectacle and the sexual practices which occurred thereafter on account of the 'strongest excitement which was elicited by the scenes'.[23] Changes in the prevailing attitudes towards animals may well have come about partly as a result of the decline of the Roman Empire as a major military power. The ritualistic slaughter in the amphitheatres was lost over time, apart from bull-fighting which remains in Spain and elsewhere; but so too were the thoughtful contributions of Rome's more humanitarian philosophers.

The ambivalence and lack of published work which prevailed over the following centuries was only brought to an end by the revival of Aristotelian thinking in the 13th century by St Thomas Aquinas (1225–74). He ascribed to humans the right to treat animals as slaves, and considered that everything on earth was placed there by God for the benefit of humans. He described humans as the 'intellectual species' with the right to do as they please with animals:[24]

> Hereby is refuted the error of those who said it is sinful for a man to kill brute animals; for by the divine providence they are intended for man's use according to the order of nature. Hence, it is not wrong for man to make use of them, either by killing or in any other way whatever. For this reason the Lord said to Noah (*Genesis* 9:3): 'As the green herbs I have delivered all flesh to you.'

It may seem to be a large chronological jump to go from the Romans to the Reformation, pausing only to examine the views of St Thomas Aquinas, but very little of note was published on the subject of animals in that period. The Reformation and the revival of learning which accompanied it led to the beginning of the 'modern' history of the philosophical analysis of the differences between humans and animals. Much of the debate can be found in the discussions between the 'rationalists' of the European continent and the 'empiricists' of Great Britain, which began in the 17th century. One of the most widely known statements by the rationalists concerning animals was made by René Descartes (1596–1650) in the 17th century. His views led to widespread abuse of animals for a considerable time. He considered animals to be the same as machines and, just as cruelty to a machine is impossible, so too, he

---

23 Turner, above n 18, p 21.
24 St Thomas Aquinas, 'Summa Contra Gentiles' in Pegis, A, (trans), *Basic Writings of Saint Thomas Aquinas*, 1945, pp 220–24, New York: Random House.

argued, it is with animals, as they do not feel pain. True to his roots in the continental European rationalist tradition, he described animals as 'automata', showing the same qualities as machines because of an absence of intellect:[25]

> ... there are no men so dull and stupid, not even idiots, as to be incapable of joining together different words, and thereby constructing a declaration by which to make their thoughts understood; and that on the other hand, there is no other animal, however perfect or happily circumstanced, which can do the like.

According to Cartesian thinking, animals are 'thoughtless brutes', unaware of the sensations of pain, suffering, heat and cold. Descartes asserted that the fact that animals appear to react to these stimuli does not indicate a conscious reaction, but merely indicated the same reaction as a machine being turned on. Any reactions to external stimuli could be attributed to the same response as a plant turning toward the sunlight: the response should not be seen as evidence of thought or intellect, but merely of reflexive mechanical action.

Another rationalist who took up the reins of denying consideration for animals was Gottfried Leibniz (1646–1716). His views were also based upon the concept of man having been created in God's image and being the sole possessor of intelligence. His notion of man as the unique animal capable of harbouring the essential sentience, or 'spirit', added to the rationalist's view of animals being created merely to serve humankind:[26]

> The difference between intelligent substances and those which are not intelligent is quite as great as between a mirror and one who sees. As God is himself the greatest and wisest of spirits, it is easy to understand that the spirits with which he can, so to speak, enter into conversation and even into social relations by communicating to them in particular ways his feelings and his will so that they are able to know and love their benefactor, must be much nearer to him than the rest of created things which may be regarded as the instruments of spirits.

The views of Descartes in particular received criticism at the time which continued for several decades after his death and into the next century as scientists and philosophers debated the validity of his theories. For example, in the 18th century La Mettrie argued that Descartes' reasoning, in terms of reflexive behaviour, could be taken a step further to explain *human* behaviour, not just animal behaviour thereby highlighting similarities rather than differences.[27] Descartes had denied this by stressing the existence of linguistic capabilities of humans as showing that they are unique in being 'conscious'.

---

25 Descartes, R, 'Discourse V' (1637), in Veitch, J (trans), *René Descartes: A Discourse on Method*, Everyman edition, 1912, Part V, pp 43–46, London: Dent.

26 Leibniz, G, 'Discourse on Metaphysics' (1710), in Veitch, J, Elwes, R and Montgomery, G (eds), *The Rationalists*, 1960, pp 450–51, New York: Dolpin Books.

27 La Mettrie, 'L'homme Machine' (1747) in Thomson, A, *La Mettrie: 'Machine Man' and other Writings*, 1996, Cambridge: Cambridge University Press.

La Mettrie had to flee, first, to Leiden and then to Berlin in order to escape the wrath of the theologians' response to this assertion. He eventually found sanctuary in the Court of Frederick the Great of Prussia. The strength of feeling which was aroused by these arguments was caused by their relationship with the very nature of mankind and our relationship with God. Soon after Descartes' influential statement, and in the centuries which followed, experimenters and commercial agriculturalists used his theories to deny that even the most minimal of humane considerations should be applied to non-human animals. Indeed, this concern of 'over-sentimentality' was given Papal support by Pope Pius XII, who considered that the cries of animals should not arouse 'unreasonable compassion'. The predominance and legacy of this Catholic view of animals goes some way to explaining the different legal and moral status accorded to non-human animals in the southern States of Europe, which has caused modern-day difficulties in framing European legislation concerning animals.[28]

Thomas Hobbes (1588–1679), although in no way as unsympathetic in his views as Descartes, found many differences between 'man and the beasts'. He used the absence of language in animals to distinguish them from humans and found differences in the fact that humans use language to name things (and even each other), to number and measure, to pass on knowledge – sometimes to even deceive themselves.[29] In the following excerpt he identifies some other differences:[30]

It is very true, that in those creatures living only by sense and appetite, their consent of mind is so durable, as there is no need of anything more to secure it, and by consequence to preserve peace amongst them, than barely their natural inclination. But among men the case is otherwise. For, first, among them there is contestation of honour and preferment; among beasts there is none: whence hatred and envy, out of which arise sedition and war, is among men; among beasts no such matter. Next, the natural appetite of bees, and the like creatures, is conformable; and they desire the common good, which among them differs not from their private. But man scarce esteems anything good, which hath not somewhat of eminence in the enjoyment, more than that which others do possess. [And] those creatures which are devoid of reason, see no defect, or think they see none, in the administration of their commonweals; but in a multitude of men there are many who, supposing themselves wiser than others, endeavour to innovate, and divers innovators innovate divers ways; which is a mere distraction and civil war. [Also], these brute creatures, howsoever they may have use of their voice to signify their affections to each other, yet want they that same art of words which is necessarily required to those motions in the mind, whereby good is represented to it as being better,

---

28 See Chapter 5 on agriculture, for example, which details the problems encountered in framing European legislation on the transportation of animals.

29 Molesworth, Sir W, *The Collected Works of Thomas Hobbes*, 1994, pp 18–19, London: Routledge/Thoemmes Press.

30 *Ibid*, pp 66–67.

and evil as worse than in truth it is. But the tongue of man is a trumpet of war and sedition; and it is reported of Pericles, that he sometimes by his elegant speeches thundered and lightened, and confounded whole Greece itself.

Despite the weight of discussion centred around the superiority of humans over animals, many writers became concerned about the philosophical questions raised by the treatment of animals. British philosophers such as John Locke (1632–1704) and David Hume (1711–76), using their direct, empirical observations of animals as opposed to the 'rationality'-based arguments of the continental Europeans such as Descartes and, later, Kant (see also Chapter 3), focused on the *similarities* that animals exhibit in relation to humans, as well as the differences.

Locke did not doubt that there are certain sentient capabilities such as memory shared by both humans and animals, with further capabilities such as abstract thinking and comparison which are better developed in humans:[31]

> ... though [brutes] take in, and retain together several combinations of simple ideas, as possibly the shape, smell, and voice of his master, make up the complex idea a dog has of him; or rather are so many distinct marks whereby he knows him: yet I do not think they do of themselves ever compound them, and make complex ideas, and perhaps even where we think they have complex ideas, 'tis only one simple one that directs them in the knowledge of several things, which possibly they distinguish less by their sight, than we imagine. ...

> ... abstraction, whereby ideas taken from particular beings, become general representations of all of the same kind; and their names general names, applicable to whatever exists conformable to such abstract ideas ... . Thus, the same colour being observed today in chalk or snow, which the mind yesterday received from milk, it considers that appearance alone, makes it a representative of that kind ...

> If it may be doubted, whether beasts compound and enlarge their ideas, to any degree: this, I think, I may be positive in, that the power of abstracting is not at all in them; and that the having of general ideas, is that which puts a perfect distinction betwixt man and brutes; and is an excellency which the faculties of brutes do by no means attain to ...

> [But] if they have any ideas at all, and are not bare machines (as some would have them) we cannot deny them to have some reason. It seems as evident to me, that they do some of them in certain instances reason, as that they have sense; but it is only in particular ideas, just as they received them from their senses. They are the best of them tied up within those narrow bound, and have not (as I think) the faculty to enlarge them by any kind of abstraction.

Locke's chief concern regarding our treatment of animals was the effect that mistreating them has on humans, particularly children: 'the custom of tormenting and killing beasts will, by degree, harden their minds even

---

31 Nidditch, P (ed), *John Locke: An Essay on Human Understanding* (1689), 1975, pp 158–60, Oxford: Oxford University Press.

towards men; and they who delight in the suffering and destruction of inferior creatures, will not be apt to be very compassionate or benign to those of their own kind.'[32]

Immanuel Kant (1724–1804) returned to the theme of the damage done to humans by heartless and brutal treatment of animals. Kant appears to have had anti-cruelty tendencies, but to call him an 'animal liberationist' would be wide of the mark. To Kant, even though he stated that having come into contact with animals it would be difficult to harbour cruel thoughts against them, the primary reasoning against cruelty is to be found in the effect it has on humanity, not in the inherent sentient qualities of animals:[33]

> Tender feelings towards animals develop humane feelings towards mankind. In England butchers and doctors do not sit on a jury because they are accustomed to the sight of death and hardened. Vivisectionists, who use living animals for their experiments, certainly act cruelly, although their aim is praiseworthy, and they can justify their cruelty, since animals must be regarded as man's instruments; but any such cruelty for sport cannot be justified. A master who turns out his ass or his dog because the animal can no longer earn its keep manifests a small mind. The Greeks' ideas in this respect were high-minded, as can be seen from the fable of the ass and the bell of ingratitude. Our duties towards animals, then, are indirect duties towards mankind.

David Hume disagreed with earlier attempts to distinguish the species on the basis of rationality: 'Next to the ridicule of denying an evident truth, is that of taking much pains to defend it; and no truth appears to me to be more evident, than that beasts are endowed with thought and reason as well as men. The arguments are in this so obvious that they never escape the most stupid and ignorant.'[34] He proposed that the depth of human reasoning goes beyond that of animals but does so merely by virtue of evolution indicating that the the differences as there are can be explained in terms of degree rather than in kind.

Throughout the 18th and 19th centuries the debate about the moral status of animals continued apace, and would eventually lead to legislation in the UK and elsewhere seeking to protect animals from the appalling treatment which was meted out to them in relation to production of food, transportation, medical experimentation, sport and recreation. Despite opposing views on the nature and extent of awareness of pain in animals and whether it could be equated with human suffering, the Cartesian view prevailed as the basis for supporting experimentation on live animal subjects

---

32 Locke, J, 'Some Thoughts Concerning Education' (1693), in *The Works of John Locke in Ten Volumes*, Vol 9, 10th edn, 1801, pp 112–15, London.

33 Kant, I, *Lectures on Ethics – Duties Towards Animals and other Spirits* (1780–81), in Infield, L (trans), 1963, p 240–41, New York: Harper and Row.

34 Hume, D, *A Treatise of Human Nature* (1739–40), Book 1, 1888, pp 176–79, Oxford: Clarendon Press.

in the 18th and 19th centuries without the use of anaesthetics. Legislation regulating this practice would not be passed until the end of the 19th century leaving dogs in particular to be the subjects of extreme cruelty due to their trusting and friendly nature even whilst being vivisected. They were often simply nailed to a board and vivisection began, despite the cries of agony from the animals. Experimentation on animals became more and more widespread as scientists strived to make medical advances by any method at their disposal.

The end of the 18th century saw many philosophers and members of the privileged classes, particularly in England, becoming more and more critical of the practices being carried out in the name of scientific progress, and of the treatment of animals in other areas such as farming and human 'sport and recreational pastimes' such as bull-baiting.[35] The most notable of these is considered to be the utilitarian, Jeremy Bentham (1748–1860). In one of the most notable contributions to the historical development of arguments used by the animal welfare movement, he asserted that the immovable lines which had traditionally been drawn between humans and animals had been drawn without any significant moral basis. There is a moral basis to the eating of animals and some experimentation, he concluded, as long as there is a speedy death. But he came out firmly against 'torment': 'a full grown horse or dog, is beyond comparison a more rational, as well as a more conversable animal, than an infant of a day, or a week, or even a month, old. But suppose the case were otherwise, what would it avail? The question is not, Can they reason? nor, Can they talk? but, Can they suffer?'[36]

Bentham's considerable contribution to a new era of human attitudes towards animals which eventually found its first significant legal recognition some years later in England is well summed up by Maehle and Tröhler:[37]

> Although Bentham did not draw any consequences for the practice of animal experimentation, his statements about the status of animals became of great importance to the modern anti-vivisectionist cause. His was probably the first serious criticism of the Christian, respectively Kantian, doctrine of man's relationship towards animals. From then on, the issue of cruelty to animals was no longer seen from a solely *anthropocentric* point of view, but also from a theriocentric one which considered the protection of animals *for their own sake*. Bentham had thrown overboard the old criterion of whether or not animals have a rational soul and replaced it with the criterion of their capacity to suffer pain.

---

35 French, R, *Anti-Vivisection and Medical Science in Victorian Society*, 1975, Chapter 2, Princeton: Princeton University Press.

36 Burns, JH and Hart, HLA, *Jeremy Bentham, An Introduction to the Principles of Morals and Legislation*, 1970, p 283, London: University of London.

37 Maehler, AH and Tröhler, U, 'Animal Experimentation from Antiquity to the End of the Eighteenth Century: Attitudes and Arguments', in Rupke, N (ed), *Vivisection in Historical Perspective*, 1987, London: Routledge.

In Chapter 3 an analysis of the writing of Tom Regan, Peter Singer and Stephen Clarke, amongst others, will illustrate how some contemporary philosophers have been much more willing to grant consideration to animals in their own right. The modern language of 'cruelty and injustice' which began in the late 18th and early 19th centuries with Jeremy Bentham, is also illustrated by Herman Daggett (1766–1832):[38]

> God has appointed to all his creatures, a certain sphere to move in, and has granted them certain privileges, which may be called their own. If we judge impartially, we shall acknowledge that there are the rights of a beast, as well as the rights of a man. And because man is considered as the Lord of this lower creation, he is not thereby licensed to infringe on the rights of those below him, any more than a King, or Magistrate, is licensed to infringe on the rights of his subjects. If the Governor of the universe has given us liberty to prepare animal food; or, if the rights of these creatures, in certain instances interfere with the rights of others, or with the rights of men, so as thereby to become forfeited; we may, in such cases, take away their lives, or deprive them of their privileges, without the imputation of blame. And I know of nothing in nature, in reason, or in revelation, which obliges us to suppose, that the unalienated rights of a beast, are not as sacred, and inviolable, as those of a man: or that the person, who wantonly commits an outrage upon the life, happiness, or security of a bird, is not as amenable, at the tribunal of eternal justice, as he, who wantonly destroys the rights and privileges, or injuriously takes away the life of one of his fellow creatures of the human race.

In Germany, Artur Scopenhauer (1788–1860) asserted that animals could suffer pain and was critical of the traditional Christian and the human-centred Kantian positions which had denied direct duties towards animals. He did, however, think that animals suffer less than humans and it could therefore be justifiable to use them in 'the chase' (hunting), but not in vivisection. Just as Bentham became an idol of the animal welfare lobby in early 19th century England, so did Artur Schopenhauer in Germany:[39]

> The right of man over the life and powers of the brutes rests on the fact that, because with the growing clearness of consciousness suffering increases in like measure; the pain which the brute suffers through death or work is not so great as man would suffer by merely denying himself the flesh, or the powers of the brutes. Therefore, man may carry the assertion of his existence to the extent of denying the existence of the brute, and the will to live as a whole endures less suffering in this way than if the opposite course were adopted. This at once determines the extent of the use man may make of the powers of the brutes without wrong; a limit, however, which is often transgressed, especially in the case of burden and dogs used in the chase; to which the activity of societies for the prevention of cruelty to animals is principally

---

38   Daggett, H, *The Rights of Animals: An Oration* (1791), 1926, pp 7–8, New York: American Society for the Prevention of Cruelty to Animals.

39   Schopenhauer, A, *The World as Will and Idea* (1819), Haldane, R, and Kemp, J (trans) in vol 2, 6th edn, 1909, pp 480–81, London: Kegan Paul, Trench, Trubner.

devoted. In my opinion, that right does not extend to vivisection, particularly of the higher animals. On the other hand, the insect does not suffer so much through its death as a man suffers from its sting. The Hindus do not understand this.

Accordingly, Schopenhauer appears to give his support to the farming of animals but not to animal experimentation. One wonders whether his attitude might have changed in light of the advent of factory farming or the advancements of human health claimed by the pro-animal experimentation lobby.

There is, however, a strong case which can be made to support the view that it was not just philosophy that brought arguments regarding the treatment of animals into the area of public debate, but the work of one man, Charles Darwin (1809–82). Darwin was not the first to notice and record similarities between the species. In 1661, Samuel Pepys noted in his diary that he had seen a 'strange creature', believed to have been a chimpanzee or a gorilla, from Guinea and commented that it was 'so much like a man in most things ... I cannot believe but that it is a monster got of a man and a she-baboon. I do believe it already understands much English; and I am of a mind it might be taught to speak and make signs.'[40] Darwin, however, provided the scientific reasoning to support intuitive observation. He explained that there are evident similarities between people and animals not only in terms of physical characteristics such as muscles, bones and reproductive systems, but also in terms of 'higher mental powers' such as memory, attention, curiosity, imitation and reason which are seen in animals to varying degrees:[41]

> If no organic being excepting man had possessed any mental power, or if his powers had been of wholly different nature from those of the lower animals, then we should never have been able to convince ourselves that our high faculties had been gradually developed. But it can be clearly shewn that there is no fundamental difference of this kind. We must also admit that there is a much wider interval in mental power between one of the lowest fishes, as a lamprey or lancelet, and one of the higher apes, than between an ape and man; yet this immense interval is filled up by numberless gradations ... there is no fundamental difference between man and the higher mammals in their mental faculties.

One attribute of humans which Darwin accepted as being a fundamental difference between the species is what he referred to as 'the moral sense'. He was of the opinion that *any* animal which had progressed intellectually would eventually have developed a sense of morality or conscience to the same extent as humans.[42] Darwin's findings opened a new era in science, attempting to prove, using empirical evidence, the existence of significant differences or

---

40 From Pepys' diary, number two, cited in Thomas, K, *Man and The Natural World: Changing Attitudes in England 1500–1800*, 1983, p 132, London: Allen Lane.

41 Darwin, C, *The Descent of Man* (1871), 1981, pp 34–35, Surrey: Princeton University Press.

42 *Ibid*, p 71.

similarities between the species which would affect our treatment of animals. Research in this area is far from complete, as new evidence of the sentient qualities of animals continues to emerge from studies across the world. There are a few scientists and philosophers who have challenged the notion of similarities begun by Darwin, but the vast majority are in accord with Darwin's notions of notable similarities with humans in terms of pain, suffering and sentient capabilities.[43]

James Rachels has argued that Darwin's theories can and have been used in two ways: the first is to use the idea of survival of the fittest to support a variety of morally unjustifiable social and political practices.[44] It is quite easy for the 'fittest' to use or abuse the weakest. As the ultimate naturally selected 'predator' on the planet, humans would be free to undertake practically any action against other species, as part and parcel of their place at the top of the evolutionary ladder; the second method of interpreting Darwin's theories, suggested Rachels, is to support the idea that evolution shows that humans are not uniquely rational beings and that animals differ from humans in degree but not in kind. This kind of thinking could suggest that 'like should be treated alike', rather than stressing the differences to justify dubious human practices in their uses of animals.

The crucial contribution of Darwin was that he clearly recognised not distinct *differences*, but rather the *similarities* between organisms which should influence whether we treat them differently. He saw the development of the moral sense of humans as being part of our own evolutionary process. In just the same way as humans had been slow to recognise other races as being our 'fellow creatures', so Darwin saw attitudes toward animals as being evidence of the evolutionary development of humankind in recognition of the similarities between the species: 'sympathy beyond the confines of man, that is humanity to the lower animals, seems to be one of the latest moral acquisitions ... This virtue, one of the noblest with which man is endowed, seems to arise incidentally from our sympathies becoming more tender and more widely diffused, until they are extended to all sentient beings.'[45] Almost overnight, Darwin had provided strong arguments which put humans alongside animals in terms of many characteristics and advocating a moral approach to our decision-making regarding animals based on scientific evidence. The historical view based on the dominance of mankind and our relationship with God largely gave way to scientific evidence of similarities and common bonds. To treat 'brute creation' in ways beneficial purely to our own species became even more morally questionable and began the move towards a new era of animal emancipation through protective legislation.

---

43 See Chapter 5 on agriculture for a discussion of different attitudes to pain and suffering in animals.

44 Rachels, J, *Created From Animals*, 1990, Oxford: Oxford University Press.

45 Darwin, above n 41, p 101.

Darwin's revelations had an immense effect on the advocates of animal rights. The thoughtful historical references to the sentience of animals from Porphyry and Plutarch through to Bentham and Schopenhauer were primarily based on observation and intuition. Darwin handed to those who came after him the invaluable and influential support of science, bringing with it the foundations for a whole new approach to the human justification for their treatment of animals.[46] The historical defences to our uses of animals which pointed to humankind being unique and made in the image of God, with absolute dominion over the animals, or arguments which concentrated on driving an immovable wedge between the sentient capacities of humans and animals based on intelligence, language and capacities for pain and suffering, were now the subjects of both philosophical *and* scientific challenge. Within 50 years of the publication of Darwin's findings, philosophical contributions began to apply Darwinism to create a new vision of our relationship with 'the beasts', as the following extract from a 1906 work of J Howard Moore illustrates:[47]

> The doctrine of organic evolution, which forever established the common genesis of all animals, sealed the doom of anthropocentricism.[48] Whatever the inhabitants of this world were before the publication of *The Origin of the Species*, they never could be anything since but a *family*. The doctrine of evolution is probably the most important revelation that has come to the world since the illuminations of Galileo and Copernicus. The authors of the Copernican theory enlarged and corrected human understanding by disclosing to man the comparative littleness of his world – by discovering that the earth, which had up to that time been supposed to be the centre and capital of cosmos, is in reality a satellite of the sun. This heliocentric discovery was hard on human conceit, for it was the first broad hint man had thus far received of his true dimensions. The doctrine of evolution has had, and is having, and is destined to continue to have, a similarly correcting effect on the naturally narrow conceptions of men.

He correctly predicted that the way in which animals were treated in his time would come to be regarded as purely anthropocentric exercises of human dominion to be replaced, in large part, by a new philosophy which recognises the 'unity and consanguinity' of all organic life.[49] He estimated a time-scale of perhaps one to two centuries for the impact of Darwin's theories to have taken their course. As we look back on the achievements of the animal welfare lobby one century later, though there are landmarks of significant progress there are

---

46 The new approach pervades contemporary philosophical support for change advocated by writers such as Peter Singer and Tom Regan, as we shall see in Chapter 3. Singer's approach, regarding the suffering of animals as being morally significant in the same way as human suffering, is based on Darwin's findings on evolution, as is Regan's notion of animals being experiencers of life in much the same way as ourselves.

47 Moore, JH, *The Universal Kinship* (1906), 1992 edn, pp 319–20, Fontwell, Sussex: Centaur Press.

48 Whereby humans create a relationship with the animals and the rest of the environment based purely on the possibilities for human gain.

49 Moore, above n 47, p 323.

still many incidences which some say carry the mark of anthropocentricism (see Chapter 2). Maybe Moore was right, and we are only half-way through a slow process of evolutionary development.

The similarities between animals and humans are certainly acknowledged by the scientific community, which is why they are keen to use them in medical experimentation. As one example of this undoubted acknowledgement, the British Association for the Advancement of Science, a body formed in 1831 to promote science in general, has stated that 'the physiology of humans and other mammals is very similar' and that there are 'similarities of development of the nervous system, particularly the brain, and reproductive structures and of the physiology, immunilogical defence systems and other characteristics, some of which are unique to humans and primates'.[50] These similarities are used as the main reason for continuing the use of primates and other animals in research. Animal welfare groups argue that the similarities should be interpreted as good enough reason to ensure that animals are not used, on the grounds that their experience may be so similar to ours as to raise moral concern over their suffering. One of the foremost scientists to continue the work started by Darwin in the search for the origins of the human species is Richard Leaky. He is in no doubt that the distance between animals and humans is not as great as some would still have us believe. As he analysed fossil evidence, particularly in Africa, he became convinced that the differences between animals and the higher primates are no more than 'an accident of history'. He believes that the differences have been consistently exaggerated because we were blinded by our own accomplishments, which in many respects appear to go beyond those of animals.[51]

Leaky is in no doubt that the fossil records still being uncovered show a complex picture of the development of *homo sapiens* from other species of apes. The qualities that some regard as being unique to humans – consciousness, emotions, language and morality, for example – would be very unlikely to emerge in a single genetic leap. This leads to the inevitable conclusion that aspects of our 'unique claims' are extremely likely to be present in other species. Humans have been shown to differ by less than 2% from chimpanzees in their genetic make-up, whereas horses and zebra – species which can mate and produce offspring – show greater genetic differences than this. A conclusion which can be drawn from this is that chimpanzees are very close to us in evolutionary terms. Unless the 2% difference can be shown to account for *all* those different characteristics claimed to be in the sole possession of human beings, then there is strong

---

50 Leaflet entitled *Animals and the Advancement of Science: Working with Animals in Medical Research*, 1994, London: British Association for the Advancement of Science.

51 Leaky, R and Lewin R, *Origins Reconsidered: In Search of What Makes Us Human*, 1992, pp 352–53, London: Abacus Books.

evidence indeed that some of those characteristics are possessed by animals other than ourselves. Just how far down the 'evolutionary ladder' these attributes might be found continues to be the subject of modern-day research.

In recent times, particularly since 1970, some scientists have started to investigate the attributes of animals which were traditionally considered to be unique to humans. Scientists are asking 'what is it actually like to be an animal; can they use language or make friends in order to determine how we should behave towards them?' These types of question, with the extreme difficulties they involve in the interpretation of behaviour, are questions from which the scientific community has traditionally strayed away. Empirical, reliable data, the core of scientific thinking, is difficult to accumulate and the scientists involved have been accused of relying too much on their own experiences and interpretation of behaviour *as humans* to make this a valid domain for exact science.

The place of emotions in the experience of pain and suffering has been dismissed by the scientific community in general as a clear case of anthropomorphism – that is, projecting the thoughts and behaviour of humans into our interpretation of animal behaviour. This is one of the central arguments of most scientists in denying the need for a change in our relationship with animals, in that we are in danger of attributing human characteristics to non-human animals, and of misinterpreting what they simply refer to as 'response behaviour' as evidence of a higher level of sentience than actually exists. Darwin, however, found no difficulty in ascribing emotions to animals, having observed their facial expressions and body language.[52]

Scientists have traditionally sought to avoid the description of animal responses in terms of emotive descriptions such as fear, mood, excitement and loneliness. Emotions are difficult enough to judge in our own species, even though we have a complex language with which to communicate with each other. Identifying and describing emotions in animals, whether they are the same as ours or not, is a task which the scientific community has yet to come to terms with. However, those working with animals, animal owners and observers seem to be in no doubt that animals have emotions, which puts them at odds with most of the scientific community: 'It is clear that animals form lasting friendships, are frightened of being hunted, have horror of dismemberment, wish they were back in the safety of their den, despair for their mates, look out for and protect their children whom they love.'[53] In response to their claims that this kind of thinking is a clear case of anthropomorphism, scientists are accused of arrogance and ignorance in their

---

52 Darwin, C, *The Expression of the Emotions in Man and Animals* (1872), 1979 edn, London: Friedman.

53 Masson, J and McCarthy, S, *When Elephants Weep: The Emotional Lives of Animals,* 1996, p 220, London: Vintage Press.

quest to assert species dominance. The general acceptance of the presence of emotions in animals might have considerable consequences for our relationship with them and, therefore, our legal provision for them (see excerpt from Jeffrey Masson in Chapter 3).

The existence of language as a primary distinguishing feature of humans from non-human animals has been the centre of controversy and debate to the present day, with dolphins and primates the subject of intense study. Studies such as those carried out by the Gardners and Duane Rumbaugh into the development of language by chimpanzees have attempted to prove higher linguistic capacities of the 'higher' animals.[54] The Gardners attempted to show that their chimpanzee, Washoe, had the ability to use a complex symbol system in order to communicate what he wanted to eat, play with or where he wanted to go. Their studies have produced convincing evidence of a rudimentary understanding of language in chimpanzees. The animals were shown to be capable of listening to, and responding to, complex verbal commands. In one of the experiments, for example, Washoe was asked to 'point to the picture of the orange', or 'point to the picture of the umbrella'. Washoe was able to do this repeatedly, without difficulty. The findings in this area of research are summarised by Richard Byrne:[55]

> There is now no doubt that these apes can understand and use the concept of *reference*; that is, the fact that one thing, a word, can be made to stand for and refer to another thing, an object or a class of objects. Nor is there doubt that they are capable of using words for real communication, requesting and offering new information when it is appropriate, as well as demanding things and commenting on performance.

> These abilities were first claimed for chimpanzees on the basis of the behaviour of Washoe, the pioneer chimpanzee taught American sign language, and this led to controversy. The Gardiners' early methods may have been less rigorous than the ideal, but their later work has repeatedly shown that their signing chimpanzees are using signs referentially and communicatively ...

> ... This took a new turn when Sue Savage-Rumbaugh discovered by accident that young apes can learn symbols entirely by observation. In trying to teach an adult pygmy chimpanzee by conventional means (she learnt little), her offspring Kanzi, happening to be present, began to pick up knowledge of the symbols spontaneously. Savage-Rumbaugh and her co-workers immediately capitalised on this, and set up a regime in which caretakers did not insist on symbol production, they merely talked about what was happening and going to happen. Pointing to symbols at the same time, they chatted about daily routines, outings and events in his varied and interesting life. Kanzi, and subsequently two other pygmy chimpanzees and one common chimpanzee, picked up the meanings of symbols and acquired large vocabularies, all

54 Gardner, RA, Gardner, BT and Van Cantfort, TE, *Teaching Sign Language to Chimpanzees*, 1989, New York: State University of New York Press; see also Blum, D, *Monkey Wars*, 1994, Oxford: Oxford University Press.

55 Byrne, R, *The Thinking Ape: Evolutionary Origins of Intelligence*, 1995, pp 166 and 168–69, Oxford: Oxford University Press.

without being taught. Kanzi even acquired the meaning of *spoken* English words, whereas extensive testing with earlier (common chimpanzee) subjects had shown that they got nothing useful from the conversations to which, they too, had been exposed.

Their results are subject to much debate and have failed to convince everyone that animals have the competence for a complex linguistic system such as that of humans.[56] If studies such as this are recognised as proving the existence of a highly developed linguistic capability in higher-order animals, then many of the arguments used by the philosophical opponents to the animal-rights lobby would, at the very least, have to be rewritten. Language, in the sense that it enables us to communicate to each other and highlights our own individuality, has been a crucial factor in ascribing the level of sentient capabilities of different species and has been the basis of the intellectual development of the human race.[57] Without it we would still be a comparatively undeveloped species; with it we have gone as far as beginning to explore space. The importance of language as a vehicle for sentient development cannot be underestimated. If higher-order animals show an ability to learn and to use language evidencing their possession of sentient capabilities similar to, if not as well developed as our own, it raises more questions about practices which use them as tools, such as experimentation. These uses rest upon the assumption that they are not the same as us. This may not be the case, as Richard Leaky explains:[58]

> [Ape-language studies] tell us that in ape brains, which are the same size and organisation as the brains of *Homo* ancestors, the cognitive foundations on which human language could be built were already present.
>
> This does not prove that those same foundations were present in our ancestors, but to me it is highly suggestive. It tells me that the 'vastness of the gulf between ... man and the brutes' is not as great as many people believe. The sentiment of the 'specialness' of *Homo Sapiens* derives, I'm sure, from the sense of wonder that emanates from human consciousness and self-awareness. But we are in danger of being tricked by its cogency. The evidence from primate language studies suggests that we are not as special as we would like to believe. For me the issue of community is clear: our language skills are firmly rooted in the cognitive abilities of ape brains.

Many other studies have looked at other aspects of non-human animal sentience but have produced less favourable results. A study carried out with baboons in Kenya by Robert Siforth and Dorothy Cheyney led the latter to comment on their sentient capacities: 'they don't know what they know'.[59] Dr

---

56   See, for example, Frey, R, *Interests and Rights*, 1980, Chapter 7, Oxford: Clarendon Press.

57   Leaky and Lewin, above n 51, p 239.

58   *Ibid*, pp 244–45.

59   From Channel Four's *Equinox*, 'Do Vampire Bats Have Friends?', 20 December 1995, UK.

Gerald Williamson, a Biologist at the University of Maryland, conducted a five-year study into whether bats shared food with fellow non-related bats. He found that young bats returned without food approximately 20% of the time and that they were able to 'beg' food from other bats. Describing this as 'friendly' behaviour is possible yet refutable, as it is difficult to say that the bats are actually 'aware' of what they are doing. However, we know from the work of Freud that humans engage in many activities without actually thinking consciously about them.

Scientists such as Dr Celia Hayes have described this type of behaviour as 'robotic', in that it does not give any real evidence of there being an 'internal light' on.[60] Other animals show a variety of complex, 'clever' behaviour: squirrels store food for long periods and know where to find it; some species of birds are able to adopt ingenious methods to get at concealed food; insects use remarkable techniques to conceal themselves or to catch prey; monkeys, birds and otters, for example, use various forms of tools to catch or consume prey. But all these instances could be attributed to the process of natural selection over the millennia, trial and error learning, or just luck.

The implications of the studies presently being carried out by scientists are potentially enormous. Are we prepared to see our legal codes based upon the sole criterion of species membership without any significant underpinning moral basis? Jared Diamond suggests that if we manage to unlock the door to determining animal consciousness then we might, at the very least, have to revise the basis of our laws governing the treatment of animals:[61]

> If our ethical code makes purely arbitrary distinction between humans and all other species, then we have a code based on naked selfishness devoid of any higher principle. If our code instead makes distinctions based on our superior intelligence, social relationships, and our capacity for feeling pain, then it becomes difficult to defend an all-or-nothing code that draws a line between all humans and all animals.

Herein lies the problem for the animal rights lobby. The scientific lobby seems to have a built-in defence to those who argue for enhanced status of animals enforceable by laws aimed at protecting animals in their own right. The question is raised: 'so you think they deserve better status because they possess sentient qualities deserving of protection? – well prove it.' On the other hand, it is argued by those such as Tom Regan, Peter Singer and Mary Midgely: should we not at least give non-human animals the benefit of the doubt?

---

60 Psychologist, University College, London, featured in Channel Four's *Equinox*, 'Do Vampire Bats Have Friends?', above n 59.

61 Diamond, J, *The Rise and Fall of The Third Chimpanzee*, 1991, p 24, London: Vintage.

WHERE MORALITY AND LAW COLLIDE – SOME PHILOSOPHICAL PROBLEMS

It cannot seriously be disputed that the development of law, at all times and places, has in fact been profoundly influenced both by conventional morality and ideals of particular social groups, and also by forms of enlightened moral criticism urged by individuals, whose moral horizon has transcended the morality currently accepted.[62]

Thus are the lines drawn in the debate over the existence or not of animal rights with those who claim to represent a 'transcendent reality' opposed to those who claim to represent prevailing and historical moral beliefs. Does it matter if we make new discoveries about the nature and extent of animal consciousness which affect our philosophical view of animals?

Few doubt that morality matters; indeed, the link between morality and law is the central theme of 'natural lawyers' who argue that they are inextricably linked.[63] Laws have been introduced as a response to specific moral problems, to create a change, and can prove difficult to enforce in the absence of a bond with public morality. It is the call to a higher source of human reason which appeals so much to those in the animal welfare lobby who claim that the present law of the land does not reflect the outcome of moral arguments involved. They argue that, in the light of contemporary philosophical and scientific evidence discussed above, the law should be changed.

Many people in the animal rights lobby claim that fundamental moral rights are being ignored by the law relating to animals, such as the right to live out a life naturally, the right to equal consideration of interests and the right to be treated according to their natural instincts (see Chapter 3). If humankind consists of moral creatures, they contend, then we should seek to fulfil our pleasures and to avoid pains but we should also recognise the consequences of our actions on the pleasures and pains of others, including animals.[64] We should recognise that just as we do not blindly seek our own individual pleasures at the expense of denying another people's pleasure or of inflicting pain upon them, so it should be with animals. We need, they contend, to recognise the inherent wrong in certain human practices and to change our customs and habits. Some people contend that we already satisfy the moral conscience. Animal welfare activists are convinced we do not.

At this point it is probably useful to contrast legal and moral rights. A legal right is reasonably straightforward to recognise. If, for example, a statute gives one the right to vote, then one can claim that right – the right is enshrined in the law and recognised by the law-making body of that country.

---

62 Hart, HLA, *The Concept of Law*, 1961, p 181, Oxford: Clarendon Press.
63 Finnis, J, *Natural Law and Natural Rights*, 1989, 6th edn, Oxford: Clarendon Press.
64 Just as Darwin suggested; see above, p 15.

The argument of those advocating 'moral rights' is that there are fundamental underlying principles which make some laws morally wrong or incomplete. Opponents of this notion argue that there is no such thing as a 'moral right', in that a claim to such a right is merely a claim for one's own preferences, and no 'fundamental truth' or 'natural rights' exist. One can understand this view if one imagines people claiming what they consider to be a 'moral right' but which others consider to be morally wrong: the disputed claims over the issue of abortion clearly show the difficulties in determining what is fundamentally wrong or right as groups assert the 'rights' of the unborn child against those of the mother, or *vice versa*.

The claims for any 'moral rights' of humans and animals, therefore, are criticised on the grounds that to recognise them is dangerous. The criticisms of natural rights by notable scholars such as Bentham[65] lead to the idea of 'legal positivism' which advocates that the only rights are *legal* rights enshrined in the law. To recognise any other rights, it is claimed, would undermine the law by giving credence to those who would subvert the law on the basis of their own self-serving interests. Indeed, Bentham described the claims to natural rights as 'simple nonsense', whilst clearly advocating that the treatment of animals should be brought more closely under the wing of the law. The claim to natural, inalienable moral rights is central to some animal rights arguments as they claim a fundamental moral case for enshrining moral rights of animals in the law. Other writers fall short of claiming rights and settle for the claim for animal *interests* to be enshrined in the law. Perhaps, in the end, what society actually calls the claims of the animal rights lobby – 'rights' or 'interests' – is of no significant consequence. What becomes crucial is that the moral foundation of the law is sound and we recognise moral claims for change where justified, whether or not we call these moral claims 'rights' or not.[66]

The following excerpts are taken from Hans Reusch's indictment of the pro-experimentation lobby, *Slaughter of the Innocent*, which illustrate why he feels that morality is a crucial determinant of the law. He seems to have little doubt that morality/philosophy should have an impact on the development of law:[67]

> Man is a moral creature. The moral sense is so deeply rooted in human beings that no thief, no murderer has ever asked the abrogation of the penalties against theft and murder.
>
> All the laws that have ruled human organisation in the past and rule them at present are based on the moral sense: on what is right and wrong. And no

---

65 Harris, JW, *Legal Philosophies*, 1980, pp 17–18, London: Butterworths.

66 See, for example, Midgely, M, *Animals and Why They Matter*, 1983, Chapter 5, Athens: University of Georgia Press.

67 Ruesch, H, *Slaughter of the Innocent*, 1983, pp 327–28 and 333, New York: Civitas Publications. By permission of Hans Ruesch.

religion, no legislature has ever deemed it necessary to define right and wrong, because no one has any doubt as to the meaning of these terms.

Only the worshippers of the pseudoscience of modern times regard morality and immorality, justice and injustice, good and evil, as anti-scientific concepts, since it is not possible to reproduce them in a laboratory.

Anybody who like Italy's Professor Silvio Garattini can declare that an artificial hormone, fabricated in a laboratory, is identical – in every respect – with a hormone produced by a living organism, will never comprehend the moral law, as the moral law can't be exposed by a surgeon's lancet nor reproduced in a test tube. And that explains also how monkey-head transplanter Dr Robert White from Cleveland can affirm that 'dehumanisation does not exist', only because, having himself lost or never possessed the notion of humaneness, he is incapable of noticing its absence; and can say that the animals don't suffer, simply because he is not sensitive to their pains – only to his own. Asked Thomas Wolfe: 'Is there no light because the blind can't see?'

The reasonings of the vivisectionists are unscientific because they don't take into account the intangible realities of life. The moral law is one such intangible reality: And it is the incomprehension of this reality that marks the inescapable failure of experimental science when applied to living beings, with its inevitable sequence of tragic errors.

He goes on to explain how profoundly this finding would effect the framework of the law:

In all countries the antivivisectionist are divided into two factions – 'controlists' and 'abolitionists', who both accuse the other of hampering the progress of the cause. The controlists include some doctors and veterinaries who claim that they want the 'abuses' of vivisection outlawed, but not the 'indispensable' experiments, usually without going on record as to which ones they consider 'indispensable'.

Abolitionists point out that the whole history of medicine hasn't brought forth one single case of an animal experiment that has been irrefutably useful for man, whereas the misleading answers, causes of immeasurable harm and endless tragedies, can't even be counted. And since vivisection is also morally wrong, it can only be outlawed, not 'regulated'.

If something is morally wrong, no amount of legislation can make it right. The abolitionists further contend that abolition would immediately cause medical science to progress, obliging it to abandon the wrong road, and to concentrate on the more dependable alternative methods of research, and especially on the far more effective preventive medicine, which harms nobody, not even the citizens' pocketbook – but is therefore financially unrewarding.

Roger Scruton, however, urges extreme caution before we embark upon legislation which dictates morality:[68]

---

68   Scruton, R, *Animal Rights and Wrongs*, 1996, pp 106–07, London: Demos. By permission of Demos, 9 Bridewell Place, London EC4V 6AP (0171 353 4479).

Even where there is substantial moral agreement, we may feel reluctant to enshrine our moral judgement in law, for fear that to do so would involve too great an encroachment on the liberties of the subject. An example of this is adultery, almost universally disapproved of but not, in our country, forbidden by law. To make this sin, to which so many are tempted, into a crime would be to bind human beings in intolerable chains and so bring the law into disrepute. Still more is it dangerous to legislate on moral grounds against activities like horse-racing or shooting, in which a substantial minority participate and in which they find a joy and fulfilment which they do not regard as immoral at all.

This does not mean that we should never legislate. It means that we should be as clear as possible concerning the ground on which we do so. And the principal ground relates, I believe, to the concept of virtue. I shall illustrate this point with a parallel example.

In our society, all kinds of sexual practices are permitted between consenting adults, provided that they take place in private. However, the publishing of certain kinds of pornographic material, even material in which normal practices are displayed, is forbidden by law. Why is this? Surely because we believe that the *interest* in pornography is corrupt. It is an interest in sex divorced from the moral context provided by human love, an interest which de-personalises the sexual act, makes the object of desire into an object *tout court*, and turns sex into a commodity. This is wrong not because it does harm to others, but because it does harm to the self. The law does not, as a rule, forbid our private actions, provided that they are mediated by consent. But it has an interest in moral corruption, since law is the guardian of society and would be ineffective in a world where the sources of social feeling had all been polluted.

Some ways of treating animals can be compared to pornography in that they minister to a comparable corruption. Dog-fights and bear-baiting, in which the object of interest is (or at any rate, seems to be) the pain, fear and helplessness of an innocent victim, can interest only a hardened heart, and one obsessed by flesh, by the machinery of suffering, and by the pornography of pain. Like sexual pornography, these practices encourage an interest in flesh as something objective, curious and without any moral claim on us. They place a veil between the world and our response to it, and poison the soul of those who watch them. Such spectacles are naturally forbidden by law, since they threaten the personality of those who attend them.

That is only one example. But it helps us to see why a civilised system of law may permit many immoralities, but nevertheless forbid deliberate cruelty. It can permit ritual slaughter, shooting and horse-racing, in which actual suffering is the known effect of what is done, while forbidding dog-fighting or bear-baiting, in which this suffering becomes an object of interest for its own sake.

... One thing is clear, however, which is that modern societies suffer from too much legislation, concerning matters in which lawyers and politicians are not necessarily the highest authorities. We are faced with a question that humanity is perhaps confronting for the first time in its true form – namely how to behave towards other species, in a world where all of us are competing for survival. The least that can be said is that we should discuss and digest the moral question, before embarking on a legislative solution to it.

The study of animal rights is, essentially, a study of what is right or wrong in our treatment of animals in light of what we know or, indeed, have yet to find out about them. This moral debate has led to the introduction of legislation regarding animals and will probably lead to more. In relation to animal rights there are clear differences in the public perceptions of whether certain practices are right or wrong. If the level of protest in 1995 is anything to go by, many people in the UK seem to have agreed in recent times that unnecessary cruelty such as long distance transportation of animals without rest or feeding is morally wrong, but many also seem to support the use of animals in, for example, experimentation or agriculture. There are conflicting, incompatible emotions which pervade our public consciousness, allowing us to accept the suffering of animals in a laboratory but not those in a lorry. The moral perceptions of the public differ quite widely, sometimes inexplicably, from one manifestation of our interaction with animals to another, and a coherent underlying principle is often difficult to find.

Other philosophical and moral questions are raised regarding many aspects of the whole animals issue. The tactics employed by the animal welfare lobby in the pursuit of their notion of 'moral justice' are frequently criticised as being morally questionable in themselves. How should they go about campaigning for revised laws and changing our relationship with animals? Should their tactics be peaceful and persuasive, or more direct and confrontational? Should animal welfare groups concentrate on seeking to influence public morality, or should they try to directly influence the legislators? There is no consensus on any of these issues; the debate is often heated and marked by public disagreements, resignations, angry written exchanges and vitriolic personal attacks. Conversely, there are those who proceed more carefully, choosing to engage in influencing incremental change by cooperative and less intimidating means. The reality of the animal welfare debate contains, it seems, a recognition of many philosophical attitudes to the whole animals debate.

The role of government in the development of the law is absolutely crucial, as a failure to influence the law-makers will usually result in a failure to secure changes in the law, despite public opinion. History tells us, however, that it is possible for Parliament to create changes in public morality, in spite of an adverse initial responses to legislation. It has been argued that it was precisely this which happened after the Wolfenden Committee Report recommended a liberalisation of the laws concerning homosexuality.[69] Lord

---

69 Warnock, M, 'Law and the Pursuit of Knowledge' (January 1986) *Conquest* (Journal of the Research Defence Society) 175.

Devlin argued against the Report, on the basis that a change in the law would fail to reflect the prevailing social attitude in this area. However, the law was changed, and with it attitudes towards homosexuals have certainly relaxed. This does appear to be a clear case of Parliament directly effecting a change in public morality.

The forthcoming chapters will examine the moral arguments surrounding some of the core human activities involving animals. There will be an examination of some of the suggested tangible improvements which could be made in the light of moral inquiry regarding facets of these practices, many of which seem to be rooted in custom and practice passed down the centuries. Humankind has not reached a consensus on the treatment of its fellow creatures, as the strength of feelings aroused by this subject will show, but the morality of these practices is at the very core of our discussion as human society continues to evolve into the 21st century.

FURTHER READING

Clarke, AB and Linzey, A, *Political Theory and Animal Rights*, 1990, London: Pluto Press. An excellent overview of the status of animals through the thoughts of many of the leading philosophers and writers in human history.

Garner, R, *Animals, Politics and Morality*, 1993, Chapter 1, Manchester: Manchester University Press. A critical overview of the various approaches to the status of animals.

Smith, J and Boyd, K (eds), *Lives in the Balance: The Ethics of Using Animals in Biomedical Research*, 1991, Chapter 11, Oxford: Oxford University Press. This chapter contains an accessible overview of the historical and contemporary discussion of the moral status of animals.

Sperlinger, D, 'Natural relations – Contemporary views of the Relationship between Humans and Other Animals', in Sperlinger, D (ed), *Animals in Research: New Perspectives in Animal Experimentation*, 1981, Chichester: John Wiley and Sons.

CHAPTER TWO

HISTORICAL AND CONTEMPORARY LEGAL ATTITUDES TO ANIMALS

HOW HAS THE LAW TREATED ANIMALS?

Humankind's use of animals stretches back into prehistory, but the protection of animals through the use of law is only a relatively recent development. Contemporary legal approaches to animals primarily attempt to protect other species from some of the more morally questionable practices of humans in the form of abuse, neglect or mistreatment; however, a glance through the pages of history shows a far different picture. For centuries animals had no legal protection, being treated merely as property, not deserving of welfare protection and even, on occasion, the recipients of harsh treatment as the result of legal proceedings against them: 'Justice, indeed, so far as animals are concerned, seems in earlier days to have dispensed altogether with her scales, and to have worn a permanent bandage over that eye which should have been turned to the wrongs [against] dumb creatures.'[1]

We shall examine four notable periods in the history of the treatment of animals in law where adequate records exist, which together provide a detailed picture of how the legal status of animals has developed: Ancient Greece; the period of Roman domination of Europe; medieval Europe, mainly from the 13th century onwards; and England in the 18th and 19th centuries. The legal status accorded to animals at these times is particularly interesting as it either illustrates a sharp contrast to modern-day legal attitudes to animals or is recognisable as providing the bedrock upon which present legal attitudes were built.

The first well-documented era which reveals a different attitude towards animals than we have today begins with the ancient Greeks. Plato (427–347 BC) produced works which put forward the ideal structure and functioning of the relationship between the State and the individual in *The Republic* and *Laws*, much of which was based upon the Athens which Plato knew. He described how the law treated animals 'accused' of murder:[2]

> If a draught animal or any other beast kill a person, unless it be in a combat authorised and instituted by the State, the kinsmen of the slain shall prosecute the said homicide for murder, and the overseers of the public lands, as many as may be commissioned by the said kinsmen, shall adjudicate upon the case and send the offender beyond the boundaries of the country.

---

1 Fairholme, E, *A Century of Work for Animals*, 1924, London: John Murray.
2 Plato (*De Leg*, IX.12).

These 'trials', along with trials where the person accused could not be traced and the prosecution of inanimate objects which had caused a death, took place outside the ancient Greek equivalent of a town hall cum community centre, the 'Prytaeneum', in the open air so that the judges would not be tainted by 'contaminated air' emanating from the accused.[3] Walter Woodburn Hyde explains:[4]

> [Regarding] the trial of animals, we know but little, only the fact that such trials were held here. They probably were based on the same principle as those of inanimate things. Not that the Greeks were obsessed, at least in the historical period, with the idea that animals any more than things were morally responsible for their acts – though this was probably at the bottom of such trials, as it certainly was in the case of things; but rather they held the general notion that the moral equilibrium of the community had been disturbed by the murder and that somebody must be punished or else dire misfortune in the form of plagues, droughts, and reverses in men's fortunes would overtake the land. So the ideal legislation of Plato on this point was based upon the same idea which was at the bottom of all the murder laws of Athens – that the Erinys or avenging spirit of the dead man must be appeased. In substance this was merely another manifestation of the *lex talionis*,[5] the oldest and deepest rooted of all human laws, axiomatic in all primitive societies, and traceable ... even in the most advanced. Greek literature furnishes many examples of the idea of 'blood for blood'. Whether the slaying was premeditated or not made no difference, for in either case a crime had been committed and a pollution had appeared in the community which must be removed.

The Greeks, Hyde suggests, were the only ancient civilisation to use such trials but the ancient Persians punished animals by decree; for example, a dog, which would be punished by: 'progressive mutilation corresponding with the number of persons or beasts bitten, beginning with the loss of the ears and ending with the amputation of the tail.'[6]

Despite their harsh attitude to their fellow creatures the Greeks extended humanitarian attitudes between each other, firstly to barbarians and then to animals. The philosophers Empedocles and Pythagoras extended the notion of 'community' as existing not just between humans but also between humans and the animal world. Indeed, Pythagoras went further than any Western legal system has ever done, by declaring the killing of an animal to be murder.[7] Despite this evidence of the diverse treatment of animals in law in Ancient Greece, the principal application of the law to animals was in relation to their status as property. There is some dispute amongst contemporary

---

3   Hyde, WW, 'The Prosecution and Punishment of Animals and Lifeless Things in the Middle Ages and Modern Times' (1916) 64 *Pensylvanian Law Review* 696–730 at 698.

4   *Ibid*, at 698.

5   Retribution and revenge.

6   Hyde, above n 3, p 700.

7   Jones, J, Law and Legal Theory of the Greeks, 1956, p 62, Oxford: Clarendon Press.

commentators on Ancient Greek law as to whether animals were considered as coming as part and parcel of the land upon which they were farmed.[8]

The Romans, whose influence dominated the period from 510 BC to AD 565, also regarded animals as being property, in a similar way to the Greeks. Animals were treated as 'things' in that they were classified as capable of being privately owned.[9] They were treated as *res mancipi* which is described by Andrew Borkowski as 'things useful or essential to the household in early Roman society.'[10] He goes on to describe the place of animals within this definition which was important in determining how *dominium* (acquisition) was obtained, as property could only be transferred in the way appropriate to its classification:[11]

> According to Gaius (*Institutes*, 2.14a) *res mancipi* comprised the following things: slaves, beasts of burden, Italic land, houses on such land and rustic praedial servitudes (ie easements and profits over land). As regards the animals, there was juristic dispute about the moment when the beasts became *res mancipi* – the Sabinians claimed it was at birth, whereas the Proulians held that it was when the animal was broken in. Gaius lists oxen, horses, mules and donkeys as examples of beasts of burden, but the list appears to be comprehensive – no other animals seem to have been regarded as *res mancipi*. Once the category of *res mancipi* was established in early law, it did not prove susceptible to amendment. For example, camels and elephants could be regarded as beasts of burden but were 'discovered' by the Romans after the list of *res mancipi* was established – so they did not qualify. The most probable reason for the reluctance to expand the list of *res mancipi* was that the formal modes of conveyancing necessary to transfer *dominium* in such things increasingly came to be seen as cumbersome and inconvenient.

Borkowski explains how acquisition of *res mancipi* could be obtained by the formal modes of conveyance – *mancipatio* and *cessio*. These modes of conveyance were indeed complicated: *mancipatio* was a mode of title transfer which, according to Gaius, required the presence of the transferor and transferee, at least five witnesses, a prescribed set of words and a set of scales;[12] *Cessio*, although similarly cumbersome to *mancipatio*, differed in that it involved a magistrate, a different set of formal words and no scales.[13]

Acquisition of wild animals could also be obtained in Roman times, but in a different way:[14]

---

8   Harrison, ARW, *The Law of Athens: The Family and Property*, 1968, p 229, Oxford: Oxford University Press.

9   Borkowski, A, *Textbook on Roman Law*, 1994, p 143, London: Blackstone Press.

10 *Ibid*, p 146.

11 *Ibid*, pp 145–46.

12 *Ibid*, p 189.

13 *Ibid*, p 190.

14 Buckland, W, *A Textbook of Roman Law from Augustus to Justinian*, 1932, pp 205–06, Cambridge: Cambridge University Press.

[*Occupatio*] was acquisition by taking. It was not of great significance, its chief importance being in relation to wild animals captured for food or other purposes. These were acquired only when effectively seized, which was true of all *occupatio*, but there was in their case the further rule that the ownership lasted only while they were effectively held, subject to the modification that of certain things, eg bees and pigeons, the ownership lasted only so long as they retained the habit of returning to their quarters – *animus revertendi*. The question what amounted to such capture as gave effect to the intent to acquire is, in effect, what amounts to gaining possession. It was agreed after disputes that a wounded animal was not 'occupied' til seized. We are not told whether killing itself was enough and, as to trapping, the matter seems to have depended somewhat on the position of the trap.

What amounted to loss of control is again a question of fact: clearly it was not lost while the owner was in close pursuit: perhaps the true account is that the beast ceased to be owned when the chance of recovering him was not materially greater than that of capturing any other wild animal. To the question why ownership was, in this case, limited by possession, the answer may be that the whole institution antedates law: it comes from a time when the strong man armed, and he alone, held his goods in peace. The rule had a curious result. If a beast escaped, and, when free from control, did damage, the owner was not responsible: it was not his beast. He need not therefore keep it securely however dangerous it was. The [edict of] aediles met the case by a provision that one who kept wild beasts of certain kinds near a highway was responsible for any damage they did. In later law this was extended to any wild animal.

Turning to the third historical chapter, the Middle Ages, records here reveal that, as early as the 9th century, animals were sometimes treated as morally culpable in the same way as people. Most of these cases appear to have been recorded from the 13th century, when animals were prosecuted for a wide range of criminal offences such as being noisy in church, murder and damage to property as well as being afforded protection normally reserved for people. Animals were prosecuted in the ecclesiastical courts with sentences ranging from banishment or excommunication, to the death penalty:[15]

The reason for indicting wild animals before ecclesiastical courts was ... purely a practical one. They were anonymous sinners. It was difficult to arrest them, and impossible to bring a whole company of them, a swarm of locusts for example, into court, although occasionally representative members of the species were caught and compelled to sit – if sit is the right word – through the proceedings. As a rule, however, it was found difficult to exercise an ordinary sentence against a multiplicity of creatures, many of them very small, and therefore the divine judgment had to be invoked upon their sins by means of a sentence of excommunication, exactly as it was invoked against human criminals whose identities were unknown. This difficulty of recognition did not, of course, occur in the case of domestic animals which committed crimes. They were in the same position as human criminals whose identity could not

---

15 Hill, R, *Both Small and Great Beasts*, 1961, p 11, London: Universities Federation for Animal Welfare.

be established, and like human criminals they could, in many parts of Europe, be compelled to stand their trials in the lay courts of justice. While awaiting trial they appear sometimes to have been confined in prison together with human beings in like case, and to have received approximately the same treatment. For example, in 1408 a pig accused of murder was shut up in the prison of Pont l'Arch and the gaoler claimed for its maintenance exactly the same sum as for each of the men who shared its captivity.

Gerald Carson has commented that: 'It requires a considerable act of imagination for a person living in the culture of the 20th century to understand the involute thought of the medieval legal mind, and the high seriousness of our ancestors in arraigning cabbageworms, he-goats, and indeed, all animal kind, domestic and wild, in a court of justice where to the solemn tolling of bells they were tried ...'.[16] The following extract from a piece by Hampton L Carson illustrates what must indeed have been, by modern day standards of animal welfare, a most bizarre scene of cruelty:[17]

In the open square of the old Norman city of Falaise, in the year 1386, a vast and motley crowd had gathered to witness the execution of a criminal convicted of murder. Noblemen in armour, proud dames in velvet and feathers, priests in cassock and cowl, falconers with hawks upon their wrists, huntsmen with hounds in leash, aged men with their staves, withered hags with their baskets or reticules, children of all ages and even babes in arms were among the spectators. The prisoner was dressed in a new suit of man's clothes, and was attended by armed men on horseback, while the hangman before mounting the scaffold had provided himself with new gloves and a new rope. As the prisoner had caused the death of a child by mutilating the face and arms to such an extent as to cause a fatal haemorrhage, the town tribunal, or local court, had decreed that the head and legs of the prisoner should be mangled with a knife before the hanging. This was the medieval application of the *lex talionis,* or 'an eye for an eye and a tooth for a tooth.' To impress a recollection of the scene upon the memories of the bystanders an artist was employed to paint a fresco on the west wall of the transept of the Church of the Holy Trinity in Falaise, and for more than 400 years that picture could be seen and studied until destroyed in 1820 by the carelessness of a white-washer. The criminal was not a human being but a sow, which had indulged in the evil propensity of eating infants on the street.

Some churchmen were of the opinion that it was wrong for the Church to prosecute animals as it was based on the assumption that animals have some relationship with God. Despite these reservations, the writings of St Thomas Aquinas[18] were certainly an influential factor in the treatment of animals in the middle ages, as described by ES Turner:[19]

16 Carson, G, *Men, Beasts and Gods,* 1972, pp 25–26, New York: Charles Scribner's and Sons.

17 Carson, HL, 'The Trial of Animals and Insects: A Little Known Chapter of Medieval Jurisprudence' (1917) 56 *American Philosophical Society Journal* 410–15 at 410.

18 See Chapter 1.

19 Turner, ES, *All Heaven in a Rage,* 1992, 2nd edn, p 26, Fontwell, Sussex: Centaur Press. By permission of ES Turner and Centaur Press.

Although they were deemed to have no souls, animals could be possessed by evil spirits. St Thomas said it was legitimate to curse animals 'as satellites of Satan instigated by the powers of Hell.' That ruling, in conjunction with the harsh law laid down in *Exodus*, was enough to authorise the custom of putting animals on trial for grievous 'crimes' and executing them with all the ignominy and high-flown sentiment reserved for human offenders. In 1386 at Falaise a pig was condemned to be mutilated and hanged on a gibbet for having killed a child; it was dressed in a man's cloths and hanged in the square. In 1408 the Russians sent a refractory he-goat to Siberia. At Basle in 1474 a cock was convicted of laying a egg (a dire offence, since cock's eggs hatched cockatrices for sorcerers) and was publicly burned along with its monstrous eggs. Pigs seem to have been the usual victims, but cows, bulls, horses and cats were also strung up. In the 15th and 16th centuries men accused of *'un crime que nous ne pouvons designer'*[20] were burned along with the violated beast, which might or might not be strangled first. Winged nuisances could not be brought before a religious tribunal, but they could be cursed collectively. After the 16th century the custom of putting animals on trial petered out and the law took action instead against the owner of the offending beast.

Animals were certainly assumed to understand the nature of what they were doing, which led one distraught pastor in Dresden in 1559 to appeal to the Elector of Saxony for help in bringing to justice sparrows for 'their incessant and extremely vexatious chatterings, and scandalous acts of unchastity committed during the sermon'.[21] As a final example of the extent to which the full ambit of legal procedure was applied to animals, it is worth considering the proceedings in a French ecclesiastical court in Autun in 1522. Some rats were summoned to appear before the court for having destroyed barley crops in the local area. When they failed to appear on the given day their counsel, Bartholomew Chassenée defended them by saying that the summons had not been circulated widely enough. In consequence, a further summons was circulated to all the parishes within the bishopric, but still not a single rat appeared on the given day. Chassenée was quick to explain this occurrence in that it would take a considerable amount of time for the rats to spread the word and gather together from their far-flung homes. The court accepted this and granted a delay in the proceedings, but not a single rat appeared. Chassenée had yet another explanation, in that the rats were disturbed by the possible presence of the plaintiffs' cats in the area and were scared to appear unless assured they would be protected. The court, naturally, accepted this, and, in consequence of a delay in further action by the plaintiffs, judgment was finally entered in default to the defendants.[22]

Records kept in churches across Europe show that the practice of prosecuting animals was not confined to any individual country but was

---

20 A crime which we cannot designate.

21 Hill, above n 15, p 10.

22 See Carson, above n 17, p 411; Carson, G, above n 16, p 31.

widespread, and persisted until as late as 1906 in one Swiss case.[23] Most recorded cases were in France, due to better record-keeping rather than a greater inclination to prosecute animals on their part. There are some 200 cases recorded on this curious chapter in the development of European jurisprudence. EP Evans discusses why animals might have been involved in judicial proceedings:[24]

> A Swiss jurist, Eduard Osenbrüggen (*Studien zur Deutschen und Schweizerischen Rechtsgeschichte*. Schaffhusen, 1868, pp 139–49), endeavours to explain these judicial proceedings on the theory of the personification of animals. As only a human being can commit crime and thus render himself liable to punishment, he concludes that it is only by an act of personification that the brute can be placed in the same category as man and become subject to the same penalties. In support of this view, he refers to the fact that in ancient and medieval times domestic animals were regarded as members of the household and entitled to the same legal protection as human vassals. In the Frankish capitularies, all beasts of burden or so-called juments were included in the King's ban and enjoyed the peace guaranteed by royal authority: *Ut jumenta pacem habent similiter per bannum regis.* The weregild extended to them as it did to women and serfs under cover of the man as master of the house and lord of the manor. The *beste covert*, to use the old legal phraseology, was thus invested with human rights and inferentially endowed with human responsibilities. According to old Welsh law, atonement was made for killing a cat or dog belonging to another person by suspending the animal by the tail so that its nozzle touched the ground, and then pouring wheat over it until its body was entirely covered. Old Germanic law also recognised the competency of these animals as witnesses in certain cases, as, for example, when burglary had been committed by night, in the absence of human testimony, the householder was permitted to appear before the court and make complaint, carrying on his arm a dog, cat or cock, and holding in his hand three straws taken from the roof as symbols of the house. Symbolism and personification, as applied to animals and inanimate objects, unquestionably played an important role in primitive legislation, but this principle does not account for the ex-communication and anathematisation of noxious vermin or for the criminal prosecution and capital punishment of homicidal beasts, nor does it throw the faintest light upon the origin and purpose of such proceedings.

Eduard Osenbrüggen's explanation, therefore, is not entirely satisfactory to Evans, who regards the prosecution of animals and witches as having arisen from the same basic superstitions as a result of the aggressive spreading of the Christian faith in northern Europe. One of the tools inevitably used in order to convert the masses was fear, and this led to 'demons' being identified in all manner of persons and animals, leading directly to their prosecution for all

---

23   Hyde, above n 3, p 709.
24   Evans, EP, *The Criminal Prosecution and Capital Punishment of Animals*, 1987 edn, pp 10–11, London: Faber & Faber. Reproduced with kind permission of Faber & Faber.

manner of 'offences'. This encouragement of superstitious beliefs combined with a peculiar sense of equity was a lethal combination which obliterated common sense:[25]

> The penal prosecution of animals, which prevailed during the Middle Ages, was by no means peculiar to that period, but has been frequently practised by primitive peoples and savage tribes; neither was it designed to inculcate any such moral lesson as is here suggested, nor did it produce any such desirable result. So far from originating in a delicate and sensitive sense of justice, it was ... the outcome of an extremely crude, obtuse, and barbaric sense of justice. It was the product of a social State, in which dense ignorance was governed by brute force, and is not to be considered as a reaction and protest against club-law, which it really tended to foster by making a travesty of the administration of justice and thus turning it into ridicule. It was also in the interest of ecclesiastical dignities to keep up this parody and perversion of a sacred and fundamental institute of civil society, since it strengthened their influence and extended their authority by subjecting even the caterpillar and the canker-worm to their dominion and control.

Whether the medieval prosecution of animals was due to the Church wishing to enhance its influence, a barbaric form of retribution and revenge, personification of animals, by way of an illustration of punishment, or to instil obedience and moral behaviour in people, may never become absolutely clear. In light of the fact that humans were also the subjects of barbaric treatment, it is no surprise to find that evidence of the medieval prosecution of animals confirms that animals were also the subjects of brutal treatment and the full weight of the law. But if anyone is of a mind to consign these incidences of inhumane or illogical treatment of animals to anomalies of distant history, it is sobering to remember, as mentioned earlier, that a dog was sentenced to death as late as 1906 in Switzerland. In present times destruction of animals, most usually dogs which have attacked people, is common even where there is no more than evidence of natural behaviour. Justification for such action is normally based upon considerations of human safety, rather than the moral culpability of the animal itself, but still represents a form of 'capital punishment' of animals which the animals themselves could never properly contemplate or understand.

In the final period of history which is examined in this chapter we encounter the protection of the welfare of animals, a much more recent phenomenon which has flourished alongside the maintenance of the status of animals as property in law. An early indication of the perceived need to protect against the unnecessary suffering of animals is illustrated by early 17th century regulations limiting the speed of postal services out of a respect for the horses and the owners thereof, and attempts in Ireland to regulate the

---

25   *Ibid*, pp 40–41.

practice of yoking horses to the plough by their tails.[26] But the first substantial early attempt to secure some kind of protection for animals occurred in the US, albeit on a small scale, when the Puritans of the Massachusetts Bay Colony passed their 'Body of Liberties'. This was the work of an Englishman, Nathanial Ward, a barrister educated in Cambridge who emigrated to New England in 1634. Accepted by the General Court of Massachusetts in 1641, the Body of Liberties included a section on animals: 'No man shall exercise any tirranny or crueltie towards any bruite creature which are usuallie kept for man's use'. There was also a section protecting animals in transit, outlining that animals should be fit before travelling and should be cared for during transit: 'If any man shall have occasion to leade or drive Cattel from place to place that is far of, so that they be weary, or hungry, or fall sick, or lambe, it shall be lawful to rest or refresh them, for a competent time, in any open place that is not Corne, meadow, or enclosed for some peculiar use.'[27]

Some writers and philosophers had shown concern about the treatment of animals in the centuries before anything was formalised in law.[28] Specific legislation came about due to significant pressure group politics. Keith Thomas explains one of the chief reasons for this climate of social change:[29]

> The triumph of the new attitude was closely linked to the growth of towns and the emergence of an industrial order in which animals became increasingly marginal to the processes of production. This industrial order first emerged in England; as a result, it was there that concern for animals was most widely expressed, though the movement was far from being peculiar to this country.

Consequently, the historical roots of modern animal welfare legislation are to be found in the UK, where the long line of legislative protection of animals began with an unsuccessful battle to secure legal protection for bulls as a result of bull-baiting in the 19th century. This activity had grown in popularity as with bear-baiting and, in addition to sites for regular meetings, could occur at almost any major public gathering. Along with cockfighting, which was associated with gambling in the taverns, these dubious practices had become entrenched aspects of English life as the general population sought entertainment and recreation: 'The bastard sport of baiting ... afforded pleasure to princes and ruffians alike. For no discernible reason, the English were more addicted to this pastime than other nations ...'.[30]

---

26 Thomas, K, *Man and the Natural World: Changing Attitudes in England 1500–1800*, 1983, p 189, London: Allen Lane.

27 For more detail see Leavitt, E, *Animals and Their Legal Rights*, 1978, p 11, Washington: Animal Welfare Institute.

28 See Chapter 1.

29 Thomas, above n 26, pp 181–82.

30 Turner, above n 19, p 33.

The campaign to improve the legal protection of animals came in the late 18th century and early 19th century when the educated classes of England became concerned about human attitudes towards each other in terms of welfare and, in a similar vein, more concerned about the treatment of animals. Welfare for animals became caught up in the debates concerning the welfare of children, the sick, the needy, the old and the insane.[31] The writing of people such as Jeremy Bentham played an influential part in this revolution in attitudes serving as a focus for widespread concern.[32] As English tourists went abroad in the late 18th century they were often shocked at the treatment of animals. After witnessing 15 or 16 bulls die at a Portuguese bullfight, William Beckford commented: 'I was highly disgusted with the spectacle'.[33]

Men had been severely punished for apparently cruel acts before the turn of the 19th century, but the perpetrators had been punished for malicious destruction or deprecation of another man's property, not because of any legal rights enjoyed by the animal itself. In 1793, for example, John Cornish was found not guilty of maliciously maiming a horse, even though he had ripped its tongue out. This followed a ruling by the judge that he could only be guilty if it was shown that the wounding occurred because of *malice shown towards the owner of it*, an attitude which continued into the early years of the 19th century.[34]

In some ways the choice of bull-baiting as the first attempt at wholesale legislative change was a strange one. At the time, the suffering of many other animals, such as horses used for transport purposes, was recognised as being of much greater magnitude in terms of the number of animals involved.[35] But the bull-baiting issue took on significance because of the distaste shown towards it as an exercise undertaken purely for human 'enjoyment and pleasure' at fairs and wakes. Indeed, many similarities can be seen in the comparison with the modern day arguments against hunting, which maintains a high public profile even though, arguably, more animals suffer in the production of food and in scientific experimentation. Figure 2.1 shows the events leading to the passing of the first major piece of animal welfare legislation in the world, and was the first move towards that '*jus animalium*' for which Bentham had pleaded.[36]

---

31 French, RD, *Antivivisection and Medical Science in Victorian Society*, 1975, pp 23–24, Princeton: Princeton University Press.

32 See Chapter 1.

33 Thomas, above n 26, p 143.

34 Turner, above n 19, p 104.

35 Evans, above n 24, p 105.

36 For a fuller account of the parliamentary struggle for the need for some animal welfare protection in the early 19th century, see Turner, above n 19, Chapters 10 and 11; Carson, above n 16, Chapter 5.

Figure 2.1 Events leading to the passing of the first major piece of animal welfare legislation.

Year	Legislative Event	Comments
1800	First Bill to put down bull-baiting.	Introduced by Sir William Pulteney and opposed by the then Secretary of War, William Windham, on the grounds that the Bill was anti-working class. Bill failed by 43 votes to 41.
1802	Second Bill to put down bull-baiting.	Introduced by William Wilberforce and opposed again by Windham who now claimed that the bulls derived satisfaction from the baiting. He also claimed that the attempt to deny the working class their pleasures was unconstitutional and that the upper-class reformers should look at their own 'rich sports' such as hunting and racing first. Bill lost 64:51.
1809	Bill to introduce 'rights' for animals.	Introduced by former Lord Chancellor, Lord Erskine, to protect 'domesticated' animals such as cattle and horses. The Bill was aimed at proscribing malicious wounding, wanton cruelty, beating and other abuse of horses and cattle. Opposed by Windham on the grounds that it might prejudice the rights of property, that men should be trusted to regulate their own behaviour and that the legislation would be too difficult and arbitrary to enforce. Bill lost after much indecision before the committee stage.
1821	Ill Treatment of horses Bill.	Introduced by the new champion in Parliament of the animal-welfare movement, Richard Martin, MP for Galway in Ireland where he was known as a 'benevolent despot' and was a follower of field sports himself. When another MP suggested it should be extended to asses the House erupted with laughter, suggesting that dogs, then cats, would be next! Bill lost.
1822	Ill treatment of Horses and Cattle Bill introduced. Royal Assent given 22 June 1822.	Introduced, once again, by Martin this Bill became the first notable legislative success of the animal-welfare lobby in the world. The Act, now referred to as 'Martin's Act' made it an offence to 'beat, abuse, or ill-treat any horse, mare, gelding, mule, ass, ox, cow, heifer, steer, sheep or other cattle.' Infringements of the Act were penalised by a minimum fine of 10s and a maximum of two months' imprisonment. The Act proved difficult to enforce, with Martin taking to the streets himself and bringing offenders to the attention of the authorities in court.

The text of the 1822 Act was as follows.

An Act to prevent the cruel and improper Treatment of Cattle. [22 July 1822.][37]

Whereas it is expedient to prevent the cruel and improper Treatment of Horses, Mares, Geldings, Mules, Asses, Cows, Heifers, Steers, Oxen, Sheep and other Cattle: May it therefore please Your Majesty that it may be enacted: And be it enacted by the King's most Excellent Majesty, by and with the Advice and Consent of the Lords Spiritual and Temporal, and Commons, in this present Parliament assembled, and by the Authority of the same, That if any Person or Persons shall wantonly and cruelly beat, abuse or ill treat any Horse, Mare, Gelding, Mule, Ass, Ox, Cow, Heifer, Steer, Sheep or other Cattle, and Complaint on Oath thereof be made to any Justice of the Peace or other Magistrate within whose Jurisdiction such Offence shall be committed, it shall be lawful for such Justice of the Peace or other Magistrate to issue his Summons or Warrant, at his Discretion, to bring the Party or Parties so complained of before him, or any other Justice of the Peace or other Magistrate of the County, City or Place within which such Justice of the Peace or other Magistrate has Jurisdiction, who shall examine upon Oath any Witness or Witnesses who shall appear or be produced to give information touching such Offence, ...

Richard Martin – 'Humanity Dick', as he was known to George IV – is a remarkable figure in the development of the law relating to animals. As Member of Parliament for Galway he deflected the ridicule aimed at him in the House of Commons because he wanted to protect animals through the use of law, and succeeded where Lord Erskine had earlier failed.[38] Known as a benevolent character, Martin was a knowledgeable and astute Parliamentarian with a sense of humour and an ability to hold the attention of the House. These 'winning ways', along with a steely character, illustrated by his brushes with *The Times* over their misquoting of him,[39] helped him accomplish what some had thought impossible and others thought ridiculous. He brought the first case under his Act himself when he had two men, Samuel Clarke and David Hyde, arrested for beating horses at Smithfield market in London. Both were convicted and fined 20 shillings each. Despite his championing the cause of animals and actively seeking out offenders, he was noted for his kindness of heart in relation to the treatment of offenders. He is known to have offered to pay the fines imposed on offenders himself, happy that they had learned their lesson, scared to death by Martin's formidable reputation.[40] He addressed the first annual meeting of the Society for the

---

37 D 1822, 3 Geo 4, C 70.

38 For an account of Erskine's early attempts to introduce legislation see Hostettler, J, 'Thomas Erskine and Animals' Rights' (November 1995) 45 *Justice of the Peace and Local Government Review*, at 159.

39 Turner, above n 19, p 126.

40 For an account of the incidents mentioned in this paragraph see Turner, above n 19, Chapter 10.

Prevention of Cruelty to Animals (the precursor to the Royal Society for the Prevention of Cruelty to Animals) in 1825. Martin defended the direction of his earlier attempts at reform, aimed as they had been at the sports of the masses, namely bull-baiting. In the following extract from the speech he gave in 1825, one can sense the essential essence of the man:[41]

> Now, although it is true enough that there is much cruelty in those gentlemanly sports (hear, hear) yet it is no reason to reject the attempt to put down a few acknowledged barbarities, because we can't put them all down. (Applause.) For my own part, I could wish to get rid of every one of them, good or bad. (Hear, hear.) But if I can't get 100%, why, then, I must be satisfied to take 50 or 25%. (Much laughter.)

> But I must say that it makes me blush, as a Member of Parliament, to be obliged to confess that the great indisposition to put an end to cruelty to animals exists in the House of Parliament itself. (Hear, hear.) I may truly say, that a greater love for, or, at least, adherence to, the principle of cruelty exists in St Stephen's Chapel than in the Bear garden itself. (Laughter.) In the House of Commons, containing six or 700 members, I am sure there are 10 to one against any measure to diminish the sufferings of the brute creation. (Hear, hear.)

Martin's hopes that his Act might prevent bull-baiting and the baiting of other animals were short-lived. The definition of the word 'cattle' was the problem, with only some magistrates allowing the Act to be used to prosecute *bull*-baiters. A Mr Adolphus, representing the accused in an 1825 case argued that the meaning of the word 'cattle' should not be extended to include the superior bull, as it was not the custom of statutory interpretation to extend the specific mention of the inferior rank to the higher. In the summer of 1825 two lions by the names of 'Nero' and 'Wallace' were baited by dogs in Warwick, an event which was criticised in the national press by *The Times* and the *Morning Post*. The reaction of *The Times* in particular shows how feelings were beginning to run against the baiters when they criticised 'the torture of a noble lion with the full consent and for the profit of a mercenary being who had gained large sums of money by hawking the poor animal about the world and exhibiting him. It is vain, however, to make any appeal to humanity where none exists or to expatiate on mercy, justice and retribution hereafter when those whom we strive to influence have never learned that language in which alone we can address them.'[42]

In 1835 the practice of baiting was finally declared illegal. Joseph Pease's amendment to the 1822 Act created several new penalties:

---

41 Fairholme, above n 1, pp 38–39.
42 For further details regarding these events, see Turner, above n 19, p 136.

An Act to consolidate and amend the several Laws relating to the cruel and improper Treatment of Animals, and the Mischiefs arising from the driving of Cattle, and to make other Provisions in regard thereto. [9 September 1835.][43]

... any Person who shall, within Five Miles of temple bar, keep or use or shall act in the Management or conducting of any Premises or Place whatsoever for the Purpose of fighting or baiting of Bears, cock-fighting, baiting or fighting of Badgers or other Animals, shall ... forfeit any Sum not exceeding Five Pounds, and in default of immediate Payment shall be liable to be imprisoned and kept to hard Labour for any Time not exceeding Two Months ...

... if any Person shall ... wantonly and cruelly beat, ill-treat, abuse, or torture any Horse, Mare, Gelding, Bull, Ox, Cow, Heifer, Steer, Calf, Mule, Ass, Sheep, Lamb, Dog, or any other Cattle or domestic Animal, or if any Person who shall drive any Cattle or other Animal shall, by Negligence or ill Usage in the driving thereof, be the Means whereby any Mischief, Damage, or Injury shall be done by any such Cattle or other Animal ... shall [pay for the damage caused and] such a Sum of Money, not exceeding 40 Shillings nor less than Five Shillings with Costs, as to such Justice shall seem meet ...

... from the passing of this Act, if any Person shall keep or use any House, Room, Pit, Ground or other Place for the Purpose of running, baiting or fighting any Bull, Bear, Badger, Dog or other Animal (whether of domestic or wild Nature of Kind), or for Cock-fighting, ... shall be liable to a Penalty not exceeding Five Pounds ...

Despite the passing of this Act its implementation had to overcome some entrenched attitudes. Some were less willing than others to give up a part of their local heritage, as ES Turner describes:[44]

The town of Stamford had no intention of ending a 600-years bull-baiting tradition merely out of deference to an Act of Parliament; still less were the townsmen willing to be dictated to by the upstart Society for the Prevention of Cruelty to Animals, whose agents had begun to circulate among them, gathering evidence. After the 1836 bait eight townsmen were prosecuted by the Society at the Lincoln Summer Assizes. There was intense indignation in the town and defence funds were readily raised, notably by a benefit performance of the play *John Bull*.

When the play opened, John Rogerson, 'a London police officer sent by the SPCA', told the court that on arrival at Stamford he went to the Carpenter's Arms, where he mingled with 50 or 60 subscribers to the baiting. They were drinking out of the horn of the bull killed the previous year. Rogerson, accused of being a spy, reluctantly paid the subscription and drank the toast of 'success to the bull'. On the day of the running he watched the bull gore one bullard and tear to shreds an effigy with which others sought to inflame it. Once again

---

43 ad 1835, 5 and 6 Will 4, C 59.

44 Turner, ES, *All Heaven in a Rage*, 1994, 2nd edn, pp 137–39, Fontwell, Sussex: Centaur Press. Printed with the permission of ES Turner and Centaur Press.

he was accused of being a 'bloody spy' and mud was thrown in his face; a woman dragged him away to safety. The proceedings began at 10.45 and the streets were unblocked at 12.30; he did not see the bull again until 3 pm, when its head was covered with blood and it could hardly stand. Rogerson's assistant watched it being baited in the meadows, in an enclosure with five-foot walls. Of the people taking part he said some were drunk, some had painted faces and most were dirty and destitute.

For the defence, a Mr Hill argued that the sport was sanctioned by its antiquity and by the tolling of a church bell to inaugurate it. He urged the Society 'to restrain their mistaken but well-intentioned zeal and to trust to the labours of the press and pulpit to accomplish the abolition of that which, but for their opposition, would gradually have fallen into disuse. You may lead men where you cannot drive them – and thank God an Englishman is not to be driven – neither is he to be hunted out of his pastimes.'

The jury acquitted five of the defendants, convicted three of riotous behaviour and one of assault. This result was regarded by the bullards as a victory and they planned another bull-running for the following November. This time the Home Secretary intervened, reminding the Mayor of Stamford of his duty to put down disorders. More than 200 special constables were sworn in, at considerable expense, but as they lacked the will to intervene the running took place as usual. In 1838 Lord John Russell took sterner measures. A troop of the 14th Light Dragoons was drafted in and 12 trusted police officers arrived from London. 'The Magistrates, although the interference of the Secretary of State had not been sought by them, were inclined on this occasion fully to perform their duty,' reported the *Stamford Mercury*. Aware of the 'strange infatuation' which afflicted even the supposedly respectable people of the town, the authorities enlisted very few special constables, but instead recruited 20 reliable tradesmen. The *Lincoln Gazette's* version was that the magistrates received a 'peremptory mandate' from the Home Office to suppress 'this relic of feudal barbarism.' As the day neared the only two bulls kept for hire in the area were moved into a hotel yard under guard and constables stood at every entrance to the town to prevent the infiltration of any others. By noon of the appointed day it looked as though the bullards had been defeated, but by chance (though some said it was not by chance) a cart containing a young bull calf entered Stamford at about one o'clock. The animal had been sold by Earl Spencer and was *en route* to its new owner. Seeing their chance, the crowd seized and unloaded the animal and began to chase it. This time the cavalry chose to uphold authority and clashed sharply with a stone-throwing mob in an effort to recapture the bull. The *Stamford Mercury* said that a brewer who seized the bridle of a horse received a sword cut in the head and neck, but the *Lincolnshire Chronicle* described the victim as an elderly person hurt by a sword while trying to escape. The *Mercury* complained: 'A serious expense on the inhabitants is occasioned by the obstinate persistence in an unlawful and barbarous custom ... It is no longer to be doubted that it can and will be put down; the Executive government having interfered will not be baffled in making the law of the land observed at Stamford as it is in the rest of the kingdom.'

In the following year, thanks to duplicity by special constables, a bull was again introduced into the town, patrolled though it was by the 5th Dragoon Guards, a draft of London police and a number of horsemen who ranged the surrounding fields. A mob, at one time 4,000 strong, threw paving stones at the police. The authorities recovered the bull 'at the expense of a few broken pates' and it was escorted to a hotel yard between two columns of cavalrymen. By now, however, the town had been called upon to pay upwards of £600 for the hire of outside forces and there was a growing feeling that the money could be spent more profitably. The mayor wrote to the Home Secretary saying that if no more forces were sent into the town he would ensure that no more bulls were run. That was the end.

The Battle of Stamford has many lessons, one of which is that cruelty can sometimes be stopped by making it too expensive. How long it would have taken 'press and pulpit' to suppress the sport nobody can say; nor can anyone be sure that the end would have come sooner if outsiders had not mounted a moral crusade. The settlement was achieved in such a way as to leave the townsfolk with some illusion of having successfully defied busybodies and tyrants.

The 1849 Cruelty to Animals Act strengthened the law protecting animals:[45]

... if any Person shall ... beat, ill-treat, over-drive, abuse or torture, or cause or procure to be cruelly beaten, ill-treated, over-driven, abused, or tortured, any Animal, every such Offender shall for every such Offence forfeit and pay a Penalty not exceeding Five Pounds.

... every Person who shall keep or use or act in the Management of any place for the Purpose of fighting or baiting any Bull, Bear, Badger, Cock, or other Kind of Animal, whether of domestic or wild Nature, or shall permit or suffer any Place to be so used, shall be liable to a Penalty not exceeding Five Pounds ...

By virtue of this Act, it became possible to prosecute both the perpetrator of the acts in question and those causing or procuring such acts, thus making it possible to prosecute the master as well as the servant. Provisions were also introduced to provide for animals going to slaughter, such as the requirement to feed and water them properly.

After 1850 the emphasis of proposed reform shifted from blatantly cruel practices to the relatively new and growing practice of experimentation involving animals (examined in detail in Chapter 4). As scientists began to see animals as the tools which would open the gateway to new discoveries to alleviate human suffering, the animal rights lobby perceived practices which violated fundamental moral principles of our relationship with animals.[46] In the UK, concerted and well-organised protests against animal experimentation led to the Cruelty to Animals Act 1876. In continental

---

45   ad 1849, 12 and 13 Vict, C 92.
46   French, above n 31, Chapter 2.

Europe, where the use of animals in this way had always been much more common, control came much later.[47]

In the UK, and continental Europe to a lesser extent, the 19th century witnessed radical changes to the law relating to animals, which led Queen Victoria to comment that during her reign she had noticed in particular, 'with real pleasure, the growth of more humane feelings towards the lower animals'.[48] But continued unease at practices *outside* the laboratory led to the passing of the principal Act which now still protects animals in the UK, the Protection of Animals Act 1911. This Act finally gave adequate protection to 'any animal', but broadly excludes wild animals,[49] animals used as 'food for mankind' and completely excludes animals used in experimentation except in certain instances which are now mainly protected by the Animals (Scientific Procedures) Act 1986 (see Chapter 4). The 19th century Cruelty to Animals Acts certainly had an effect on a number of cruel practices including 'leisure and sporting pursuits', but it was the 1911 Act which finally made illegal practices which had caused concern throughout the 19th century such as abuse of horses or using dogs as draught animals:

The Protection of Animals Act 1911 (as Amended)

Section 1. Offences of cruelty

(1) If any person:

(a) shall cruelly beat, kick, ill-treat, over-drive, over-load, torture, infuriate, or terrify any animal, or shall cause or procure, or, being the owner, permit any animal to be so used, or shall, by wantonly or unreasonably doing or omitting to do any act, or causing or procuring the commission or omission of any act, cause any unnecessary suffering, or, being the owner, permit any unnecessary suffering to be so caused to any animal; or

(b) shall convey or carry, or cause or procure, or, being the owner, permit to be conveyed or carried, any animal in such a manner or position as to cause that animal unnecessary suffering; or

(c) shall cause, procure, or assist at the fighting or baiting of animal; or shall keep, use, manage, or act or assist in the management of, any premises or place for the purpose, or partly for the purpose of fighting or baiting any animal, or shall permit any premises or place to be so kept, managed, or used, or shall receive, or cause or procure any person to receive, money for the admission of any person to such premises or place; or

(d) shall wilfully, without any reasonable cause or excuse, administer, or cause or procure, or being the owner permit, such administration of,

---

47 See Chapter 4, which contains more detail on the development of the law relating to experimentation on animals.

48 Thomas, above n 26, pp 149–50.

49 See Chapter 8; Wild Mammals Protection Act 1996, p 351.

any poisonous or injurious drug or substance to any animal, or shall wilfully, without any reasonable cause or excuse, cause any such substance to be taken by any animal; or

(e) shall subject, or cause or procure, or being the owner permit to be subjected, any animal to any operation which is performed without due care and humanity.

(f) shall tether any horse, ass or mule under such conditions or in such manner as to cause that animal unnecessary suffering; such person shall be guilty of an offence of cruelty within the meaning of this Act, and [shall be liable on summary conviction to imprisonment for a term not exceeding six months or to a fine not exceeding level 5 on the standard scale, or both].

(2) For the purposes of this section, an owner shall be deemed to have permitted cruelty within the meaning of this Act if he shall have failed to exercise reasonable care and supervision in respect of the protection of the animal therefrom.

Provided that, where an owner is convicted of permitting cruelty within the meaning of this Act by reason only of his having failed to exercise such care and supervision, he shall not be liable to imprisonment without the option of a fine.

(3) Nothing in this section shall render illegal any act lawfully done under [the Animals (Scientific Procedures) Act 1986], or shall apply:

(a) to the commission or omission of any act in the course of the destruction, or the preparation for destruction, of any animal as food for mankind, unless such destruction or such preparation was accompanied by the infliction of unnecessary suffering; or

(b) to the coursing or hunting of any captive animal, unless such animal is liberated in an injured, mutilated, or exhausted condition; but a captive animal shall not, for the purposes of this section, be deemed to be coursed or hunted before it is liberated for the purpose of being coursed or hunted, or after it has been recaptured, or if it is under control, [and a captive animal shall not be deemed to be coursed or hunted within the meaning of this subsection if it is coursed or hunted in an enclosed space from which it has no reasonable chance of escape].

Section 2

Where the owner of an animal is convicted of an offence of cruelty within the meaning of this Act, it shall be lawful for the court, if the court is satisfied that it would be cruel to keep the animal alive, to direct that the animal be destroyed, and to assign the animal to any suitable person for that purpose; and the person to whom such animal is so assigned shall, as soon as possible, destroy such animal, or cause or procure such animal to be destroyed, in his presence without unnecessary suffering. Any reasonable expenses incurred in destroying the animal may be ordered by the court to be paid by the owner, and thereupon shall be recoverable summarily as a civil debt.

Provided that, unless the owner assent, no order shall be made under this section except upon the evidence of a duly registered veterinary surgeon.

Section 3

If the owner of any animal shall be guilty of cruelty within the meaning of this Act to the animal, the court, upon his conviction thereof, may, if they think fit, in addition to any other punishment, deprive such person of the ownership of the animal, and may make such order as to the disposal of the animal as they think fit under the circumstances.

Provided that no order shall be made under this section, unless it is shown by evidence as to a previous conviction, or as to the character of the owner, or otherwise, that the animal, if left with the owner, is likely to be exposed to further cruelty.

Section 7

(1) Any person who impounds or confines, or causes to be impounded or confined, any animal in any pound shall, while the animal is so impounded or confined, supply it with a sufficient quantity of wholesome and suitable food and water, and, if he fails to do so, he shall be liable upon summary conviction to a fine not exceeding [level 1 on the standard scale].

(2) If any animal is impounded or confined in any pound and is without sufficient suitable food or water for six successive hours, or longer, any person may enter the pound for the purpose of supplying the animal therewith.

(3) The reasonable cost of the food and water supplied to any animal impounded or confined in any pound shall be recoverable summarily from the owner of the animal as a civil debt.

Section 11

(1) If a police constable finds any animal so diseased or so severely injured or in such a physical condition that, in his opinion, having regard to the means available for removing the animal, there is no possibility of removing it without cruelty, he shall, if the owner is absent or refuses to consent to the destruction of the animal, at once summon a duly registered veterinary surgeon, if any such veterinary surgeon resides within a reasonable distance, and, if it appears by the certificate of such veterinary surgeon that the animal is mortally injured, or so severely injured, or so diseased, or in such physical condition, that it is cruel to keep it alive, it shall be lawful for the police constable, without the consent of the owner, to slaughter the animal, or cause or procure it to be slaughtered, with such instruments or appliances, and with such precautions, and in such manner, as to inflict as little suffering as practicable, and, if the slaughter takes place on any public highway, to remove the carcass or cause or procure it to be removed therefrom.

(2) If any veterinary surgeon summoned under this section certifies that the injured animal can without cruelty be removed, it shall be the duty of the person in charge of the animal to cause it forthwith to be removed with as little suffering as possible, and, if that person fail so to do, the police

constable may, without the consent of that person, cause the animal
forthwith to be so removed.

Elsewhere, in continental Europe, the French were the first to follow the
British lead in respect of animal welfare legislation when, in 1850 after much
work by Jaques-Phillipe Delmas de Grammont, they passed the 'Loi
Grammont', an Act which was similar in its aims to the British legislation
regarding cruelty. So began the modern history of legislative recognition for
the 'rights' of animals protected by statute. Other countries took time to fall in
behind the lead taken in the UK and France. In the US, for example, there are
large discrepancies regarding the date of introduction of the first anti-cruelty
laws, ranging from, for example, 1828 in New York, 1859 in Washington, 1868
in California to 1889 in Florida.[50]

The 1911 Act marks the beginning of contemporary legal attitudes to
animals. Legislation after that date will be examined in Chapters 4–10.

CONTEMPORARY ANOMALIES

Property status

The basis for the introduction of legislation concerning animals has not always
been a straightforward concern for animal welfare; indeed, a great deal of
legislation regarding animals has been introduced to protect human property
interests. Even where law has been developed to protect animals it rarely goes
so far as law protecting humans. For example, if one person inflicts pain upon
another person, then they are usually subject to criminal prosecution by the
State, which might impose financial or more serious penalties. There might
also be a civil action which would result, possibly, in financial compensation
being awarded to the victim. In the case of animals, however, the animal is
never the recipient of any financial penalties awarded against the perpetrator.
It is the owner who is the recipient of damages for the *damage incurred to
property*.

The treatment of animals as property without rights is a common feature
of the law relating to animals: an abuse of an animal is an abuse of the human
interest in the animal concerned; over-fishing the Atlantic fish stocks is the
loss of a public environmental resource; poaching results in the loss of
possible financial gain through sale; the hunting of a species to near extinction
raises concerns about the loss of rare species to be enjoyed by future
generations, and so on. Therefore, it has been argued, animals do not have
legal 'rights' as such, despite the appearance in much legislation that they do:
they are the 'subjects' of protection in various laws, but they do not have the

---

50   Leavitt, above n 27, p 13.

right to the benefits of legal action, merely the right to welfare protection as a result of it.[51] Animals are not protected as independent entities deserving of intrinsic inviolable rights but as objects to be used by people within certain boundaries which we term 'welfare', a notion which is bound up in the roots of our legal treatment of animals as property, as illustrated here by this 1690 contribution of John Locke:[52]

> Though the Earth, and all inferior creatures be common to all men, yet every man has a property in his own person. This no body has any right to but himself. The labour of his body, and the work of his hands, we may say, are properly his. Whatsoever then he removes out of the state that nature hath provided, and left it in, he hath mixed his labour with, and joyned to it something that is his own, and thereby makes it his property. It being by him removed from the common state nature placed it in, it hath by his labour something annexed to it, that excludes the common right of other men. For this labour being the unquestionable property of the labourer, no man but he can have a right to what that is once joined to, at least where there is enough, and as good left in common for others.

In his historic contribution to the documentation on the development of English law, Sir William Blackstone, in the 1794 edition of *Commentaries on the Laws of England*, outlines the basis of the legal status of animals, which remains largely intact today:[53]

> In the beginning of the world, we are informed by holy writ, the all-bountiful creator gave to man 'dominion over all of the earth; and over the fish of the sea, and over the fowl of the air, and over every living thing that moveth upon the earth'. This is the only true and solid foundation of man's dominion over external things, whatever airy metaphysical notions may have been started by fanciful writers upon this subject. The earth, therefore, and all things therein, are the general property of all mankind, exclusive of all other beings, form the immediate gift of the creator.

On the importance of the property status of animals in pre-history, Blackstone comments:[54]

> The article of food was a more immediate call, and therefore a more early consideration. Such, as were not contented with the spontaneous product of the earth, fought for a more solid refreshment in the flesh of beasts, which they obtained by hunting. But the frequent disappointments, incident to that method of provision, induced them to gather together such animals as were of a more tame and fequacious nature; and to establish a permanent property in

51 For a full discussion of the nature of 'rights', arguments as to whether animals can acquire them or whether they already have them enshrined in law, see Chapter 3, p 79.

52 Laslett, P (ed), *John Locke: Two Treatises of Government*, 1988 edn, pp 287–88, Cambridge: Cambridge University Press.

53 Blackstone, Sir W, *Commentaries on the Laws of England*, 1794, 12th edn, Book II, pp 2–3, London: T Cadell.

54 *Ibid*, p 5.

their flocks and herds, in order to sustain themselves in a less precarious manner, partly by the milk of the dams, and partly by the flesh of the young.

Finally he provides justification for the treatment of animals as property:[55]

> As the world by degrees grew more populous, it daily became more difficult to find out new spots to inhabit, without encroaching upon former occupants; and, by constantly occupying the same individual spot, the fruits of the earth were consumed, and its spontaneous produce destroyed, without any provision for a future supply or succession. It therefore became necessary to pursue some regular method of providing a constant subsistence; and this necessity produced, or at least promoted and encouraged, the art of agriculture. And the art of agriculture, by a regular connexion and consequence, introduced and established the idea of a more permanent property in the soil, than had hitherto been received and adopted. It was clear that the earth would not produce her fruits in sufficient quantities, without the assistance of tillage; but who would be at the pains of tilling it, if another might watch upon an opportunity to seize upon and enjoy the product of his industry, art, and labour? Had not therefore a separate property in lands, as well as moveables, been vested in some individuals, the world must have continued a forest, and men have been mere animals of prey; which, according to some philosophers, is the genuine fate of nature.

The term 'animal' for the purpose of current laws usually covers any creature which is not a human being, but specific statutes such as the Animals (Scientific Procedures) Act 1986 may give a slightly amended definition of 'animal' in line with its purpose. Legislation relating to animals divides them into *domestic, captive* and *wild* animals for the purposes of different levels of protection, with domestic animals being deemed as absolute property and the ability to treat wild animals as property being strictly limited (see Chapter 6). The treatment of domestic animals does not differ significantly from the treatment of other chattels in English law.[56]

Limited property rights in wild animals can arise by lawfully taking, taming or reclaiming them, as a result of their being born on a person's land until they can fly or run away, as a right of an owner of land who has retained exclusive right to hunt, take and kill animals on his own land or as a result of being granted those rights by the owner. These qualified rights are usually only important in relation to actions for trespass to property, and do not grant unlimited property rights.[57] This branch of the law relating to wild animals presents more difficult problems than that of domestic animals, for several reasons:[58]

---

55 *Ibid*, p 7.

56 Holdsworth, Sir W, *A History of English Law*, 1973, 2nd edn, vol VII, pp 488–89, London: Sweet & Maxwell.

57 For further detail see *Halsbury's Laws*, vol 2: Animals.

58 Holdsworth, above n 56, p 490.

The law as to the original acquisition of the ownership and possession of animals *ferae naturae* has, at different periods, been affected by four different sets of influences. Those influences are the Roman rules as to the acquisition of such animals, the rights of the Crown, the rights of landowners, and the Game Laws enacted in the interest of larger landowners. All these influences have combined to make the history of this branch of law very complex.

Although extremely valuable to the progress of humankind, the treatment of animals as property has, arguably, been extremely damaging to the fate of animals. As 'property', animals' 'owners' have been able to dispose of their animals as they wish. Not only has it been difficult for the law to reach into areas of welfare concern where there were human property interests at stake, such as farming, but the continuing status of animals as property means that, as Gary Francione has noted: 'animals are regarded merely as means to human ends, which means that the law embodies the instrumentalist view of animals.'[59] Francione suggests that as a society, our laws reject the notion of intrinsic value in animals, in favour of allowing their owners to do broadly as they please with their 'possessions'.[60]

The courts of many countries have sometimes been asked to consider whether animals can be attributed with legal personality or status. Dolphins have attracted particular attention for centuries because of their apparent desire to actively seek out human contact, and their obvious intelligence. The history of seafaring nations records many tales of dolphins coming to the aid of sailors in trouble. More recently, philosophers and, indeed, courts of law have been asked to consider whether a dolphin is a legal 'person'. In 1977 two men were tried in the US for releasing two bottle-nosed dolphins from the University of Hawaii's Institute of Marine Biology.[61] It is a classic contemporary incidence of the philosophical questions being asked about the sentient status of higher-order animals. It is particularly interesting because it was a crucial question asked in a case which would decide on the continuing liberty of two men, Kenneth Le Vaseur and Stephen C Sipman. They were attempting to raise the defence of necessity where the law 'allows' the commission of an offence if the action is done for the avoidance of imminent and more serious harm to oneself or 'another'. The defence is common to most legal systems around the world. The question which came up for consideration was whether a dolphin could be defined as 'another' for the purposes of the defence. Judge Doi declined to designate a dolphin as

59   Francione, G, *Rain Without Thunder: The Ideology of the Animal Rights Movement*, 1996, p 25, Philadelphia: Temple University Press.

60   Proposed alternatives to the classification of animals as property and for them to be attributed with 'rights' or 'interests' are examined in detail in Chapter 3.

61   The writers have been unable to find an official UK case report reference for this case. These details were compiled from several other references in books and articles, the best being Midgley, M, 'Persons and Non-Persons', in Singer, P (ed), *In Defence of Animals*, 1985, pp 52–62, Oxford: Basil Blackwell.

'another', and defined them purely as property. He also decided that any possible cruelty to the animals in terms of isolation and behavioural change would not outweigh the more serious 'offence' in this case, namely theft, thus reinforcing the property status of animals. A further attempt to obtain leave to appeal to the Federal Court in order to claim the Thirteenth Amendment in respect of involuntary servitude was also rejected by the judge.

The philosophical basis of Judge Doi's decision has been questioned by Mary Midgley, who pointed out that corporations can be termed 'legal persons' in law in order to sue and be sued. She compared the decision in this case to the difficulties women had in the US in bringing themselves within the definition of 'person' for the purposes of being able to practise law and to sit on a jury.[62] There are, it is claimed by those such as Mary Midgley, philosophical anomalies in a legal system which allows a sentient animal such as a dolphin to be treated as having less legal status than a corporation which benefits from the legal fiction of being treated as a 'legal person'. The proposition that there is a need to grant animals an enhanced new legal status above and beyond their current status as property is discussed in detail in Chapter 3.

Not only have animals themselves been treated as property, but property interests in relation to the ownership of land are often considered to be more important than animals. In the UK and elsewhere there are several statutes which give wide discretionary powers to landowners or their employees to kill or injure animals where there is conflict with human interests. Even though the *indirect* effect of the Animals Act 1971 might be to protect livestock, Les Brown proposes that this is clearly not the actual intention of the Act, which is actually in place to protect property interests in the animals:[63]

> Property interests have long been protected in English and US law, sometimes in ways which do not consider the interests of all animals involved. For instance, the Animals Act 1971 gives the occupier of land, or the landowner, wide powers in protecting livestock from any dog found on his property, but excessive trust seems to be placed in both his rational powers and the morality of his motives and attitudes. This Act, replacing the common law rules relating to the protection of livestock against dogs (s 9) requires, to absolve from liability, only that the killing or injuring of a dog found wandering on land and supposedly threatening livestock be notified to the police within two days. The occupier so killing or injuring a dog is said to be acting for the protection of the livestock if either (a) 'the dog is worrying or about to worry the livestock, and there are no other reasonable means of ending or preventing the worrying; or (b) the dog has been worrying livestock, has not left the vicinity and is not under the control of any person and there are no practical means of ascertaining to whom it belongs'. The condition of either (a) or (b) is 'deemed

---

62   *Ibid*, n 61, pp 54–55.
63   Brown, L, *Cruelty to Animals: The Moral Debt*, 1989, pp 160–61, London: Macmillan.

to be satisfied if the defendant believed that it was satisfied and had reasonable ground for that belief' (s 9(4)). It is noted that under this provision 'the dog need not actually have attacked or worried the livestock or be renewing an attempt'. All the occupier or landowner needs is 'reasonable ground for believing that an attack on the livestock is imminent and no other reasonable means of dealing with the situation is available'. Under this Act the dog would have little chance against a person who believed that all dogs found on properties are marauders, who ruled out the possibility of mistakes of judgement, who was malicious towards a dog known to belong to an unfriendly neighbour and who acted without witnesses. In its protection of property rights the Act leaves open the possibility of an infliction of unnecessary suffering on an animal.

Some apparently protective statutes, even though they cater for the welfare of animals, sometimes remove this protection if occupiers or landowners use their discretion to do so in order to protect their property. The Protection of Badgers Act 1992 prohibits the taking, injuring or killing of badgers (s 1), cruelty to badgers (s 2), interfering with their sets (s 3) and selling badgers (s 4). But s 7 provides exceptions if the person shows that 'his action was necessary for the purpose of preventing serious damage to land, crops, poultry or any other form of property'. There are strict licensing provisions in s 10 to allow the killing or taking of badgers, and normally an occupier would have to comply with these. There is, however, an exception to this where it was not apparent before the time of the killing that such action was necessary. An occupier is thus protected if he can show that the action was immediately necessary to protect his property.

Are we protecting animals or humans?

In 1996 the UK introduced new legislation concerning wild animals. The Wild Mammals (Protection) Act 1996 marks a new departure in the range of protection afforded to animals in the UK and is examined in detail in Chapter 8. The mutilation, kicking, burning, stabbing, etc of wild mammals is now an offence under the Act, giving the generality of animals, for the first time, protection under English law. But further anomalies in our treatment of animals under the law are introduced by the Act:[64]

> [T]here exist a number of different regimes which provide markedly different degrees of protection depending on the situation in which the animal finds itself, without reference to the need of the particular animal. A captive wild mammal will still enjoy greater protection from cruelty than an individual of the same species which is living wild.

64   Radford, M, 'Protecting Wild Mammals' (1996) 146 NLJ 458.

The only difference between a captive animal and a wild animal of the same species is the human interest in the captive animal. Thus, the captive animal retains greater protection and the human interest in the captive animal is maintained beyond the interests of wild animals. In addition, s 2 provides protection for hunters who kill wild animals and those who lawfully trap animals with snares and dogs, etc. Thus, despite providing a degree of protection which wild animals have never had before, the Act is human-centred in as much as activities which are to the benefit of humans and to the detriment of wild animals are actually protected by the Act.

The Protection of Badgers Act 1992 also contains specific protection of human interests at the expense of wild animals. It can be cited as another example of legislation aimed at the protection of animals which actually contains contrary protection of humans in one form or other. If another example is needed to confirm this point then an examination of the provisions of the Animals (Scientific Procedures) Act 1986 in Chapter 4 also reveals protection for scientists performing experimental procedures on animals which may or may not involve severe pain, if they are in possession of personal and project licences issued by the Home Office.

Moral concern for animals v legitimate human interests

The law not only reflects what humans think animals need or want, but also finds problems in incorporating moral concerns for animals against lawful human activities. In the following three cases, moral concern for the welfare of animals was subsumed by the pursuit of legitimate human interests. In *R v Coventry Airport, ex p Phoenix Aviation* (1995)[65] the Court of Appeal was asked to consider whether it was lawful for public authorities operating airports and docks to ban the flights or shipments of livestock by exporters because of problems caused by public demonstrations against such flights or shipments. It was held that the respective authorities have no powers to distinguish between these flights or shipments and other lawful trades, and even if they did they would not be allowed to ban the export of live animals, which is protected by the fact that the practice is considered to be lawful. In the excerpt below, Simon Brown LJ not only illustrates how direct action by groups such as animal rights groups will not be allowed to affect lawful activities, but also clearly distinguishes moral considerations of human rights as against those of animal rights. In short, the court maintained limits on the ability of the authorities to respond to moral judgments on account of animals' welfare where legitimate financial and property interests are protected by law as they were here:[66]

---

65   *R v Coventry Airport, ex p Phoenix Aviation* [1995] 3 All ER 37; (1995) 145 *New Law Journal*, No 6689, p 559.

66   *R v Coventry City Council*, above n 65, [1995] 3 All ER 37 at 62.

One thread runs consistently throughout all the case law: the recognition that public authorities must beware of surrendering to the dictates of unlawful pressure groups. The implications of such surrender for the rule of law can hardly be exaggerated. Of course, on occasion, a variation or even short-term suspension of services may be justified. As suggested in certain of the authorities, that may be a lawful response. But it is one thing to respond to unlawful threats, quite another to submit to them – the difference, although perhaps difficult to define, will generally be easy to recognise. Tempting though it may sometimes be for public authorities to yield too readily to threats of disruption, they must expect the courts to review any such decision with particular rigour – this is not an area where they can be permitted a wide measure of discretion. As when fundamental human rights are in play, the courts will adopt a more interventionist role.

The lower status of moral concerns for animals has also been espoused by the European Court of Justice in *Hedley Lomas (Ireland) Ltd v Ministry of Agriculture, Fisheries and Food* (1996). The Court held that the temporary ban on the export of live sheep to Spain (1992–94), because of fears over whether they were complying with rules regarding the stunning of animals before slaughter, was a breach of EC requirements regarding the free movement of goods. The Ministry was not allowed to invoke moral concern for the animals' welfare to support their action, and was compelled to depend on the enforcement of regulations in the member State concerned. Much to the dismay of the animal welfare lobby the case once again confirmed the supremacy of matters of economics over animal welfare in the EC. It is because of cases such as this that the EC is criticised by welfare groups as being the cause of much animal suffering, leading to calls for specific articles on animal welfare to be incorporated into the Treaty of Rome (see Chapter 5). This would compel authorities to take animal welfare into account at all times in interpreting current EC or domestic legislation and might lead to the rewriting of many specific legal provisions.

The strict application of the rule of law, leading to a frustration of attempts to invoke welfare concerns, occurred in 1995 in *R v Somerset County Council, ex p Fewings*,[67] when the Court of Appeal was asked to consider whether a local authority could lawfully ban hunting on its land on moral grounds. It was held that, unlike private landowners where the use of land starts from the principle that one may do what one likes with one's own land, a local authority's decision to act must be done in response to specific powers given to them by Parliament (see also Chapter 7, pp 306–15). Somerset County Council's attempt to use s 122(1) of the Local Government Act 1972, which allows them to appropriate land for the purpose of the 'benefit, improvement or development' of that area, could not be used as a means to ban hunting as this purpose did not come within the meaning of the section. Sir Thomas Bingham left open the question as to whether the Council was morally correct

---

67   *R v Somerset County Council, ex p Fewings* [1995] 1 All ER 513; (1995) 145 NLJ 6689 at 450.

in its intentions, but a strict interpretation of the legislation frustrated the Council's intentions.

Some other bodies trying to advocate improved animal welfare have also faced problems when there is a conflict with human interests. The RSPCA, for example, depends upon the fact that it is recognised as a charity to avoid taxation of its funds and to be able to commit those funds to the cause of advancing animal welfare. In a decision which the RSPCA described as 'absolutely devastating'[68] the Charity Commissioners ruled that the RSPCA would be acting in a way inconsistent with its charitable status if it opposed animal suffering where there are human benefits. The Charity Commissioners issued the following press release:

> In view of recent publicity, the Charity Commission is glad to be able to announce that it has reached a satisfactory conclusion to discussions with the RSPCA about the scope of its activities. RSPCA's charitable status places some limit on what it can do in relation to animal issues. These limits do not impede the important welfare work for which the RSPCA is well-known. The discussions have led the RSPCA to review its promotional literature and to withdraw some leaflets in response to public concerns that the Society had engaged in the promotion of animal rights issues.
>
> The RSPCA has also removed all restrictions on membership, save those which require aspiring members to affirm their support of the registered objects of the charity.
>
> The Commission is satisfied that the projects and operations conducted by the RSPCA are legitimate and consistent with the published guidelines on campaigning by charities.
>
> Chief Charity Commissioner Richard Fries said today:
>
>> 'I welcome the outcome of the discussions we have been having with the RSPCA. The law allows charities operating in the field of animal welfare the scope they need to raise awareness of cruelty issues and campaign for better standards of animal care. Charities must of course act within the limits of their objects and charity law, if they are not to invite criticism which damages their reputations and detracts from their achievements'. ...
>
> To be charitable an organisation must exist for public benefit. In the case of animal welfare charities, long standing legal decisions have made it clear that public benefit is understood in terms of the promotion of human morality. Thus the benefit to animals is an indirect rather than a direct basis for animal bodies being charitable. The significance of this is that the benefit to animals can be outweighed by the interests of mankind, for example, in relation to medical knowledge. An animal welfare charity may not therefore seek to protect animals in ways which would have adverse consequences for mankind.
>
> Various articles have appeared in recent months which have suggested that the RSPCA, rather than confining itself to legitimate animal welfare had engaged

---

68   *The Guardian*, 27 March 1996, p 1.

in the promotion of 'Animal Rights'. Taking 'Animal Rights' to mean the furtherance of the interests of animals without regard to the question of the impact on man, the Charity Commission raised the issue with the Society. Also, restrictions on membership had given the impression that those who disagreed with the policy set out in its promotional literature would be excluded despite being able to support the RSPCA's objects.

Were the Society to campaign against the use of animals in scientific research or agriculture where there is benefit to humans, it might well step outside the boundaries of its charitable status. The full effects of this ruling have yet to be tested, but there were fears that the ruling might amount to a gagging order and be to the benefit of the field sports and experimentation communities by restricting RSPCA challenges to their work. The first casualty of the ruling was a campaign against the British-financed use of chimpanzees for vivisection in the Netherlands.[69] The Charity Commissioners' ruling illustrates not only the predominance of human interests over animals' interests as reflected in the law, but is also evidence of the difference in legal status granted by the courts to different species.

A 'charity' is extremely difficult to define and 'excludes some benevolent or philanthropic activities which a layman might consider charitable.'[70] Certainly, the decision of the Charity Commissioners in relation to the RSPCA is in keeping with the decision in *National Anti-Vivisection Society v Inland Revenue Commissioners* (1947),[71] where it was held that the main objective of the society, namely the total abolition of vivisection, meant that it could not be accorded the status of a charity and the resulting tax benefits this would bring.[72] In one of the judgments in that case, Lord Wright clearly elucidates the reasoning which has traditionally been adopted by the courts in relation to animals, placing moral concern for animals below the pursuit of human interests:[73]

> There is not, so far as I can see, any difficulty in weighing the relative value of ... the material benefits of vivisection against the moral benefit which is alleged or assumed as possibly following from the success of the society's project. In any case the position must be judged as a whole. It is arbitrary and unreal to attempt to dissect the problem into what is said to be direct and what is said to be consequential. The whole complex of resulting circumstances of whatever kind must be foreseen or imagined in order to estimate whether the change advocated would, or would not be, beneficial to the community. The commissioners have abstained from any but the vaguest finding on the

---

69   *Ibid.*

70   *Halsbury's Laws,* vol 5(2): 'Charities', para 2.

71   *National Anti-Vivisection Society v Inland Revenue Commissioners* [1947] 2 All ER 217.

72   See also the Charity Commissioners' decision in relation to the the Animal Abuse, Injustice and Defence Society (Animal AID), reported in the *New Law Journal,* Christmas Appeals edition, No 65, 16 December 1994.

73   *National Anti-Vivisection Society v IRC,* above n 71 at 223–24.

possibility of moral benefit. They had no evidence, they said, on the point, but, at the highest, the assumed or alleged benefit is indirect and problematical. There is clearly no general consensus of public opinion or understanding against the practice of vivisection which has been permitted by Parliament as regulated under the Act of 1876.[74] The Act has stood all these years substantially without any serious attack. It seems that people's moral feelings are not weakened by the existence of the Act. If they think about it at all they think about the immense and incalculable benefits which have resulted from vivisection. If that involves some measure of pain at times to some animals, notwithstanding the Act, they feel that it is due to regrettable necessity. Similarly, a man who has a beefsteak for dinner, if he thinks at all about the slaughter of the beast, reflects that it is inevitable in the present constitution of society. I do not question that a high degree of regard for animals is a good thing, but it must be a regulated regard. Cruelty, that is purposeless cruelty, whether through brutality or through a purpose to satisfy our pleasure or our pride, cannot be forgiven. It is, indeed, also a penal offence at law, but it is impossible to apply the word cruelty to the efforts of high-minded scientists who have devoted themselves to vivisection experiments for the purpose of alleviating human suffering. Harvey was only able to publish in 1628 his great work, *De motu cordis*, because he had been given deer from the Royal park for the purposes of vivisection. Countless millions have benefited from that discovery. I do not minimise the sufferings of the unfortunate deer. The subject of vivisection is not a consenting party nor does it benefit, but I put that against the benefit to humanity. It has been argued that a court cannot weigh moral and material benefits against each other. This is not the place to accept or reject Bentham's pronouncement that 'measure for measure pushpin is as good as poetry,' or debate whether utilitarian or intuitionist ethics is the truer theory, but in ordinary life people often have to decide between moral and material benefit. However, I do not think that is a fair statement of the issue. The scientist who inflicts pain in the course of vivisection is fulfilling a moral duty to mankind which is higher in degree than the moralist or sentimentalist who thinks only of the animals. Nor do I agree that animals ought not to be sacrificed to man when necessary. A strictly regulated amount of pain to some hundreds of animals may save and avert incalculable suffering to innumerable millions of mankind. I cannot doubt what the moral choice should be. There is only one single issue. I have great sympathy with much that Lord Greene, MR, has said in his powerful dissenting judgment. I have a great love for animals and some familiarity with certain classes. I am sorry that rabbits, a weak and innocent but monstrously destructive race, should have been destroyed in great numbers as they were and are being, to save our people from qualified starvation. I agree with the Master of the Rolls that rats, beetles and other pests, if they have to be destroyed, should be destroyed with as little cruelty as possible, but destroyed they must be. The lives of animals at the best are precarious. Millions have perished in the last frost. That is a regrettable necessity, but, however it is looked at, the life and happiness of human beings must be preferred to that of animals. Mankind, of whatever race or breed, is on

74 The Cruelty to Animals Act 1876 (now replaced by the Animals (Scientific Procedures) Act 1986).

a higher plane and a different level from even the highest of the animals who are our friends, helpers and companions. No one faced with the decision to chose between saving a man or an animal could hesitate to save the man.

I have turned for a while to considerations of fact because that is inevitable in balancing conflicting value. To my mind, the scale of the anti-vivisectionist mounts up and kicks the beam. A statesman is constantly weighing conflicting moral and material utilities. I must add that I have great doubt ... that the object of abolishing vivisection can on any view be regarded as being in law a public charitable object.

Deciding what animals need

When society has legislated in favour of animals, it has tended to take an anthropomorphic[75] view of what needs protection. This tendency was noted by Laurence H Tribe in relation to the Federal Laboratory Animal Welfare Act 1970:[76]

> [T]he legislative history of the 1970 amendments to the Act ... provides a graphic illustration of the process of anthropomorphic validation: The House committee report proclaims that the purpose of the legislation is to ensure that animals are 'accorded the basic *creature comforts* of adequate housing, ample food and water, reasonable handling, *decent sanitation* ... and adequate veterinary care including the appropriate use of *pain*-killing drugs ... .' The statutory terms reveal an obvious transfer of human values to the non-human rights-holders: The words 'comfort', 'decent sanitation' and indeed 'pain' refer to human experiences and perceptions. By incorporating such terms into legislation protecting animals, the draftsmen are equating the perceptions of animals with those of humans; the terminology subliminally reinforces our sympathy for the plight of mistreated animals by evoking images of human suffering. As a result, the propriety of legal protection in the interest of the animals themselves becomes more apparent.

To a large extent this anthropomorphic tendency is inevitable as humans have had great difficulty in finding out what animals actually need or want. Science continues to add to the sum of knowledge on the experience and requirements of animals particularly in relation to scientific experimentation and farming and new domestic or EC legislation has often been introduced in recognition of evidence regarding animal's suffering, physiological and ethological requirements.[77]

---

75 Projecting the thoughts and feeling of humans into animals in order to determine what animals want or need. Scientists have often criticised this tendency as being an unreliable practice to determine *actual* requirements. On the other hand, reliable alternative methods of determining animal needs have yet to come to light, since we cannot communicate with them.

76 Tribe, LH, 'Ways not to Think About Plastic Trees: New Foundations for Environmental Law' (1974) 83 *Yale LJ* 1344.

77 See Chapters 4 and 5 for more discussion on how scientific discovery in relation to the experience of animals continues to influence changes in the law.

A CASE STUDY IN ANIMAL LAW: GENETIC ENGINEERING AND BIOTECHNOLOGY

The conflict arising from the current legal status of animals is nowhere more clearly illustrated than by the situation in relation to patenting advanced breeding techniques, which is at the forefront of the current debate regarding animals. The law in this area represents a contrasting mixture of property and welfare-based legal provision surrounded by moral debate. For some, the whole issue of patenting in this area raises moral reprehension at any idea of treating animals as mere products or artefacts. Others argue that patenting laws are necessary to protect financial investments and to allow them to seek profits for their hard work.[78] The issue illustrates the treatment of animals in law as property, which allows them to be used to fulfil human wants by 'designing' animals better able to fulfil those wants. Official bodies have sometimes been unsure in their handling of cases in which these issues are raised, due to a combination of public pressure and moral concern. In 1988, for example, the US Patent and Trademark Office granted Harvard University researchers a patent for a genetically engineered mouse specially susceptible to cancers for research into carcinogens. After a storm of protests they created time for discussion of the moral implications by placing a moratorium on the issuing of like patents, which was not lifted until 1993. A similar request to the European Patent Office to patent the Harvard mouse was rejected in 1989 on the grounds that it was contrary to *'ordre publique* or morality'. At the time of writing the EC was itself embroiled in a long-running dispute over how to frame legislation in this area which would satisfy both moral anxieties and the desires of business.

The use of patents in relation to developing new genetically altered animals in the UK is presently governed by the Patents Act 1977 and the European Patent Convention.[79] The traditional view of animals as property is quite clearly shown by the ability of those involved in genetic engineering to patent a novel, non-obvious genetic step in order to protect it from those who would poach the idea for economic gain.[80] Conversely, there are requirements to take heed of the welfare of the animals in relation to patenting through provisions of the Animals (Scientific Procedures) Act 1986 or the various farm animals protection statutes where they apply (see Chapter 4).

There is considerable apprehension about the morality of what scientists are attempting and whether the law in this area adequately protects against

---

78 See the *Report of the Committee to Consider the Ethical Implications of Emerging Technologies in the Breeding of Farm Animals*, 1995, paras 5.7 and 5.8, London: HMSO, below, p 65.

79 *Ibid*, para 5.2, p 41.

80 For a good overview of the technical nature of genetic engineering in relation to animals, and a clear indication of their property status to be used as their owners see fit, see Peace, N and Christie, A, 'Intellectual Property Protection for the Products of Animal Breeding' (1996) 4 *EIPR* 213 at 213–33.

possible mistreatment of animals which have been specifically 'designed' by humans. There are concerns that law is not keeping pace with advances in technology, that we are tampering with the gene-pool and the unforeseeable side-effects this involves, and there are more immediate concerns about the current welfare of such animals:[81]

> Genetic engineering of animals, indeed all of biotechnology, is a tool, like all tools humans have deployed, from clay pots to nuclear reactors. In and of themselves, tools are neutral – pistols, surgical saws, and collection plates are not good and not bad. But tools are not just, or even primarily, in and of themselves. They are, as Heidegger says, ready at hand. They exist as tools in relation to humans who deploy them, and they derive their 'toolness', their *telos*, from the uses to which they are put. Unlike humans or animals, whose *telos* is in them, tools gain their natures from the real set of possibilities for their deployment. One can, I suppose, plough one's garden with a samurai sword, or crush garlic with an Uzi. But these are not part of the normal set of possibilities these instruments carry.
>
> What in large part determines the normal set of possibilities for tools are the valuational contexts that surround them. A society whose values preclude any violence at all will, when encountering a cache of swords, either leave them untouched or develop its own set of possibilities for them, perhaps as garden or kitchen implements, but certainly not as weapons. Genetic engineering of animals stands us and our society in something like that pristine relationship. There are those who would deploy it as a shortcut to profit, efficiency, and animal exploitation. If their views prevail, the technology will be bad for people and animals. On the other hand, its use can be informed by values and by notions of sustainability and awe at its potential. Which option develops is not something that will happen to us, but something we will do, be it by commission or forbearance.

At the end of 1996, preliminary evidence from a pending report by a group commissioned by ministers to investigate the potential problems of transplanting animal organs into humans and then suppressing the human immune system responses to the 'invader', caused such concern in governmental circles as to lead to a delay in the approval of pig heart transplants. At the time of writing the full implications were unclear but some of the concerns were illustrated by an article in *The Guardian*:[82]

> Pigs were chosen because surgeons already have a lot of experience with pig heart valves, because they were mammals of about human weight, and because they were easy to breed ...
>
> But research into new infections has also been accelerating. The first concern was that animal-to-human transplants could introduce into the human population afflictions which would take on a new ferocity.

81   Rollin, B, *The Frankenstein Syndrome: Ethical and Social Issues in the Genetic Engineering of Animals*, 1995, pp 213–14, Cambridge: Cambridge University Press.

82   Radford, T, 'Virus fears raised over pig organ transplants', *The Guardian*, 16 December 1996, p 3. Reproduced with kind permission of Guardian Newspapers.

There are a number of examples already. The influenza virus was first identified not in humans but in a ferret: flu mutates in the duck and pig populations of the crowded villages of southern China and emerges every two or three years with a different virulence. The Aids virus was almost certainly introduced from an African monkey host. And the government is haunted by the lesson of BSE, a still-puzzling infection which spread from sheep to cattle to zoo animals and finally – it was admitted this year – to 14 Britons to become a new and alarming form of Creutzfeldt-Jakob disease.

There may be more shocks in store: in the past decade virologists and health workers have identified more than 20 new and emerging diseases, many of them spread by animals.

In its leading article *The Times* was drawn to comment that further research was required: 'The proponents of xenotransplantation are confident that the risks are small; but so were the scientists who dismissed the dangers of BSE infecting man'[83] In January 1997 the government confirmed that it would be delaying its acceptance of pig organ transplants until the procedure's safety and effectiveness had been examined.[84] Concerns in this area are nowhere more clearly illustrated than in the response to the cloning of 'Dolly' the sheep in February 1997.[85]

A 1989 draft proposal for a European Parliament and Council Directive on the Legal Protection of Biotechnological Inventions provided in Article 2.3 that 'inventions shall be considered unpatentable where publication or exploitation would be contrary to public policy or morality'.[86] But the proposed Directive ran into difficulties in the European legislative process because of European Parliament concerns partly over whether it adequately protected the interests of animals. At the time of writing, some seven years on, the proposed Directive was still struggling through the European legislature after having been reintroduced, subject to many amendments, in December 1995. Amendments included those in relation to proposals regarding, for example, the patentability of human body parts and the patenting of genetically engineered animals. It has been suggested that the proposal might, conceivably, not come into effect for another three years, taking it into the year 2000, and that the European 'green lobby' was going to be difficult to convince.[87]

The 1989 proposal defined which advances would be declared unpatentable under Article 2.3 as any 'processes for modifying the genetic

---

83 *The Times*, 16 December 1996, p 19. On the same day *The Times* led with an article on p 1 about concerns regarding pig organ transplants.

84 *The Guardian*, Friday 17 January 1997, p 7.

85 *The Observer*, 23 February 1997, p 1.

86 'Proposal for a Council Directive on the Legal Protection of Biotechnological Inventions', COM (88) 496 final, OJ 1989 C10/3.

87 Jones, N, 'The New Draft Biotechnology Directive' (1996) 6 *EIPR* 365 at 363–65. At the time of writing the new version of the proposed directive had not been reported on the Official Journal of the EC.

identity of animals which are likely to cause them suffering or physical handicaps without any *substantial benefit* to man or animals resulting from such processes'. This might well have resulted in greater protection for genetically altered animals, but the notion of 'substantial benefit' caused concern as it was felt that it would serve merely to protect scientists by involving a wide discretion to avoid prohibition of certain procedures. It was this which led the European Parliament to reject the proposed directive as it stood, invoking its new powers of veto under the Maastrict Treaty for the first time.[88]

The current position of the UK authorities in relation to genetic engineering and biotechnology is that of the middle ground, accepting neither an absolute prohibitionist nor an entirely free-market approach. It is also the approach which was supported by the Ministry of Agriculture, Fisheries and Food's Report of the Committee to Consider the Ethical Implications of Emerging Technologies in the Breeding of Farm Animals, 1995, before the new proposal was introduced:[89]

5.6 Though it is not possible under existing UK law to claim a patent on animal varieties or on offspring produced as a result of 'essentially biological processes' (for example, those produced by normal breeding), it is possible to obtain a patent for animals if an inventive step has been involved in obtaining it. Thus, where an animal has had its genetic identity modified by artificial techniques, a patent may be claimed. The patent may relate to the modified gene or genes (the gene construct), the process by which the modification is made and/or the modified gene or genes are inserted into the target genome, and the resulting transgenic animal. The patent could be claimed for a single step in the process if it were inventive. The same patent could also be claimed in (subordinate claims) for that step in combination with other steps – up to and including the whole process. The scope of the patent will depend on how it has been drawn up and each patent claim is dealt with on a case by case basis.

5.7 Is this state of affairs satisfactory? Those who have replied on behalf of the biotechnology industry have naturally claimed that it is, and any attempt to single out inventions in this area and deny them patent protection which is given to other technology should be resisted. It is argued that without such protection investment in biotechnology will be discouraged: that any work which did nonetheless go on in this area would necessarily be conducted in secret; and that were the UK or the EU to limit the scope of patent protection so that work aimed at genetic modification were not capable of protection, the such work would simply move to countries with more favourable patenting regimes with the resulting economic loss. It is further argued that any attempt to import moral considerations into the

---

88 *Ibid*, at p 365.

89 *Report of the Committee to Consider the Ethical Implications of Emerging Technologies in the Breeding of Farm Animals*, 1995, London: HMSO. Crown copyright is reproduced with the permission of the Controller of Her Majesty's Stationery Office.

patent system (allowing grants of patents to some, but not all biotechnological advances) should be resisted as adding an inappropriate element. The patent system is not the right forum, it is said, for achieving moral or social objectives such as the protection of animal welfare.

5.8 Those who are unhappy with the present situation express a number of different concerns. Some argue that the extension of patenting rights to animals is offensive as such, in that it encourages us to view and treat animals as if they were simply products of human ingenuity or inventions, and thus to confuse living things with artifacts. Others, who may not object to patenting of animals on these grounds, but who are opposed to all experiments on animals, or who believe that genetic modification is in general likely to be harmful to animal welfare, contend that a denial of the possibility of obtaining patents will be an effective means of discouraging such work. And there is also concern that patenting will allow the concentration of ownership of genetically superior stock in fewer and fewer hands, to the detriment of Third World farmers and perhaps also to the detriment of smaller farming enterprises in general, and that for this reason it should be disallowed. ...

5.13 In UK law animals are already a form of property since they can be bought, sold and stolen, and are treated as 'goods' under the provisions of the Sale of Goods Act 1979 – indeed, it is the fact that animals are owned which is the basis for the attribution of various duties to their owners in relation to their welfare. Now, just as laws relating to theft protect a certain property interest, so patents are a means of protecting another form of property interest (an interest in so-called intellectual property), and there is no reason why intellectual property should not reside in animals. It is, after all, human ingenuity or invention which is responsible for the existence of a genetically modified animal in just the form which it has. Thus, the extension of patenting to genetically modified animals does not introduce a new doctrine as regards the status of animals as property, but is a logical extension of existing practice. Nor do we find this practice offensive as such, so long as it is understood (as in UK law) that a property interest is not a licence to treat what one owns in any manner one sees fit. There is nothing incompatible then, in recognising property interests in animals, genetically modified or otherwise, at the same time as one requires of their owners conformity to a rigorous welfare regime. ...

Conclusion

5.31 The question we have considered is whether work relating to the genetic modification of animals should be denied the possibility of gaining protection by patent. Such work may be protected by patents relating to the gene construct, the process of modification, the techniques for inserting the modified genes, or to the modified animal itself. Some members of the Committee take the view that patents should not be granted on transgenic animals for the reasons we have explained. The majority does not regard such patents as objectionable in principle. All of us accept that the case for denying protection by patents to all work relating to genetic modification of animals is not wholly persuasive, but believe that a moral criterion does have a proper place in the consideration of patent applications. The draft EU Directive has such a criterion and though we have reservations about this Directive, we nonetheless recommend that Ministers support it as it relates to animals. Though it may need revision at a later stage, the Directive establishes an important principle which will serve to protect animals to some extent, and for that reason it is to be welcomed.

The Committee was, however, concerned that the use of wording such as 'substantial benefit' in the 1989 proposal would leave too many doors open to the patent-seeker and would not protect the animal's 'natural integrity',[90] but they were still willing to support it in para 5.31. The new proposal for a directive, introduced after the MAFF Committee reported, uses a concept of proportionality to protect animals by providing that the suffering which may be caused to the animal by genetic alterations must be proportional to the benefits that can be derived from the invention. At the end of 1996 it was unclear as to whether this was going to satisfy the European Parliament Greens. The whole episode illustrates deep moral concern over biotechnological advance in contrast to enthusiasm within the scientific and business communities to see a legal framework introduced which allows them to move forward.

Without a new directive there is a danger that the law in relation to patenting might become extremely confused from country to country as businesses seek to exploit this new resource. This would not create the economic 'level playing field' that the Community is so keen to promote. More seriously, perhaps, animals' welfare requirements might be lost in a quest for profit without controls exerted by a national or supranational body such as the proposed Directive provides. Technological advance in relation to animal breeding represents a classic contemporary example of moral and philosophical concerns over the provision for the welfare of animals conflicting with a desire on the part of business to assert property rights to the full.

Fortunately for animals, they are no longer prosecuted in the ways practised by the Greeks and in medieval Europe. The notion of animals as property introduced by the Ancient Greeks and continued by the Romans, remains and is the subject of intense controversy. It is only over the past 170 years that humans have tried to improve their relationship with animals by preventing members of our own species from abusing or mistreating animals in a number of different ways. Now, as awareness of animal sentience and needs develops and technological possibilities increase, questions have been raised regarding the morality underpinning the laws that have been introduced or are planned in relation to biotechnological advances. In law,

---

90 *Ibid*, para 5.30. See pp 178–79 for a detailed account of the recommendations of the Committee.

companion animals are perceived as deserving of better protection than wild animals. Some laws appear to protect humans as much as or more than the animals who are the supposed objects of the legislation, and legitimate human interests regularly override attempts to invoke moral concern for animals. An examination of whether we treat other species in a morally consistent way reveals allegations of arbitrary distinctions being made between the species, anthropocentric[91] tendencies and legal systems which, some say, fail to keep up with moral debate and scientific advance.

---

91 Human-centred actions.

FURTHER READING

Evans, EP, *The Criminal Prosecution and Capital Punishment of Animals: The Lost History of Europe's Animal Trials*, 1906, reprinted 1988, London: Faber & Faber. A very stylised account of some remarkable occurrences throughout Europe, with the author's explanation for those practices.

Francione, G, *Rain Without Thunder: The Ideology of the Animal Rights Movement*, 1996, Philadelphia: Temple University Press. At around £50 this book may be beyond most budgets, but if obtained through a library it contains a good overview of the property status of animals and the consequences this brings, along with an interesting blueprint of the philosophical basis to campaigning which the writer urges the animal rights movement to adopt.

Turner, ES, *All Heaven in a Rage*, 1992, 2nd edn, Fontwell, Sussex: Centaur Press. An excellent overview of the development of British attitudes towards animals through social change, philosophical discussion and legislation. Recognised as a classic.

Hyde, WW, 'The Prosecution and Punishment of Animals and Lifeless Things in the Middle Ages and Modern Times' (1916) *Pensylvanian Law Review* 696–730. Along similar lines to Evans' book but in a more modern style and very readable.

CHAPTER THREE

HOW SHOULD THE LAW TREAT ANIMALS?

INTRODUCTION

The aim of this chapter is to draw together the main contemporary philosophical and scientific contributions to the debate over the status of animals which seek to influence the development of the law. Many of the historical contributions discussed in Chapter 1 remain as pertinent today as they were when first published. The influence of scientific discovery, however, has added a new dimension to the weight which can be attributed to credibility of contemporary philosophical contribution. Science and philosophy have certainly influenced legislators in the UK and Europe over the last 20 years.

Before we turn to contemporary arguments, it is worth considering two historical contributions which specifically examine how the law should treat animals. In the final work of his life, *Laws,* Plato created a picture of his Utopian State, which was to be called Magnesia. He was a great believer in government closely linked to philosophy, and within his ideas it appears that animals may have been viewed as being morally culpable and to be held responsible within the criminal law:[1] 'If a beast of burden or any other animal kills anyone (except when the incident occurs while they are competing in one of the public contests) the relatives must prosecute the killer for murder; the next of kin must appoint some Country Wardens, and they must try the case; if the animal is found guilty, they must kill it and throw it out beyond the frontiers of the country.'[2] Moral culpability of animals certainly seems to run contrary to modern consensus and it is doubtful whether there is any contemporary philosophical or scientific support.

In the following extract, which sharply contrasts with the theory suggested by Plato, EP Evans is in no doubt as to whether animals should be treated as being morally culpable in exactly the same way as humans:[3]

> [W]hy should not animals be held responsible for their conduct as well as human beings? There are men apparently less intelligent than apes. Why then should the man be capitally punished and the ape not brought to trail? And if the ape be made responsible and punishable, why not the dog, the horse, the

---

1   See the contribution of Walter Woodburn Hyde in Chapter 2, p 32 for an alternative explanation as to why animals were apparently tried and punished.

2   Saunders, TJ, *Plato: The Laws,* 1970, p 392, Harmondsworth: Penguin Books.

3   Evans, EP, *The Criminal Prosecution and Capital Punishment of Animals* (1906), 1987 edn, pp 236–37, London: Faber & Faber.

pig, and the cat? In other words, does evolutionary criminology justify the judicial proceedings instituted by medieval courts against animals or regard the typical human criminal as having in this respect no supremacy over the beast? Does modern science take us back to the barbarities of the Middle Ages in matters of penal legislation, and in abolishing judicial procedure against quadrupedal beasts is it thereby logically forced to stay the hand of justice uplifted against bipedal brutes? The answer to these questions is unhesitatingly negative. Zoöpsychology is the key to anthropopsychology and enables us to get a clearer conception of the genesis of human crime by studying its manifestations in the lower creation; we thus see it in the process of becoming, acquire a more correct appreciation of its nature and origin and learn how to deal with it more rationally and effectively in bestial man.

Not all writers have been quite so rational in their approach to animals' culpability. There are two primary functions of the criminal law, namely to deter others from committing crimes and to punish the offender. It is quite clear that an animal would not be able to recognise a link between crime and punishment. But Hierolymus Rosarius, writing in the 16th century, was convinced that killing an offending animal and then placing its body where it could be seen by others of its kind would be certain to act as a deterrent – a surprisingly punitive suggestion; Rosarius also wrote a book which detailed how animals were frequently superior to men in their rationality.[4]

Many of the laws which have been introduced in the last 150 years or so have been based on the notion of 'cruelty', which started to attract notable public concern at the end of the 18th century. Jeremy Bentham refers in the passage below to 'cruelty towards animals', a notion which remains at the core of protective legislation in every country which has it. Only our definitions of what actually amounts to 'cruelty' have changed as science has made discoveries as to what actually causes animal pain and suffering:[5]

> The legislator ought to interdict everything which may serve to lead to cruelty. The barbarous spectacles of gladiators no doubt contributed to give the Romans that ferocity which they displayed in their civil wars. A people accustomed to despise human life in their games could not be expected to respect it amid the fury of their passions. It is proper for the same reason to forbid every kind of cruelty towards animals, whether by way of amusement, or to gratify gluttony. Cock-fights, bull-baiting, hunting hares and foxes, fishing, and other amusements of the same kind, necessarily suppose either the absence of reflection or a fund of inhumanity, since they produce the most acute sufferings to sensible beings, and the most painful and lingering death of which we can form any idea. Why should the law refuse its protection to any sensitive being? The time will come when humanity will extend its mantle over everything which breathes. We have begun by attending to the condition

---

4   *Ibid*, pp 251–52.
5   Bentham, J, 'The Principles of Modern Penal Law', Part III, Chapter XVI, in Bowring, J, *The Works of Jeremy Bentham*, 1859 edn, vol 1, p 562, Edinburgh: Willaim Tait.

of slaves; we shall finish by softening that of all the animals which assist our labours or supply our wants.

The belief in the 'prevention of cruelty' advocated by Bentham still forms the main basis of current legislation and the incremental changes which are regularly introduced. The current debate regarding animals centres on how far society should recognise 'cruelty', as illustrated in the following piece by Michael Leahy:[6]

The law: stability and animals

Individual moral decision although capable of exemplification has, because of its circumstantial and often impulsive nature, been shown to be impossible to pin down for classification. But the system of laws in place at one time in a democracy worthy of the name has a permanence about it: partly due to the formality and bureaucracy of the institutions which sustain it, but, more importantly, because of the hydra-headed nature of the social processes which it facilitates. If income tax, the armed services, or even the Royal Family had to be revolutionised, it would be achieved by degrees with the countless checks and balances. In addition, the everyday activities of the courts, in handing down precedents, and the workings of legislative assemblies like the US Congress and British Parliament, ensure constant modification and renewal at, as it were, the edges. But what remains at any one time provides a crystallised record of society's received wisdom transmuted to some extent, of course, by the political intrusions of the democratic process and Christian tradition. (Christian belief was the forming influence of the law of equity which, in part, has to do with those legal 'persons' unable to help themselves.)

Now if we consult this record, and remember the success, in giving its modern form, of a gallery of reformers of roughly utilitarian hue from Tom Paine, Bentham, JS Mill, Tolstoy, to Bernard Shaw, Sidney and Beatrice Webb, and Evelyn Strachey, we might wonder why its provisions for animals do not embody more closely the ideals of that theory. Yet public opinion, as it is reflected in British law, has steadfastly refused to enlarge upon the spirit of pioneering legislation of the early 1820s and 1830s, updated 50 years later, which introduced the protection of animals against cruelty. The most recent legislation, the Animals (Scientific Procedures) Act 1986, as its title implies, is not a liberationist document. In my view this is as it ought to be. That animals should be treated humanely, and with this proviso, that they may be killed, experimented upon, hunted, raced, or petted is both the legal, and perfectly defensible, position to hold. It is no accident that it seems to confirm the position of animals near the foot of our thumbnail hierarchy or 'order of obligation' ... Furthermore, the ordering, in general, is supported by legal requirements in numerous other areas. A parent is legally bound to feed, clothe, house, not to mistreat, and to see to the education of his own children, but not those of his neighbour; although those next door are legally protected against anyone's abuse or assault. It can be an offence, however, not to assist

---

6   Leahy, M, *Against Liberation: Putting Animals in Perspective*, 1991, pp 176–78, London: Routledge. By permission of Routledge.

strangers, injured or in acute danger, where an obvious remedy is at hand such as pulling someone from wreckage or issuing a warning. But there is no legal obligation to assist people in general nor the world at large. The laws of citizenship provide a complete portfolio of legal entitlements which frequently elevate the members of a particular nation into a favoured species and the envy of a less fortunate world at large. In a less flamboyant way, numberless provisions of State law, county councils, local authorities, regulate and make possible the wealth, power, and by most people's lights, the reasonable and necessary exclusivity, of clubs, societies, schools, and universities which foster fraternal and even class loyalties.

Reformers and those with axes to grind will argue that much of this is all wrong despite its being the case. But my argument has been that it is not difficult to defend something roughly resembling the *status quo* rather than being bludgeoned into a guilt conscience by accepting that one is a covert elitist or racist. The animal liberationists certainly think that the 'cruelty-kindness view', as Regan calls it,[7] is speciesist since it ignores the extent to which animal awareness is akin to that of human beings. But if this is a mistake and animals are properly to be understood as primitive beings, at least as different from us as they are similar, then their modest entitlement to humane treatment, accorded them by commonsense and enshrined in the law, might well be vindicated.

WHAT NEEDS PROTECTION?

Two leading theories have emerged in relation to contemporary arguments for greater account to be taken of the moral position of animals. The first is the inherent value theory which has been put forward by Tom Regan in his book *The Case for Animal Rights*. This is, broadly speaking, a *rights*-based theory which looks upon some animals at least as possessing *inherent value* in that they have desires, an identity, a memory and sense of the future in a similar way to humans. This, in turn, can give them moral standing which needs to be taken into account by humans. Thus, in relation to animal use in agriculture or experimentation, for example, animals should have their inherent value as the 'experiencers of life' taken into account, and it would be difficult to justify using them because of their inherent moral claim, or 'right', to certain treatment. Thus, animals would be accorded *moral rights* which could then be reflected by giving them *legal rights*. This 'strong animal rights position' is certainly the philosophical blueprint which would have the most far-reaching effect on the relationship of humans to animals.

The second broad area of discussion occurs through the philosophical concept of 'utilitarianism', which rejects the notion of intrinsic moral rights

---

[7] Regan, T, *The Case for Animal Rights*, 1983, pp 195–200, Berkeley: University of California Press.

held by animals and embraces the notion of taking into account morally significant 'interests' instead. The utilitarianist proponent of improved animal welfare provision argues that animals have an 'interest' in not suffering which should be taken into account in our treatment of them.[8]

Both arguments agree on the principle that animals possess some qualities in common with humans which give rise to the need for better protection than we have been prepared to give. Proponents of both arguments use the cases of infants and severely mentally disabled or senile adults and find interests or inherent value in animals which might be said to go beyond those of these particular humans. This is based on the apparently superior sentience of some animals over humans in those situations. It is argued that if we accord interests or inherent value to those humans, then it would be morally inconsistent not to do the same for the analogous qualities of animals.[9]

Perhaps the critical difference between inherent value theory and the equal consideration theory of utilitarianism is as follows: inherent value theory recognises that there is an inbuilt quality of the individual which should not be surrendered except in the most extreme of circumstances; utilitarianism demands equal treatment and consideration but is willing to override this if the needs or desires of the many outweigh the needs or desires of the few. Therefore, as an example, inherent value theory would say that a sentient animal such as a chimpanzee should never be allowed to be used in experimentation. Its apparent self-awareness and undoubted sentience would ascribe to it inherent value which should not be sacrificed, in much the same way as we would not sacrifice individual humans for the sake of collective benefit, as inviolable 'rights' of the individual are not tradable in this way. Utilitarianism, as it is applied to the animals issue, proposes that as animals are able to suffer and feel pain in much the same way as humans, their interests should be considered as part of the equation. To ignore them on the basis of no more than membership of a species ignores comparable sentient qualities. This is illustrated by the demand that we should first consider using the insensate human in experimentation on account of their 'missing sentience', or we would be accused of 'speciesism'. For some in the animal welfare lobby the main problem is that the theory might, in the final analysis, allow the interests of the chimpanzee (or human) to be overridden by the consequential benefits which might be obtained by performing the experiment. Individuality would not carry the same weight as it does as a part of 'strong' animal rights theory.

8   See section on 'Utilitarianism' below, p 91.
9   Singer, P, *Animal Liberation*, 1995, 3rd edn, p 18, London: Pimlico.

INHERENT VALUE

It has been suggested that: 'what differentiates the modern animal protection movement from its predecessors is the acceptance by the former of the notion of animal rights.'[10] The crucial feature of the 'inherent value' argument is that it is an uncompromising denial of the modern-day arguments regarding the benefits that we obtain from the use of animals. It is the ultimate argument in favour of the individual animal by replacing the notion that 'the needs of the many outweigh the needs of the one' with the notion that 'the needs of the one are equivalent to the needs of the many'. There is evidence of this notion in human attitudes to 'the gift of life'. No one, it appears, feels such a burning desire to benefit the whole of mankind that they willingly allow themselves to be sacrificed in the cause of medical advance.

It could be argued that Albert Schweitzer was one of the 'grandfathers' of the modern 'rights' movement in relation to animals. Writing in the 1920s and 1930s he coined the phrase 'reverence for life' which arose out of a search for a common theme in his pursuit of the 'ethic of universality' and his critical evaluation of previous attempts at defining morality:[11]

> A Man is really ethical only when he obeys the constraint laid on him to help all life which he is able to succour, and when he goes out of his way to avoid injuring anything living. He does not ask how far this or that life deserves sympathy as valuable in itself, nor how far it is capable of feeling. To him life as such is sacred. He shatters no crystal that sparkles in the sun, tears no leaf from its tree, breaks off no flower, and is careful not to crush any insect as he walks.

There are elements of Schweitzer's 'life-centred' approach, and its recognition of the value of all life, in much of the contemporary work on 'animal rights', although there are considerable differences in the substance of the respective arguments. Tom Regan has continued the theme into modern times, although he would not accept 'inherent moral value' for *all* forms of life as Schweitzer did, but only to those animals who are 'subjects of a life', which would exclude lower lifeforms. Regan regards at least some animals, as having *enhanced* moral status. Schweitzer was critical of the use of animals in experimentation, but he stopped short of condemning it outright, by saying that those involved should 'care to alleviate as much as possible the pain which they cause'.[12] Modern 'inherent value' proponents such as Regan go much further by calling for an end to *all* animal experimentation. This applies particularly to experiments involving mammalian animals which are 'subjects

---

10 Francione, G, *Rain Without Thunder: The Ideology of the Modern Animal Rights Movement*, 1996, p 31, Philadelphia: Temple University Press.

11 Schweitzer, A, *Civilisation and Ethics*, 1923, p 254, London: A & C Black Ltd.

12 *Ibid*, p 264.

of a life'.[13] In spite of these differences, Schweitzer's argument constituted one of the stepping stones to the present-day discussion.

The attractive element of the inherent value argument, argue its proponents, is that it gives due weight to the interests of the *individual animal*. As discussed in Chapter 2, the chief problem for some proponents of animal rights is that any legislation we pass, even regarding animal 'welfare', only protects animals in relation to allowing our continued use and disposal of them as property.[14] Using his basic formula, legislation is framed in terms of protecting *human* interests rather than those of the animal. The central proposal in Regan's writing is that he sees inherent value in animals, specifically mammals of one year of age or over, which should accord to them a moral 'right to life' and a right to be treated properly in our dealings with them. He sees them as possessing beliefs, desires, perception, memory, self-consciousness and a sense of future which should be protected in the same way that we protect those moral claims for people. If it were accepted as the basis for future legislation, inherent value arguments would give animals the *right* to better fundamental treatment irrespective of their value as resources to humans, thus ending farming, experimentation involving animals, hunting and trapping. Intrinsic moral rights would become rights enshrined in the law. He points to the basic moral discrepancies in our treatment of animals to support a radical remodelling of law relating to them:[15]

> On the one hand, human beings, of whatever colour, gender, or religious persuasion, are recognised as having interests; are understood to be subjects who can themselves be benefited or injured; are viewed as individuals who can themselves press their claims or have them pressed by others acting on their behalf; are acknowledged to be possessors of a life that is better or worse for them considered as individuals, logically independently of their value to others; and are not relegated to the legal status of property but themselves have legal rights. On the other hand, we have non-human animals, members of many species which are now known to be like humans in the relevant respects – for example, they have interests and can be benefited or injured – but who are relegated to the legal status of property and who are denied legal rights. And my question is: Is there any satisfactory way to explain this discrepancy that does not itself bespeak the very prejudice at issue? Not surprisingly, I think not.

Regan looks to protect animals in the sense that they are experiencers of a life and deserving of protection in their own right. He rejects the positivist's view that the only real 'rights' are those given specifically by statute or a person's voluntary act. Regan appeals to us to base our legal protection of animals on the, presently, unquantifiable qualities of animals leading to moral rights. On

---

13 Regan, above n 7, p 392 and p 397.
14 See Francione, above n 10, Chapter 1.
15 Regan, T, *All That Dwell Therein*, 1982, pp 159–60, Berkeley: University of California Press.

a practical level this would, obviously, have significant effects on the interpretation of current legislation. It would require the introduction of new legislation at both national and international levels. At the moment, for example, one of the chief reasons that we protect endangered species is for the benefit of future generations. Using Regan's model would switch the emphasis of law from the benefit of future generations to protecting the animals in their own right:[16]

> Animals, it is true, lack many of the abilities humans possess. They can't read, do higher mathematics, build a bookcase or make *baba ghanoush*. Neither can many human beings, however, and yet we don't (and shouldn't) say that they (these humans) therefore have less inherent value, less of a right to be treated with respect, than do others. It is the *similarities* between those human beings who most clearly, most non-controversially have such value (the people reading this, for example), not our differences, that matter most. And the really crucial, the basic similarity is simply this: we are each of us the experiencing subject of a life, a conscious creature having an individual welfare that has importance to us whatever our usefulness to others. We want and prefer things, believe and feel things, recall and expect things. And all these dimensions of our life, including our pleasure and pain, our enjoyment and suffering, our satisfaction and frustration, our continued existence or our untimely death – all make a difference to the quality of our life as lived, as experienced, by us as individuals. As the same is true of those animals that concern us (the ones that are eaten and trapped, for example), they too must be viewed as the experiencing subjects of a life, with inherent value of their own.

> Some there are who resist the idea that animals have inherent value. 'Only humans have such value,' they profess. How might this narrow view be defended? Shall we say that only humans have the requisite intelligence, or autonomy, or reason? But there are many, many humans who will fail to meet these standards and yet are reasonably viewed as having value above and beyond their usefulness to others. Shall we claim that only humans belong to the right species, the species *Homo sapiens*? But this is blatant speciesism.

Some might argue that current laws in relation to, for example, farming or experimentation already protect animals and gives them 'rights', but Regan denies this and uses the example of a protected painting to illustrate why this is not necessarily the case: a law may protect a painting but it would be ridiculous to state that the painting is the possessor of 'rights'. Regan sees the claim for 'moral rights' of animals to be a separate issue from the resulting 'legal rights' which might be introduced. Regan is of the view that morality will accept nothing short of the granting of legal rights to animals. This would not mean legislating for them to have the right to go to school or to have a bus pass, but would recognise the inherent value and natural lives of animals distinct from our own prejudices towards them. In cases involving pain,

---

16 Regan, T, 'The Case for Animals Rights', in Singer, P (ed), *In Defence of Animals*, 1985, pp 22–23, Oxford: Basil Blackwell.

suffering or other 'abuse' a court would consider the situation from the animals' perspective not from the perspective of any *human* benefits to be gained. For Regan the importance of inherent value means that 'a legal system that excludes it is blind.'[17]

As we shall see later, Regan's views have been criticised from several sources. Some writers such as Frey deny Regan's use of the word 'right' at all, arguing that such a moral claim is only suitable for 'rational agents', namely humans. Other writers from within the animal rights movement itself, although agreeing with Regan's basic aim of improving the treatment of animals, find themselves unable to equate animal rights with human rights on the scale demanded by Regan. Most settle for a pragmatic and, probably, more widely accepted view that the pain and suffering of animals needs further protection. But the argument that a 'right to life' is comparable with a human's 'right to life' may contribute to the obscurification of the core issues caused by trying to define 'human rights', let alone 'animal rights'.

Perhaps the greatest strength of a 'rights'-based argument is that, unlike the utilitarianist argument, it brings home the importance of individuals by focusing on the fact that the needs of the one may outweigh the needs of the many. The notion of 'strong animal rights' as opposed to notions of interests or improved welfare has certainly attracted much interest, as is examined in the following section.

CAN ANIMALS HAVE 'RIGHTS'?

Unfortunately, the word 'rights' has been 'hijacked' by some philosophers who have struggled to find a definition of what a moral 'right' actually is in relation to humans and whether 'rights' exist at all. Therefore, when engaged in discussion about animal rights, the proponent of classical rights theories responds that 'animals can't have rights'.[18] Why is there so much disagreement concerning the granting of 'rights' to non-human animals?

The first problem occurs with the everyday usage of the word 'right'. When we speak of rights, what are we actually referring to? 'Human rights' would probably be the first definition of 'rights' which would come to mind if one were asked, and these would encompass the classical 'rights' embodied in the European Convention on Human Rights, including, for example, the right to a fair trial, the freedom to express oneself, and the freedom to associate with others. In addition to this extremely important, fundamental protection of what we consider to be the qualities which make the living of life richer by keeping us free from oppression and retaining our liberty, there are less

---

17   Regan, above n 15, p 163.
18   See the arguments of R Frey, below.

fundamental 'rights' which are also protected in various ways. These might include, for example, the 'right' to a free bus-pass and the 'right' to a pension. The 'fundamental moral rights' claimed for animals are different to these kinds of 'human rights' which, in most cases, would have no value to animals. The moral rights claimed for animals include those to protect their physiological, emotional and psychological attributes, which they claim gives us a moral reason for that protection. This lies at the heart of many arguments for improved animal protection. Some call this a 'right'; others refer to 'interests', or dismiss altogether any moral claim for enhanced or equal consideration.

The second problem occurs at a more fundamental philosophical level in the way that 'rights theory' has developed in relation to people. In classical philosophy, as espoused by Immanuel Kant, 'rights' cannot be attributed unless the subject of those rights has the will or capacity to enforce them and to attach a duty to another not to infringe those rights – rights are only granted to those who are able to fulfil the 'social contract', to claim the right and fulfil the corresponding duty to others, which animals plainly cannot: animals have no concept of duties towards others, and because animals are incapable of actually exercising their will in relation to *duties*, the claim for 'animal rights' has been criticised. This may be part of the reason for the emergence of other arguments within the modern animal welfare movement which avoid the use of the word 'rights'. Writers such as Peter Singer have embraced an alternative theory of the animal rights movement; namely interest theory which avoids this confrontation with the classical definition of 'rights' for humans. The traditional notion of the meaning 'rights' is itself criticised, because it is claimed that there is little logic in attaching rights to duties in an arbitrary manner. It is also pointed out that animals given enhanced legal protection would, presumably, have that law enforced by certain bodies, thereby creating that which, in all but name, has the attributes of a legal 'right'. If animals can have legal rights, it is argued, then surely they can have moral ones?

A third problem occurs when we try to equate human and non-human animal 'rights'. It is argued that when we talk of 'animal rights' we cannot ascribe to animals 'rights' which could be equated with 'human rights'. An animal's right to life, for example, would be lost if it came into conflict with the right to life of a human. An example of this is the 'lifeboat scenario' which has been used as the basis of theoretical discussion between philosophers to determine the nature of 'animal rights'.[19] The scenario involves humans and a dog in a lifeboat; one has to be cast overboard in order to secure the safety of the others. If we ascribed to the dog the same right to life as the humans, then the decision as to which would be cast overboard would have to depend on

19 See, for example, discussion in Regan, T and Singer, P (eds), *Animal Rights and Human Obligations*, 2nd edn, 1989, Englewood Cliffs: Prentice-Hall.

drawing lots. Most people would probably agree, however, that it would be the dog who should go first, illustrating that the right to life of a dog does not match that of humans.

This highly unlikely scenario involving a direct threat might merely show that in such an 'ultimate situation' the animal would be likely to lose out. It may be that we could plausibly and logically ascribe limited rights to animals which might be lost in such 'ultimate situations'. The third argument against animal 'rights' might not preclude animal rights but merely be indicative of their difference.

What is clear is that the traditionalists argue that, for the sake of consistency of argument, animals might best be described as having 'interests' which need to be taken into account, rather than 'rights'. But this is not accepted by everyone, and there are authoritative arguments that 'rights' already attributed to animals by law (in relation to scientific experimentation, for example), do not need to give rise to corresponding duties or need to be claimed by individuals themselves, as they can be claimed by another on their behalf.[20]

The foregoing discussion assumes that 'rights' are something which humans have, as yet, been unwilling to grant to animals on account of their sentient capacities. Joel Feinberg, on the other hand, argues that animals have 'rights' enshrined in the law already, in order to counter arguments by classical philosophers that animals do not have the necessary sentient attributes to become rightholders:[21]

> Almost all modern writers agree that we ought to be kind to animals, but that is quite another thing from holding that animals can claim kind treatment from us as their due. Statutes making cruelty to animals a crime are now very common, and these, of course, impose legal duties on people not to mistreat animals; but that still leaves open the question whether the animals, as beneficiaries of those duties, possess rights correlative to them. We may very well have duties *regarding* animals that are not at the same time duties *to* animals, just as we may have duties regarding rocks, or buildings, or lawns, that are not duties *to* the rocks, buildings, or lawns. Some legal writers have taken the still more extreme position that animals themselves are not even the directly intended beneficiaries of statutes prohibiting cruelty to animals. During the 19th century, for example, it was commonly said that such statutes were designed to protect human beings by preventing the growth of cruel habits that could later threaten human beings with harm too. Professor Louis B Schwartz finds the rationale of the cruelty-to-animals prohibition in its protection of animal lovers from affronts to their sensibilities. 'It is not the mistreated dog who is the ultimate object of concern,' he writes. 'Our concern is for the feelings of other human beings, a large proportion of whom,

---

20 Feinberg, J, 'The Rights of Animals and Unborn Generations', in Blackstone, W, *Philosophy and Environmental Crisis,* 1974, Athens, Georgia: University of Georgia Press. With kind permission of the University of Georgia Press.

21 *Ibid,* pp 43–68.

although accustomed to the slaughter of animals for food, readily identify themselves with a tortured dog or horse and respond with great sensitivity to its sufferings.' This seems to me to be factitious. How much more natural it is to say with John Chipman Gray that the true purpose of cruelty-to-animals statutes is 'to preserve the dumb brutes from suffering.' The very people whose sensibilities are invoked in the alternative explanation, a group that no doubt now includes most of us, are precisely those who would insist that the protection belongs primarily to the animals themselves, not merely to their own tender feelings. Indeed, it would be difficult even to account for the existence of such feelings in the absence of a belief that the animals deserve the protection in their own right and for their own sakes.

Even if we allow, as I think we must, that animals are the intended direct beneficiaries of legislation forbidding cruelty to animals, it does not follow directly that animals have legal rights, and Gray himself, for one, refused to draw this further inference. Animals cannot have rights, he thought, for the same reason they cannot have duties, namely that they are not genuine 'moral agents.' Now, it is relatively easy to see why animals cannot have duties, and this matter is largely beyond controversy. Animals cannot be 'reasoned with' or instructed in their responsibilities; they are inflexible and unadaptable to future contingencies; they are subject to fits of instinctive passion which they are incapable of repressing or controlling, postponing or sublimating. Hence, they cannot enter into contractual agreements, or make promises; they cannot be trusted; and they cannot (except within very narrow limits and for purposes of conditioning) be blamed for what would be called 'moral failures' in a human being. They are therefore incapable of being moral subjects, of acting rightly or wrongly in the moral sense, of having, discharging, or breeching duties and obligations.

But what is there about the intellectual incompetence of animals (which admittedly disqualifies them for duties) that makes them logically unsuitable for rights? The most common reply to this question is that animals are incapable of *claiming* rights on their own. They cannot make motion, on their own, to courts to have their claims recognised or enforced; they cannot initiate, on their own, any kind of legal proceedings; nor are they capable of even understanding when their rights are being violated, of distinguishing harm from wrongful injury, and responding with indignation and an outraged sense of justice instead of mere anger or fear.

No one can deny any of these allegations, but to the claim that they are the grounds for disqualification of rights of animals, philosophers on the other side of this controversy have made convincing rejoinders. It is simply not true, says WD Lamont, that the ability to understand what a right is and the ability to set legal machinery in motion by one's own initiative are necessary for the possession of rights. If that were the case, then neither human idiots nor wee babies would have any legal rights at all. Yet it is manifest that both of these classes of intellectual incompetents have legal rights recognised and easily enforced by the courts. Children and idiots start legal proceedings, not on their own direct initiative, but rather through the actions of proxies or attorneys who are empowered to speak in their names. If there is no conceptual absurdity in this situation, why should there be in the case where a proxy makes a claim on behalf of an animal? People commonly enough make wills leaving money to trustees for the care of animals. Is it not natural to speak of the animal's right to his inheritance in cases of this kind? If a trustee embezzles money from the animal's account, and a proxy speaking in the dumb brute's behalf presses the animal's claim, can he not be described as asserting the animal's *rights?* More exactly, the animal itself claims its rights through the vicarious actions of a human proxy speaking in its name and in its behalf. There appears to be no reason why we should require the animal to understand what is going on (so the argument concludes) as a condition for regarding it as a possessor of rights.

It may be that the argument over the recognition of 'rights' for animals and whether animals can actually have them is a 'red herring'. 'Rights' have been ill-defined for humans let alone animals and to become embroiled in that argument may be distracting us from the essential issues, as Henry Salt explains:[22]

The principle of animals' rights

Have the lower animals 'rights'? Undoubtedly – if men have. That is the point I wish to make evident ... But have men rights? Let it be stated at the outset that I have no intention of discussing the abstract theory of natural rights, which, at the present time, is looked upon with suspicion and disfavour by many social reformers, since it has not infrequently been made to cover the most extravagant and contradictory assertions. But though its phraseology is confessedly vague and perilous, there is nevertheless a solid truth underlying it – a truth which has always been clearly apprehended by the moral faculty, however difficult it may be to establish it on an unassailable logical basis. If men have not 'rights' – well, they have an unmistakable intimation of something very similar; a sense of justice which marks the boundary-line where acquiesence ceases and resistance begins; a demand for freedom to live their own life, subject to the necessity of respecting the equal freedom of other people.

Such is the doctrine of rights as formulated by Herbert Spencer. 'Every man', he says, 'is free to do that which he wills, provided he infringes not the equal liberty of any other man'. And again, 'whoever admits that each man must have a certain restricted freedom, asserts that it is a *right* he should have this restricted freedom ... And hence the several restricted freedoms deducible may fitly be called, his *rights'*.

The fitness of this nomenclature is disputed, but the existence of some real principle of the kind can hardly be called in question; so that the controversy concerning 'rights' is little else than an academic battle over words, which leads to no practical conclusion.

---

22 Salt, H, *Animals' Rights: Considered in Relation to Social Progress,* 1980 edn (original edn 1892), pp 1–3, Pennsylvania: Society for Animal Rights, Inc. By permission of the International Society for Animal Rights.

A similar theme has been proposed more recently by Stephen Clark:[23]

> Either those laws, from Martin's Act of 1822 to modern legislation against gin-traps and spring-traps, recognise that animals can be wronged or else they are laws of manners, dealing with the vice or virtue of the State's citizens. Either the evil they seek to prevent is the suffering of animals, as Hart supposes that he supposes,[24] or it is the moral corruption of human beings. If it is the latter we must decide if we are willing to retain such illiberal laws at the price of abandoning any objection of principle to further moralistic legislation. If it is the former, if animals are wronged – a wrong is committed – when they are treated with cruelty or negligence, how can we pretend to excuse the fate of those creatures tortured for their flesh, their fur, our pleasure, our convenience? My own opinion, indeed, is that a community has as much right to protect its moral as its material heritage, but most modern humanists seem to disagree. In that case 'if these laws have not been founded on a silent recognition (that *some* animals have at least *some* rights), they are unwarrantable curbs on the rights of men'.[25]

> And if some animals have some rights, even of this negative sort, to be spared wanton ill-treatment, on what grounds do we deny them other rights, to life and happiness within their kind? On what grounds can other animals be fair game? ...

> ... there has been no fully satisfying account even of human rights, let alone animal. All sorts of problems might arise: men can waive their rights, but animals either cannot do so or at least cannot be assumed to have done so; some human rights at least are positive, embodying the rightfulness of some claim upon society's resources, yet animals, perhaps, can make no such claims.[26] If animals have rights that can be disregarded, are they not disregarded also by other non-human animals, and do we not therefore have a duty to protect each creature's rights against all comers? And where do such *rights* lie in the relation of prey and predator? One law for the lion and the ox is oppression, and to save the ox may be an affront to the lion. To the extent that these queries embody real issues I shall attempt to deal with them in what follows, but it is well to remember that they may too easily be mere devices to distract attention from the main point.

> There are laws to protect animals even against their owners, laws which some judges at least have interpreted as according rights to the animals. It may be, however, that better legal opinion would hesitate to speak of rights in this

---

23 Clark, S, *The Moral Status of Animals*, 1977, pp 12–15, Oxford: Oxford University Press. By permission of Oxford University Press.

[24] For if Hart truly believed that avoidable suffering should be avoided, and the law invoked to ensure this, he would be an advocate of vegetarianism: in fact he plainly disapproves not of the infliction of *unnecessary* suffering, but of suffering inflicted in the course of human practices of which he disapproves for other reasons.

[25] Nicholson, EB, *The Rights of Animals*, 1879, p 16, London.

[26] Though Graham Haydon has remarked to me that if the right to an education is founded on the possession of certain educable capacities, it seems to follow that chimpanzees, dolphins et al have a right to an education. It also seems likely that experimental animals in particular have a claim in natural justice to care and protection at society's expense.

context, or would wish to make some subtle distinction between different varieties of rights. Such distinctions may be useful, but they do not contradict the simple claim that it is *wrong* to treat animals badly: *wrong,* not because of some damage to the human psyche (though such damage may indeed be grave) but for the very same reason that it is wrong to treat human beings badly. Animals can be wronged, *injured,* not merely metaphorically but in fact. The very fact that we do speak of *injuring* animals, whereas we can only damage the inanimate, is a symptom of our recognition that animals are the proper subjects of our moral concern. If we are mistaken in this, as Thomists and Kantians must suppose, and our relations with animals are without moral significance, then the protective laws are indeed merely laws of manners. If on the other hand, Thomists and Kantians are merely the mistaken heirs of Stoic thought, and animals are moral objects, how can we excuse our treatment of them?

Stephen Clark suggests that the use of the word 'right' has its problems for the proponents of animal welfare improvements. If this is so, the case is made to change the language used. Perhaps we are left with the notion that the person who says 'animals can't have rights' should be judged on whether they mean classical 'rights', or that animals don't deserve any moral consideration. Animal welfare campaigners might agree with the technical problems encountered by the former but not the apparently inhumane motives of the latter.

ENHANCED LEGAL STATUS FOR ANIMALS – HOW FAR SHOULD WE GO?

The question of whether animals have intrinsic moral rights gives rise to the further question of how far we should accord to them a status as 'persons'. The theory of 'rights' advocated by Regan only goes as far as making out a case for prohibiting exploitative relations with animals. Should we go further by enabling them, for example, to instigate legal proceedings through 'another' and to become the sole beneficiaries of any financial awards?

Aside from the conflict involving the very meaning of the word 'rights', many have argued that animals should have their inherent rights and interests recognised in the law beyond the current situation which views them as property in common law, objects of interest for future generations in environmental law, and the recipients of limited protection in animal welfare law. Comparisons are drawn with the situation of ethnic minorities throughout the Western world who struggled for centuries to attain rights comparable with those of the white man. The lack of legal recognition of those rights led to one American court finding that the black man had no legal rights which the white man need respect. This now seems absurd and in violation of basic humanitarian philosophy.[27]

The critical question that the law has asked in granting rights to individuals or groups of individuals is whether those entities are 'persons' deserving of the granting of 'rights'. Animals have never been granted legal status and the corresponding rights which would recognise their similarities to us. Yet the law has granted very specific legal rights to entities which in no way could claim to have the equivalent sentience to even the lowest order animals. Corporations, partnerships, central and local government, clubs and societies all operate through their representatives or legal counsel to uphold their 'rights' – for example, to damages for negligence and protection of their business interests. It is suggested that to deny animals rights on the basis that they are different and lack the essential qualities necessary as 'persons' denies the fact that we have already bypassed this requirement in these instances.

In an article which examines the nature of 'rights' which are granted to 'legal persons' such as human beings or, indeed, corporations, Roger W Galvin goes on to argue why 'rights' should be granted to non-human animals too:[28]

> If the criteria used to define 'personhood' are objectively shown to be satisfied by other species besides man, we simply must accept the fact that we are not unique. We cannot ignore our physical, mental and emotional evolution.[29] Logic dictates that if a species shares with us those attributes that we believe make us essentially human, we must conclude that we believe that the species in question is entitled to 'personhood'. The alternative is to discard the term altogether because it has no scientific, moral or legal justification; it is a term with no descriptive content. By clothing animals with the mantle of 'personhood' we recognise both their legal existence and the concurrent entitlement of legal protection, to the extent consistent with their nature. Such protection can only be effective if animals possess the right to have their interests judged independently of the subjective values that humans place upon them.

Galvin sees these rights in three forms: the right to live a life according to their nature, instincts and intelligence; the right to live in an ecologically sufficient habitat; and the right to be free from exploitation. This would create the corresponding duty upon humans not to infringe those rights and would lead where necessary to those rights being upheld by advocates for animals in a court of law. If animals were given legal status this would open the way for representatives to take legal action on their behalf, allowing them, for example, to become the direct beneficiaries of any award of damages or

---

27   *Dred Scott v Sandford* (1856) 60 US (19 How) 393.

28   Galvin, R, 'What Rights for Animals?: A Modest Proposal' (1985) 2 *Pace Environmental Law Review* 245 at 245–54.

[29] See Darwin, C, *The Evolution of the Emotions in Man and Animals*, 1979; Gruter, M, and Bohannan, P (eds), *Law, Biology and Culture: The Evolution of Law*, 1983.

injunctions against humans. Alternatively the money awarded might be used to fund animal welfare groups or the creation of a new 'Ministry for Animals', (as suggested by Sid Jenkins in Chapter 10) if it was felt to be frivolous to hold money on trust for individual animals.

Allowing actions on behalf of animals in contract is a pointless exercise, as animals do not possess the mental capabilities to enter a contract. Henry Cohen suggests another possibility:[30]

> [T]he concept of quasi contract might be invoked on behalf of animals who were injured as a result of justified reliance on another's acts. An example might be a pet animal or a zoo animal that was abandoned after having lost its ability to survive on its own, or that it was abandoned in a locale where survival on its own was impossible. The monkeys who were taught to use sign language and who were recently threatened with becoming the subjects of laboratory experiments also might have had a cause of action under this theory. Could not having taught these monkeys to use language be viewed as having created an obligation to keep them in an environment in which they could use this skill?

If the arguments of some proponents of animal rights such as Peter Singer are accepted to the full, then why should not the notion of obligation be extended to animals? Another aspect of this proposed creation of 'strong animal rights' is the proposal that an animal might have *tortious* damages awarded to it. A good example of this is an award of damages to an animal injured in a road accident where, for example, both dog and owner are injured, as Henry Cohen continues:[31]

> Under the present law, the man could recover veterinary expenses and any loss of income that resulted from the dog's injury (assuming the dog did television commercials or the like). But there could be no recovery for the dog's pain and suffering, even though the dog's pain and suffering might have been greater than the man's. Yet, as Peter Singer showed in *Animal Liberation*, there is no relevant difference between humans and animals that would justify considering the pain of one more important than the pain of the other. Incidentally, measuring a dog's pain and suffering would seem only slightly more difficult than measuring a man's.

To the philosophers who reject any rights for animals, such an idea will seem absurd, but there is a great deal of moral consistency in its favour *if* one accepts arguments from proponents of 'strong' animal rights.

Another controversial suggestion involves enhancing the legal status of some animals so as to bring them within the definition of murder. Under English law the definition of murder contains the phrase 'unlawful killing of a *reasonable person* who is in being and under the King's Peace.' In the US the

---

30 Cohen, H, 'Some Preliminary Thoughts on Permitting Animals to Sue in Contract and Tort' (1983) 4 *International Journal for the Study of Animal Problems* 284–85 at 284.

31 *Ibid*, at 284.

definition of murder follows the lines of this example from Tennessee: 'If any person of sound memory and discretion, unlawfully kills any *reasonable creature* in being, and under the peace of the State, with malice aforethought, either expressed or implied, shall be guilty of murder'.[32] Edwards and Marsh have pointed out that there is no precise definition of 'reasonable being', based as it is on the Aristotelian concept of humans as 'rational beings', which would necessarily exclude the higher primates. There is no requirement that the being in question be *highly* reasonable or a specific reference to humans. Edwards and Marsh propose not only that the definition of murder has probably been misinterpreted to exclude the higher primates, but also that there is a very good case for including them in the definition now:[33]

> Are all men reasonable creatures in being; and, are all reasonable creature in being men? It would seem that with a proper examination of the terms 'reasonable' and 'rational' a termination of a profoundly retarded child's life or the life of an irreversibly comatose patient under our murder statutes would not be murder, while the killing of the educable chimpanzee ... could be considered murder. The law is notoriously slow to move or change; however, this fact has its meritorious moments as well as its negative moments. Even if our courts should decide by arbitrary fiat that our murder laws do cover the profoundly retarded and the comatose human and do not cover the chimpanzee, the theoretical and moral issues concerning rationality ... would still remain to be resolved.

Edwards and Marsh suggest, therefore, that it would be morally questionable to redefine 'murder' in light of changes in our knowledge of the rationality of certain animals. This definition has been entrenched in many legal systems and has represented the moral basis of the law in that it is wrong to take a 'rational life'. If the definition was suddenly considered to be inadequate because it brings primates within its coverage, it would appear to be arbitrary and illustrative of human prejudice by suddenly moving the goal-posts. If Edwards and Marsh's proposal is accepted, then the moral consequences for experimentation involving primates would certainly be subject to further examination.

In the following extract Rosemary Rodd gives an overview of how enhanced legal status might work, and why it need not necessarily be seen as an unworkable abstract theory:[34]

> [L]egal personhood would mean that anti-cruelty laws would cease to appear more like laws of manners than the protection of individuals and it would no longer be possible to equate cruelty with 'victimless crimes', as Lord Patrick

---

32 *Tennessee Code Annotated*, Chapter 24, s 39–2401, Indianapolis: Bobbs Merrill Co, Inc.

33 Edwards, RB and Marsh, F, 'Reasonableness, Murder and Modern Science' (1978) 58 *Phi Kappa Phi Journal* 24–29.

34 Rodd, R, *Biology, Ethics and Animals*, 1990, pp 254–55, Oxford: Clarendon Press. By permission of Oxford University Press.

Devlin does in his book on the enforcement of morality.[35] Since the justifiability of legislating against behaviour purely because we happen to disapprove of it, rather than in order to protect its victims, is highly controversial, it appears that the legal recognition of animals as persons, ie as individuals who deserve protection for their own sakes, could be an important safeguard for their continued legal protection. It would also pave the way for further improvements. Proposals for the ending of ritual slaughter in Britain, for example, have been strongly criticised as mere prejudice against the customs of minorities:

'If ritual slaughter is cruel ... it is for the minority communities themselves to sort the matter out according to their own customs and priorities. Members of the majority community have no right to lecture them.'[36]

In ritual slaughter according to Jewish and Islamic custom pre-stunning is not permitted and the animal's throat is cut while he is still conscious. There is evidence that the cut does not produce immediate loss of consciousness, particularly in young animals, and that there may be a period of severe pain.[37] If animal protection were not seen as an attempt to protect a particular group of society members, reformed legislation need not be seen simply as prejudiced interference with a minority culture.

The 'personhood' of some species need not mean that all animals would have to be granted equal status ... some species, such as sponges, are unlikely to have subjective experience. Nor need it mean that animal persons must necessarily have exactly the same legal rights as normal adult humans. In some instances this might not be in the animal's own best interests, as in the case of euthanasia, where it arguable that the animal's inability to comprehend his suffering is a crucial reason why it should be permissable to end his life painlessly if there is no reasonable hope of his recovery. However, it does not seem to be the case that present laws necessarily compel us to treat different types of legal persons as if they were exactly the same. No one would treat the dissolution of a limited company as murder, even though companies are treated as legal persons in certain circumstances. Thus, legal classification of some species of animal as persons need not rule that their interests might never be sacrificed to the welfare of the general community (as indeed the interests of human persons are sometimes sacrificed in times of great necessity). However, we might no longer feel so easily justified in killing them, as the Nuer say, 'just for nothing' (ie merely to eat, not out of necessity).

In the following extract, Helena Silverstein also examines the advantages of moving towards a notion of rights and the effect this has on *human* rights. She also explains how the movement lies close to other claims for 'rights' and the advantages this brings:[38]

[35] Develin, P, *The Enforcement of Morals*, 1965, p 17, London: Oxford University Press.

[36] Redfern, N, letter published in *The Guardian*, 2 September 1985.

[37] Farm Animal Welfare Council, *Report on the Welfare of Livestock when Slaughtered by Religious Methods*, 1985, London: HMSO.

38 Silverstein, H, *Unleashing Rights: Law, Meaning, and the Animal Rights Movement*, 1996, pp 231–32, Ann Arbor: The University of Michigan Press. By permission of The University of Michigan Press.

The notion of animal welfare subscribes to specific identity images of humans and non-humans. Rationality separates humans from non-humans and creates a hierarchy of identity in which human identity is superior to non-human identity. Although superior, human identity is also compassionate and considerate. Thus, treatment of non-humans is guided by the dual sides of human identity: compassion and rationality. Aside from the fact that non-humans lack rationality, non-human identity is of little relevance; human identity is what matters for animal welfare.

The notion of animal rights puts forth alternative identity images for both humans and non-humans by suggesting a relative equality between the two. Sentience becomes the crucial identifying characteristic that dissolves the gap between humans and non-humans. With sentience, activists maintain that animals gain an identity worthy of rights. Not only must humans be caring and considerate to animals, but they must also be restrained by the rights of animals. These alternative identity images contained within animal rights are noteworthy because they resist the dominant conception of rights and the identity images normally associated with rights.

The alternative identity images of humans and non-humans are noteworthy because not only do they elevate animals to the level of rights-bearing entities, they further speak to human rights. On the one hand, identifying animals as rights-bearing beings places considerable limits on what we now take to be human rights. If animal rights are accepted, the right of humans to eat and wear what we choose is no longer viable. On the one hand ... animal rights reinforce certain human rights and, in turn, human identity. Because the notion of human rights goes beyond rationality, it maintains the rights and identities of those humans who lack rationality, including the rights of the mentally disabled and children.

Movement identity is also significantly influenced by these alternative identity images. With the move to rights, animal advocates seek to cast their movement's identity in a new light. From the animal advocate's perspective, the choice of rights creates a positive, progressive, and life-affirming identity for the movement. It is an identity that stresses the values of liberation, equality, community, relationship, and caring. In addition, for animal advocates the movement's identity does not diminish human identity but uplifts animal identity.

The movement to rights attempts to align the identity of the animal rights movement with the identities of movements for civil, women's, and gay and lesbian rights. Like these movements, the animal rights movement seeks to extend moral and legal rights to a group that has been excluded from consideration. But the animal rights movement is, in an important sense, distinct from these other movements. Since the concept of animal rights moves beyond the prevailing notion of rationality, the movement's identity lies closer to the identities of the movements for the rights of children and the mentally disabled.

However, animal rights go beyond all of these movements by steering away from the strict emphasis on human rights. The identity of the animal rights movement is therefore unique. To be sure, this movement, like others, has appropriated and internalised a dominant mode of speaking. As such, its identity has certainly been shaped by the prevalence of rights language and its commonplace meaning. But this movement's uniqueness suggests that a movement's identity can resist dominant constructions of meaning. The movement, assuming a rights-oriented identity, has not straightforwardly subscribed to accepted notions of rights. The indeterminate meaning of rights thus provides the movement with space in which to shape its own identity.

UTILITARIANISM

Despite being regarded as one of the 'fathers' of the modern animal rights movement Peter Singer, as a utilitarian, does not in fact present an argument for 'animal rights' at all. This apparently strange anomaly occurs because of the inherent confusion, left untouched, between a notion of 'rights' for animals as espoused by Tom Regan, and the broad spectrum of philosophical ideals covered by the term 'animal rights movement'. This term is a misleading historical error which has never been rectified. Singer does not call for the recognition of moral 'rights' leading to the necessity for 'legal rights', but uses utilitarian principles which would have the effect of creating enhanced protection for animals.

Utilitarianism, as applied to humans in the tradition of Jeremy Bentham, applies two basic criteria to moral decision-making. The first is that everybody's interests, whether black or white, male or female, European or African, carry the same significance. The second principle is that any act should be undertaken having given due consideration to all competing interests and recognising the best possible equilibrium between the satisfaction and frustration of the interests of those affected by the action. Utilitarianism is not, therefore, a philosophical tool which was been devised purely to advocate the animal rights argument. In fact, the whole basis of our present moral attitude to animals, and accordingly the way in which the law protects them, is actually based upon the notion that society feels able to say that the benefits we gain from using animals for food, experimentation or whatever outweigh the disadvantages to the animals themselves. Utilitarianism can in some ways be regarded as the philosophical *cause* of our treatment of animals, not just as one suggested route to a remedy for its perceived ills. Peter Singer is the foremost contemporary advocate of using the principles of utilitarianism to promote a different approach to our treatment of animals. He claims that this would have much the same effect as using a 'rights'-based approach by prohibiting many of our present uses of animals because the present ends do not justify the present means.

Utilitarianism, as applied to the animal welfare debate, claims that animals' interests, principally the interest in not suffering or being subjected to pain, should be given much greater weight by humans in deciding whether to proceed with a certain course of action, such as farming animals for food or using them as the subjects of experimentation. In the case of experimentation, for example, there are the competing interests of the animal not to suffer and the possible benefits to be obtained from the experiment. Utilitarianism imposes a degree of egalitarianism to all conflicts, in that *all* competing interests have to be taken into account in order to decide upon a course of action. The argument of the utilitarian in relation to animals is that animals have interests which should be taken into account where they are similar to our own – such as the interest in not suffering pain.

As will be discussed later, classical 'rationalist' theories hold that animals cannot be accorded 'rights' for a variety of reasons. Depending on how the term 'interest' is defined, utilitarian theories can remove the need for claiming 'rights' at all, and assert the moral claim to have *interests* taken into account instead. Of course, it is still a moot point as to whether an 'interest' protected by law might reasonably be interpreted as a legal right being accorded to the animal. The attraction of utilitarianism here is that it removes us, in part, from the need to consider whether animals can have rights, and stops that area of uncertainty distracting us from the core issues of sentience, pain and suffering leading to claims for equal consideration.

The interest theory of the utilitarians is subject to much controversy and debate with writers such as RG Frey arguing that animals cannot have interests because they have no desires or emotions which are based on thoughts which, in turn, animals are incapable of having because of their lack of language (see later in this chapter).

The interest argument from the utilitarian point of view is argued extremely powerfully by Peter Singer in his highly respected book, *Animal Liberation*. Singer is regarded by many as starting a new era in the development of the law concerning animals.[39] He does not argue for the *same* rights for animals as we give to humans, just for their interests in avoiding suffering to be adequately considered:[40]

> Jeremy Bentham, the founder of the reforming utilitarian school of moral philosophy, incorporated the essential basis of moral philosophy into his system of ethics by the means of the formula: 'Each to count for one and none for more than one.' In other words, the interests of every being affected by an action are to be taken into account and given the same weight as the like interests of any other being. A later utilitarian, Henry Sedgwick, put the point in this way: The good of any one individual is of no more importance, from the point of view (if I may say so) of the Universe, than the good of any other.' More recently, the leading figures in contemporary moral philosophy have shown a great deal of agreement in specifying as a fundamental

---

39 See, for example, Rowan, A, in *Of Mice, Models and Men*, 1984, p 151, Albany: State University of New York Press; Francione, G, *Rain Without Thunder: The Ideology of the Animal Rights Movement*, 1996, p 14, Philadelphia: Temple University Press.

40 Singer, P, *Animal Liberation*, 1995 edn, pp 4–5, London: Pimlico. By permission of Random House.

presupposition of their moral theories some similar requirement that works to give everyone's interests equal consideration – although theses writers cannot agree on how this requirement is best formulated.[41]

It is an implication of this principle of equality that our concern for others and our readiness to consider their interests ought not to depend on what they are like or on what abilities they may possess. Precisely what our concern or moral consideration requires us to do may vary according to the characteristics of those affected by what we do: concern for the well-being of children growing up in America would require that we teach them to read; concern for the well-being of pigs may require no more than that we leave them with other pigs in a place where there is adequate food and room to run freely. But the basic element – the taking into account of the interests of the being, whatever those interests may be – must, according to the principle of equality, be extended to all beings, black or white, masculine or feminine, human or non-human.

Thomas Jefferson, who was responsible for writing the principle of the equality of men into the American Declaration of Independence, saw this point. It led him to oppose slavery even though he was unable to free himself fully from his slaveholding background. He wrote in a letter to the author of a book that emphasised the notable intellectual achievements of Negroes in order to refute the then common view that they had limited intellectual capacities:

'Be assured that no person living wishes more sincerely than I do, to see a complete refutation of the doubts I myself have entertained and expressed on the grade of understanding allotted to them by nature, and to find that they are on a par with ourselves ... but whatever be their degree of talent it is no measure of their rights. Because Sir Isaac Newton was superior to others in understanding, he was not therefore lord of the property or persons of others.'[42]

Similarly, when in the 1950s the call for women's rights was raised in the US, a remarkable black feminist named Sojourner Truth made the same point in more robust terms at a feminist convention:

'They talk about this thing in the head; what do they call it? ["Intellect", whispered someone nearby.] That's it. What's that got to do with women's rights or negroes' rights? If my cup won't hold but a pint and yours holds a quart, wouldn't you be mean not to let me have my little half-measure full?'[43]

---

[41] For Bentham's moral philosophy, see his *Introduction to the Principles of Morals and Legislation*, and for Sidgwicks's see *The Methods of Ethics*, 1907 (the passage is quoted from the 7th edition, 1963, p 382, London: Macmillan). As examples of leading contemporary moral philosophers who incorporate a requirement of equal consideration of interests, see Hare, RM, *Freedom and Reason*, 1963, New York: Oxford University Press, and Rawls, J, *A Theory of Justice*, 1972, Cambridge: Harvard University Press, Belknap Press. For a brief account of the essential agreement on this issue between these and other positions, see Hare, RM, 'Rules of War and Moral reasoning' (1972) 1(2) *Philosophy and Public Affairs*.

[42] Letter to Harry Gregoire, 25 February 1809.

[43] Reminiscences by Gage, FD, from Anthony, SB, *The History of Woman's Suffrage*, vol 1; the passage is to be found in the extract in Tanner, L (ed), *Voices From Women's Liberation*, 1970, New York: Signet.

It is on this basis that the case against racism and the case against sexism must both ultimately rest; and it is in accordance with this principle that the attitude that we may call 'speciesism,' by analogy with racism, must also be condemned. Speciesism – the word is not an attractive one, but I can think of no other – is a prejudice or attitude of bias in favour of the interests of members of one's own species and against those of members of other species. It should be obvious that the fundamental objections to racism and sexism made by Thomas Jefferson and Sojourner Truth apply equally to speciesism. If possessing a higher degree of intelligence does not entitle one human being to use another for his or her own ends, how can it entitle humans to exploit non-humans for the same purpose?

For Singer the only answer is to ban animal experiments until we are ready to consider the use of human infants and brain-damaged humans who possess no more significant sentient qualities than some of the animal subjects of experimentation. In the same way that the 'rights' arguments cause problems, so also do the utilitarians come under scrutiny for various reasons. Utilitarianism requires a cost/benefit analysis, and a problem here is to decide what should be taken into account in that analysis. Bentham suggested that the pleasure and pain outcomes of an action would be the best approach, but in recent times writers such as Singer have preferred to talk of the 'maximisation of preferences' or 'interest satisfaction'. As with most moral theories, the reason for the changing language is the dissatisfaction or inadequacies of earlier descriptions of theories. Despite the use of language as the primary historical tool to distinguish 'man from the beasts', ironically, we constantly come across the inadequacies of language in describing the crucial moral concerns, emotional responses and intuitive responses of humankind of our interactions with each other and animals.

Utilitarianism as applied to the claims for 'animal rights' also fails to satisfy some of those within the movement itself. Robert Nozick, for example, illustrates the reason why there are those who dislike the theory of utilitarianism as it is applied to any given situation involving people or animals when he raises the possibility of 'utility monsters who get enormously greater gains in utility from any sacrifice than these others lose', which would satisfy the acceptance of some very dubious practices.[44] Tom Regan is also critical and has consistently attacked utilitarianism in that, in the final analysis, it allows any human or animal to be used where the benefits outweigh the costs, thereby sanctioning a 'good end' by 'evil means'. This, he argues, fails to accord the necessary value to *individuality* which exists irrespective of that creature's value to other creatures and amounts to a violation of individual rights.[45] In response to these claims that he would sanction experimentation on animals *or humans*, where the benefits were

---

44 Nozick, R, *Anarchy, State and Utopia*, 1974, p 41, Oxford: Basil Blackwell.
45 Regan, above n 16, p 21.

proved to lead to a cure for diseases, Singer responds that he is very doubtful as to whether this could ever be proven to a satisfactory level. He doubts whether any experiments would be valuable enough to warrant experiments involving humans or animals and, to all intents and purposes, the application of the utilitarian animal rights theory would amount, in practice, to total prohibition.

Utilitarianism is faced with other challenges, such as the difficulty in deciding what preferences or satisfaction of interests should be taken into account in given situations. It is very difficult to pick out all the potential benefits in a given situation. Do we look one week, one month, or years ahead? Utilitarianism is dependent on being able to accurately compare the different experiences of different animals. But in relation to comparing the pain and suffering of animals, how do we go about identifying the *nature* of this in different species in order to be able to compare it? Singer has trouble in protecting the lives of certain animals for their own sake. In agriculture, for example, Singer explains how the knowledge of the future is essential in making the taking of certain lives wrong. But if some animals cannot appreciate the future, then the painless taking of their lives and their replacement by another animal might be considered to be acceptable. For 'inherent rights' advocates, this capacity for sensing the future is only one indicator of 'sentience' which would not carry the significance which Singer applies to it in relation to farm animals. There are other capacities in being an 'experiencer of life', such as the ability of memory or perception, which are relevant to creating 'rights'. The possibility left by utilitarianism for experimentation or the use of animals in agriculture leaves the theory unacceptable to many within the animal rights lobby, despite its historical significance in the creation of the movement itself.[46]

OTHER THEORIES

The problem encountered by the proponents of increased protection for animals has been to try and fit the reasons in favour of this into any single moral theory such as inherent value theory or utilitarianism. This is illustrated by the problem that Tom Regan had in trying to include the acceptance that a dog would not survive at the expense of the human in the 'lifeboat scenario' (discussed below) within a theory based on the inherent value of all species of a certain level of sentience. Singer's utilitarian stance has also found difficulty in defining a moral code for all times and all places.

This has led other philosophers to approach the issue of a change in our relationship with animals in ways less dependent on a single moral theory.

---

46 Garner, R, *Animals, Politics and Morality*, 1993, p 129, Manchester: Manchester University Press.

Stephen Clark, sympathising with a hypothetical 'amoralist', embraces many different philosophical approaches to the consideration of the fate of animals in the search for a practical outcome rather than a single theoretical device:[47]

> I have not offered any consistent moral system in the course of my explorations. The first reason for this is purely practical: I am very much more interested in achieving a practical issue than in the details of abstract philosophy, and am willing to argue on almost any basis to achieve that end. The second reason is Aristotelian: I doubt if there is any set of rules, any clear and compendious system, that does full justice to the vagaries and unformalisable sensitivities of our moral experience.

He accepts, for example, the Kantian notion that improving the human attitude to non-human animals might improve human attitudes towards our own species.[48] He also concurs with the criticism of utilitarianism in that the doctrine, based as it is on the calculus of outcomes in terms of pleasures and desires, supposes that the pleasures and desires of different species are *actually* comparable.[49]

Mary Midgeley also avoids the use of a single moral theory to underpin her claims for animals. She supports the animal rights cause to a large extent but, whilst she dismantles the absolute denial theories of writers such as Descartes and Leibniz (see Chapter 1), she appears wary of 'rights' arguments. Midgeley seems to support positivist theories that 'rights' might only exist as far as they are given to those who can understand and claim them.[50] She also recognises the important part which has been played by the proponents of utilitarianism such as Bentham and Singer but finds Singer's case for dropping species barriers in favour of considering the pain and suffering of animals and humans as morally equivalent, to be unacceptable. Instead, she defends the notion of 'our tendency to respond differentially' as being a natural one.[51]

Midgely tends towards a recognition that we treat animals in morally questionable ways, but she does not feel able to embrace a single moral theory to explain why. Midgely's more pragmatic approach is certainly one favoured by many of those in the animal rights movement, who often agree with the strands of several moral arguments against our present treatment of animals. As an example of how Midgely's all-embracing pragmatic approach reflects what happens in practice, we can quote her vigilant attitude to both the pro- and anti-animal experimentation lobbies:[52]

---

47   Clark, above n 23, p 186.

48   *Ibid*, p 182.

49   *Ibid*, p 70.

50   Midgely, M, *Animals and Why They Matter*, 1983, p 62, Athens: University of Georgia Press.

51   *Ibid*, p 105.

52   *Ibid*, p 28.

Both sides now acknowledge the need to meet each other's arguments. It must emerge that some experiments are much more justifiable than others. The feat of justification cannot, in any case, be performed merely by raising an umbrella marked 'Science'. It demands attention to the actual benefits which can reasonably be expected, and serious comparison of the conflicting values involved.

THE INFLUENCE OF SCIENCE AFTER DARWIN

The place of science in the moral argument concerning animals is currently undergoing a change. In the 18th and 19th centuries scientists were seen as the opposition by the animal welfare campaigners – ruthless pursuers of medical advance with little or no regard for the animals they used as the subjects of live experiments. But the work of Charles Darwin brought about a radical change in the role of science in attributing new protection to animals. The ramifications of Darwin's revolution in science are increasingly becoming apparent. Darwin saw evidence for the clear relationship between humans and other species but others have always denied just how far these similarities extend. Scientific evidence is beginning to reveal more conscious awareness down the evolutionary ladder evidenced by long and painstaking research involving close observation of animals over months and sometimes years. Without the aid of language it is very difficult to reveal the thoughts of a monkey, cow, dog or rat, without long-term observation.

As evidence of suffering comes to light, such as that revealed by the scientists discussed in Chapter 5 regarding farm animals, there are indications that legislation should change if it is to remain morally consistent. We might leave in place laws which protect purely on the basis of species membership – this is favoured by many such as Frey and Carruthers, as examined in the next section. On the other hand, as suggested here by Jeffrey Masson, the moral case for change based on science might be overwhelming:[53]

> What are the implications of finding that animals lead emotional lives comparable to our own? Must we change our relationship with them? Have we obligations to them? Is animal testing defensible? Is experimentation on animals ethical? Can we confine them for our edification? Can we kill them to cover, sustain and adorn ourselves? Should we cease eating animals who have complex social lives, passionate relations with one another, and desperately love their children?

> Is something like us more worthy of respect than something not like us? Humans often behave as if this were the case with respect to other human beings. Racism can partly be described, if not explained, in this way. Men treat other men better than they treat women, based in part on their view that

---

53 Masson, J and McCarthy, S, *When Elephants Weep: The Emotional Lives of Animals*, 1996, pp 215–23 (abridged), London: Vintage.

women are not like them. Many of these so-called differences are disguises for whatever a dominant power can impose. Think, for a moment, of how human beings treat trees, the rationales used. As John Fowles put it: 'Unlike white sharks, trees do not even possess the ability to defend themselves when attacked; what arms they sometimes have, like thorns, are static and their size and immobility means they cannot hide, they are the most defenceless of creations in regard to man ...'. Which is why they are destroyed in such large numbers.

The basic idea seems to be that if something does not feel pain in the way a human being feels pain, it is permissible to hurt it. Even though this is not necessarily true, the illusion of differences is maintained out of fear that seeing similarity will create an obligation to accord respect and perhaps even equality. This appears to be especially true when it comes to suffering, pain, sorrow, sadness. We do not want to cause these things in others because we know what it feels like to experience them ourselves. No one defends suffering as such. But animal experimentation? The arguments revolve around their utility, pitting the greater good against the lesser suffering. Implicit, usually, is the greater importance of those who stand to gain, compared with the lesser importance of those who are sacrificed to their benefit.

An animal experimenter, almost by definition, is going to deny that animals suffer in the same way that a human does. If that were not so, then an admission of cruelty would be implicit. Experimental suffering is not randomly imposed without consent on human beings and defended as ethical on the grounds that it would bestow enormous benefits to others. Animals suffer. Can we, should we, measure it, compare it to our own? Why should the suffering have to be like ours? It has been argued that humans experience pain more acutely because we remember and anticipate it. It is not apparent that an animal cannot do both. But even if it could not, there is no reason to suppose that some may suffer more. Brigid Brophy, for example, points out that 'pain is likely to fill the sheep's whole capacity for experience in a way it seldom does in us, whose intellect and imagination can create breaks for us in the immediacy of our sensations'. But isn't the fact that they suffer at all enough? ...

... When humans refuse to inflict pain on others, surely it is because they assume they feel. It is not because another person can think, nor because they can reason, nor even because they can speak that we respect their physical boundaries, but because they feel. They feel pain, humiliation, sorrow and other emotions, perhaps even some we do not yet recognise. We do not want to cause suffering. If, as I believe, animals feel pain and sorrow and all other emotions, these feelings cannot be ignored in behaviour towards them. A bear is not going to compose Beethoven's 9th Symphony, but then neither is our next-door neighbour. We do not for this reason conclude that we have the freedom to experiment upon him, hunt him for sport or eat him for food ...

... Reciprocity on the level of Androcles and the lion, this dream of equality, may be closed for us now; whether or not it can be realised, we do owe animals something. Freedom from exploitation and abuse by humankind should be the inalienable right of every living being. Animals are not there for us to drill holes into, clamp down, dissect, pull apart, render helpless and subject to agonising experiments. They are, like us, endangered species on an endangered planet, and we are the ones who are endangering them, it and ourselves. They are innocent sufferers in a hell of our making. We owe it to them, at the very least, to refrain from harming them further. If no more, we could leave them be.

THE REJECTION OF MORAL RIGHTS AND THE INTERESTS OF ANIMALS

Different writers in the rationalist and contractualist traditions have sought, to varying degrees, to discount animals from moral consideration. Some rationalists such as Descartes (see Chapter 1) and Spinoza writing in the 17th century, stressed a human's rationality as setting them apart from the rest of the animal kingdom. They sought to discount all consideration regarding animals. Spinoza went as far as seeing pity as an evil, because it is a feeling and causes pain.[54] The associated theory of contractualism, in the tradition of Locke, Rousseau and Kant attempts to define how the fundamental underpinning moral values of society are to be decided. The contents of the 'contract' are described by John Rawls as 'the principles that free and rational persons concerned to further their own interests would accept in an initial position of equality as defining the fundamental terms of their association.'[55]

Contractualists have tended to avoid ascribing moral rights to animals as the theory is aimed at governing the principles of the dealings – the rights and duties – that exist between articulate, self-interested 'rational agents', a term which, by its definition, excludes animals. Whereas some writers from these traditions deny that animals should be the subjects of our moral concern at all, Rawls uses these philosophical tools to distinguish humans and animals and the degree to which the laws of society should protect them, but falls short of an absolute dismissal of their interests. In his eyes, the rules of society are to be decided upon by rational agents who would choose the rules to govern their interaction from behind a 'veil of ignorance'. This term refers to the need to make the rule-makers ignorant of some things such as their relative intelligence, physical strength and personal desires. Otherwise, they would create rules which reflected their own strengths at the expense of other rational agents – strong people might have certain benefits bestowed upon them, or people of wealth only might be entitled to a fair hearing in a dispute. They would, however, have to be aware of certain broad concepts such as happiness and freedom in order to be able to create a set of rights and duties which would be applicable and relevant to all those rational agents.

What then of the place of animals in this equation? It is clear that animals, lacking the necessary linguistic skills, could not take part in the fictitious

---

54   Rhys, E (ed), *The Ethics of Spinoza and De Emendatione*, 1913 edn, pp 175–76, London: Dent.
55   Rawls, J, *A Theory of Justice*, 1972, p 11, Oxford: Oxford University Press.

'discussion'. However, the question remains as to whether animals might be accorded any rights in this decision-making process occurring behind the 'veil of ignorance'. The rationalists have generally argued that animals should not be accorded rights for three main reasons: first, they cannot be accorded rights because they could not be part of the decision-making process, not being rational agents; secondly, because of the fact that they are not rational, they could not recognise the duties that they themselves should owe to the other possessors of rights; and thirdly, to accord them the same status as humans would be against a 'common sense' rationale which should lead us to accord greater status to our own species.

One of the first philosophers to look at the moral status of animals in this way was Immanuel Kant (1724–1804), who regarded the 'rational bond' between humans as creating duties towards each other. He denied that similar duties are owed to animals,[56] but still managed to find a route to allowing them some consideration:[57]

> So far as animals are concerned, we have no direct duties as animals are not self-conscious, and are there merely as a means to an end. That end is man. We can ask, 'Why do animals exist?' But to ask 'Why does man exist?' is a meaningless question. Thus, if a dog has served his master long and faithfully, his service, on the analogy of human service, deserves reward, and when the dog has grown too old to serve, his master ought to keep him till he dies. Such action helps to support us in our duties towards human beings, where they are bounden duties ... If a man shoots his dog because the animal is no longer capable of service, he does not fail in his duty to the dog, for the dog cannot judge, but his act is inhuman and damages in himself that humanity which it is his duty to show towards mankind ... He who is cruel to animals becomes hard also in his dealings with men ... The more we come in contact with animals, and observe their behaviour, the more we love them, for we see how great is their care for their young. It is then difficult for us to be cruel in thought even to a wolf. Leibnitz used a tiny worm for purposes of observation, and then carefully replaced it with its leaf on a tree so that it should not come to harm through any act of his. He would have been sorry – a natural feeling for a humane man – to destroy such a creature for no reason.

Thus, Kant explains why we owe no direct duties to animals, but only indirect duties to those humans who might be upset, angry or merely affected financially by our actions. Such a philosophy certainly has no room for the ascription of rights to animals which is argued by Regan, or the similar value placed upon the pain and suffering of animals in the utilitarian balancing act performed by Singer. In Kant's view, humans are the only beings which carry any inherent reason for direct moral concern.

---

56 See p 12, above.

57 Kant, I, *Lectures on Ethics – Duties Towards Animals and Other Spirits* (1780–81), Infield, L (trans), 1963, pp 239–40, New York: Harper & Row.

In response to the inability of animals to be at the imaginary bargaining table to emphasise their interests, many have argued that representatives could argue on their behalf for some recognition of the status of animals when the decisions were being made behind this 'veil of ignorance'. The idea of representation is a fundamental pillar of the legal system in relation to those who cannot represent themselves, such as the very young, the mentally subnormal and indeed all those who choose an advocate better equipped to state their argument than they are themselves. To philosophers in the rationalist tradition, it appears that representation for animals behind the veil of ignorance is disallowed as the 'rational' deny the claims of all other species to have a case presented on their behalf.

In his highly respected book *A Theory Of Justice*, John Rawls applies a general theory of contractualism to determine how the rules which govern the interaction of rational agents are to be created and enforced. His ideas appear much more sympathetic to the 'animal rights' movement than others writing within this tradition. He argues that the 'initial contractors' should be ignorant of 'accidental features' such as race, gender and intelligence, so as to avoid bias or prejudice in determining the contract. In that case, it might only be a small step to include 'species' in the list of accidental features. However, Rawls argues that his notions of 'justice based upon fairness' are limited, in that they cannot embrace all moral relationships, including the way in which humans conduct themselves towards animals. He goes on to explain why he feels that his theory does not allow for animals to be considered as the recipients of the right to 'justice':[58]

> On what grounds then do we distinguish between mankind and other living things and regard the constraints of justice as holding only in our relations to human persons? We must examine what determines the range of application of conceptions of justice.

> To clarify our question, we may distinguish three levels where the concept of justice applies. The first is to the administration of institutions as public systems of rules. In this case justice is essentially justice as regularity. It implies the impartial application and consistent interpretation of rules according to such precepts as to treat similar cases similarly (as defined by statutes and precedents) and the like. Equality at this level is the least controversial element in the common sense idea of justice. The second and much more difficult application of equality is to the substantive structure of institutions. Here the meaning of equality is specified by the principles of justice which require that equal basic rights be assigned to all persons. Presumably this excludes animals; they have some protection certainly but their status is not that of human beings. But this outcome is still not explained. We have yet to consider what sorts of beings are owed the guarantees of justice. That brings us to the third level at which the question of equality arises.

---

58 Rawls, J, *A Theory of Justice*, 1980, pp 504–06, Oxford: Oxford University Press. By permission of Oxford University Press.

The natural answer seems to be that it is precisely the moral persons who are entitled to equal justice. Moral persons are distinguished by two features: first they are capable of having (and are assumed to have) a conception of their good (as expressed by a rational plan of life); and second they are capable of having (and are assumed to acquire) a sense of justice, a normally effective desire to apply and act upon the principles of justice, at least to a certain minimum degree. We use the characterisation of the persons in the original position to single out the kinds of beings to whom the principles chosen apply. After all, the parties are thought of as adopting these criteria to regulate their common institutions and their conduct to one another; and the description of their nature enters into the reasoning by which these principles are selected. Thus equal justice is owed to those who have capacity to take part in and to act in accordance with the public understanding of the initial situation. One should observe that moral personality is here defined as a potentiality that is ordinarily realised in due course. It is this potentiality which brings the claims of justice into play ...

We see, then, that the capacity for moral personality is a sufficient condition for being entitled to equal justice.[59] Nothing beyond the essential minimum is required. Whether moral personality is also a necessary condition I shall leave aside. I assume that the capacity for a sense of justice is possessed by the overwhelming majority of mankind, and therefore this question does not raise a serious practical problem. That moral personality suffices to make one the subject of claims is the essential thing. We cannot go far wrong in supposing that the sufficient condition is always satisfied. Even if the capacity were necessary, it would be unwise in practice to withhold justice on this ground. The risk to just institutions would be too great.

It is clear from what Rawls says that even though his arguments, based as they are upon the implicit acceptance that rationality is the essential quality necessary to be considered as a recipient of 'justice', he does not reject the claims of the animal rights movement for *some* consideration for animals. He suggests that: 'the capacity for feelings of pleasure and pain and for the forms of life of which animals are capable clearly impose duties of compassion and

---

[59] This fact can be used to interpret the concept of natural rights. For one thing, it explains why it is appropriate to call by this name the rights that justice protects. These claims depend solely on certain natural attributes which can be ascertained by natural persons pursuing common-sense methods of inquiry. The existence of these attributes and the claims based upon them is established independently from social conventions and legal norms. The propriety of the term 'natural' is that it suggests the contrast between the rights identified by a theory of justice and the rights defined by law and custom. But more than this, the concept of natural rights includes the idea that these rights are assigned in the first instance to persons, and that they are given a special weight. Claims easily overridden for other values are not natural rights. Now the rights protected by the first principle have both of these features in view of priority rules. Thus, justice as fairness has the characteristic marks of a natural rights theory. Not only does it ground fundamental rights on natural attributes and distinguish their bases from social norms, but it assigns rights to persons by principles of equal justice, these principles having a special force against which other values cannot normally prevail. Although specific rights are not absolute, the system of equal liberties is absolute, practically speaking, under favourable conditions.

humanity in their case'.[60] It is unclear whether this would leave animals with 'rights' which fall a long way short of those accorded to humans or of the nature of the rights advocated by Regan. This is highlighted by a recent contribution to the debate by Roger Scruton. He is unwilling to accord to animals the status of 'personhood':[61]

> The concept of the person belongs to the ongoing dialogue which binds the moral community. Creatures who are by nature incapable of entering into this dialogue have neither rights nor duties nor personality. If animals had rights, then we should require their consent before taking them into captivity, training them, domesticating them or in any way putting them to our uses. But there is no conceivable process whereby this consent could be delivered or withheld. Furthermore, a creature with rights is duty bound to respect the rights of others. The fox would be duty-bound to respect the right to life of the chicken, and whole species would be condemned out of hand as criminal by nature. Any law which compelled persons to respect the rights of non-human species would weigh so heavily on the predators as to drive them to extinction in a short while. Any morality which really attributed rights to animals would therefore constitute a gross and callous abuse of them.

Like Rawls, Scruton does not deny that animals have no moral status – he just denies them the status of having rights. He is willing to say that certain animals are owed some duties which protect them against some forms of ill-treatment but that the institutions of food production and scientific experimentation are defensible and necessary: 'virtuous people may engage in activities like raising pigs for slaughter, eating meat, fishing with a line, wearing furs, or shooting crows and rabbits, which many observers of the human world have denounced as depraved'.[62]

A similar theme is proposed by John Finnis, once again on the basis that humans possess the fundamental capacities to be treated differently to animals:[63]

> Those who propose that animals have rights have a deficient appreciation of the basic forms a human good. At the root of their contention is the conception that good consists essentially in sentience; for it is only sentience that is common to human beings and the animals which are said to have rights. (For they do not have regard to life as such, or even to animal life as such: they do not propose to stop the phagocytes in their blood from destroying alien life.) Even if we consider the bodily human goods, and those simply experienced, we see that the quality of this experience is very different from a merely animal consciousness, since it is experienced as expressive of decision, choice, reflectiveness, commitment, as fruition of purpose, or of self-discipline or self-abandonment, and as the action of a responsible personality. The basic human

---

60   Rawls, above n 58, p 512.
61   Scruton, R, *Animal Rights and Wrongs*, 1996, pp 66–67, London: Demos.
62   *Ibid*, p 99.
63   Finnis, J, *Natural law and Natural Rights*, 1980, pp 194–95, Oxford: Clarendon Press.

goods are not abstract forms, such as 'life' or 'conscious life': they are good as aspects of the flourishing of a person. And if the proponents of animal rights point to very young babies, or the very old and decayed or mentally defective persons (or to someone asleep?), and ask how their state differs empirically from that of a flourishing, friendly, and clever dog, and demand to know why the former are accorded the respect due to rights holders while the latter is not, we must reply that respect for human good reasonably extends as far as human being, and is not to be extinguished by the circumstance that the incidents or 'accidents' of affairs have deprived a particular human being of the opportunity of a full flourishing.

Other contractualist writers have been less willing than Rawls to accept that the theory can still leave room for more account to be taken of specific claims of the animal rights movement. Peter Carruthers stresses the claim that animals are not rational agents and therefore cannot sign up to any 'social contract' based upon rights and duties.[64] They have no appreciation of duties and, therefore, should have no rights. He argues that animals matter only when cruelty towards them exhibits a trait in us which may be manifested against humans, which would seem, at first glance, to be following the Kantian tradition. But the Kantian idea that we should not harm animals because it harms humans who care about animals is also rejected. It is only when the harm inflicted upon animals is of a 'trivial nature', such as wanton cruelty, that we should censure the harmer. He goes to great length to show that it is humans who are the rational agents and therefore it is humans who should be our prime concern. If the animal rights lobby's activities disturb the interests of humans by, for example, affecting employment opportunities, then that would be morally wrong:[65]

> There would be economic and social costs in placing further restrictions on our use of animals, particularly if factory farming and scientific experiments on animals were forbidden. But I do not wish to focus especially on these. More important is that the increasing cost of increasing concern for animal welfare is to distract attention from the needs of those who certainly do have moral standing – namely human beings. We live on a planet where millions of fellow humans starve, or are near starving, and where many millions more are undernourished. In addition, the twin perils of pollution and exhaustion of natural resources threaten the futures of ourselves and our descendants. It is here that moral attention should be focused. Concern with animal welfare, while expressive of states of character that are admirable, is an irrelevance to be opened rather than be encouraged. Our response to animal lovers should not be 'If it upsets you, don't think about it', but rather, 'If it upsets you, think about something more important'.

RG Frey argues against both the claim to accord animals with moral 'rights' and the claims that animals have interests.[66] His theories amount to a rejection

---

64   Carruthers, P, *The Animals Issue*, 1992, Cambridge: Cambridge University Press.

65   Ibid, p 168.

66   Frey, RG, *Interests and Rights: The Case Against Animals*, 1980, Oxford: Clarendon Press.

of any notion of 'natural rights'. He asserts that because people have widely differing views on what is morally right or wrong, to claim that one has a 'moral right' to something is merely stating one's own preference; there are no such things as underlying 'natural moral rights'. In that case, he argues, to point to some divine 'moral right' to something is pointless and we are better concentrating on the treatment of animals by working out 'principles of rightness and justification of treatment'. Unfortunately, Frey's arguments do not define what should be considered to be a moral right for humans or animals, as he merely rejects the notion of 'moral rights' altogether.

Frey also attacks the second primary tool of the animal welfare movement, the claim for animal 'interests'. He denies Singer's claim that the interests of animals in not suffering pain are morally supportable. Frey suggests a 'ladder' to deny claims for animal rights and interests which works like this:

- Animals cannot speak.
- Because they cannot speak they cannot have thoughts.
- Because they don't have thoughts they cannot have desires or emotions.[67]
- Because they don't have desires or emotions they cannot have interests.

His book appears, at first sight, to be an indictment of any attempt to consider the plight of animals from a moral standpoint. But in spite of subtitling the book *The Case Against Animals*, he concludes that one should look to another source for justifying welfare claims for animals. He appears to cast doubt on the human moral right to confine animals in zoos or to use them for experimentation, but does not provide any positive framework around which legislation could be framed except for a reference to the 'higher' animals' ability to 'suffer unpleasant sensations':[68]

> The truth is that I am out of sympathy with the present trend of suddenly discovering this or that, which it so happens that one has wanted or wanted to be the case all along, to be a moral right, a trend which increasingly knows no bounds, what with the recent formation of pressure groups to lobby and demonstrate on behalf of our moral right to sunshine, a car-free environment, a degree for university (failure produces avoidable mental anguish and often physical distress and so avoidable unhappiness, freedom from which is a right), and a society completely rid of aerosol sprays. So far as I can see, our alleged moral rights proliferate daily; and though some claims for moral rights, such as a moral right to abortion on demand, are obviously much more momentous than others, all such claims, including the momentous ones, presently are foundering in a sea of charges and counter-charges over the existence of moral rights and thereby over the acceptability of the particular normative theses, standards, or principles in which these claims are allegedly

---

67   For a rebuttal of this claim, see Masson and McCarthy, above n 53.

68   Frey, RG, *Interests and Rights: The Case Against Animals*, 1980, pp 168–71, Oxford: Oxford University Press. By permission of Oxford University Press.

grounded and upon which they rely and especially over the adequacy of the normative ethical theories of which these theses, etc form a part.

As I say, I strongly suspect that such claims have become nothing more than a means to the end of securing what one or one's group wants; they have become attempts, and not very subtle attempts, to extract by force concessions from those who do not agree with one's view of the rightness or wrongness of this or that. But even where there is agreement in this regard, it by no means follows that there are moral rights lurking somewhere in the shadows: to cite the standard example in this context, I may perfectly well agree and think it right to give part of my salary each month to charities for the poor in London without in the least having to concede that the poor of London have a right to part of my salary.

My conclusion ... with respect to animal rights, then, may be seen as part of – certainly, it coheres with – my overall view about moral rights generally. The implications of this overall view, however, do not run merely to the denial of moral rights to animals: they extend also, and doubtless more unpalatably, to a denial of moral rights to human beings. And one important thing this means is that we have no moral right to an animal's confinement in zoos, to its ceaseless drudgery and labour on our behalf, to its persistent exploitation in the name of cosmetics, clothing, entertainment, and sport, to its blindness, dismemberment, and ultimate death in the name of science, and, to be sure, to its appearance on our dining tables. For anyone with my views, to pretend otherwise is obviously to be inconsistent, a point Stephen Clark presses with force and vigour.[69]

On the other hand, it is a nonsense to suppose, as many animal rightists do, that the denial of moral rights to animals leaves them utterly defenceless; it no more does this than the denial of a right to abortion on demand leaves a pregnant woman defenceless. In each case, even on my view, the question of whether our treatment of them is morally right can be raised and argued; it is not as if, as both Singer and Clark would agree, the only way we can wrong them is by infringing their putative rights, not as if, for example, Singer's book or Smart's utilitarianism or Hare's two levels of moral thinking or my view here must be dismissed out of hand simply because it does not agree that what makes wrong acts wrong is that they infringe this or that alleged right ... With no moral rights posited at all, we can still argue with the feminist about whether it is wrong to deprive a woman of an abortion when she wants one; even with no moral rights posited, acts can still be morally wrong, though we do well to remind ourselves, whatever the pressure from feminists, animal rightists, and others, that they can also be morally right. But can animals be wronged, even if they have no interests? Yes, they can. For I have allowed that the 'higher' animals can suffer unpleasant sensations and so, in respect of the distinction between harm and hurt, can be hurt; and wantonly hurting them, just as wantonly hurting human beings, demands justification, if it is not to be condemned. I do not mean to deny that, even here, fundamental questions of value will not have to be thrashed out; after all, one is only going to agree that wantonly hurting animals amounts to wronging them if one can be brought to

[69] Clarke, S, *The Moral Status of Animals*, 1977, p 27, Oxford: Oxford University Press.

agree that wantonly inflicting unpleasant sensations upon them is wrong, and, here, as elsewhere, simply presenting some *unargued* value judgement in this regard is unlikely to bring this about. So, even here, problems may remain; but, importantly, they are not problems about moral rights. The point is that once the question is raised of whether our treatment of animals or our treatment of women is right and/or justified, we begin to set about the task not only of working out acceptable theses of rightness and justification of treatment but also of developing and working out answers to those absolutely critical questions about the adequacy of the normative ethics of which these theses are a part ...

On my view, then, questions can still be raised about our treatment of animals; but the answers cannot now consist in appeal to our reliance upon moral rights, claims to which have never really settled questions about our treatment of other creatures anyway.

In summary, the chief criticism of contractualist or rationalist theories as applied to animals is that they deny animals moral rights which could be bestowed upon them in light of their sentience. The influence of the contractualists with their notion of the suffering of animals as being different and of substantially less moral concern to that of people, has meant that advances in the welfare of animals or the proposals to grant them distinct rights have been slow to develop. Historically, the claims of significant differences between the species to the effect that humans can rule without significant interference from moral philosophy finds its roots in the theological teachings of the world's religions. The proponents of the denial of any significant cognisance of the claims of the animal rights lobby have constantly defined differences which are being questioned as science makes new discoveries about animals. There has been considerable movement in relation to the law protecting animals in the past 20 years or so. But scientific evidence about the existence of pain and suffering or 'lifestyle' requirements of animals and their significant similarities to ourselves has only been partially recognised by the legislators, due to our traditional reliance upon highlighting differences between ourselves and animals rather than similarities. Contemporary theories of the animal rights movement's campaigners, most notably Regan and Singer, propose that similarities between humans and animals demand a re-evaluation of our laws relating to animals. Critics of these campaigns deny that animals have a moral status in any way approaching that of humans.

FURTHER READING

Clark, S, *The Moral Status of Animals*, 1977, Oxford: Oxford University Press. Recognised as being one of the foremost contemporary contributions to the animals debate, without relying on a single philosophical tool such as utilitarianism or inherent rights theory.

Francione, G, *Rain Without Thunder: The Ideology of the Animal Rights Movement*, 1996, Philadelphia: Temple University Press. The author is critical of current trends in support of incremental welfare reforms, and thoroughly endorses a shift to a rights-based approach. A excellent discussion of the ideological inconsistencies of the present animal rights movement.

Midgley, M, *Animals and Why they Matter*, 1983, Athens, Georgia: University of Georgia Press. An excellent contribution to the animals debate examining many aspects such as its relationship with claims for the rights of women and the theories which deny enhanced status of animals.

Singer, P (ed), *In Defence of Animals*, 1985, Oxford: Basil Blackwell. Excellent contributions from some of the leading figures in the animal rights debate, covering issues such as experimentation, zoos, vegetarianism and endangered species.

CHAPTER FOUR

THE LEGAL CONTROL OF EXPERIMENTATION

INTRODUCTION

The root question, whether animal experimentation is, for certain benign purposes of man, permissible, has long since been answered in the affirmative. It is permissible, whether or not you happen to think it is moral. The correctness of the answer is not in doubt, except among a small number of committed philosophers, abstract moralists and eccentrics with minds of a certain cast. We do not say they are wrong; for that would be presumptuous. We merely say that, for the time being, they have lost the argument. And though the question is a proper one to be re-examined from time to time, the answer is likely to remain the same for a while. It will be ratified and legitimised by the law which as a community we make for ourselves, with the intention to observe it, and trusting others to observe it also.[1]

Since the subject of animal rights moved back into the public arena in the mid-1970s, there has been no issue which has received more attention than the use of animals in scientific experimentation. The contrasting emotions raised by the visually shocking images of animals in the laboratory and the continued focus on the advances claimed by the scientific lobby and those who have benefited from animal experimentation, has ensured that the debate has never been far away from the headlines, in one form or another. Many protagonists in the animal welfare lobby see this as being the ultimate argument as far as the interaction of humans and animals is concerned, because the advances claimed to have been brought about by the use of animals in experimentation are extremely compelling.[2] It is one thing to complain about the wearing of furs to serve human vanity, quite another where scientists claim that they are saving or significantly improving the quality of human lives. If there is change in prevailing attitudes towards animal experimentation it might seem morally inconsistent not to also change attitudes to agriculture, hunting and trade, where the claimed benefits to humans are less significant or cater merely to human lifestyle.

Specific interest in the animal experimentation debate[3] is evidenced by the number of pressure groups worldwide, such as the National Anti Vivisection

---

1   Carter, G, 'The Law of the Matter, Viewed in Relation to its Ethics', the 49th Stephen Paget Memorial Lecture, 8 October 1980, *Conquest*, no 171, January 1981.

2   Paton, Sir W, *Man and Mouse*, 2nd edn, 1993, Oxford: Oxford University Press.

3   For the sake of uncomplicated language, the terms 'animal experimentation' and 'vivisection' will be used interchangeably in this chapter, despite the fact that each is, in fact, quite different. 'Vivisection' actually means experimentation by *cutting or wounding* a live animal, a graphic term which appealed to animal rights activists. 'Animal experimentation' in general uses many more techniques in addition to cutting or wounding, but the term has now assumed common usage and is a convenient shorthand for the somewhat more clumsy term, 'animals used in experimentation'.

Society in the US, Beauty Without Cruelty in Australia and the British Union for the Abolition of Vivisection, which have been formed to tackle this one issue. This is mirrored on the pro-experimentation side by the creation of pressure groups such as the UK-based Research Defence Society, the Research for Health Charities Group and the Biomedical Research Education Trust, which provide materials to schools, universities and the public at large, and were formed to actively lobby in support of animal experimentation.

Many countries throughout the world have implemented varying degrees of control over animal experimentation, some of which will be discussed in more detail below. The use of animals in the search for significant medical advances, although questioned by many,[4] continues to receive wide political and public support. The issue of experimentation provokes extreme passion on both sides of the debate. Letter-bombs, death-threats, parcels of razor blades and obscene telephone calls have been some of the more extreme tactics used by a hard-core of animal rights activists. Catherine Bennett noted that 'the degree of violence and threats in animal rights activity has been enough to reduce most researchers to a cowed silence, and to turn laboratories into grim-looking, windowless bunkers, bristling with security cameras, locks, entry points and infra-red alarm systems'.[5] But most activists remain committed to non-violent protest and a thorough debate of the moral issues involved, rather than engaging in more controversial tactics. As we shall see, scientists are accused of performing unnecessary experiments and arrogance. In many counties, there is criticism regarding weakness in enforcing legislation and an unwillingness to adopt good practices from other countries. No country, it seems, has come up with the perfect system which satisfies all sides and, considering the intensity of opposing views on the matter, reaching a compromise to satisfy all the competing interests and claims, both human and non-human, seems a distant prospect.

Despite the continuous interest in the anatomy of animals throughout history, it was only in the 17th and 18th centuries that animal research became widespread. There had been incidents before, but they were comparatively modest affairs compared with what came later:[6]

> From the very beginning of Western scientific medicine, physicians interested in the anatomical structures as well as in the functions of the human body did not confine themselves to the dissection of corpses, but also occasionally made use of the method of vivisection. Thus, about 450 years BC Alcmaeon of Croton was able to find the function of the optic nerve by cutting through this structure in the living animal and recording the ensuing blindness. In a similar

---

4   See Ryder, R, *Victims of Science*, 2nd edn, 1983, Fontwell, Sussex: Centaur Press; Sharpe, R, *The Cruel Deception*, 1988, Wellingborough: Thorsons Publishing.

5   Bennett, C, 'The Human Factor', *The Guardian Weekend Supplement*, 4 February 1995, p 12.

6   Maeler, A and Tröhler, U, 'Animal Experimentation from Antiquity to the End of the Eighteenth Century: Attitudes and Arguments', in Rupke, N (ed), *Vivisection in Historical Perspective*, 1987, pp 15–16, London: Routledge.

way the author of the Hippocratic text *On The Heart* (about 300 BC) cut the throat of a pig which was drinking coloured water, in order to study the act of swallowing. He also opened up the chest of another living animal and described how the auricles and ventricles of the heart were beating alternately. It was in ancient Alexandria that anatomical and physiological research first reached a climax. After Herophilos (about 330–250 BC) had shown the functional difference between tendon and nerve, Erasistratos (about 305–240 BC) succeeded in making the distinction between sensory and motor nerves by means of vivisection ...

... In his treatise *De anatomicis administrationibus, Galen of Pergamon* (c. 130–210), physician to the Roman emperor Marcus Aurelius, described techniques of dissecting living animals and improved these techniques to a hitherto unknown degree. Using vivisection, he tried to unveil the ever intriguing secrets of respiration and heart action, of the function of the brain and spinal cord. In his text Galen also expressed his feelings during the performance of such experiments. For the exposure of the brain or the experimental cutting of the recurrent laryngeal nerves, he recommended the use of pigs or goats rather than apes, because 'you avoid seeing the unpleasing expression of the ape when it is being vivisected'. As Galen further stated, the 'loathsomeness of the expression in vivisection' was not the same in all animals. Nevertheless, the dissection, once started, should proceed just as with a dead animal, penetrating into the deep tissues without pity or compassion. The physician should not allow himself to be discouraged from repeating the procedure by the frequent outflow of blood.

Galen is also credited with discovering that the veins contain blood, not air, yet he made some startling errors which were supported for centuries, including women having two wombs – one for male and one for female embryos – and the eating of fruit being harmful.

The scientific revolution which accompanied the Renaissance saw the birth of the modern era of animal experimentation; René Descartes' philosophical treatment of animals was a large contributory factor in the considerable increase in the numbers of animals being used in scientific discovery in the 18th and 19th centuries.[7] Despite the fact that the number of animals used paled into insignificance compared with the explosion in their use in the 20th century, considerable competition developed between the scientific communities of France, including Claude Bernard (1813–78) and Francois Magendie (1783–1855), and England, including Marshall Hall (1790–1857) and Sir Charles Bell (1774–1847). Along with this, gathering pace throughout the 18th century, came the growth of the animal welfare lobby, particularly in England, which began to exert pressure on the scientists to alter their practices. This lobby was fuelled by the continuing philosophical questioning of our attitude towards animals, particularly notably by Jeremy Bentham. His simple yet compelling focus on the suffering of the animals, rather than

---

7   See Chapter 1, p 12.

differences between humans and animals, served as a rallying call to the antivivisection movement.[8] Scientists were subjected to intense scrutiny of their practices, whereas in France and Germany, to the consternation of English scientists arguing that our science was being left behind, there was far greater use of animals.[9]

The move towards more animal experimentation was also criticised by those who saw better sanitation and more effective health policies generally as a means of improving the health of the nation. The continuous 19th century battle between the scientific and antivivisection lobbies eventually led to success for the animal rights lobby in the UK where the Cruelty to Animals Act 1876 was passed (see below). In other parts of the world, success was practically non-existent until much later. Some European countries were forced to introduce legislation in the 1980s by the very fact of their membership of the European Union, illustrating how a consensus on the treatment of animals in experimentation and other uses has been very slow to emerge internationally, if indeed it has emerged at all.

The antivivisection lobby might have managed to significantly shift the debate in their direction were it not for the fact that the scientific lobby began to fight back in the late 19th century by forming its own groups, which managed to influence governments much more effectively than those opposing animal experiments. It has also been suggested that because the antivivisection movement decided to compromise with the experimentation lobby after their limited successes of the late 19th century, they became less effective as radical proponents of change in the 20th century.[10] They sought to police the changes that had taken place, rather than looking for further restrictions on the use of animals, which continued with relative ease. To this day there is a considerable distance between the various degrees of acceptance of animal experimentation. The chief aim of many governments is to reduce, refine and replace experiments ('the three Rs') and all pro- and anti-experimentation groups are seen as forming an invaluable part of that process.

ARGUMENTS FOR AND AGAINST ANIMAL EXPERIMENTATION

Should we continue with animal experiments? Are animal experiments necessary? When we examine these sorts of questions it is important to consider the great variety of different kinds of experimentation involving

---

8   For further detail of Bentham's contribution, see above, p 13 and p 72.

9   French, RD, *Anti–vivisection and Medical Science in Victorian Society*, 1975, pp 38–41, 91 and 236–37, London: Princeton University Press.

10   See Rodman, J, 'The Liberation of Nature' (1977) 20 *Inquiry* 83–145.

animals, which arouse different levels of opposition or support. Peter Singer outlines one type of experiment which tends to attract severe criticism:[11]

> At a prestigious institute in the US, monkeys were trained to run in a cylindrical treadmill. The monkeys received electric shocks unless they kept the treadmill moving. Once the monkeys had received initial training at keeping the treadmill in motion, they were subjected to varying doses of radiation. Monkeys receiving the higher doses vomited repeatedly. They were then put back into the treadmill to measure the effect of the radiation on their ability to keep it moving. During this period, if the monkey did not move the treadmill for one minute, shock intensity was increased to 10 mA. (This is an intense electric shock, causing severe pain.) Some monkeys continued to vomit while in the treadmill. The irradiated monkeys took up to five days to die.

The 1994 Home Office *Statistics of Scientific Procedures on Living Animals* lists other common types of experimental procedure such as application of substances to the eye, direct mechanical interference with brain centres controlling the senses, direct injection of micro-organisms or material suspected of containing micro-organisms, exposure to ionising radiation and inhalation experiments.[12]

Arguments in favour

The proponents of continued animal experimentation have become much more vociferous in recent times as a response to the increase in momentum built up against it by the 'animal rights' lobby since the 1970s. It is argued that experiments on animals have provided an important contribution to medical and surgical advances, bringing about major improvements to the health of humans and animals.[13] Many examples are cited, such as the development of insulin for diabetes, whooping cough vaccine, heart-lung surgery, kidney transplants, polio vaccine, drugs to treat asthma and anaesthetics for surgery. The pro-experimentation lobby has continued a concerted campaign in order to counter the antivivisection lobby's successes in turning people against the scientists.

The claims of the advocates of animal experimentation are substantial. Dr Mark Matfield, Executive Director of the Research Defence Society, commented that:[14]

> During this century there have been tremendous advances in medical research, much of it dependent upon animal experimentation. The result has been

---

11 Singer, P, 'To Do or Not to Do', in Baird, R and Rosenbaum, S (eds), *Animal Experimentation: The Moral Issues,* 1991, p 147, Buffalo: Prometheus Books.

12 *Statistics of Scientific Procedures on Living Animals,* 1994, p 46, London: HMSO.

13 Paton, above n 2, Chapter 5.

14 Matfield, Dr M, 'Animal research within an ethical framework', from a lecture given to the Parliamentary and Scientific Committee on 19 November 1991, (December 1991) 48 *Science in Parliament* 5.

enormous progress in our ability to diagnose, prevent and treat a wide range of diseases and injuries, both for humans, and, with veterinary medicine, for animals as well. The total amount of death and suffering which has been alleviated or prevented has never been calculated. However, one study measured this in terms of life expectancy and proposed that modern medical research had added twenty years on to the average western lifespan. That would be the approximate equivalent of saving 100 million human lives.

It is argued that research involving animals should continue in the future in order to combat as yet unsolved medical problems such as cancer, AIDS and other genetic, psychiatric and neurological conditions. The advocates of experimentation point to the possibilities for treatment to which animal-based studies will provide a large contribution:[15]

[I am] led to the same question: 'How can any rational, compassionate, and thoughtful person oppose the use of animals in medical research?' Have those who oppose such research watched one grandchild die because of a lack of medical knowledge and then, a few years later, watched two other grandchildren be saved by medical procedures that could not have been developed without research on animals? Would they have a young medical officer bleed to death somewhere in war-torn France rather than allow the experiments on dogs that were essential to the development of effective treatment of shock due to massive loss of blood? Are they so blindly opposed to the use of animals in medical research that they would prevent Dr Sabin's experiments on his 'thousands of monkeys and hundreds of chimpanzees' that were necessary to perfect the vaccine that conquered poliomyelitis? Will they tell the thousands of patients who today suffer from AIDS to give up hope because monkeys should not be used in the laboratory in our fight against this plague? Are those who oppose my view on the use of animals in medical research willing to tell my grandsons that it would have been preferable to let them and thousands of other children die rather than allow research on animals? I hope not.

But the fact is, there are people who would let my grandsons die rather than allow any animal to be used in medical research. These are not people who will press only for the humane treatment of animals in the laboratory, a cause that no reasonable person can oppose. These are anti-vivisectionists who will, if they have their way, put a stop to all experimentation on animals no matter the cost to the advancement of health care. The number and the political influence of people in this movement have grown alarmingly in recent years. They have lobbied successfully for a law in Massachusetts to forbid the use of pound animals in biomedical research. If such federal legislation is passed, it will seriously hamper all medical research in this country and will make the cost of some research prohibitively high, as it already has done in Massachusetts.

The following extracts from information produced by the British Association

---

15   White, R, 'Beastly Questions', in Baird, R and Rosenblum, S (eds), *Animal Experimentation: The Moral Issues*, 1991, p 22, Buffalo: Prometheus Books.

Promoting Science and Technology highlight the past benefits of research involving animals and the need for this research to continue:[16]

> Over 100 eminent doctors and scientists, including 31 Nobel Prize winners, and all the Royal Medical Colleges, have signed the declaration [below] on the use and welfare of animals in biomedical research ...

> The incalculable benefits of past advances in medicine and surgery are often taken for granted. When we go to the doctor few of us think of the years of biomedical research, maybe spread over generations, which led to the treatment that we receive ...

> ... the milestones marking the history of biomedical research map a long and successful journey. They include immunisation with vaccines; antiseptic surgery and anaesthetics; insulin for diabetes; the discovery of antibiotics; the development of transplantation; and the vast array of medicines for illnesses from asthma to ulcers ...

> Progress with anti-cancer treatments is especially remarkable. A decade ago medical researchers were reluctant to talk of the possibility of cures for cancer. Surgery, chemicals and radiation struggled to keep the illness at bay.

> Now there are effective anti-cancer drugs and other therapies. They have all depended on animal-based research at some stage ...

> The improvement in human life produced by modern medicine is also well illustrated by the statistics showing dramatic improvement in the life expectancy of heart disease sufferers. Animal studies play a crucial part in research into heart disease. As a result of this research, over 10,000 heart attack victims will be saved in the UK this year by the new clot-busting drugs.

Declaration on Animals in Medical research

1. Experiments on animals have made an important contribution to advances in medicine and surgery, which have brought about major improvements in the health of human beings and animals.

2. Continued research involving animals is essential for the conquest of many unsolved medical problems, such as cancer, AIDS, other infectious diseases, and genetic, developmental, neurological and psychiatric conditions.

3. Much basic research on physiological, pathological and therapeutic processes still requires animal experimentation. Such research has provided and continues to provide the essential foundation for improvements in medical and veterinary knowledge, education and practice.

4. The scientific and medical community has a duty to explain the aims and methods of its research, and to disseminate information about the benefits derived from animal experimentation.

5. The comprehensive legislation governing the use of animals in scientific

---

16 British Association Promoting Science and Technology, *Animals and the Advancement of Science: Working with Animals in Medical Research*, 1994, London: BAPST.

procedures must be strictly adhered to. Those involved must respect animal life, using animals only when essential and as humanely as possible, and they should adopt alternative methods as soon as they are proved to be reliable.

6. Freedom of opinion and discussion on the subject must be safeguarded, but violent attacks on people and property, hostile campaigns against individual scientists, and the use of distorted, inaccurate and misleading evidence should be publicly condemned.

One of the most detailed examinations of the cases for and against animal experimentation was the report produced by a Working Party of the Institute of Medical Ethics on *The Ethics of Using Animals in Biomedical Research*, in 1991.[17] The 16 members of the Working Party, including RG Frey and Clive Hollands (well-known adversaries in the animal experimentation debate), represented a cross-section of differing views mainly from the 'centre-ground' of the debate, but did not include any representatives from specifically 'absolute rejection' groups such as the British Union for the Abolition of Vivisection. Had it done so, agreement might have been more difficult to reach. The group examined the full range of moral arguments and highlighted the 'tragic conflict' involved in using undoubtedly sentient animals against the lack of viable alternatives at present. In light of this, and conscious of the need to come up with a workable conclusion in spite of their moral differences, the group supported the use of animals in experimentation, backed up by suitable legislative regulation. They supported the view that animal experimentation had 'proved worthwhile for human purposes' in terms of advanced health levels, and doubted whether the advances in human health might all have been achieved without the use of animals. Therefore, they supported the use of animals as long as there are continued efforts to reduce, refine and replace the use of animals in experimentation.[18]

Arguments against

The antivivisection lobby has attracted many leading historical figures to the fold for humanitarian reasons and due to fears regarding the effect on the experimenters themselves of performing the experiments. The passions aroused and the depth of feeling are clearly illustrated by the following extract from George Bernard Shaw alluding to the advances in knowledge gained by animal experimentation:[19]

---

17 Smith, J and Boyd, K (eds), *Lives in the Balance: The Ethics of Using Animals in Biomedical Research*, 1991, Oxford: Oxford University Press.

18 *Ibid*, pp 310–13.

19 Shaw, GB, in Bowker, GH (ed), *Shaw on Vivisection*, 1949, pp 29–31, London: George Allen & Unwin. Reproduced with kind permission of George Allen Unwin.

The right to know is like the right to live. It is fundamental and unconditional in its assumption that knowledge, like life, is a desirable thing. But no government dares exempt the pursuit of knowledge, or any other pursuit, from all moral obligation. No man is allowed to put his mother in a stove because he desires to know how long an adult woman will survive at a temperature of 500 Centigrade, no matter how important or interesting he may deem that addition to the store of human knowledge. A man who did so would have short work made not only of his right to knowledge but of his right to live and all his other rights at the same time. The right to knowledge is not the only right; and its exercise must be limited legally like other rights.

When a man says to society, 'May I torture my sister or her baby in pursuit of knowledge?' society replies. 'No.' If he pleads, 'What! Not even if I have a chance of finding out how to cure cancer by doing it?' Society still says, 'Not even then.' If the scientist, making the best of his disappointment, goes on to ask may he torture a dog, the stupid and callous people who do not realise that a dog is a fellow-creature, and sometimes a good friend, may say 'Yes.' But even those who say, 'You may torture a dog' never say. 'You may torture my dog.' And nobody says, 'Yes, because in the pursuit of knowledge you may do as you please.' Just as even the stupidest people would say. 'If you cannot attain to knowledge without boiling your mother you must do without knowledge' so the wisest people say, 'If you cannot attain knowledge without torturing a dog, you must be literally a damned fool, incapable of putting knowledge to any good use.'

It will now, I hope, be clear why the attack on vivisection is not an attack on the pursuit of scientific knowledge: why, indeed, those who have the deepest conviction of the sacredness of that pursuit are the leaders of the attack. But knowledge must not be confused with methods of its pursuit. No method of investigation is the only method; and no law forbidding any cruel method can cut us off from the knowledge we hope to gain by it. We have only to find a humane one. The knowledge we lose by forbidding cruelty is knowledge at first hand of cruelty itself, which is precisely the knowledge we wish to be spared.

The truth is, if the acquisition of knowledge justifies every sort of conduct, it justifies any sort of conduct, from the illumination of Nero's feasts by burning human beings alive (another interesting experiment) to the simplest act of kindness. And in the light of that truth it is clear that the exemption in the pursuit of knowledge from the laws of honour is the most hideous conceivable enlargement of anarchy, worse, by far, than an exemption of the pursuit of money or political power, since these can hardly be pursued without some regard for at least the appearance of human welfare, whereas a curious devil might massacre multitudes in torment, acquiring knowledge all the time from his highly interesting experiments.

Despite the contribution to increased human and animal welfare claimed by the scientific lobby, Henry Salt wondered as to whether this would, were it possible, affect an animal's possible agreement to become the subject of experimentation: 'Can we doubt that the victims themselves, if once they could realise the noble object of their matyrdom, would vie each with the other in rushing eagerly on the knife? The only marvel is that, where the cause is so meritorious, no *human* volunteer has as yet come forward to die under the hands of the vivisector!'[20]

One of the leading protagonists in the cause of animal welfare in the 1960s and 1970s was Brigid Brophy, who was in no doubt that the only way forward was to ban animal experimentation. Circumstances and regulation may have changed since 1971, when the piece was published, but the sentiments expressed remain just as relevant for many in the antivivisection lobby today:[21]

> [A]s a matter of fact, society must forbid the vivisection of the other animals, because it is on society as a whole that the moral obligation falls to circumvent vivisection, and science as a whole, and the capitalists and administrators behind it, are not paying attention to the problem and are therefore not, as an instrument of society, meeting society's obligation. Scientific expertise and enthusiasm have not been volunteered since 1908 towards a society for devising alternatives to vivisection. They have been put in a society for defending and extending vivisection. The many alternatives which have already been devised often go unused or even unknown. While vivisection remains possible (legal, respectable, easy in practical ways because it is the established system, mentally easier because it requires no new thought, clumsy and costly but traditional and academically safe), the bubble of superstition will not just spontaneously burst. Society must burst it.

> Continue to permit vivisection, and scientists will continue to mislead themselves and the public by claiming that there are no alternatives – a claim made plausible only by their contriving to remain ignorant if the work of fellow-scientists who have discovered alternatives. Forbid vivisection, and necessity will mother invention. Science and society will alike be freed from a superstition which is making nonsense of our professional morality, subverting our science and corrupting our very use of language by hypocrisy. By the monstrously sized and systematic machinery which technology makes possible, we vivisect one animal a year for every 10 humans in the population: a monstrous attempt to plumb the present, carried out on principles no more moral and barely more rational than those on which the ancients tried to divine the future from the entrails of animals who were at least killed first. We seek cures almost as blindly as the ancients sought a propitious future by the same propitiatory method.

One of the main justifications for the continued use of animals is the possibility of discovering significant benefits for mankind or animals. Defining 'significant benefit' is subject to controversy, as illustrated by the public outcry which arose in the US in 1996 when the Bion Space Project, funded by Russia, France and the US, announced that it was going to send monkeys into space in order to study why spaceflight takes such a severe toll

20 Salt, H, *Animals' Rights: Considered in Relation to Social Progress*, 1915, pp 72–73, London: Bell & Sons.
21 Brophy, B, 'In Pursuit of a Fantasy' in Godlovitch, S, Godlovitch, R and Harris, J (eds), *Animals, Men and Morals*, 1971, pp 143–44, London: Victor Gollancz Ltd.

118

on humans. The effects of space travel are well documented by human experience, but the causes have not been pinpointed. The monkeys were sent up in straitjackets to stop them pulling out electrodes which were inserted into their brains and under the skin. Animal welfare groups in the US were vociferous in opposing these experiments as unnecessary in light of what is already known from human experience of spaceflight and the pain and suffering to be endured by the animals, and criticised the experiment as being a waste of money. Some scientists criticised the experiments because restrained monkeys would hardy produce results comparable to active humans in space. What was considered, and supported by an independent task force investigation chaired by a Yale University surgeon, to be an essential use of sentient creature for the significant benefit of mankind, was considered by welfare groups to be a 'pointless exercise that is indisputably cruel'.[22]

Aside from this high-profile case, many antivivisection groups have consistently argued that animal experiments are either morally wrong, harmful to humans as well as the animals or, at best, of limited use: 'a large amount of the research which is done is trivial and the knowledge has no medical importance'.[23] Opponents of animal experimentation have often pointed to the notable failures of some drugs, released publicly after having been tested on animals, which turned out to have catastrophic effects. For example: Thalidomide was given to women to prevent morning sickness and caused as many as 10,000 birth defects;[24] Opren, an anti-arthritis drug, caused 70 deaths and some 3,500 cases of serious side-effects in Britain before being withdrawn; and Osmosin, an anti-inflammatory drug caused 650 cases of serious side-effects and 20 deaths.[25] The suffering of humans brought about by the mistaken belief in the safety of these drugs is one of the human costs which society has paid. Some people have been the unwilling victims of the utilitarian calculus of the potential benefits to be gained by animal experimentation against the potential risks to humankind.

The claims of the scientific lobby regarding advances in human health are also disputed by some scientists such as Dr Robert Sharpe, who doubts whether experiments involving animals have been the source of the advances in human health as claimed by the scientific community:[26]

> [N]ot only does [experimentation] cause suffering to animals, its overall contribution to our health is negligible. Since 1876 when the [now replaced] Cruelty to Animals Act was passed, over 170 million animal experiments have

---

22 McKie, R, 'The Animal Astronauts', *The Observer 'Life' Magazine*, 13 October 1996, p 4.

23 Ryder, R, *Victims of Science*, 1983, 2nd edn, p 11, Fontwell, Sussex: Centaur Press.

24 *Ibid*, p 32.

25 See Singer, P, *Animal Liberation*, 1995, 3rd edn, p 57, London: Pimlico.

26 Sharpe, R, *The Cruel Deception: The Use of Animals In Medical Research*, 1988, pp 238–39, Wellingborough: Thorsons Publishers.

been carried out in the UK alone. Of these, 85% were performed since 1950 yet, by then, the rapid fall in deaths that commenced more than a hundred years earlier, had largely levelled out. So the vast majority of experiments can have had little impact and today we know that society's control of the infectious epidemics rests primarily on efficient public health services and a good standard of living. The increase in life-expectancy, then, can be directly traced to those sources. Even now infectious diseases like TB and whooping cough are far more common amongst working-class people than in the professional workers of social class I, despite the availability of modern drugs and vaccines. And, despite the huge increase in animal experiments since 1950, our overall health could now be deteriorating.

The conclusion is inevitable: when it comes to real advances in health, animal experiments are irrelevant. To make matters worse, vivisection has constantly proved misleading, diverting attention and resources from more reliable sources of information, much of which focuses on preventing disease rather than treating its symptoms. So it is not surprising that the really important advances have come not by experimenting on animals but through methods that directly relate to people.

Some of the methods of research put forward as an immediate alternative to the use of animals are: epidemiology which involves the study of diseases; cell tissue and organ culture from human sources; quantum pharmacology which involves computer predictions of reactions from knowledge already gained; and clinical trials involving the study of people who have spontaneously contracted a disease, and their response to therapy or drug treatments.

Moral and practical arguments have been put forward to replace the use of animals in experimentation with the use of humans who are in a permanent vegetative state (PVS). One advocate of this is Professor David Morton of Birmingham University, whose proposal along these lines brought criticism from religious leaders and the relatives of those who remain in a PVS. Not using PVS humans is considered by some to be another illustration of speciesism – failing to use what is, in effect, a 'human shell' and no longer a person, in favour of sacrificing the contrastingly superior sentience of animals. Dr Morton suggested that an obvious extension of the wishes of a person to leave their bodies to science would be to allow them to leave a living body to experimentation which, far from being abhorrent and 'the thin end of the wedge' would be a sensible step for science to take.[27] The same philosophical dilemma facing the pro-animal experimentation lobby has been noted by RG Frey who, in defending the continued use of animals, perceived the compelling nature of this demand:[28]

The case for antivivisectionism, I think, is far stronger than most people allow: so as far as I can see, the only way to avoid it, if you are attracted by the appeal to benefit and are not religious, is *either* to have in your possession some means

27   *The Guardian*, 8 April 1996, p 8.
28   Frey, RG, 'Vivisection, Morals and Medicine' (1983) 9 *Journal of Medical Ethics* 94 at 96.

of conceding human life of any quality greater value than animal life of any quality or to condone experiments on humans whose quality of life is exceeded by that of animals.

WORLDWIDE CONTROL

In 1985 the Council for International Organisations of Medical Sciences (CIOMS) published the International Guiding Principles for Biomedical Research Involving Animals, aimed at helping those countries lacking any legislative control regarding animal experimentation to introduce new controls. The principles embrace the need to 'recourse to experimentation on intact live animals of a wide variety of species'. They then go on to recommend several fundamental standards which have been embraced in many legal controls: the need to use alternatives where possible; proper housing and care of subjects; to ask whether the experiments are really necessary; and minimising pain and suffering. The principles also highlight the need for a suitably constituted review body where it is necessary to override any of the basic standards, but do not give any substance as to what would amount to one that is 'suitably constituted'.[29] As shall be examined later from the experience of various different countries, the methods employed to review and control animal experimentation are diverse in their guises, drawing some praise and, invariably, plenty of criticism.

EUROPEAN CONTROL

At a European level there have been two major international initiatives aimed at the protection of animals used in experimentation. In 1985 the Council of Europe adopted a Convention for the Protection of Vertebrate Animals Used for Experimental and Other Scientific Purposes. Countries ratifying the convention are required to give legislative force to its provisions. It contains similar basic guidelines to the 1985 CIOMS Guidelines (see above) encouraging humane care and termination of animals in pain as well as encouraging the search for alternatives.

In 1986 the EU introduced a directive based on the 1985 Convention covering the 'approximation of laws, regulations and administrative provisions of the Member States regarding the protection of animals used for experimental and scientific purposes.'[30] This laid down a time-scale up to

29 Smith and Boyd, above n 17, pp 258–59.
30 Council Directive (86/609) of 24 November 1986 on the approximation of laws, regulations and administrative provisions of the Member States regarding the protection of animals used for experimental and other scientific purposes (OJ L358/1 pp 1–13).

November 1989 within which Member States were required to comply with its provisions by strengthening where necessary or indeed introducing a legal framework from scratch. The main provisions are outlined below:

– The animals covered by the directive are live non-human vertebrates (not embryos) used in product development and testing, or in research for the benefit of the health and welfare of man/animals (Article 2).

– 'Experiment' means any procedure which may cause pain, distress, suffering or lasting harm (Article 2).

– Animals should be appropriately housed and cared for (Article 5).

– The minimum number of animals possible should be used (Article 7).

– Pain and suffering should be avoided, or kept to a minimum if unavoidable (Article 7).

– Animals with the lowest possible degree of neurophysiological sensitivity should be used and animals from the wild are not to be used, unless no alternative exists (Article 7).

– Alternatives should be used where possible (Article 7).

– Anaesthesia or analgesics should normally be used (Article 8).

– Animals should not normally be re-used (Articles 9 and 10).

– Procedures should be notified to the appropriate authority (Article 12).

– Statistical information should be made available by Member States regarding the numbers and types of animals involved as well as the purposes of the work (Article 13).

– Only competent/trained personnel should perform procedures (Article 14).

– Normally, only purpose-bred animals should be used, not strays or wild animals, and to this end supplying establishments should be registered (Article 15).

– Establishments using animals should be appropriately registered and provide suitable premises, personnel and veterinary back-up (Article 19).

Despite the fact that the 1986 Directive is the most stringent international attempt at regulation to date, there are concerns on both a moral and practical basis that there is still much to be done, which will be examined later. Some EU Member States already complied with or went beyond the provisions of the directive, but two Member States, Spain and Portugal, both of which had no specific laws concerning the use of animals in experimentation subjects, were required to introduce new legislation to comply. A project carried out for the Eurogroup for Animal Welfare in 1992 revealed how slowly some Member States reacted: Belgium, Greece, Italy, Portugal and Spain were still in the process of implementing the directive, and poor and inadequate administrative support was also reported in Greece, Italy, Portugal and Spain.[29] The concern of animal welfare groups seemed to be vindicated by the

31 *Analysis of Major Areas of Concern for Animal Welfare in Europe,* June 1994, p 88, Brussels: Eurogroup for Animal Welfare.

recent action which was taken against Luxembourg for failing to implement the directive. However, the action was unsuccessful on account of a technicality, and a full examination of the provisions of Luxembourg law in relation to animals used in experimentation was never undertaken by the European Court.[32]

Another problem encountered by the directive is that it fails to reach beyond the boundaries of the EU; several types of animal are still imported or arrive whilst in transit to other global destinations. Some protection is provided, particularly for non-human primates, by the Convention on International Trade in Endangered Species[33] and EU wildlife trade legislation[34] but several species are not covered and suffer cruel methods of trapping or high mortality rates in transit. Without further control on the use of animals from unregulated sources there is always the danger that the protection fails in these cases, and European experimentation on animals continues to contribute to the decline of many species. Despite the apparent willingness of the EU to involve itself in a measure of animal protection in this area, the anomaly remains that other EU laws such as those dealing with chemical testing actually *require* animal experimentation.[35]

The fact remains that the EU is committed to the use of animals in experiments because of their perceived role in improving the economic success of the Community. Reliance on product innovation and consumer confidence has in some circumstances led EU and domestic legislation to require animal experimentation. If the EU is to fulfil its obligations under the Treaty of Rome, then animal testing is seen as being an essential part of the jigsaw, not to be banned or further restricted unless there are suitable alternatives in place. Whether this is morally justifiable would be doubted by some in light of the philosophical arguments of the animal welfare lobby (see previous section and Chapter 1), but appears to represent underlying Community economic philosophy. On the other hand, it may be that future developments in the use of alternative methods will produce more cost effective methods of testing that are less reliant on the housing, care and feeding of animals. This would ensure that the economic arguments removed the European Union's reliance on animal testing before the moral arguments have been decided.

---

32 *Commission of the European Communities v Grand Duchy of Luxembourg* (1996), Case C–274/93, OJ 1996 I2079.

33 Council Regulation (EEC) 3626/82 on the implementation in the Community of the Convention on International Trade in Endangered Species allows the import and export of otherwise strictly protected species for research. The proposed regulation which will update and replace this would also allow the import of highly protected species for 'essential biomedical purposes'.

34 The shipment of all laboratory animals from and within the Community is covered by Council Directive (91/628/EEC) of 19 November 1991 on the protection of animals during transport. This gives legal force, at least as far as EU countries are concerned, to the transport for wild animals established by CITES and IATA.

35 *Analysis of Major Areas of Concern for Animal Welfare in Europe*, above n 31, p 96.

It has been suggested that since the European Convention was drawn up in the early 1980s, scientific advances and research have shown more evidence of the suffering and pain experienced by animals.[36] Welfare concerns such as the need for social interaction, adequate space, a suitable environment and being able to exhibit natural behaviour have been recognised and discussed at length, particularly in relation to farm and experimental animals.[37] In 1991, partly as a response to these new findings, the European Commission set up the European Centre for the Validation of Alternative Methods, with the responsibility to recommend action to be legislated upon by 1997.

Animal welfare groups have been campaigning for clear references to be made to animal welfare in the Treaty of Rome (see Chapter 5). This is supported by the Eurogroup for Animal Welfare, which has argued that this would enable legislation to be put in place more easily and allow impingements to remedied more quickly. It would also be of considerable benefit to various animals, particularly those used in agriculture and experimentation. The Eurogroup has suggested that a new reference to animal welfare in the Treaty of Rome would 'enhance the status of legislation concerning animals and might therefore lead to optimum and better implementation.'[38]

DOMESTIC CONTROLS

The UK

Historical development

In the 19th century, the RSPCA tried, unsuccessfully, to prosecute people for cruelty in animal experimentation under the 1849 successor[39] to Martin's Act 1822 for cruelty to domestic animals. The first prosecution took place in 1874 when Eugenne Mangan and three organisers were prosecuted for the manner in which they induced epilepsy in two dogs at the annual meeting of the British Medical Association in Norwich in August 1874. The prosecution was unsuccessful as Mangan had returned (or fled) to France, and the organisers had not actually taken part in the demonstration. The main problem encountered in other instances was the qualification 'unnecessary', which required an experiment to be proved to be completely unnecessary, an almost impossible task. Therefore, throughout the greater part of the 19th century any alleged instances of cruelty in animal experimentation went entirely unpunished, serving merely to intensify the anger of the antivivisectionists,

---

36   *Ibid*, p 89. See also the proposals of *Compassion in World Farming* in Chapter 5, pp 217–19.

37   See the section 'Do animals suffer in modern farming practices?' in Chapter 5, pp 174–89.

38   *Analysis of major Areas of Concern for Animal Welfare in Europe*, above n 31, pp 127–28.

39   See p 46 above.

frustrated that the law appeared to offer little, if any, protection to animals used in experimentation.[40]

Since the latter half of the 19th century animals involved in experimentation have been protected, firstly, by the Cruelty to Animals Act 1876 and subsequently by the Animals (Scientific Procedures) Act 1986 whereby experimenters have been able to carry out experiments on animals by obtaining Home Office licences. It is interesting to note that the effect of the introduction of legislation was not to *reduce* the number of animals used in experimentation. In 1878 less than 300 experiments were being performed on animals; by 1970 there were more than five million.[41]

Regarded by many as one of the most stringent pieces of legislation of its type in existence in the world, the Animals (Scientific Procedures) Act 1986 replaced the 1876 Cruelty to Animals Act,[42] which had been widely criticised because of its ineffectiveness in dealing with the treatment of animals in relation to medical experimentation. The introduction of the 1876 Act came about as a result of successful antivivisectionist lobbying in response to changes in policy by the scientific community. For example, in 1870, scientists from leading UK institutions decided to use animal experimentation to the same extent as their French and German counterparts. In the same year the Royal College of Surgeons began a reform of examinations which required greater use of animals in training, thus setting the scene for the intervention of Parliament.[43] In May 1875 there were two unsuccessful attempts at introducing legislation, but both were poorly worded and introduced into the Parliamentary session too late.[44]

The Cruelty to Animals Bill introduced through the House of Lords on 20 March 1876 was a much stricter version than eventually reached the statute books. Effective lobbying and a Royal Commission report[45] had created the potential for far-reaching reform of the law. Dr George Hoggan, an English physiologist, had been working in France with Claude Bernard, the notorious French scientist, and returned appalled by the experiments he had witnessed. In a letter to the *Morning Post* on 1 February 1875 he described dogs which would 'make friendly advances to each of the three or four present, and as far as the eyes, ears, and tail could make a mute appeal for mercy eloquent, they

---

40 For further detail of this period see Turner, ES, *All Heaven in a Rage*, 1992 edn, Chapter 15, p 44, Fontwell, Sussex: Centaur Press.

41 Ryder, above n 23, p 17.

42 For a description of events leading up to the passing of the Animals (Scientific procedures) Act 1986 see Ryder, R, *Animal Revolution*, 1989, Chapter 7, Oxford: Blackwell.

43 French, above n 9, pp 42–43.

44 Ryder, R, 'British Legislation and Proposals for Reform', in Sperlinger, D (ed), *Animals in Research: New Perspectives in Animal Experimentation*, 1981, pp 11–38, Chichester: John Wiley and Sons.

45 *Report of the Royal Commission on the Practice of Subjecting Live Animals to Experiments for Scientific Purposes*, 1876, London: HMSO.

tried it in vain.'[46] The letter stirred up a groundswell of opinion against research involving animals and an antivivisection league was founded, which came to be known as the Victoria Street Society. It had the support of Tennyson, Ruskin, Victor Hugo and Lord Shaftesbury, amongst others. In addition, Queen Victoria used her influence on Prime Minister Disraeli[47] to instigate a Royal Commission, which set about cross-examining several notable scientists of the time, including Charles Darwin.

The Royal Commission Report of January 1876 noted the concern of the British public and recommended that animal experimentation should be subject to regulation and control because of possible abuse. The report supported the continued use of animals, which the Commission felt had already improved public health, but only within a framework to promote humane practice. This build up of momentum led the following year to the introduction of a parliamentary Bill, with the original aim of severely curtailing animal experimentation. But the effectiveness of the animal research lobby was demonstrated by last-minute lobbying of the Home Secretary by the General Medical Council whilst the Bill's sponsor, Lord Carnarvon, was away from London after the death of his mother. The science lobby proceeded to lobby the Commission chairman, Lord Cardwell, members of the Cabinet and members of both Houses of Parliament, saying that the Bill was too restrictive to allow significant medical progress. The resulting one-month delay led to the introduction of a new Bill containing provisions which were to prove more favourable to the research community than the provisions of the original Bill, and difficult to enforce, receiving Royal Assent only five days later. Experiments to alleviate either human or *animal* suffering would now be allowed, and cats and dogs could be used as could asses, horses or mules. It has been argued that this series of events marked the beginning of a new relationship between scientists and politicians, whereby the view that 'scientists know best' began to take hold.[48]

The 1876 Act introduced a licensing system in order to perform experiments upon living vertebrates issued after an application made to the Home Secretary. The place to be used for the experimentation had to be registered, as did the proposed experiments, which had to be shown to be for the 'advancement by new discovery of physiological knowledge or of knowledge which will be useful for saving or prolonging life or alleviating suffering'. In addition there was a controversial list of exemptions to the coverage of the Act which could be performed with specific certification, such as the use of cats and dogs. The introduction of the Act may have been

---

46 French, RD, *Antivivisection and Medical Science in Victorian Society*, 1975, p 414, London: Princeton University Press.

47 *Ibid*, p 123.

48 Ryder, above n 42, p 120.

considered to have been a great victory for the antivivisection lobby in England, and for short time, up to 1882, it probably was:[49]

> [It] is certain that the administration of [the Cruelty to Animals Act 1876] interfered significantly with research in experimental medicine in Britain between 1876 and 1882. The vivisectionial approach had become an integral part of the research method of physiology, pharmacology, pathology, and bacteriology; in so far as experiments on living animals were prevented, advance in these sciences was frustrated ... During its first years of operation, therefore, the Act probably did not completely merit the blanket condemnation it received from antivivisection interests.

In 1883 the scientific lobby managed to obtain a significant foothold in the operation of the Act. The newly formed Association for the Advancement of Medicine by Research (AAMR), composed entirely of scientists, had the principal objective of representing experimental medicine on the political front. They were invited by the then Home Secretary, Sir William Vernon Harcourt, to advise on the administration of the Act, which resulted in far more applications for Home Office licences being successful and radically transformed the Act's operation helping to bring about a rapid growth in the use of animals in research. The number of licences increased from 42 in 1882 to 638 in 1913 as experimental medicine burgeoned. Antivivisectionists saw the Act as a scientist's charter, but were unable to bring about significant change for 110 years. Despite attracting a committed and impassioned membership, the antivivisection lobby suffered from many of the problems, including conflict within its own ranks and an inability to attract public support for their tactics, which led the 1876 Act to be entrenched in practice before united opposition could force a change.

Throughout its life the animal rights lobby was concerned about several perceived flaws in the structure and operation of the 1876 Act:[50]

– There were suspiciously few prosecutions under the Act.[51]

– Little investigation was required into the extent of the potential benefits to be gained from carrying out the procedure for which a licence was being sought. The experimenters merely had to show that the experiments were for a purpose which was allowed for the by the Act and this, it was argued, meant that far from experiments being motivated by the wish to

49 French, above n 9, p 191.

50 For a good overview of the criticisms of the functioning of the 1876 Cruelty to Animals Act in relation to experimentation, see Ryder, above n 4, pp 96–107. Ryder updated these arguments in 'British legislation and proposals for Reform', in Sperlinger, D (ed), *Animals in Research: New Perspectives in Animal Experimentation*, 1981, Chichester: John Wiley and Sons.

51 ES Turner commented that 'humanitarian and sceptic alike join in wondering whether any other Act in history has been so scrupulously observed': *All Heaven in a Rage*, above n 40, p 218. SRL Clarke commented that the Research Defence Society showed 'startling lack of integrity' in basing their support for the 1876 Act on the lack of prosecutions under it, in *The Moral Status Of Animals*, 1977, Oxford: Oxford University Press.

prolong or improve the quality of human life, as required by the Act, they were motivated by a desire for profit, mere curiosity, or trivial purposes.

– Even though the Act, on the face of it, severely limited the scope of experimentation, the system of licences to avoid these restrictions made the Act much less effective than would at first appear.

– The Act failed to encourage alternatives to the use of animals in experimentation.

– The species covered by the Act were too narrowly defined.

– Certain experiments, such as psychological experiments, were not covered at all.

– The Act did not cover the rearing or housing of the animals before the experiments began.

– The requirement for euthanasia of an animal in pain was vague and left scope for continued unnecessary suffering.

– There were too few inspectors to ensure compliance with the Act, and training needed to be improved.

– The Home Office Advisory Group set up following a second Royal Commission investigation of 1906–12 was not fulfilling its brief to reassure the public that adequate supervision of experimentation was taking place.

– Inadequate information on the number of animals used and the purposes of those experiments was being provided to the public.

The second Royal Commission reported in 1913 and recommended an increase in the inspectorate, better provision for anaesthetising animals, and the power of inspectors to be widened to order the termination of animals suffering pain. It also recommended the replacement of the AAMR with a more independent advisory body selected by the Home Secretary from a list of names not involved in scientific research. These recommendations were accepted with no legislative amendments required.

Despite the continuing work of the RSPCA, it was not until the 1960s that the movement against the use of animals in experimentation found an effective voice through the work of an increasing number of organisations opposed to the use of animals in experimentation. Tighter controls were demanded to prevent the use of animals in research, and there was campaigning for the use of alternative methods of research, or to at least bring down the numbers of animals used. The impetus for change was spurred on by the publication of the Littlewood Report[52] in 1965, which recommended 83 changes to the control of animal experimentation. However, by the time of the 1979 general election, only 20 of these recommendations had been implemented.[53] The movement attracted increasing numbers of people and the

52 *Report of the Departmental Committee of Experimentation on Animals (The Littlewood Report)*, 1965, Cmnd 2641, London: HMSO.

53 House of Lords, 25 October 1979, Reported in *Hansard*.

cause began to increase the momentum for change. In the 1970s two particular incidents brought the issue back into the public arena. These were a *Sunday People* story about 'smoking beagles' in 1975 and the imprisonment of two animal rights activists from the Animal Liberation Front (Ronnie Lee and Clifford Goodman) for damage to property used by animal experimenters. These incidents, along with the plethora of new writing on the subject which began to appear at this time, helped to create a climate for a change at a political level. The scientific community also appeared to recognise that there was a groundswell of public opinion and academic argument which needed addressing. On 16 July 1979 the Research Defence Society's President, Lord Halsbury, tried to head off criticism by introducing the Laboratory Animal Protection Bill into the House of Lords, which covered some of the criticisms of the animal welfare lobby (although it was still considered inadequate), but the Bill failed to become law.

During the general election campaign of 1979 the animal welfare movement succeeded in obtaining a commitment to new legislation from a incoming government when the Conservatives promised to 'update' the existing legal framework. The Home Secretary asked the Advisory Committee set up under the 1876 Act to consider a new legal framework. In 1985, the government introduced its Animals (Scientific Procedures) Bill with David Mellor as its main sponsor. It contained many changes to the original version of the Bill produced in 1983 which had been secured by an alliance of the Committee for Reform of Animal Experimentation (CRAE), the Fund for the Replacement of Animals in Medical Experimentation (FRAME), and the British Veterinary Association (BVA) following several meetings.[54] These included the grading of experiments according to severity, to determine whether the experiment should go ahead, and the inclusion of a termination requirement if animals were found to be in severe pain.[55] But the animal welfare lobby was far less successful in securing further changes as the Bill proceeded through Parliament. This was partly as a result of considerable differences in opinion as to what they should accept in the legislation, and because of a fear of alienation from proceedings if they were considered to be too 'radical'.

The Bill proceeded through Parliament without the antivivisection movement being able to mount effective, united opposition against it, despite the reservations of many. The Bill was supported by the Labour Party, a factor which was critical in ensuring that its passage through Parliament was a relatively straightforward affair. The Bill was, however, opposed by many

---

54 Hollands, C, 'Animal Experimentation', *The Lancet*, 5 July 1986.

55 Judith Hampson notes in her essay 'Legislation: A Practical Solution to the Vivisection Dilemma', in Rupke, N (ed), *Vivisection in Historical Perspective*, 1987, p 318, London: Routledge, that 'the receipt by the Home Secretary of a 300-page report from the RSPCA on the pain and suffering in recent British experiments, forwarded by Patrick Wall, editor of the international journal, *Pain*, also played a part in changing government thinking on this issue during these deliberations.'

such as the Liberal/Social Democratic Alliance parties in Parliament, most of the animal welfare organisations, some church leaders and many academics on the grounds that it did not go far enough. The RSPCA was less vocal in its opposition to the Bill than the other welfare organisations, as it had decided quite early on to support the Bill as the best way of securing at least some improvement in the treatment of animals. But they were clearly hopeful throughout the passage of the Bill of securing more than the Bill finally delivered.[56]

The main provisions of the Animals (Scientific Procedures) Act 1986

One of the major changes brought about by the 1986 Act is the range of coverage it introduced. The Act covers *procedures,* bringing experiments where the outcome is known, such as the production of antisera, previously uncovered, within its coverage. The care and welfare of animals is covered not just when they are being used in procedures, but also in their care and housing before and after those procedures. Centres being used must be registered, as must the person responsible for the day-to-day care of the animals and a vet with the responsibility of looking after the animals' well-being. A Code of Practice for the Housing and Care of Animals Used in Scientific Procedures was issued in 1989 to provide detailed guidance to those involved, based on knowledge of the requirements of different animals. The Code does not set mandatory guidelines, but is used to enable the Home Office to require programmes for improvement by establishments which do not meet the Code's definitions.

Mice, rats, guinea-pigs, hamsters, rabbits and primates used in procedures must be obtained from designated establishments involved in breeding or supplying of animals, as must cats and dogs (s 10).

The Act replaced the Advisory Committee established under the 1876 Act with the Animal Procedures Committee (APC) which has to issue a yearly report on matters of policy and practice or on matters referred to it by the Home Secretary (s 19). They describe their role as follows:[57]

> We believe that the Animal Procedures Committee has a two-fold role. In advising the government on the implementation of the Animals (Scientific Procedures) Act 1986, it performs a conserving role; ie the committee is a creature of the Act and it has an interest in ensuring that the Act operates effectively, retains public confidence and, therefore, minimises the pressure for new legislative controls over animal experimentation. It also has a more reforming, or proactive, role when it acknowledges and quantifies the tensions

---

56 On 26 March 1986 the RSPCA council chairman, Anelay Hart, wrote to *The Times* criticising the Bill and indicating that it would only receive their full support if there were changes to it.

57 *Report of the Animal Procedures Committee for 1995,* May 1996, p 6, para 36, London: HMSO.

between the changing attitudes of society to animal usage on the one hand and society's aspirations for increased health and safety on the other and influences the inevitable steps towards change.

The APC has powers to report on any matter relating to the operation of the Act or as directed by the Home Secretary. Examples of their functions and recommendations range quite widely, as illustrated in the following small number of instances.

– They receive limited resources (£242,000 in 1996–97) to award to projects looking to reduce, refine or to replace animal procedures – a very small sum indeed, as they have often pointed out to the Home Secretary.

– In chapter three of the 1992 Report the Committee recommended the extension of the Act to cover cephalopods, because of the evidence of pain and suffering noted in these animals.[58] This was implemented by an order which came into effect on 1 October 1993 extending the Act to cover Octopus Vulgarisis and was a remarkable change, in light of the fact that evidence was inconclusive and based on 'doubts'.

– They have regularly shown concern regarding the number of 'inadvertent infringements' due to a lack of understanding generally or the ignorance of new staff.

– They are consulted about licence applications involving procedures of substantial severity on non-human primates and the use of any wild-caught, non-human primates. Their recommendations to refuse approval have the effect of leading to some applications being withdrawn.

– Examples of continuing or specific areas of concern examined by the APC include the use of primates in research, the use of animals in toxicity testing and the use of animals in the safety testing of cosmetics.

The main aim of the Act is to try and balance the aims of research considered to be essential and necessary against the possible harm to the animals. Section 5(3) outlines the permissible purposes of scientific procedures with this aim in mind:

- the prevention (whether by testing of any product or otherwise) or the diagnosis or treatment of disease, ill-health or abnormality, or their effects, in man, animals, or plants;

- the assessment, detection, regulation or modification of physiological conditions in man, animals, or plants;

- the protection of the natural environment in the interest of the health or welfare of man or animals;

- the advancement of knowledge in biological or behavioral sciences;

- education or training otherwise than in primary or secondary schools;

---

58   *Report of the Animal Procedures Committee for 1992*, 1993, Chapter 3, London: HMSO.

–   forensic enquiries; and
–   the breeding of animals for experimental or other scientific use.

The chief method of regulation used by the 1986 Act is a two-tier licensing system of individuals (s 4) and of projects (s 6). The personal licence allows experimenters to carry out individual programmes of work. As of 1 April 1994 all applicants seeking a personal licence must successfully complete an accredited training programme. The second tier is the project licence procedure, which now requires separate authorisation for each individual programme, in contrast to the 1876 Act which had merely required the registration of a technique, which could be repeated time and again with a new project and new animals. The greater use of licences specifically for each project aims to allow the Home Office to exert greater control of experimentation involving animals, including the conduct of the experiment itself.

A critical tool to enable the Home Office to make its decision is the requirement created by s 5(4):

> In determining whether and on what terms to grant a project licence the Secretary of State shall weigh the likely adverse effects concerned against the benefit likely to accrue as a result of the programme to be specified in the licence.

Thus, the Act requires applicants to justify the severity of the procedures and the species of animals they propose to use. They must also sign a declaration to the effect that no alternatives will achieve the objectives of the project. In respect of the special relationships humans have developed with some species of animal, s 5(6) provides that cats, dogs, primates or equidae are not permitted to be used unless there is proof that no other species will be suitable.

The primary sanction available under the Act is the removal of either the project or personal licence if there is a breach of a condition of the licence, or where it appears appropriate to the Secretary of State to do so (s 11). The licence-holder is entitled to make representations if they are told that their licence is to be revoked (s 12). The Act also provides for the imprisonment and/or fining of an offender if they are convicted on indictment, for a maximum of two years.

Only a handful of infringements are reported each year: in 1995, for example, there were 19 infringements of the Act, ranging from performing procedures without one of the licences required, to lack of approval for premises used for the experiments. The resulting actions consisted of revoking three personal and three project licences, 10 licence-holders were required to undergo accredited training before being allowed to undertake further work, and 18 licensees were cautioned.

Has the Act been effective?

The Act has received praise from several sources around the world[59] and has variously been described as 'draconian' and 'the best legislation of its kind in the world.'[60] Most scientists and pro-experimenters are at pains to stress that the Act provides the best possible framework to ensure that animals are well looked after and used in the smallest possible numbers. The coverage of the Act is certainly very wide in comparison to other major animal experimentation countries such as the US. The Code of Practice for the Housing and Care of Animals used in Scientific Procedures adds specific non-mandatory welfare recommendations. A 1995 audit conducted by the Animals (Scientific Procedures) Inspectorate found that 312 of the 487 sites covered by the audit complied with the requirements, but 20% (95 facilities) did not because it was considered that 'the conditions had the potential to compromise either the welfare of the animals or the quality of the scientific work.'[61]

One of the leading proponents of experimentation using animals in the UK is Sir William Paton, who discovered the hypotensive drug hexamethonium and who also served on the Medical Research Council and other bodies associated with support for animal research. One of his chief arguments is his 'test of deletion', which invites those who oppose medical research involving animals to choose a date in history from which they would have banned such testing, in order to see which medical advances would have been lost. After pointing out the discoveries made after various dates of deletion which might have been forsaken as a result, he urges support for continued testing on animals for the advances yet to come. Paton is supportive of the 1986 Act and, to a certain extent its predecessor:[62]

> It has been contended that because there were no prosecutions under the 1876 Act, the inspectors must have been failing to provide the control required, and that in effect experiment had been uncontrolled. Historically the statement about prosecutions is not correct. There have been, so far as I am aware, three prosecutions, which are worth a brief summary. The first was in 1876, when a certain Dr Arbrath was prosecuted for advertising a public lecture on poisons in which (unspecified) experiments would be shown. The advertisement went to press before, and appeared after, the passing of the Act. Although in the end no experiment was performed, Dr Arbrath was convicted with a nominal fine. It is also noted that he belonged to the local branch of the SPCA (as it then was), and that it refused itself to prosecute. A second case was in 1881, when

59 See, for example, *Alternatives to Animal Use in Research, Testing, and Education*, 1988, p 28, New York: Office of Technology Assessment, Congress of the US.

60 See, for example, the contribution of Dr M Matfield to the 1996 review of the Animals (Scientific Procedures) Act 1986, below p 142.

61 *Report of the Animal Procedures Committee for 1995*, May 1996, Cmnd 3280, para 10, London: HMSO.

62 Paton, Sir W, *Man and Mouse*, 1993, 2nd edn, pp 212–14, Oxford: Oxford University Press. By permission of Oxford University Press.

the Victoria Street Society (precursor of the NAVS) prosecuted Dr David Ferrier for performing experiments on the brain while unlicensed and uncertificated for such experiments. The prosecution failed, however, because the operations were in fact preformed by Dr GF Yeo, who held the required licence and certificates. Ferrier is famous for his work on cortical localisation, fundamental to modern neurosurgery; and a Royal Society lecture is named after him. A third case was in 1913. This was a prosecution by the RSPCA of Dr Warrington Yorke for cruelty to a donkey. It involved an experiment in which a drug possibly useful against sleeping sickness produced a type of paralysis. The prosecution failed, because Dr Yorke was properly licensed and the suffering involved was judged not to be unnecessary. Dr Yorke, later a fellow of the Royal Society, was a pioneer in tropical medicine, and with Kinghorn discovered the insect vector of one of the sleeping sickness parasites (*Trypanosoma rhodesiense*), an essential piece of knowledge for its control. One further case is of historical interest, since it probably contributed to the movement which resulted in the 1876 Act. This concerned Dr Mangan, a French investigator who demonstrated at a public meeting of the Medical Association in 1874 that whereas injection of alcohol into a dog produced anaesthesia, injection of absinthe produced convulsions. He did this to draw attention to what are now well-recognised dangers of absinthe. The RSPCA prosecuted under Martin's Act (the first in this country dealing with cruelty to animals), but Mangan had by then left the country.

In fact, prosecutions are rather beside the point. There is an immediate sanction available: namely, the withdrawal of licence or certificates from an individual or from premises. For the vast majority of scientists who do animal experiments, such a withdrawal would radically affect their careers and could lead to some losing their jobs. No data exist on how often this has been done, but it is clearly rare. This could be taken as reflecting the lack of abuse of the law; or it could show the lack of effectiveness of the inspectorate. The former seems the more probable, in the light of the Annual Reports which record each year their detection of a series of infringements. In the great majority of cases, these are technical, such as allowing a licence or certificate to run out while experiments continue. The essential point to which the inspectors' attention is directed is whether any unnecessary suffering was caused by the infringement. Appropriate warnings are given, and in two recent cases the facts were brought to the attention of the Director of Public Prosecutions. Infringements sometimes arise in the course of work by visitors to this country from other countries with less stringent regulations.

It has also been contended that adequate supervision cannot possibly be conducted by the 15–20 inspectors. This implies some misunderstandings, and some figures are quite enlightening, if one compares 1982, say, with 1988. First, experiments take place in a relatively limited number of recognised places: 518 in 1982, 381 in 1988. The inspectorate made 6,531 visits, mainly without notice, in 1982; 7,640 in 1988 (figures are not given for later years). The number of centres has therefore declined by 28%; visitation has increased by 17%; and the average number of visits per year to a centre has risen from 12.6 to 20. In 1982 there were 11,800 active licences, an average of 23 at each centre. (This information also is no longer given – only project licensees.) The inspector already knows the nature and purpose of the experiments to be done, and has usually discussed them with the licensees, whom he knows personally. It must be appreciated that the inspector is not a policeman, and that it would be futile to attempt to oversee every one of a series of experiments. The practice has been, in fact, to get to know the scientists concerned and to act so as to prevent infringements.

It is interesting to compare all this with any other inspectorate activity. One case for which some figures are available is factories, where considerable human hazard may exist; inspection was found to take place about once a year at each establishment. But inspection of pet shops, animal dispensaries, pet-owners, stables, or (perhaps) children's homes, 20 times a year? No. The irony about animal experiment is revealed yet again: the less there is, the more it is inspected; and of all the activities in which suffering may arise, it is that which offers the prospect of less suffering in the future which is most frequently examined.

Not everyone accepts Paton's view of trustworthy scientists working under stringent regulation, a lack of prosecutions illustrating how responsible the scientists are and a system working well. There has been criticism from a variety of sources about the lack of prosecutions in the UK since it first created regulation in 1876. The Working Party of the Institute of Medical Ethics into the Ethics of Using Animals in Biomedical Research in 1991 was not quite as convinced as Paton that the system was working well:[63]

There are several ways in which the public might be reassured that the law really is protecting the animals. One way might be to pursue more prosecutions under the law. These would help to assure people that the legislation has 'teeth'. In the UK, however, (and probably elsewhere in the world) there seems to be a reluctance to bring transgressors before the courts. Although, over the years, a number of infringements of the 1876 Act and now the 1986 Act have been brought to the attention of the Director of Public Prosecutions, there have been no prosecutions under either Act. The number of infringements and action taken are recorded in the Annual Home Office Statistics, which are available to the public. Examination of these records over the period 1978–89 shows that all those infringing the Act were 'admonished' or 'warned about their future conduct'. In each year except 1987 and 1989, some cases were referred to the DPP, who, after consideration, chose not to prosecute. In some cases licences were revoked and in one case the DPP instructed the police to issue a Caution.

As criticism of the Canadian system illustrates, the public may have little faith in a system that is not seen to be enforced. In a similar way, the lack of prosecutions under UK law has caused some public concern. Indeed, the UK statutory advisory committee, the APC has stated in its report for 1987 that it is 'concerned ... that, where appropriate, people who offend against the Act should be prosecuted'. The Committee endorsed a 1986 letter from the Advisory Committee under the 1876 Act to the Secretary of State, which included the following points:

63   Smith, J and Boyd, above n 17, pp 279–80. By permission of Oxford University Press.

'Administrative sanctions can no doubt be effective, but discretion to enforce the criminal law should not mean that it is never enforced in the courts ... The Animals (Scientific Procedures) Bill rightly makes provision for substantial penalties for the most serious offences involving animals used in scientific procedures. We are concerned that the new legislation will fail to command the respect it deserves, unless there is a willingness to bring its full force to bear when the circumstances warrant it ... It is the hope of the Committee that the official procedures for dealing with serious infringements may be improved so that the possibility of prosecution is more vigorously explored. We believe this will be of particular importance for the public credibility and the effectiveness of the legislation now before Parliament, which has your Committee's full confidence and support.'

'It is clear that there may be a gradation in the culpability of offences under laboratory protection laws, from the most minor, inadvertent infringements, to more substantial neglect or irresponsibility and even deliberate evasion of the law. It would seem important that this gradation of offence is matched rigorously with the gradation in penalty, including prosecution for the most serious offenses. For other, less serious offences, the removal of licences may be a sufficiently severe sanction, since this can mean that offenders may never again be allowed to perform experiments involving animals.'

There have been many who have argued that the 1986 Act did not go far enough and represented too much of a compromise between the competing interests of the scientific and animal welfare communities. Antivivisection groups have continued to investigate the operation of establishments under the Act and have presented evidence that guidelines are being broken on a regular basis. For example, in 1996, the British Union for the Abolition of Vivisection alleged 'rough handling and lack of regard for the welfare of animals' at the Huntington Research Centre. In 1993, as a result of an investigation into the trade in primates for research, they had alleged 'misery, suffering and death on a massive scale, with as many as eight out of 10 wild-caught primates dying before reaching the laboratory'.[64]

In March 1996 Crispin Iles, a member of the Anti-Vivisection Society, presented evidence which was shown on television indicating that animals were being subjected to considerable suffering at the laboratory under investigation.[65] The AVS pointed out that the reasons they felt that they had to undertake these clandestine investigations were the absence of effective legislative control of such work and the insufficiency of ensuring compliance with the Act when only 20 inspectors were provided to regularly visit the institutions involved. The Home Office response was to request that the details be presented to them for investigation. The clear undertone throughout

---

64 *Insight into the Animals (Scientific Procedures) Act 1986*, 1996, p 2, London: British Union Against Vivisection.

65 *The Guardian,* 13 March 1996; *Here and Now,* BBC 1, Wednesday 13 March, 1996.

the presentation of the evidence by the AVS was their considerable distrust of the scientists involved in the research and their justification for carrying out experiments. Experiments investigated included a monkey with metal plates and electrodes attached to its skull and the gassing of thousands of surplus rats and dogs implanted with pacemakers to induce mild heart attacks. For their part the institutions themselves stressed the effectiveness of Home Office regulation and inspections in ensuring that the experiments were only performed as a part of essential research where no alternatives would be effective. It still remains the case that the Act and the way it has been implemented have failed to attract the full backing of animal welfare groups.

In the face of a history of sometimes violent tactics scientists, perhaps understandably, have developed a reluctance to come out in the open on an individual basis to support the use of animals in scientific research. It is all too easy for them to be portrayed as the 'hand of evil', when the visual images of animals used in experimentation are so emotive. Even though they justifiably fear reprisals, antivivisection groups still suspect, as indicated by their continued use of radical undercover operations such as those in the Iles affair, that scientists have something to hide. It is suggested that the use of Ethics Committees including members from the antivivisection societies might benefit the whole debate. This seems to have the two sides tagged with the impressions of 'radical vegan revolutionaries' on the one hand and 'uncaring, unemotional pursuers of scientific advances at any cost' on the other. It is suggested, for example, that it might improve the transparency of the operation of the regulation of laboratory use of animals, by improving the perception of the need for animal usage as the scientists would have them believe, or by bringing possibly suspect justification arguments into the open to be properly debated, as sought by the antivivisection lobby.[66]

The Act has been criticised from official sources such as the Ministry of Agriculture, Fisheries and Food's *Report of the Committee to Consider the Ethical Implications of Emerging Technologies in the Breeding of Farm Animals* (1995) (the Banner Committee). The Committee examined the protection afforded by the Act to farm animals used in genetic modification experimentation and produced the strongest official indication to date that the Act has its flaws. Although the report concerned emerging technologies, the Committee's concerns extended to all types of experiments involving animals. In relation to the s 5(4) requirement to weigh the likely benefits against the adverse effects on the animal, the Committee felt that sometimes not even profound benefits could be justified:[67]

---

66 It is also suggested by Hampson, J, p 337, above n 52, that this would assist the small inspectorate to ensure compliance, allow more peer review and assist project refinement.

67 Ministry of Agriculture Fisheries and Food's *Report of the Committee to Consider the Ethical Implications of Emerging Technologies in the Breeding of farm Animals*, 1995, para 4.98, London: HMSO. Crown Copyright is reproduced with the permission of the Controller of HMSO.

Some would wish to see a more prohibitive provision here – it might be said, and we would be inclined to agree, that where an experiment risks serious and profound harm to an animal that is reason enough to warrant its prohibition – as would be the case with experiments on humans. Even those who do not go along with such a strong principle might hold that if the harm which was done to the Beltsville pigs, for example, was not merely risked by a particular experiment but was a foreseen or reasonably likely consequence of it, such an experiment ought to be forbidden no matter any results which are reasonably anticipated.

In relation to the s 15(1) requirement that any protected animal which, at the end of the regulated procedures, 'is suffering or likely to suffer adverse effects' must be killed and cannot be released from the Act's control, the Committee commented:

Para 4.102. There are, however, ... grounds for concern as to the adequacy of the protection that the ASPA affords ... the interpretation and application of the phrase 'adverse effects' is a matter of some uncertainty. It may be that the modifications we considered objectionable (such as the one aimed at reducing the sentience of a pig so as to increase the efficiency of its conversion of food), would not be covered by the interpretation of this section. Or it may be that the range of welfare and other indications which are considered in the application of s 15(1) are insufficiently wide, and that those which are considered are not assessed with the scientific rigour which is in some cases possible and appropriate. Or it may be that animals are not observed in the range of conditions they may experience in commercial settings, but only in the highly controlled and protected settings of experimental research institutions. At root, then, the difficulty is that what is meant by 'adverse effects' in s 15(1), and how the existence of such effects is determined, are matters which are within the discretion of the Secretary of State, and, in turn, those who administer the Act. This discretion is doubtless exercised after the widest consultation and consideration, but it remains the case that the adequacy of the Act in relation to the problems posed by genetic modification is not easily established. ...

Para 4.104. [This] concern could be dealt with were the Home Office to give an account of how the existence of 'adverse effects' is established, and an indication of whether genetic modifications which could be judged intrinsically objectionable would be held to have caused 'adverse effects'. We recommend, therefore, that the Animal Procedures Committee be invited to address this issue – our view is that if 'adverse effects' are held to include damage to the natural integrity of the animal subject to modification, then ASPA is sufficient to preclude intrinsically objectionable genetic modification.[68]

One of the most crucial tasks taken on by the APC was the 1996 review of the operation of the Act. They invited interested parties to submit their comments on the strengths and weaknesses of current arrangements with a view to recommending changes to the Home Secretary. There follow some extracts from those responses.

---

68 At the time of writing the APC was considering its response and was due to give its response to this request by the Banner Committee.

The RSPCA[69]

1. The RSPCA recommends that the Home Office and/or the Animal Procedures Committee consults with the interested parties – both welfarists and researchers – to find a way of presenting information on procedures conducted on animals that clarifies what is actually done to which animals and why, without compromising the safety of researchers or their establishments. ...

6. The RSPCA considers the length of time taken for the Home Secretary to reply to the Animal Procedures Committee on matters such as the use of non-human primates and regulatory toxicity to be totally unacceptable. The Society recommends that the Home Secretary give higher priority to the advice given to him or her by the Animal Procedures Committee. ...

8. The RSPCA recommends that composition of the Animal Procedures Committee should be reviewed and that a higher proportion of members should be animal welfare specialist and/or have expertise in alternatives or refinement techniques. ...

15. The RSPCA recommends that the ethics of using animals in research and testing – including the concepts of justification and necessity as well as the costs and benefit – should be kept constantly under review by the Animal Procedures Committee, since practices which were acceptable twenty years ago would not be regarded as such today, and today's practices may well be criticised as inhumane or unjustified 10 years from now. In particular, the costs to animals may need on-going reappraisal, as awareness of the needs of animals progresses through behaviourial and other studies. ...

18. The RSPCA recommends that the government should provide a more appropriate level of funding for the Animal procedures sponsored grant programme in the 3Rs,[70] both in order to act as an incentive to developing and implementing the 3Rs and to demonstrate their own commitment to this principle. ...

27. The RSPCA believes the education and training, both initially and as continuing development, are crucial to the operation of the Act. The RSPCA recommends, therefore, that all people carrying out regulated procedures, or who are responsible for a project licence, should have to attend a training course regardless of when their licence was awarded. Furthermore, since laboratory animal science is a continuing discipline, everyone, including experienced persons, may benefit from attendance at refresher course at appropriate intervals (eg five years) to keep them up to date with current thinking. ...

37. The RSPCA recommends that information provided by the Home Office Statistics regarding primates should at the very least include a breakdown

---

69   *The Animals (Scientific Procedures) Act 1986: A Review of the first 10 Years of the Operation of the Act,* May 1996, Horsham, Surrey: RSPCA. The RSPCA's response to the APC review contains 58 recommendations for action, including the ones selected here.

70   Reduction, refinement and replacement.

into individual species, details of the number of wild-caught and captive-bred animals used, and information on the severity of procedures carried out. ...

40. The RSPCA believes that the consistent occurrence of infringements under the Animals (Scientific Procedures) Act 1986 in unacceptable and recommends that such infringements should be dealt with more forcefully by the Home Office, either by the immediate revocation of the licence of the perpetrator of the offence or by prosecution by the Director of Public Prosecutions. Serious letters of admonishment are clearly not sufficient in all cases.

41 The RSPCA recommends that to ensure effective implementation of the Animals (Scientific Procedures) Act 1986, including full attention to the cost-benefit assessment and to ensure that animals are use 'only when necessary and with the minimum possible suffering', it is essential that the government increase the number of Home Office Inspectors and the resources available to them in terms of support staff and finance. ...

50 The RSPCA believes the effective fulfilment of the roles of named persons, in particular the day-to-day care person and the named veterinary surgeon, are crucial to the proper functioning of the Animals (Scientific Procedures) Act 1986. It is therefore important for all those working under the Animals (Scientific Procedures) Act to have clearly defined lines of responsibility and good management structures in place at a local level. The Society recommends that local ethics/ethical review/animal care and use committees, as described in the reports of the RSPCA and the Boyd Group should be encouraged by the Home Office. ...

55. The RSPCA considers that exporting research and testing to countries where it can be done with less restrictions and less concern for animal welfare is immoral and shows little consideration for the animals involved. The RSPCA recommends that the issue of the export of animal use be considered by the Animal Procedures committee to assess the scale of the problems and to discuss possible solutions. ...

58. The RSPCA recommends that the Animals (Scientific Procedures) Act be amended to protect all cephalopods and not just *Octopus Vulgaris*.

British Union for the Abolition of Vivisection

The British Union for the Abolition of Vivisection (BUAV) has been critical of the 1986 Act from its inception.[71] They are suspicious of the scientific community which is given the power to implement the pain versus benefits requirements – it is they who are required to assess the likely pain to be endured and to rank it according to the Act, so that the Home Secretary can decide whether or not to grant a licence. The lack of independent scrutiny in the absence of ethics committees adds to their suspicions. BUAV, in common

---

71 *The Animals (Scientific Procedures) Act 1986,* a fact sheet produced in 1992, London: British Union for the Abolition of Vivisection.

with the Working Party of the Institute of Medical Ethics, questions why there have been so few prosecutions under the Act, suggesting this is not evidence of compliance, but rather of a lack of willingness to prosecute.[72]

Almost three million experiments are still carried out in Great Britain each year. In around two-thirds of these experiments no anaesthetic is used. No category of experimentation has been banned. Cruel and unscientific tests such as the draize eye test and the LD50 (which involves poisoning a group of animals in order to find the dose of a test substance necessary to kill half of them) continue ...

Section 5(4) of the Act states that licences should only be awarded after the suffering caused to animals has been weighed against the 'likely benefit' of carrying out the experiment. If even tests for cosmetics pass this assessment it is hard to see exactly what tests, if any, were meant to be prevented under this clause ...

Not only do animals continue to suffer in Draize tests but the use of LD50 style tests has actually increased. The Draize eye test was carried out on 3,330 rabbits and 32 monkeys in 1994, and 116,493 LD50 style tests took place.[73] Other trivial or particularly controversial areas of testing include those for alcohol, household products and weapons research ...

Although a licence must be issued before an experiment can be carried out on an animal these licences do not usually cover individual projects but just seem to give researchers blanket permission to carry out any number of experiments of a given type, without each project necessarily being individually assessed. For example, only six project licences were issued to cover over 12,000 cosmetic experiments in 1989 ...

A BUAV investigation into Wickham Laboratories revealed that rabbits were being used in pyrogenicity tests for which a recognised alternative was not only available but recommended by UK regulators. This raises the key question of how s 5(5) is being interpreted ...

The APC is heavily dominated by individuals who are either researchers themselves or work for bodies which carry out or fund animal research. This has contributed to a situation in which the committee continues to defend even the continuation of cosmetic tests with only two from a 20 strong committee objecting to these tests.[74] The APC has yet to come forward with any major proposals for improving the increasingly unsatisfactory implementation of the 1986 Act ...

The Home Office Inspectorate is also overwhelmingly dominated by former animal researchers. It is also under strength for the job expected of it. For example, there were only 19 inspectors to monitor almost three million experiments in 1994. The situation has become worse since the Act was passed, with the number of visits by inspectors having declined by over 20%.[75]

---

72   *Ibid*, p 3.

[73] *Statistics of Scientific Procedures on Living Animals in Great Britain*, 1994, London: HMSO.

[74] *Report of the Animal Procedures Committee for 1987*, December 1988, London: HMSO.

75   *Statistics of Experiments on Living Animals in Great Britain*, 1986, London: HMSO; *Statistics of Scientific Procedures on Living Animals in Great Britain*, 1994, London: HMSO.

BUAV indicated that they felt that the Act could become workable with the inclusion of the following strategies: ending the most cruel, trivial and discredited experiments such as cosmetic testing; creating a strategy to reduce the number of animals used in experimentation by 50% by the year 2000; and encouraging the development of alternatives and strengthening the institutions and guidelines set up under the Act.

The Research Defence Society had a different view in their contributions to the review of the Act:[76]

> Regrettably, this review of the Act is certain to be used by the antivivisection groups as an opportunity to attempt to undermine public confidence in the legislation and the way it is implemented. Organisations which have the sole objective of ending any and all animal experimentation will necessarily find that this objective determines the content of any objection they might make. Since they are fundamentally opposed to the 1986 Act on the ground that it does not ban animal experiments, it is difficult to see how they can avoid being entirely one-sided in their comments ...

> ... When the UK legislation is compared to that of other countries, it is clear that our system of regulation is more stringent than that of any other country in the world. The UK is the only country in the world to require licences for the person, the project and the premises. Researchers who have worked abroad confirm that the degree and justification required by the UK project licence is greater than required in any other country. Whilst several other countries include a requirement to consider costs and benefits, the UK is the only country to have the benefit-suffering principle as the fundamental basis of regulating animal experiments. This is the only country to have an inspectorate which routinely pays unannounced visits to laboratories.

> The overwhelming impression of the scientists and technicians involved with animal research in the UK is that laboratory animal welfare has improved considerably over the last decade ...

> The level of serious infringements (ie those serious enough to result in a personal or project licence being revoked) has been very low indeed, with an average of two per year. Whilst this is obviously two too many, it provides evidence that the general level of compliance must be very high ...

> Since the 1986 Act is already the most stringent and, it would seem, the most complex regulatory system of its type, of any country in the world, one should question the idea of merely making it more stringent and more complex.

The APC has referred many times in its annual reports to the inadequacy of their budget to fund research into alternatives and, perhaps more seriously, they occasionally criticise the fact that some of their recommendations are rejected without good cause by the Home Office.[77] On a local institutional

---

76   Matfield, M, 'Ten years of the Animals (Scientific Procedures) Act' *RDS News*, April 1996, London: Research Defence Society.

77   See for example, the *Report of the Animal Procedures Committee for 1992*, September 1993, p 2, para 1.9, London: HMSO; *Report of the Animal Procedures Committee for 1995*, May 1996, p 17, London: HMSO.

basis they have had very little impact and only a few individual occurrences of infringements or bad practice have been specifically investigated, in line with the general lack of recorded infringements of the Act. Some welfare groups see this as one of the reasons that local ethics committees are an essential addition needed by the UK system. Indeed, the 1995 APC report recommends that the Home Secretary should provide advice to licence holders on the use that might be made of ethics committees. It indicated that an 'ethical review process' would be a useful addition to the UK system but was unwilling to recommend compelling their creation nor the form they should take.[78]

The RSPCA and BUAV submissions to the 1996 Review of the 1986 Act reveal that they are critical of the composition of the APC. Current membership includes people who could certainly be described as being from backgrounds supporting animal welfare stances: a member from the RSPCA, a member from the World Society for the Protection of Animals and the Director of Advocates for Animals. They number three from 17 members of the Committee (as of 1996), but do not include members from groups which hold absolute prohibition views on the use of animals in experimentation. It is a moot point as to whether the present 17 members of the APC represent all the diverging attitudes towards animal use in experimentation. It might be better to assess their record of achievement in order to observe whether they are effective bearing in mind that for some opponents, any underlying acceptance of the need to continue to use animals will always attract criticism.

The group which the APC replaced, namely the Home Office Advisory Committee, was criticised because of its lack of effectiveness. In the House of Lords, Lord Platt said: 'I was on the Advisory Committee for eleven years and we met only five times and advised on 19 cases.'[79] The APC now meets at least this many times in a single year, but they appear to have a long way to go to convince everyone that they are an entirely objective and effective forum of review.

Germany

Originally passed in 1934 and revised in 1972, 1986 and 1993, Germany's Animal Protection Act is considered to be an advanced piece of protective legislation. The Act's principal method of control is by means of a requirement to obtain authorisation from the Ministry of Food, Agriculture and Forestry for experiments on vertebrates which involve pain, suffering or injury. Licences are granted only where there is evidence that alternatives have been considered. There are several types of experiment which are not covered by the Act including experiments on embryos or fetuses, breeding and behavioral

---

78 *Report of the Animal Procedures Committee for 1995,* above n 74, p 7, para 44.
79 House of Lords, 14 May 1975, reported in *Hansard.*

experiments not involving stress and experiments carried out to conform with other statutory requirements.

The Act is underpinned by the familiar basic principles that higher animals are not to be used unless absolutely necessary and warm-blooded animals should only be used where cold-blooded animals would not suffice. The Act also stresses that pain and suffering should only be inflicted if they are inevitable consequences of the experiments.

There are certain types of animals which are given extra protection under the Act, most of which are domestic animals. At the end of an experiment the Act requires that animals such as cats, dogs, rabbits and non-human primates be examined by a veterinary officer to determine whether the animal should be kept alive or not. For other types of animal the experimenter is permitted to make the decision. The Act also requires the establishments concerned to keep detailed records of all experiments for a period of three years which should made available for inspection as required by the supervising body.

German law does not require animals to have been specialist bred for the purpose which is common in other countries in Europe.

The Netherlands

The Netherlands, by virtue of the Law for Animal Experiments 1977, uses a system of licences supervised by the Ministry of Public Health covering experiments which involve vertebrates and are likely to cause pain or injury. Licences are issued to the head of the institution involved who is held responsible for all the activities at that institution. Government appointed inspectors work closely with the personnel involved within the institution to provide the best conditions possible for the animals. An interesting and radical constituent of the Dutch system is that the people involved in experimentation are required to undertake an ethics course at the University of Utrecht.

Unlike the German system, the Dutch system also pays some attention to the rearing of animals by giving the Minister of Public Health the power to specify requirements for the source of or the rearing of animals. As with some other countries the Act recognises public sentiments for particular species by requiring that dogs, cats, horses and apes should not be used where other animals would suffice. The Act is also notable for its absolute prohibition of the use of animals where the results can be obtained by alternative experimental techniques. The pain suffered by animals is regulated by the requirement that persistent pain must be alleviated by euthanasia immediately after the experiment.

The Netherlands uses a similar system to the UK in relation to the advice given to the relevant Minister in government. It creates an advisory committee to look at all aspects of the Act and is comprised of experts from both scientific and animal welfare groups. Also in common with the UK is the requirement for the publication of detailed information regarding the number of animals used and the purposes for which they are used. In this regard the Netherlands joins the ranks of the few countries that release detailed figures for public scrutiny.

Sweden

Sweden was one of the first countries in Europe to tackle all forms of animal abuse. There was considerable debate in the 1880s with the anti-animal experimentation lobby being led by the highly respected Adolf Leonard Nordvall: 'Can love of the truth so demoralise human beings that they can carry out experiments with cold-blooded calmness – nay, with unspeakable pleasure, and so openly mock at all justice and mercy?'[80] His influence on the future of Swedish animal welfare groups was considerable even if his actual attempts at introducing legislation through the Riksdag were unsuccessful.

The relevant piece of legislation here is the Animal Protection Act 1988. It replaced the Protection of Animals Act 1944 which had been amended several times. The new Act is supported by more detailed provisions in the Animal Protection Ordinance 1988 and by regulations issued by the National Board of Agriculture:

The Animal Protection Act 1988

Section 19

(1) Animals must not without permission from the government or, where the government so decides, from the National Board of Agriculture, be used for scientific research or education, the diagnosis of disease, the production of drugs or chemical products or for other comparable purposes if the animals are subjected to surgery, injections, bleeding or other suffering. Only animals bred for such purposes may be used. Such breeding may not take place without permission from the National Board of Agriculture.

(2) In considering applications, special attention shall be paid to the question of whether the applicant can be considered to have the qualifications required to engage in the activity and whether the premises in which the activity is to take place are suitable from the point of view of animals protection. In considering applications for the breeding for experimental purposes, the necessity of using such animals shall also be taken into account.

Section 21

(1) The use of animals for the purpose referred to in s 19(1) shall be subject to an ethical review before commencement of the activity.

---

80 Quoted in Bromander, L, 'The Vivisection Debate in Sweden in the 1880s', in Rupke, above n 55, p 219.

The Animal Protection Ordinance (1988) (as amended)

Section 41

Ethical reviews pursuant to s 21(1) of the Animal Protection Act 1988 shall be conducted by local committees for ethical review of animal experiments.

Section 43

(1) Each committee shall have a chairman and a vice-chairman and include laymen, research workers and representatives of personnel who handle laboratory animals.

(2) The National Board for Laboratory Animals shall appoint the chairman and vice-chairman, who shall be impartial and shall preferably have legal training and experience as judges.

(3) Half of the other members of the committee shall be laymen. The number or representatives for animal protection organisations on the committee shall number less than half the lay members of the committee.

Section 48

(1) The local committees for the ethical review of animal experiments shall have an advisory role. They shall provide advisory services to those responsible for animal experiments.

(2) Ethical reviews of experiments shall take place every three years.

Section 49

(1) In considering a case the committee shall weigh the importance of the experiment against the suffering inflicted on the animal.

(2) The committee shall advise against the use of animals for scientific purposes if this cannot be regarded as being in the public interest. The committee shall also advise against the use of animals for such purposes where it is possible to acquire comparable information by other means.

(3) Ethical reviews shall also take into account the care and housing of animals in connection with their use for experimental purposes.

Section 50

The National Board of Agriculture may adopt provisions granting exemptions from the provisions relating to the breeding of laboratory animals in the second sentence of s 19(1) of the Animal Protection Act 1988.

Section 53

Before the performance of surgery of any significance on a warm-blooded animal pursuant to s 19(1) of the Animal Protection Act 1988, the animal shall be anaesthetised. However, if necessary in view of the purpose of the surgery, it may be performed under partial anaesthesia or without an anaesthetic. Where possible, an analgesic or tranquilliser shall be used in such cases in order to alleviate the animal's suffering.

Section 54

A person using animals for the purposes referred to in s 19(1) of the Animal Protection Act 1988 shall, pursuant to the rule adopted by the National Board for Laboratory Animals:

1. supply information about the numbers and kinds of animals used;

2. keep records of the purchase of animals; and

3. keep records of the measures taken.

Section 55

(1) Premises for laboratory animals must not be built, extended or rebuilt without the prior approval, with reference to animal protection, of the National Board of Agriculture. The same shall apply to modifications of such premises with significant implications for animal protection or when premises which have previously been used for other purposes are put to use or fitted up as premises for laboratory animals.

Regulation has much in common with Norway and Denmark and provides for a system of licensing individuals and institutions in the form of research establishments, universities and hospitals. As with some other countries it is the head of the establishment who is made responsible for the activities within the institution. The Act requires that experiments must be permitted by the National Board of Agriculture and is unusual in that it regulates experiments which involve 'fear'. Higher animals are again afforded greater protection by not being used where alternative animals could be used and non-human primates, cats, dogs and horses are given the added protection of registration of their origin and their use in experimentation.

An unusual aspect of the Swedish legislation is its decentralised organisation of supervision through tiers of responsibility. The 1988 Act created seven ethics committees on a regional basis which have responsibility for examining all requests for permission to use animals in experimentation. Each has 12 members, half of whom are lay members. A National Board for Laboratory Animals (NBLA) advises and oversees their work and these two levels of review are ultimately overseen directly by the Ministry of Agriculture. A Board of Agriculture awards the licences to laboratories and institutions to house laboratory animals and to conduct experiments as well as appointing the individual with overall responsibility. Unlike the UK, no specific licence is required for each experiment but it must have undergone a review by one of the ethics committees. These committees are only advisory and a project can go ahead even if the committee has recommended otherwise. Judith Hampson notes that, as seen in the Australian experience of the use of ethics committees, the end product has not always been entirely satisfactory in Sweden:[81]

81   Hampson, J, 'Legislation: A Practical Solution to the Vivisection Dilemma', in Rupke, above n 55, p 337.

> The scheme in Sweden has been rendered almost ineffective by the adoption in many regions of antivivisectionists among the lay members. Since these persons are opposed to all animal experimentation, they are less interested in refining protocols than in impeding research by holding it up. This has lead to a generally poor attendance at full committee meetings and loss of faith by scientists in the system. Thus, rather than contributing directly to a system which could improve the lot of laboratory animals, the radical vivisectionists have brought that system into disfavour and threatened its continuance.

This criticism is not, however supported by those working within the system. Karin Gabrielson of the Swedish Society Against Painful Experiments responded to these criticisms by saying: '... the criticism mentioned by Judith Hampson is unfounded, and as far as I'm aware, has not even been raised in Sweden. On the contrary, criticism from animal welfare groups involved in the ethics committees has led to several amendments of the system, most notably in 1988.'[82] The Swedish legislation certainly does seem to undergo frequent revisions and updates. At the time of writing (late 1996) the Animal Protection Act 1988 was being revised with new amendments and due to be published for public consultation in the winter of 1996–97.

The Animal Protection Act 1988 also provides that animals used in experimentation must have been bred for that purpose, regulates who can be registered as a breeder, requires those involved in experimentation to be adequately trained, can order improvements to be made at the experimenter's expense and requires institutions to provide statistical information when required to do so. Inspections and enforcement of animal protection legislation is the responsibility of the local authorities. Finally, in addition to this legislative control, mention should be made of the Swedish Medical Research Council which also exercises considerable ethical control over experimentation and only allocates funds to those projects which are considered to be ethically sound.

Australia

The Australian experience of the regulation of animal experimentation, the primary tool of which is the use of Animal Experimentation Ethics Committees (AEECs) has been viewed by other animal welfare groups worldwide, such as the RSPCA, as an example of good practice in the absence of a total ban on experiments as many organisations would like to see. All States have some form of legislation which makes it an offence to inflict cruelty on an animal but specific regulation of research differs between States. Some have altered regulation recently, whereas others rely on comparatively old legislation. New South Wales has the tightest legislation of animal experimentation where both personal and institutional licences are required.

82   From a letter to Simon Brooman, 28 October 1996.

Despite disparate legislative control, the second method of regulation, and some would argue more effective, is the use of a national code of practice and its requirement for the setting up of AEECs.

The prime mover in creating and enforcing the system of AEECs in Australia is the National Health and Medical Research Council (NHMRC) which is the main funding body for bio-medical research in Australia. In the past 25 years, the NHMRC has been the leading light in the control of animal experimentation in Australia with the publication of the *Australian Code of Practice for Care and Use of Animals for Scientific Purposes* which is published with the Commonwealth Scientific and Industrial research Council (CSIRO) and the Australian Agriculture Council. In 1985 the NHMRC established the Animal Experimentation Ethics Committee, now the Animal Welfare Committee (AWC), which has a proactive role in advising on ethical matters relating to the conduct of research involving animals, to monitor compliance, investigate some alleged breaches and recommend amendments to the Code. The NHMRC requires institutions receiving its funding to comply with the Code and can withdraw funding from those who do not. Some States' legislation incorporates or refers to the Code specifically making it the chief method of regulation in Australia.[83]

The responsibilities imposed by the Code are aimed at institutions, investigators (experimenters) and AEECs themselves; institutions must set up and provide resources for AEECs; experimenters must comply with welfare requirements and liaise and respond to AEEC concerns; and AEECs are compelled to effectively oversee, review and maintain records of the their operation. The Code provides that the crucial issue of membership must include a vet, a person experienced in experimentation, a person committed to animal welfare and not involved in research who is not an employee of the institution. AEECs, the first modern version of which appeared at the University of Adelaide in 1973, are part of the self-regulatory process under which institutions approve research involving animals. Institutions wishing to conduct animal experimentation must align themselves to an AEEC to receive NHMRC funding. In order to approve a programme of research an AEEC is required to take into account questions which are echoed in the regulation of research in many other countries: what alternatives are there?; is duplication of research involved?; is the research really necessary and important?

The Australian use of AEECs receives widespread support, both from home and abroad and bodies such as the RSPCA in the UK have looked very closely at how effectively the system operates with a view to advocating the incorporation of its best features into UK regulations. In the opening address

---

83   Anderson, W, 'A New Approach to Regulating the Use of Animals in Science' (1990) 4 *Bioethics* 1, at 51.

to a conference on the effectiveness of AEECs in Adelaide in 1992, Loane Skene examined the advantages of the system:[84]

Functional Factors – how AEEC's operate

AEEC's have a special function within the total regulatory framework. This arises from their constitution and also from the way they operate. The differences can be best illustrated by comparing AEEC's with licensing authorities and their inspection process.

AEEC's include an in-house member.

The categories of membership of AEEC's are similar in most respects to those of licensing authorities. Under the Code, AEEC members must include a veterinary surgeon, a person experienced in animal experimentation, a person committed to and experienced in animal welfare who is not involved in animal research, and an independent person not involved in animal research, who is preferably not an employee of an institution. The significant difference is that the first category member, the veterinary surgeon, is to be a person 'preferably with experience relevant to activities of the institution'. This means that one member of most AEEC's is someone with familiar with the institution and its staff and who is likely to be on-site. This not only assists monitoring; it also means that this members has a particular interest in preserving the reputation, and the funding, of the institution. And investigators may be more amenable to instructions from someone they know than from an outside 'policeman'.

AEEC's help develop procedures.

The role of AEEC's is not confined to monitoring and policing. Indeed, that is not the sole function of licensing authorities either – they also provide advice. In New South Wales, for example, the Animal Research Review Panel is there as much to advise and help the AEEC's as to inspect. It intends to have two advisory visits for every inspection and Panel members often accompany the inspectors. The Panel's other function is to draw up guidelines for the AEEC's, who are requesting this at the moment.

However, AEEC's are also required by the Code to develop procedures for the humane care of animals within the institution – to be proactive. That is, they co-operate with the institution in developing its procedures and in revising them from time to time. The focus is on education – on learning together – rather than on making rules and policing them. People are more likely to observe procedures that they have been involved in developing, and for which they can see the justification.

AEEC's monitor on a day-to-day basis.

Although inspectors can visit without notice, AEEC's are on the spot all the time. Institutions and investigators know that someone is looking over

84   Skene, L, 'Animal experimentation ethics committees – what are we trying to achieve?', in Baker, R, Burrell, J and Rose, M (eds), *Effective Animal Experimentation Committees*, 1994, pp 5-6, Glen Osmond, South Australia: Australian and New Zealand Council for the Care of Animals in Research and Teaching (ANZCCART).

their shoulder. Most AEEC's meet monthly, and, if something is wrong, it will be brought up at the next meeting. This is a more rigorous form of surveillance than monitoring by someone from a distant bureaucracy who periodically appears and disappears. This is illustrated by a recent incident in New South Wales, where an AEEC closed down a whole research program at a major institution on a Saturday morning until they could investigate a possible problem. This was a more immediate and stringent response than might be expected from a central licensing authority.

Non-veterinary surgeons more involved in monitoring

Because all AEEC members are local, visits are more likely to be conducted by members who are not veterinarians, than non-veterinary members of licensing authorities. For cost reasons, most inspections by licensing authorities are conducted by veterinary surgeons alone. Their expertise is obviously more than sufficient for the task, but community concerns may be better satisfied by visits from concerned community representatives ... Non-veterinarians who are sufficiently concerned about animal welfare to join an AEEC are likely to be particularly sensitive to any problems.

AEEC's are more cost-efficient

The administrative costs of external regulation and monitoring are very high. Inspections need to be done regularly to be effective, and when 80–100 institutions are involved (as in Victoria and New South Wales), often in distant locations, this requires considerable time and resources. In New South Wales, licenses are currently granted subject to an inspection, which is done up to 12 months later. Inspections can take up to a week, and follow-up visits may be required. This involves considerable costs and ongoing inspections are difficult. AEEC's, on the other hand, involve little expense. Their members serve on a voluntary basis or are paid by the institution. Because they are on-site, costly travelling expenses are avoided.

Criticisms of AEEC's

Monitoring by AEEC's may also have disadvantages

Lack of objectivity

If AEEC's include members from within an institution, can they be trusted to police their own premises and personnel effectively? Although the committee also has lay members, they may not be sufficiently confident, or vocal, to voice their concerns to people who appear to have greater expertise or experience than they do.

Lack of consistency

If monitoring is conducted by individual in-house committees, they may be a piece-meal approach to monitoring and inspections. Each institution may be different to others.

The way forward

To overcome these concerns, it is obviously essential that measures should be developed to increase the knowledge and confidence of AEEC members, especially the lay members. All people who are concerned with animal welfare, especially in the scientific area, must be able to share their knowledge and experience in order to develop consistent policies. This can be achieved through training programs, information and educational materials, publications, meetings and conferences. ANZCCART has a particularly valuable role in providing information of a general or specific kind, in answering questions from researchers and the public about animal welfare, and in sponsoring conferences to enable people to inform themselves and to share their knowledge and experience.

One of the chief problems the Australian system has experienced is the lack of confidence expressed by some regarding its effectiveness and propriety. Many groups in the Australian animal welfare lobby such as Humane Society International argue that AEEC members, often people actually involved in research themselves, do not take an unbiased view of their function and this leads to abuse of the system. The Humane Society International reported that of 47,781 animals used in research in 1993–94 in New South Wales only 14 alternatives were implemented and suspected a 'lack of impetus on researchers' to find and use alternatives. One might have thought that the requirement to have a person committed to animal welfare, preferably from outside the institution would have alleviated this possibility. But Glenys Oogjes of the Australian and New Zealand Federation of Animal Societies (ANZFAS) identifies associated problems which might have led AEECs to be less effective than the animal welfare lobby would have liked:[85]

> The current regulatory system in Australia, which relies heavily on Animal Experimentation Ethics Committees (AEEC's), can operate effectively. A properly constituted and well managed institutional AEEC can reduce reliance on animals, improve experimental design leading to fewer animals and more humane techniques being used, and can improve the housing and husbandry of animals used in research.

> Unfortunately, due to the unwillingness of many institutions to seek AEEC members from established animal welfare organisations, those welfare organisations have no confidence that the research community wish to abide by the spirit of the Code of Practice in other respects. Further, it is critical that AEEC members, particularly animal welfare and other outside members, are assured of adequate assistance through written material, tours of institution facilities, regular workshops conducted on a regional or State basis, and the exchange of AEEC annual reports which summarise significant advances or problems. Due largely to neglect and, perhaps, to inadequate staffing on the part of the relevant State Government Departments, AEEC's are rarely offered sufficient support or assistance.

> Compounding the problems arising from the failure of many institutions to invite representatives from major animal welfare bodies onto AEECs, is the absence of any alternative means of providing public accountability. A

---

85 Oogjes, G, 'Are animal Experimentation committees Delivering?', in Baker, Burrell and Rose, above n 84, p 65.

national register of meaningful animal research statistics is required and an increase in government monitoring of the operation of AEECs is now overdue.

As a result of observations such as these, there have been concerns raised regarding the public accountability and credibility of AEECs. Some groups in Australia have regarded them purely as 'rubber stamps' to the purposes of the scientific community, a perception which is damaging to the function of the legislation, and have proposed increased external monitoring of the effectiveness of individual AEECs which would probably require legislation at a State or federal level to create a government-sponsored inspection system. The attitude of researchers to 'outside interference' by those on AEECs has also been suggested as being a barrier to their effectiveness. AEECs may lack teeth for non-compliance with the use of Code of Practice, as they are dependent on a continuing relationship between AEEC members and experimenters. By way of contrast, external bodies provide independent and objective assessments of legality.

Because the Australian States each have different laws and codes to regulate experimentation, providing a conclusive national picture is also extremely difficult. A national study of, for example, the number of animals involved in experimentation, is extremely difficult as there so many different organisations and public bodies at State and national level producing statistics. The Humane Society International (HSI) conducted national research in 1995–96 into the use of primates in experimental research.[86] They found gathering information regarding the type of use and number of animals involved an extremely difficult task. In the UK, information is comparatively easy to obtain through the comprehensive Home Office/Animal Procedures Committee annual reports which are readily available. The lack of centrally produced statistical information is a barrier in any country for groups trying to highlight the effectiveness or otherwise of control. Even where it has been produced, statistical information in Australia lacks the detail necessary to ensure that duplication of experiments is not occurring, and makes moves towards the replacement, refinement and reduction of experiments more difficult to monitor. Where statistical information is weak, there is a fear that experimenters avoid effective accountability for the numbers of animals used in different types of research and there is no concrete evidence of reduction and replacement.[87]

---

86   *Human Society International Australia Newsletter*, 1995, vol 2, Issue 4, p 7.

87   Oogjes, G, 'Expectations of ANZFAS Member Societies', in *Farm Animals in Biomedical and Agricultural Research*, 1996, p 89, Australia: Australian and New Zealand Council for the Care of Animals in Research and Teaching.

One feature of Australian animal experimentation which can be contrasted with the situation in the UK is the use of domestic animals from pounds. In 1993 the Senate Select Committee supported the continued use of pound animals, in response to the advantages put forward by the scientific community.[88] They see the use of these animals as avoiding waste when animals are destroyed, and as preventing the need to breed animals. Animal welfare groups are opposed to the use of such animals because of the fear experienced by these animals outside the domestic environment they have been used to, the concerns of people over the fate of their pets, and the fact that the continued use of these 'cheap' animals subverts the government's stated intention of reducing the numbers of animals in research. At the time of writing, the practice seems set to continue.

New federal legislation seemed possible with the introduction of a National Animal Welfare Bill in 1995, which would have contained far-reaching provisions for animals used as the subjects of experimentation or being transported or exported, and would also have extended protection to wild animals. The Bill proposed that the use of non-human primates in research be phased out within five years, together with an end to Commonwealth support for the use of animals in education, and a licensing system similar to that already in use in the UK. It would also have required the production of an annual report indicating the number and types of animals being used in registered institutions. Perhaps the most far-reaching and potentially most effective provision would have been the creation of National Animal Welfare Authority based in Canberra, given responsibility to initiate changes in policy where necessary. However, without the support of the Labour or Liberal parties, the Bill was lost at the end of 1996.

The US

The US became a major world centre for animal experimentation in the 1880s and 1890s. Protest by a growing number of antivivisection groups in the latter part of the 19th century led to the first Bill attempting to regulate animal experimentation being introduced in 1880. Based on the UK's Cruelty to Animals Act 1876, it was undone by successful lobbying by the scientific community.[89]

Perhaps a turning point in the development of US control of experimentation can be found in the number of new 'pound seizure laws' which came into being after the Second World War in order to feed the ever-increasing demand for experimental animals. These new laws, which allowed

---

88 *Report of the Animal Welfare Committee,* 1993, Australia: National Health and Medical Research Council.

89 Stevens, C, 'Laboratory Animal Welfare', in *Animals and Their Legal Rights,* 1990, p 70, Washington: Animal Welfare Institute.

the seizure of animals kept in animal welfare sanctuaries or pounds to be used for experimentation, had the support of the public as the result of the Los Angeles referendum on the matter in 1949 illustrates.[90] This left the animal welfare institutions of the US without the ability to succeed in their basic mission, as they saw it, of providing a sanctuary from human use or abuse, and led to an increase in their protest activities. The main reason for the use of pound animals in research was their low cost in comparison to purpose-bred animals. It is still argued, as it is in Australia, that this is a reasonable use of animals which have to be put down anyway, rather than just letting them go to waste. But the issue of the use of pound animals provoked heated public criticism of the regulation of animal use, possibly because of the additional emotions stirred by the thought of the family pet eventually ending up as a subject of research. Antivivisection groups opposed the practice, along with all other forms of vivisection, but this issue intensified an already heated debate surrounding animal welfare in the US.

As regards general regulation of animal research, the US medical profession remained very sceptical of UK-type regulation, with its requirement for licensing of individual researchers and the monitoring of their activities. Scientists were convinced that advances such as open heart surgery, the development of pacemakers and kidney transplantation, had taken place as a result of less stringent regulation of experimentation.[91] At the same time as the UK government appointed Sir Sydney Littlewood to look into the whole question of the use of animals in research, two events in 1966 conspired to catapult the whole question into a full-scale political debate in the US. The first was the case of the loss of the Lakavage family's dog, Pepper, the pursuit of which was taken up by Congressman Resnick in New York. The trail eventually led to a laboratory incinerator and the Congressman was extremely concerned about the attitude of those involved, leading him to introduce a Bill to regulate the trade in dogs. The second event was the publication of photographs by *Life* magazine which exposed the cruelty involved in the handling of dogs as a result of the pound seizure laws. There was a public outcry, and the momentum behind Resnick's Bill gathered pace. Two random events had conspired to ensure that the Animal Welfare Act became law on 24 August 1966.[92] The Act certainly gives protection to the abuses uncovered by Pepper's case, by requiring that animals be obtained from licensed dealers, but scientists retained most of their control of procedures and decision-making in the laboratory itself. Although the practice is now much more regulated than it was, the use of ex-pets through 'pound seizure', so much a

90 The vote was 357,393 to 261,699 in favour of the new animal procurement orders.

91 See Dennis, C, 'America's Littlewood Crisis: The Sentimental Threat to Animal Research' (1966) 60 *Surgery* 827–39.

92 Stevens, above n 89, pp 73–75. For further background to the passing of the 1966 Act, see Francione, G, *Rain Without Thunder: The Ideology of the Animal Rights Movement,* 1996, pp 87–90, Philadelphia: Temple University Press.

part of the introduction of the 1966 Act, still continues in the US.[93] Thirteen States prohibit the release of 'pound animals', but others either require it or allow it.[94] The chances of the family pet being stolen and then sold to a laboratory have receded, but the use of pound animals in experimentation remains a possibility.

The Act has since been amended, in 1970, 1976, 1985 and 1990. It now requires that dealers and laboratories are licensed and that pain-relieving drugs are used where possible. Despite this development, however, US legislation falls a long way short of the legislation of the UK.[95] Two examples of this can be found in the fact that US legislation does not cover the actual procedures involved, but only the housing, handling and transportation of the animals to be used. US legislation also fails to cover rats and mice, approximately 80% of the subjects of US laboratory experiments. On both these counts UK legislation gives more protection to animals. There follows an abridged version of some of the main provisions of the Act:

The Animal Welfare Act 1966 (as amended)

Section 1

> (b) ... the regulation of animals and activities ... is necessary to prevent and eliminate burdens upon such commerce and to eliminate such commerce, in order:
>
> > (1) to ensure that animals intended for use in research facilities or for exhibition purposes or for use as pets are provided humane care and treatment;
> >
> > (2) to ensure the humane treatment of animals during transportation in commerce; and
> >
> > (3) to protect the owners of animals form the theft of their animals by preventing the sale or use of animals which have been stolen. ...
>
> (1) the use of animals is instrumental in certain research and education for advancing knowledge of cures and treatment for diseases and injuries which affect both humans and animals; ...
>
> (4) measures which help meet the public concern for laboratory animal care and treatment are important in assuring that research will continue to progress. ...

Section 4

No dealer or exhibitor shall sell or offer to sell or transport or offer for transportation, in commerce, to any research facility or for exhibition or for use as a pet any animal, or buy, sell, offer to buy or sell, transport or offer for

---

93 The 1990 amendment to the Act requires that a shelter or pound holds an animal for at least five days, to allow time for it to be reclaimed.

94 Stevens, above n 89, p 66.

95 The Animal Welfare Institute reported in *Beyond the Laboratory Door*, 1985, Washington DC, that abuse or neglect of animals occurred in 80% of places visited.

transportation, in commerce, to or from another dealer or exhibitor under this Act any animal, unless and until such dealer or exhibitor shall have obtained a license from the Secretary and such license shall not have been suspended or revoked.

Section 5

No dealer or exhibitor shall sell or otherwise dispose of any dog or cat within a period of 5 business days after the acquisition of such animal ...

Section 10

Dealers and exhibitors shall make and retain for such reasonable period of time as the Secretary may prescribe, such records with respect to the purchase, sale, transportation, identification, and previous ownership of animals as the Secretary may prescribe ...

Section 13

(1) The Secretary shall promulgate standards to govern the humane handling, care, treatment and transportation of animals by dealers, research facilities, and exhibitors.

(2) the standards described in paragraph (1) shall include minimum requirements:

   (A) for handling, housing, sanitation, ventilation, shelter from extremes of weather and temperatures, adequate veterinary care, and separation by species where the Secretary finds necessary for human handling, care, or treatment of animals; and

   (B) for exercise of dogs, as determined by an attending veterinarian in accordance with the general standards promulgated by the Secretary, and for a physical environment adequate to promote the psychological well-being of primates.

(3) In addition to the requirements under paragraph (2), the standards described in paragraph (1) shall, with respect to animals in research facilities, include requirements:

   (A) for animal care, treatment, and practices in experimental procedures to ensure that animal pain and distress are minimised, including adequate veterinary care with the appropriate use of anaesthetic, analgesic, tranquillising drugs, or euthanasia;

   (B) that the principal investigator considers alternatives to any procedure likely to produce pain to or distress in an experimental animal ...

There have been several cases where animal rights activists have uncovered some unpleasant examples of a lack of care where legislation has failed to provide a remedy. One of the most infamous cases is that of Dr Edward Taub of the Institute of Behavioral Research in Washington, in 1981. Dr Taub crippled the arms of monkeys to see whether they could be taught to reuse them, as part of his research into the effects of strokes. His treatment of monkeys was revealed by an undercover animal rights activist; he was prosecuted for the housing and conditions in which the monkeys were kept, not for the procedures carried out on the animals. He was initially found guilty of providing inadequate veterinary care, and the case led to an investigation as to how an institution supported by the National Institute of Health and inspected by the Department of Agriculture could have 'slipped through the net' in such a manner. Taub was eventually acquitted – not because the alleged cruelty was disproved, but because the Maryland State anti-cruelty law under which he was convicted was held not to apply to animals in research. Problems regarding the meaning of the word 'unnecessary' arose again, just as they had in relation to Martin's Act in the UK. But as Andrew Rowan commented, the case 'served dramatic notice on members of Congress that things are not all they could be in the nation's laboratories'.[96]

Following incidents such as that involving Taub, the US Congress passed the Improved Standards for Laboratory Animals Act 1985 amending the 1966 Act which provided that, for the first time, pain and distress should be minimised. It also stressed the need to search for alternatives and that 'institutional care committees' should be set up in institutions involved in animal experimentation. They should have at least one lay member and should regularly inspect research facilities in question. Despite the success of ethics committees elsewhere, the problem remains in the US that they are unable, in contrast to Australia and Sweden, to exert any influence over the actual conduct of the experiments, thus greatly reducing their effectiveness.[97]

Federal law in the shape of the Animal Welfare Act and various controls, mainly relating to the procurement of animals, introduced at State level make the US coverage extremely complex and diverse. The primary tool of protection remains the 1966 Act (as amended), the enforcement of which is the responsibility of the US Department of Agriculture's Animal and Plant Inspection Service (APHIS). Institutions must register with APHIS and are inspected at least once a year, but only as regards professionally acceptable standards being in place to relieve pain and stress. The actual conduct of research in terms of design and performance is not affected by APHIS, leaving its coverage short of that in the UK and elsewhere. Most other countries such as the UK and Australia seem to be favouring the specific justification of individual studies, including the techniques used, in contrast to the US which specifically excludes this.

Control of specific studies and techniques at a local level is better catered for by the further protection provided for animals used in establishments which obtain Public Health Service research funds. They have to comply with the National Institute of Health's *Guide for the Care and Use of Laboratory Animals*. This brings most research facilities within its coverage which requires institutions to set up Institutional Animal Care and Use Committees.

---

96 Rowan, A, *Of Mice, Models and Men: A Critical Evaluation of Animal Research*, 1984, p 63, Albany: State University of New York Press.

97 Francione, above n 92, pp 91–93.

During the 1970s and 1980s the US experienced some of the most notorious incidences of animal experimentation, such as those involving Edward Taub, but some of the present advocates of research involving animals in the US have suggested that such experiments would be unlikely to be approved by such committees today: one proposed experiment in 1990 to look at the effects of isolation on primates by taking 21 infant monkeys away from their mothers for a year to induce self-mutilation was vociferously opposed by animal activists at the meeting of the University of Washington in Seattle's animal care committee. The NIH refused to fund the project, leading the experimenter, Gene Sackett, to accuse them of 'cowardice' in the face of the very public criticism at the meeting. Ironically the activists had been in attendance to complain about a different experiment, involving rats.[98]

Whether this combination of legislation and persuasion is effective remains doubtful: the 1985 amendments have been described as 'representing nothing but complete capitulation to the desire of the research community to continue doing business as usual'.[99] The US does not provide the same degree of welfare protection that is seen in Europe and Australia. The Office of Technology Assessment's report to the US Congress in 1988 highlighted considerable problems in implementing the new controls of the use of animals in experimentation. Not least of these was the doubt over whether the federal government had constitutional authority to enter the domain of control which was traditionally regulated by the States themselves:[100]

> A legislative reluctance to invade the actual conduct of research is clear. The Secretary of Agriculture is forbidden to enact any regulation that could be so construed. The closest the law comes is to require the Secretary to establish and enforce standards for care and treatment of experimental animals outside the laboratory door, and to require covered research facilities to certify that professionally acceptable standards of care, treatment, and use are being followed in the laboratory, including 'appropriate' use of anaesthetics and pain relievers, except when their use would interfere with experimental objectives. In addition, large classes of experimental animals – principally mice and rats – are not covered by the Act as it is currently enforced by the Department of Agriculture, and the law's provisions remain weighted toward traffic in pet species. Since interstate regulation constitutionally requires some connection to interstate commerce, research institutions that use animals protected by the Act but that receive no Federal funds and that maintain their own breeding colonies cannot be regulated. To date, there has been no significant judicial test of the provisions regulating research.

---

98 Blum, D, *Monkey Wars*, 1994, pp 99–100, Oxford: Oxford University Press.

99 Francione, above n 92, p 94.

100 See the Office of Technology Assessment's Report *Alternatives to Animal Use in Research, Testing, and Education*, above n 59, p 34.

In addition, regulation has been criticised in 1985 by the General Accounting Office which reported that training of USDA inspectors is insufficient and that APHIS did not follow up serious deficiencies in a satisfactory manner. There are also concerns from the USDA Office of the Inspector General that researchers are obtaining animals from shelters before the required waiting period has elapsed.[101]

Canada

From the point of view of self-regulation, one of the most interesting examples to examine is that of Canada, which uses an entirely voluntary system of national regulation.[102] Certain States, for example, Ontario, have implemented their own State regulation of certain aspects of research such as the use of unclaimed pound animals. But these regulations are extremely limited in their ambit.

The voluntary programme is run by the Canadian Council on Animal Care (CCAC) which was formed in 1968 as an independent agency with a wide range of interest groups represented by its membership of 21. The basic tool of implementation is a guide which is produced by CCAC, the *Guide for the Care and Use of Experimental Animals*, which is provided free to every researcher using animals. This guide requires that institutions should set up Animal Care Committees (ACCs) to oversee experimentation to ensure that the animals concerned are dealt with as humanely as possible.

The obvious problem that a system such as this might encounter would be its lack of teeth in implementation, as there are no sanctions for violation of the CCAC standards. To this end the CCAC chooses assessment panels to investigate whether the basic guidelines are adhered to. They visit institutions at least every three years and report on the training and qualifications of staff concerned, the standard of the facilities, the care of the animals, and procedures for the welfare of the animals generally. This has led to the CCAC recommending national changes in practice on, for example, poor surgical or anaesthesia techniques. In addition to this, other national bodies such as the Health Protection Branch of the Department of National Health and Welfare have used their position in relation to the awarding of contracts by requiring institutions to demonstrate compliance with the CCAC standards or lose their funding.

In 1982 a government-initiated review of the effectiveness of the CCAC in policing animal welfare in relation to experimentation found that it was

---

101 Francione, G, *Rain Without Thunder*, above n 92, pp 115–16.

102 For more details on the Canadian system of regulation, see Smith, J and Boyd, K, *Lives in the Balance: The Ethics of Using Animals in Biomedical Research, a summary of the Report by a Working Party of the Institute of Medical Ethics*, 1991, pp 268–71, Oxford: Oxford University Press.

effective and carried considerable influence in eliminating bad practice. It should be said, however, that criticism still remains and legislative back-up is considered desirable by some so as to ensure consistency of the operation of Animal Care Committees.[103]

Critics have claimed that the system merely protects the scientists and not the animals. Considerable variation in the functioning of the committees has been noted and it has been argued by Tatum that it is very difficult for the members of the committees to regulate the actions of colleagues. Tatum argued that the Canadian system of self-regulation merely served to protect the scientists and he resigned from any involvement in the operation of ACCs. He argued that the best method of protecting the animals would be 'legislation enacted in Parliament – legislation which must be enforced and of which the experimenter must be afraid, and which provides for his or her punishment if he or she contravenes the Criminal Code of Canada.' The CCAC is well aware of this, and strongly and actively opposes any attempt to secure such legislation, leading one writer to point out that a system which so 'well protects the scientists, is the "envy" of scientists abroad'.[104] The working party of the Institute of Medical Ethics commented on the Canadian system that 'it seems that implementation of legislation might help improve public confidence in the system of control'.[105]

WHAT IS THE BEST WAY TO REGULATE ANIMAL EXPERIMENTATION?

The more 'extreme' elements of opposition to the use of animals in experimentation argue that the only satisfactory moral solution to adequately protect animals is its complete abolition. This would force scientists, they claim, to rapidly come up with new methods of research. They point to evidence that, in the face of united opposition to certain practices, new methods tend to appear more quickly. In Australia, for example, all sides of the animal rights debate have broadly supported the need to protect indigenous species against predators or other successful species such as foxes, which were introduced recently by humans. There is unease at mass destruction of animals, leading to a focusing of energy on new methods of control such as introducing infertility so that the animals concerned can at least live out a relatively natural life without reproducing.[106] Whether these

---

103 See Clark, J, 'Public concerns for animals in research', *Laboratory Animal Science*, Special Issue, January 1987, pp 120–21; Hampson, J, 'Legislation: A Practical Solution to the Vivisection Dilemma' in Rupke, above n 55.

104 Tatum, J, 'On The Ineffectiveness of Canadian Animal Care Committees', *PsyETA Bulletin*, Fall 1988, pp 3–5.

105 Smith, and Boyd, above n 17, p 271.

106 BBC Television, '20th Century Fox', *Nature Special*, October 1996.

new methods would have been developed as quickly without consolidated opposition to traditional methods of control such as shooting or trapping is a moot point. However, complete abolition of experiments on animals appears to be extremely unlikely, despite what this might achieve in the search for alternatives. This leads many groups to stress the need for the achievable rather than the impossible, without giving up the objective of total abolition. Better control now, it is argued by groups such as the RSPCA, helps alleviate present suffering, rather than keeping the proponents of welfare change away from the negotiating table if their views are considered to be too radical to be acceptable.

There are two broad methods of regulation which appear to be possible in the absence of total abolition: the first is to put in place an extensive body of legislation at country-wide or State level which is monitored by external agencies of local or central government, supported by a system of licensing and/or fines. The second is a more localised use either of entirely voluntary regulation or of compelling institutions to use ethics committees. The sanctions available under these systems vary, from a withdrawal of funding to adverse publicity and professionally related disciplinary action. Australia employs a mixed system incorporating both types of regulation, with some States having specific legislation combined with the use of AEECs whilst others rely primarily on the use of AEECs alone. The UK uses a formal legislative system for the most part, and Canada uses a voluntary system incorporating the use of ethics committees.

One radical suggested complement to a formal system of regulation would be to allow proposed experiments to be challenged in the courts if groups felt they were not directly relevant to human or animal health. This was the subject of a referendum in Switzerland in 1992, where the pharmaceutical companies, universities and pro-experimentation groups had argued that the introduction of such a facility for antivivisectionist groups would cause the cessation of most Swiss animal research. The Swiss electorate voted 56% against the introduction of this initiative in a referendum on 16 February 1992.[107] Whether this is a suitable subject for traditional courts is a debatable point. One doubts whether judges lacking sufficient expertise would be happy to be thrust into the limelight as the final adjudicator in an area which arouses such extreme emotions. Reports also suggest quite strongly that the courts are already particularly overstretched, and the addition of this new cause to the arena would see further delays in all cases coming to court. There is the further possibility that research might be forced out of the country in question and set up in a country with less stringent regulation. A review body outside the mainstream courts process would appear to be more suitable, consisting of a wide cross-section of interested parties similar to the present tribunal systems for employment and other matters.

---

107 See *Nature*, vol 335, 13 February 1992, p 575; vol 355, 20 February 1992, p 664.

As seen earlier in the cases of Australia and Sweden, many countries have opted for the formation of 'ethics committees' in the institutions involved as a means of regulating experimentation, either as the main means of control or as a supplement to more centralised legislation. Loane Skene commented of Australian Animal Experimentation Ethics Committees that, in contrast to external licensing systems such as that in the UK:[108]

> [S]elf regulation through AEECs ensures that animal experimentation issues are an integral part of all research programmes, and a constant consideration for investigators. AEECs are on-site and generally meet monthly. Many AEEC members are associated with the institutions and investigators they oversee. They are therefore more aware of the research and the individuals involved. This should result in more sensitive monitoring and advising, and more responsiveness from the investigators.

> However, a central authority still has an important role to play in a localised monitoring system. AEECs should be answerable to someone who can ensure that they are functioning properly, can advise and help them, and can co-ordinate interaction with other AEECs. Central authorities can formulate policies, draft guidelines, and collect information regarding the functioning of AEECs. All of these assist in achieving a consistent approach and in ensuring that institutions, investigators and AEECs themselves are publicly accountable for their acts and decisions. In order to avoid unnecessary duplication with the extra costs and effort that involves, thought might be given to even more delegation of monitoring and inspection from licensing authorities to AEECs.

All systems in operation have their critics and supporters. There does, however, appear to be a consensus developing amongst some commentators that ethics committees provide the best single control available, although there seems to be room for improvement regarding, for example, the appointment, training, continuing support of, and scientist's attitudes to, welfare group representatives.[109] The committees are praised because they bring together diverse opinions, create a mechanism for the discussion of ethical and scientific considerations, provide more involvement of local communities, lead to effective accountability and contribute to public confidence.[110] The Swedish system, for example, seems to have a dynamism and level of support from all sides of the animal welfare debate which contrasts quite significantly to the UK system, which contributions to the 1996 review of ASPA suggest is viewed with some suspicion even by moderate groups such as the RSPCA.

---

108 Skene, L, 'Animal experimentation ethics committees – what are we trying to achieve?', in *Effective Animal Experimentation Ethics Committees*, 1994, p 1, Australia: Australian and New Zealand Council for the Care of Animals in Research and Teaching (ANZCCART).

109 See the responses of the RSPCA and BUAV to the 1996 APC review of ASPA, above p 139; compare these with concerns of Hampson, J, above n 81, in relation to Swedish experience of regional ethics committees with radical antivivisectionist membership.

110 Rose, M, 'Regulation of Animal Research – The Australian Experience', in Paterson, D and Palmer, M (eds), *The Status of Animals: Ethics, Education and Welfare*, 1991 edn, pp 123-35, Oxon: CAB International.

The critical factor for the success of the Swedish system, it is claimed, is the involvement and influence of animal welfare groups which are exercised in an atmosphere of cooperation and consensus, as opposed to the UK system which leaves such groups on the outside of the day-to-day operation of legislation and without direct influence. Birgitta Forsman suggests that the Swedish system has resulted in significant benefits:

> [T]here is by and large a consensus that the committees have served a purpose and have had mostly good consequences, both for science and for animals. The main consequences I have found are these: The discussion in the AECs has lead to a *rise in the perception* of animal experimentation as a moral problem. Within the laboratories, this has entailed *enforced self-policing* and an improvement of the experimental procedures and care of animals. Outside the laboratories it has *generated a discourse* regarding animal experimentation as a morally significant issue. At the same time, animal experimentation has been consolidated as an enterprise that is here to stay. The abolitionist protests have abated, and a *convergence* of opinions has come about. The discussion of animal experimentation has been depoliticised and turned into a more technical discussion concentrating on scientific and animal-welfare details. The AECs have led to *no pernicious consequences* for science and research.[111]

There is the problem that some of those in the radical wing of the animal rights movement refuse to have any involvement with ethics committees, because of the inherent acceptance of animal experimentation that this involves. Peter Singer, for example, noted that any decisions made by these committees would be bound to be speciesist by considering human interests above and beyond those of animals. Despite this reservation he suggested that in countries where regulation is weak or flawed 'a minimal first step' would be a requirement that no experiment be conducted without prior approval from an ethics committee that includes animal welfare representatives and which is authorised to refuse approval to experiments when it does not consider that the potential benefits outweigh the harm to the animals.[112] It has also been suggested that ethics committees would be a useful addition even where detailed legislation exists. This is supported by the findings of the Working Party of the Institute of Medical Ethics on the ethics of using animals in biomedical research:[113]

> In some countries, such as Canada, the Netherlands, Denmark and Sweden, local committees are responsible for deciding whether or not, on ethical grounds, particular proposals for scientific work using animals should be allowed to proceed. In other countries local ethics committees may not play such a decisive role, either because the law requires that such decisions are

---

111 Forsman, B, 'Research Ethics in Practice: The Animal Ethics Committees in Sweden 1979–89' *Studies in Research Ethics*, 1993, no 4, Göteborg, Sweden: Centre for Research Ethics.

112 Singer, above n 25, p 86.

113 Smith and Boyd, above n 17, pp 273–75. By permission of Oxford University Press.

made by the relevant government authority (for example, in the UK the Home Office inspectors make these decision, except in marginal cases) or because they are *ad hoc* committees in countries with no special legal or legalistic control of laboratory animal use. In both situations local committees would have no powers to impose their decisions on researchers, so that, whilst they may advise, they cannot formally decide whether or not particular pieces of work should take place. In these cases (and also in cases where the committees can take binding decisions) local review committees might play a number of other important roles.

1. Such committees could provide clearly identified forums for ethical discussion of proposed research (or research in progress), which might otherwise be lacking within an institution. The committees might also engage in post-study review and so build up valuable case history experience which would help in future discussions and decisions.

2. In the context of ethical discussion, the committees might also be seen as educative bodies: they might play a part in informing the consciences of researcher, by providing a variety of independent opinions on a particular protocol or aspect of animal use, and so helping investigators to develop a balanced and humane attitude towards their use of animals. Although it might be argued that scientists already have well-informed consciences, it should be noted that it has sometimes been found necessary for ethics committees to fill this role in the field of medical research involving humans. Care should be taken, however, to ensure that the committee does not have an opposite effect, providing a refuge from conscience for the researcher ('if the committee has said it's alright, then it must be alright!').

3. Lay representation on institutional committees could provide reassurance about what is going on in that institution within that community. One example of the way in which review committees might help to reassure the public concerns the vetting of all applications for project licences for cosmetic testing by the UK Animal Procedures Committee (a kind of national research review committee). All such applications are referred to the APC because the government has taken note of public anxiety about cosmetics testing. Lay representation can, however, be a difficult business – choosing the right person is not always easy. It is not possible to describe the ideal lay member or to give general criteria which would assist in a suitable choice: it is clear, however, that individual committees would need to think very carefully about any choice of lay representative. If, for instance, an ardent anti-vivisectionist was elected to the committee this could hold up research (a problem which has been encountered in Sweden, where there is a strong anti-vivisection movement.[114]

4. Research review committees could be concerned with all forms of animal use within an institution, not only those covered by local laws and codes of practice. In the UK, for instance, ethics committees could consider the use of invertebrates in scientific procedures, or the killing of animals (by

[114]Britt, D, 'Local committees for the review of experiments involving animals' (1985) 12 *Alternatives to Laboratory Animals* 171–74.

Schedule 1 methods) in order to obtain parts of their bodies for in vitro work, neither of which uses requires a licence under the Animals (Scientific Procedures) Act. The committees might also have the option of setting standards higher than those of the local laws or codes.

5. Such committees could also concern themselves with the wider aspects of animal use within the institution – making sure, for instance, that the animal care and breeding facilities are meeting the needs of both the researchers and animals; coordinating animal use between different research groups within an organisation (so that, for instance, organs and/or tissues for in vitro work can be taken from animals being used in terminal studies); providing a focal point for the exchange of information on local facilities and expertise, so helping to ensure that researchers are able to carry out procedures using the best available equipment and techniques; and acting as resource centre on animal welfare issues.

Some conclusions regarding research review committees

In countries where there is no legal control, local research review committees could be established as a way forward, providing an opportunity for discussion and review of research proposals, so as to help sort out a coherent ethical position, delineating what is and not thought to be acceptable practice in that country. Learned society and journal ethics committees could also play a valuable part in this process. As discussed above, in some countries research review, or ethics, committees are already apart of the system of statutory control, where they play a central role in deciding whether particular pieces of research should or should not be allowed. In countries such as the UK, where such decisions are taken by representatives of the government, local committees could have an important complementary role. They could, for instance, act as a preliminary screen, by reviewing research proposals before application to the Home Office, and could consider the uses of animals which are not covered by current legislation, as well as giving some local accountability and public relations coverage.

Problems are encountered by purely external systems, such as the monitoring of day-to-day enforcement with a small number of inspectors and the apparent reluctance of authorities to prosecute. In Australia, some critics want to encourage better practice by applying *more* external pressure on AEECs which is most likely to involve the creation of a new tier of publicly funded bodies.[115]

Much of the worldwide control of animal experimentation has now been in force for some time, and in light of the substantial body of material which has been written on the subject it is possible to identify those aspects of the various methods of control which are considered to be most effective. A consensus of opinion on this can only help in the continued goal of refinement, replacement and reduction of animal experimentation. In the

---

115 Oogjes, above n 85, p 67.

absence of a total ban, which appears to be an unrealistic expectation at present, these essential aspects might include:

- a legislative framework which outlines functions, procedures covered and the animals covered;
- an effective range of sanctions, including formal prosecution of offenders and the removal of licences and/or funding in appropriate circumstances;
- a national review and data-collection body which can oversee the 'wide-picture' and recommend or directly implement changes;
- ethics committees representing a wide range of interests and opinions at a local level and with power to stop an experiment from going ahead; and
- adequate representation and influence for different interest groups at all levels to ensure public confidence.

In the absence of comprehensive and effective legislation in countries such as the US, where constitutional issues may not allow for federal control similar in content to arrangements in the UK, there are a variety of other ways in which animal experimentation is actually controlled, or ways in which it could be improved. One interesting possibility which was considered by the Working Party of the Institute of Medical Ethics on the ethics of animal experimentation was the use of an ombudsman scheme such as is used in local government and banking cases in the UK.[116] There is evidence that effective accountability can be introduced when an ombudsman becomes involved. No formal sanctions are used, but the ombudsman does have at his disposal the important weapon of publication. The Institute of Medical Ethics report of the ethics of using animals in biomedical research considered the introduction of an ombudsman for laboratory animals to be deserving of further investigation, as it would enable concerned members of the public to air their complaints on behalf of animals and thereby strengthen public confidence in the legislation.[117]

In the UK, the Animal Procedures Committee has the power to initiate an investigation and to report to the Home Secretary on any matter which comes to their attention. Their findings in relation to cephalopods and their subsequent inclusion under the protection provided by the 1986 Act illustrate that the APC can be effective, but it does not have the resources to investigate individual alleged incidences of cruel or unnecessary procedures. It also lacks the more independent profile of an ombudsman with the focus of protecting the citizen (or in the proposed case, the animal) against abuses of authority, inaction, or unreasonable or oppressive behaviour.

The Institute's investigation also examined the possibility of tightening up control by encouraging non-legislative methods of regulation which are

---

116 Smith and Boyd, above n 17, p 282.
117 *Ibid*, p 283.

already employed in the control of animal experimentation worldwide, and which have influence throughout the scientific community of the world.[118] For example, there is a degree of peer review in the institutions involved themselves as part of the ongoing scientific process, and in many countries this is has been formalised by the use of review committees. Guidelines may also be produced by societies to their members giving specialist advice on particular areas of work.

Scientists who research like their findings to be published in journals, and the editorial boards of these journals can play a crucial part in ensuring that the methods used in obtaining the findings do not involve the use of illegal or immoral practices. Most of the reputable scientific journals use either a formal statement of moral principles to which contributors should adhere, or use peer review of findings to try and ensure that standards of welfare are maintained. Whether these editorial policies are completely effective in the absence of other forms of control is doubtful, but they do provide a useful supplement to other forms of regulation. One of the most reputable journals in the scientific community, *Nature*, admitted in response to criticism from Clive Hollands, the former head of the RSPCA, that the decision whether to publish findings or not would not always depend on whether the results had been obtained in a morally acceptable manner, but might depend on the nature of the findings themselves and other 'pragmatic' considerations.[119] In light of this it is doubtful whether editorial boards will ever perform more than a peripheral function.

Scientists are also dependent on money given by grant-awarding bodies and there is evidence from the US, Australia and Canada that these bodies can provide one of the best forms of control, particularly in those countries where specific legislation is a little thin. Bodies awarding research funding, such as the Medical Research Council in the UK and the National Institutes of Health (NIH) in the US, lay down criteria to be met in order to receive funding. Bernard Rollin, an advocate of incremental change in relation to the use of animals sees an opportunity here to involve the public at large more closely in the decision-making process which echoes one of the benefits claimed for ethics committees:[120]

> Currently ... competing claims for funding are adjudicated by panels of experts in the given field. It is well-known that such procedures tend towards conservatism, towards favouring the status quo, toward preserving established paradigms and approaches, and towards in-group domination of a field. Such an approach therefore is unlikely to implement the new sort of calculation we have argued for. I would therefore argue that funding decisions should be

---

118 *Ibid*, pp 284–89.

119 *Nature*, 1 June 1989, p 324.

120 Rollin, B, 'Some Ethical Concerns in Animal Research: Where Do We Go Next?', in Baird, R and Rosenbaum, S (eds), *Animal Experimentation: The Moral Issues*, 1991, pp 155–56, Buffalo: Prometheus Books.

made not by experts, but by the citizenry that pays for the research. I would defend the development of panels – grand juries as it were – of intelligent, interested citizens who would look at research proposals and decide if the benefits exceeded the costs, or if the question being asked was the sort that truly needed to be answered. Obviously, such panels would need expert advice to assure that the project was technically feasible, and to translate what was being proposed into non-technical notions. But, having gotten such information, they would be asked to judge the project in accordance with emerging concern for animals and the cost-benefit notions outlined above. Such a mechanism would do much to move science away from elitism and old boyism and closer to its democratic funding base. It would also assure the ingression of changing ethical ideas into the fabric of science and hasten the erosion of the idea that science was 'value-free'.

It might be too optimistic to expect peer review or any other of these less formal methods of supervision to provide a comprehensive and reliable system of regulation commanding public support and ensuring scientific accountability. A formal encasement of these control methods in law would require the passing of complex and practically unenforceable legislation. The best that can be hoped is for the journals and bodies involved to continue to encourage scientists to adopt new techniques whilst retaining a structured system of legislative management.

FURTHER READING

Baird, R and Rosenbaum, S (eds), *Animal Experimentation: The Moral Issues*, 1991, Buffalo, New York: Prometheus Books. Some excellent contributions from a variety of standpoints bringing home some of the moral dilemmas involved in animal experimentation.

Effective Animal Experimentation Ethics Committees, 1994, Australia: Australian and New Zealand Council for the Care of Animals in Research and Teaching.

French, R, *Antivivisection and Medical Science in Victorian Society*, 1975, London: Princeton University Press. Essential for anyone wishing to see the background to, and the problems encountered by, the introduction of the Cruelty to Animals Act 1876.

Ruesch, H, *Slaughter of the Innocent*, 1983, US: Civitas Publications. An unremitting attack on the vivisection lobby with plenty of historical and contemporary evidence against the claims of the pro-experimentation lobby.

Smith, J and Boyd, K, *Lives in the Balance: The Ethics of Using Animals in Biomedical Research*, 1991, Oxford: Oxford University Press. A superb book for anyone interested in the issues surrounding experimentation, covering all aspects of the Working Party of the Institute of Medical Ethics Report into the subject.

Sperlinger, D (ed), *Animals in Research: New Perspectives in Animal Experimentation*, 1981, Chichester: John Wiley and Sons. Although a little out of date in some sections, the coverage of the historical development of the law in relation to experimentation remains a valuable contribution.

CHAPTER FIVE

ANIMALS IN AGRICULTURE

INTRODUCTION

The place of agriculture in the development of humankind, including the organised farming of animals, cannot be doubted. Richard Leaky, the world-famous palaeoanthropologist, has noted that:[1]

> [B]etween 20,000 and 10,000 years ago, people began to organise their practical lives differently, sometimes exploiting plentiful food resources in a way that allowed less mobility, more stability, perhaps more possessions. Finally, from ten thousand years onward, food production – as against food gathering – became more common, villages sprang up, small towns, cities, city-States, and eventually nation States.

Although animals have been closely associated with human development for thousands of years, the causes of modern welfare problems for farm animals are the result of much more recent events in human history. With the end of the Second World War in 1945 came the beginning of a new era of increased demand for the production of meat and other animal products.[2] This demand led the farming community to search for methods to produce that food at the cheapest possible price for the consumer:[3]

> In the post-war period the overwhelming priorities were for yields in agriculture to be increased and prices to be brought down. These factors encouraged the development of a particular kind of agriculture so that in quite subtle ways the rules and resources of society militated against the organic option. Thus, although exercises of power have not been absent – for instance, advocates of organic methods have been denied the funds to pursue effective research – of far greater significance has been the overwhelming prominence of presuppositions which have, as it were, denied the organic option any space in which it could be articulated.

Farming techniques were introduced which were designed to maximise productivity and to drive down the chief production costs of manpower and land required for traditional expansive husbandry systems. Intensive

---

1 Leaky, R and Lewin, R, *Origins Reconsidered: In Search of What Makes Us Human*, 1992, pp 351–52, London: Abacus Books.

2 *Report of the Technical Committee to Enquire into the Welfare of Animals kept under Intensive Husbandry Systems, The 'Brambell Committee'*, December 1965, para 11, London: Ministry of Agriculture Fisheries and Food, Cmnd 2836.

3 Clunies-Ross, T and Cox, G, 'Challenging the Productivist Paradigm: Organic Farming and the Politics of Agricultural Change', in Lowe, P, Marsden, T and Whatmore, S (eds), *Regulating Agriculture*, 1994, p 55, London: David Fulton Publishers.

husbandry farming in the 20th century has caused a series of encounters between the animal welfare lobby, on the one hand, and most farmers and the government on the other. This has been based on concern that the technological and other scientific advances used in agriculture have been employed at the expense of the welfare of farm animals, as well as being damaging to the environment and human health. The number of practices which have been the focus of animal welfare concern include those in the following non-exhaustive list.

–   In the case of the production of eggs and broiler hens (for eating), the use of battery cages or group-housing of birds, debeaking and the mass-production of chicks.

–   In the production of pigs, the use of 'farrowing crates' (a tubular iron stall where the sows give birth), castration of piglets, close confinement of animals, and the psychological problems they sometimes exhibit.

–   In the production of milk and beef, the reduced lifespan due to use of hormones, close confinement of cattle (particularly in the US), the premature weaning of calves and the notorious use of veal-crates for those calves.

–   In relation to the transportation of animals, the use of overcrowded vehicles, over-long journey times and the husbandry of animals throughout the journey.

–   The slaughter techniques used for all animals have been examined in terms of whether the animals remain conscious through the experience, are affected by seeing other animals slaughtered and are handled in a humane way before slaughter.

–   The effects of emerging technological advances on breeding practices and the effect that this will have on the general welfare of animals.[4]

Many scientists and animal welfare observers claim that animals can suffer through the physical and psychological pressures placed upon them, as discussed below, although some intensive farmers, as well as philosophers and scientists, dispute this.[5] In many countries, agricultural practices in relation to animals have been affected by the introduction of domestic and international controls in the second half of the 20th century. The increased use of antibiotics and other health products has enabled farmers to place more animals into close confinement conditions which, as Bernard Rollin notes, might have been a recipe for disaster in preceding times:[6]

---

4   See Chapter 2 – A Case Study in Animal Law – biotechnology and genetic engineering.

5   See section below on issues of pain and suffering, for a further development of these arguments.

6   Rollin, B, *Farm Animal Welfare: Social, Bioethical, and Research Issues*, 1995, p 7, Iowa: Iowa State University Press.

If a 19th century agriculturalist, let alone an ancient one, had dreamed of keeping thousands of chickens in one building, such a scheme would have been corrected by nature, for it would be a rapid path to ruin, bringing quick spread of animal disease, death, and financial disaster. Producers did well if and only if animals did well, and – this is critical – 'did well' for the animal meant playing out its biological nature in an environment for which those powers had been selected by both natural and artificial selection.

Society, therefore, did not need laws mandating good husbandry for animals – that was dictated by self-interest and reinforced by the ancient ethic of care. If a person did not care about self-interest, he or she was unlikely to be persuaded by laws. Punishing bad husbandrymen was redundant, for they were effectively self-punishing. This, in turn, explains why the traditional social consensus ethic for the treatment of animals – the anticruelty ethic and, later, the laws expressing it – could be so minimal yet so socially adequate. Normal people cared for their animals: failure to care for animals; failure to provide food, water, and shelter; or eagerness to inflict pain and suffering bespoke sadism or pathology that was irrational, deviant, and needed to be socially punished. To this day, a powerful aversion to animal cruelty – that is, wilfully and uselessly harming an animal, or harming an animal for frivolous reasons – is ingrained in virtually all agriculturalists, especially those who come from an extensive background.

A major reason that animals are still reared in huge numbers in intensive farming systems is that consumer demand for meat and other animal products at the cheapest possible price remains strong. Many surveys have found that the public find factory farming practices abhorrent and would like to see them stopped. Yet, at the same time, evidence shows that roughly the same number would vote in favour of retaining an ability to buy inexpensive animal products.[7] Consumers, it seems, want to have the welfare benefits for animals advanced by the proponents of organic or more extensive farming without the use of chemical enhancers of production, as well as a cheap product.[8] Recent experience shows that organically produced meat is 15–20% more expensive than intensively farmed animal produce. This, despite the apparently good intentions of consumers, initially resulted in low demand for organically produced food. One leading British high street retailer, Marks and Spencers, abandoned its attempt to sell organic products in 1995, although they, along with other retailers, are supplying meat which is farmed extensively. Consumers, it seems, were reluctant to spend extra money on organic produce, despite what they felt about factory farming. However, the

7   See, for example, a telephone survey for *You Decide,* BBC Television, 19 September 1996 in which 90% were in favour of ending factory farming. After the programme, having heard the case *for* intensive farming, this dropped to 70% in favour of ending factory farming.

8   It should be noted that these terms, 'organic' and 'extensive', do not refer to the same kinds of farming. Organic farming embraces both extensive farming systems and the drastically reduced or complete absence of the use of drugs. An animal which is extensively farmed might not, therefore, necessarily be an organically farmed animal.

BSE[9] crisis of 1996 changed this situation beyond recognition: 'after BSE and other health scares, the organic market has become so bullish that one farm in five could profitably convert right now, even though government support is minimal.'[10] Figures reproduced in *The Guardian* in early 1997 suggested that demand for beef meat products had fallen by up to 37%, in the case of steak pies, as compared to the end of 1995, before the BSE crisis.[11]

DO ANIMALS SUFFER IN MODERN FARMING PRACTICES?

It is generally recognised and provided for by law that we should prevent animal 'pain and suffering' and provide for their 'welfare'. But what is meant by these terms, and can suffering in animals ever be identified or proved? To what extent should we legislate, and against which practices in particular?

Defining prohibited farming techniques, providing against 'pain and suffering' or providing for 'welfare' requires precise definitions of those words. The word 'welfare' is actually used to cover different types of treatment of animals – direct or indirect ill-treatment of farm animals involving *abuse* or *neglect* alongside the comparatively recently recognisable form of welfare concern, quality of life. As a basic illustrative guide to terms which are extremely difficult to pin down to specific practices, abuse might be said to involve direct and deliberate actions resulting in actual injury/pain, fear or distress in an animal, whereas neglect is an indirect form of welfare violation involving either overworking animals or simply being negligent in, for example, their dietary requirements. Alongside the forms of physical abuse which have been recognised in legislation since the Protection of Animals Act 1911, has come legislation aimed more at the quality of life given to farm animals to provide for their physiological and other needs, in the form of the Agriculture (Miscellaneous Provisions) Act 1968. Together, these pieces of legislation try to ensure that animals are subjected to as little pain and suffering as possible.

It should be noted that not everyone agrees that animals experience 'pain' or 'suffering' which can be equated with the pain and suffering of humans. Peter Carruthers, for example, distinguishes between 'conscious' and 'non-conscious' mental processes in relation to pain, as well as the levels of suffering endured by different species, claiming that the capacity for pain and suffering is much greater in humans because of their greater intelligence. Carruthers proposes that animals think in an 'non-conscious' way, somewhat akin to the way humans can perform a task, such as driving or washing-up,

---

9   Bovine spongyform encaphalopathy, or 'mad cow disease', which began to appear in humans in the shape of Creutzfeld Jacobs Disease (CJD) in 1995/96.

10   *The Guardian*, 'Society' supplement, 8 January 1997, pp 4–5.

11   *The Guardian*, 21 January 1997, p 9.

without really thinking about the specifics of the task in hand, and whilst *consciously* thinking about what they are going to do that evening. This leads him to conclude that, as there are no reasons to protect non-conscious thoughts, animals are not worthy of our moral concern. Applied to intensive farming, he regards the apparent suffering or pain of animals, evidenced by the observation of measurable physiological changes, as amounting to no more than non-conscious reactions which carry no moral weight.[12]

Peter Singer, however, is of the opposite view:[13]

Nearly all the external signs that lead us to infer pain in other humans can be seen in other species, especially the species most closely related to us – the species of mammals and birds. The behavioral signs include writhing, facial contortions, moaning, yelping or other forms of calling, attempts to avoid the source of pain, appearance of fear at the prospect of its repetition, and so on. In addition, we know that these animals have nervous systems very like ours, which respond physiologically as ours do when the animal is in circumstances in which we would feel pain: an initial rise in blood pressure, dilated pupils, perspiration, an increased pulse rate, and, if the stimulus continues, a fall in blood pressure. Although human beings have a more developed cerebral cortex than other animals, this part of the brain is concerned with thinking functions rather than with basic impulses, emotions, and feelings. These impulses, emotions, and feelings are located in the diencephalon, which is well developed in many other species of animals, especially mammals and birds.

Identifying whether an animal's welfare requirements are being fulfilled or whether it is 'suffering', 'under stress' or 'illustrating abnormal behaviour' is certainly not easy.[14] In its report of 1970, *The Welfare of Livestock*, the Farm Animal Welfare Advisory Committee[15] was so split as to the extent of animal suffering that the 'ethical' and 'scientific' members had to offer their findings in separate sections, as they were unable to reach agreement. The scientific group referred to the lack of substantial and verifiable evidence as to whether, for example, the inability to turn around in tethering stalls, actually causes distress in animals.

A chief indicator of a breach in the welfare requirements concerning an animal is the presence of 'stress'. Biologically, a mere increase in the activity of the adrenal cortex which is the main scientifically measurable indicator of stress is insufficient to prove stress and it must be accompanied by other factors such as increased heart-rate. It has been suggested by Roger Ewbank that the use of the term 'stress' is probably insufficient and we should be talking of 'overstress' to indicate medium-level responses which may be

12 Carruthers, P, *The Animals Issue*, 1992, Chapter 8, Cambridge: Cambridge University Press.

13 Singer, P, *Animal Liberation*, 1995, 3rd edn, p 11, London: Pimlico.

14 Carey, M and Fry, J, 'Evaluation of Animal Welfare by the Self-expression of an Anxiety State' (1995) 29 *Laboratory Animals* 370–79.

15 The then Secretary of State for Agriculture, Peter Walker, replaced the Farm Animal Welfare Advisory Committee with the Farm Animal Welfare Committee in 1980.

accompanied by biological damage to the animal, and 'distress' where there is a high response and a high biological cost to the animal. This helps to define more precisely what we are protecting against in legislation:[16]

> This use of the term *distress* fits in with the legal terminology of the Agriculture (Miscellaneous Provisions) Act 1968 where the main offence is to cause 'unnecessary pain or distress'. Pain (an internal physical/psychological process causing suffering) in animals is usually noticed by the human observer when the animals show outward signs of distress. It is possible also that animals suffer from emotional distress which is not associated with pain. Most stock keepers would probably agree that their charges feel and probably suffer from fear. If farm animals experience one emotion, could they not have others? The ewe separated from its lamb shows physiological and behavioral changes indicative of distress. How does the ewe's reaction compare with the response of a human mother forcibly separated from her child? There are no real answers to these questions but practical experience, common sense and humaneness suggest that, in the absence of positive proof to the contrary, animals must be given the benefit of the doubt. If an animal is in a situation that would induce unpleasant emotions in humans, and shows behavioral signs of distress, then it is probably undergoing an unpleasant emotion process – in other words it is probably suffering. It is interesting to note that emotional suffering in animals has been recognised for many years. The Protection of Animals Act 1911 stipulates that it is an offence to 'infuriate or terrify any animal'.

Since 1970, many scientists have provided a considerable weight of evidence that points towards the existence of animal suffering. Studies such as those carried out in 1980 by Marion Stamp-Dawkins of the Animal Behaviour Research Group at the Department of Zoology in Oxford, lend support to this hypothesis. Having conducted 'preference testing' with hens to establish which kind of environment they preferred, she found that, despite an initial reluctance to move away from the close confinement of the battery cages, the birds' curiosity eventually led them to investigate and then to move into a more free-range environment.[17] She believes that no single scientific test can be used to determine the subjective experiences of animals. She does, however, believe that it is possible to examine a variety of evidence such as physical health, productivity, comparing them to their wild counterparts where possible, examining behaviour or the animals' preferences as above, in order to determine whether the animals are 'suffering'.

Another example of suffering in modern farming practice is the use of growth enhancement techniques which aim to have chickens reach their slaughter weight within six weeks of hatching, twice as quickly as they did 25–30 years ago. One consequence of this is that the birds become too heavy

---

16 Ewbank R, 'Animal Welfare', in *Management and Welfare of Farm Animals*, 1994, p 3, Potters Bar, Hertfordshire: Universities Fund for Animal Welfare.

17 Stamp-Dawkins, M, *Animal Suffering*, 1980, London: Chapman & Hall.

too quickly, resulting in leg deformities and suffering. The mortality rates during this maturing period are also a cause for some concern, in that around 5% of the birds may die during this time, some 30 million birds each year.[18] In June 1994, Dr Mike Baxter of Brunel University concluded that there is decisive evidence that battery hens do suffer in a variety of different ways.[19]

There is also ample evidence regarding the stress suffered by animals in transit to, waiting for and during slaughter, which was recognised at Parliamentary level as long ago as 1904 by the *Report of the Committee on Humane Slaughtering of Animals*. In light of their findings regarding the potential suffering of animals, they recommended that animals should be stunned and rendered unconscious, and be spared the sight, sounds and smells of the slaughter as far as possible. No one would doubt that the situation regarding slaughter is far better in many respects than in 1904, but, over 90 years later, many problems are still said to exist. Not only does the transportation of animals to slaughter continue to occupy minds in the EU and the UK, but also methods of religious slaughter of animals without stunning and the general conditions of slaughter endured by many animals.[20]

An ever-increasing number of studies of animal suffering suggest that the law as it is presently framed merely gives the green light to practices which are inhumane, and that it fails to protect farm animals. Regulations in relation to intensive farming, it is argued by some, are not only inadequate but should not exist because the practices they 'protect' should themselves not exist.

Some farmers and scientists argue that the use of intensive farm systems is actually to the welfare benefit of the animals in that, for example, aggressive behaviour and diseases are much easier to control in confined conditions. Wild animals have also been known to pass on diseases to farm animals, which all leads to concerns about a shift to free-range methods of rearing animals, as mortality rates for animals raised in extensive systems have been reported to be twice that of animals raised in intensive systems.[21] The argument then centres on whether the increased risks to extensively farmed animals are significant enough, as opposed to their possible 'suffering', to outweigh the deprivation alleged in intensive systems. Certainly many farmers now see the use of intensive rearing techniques as the 'natural' way to farm, in the light of consumer demand and tight profit margins, and they use mortality rates as evidence of better welfare for intensively farmed animals.

---

18   Moore, P, 'Farming: meat 'n' veg: at what price?', *The Guardian*, 30 May 1996, p 12.

19   *The Observer*, 12 June 1994, p 2.

20   Garner, R, *Animals, Politics and Morality*, 1993, p 103, Manchester: Manchester University Press.

21   Hignett, A, 'Free Range egg production – A producer's View' in, Universities Federation for Animal Welfare, *Extensive and Organic Livestock Systems*, 1993, p 21, Potters Bar, Hertfordshire: UFAW.

Farmers also point out that unhappy animals would not produce as well as they do, indicating that the animals are 'lean and healthy'.[22]

In recent times, new evidence has suggested another form of ill-treatment which animals are said to suffer, namely deprivation, which involves the denial of physiological or behavioural needs and thus affects their quality of life. The most contentious practices alleged to cause suffering through deprivation in intensive factory-farming systems are those involving veal-crates, pig confinement in stalls and close confinement of egg-laying hens. Many studies, particularly in the past 20 years, have suggested that this form of deprivation may cause suffering which is comparable to the more recognisable forms of animal suffering – abuse and neglect. A study in 1981 by Wood-Gush and Stolba, for example, found evidence of highly complex behaviour in sows, such as forming social groups, building communal nests in a cooperative way far away from feeding sites, and walking at least seven metres away from those nests before urinating and defecating.[23] It is suggested by groups such as Compassion in World Farming that restrictive crates frustrate this behaviour.[24]

Legislation in many countries or from extranational bodies such as the EU (see below) now recognises the welfare concerns arising from deprivation, as well as the more scientifically verifiable forms of ill-treatment. Whatever the problems with terminology, regulations and codes of practice now protect against these extended forms of welfare concern: 'The basic requirements for the welfare of livestock are a husbandry system appropriate to the health and, so far as practicable, the behavioural needs of the animals and a high standard of stockmanship.'[25]

Recent scientific developments regarding new technologies employed in the breeding of farm animals have resulted in concern over the welfare implications. In 1995 the Ministry of Agriculture, Fisheries and Food produced its *Report of the Committee to Consider the Ethical Implications of Emerging Technologies in the Breeding of Farm Animals*. This Committee used a wide definition of 'harm' which would need to be taken into account in the definition of acceptable practice, which illustrates the modern extension of the term 'suffering': 'We would contend that animals can be harmed or wronged in other ways than simply by physical mistreatment. An animal can be harmed, for example, by treatment which is degrading.'[26] The Committee

---

22 For details of the defence of intensive farming techniques put forward by the farming lobby, see the extract from the National Farmers' Union below, p 182.

23 Wood-Gush, DGM and Stolba, A, 'The Behaviour of Pigs and the Design of New Housing System', 1981, 80 *Applied Animal Ethology* 583–85.

24 See excerpt from Compassion in World Farming literature in relation to pigs below, p 181.

25 *Code of Recommendation for the Welfare of Domestic Fowls*, 1987, p 1, London: Ministry of Agriculture, Fisheries and Food.

26 *Report of the Committee to Consider the Ethical Implications of Emerging Technologies in the Breeding of Farm Animals*, 1995, para 2.9, London: HMSO.

examined the range of total-abolitionist and total-deregulation arguments and the majority concluded that the use of animals is acceptable provided that the use is humane. It was upon this basis of acceptance in principle that the Committee analysed specific concerns of the animal welfare lobby.[27]

Of particular concern to the Committee was the whole range of new technologies and techniques being used in the UK in relation to breeding. They examined the welfare concerns and existing welfare controls of selective breeding, artificial insemination, superovulation (increasing the number of eggs available for fertilisation, and hence offspring), embryo transfer, *in vitro* fertilisation, cloning and genetic modification. The Committee's specific findings on the morality of using the new biotechnological techniques can be found in Chapter 2, and their findings regarding experimentation in Chapter 4. Several other points were made specifically in relation to agricultural breeding techniques which are relevant to any country using new breeding technologies: the Committee objected in principle to the use of genetic modification which results in an attack on the animal's essential nature; they disapproved of the use of non-therapeutic surgery in routine breeding programmes of sheep, goats and deer, but were happy with it continuing in relation to cattle; and the Committee considered certain uses of new technologies such as artificial insemination, embryo transfer, cloning and superovulation to be generally acceptable.

The Committee's concerns regarding the protection of the 'essential nature' of animals illustrate gradual changes to the demarcation of what society should legislate for far beyond traditional notions of pain, suffering and welfare and into new areas encompassing lifestyle and 'natural existence'. A wider definition of 'welfare' than recognised in early attempts to prevent more obvious forms of abuse such as beating and neglect of an animal has led some groups to note that studies of what it is like to *be* an animal will be an ever more important influence on legislation.[28]

One of the biggest international groups leading the campaign for improved conditions for farm animals is Compassion in World Farming (CIWF) which is in no doubt that intensive factory farming techniques cause health problems in animals and stop them from exercising their normal behaviour, thereby breaching the animals' welfare requirements. The following extracts illustrate areas of welfare concern for three types of farm animal and are followed by the approach taken by a defender of modern farming practices, the National Farmers' Union:

---

27   For extracts from the committee's findings, see Chapter 2.
28   Farm Animal Welfare Council, *Report on Priorities for Animal Welfare Research and Development,* May 1993, Tolworth, Surrey: Farm Animal Welfare Council.

The welfare of laying hens in battery cages[29]

Hens need to have sufficient exercise.[30] In natural conditions hens stretch their wings and flap them. They walk, run when required and fly up to and off their perching places. In the cage all these behaviours are made impossible by lack of space.[31] Wing flapping is necessary for good hen welfare.[32] Much of what we know comes from preference studies. In one such study, hens in percheries flapped 1.9 times per hour and flew twice in every five hours.[33] In the cage, hens can neither flap nor fly.

Inability to perform normal pre-laying behaviour is generally regarded as one of the most important problems for the welfare of battery hens.[34] In natural conditions hens will build a nest in which to lay their eggs in privacy and comfort. Nest building is a fairly complex activity. It involves gathering material, transporting it and then constructing the nest. In the cage, nest building is impossible. Hens have neither sufficient space to perform pre-laying movements nor any nesting materials. As a result, caged hens will show high levels of abnormal behaviour. Some will perform vacuum nest building, others will engage in stereotyped behaviour or pecking.[35]

The welfare of dairy cows[36]

With over one-third of the UK (and EC) dairy herd contracting mastitis every year, it would be reasonable to ask – how many cows actually make it through three lactations *without* getting mastitis? Mastitis may be an obvious health problem for the cow and an economic problem for the farmer, but it is also a welfare problem. Cows with mastitis *suffer*. Should the infection remain untreated for any length of time it is likely that subjecting an infected quarter to the relentless pulsating of the milking machine can be little less than agony. Although careful observation of symptoms, prophylactic medication in dry cows and prompt treatment are obviously essential to prevent or minimise suffering, it is vital that good preventive measures are practised. Cubicles which are too short make teat injuries and mastitis more likely.[37] Clean bedding in cow cubicles, regular cleaning of cubicle passages and good teat

29 Compassion in World Farming, *The Welfare of Laying Hens in Battery Cages*, 1996, Petersfield: CIWF.

[30] Broom, D, 'The needs of laying hens and Some Indicators of poor Welfare', *The Laying Hen*, 1992. Proceedings of a seminar held in Brussels 24–25 March 1992, organised by the Eurogroup on the Protection of Farm Animals.

[31] *Report of the European Commission's Scientific Veterinary Committee* (Animal Welfare Section), 1992.

[32] Broom, above n 30.

[33] Knowle, T and Broom, D, 'Limb bone strength and movement in laying hens from different housing systems' (1990) 126 *Veterinary Record* 354–56.

[34] Farm Animal Welfare Council, *An Assessment of Egg Production Systems*, 1986, Tolworth: FAWC.

[35] Wood-Gush, DGM and Gilbert, AB, 'Observations on the laying behaviour of hens in battery cages' (1969) 10 *British Poultry Science* 29–36.

36 Compassion in World Farming, *The Welfare of Dairy Cows*, 1996, Petersfield: CIWF.

[37] Jones, TO, 'A review of teat factors in bovine E coli mastitis' (1986) 118 *Veterinary Record* 507–09.

hygiene both pre and post-milking are vital. Perhaps it is also time that genetic selection for high yields/large udders was reversed.

As Webster has pointed out, the modern dairy cow is 'an exploited mother',[38] but he might equally have said she is a 'frustrated mother' as she has her mothering instincts totally frustrated every year when her day-old calf is taken from her. Behaviourists point out that leaving cow and calf together for longer only makes the separation more painful for both. That may be so, but again begs the whole question of whether modern dairy practice is sustainable on welfare grounds.

The welfare of pigs[39]

With the legislative phase-out of dry sow stalls and tether systems in the UK, pregnant pigs will endure close confinement for the first time when moved into the farrowing crate. This narrow, metal crate confines the sow, usually from up to a week before birth (farrowing) until the piglets are weaned. Most piglets are currently weaned at 3–4 weeks old. Farrowing crates are widely used throughout the industry. About four-fifths of the British breeding herd of about 800,000 sows are housed indoors. Of these, about 95% give birth in farrowing crates.

Under normal, unrestrained conditions, sows show a general increase in activity and a strong pre-natal instinct to nest build. Between 24–36 hours before giving birth a marked increase in activity takes place and sows spend much time showing nesting behaviour such as gathering, rooting and pawing straw or other bedding material. Researchers have found that within a period of about 20 hours of pre-natal activity, the sow can travel a distance of up to 30 km.[40] In the farrowing crate, sows' movements are restricted so much that only standing, sitting or lying are possible. Often litter or straw is not provided, completely denying any fulfilment of nesting behaviour. Researchers described the behaviour of restrained sows during the 36 hours prior to parturition as follows:

> '... when the unrestrained sows exhibited nesting behaviour, the behaviour of the restrained sows changed considerably. Intense stereotyped bar gnawing and pawing behaviours were accompanied by strenuous attempts to escape from the crate, copious frothing at the mouth and pupillary dilation'.[41]

The researchers concluded that the stereotyped behaviour was frustrated and displaced nesting behaviour, and was 'accompanied by clear signs of stress'. From these behavioural observations it seems reasonable to suggest that close confinement at farrowing is aversive to sows.

[38] Webster, J, *Understanding the Dairy Cow*, 1987, Oxford: BSP Professional Books.

39 Compassion in World Farming, *The Welfare of Pigs*, 1996, Petersfield: CIWF.

[40] Baxter, M, 'The "Freedom" Farrowing System' (1991) 107 *Farm Building Progress* 5–7.

[41] Baxter, MR and Petherwick, JC, 'The effect of restraint on parturition of the sow' in, Nielson, N, Hogh, P and Billie, N (eds), 1980, *Proceedings of the International Pig Veterinary Society Congress*, June–July 1980, p 84.

Some of CIWF's other concerns include: suffering endured during transportation of animals;[42] restrictive conditions of veal crates and the calves' poor diets; and the effects of genetic engineering on the natural characteristics and physical well-being of animals.

The following extracts are taken from a report presented to the National Farmers' Union Council in June 1995 by the Animal Welfare Working Group:[43]

Transport of live animals

22. All journeys entail some stress for animals, notably during loading and unloading, and therefore we must ensure that transport of animals is conducted according to the highest standards.

23. The Group firmly believes that transport rules must be based on the best scientific findings available. In our view, scientific evidence clearly shows that transport rules must clearly differentiate between species of animals.

Travel times and feeding, watering and rest periods

24. There continues to be a good deal of confusion over definitions. There are two basic concepts in the transport of live animals. These are:

   – the maximum journey limit beyond which further travel does not take place;

   – journeys which include prescribed feeding/watering/rest intervals after which the journey may resume.

We reject the concept of maximum journey limit and recommend that the NFU maintains its support for the feeding/watering/resting approach. ...

Cattle

28. There are indications that calves may be able to travel satisfactorily for up to 24 hours without water or food provided they are rested and well-fed prior to the start of the journey. The minimum rest period between 24-hour travel periods should be 24 hours in order to allow recovery. While calves normally feed fairly frequently, there is some evidence to suggest that it is better to continue the journey for up to 24 hours, though interrupting the animal's normal feeding pattern, than to cause the stress of unloading (and subsequent reloading) in order to allow for feeding. Calves should be transported with adequate straw and bedding and at a stocking density which allows all calves to lie down at the same time. ...

Pigs

31. For pigs, the length of journey and rest periods are less critical than the quality of the environment within the vehicle, heat and cold stress being

---

42 See, for example, The Proceedings of the Animal Welfare Foundation's Third Symposium, *The Welfare of Animals in Transit*, 1986, London: British Veterinary Association. This set of papers details many concerns over animal suffering which have been repeated many times: from injury through loading and unloading, overheating, distress caused by being moved from familiar surroundings, injuries caused during transit, overlong journey times to a lack of adequate feeding and watering during transit.

43 *Caring for Livestock: Report of the Animal Welfare Working Group*, presented to the NFU Council, June 1995. By permission of the National Farmers' Union.

key factors. Our investigations point to the need for more research on transport arrangements for pigs but suggest that travel periods should be no longer than eight hours in temperate climatic conditions and possibly somewhat less in hotter climates. Further investigations are required into the desirable length of rest periods for pigs.

32. Where pigs are transported in very high quality, specially designed vehicles, journey times can be significantly extended.

Poultry

33. As poultry are also particularly susceptible to heat and cold, environmental conditions rather than the length of the journey are the most important factors.

34. Because of the limited number of facilities which are able to handle end-of-lay hens, it is important that they are transported in suitable conditions and are processed promptly at the end of their journeys. ...

Welfare of animals at slaughter

44. It is paramount that the slaughter of animals is carried out humanely and efficiently by properly trained and licensed slaughtermen in order to minimise pain and fear. We are satisfied that the general standard of slaughter methodologies in this country is satisfactory. We are also confident that abattoir operators recognise their role in maintaining high welfare standards beyond the farm gate. It is essential that abattoir operators strive to achieve the highest possible standards amongst their workforce.

Stunning techniques

45. Electrical stunning is largely carried out on poultry and 75% of pigs. We welcome continuing research on improved methods of electrical stunning which is being carried out. Research on electrical stunning of pigs has resulted in the commercial application of fail-safe stunning systems and improved positioning of electrodes.

46. In the UK, most cattle, up to 35% of sheep and goats and a small percentage of pigs are stunned by captive-bolt pistol. Properly carried out, captive-bolt stunning is humane and effective. But the well-respected Humane Slaughter Association has expressed concern over what it considers to be the high incidence of the misuse of equipment (eg incorrect bolts and cartridges) and poorly-maintained guns. We support the HSA in seeking to monitor regularly the accuracy of bolt stunning in order to identify and rectify any deficiencies in operating procedures.

47. Around 25% of pigs are stunned prior to slaughter using CO_2 gas. However, there are some indications that for a brief period before loss of consciousness CO_2-stunned animals may experience distress caused by choking. This is a serious welfare concern. Researchers are investigating alternative gas stunning methods for both pigs and poultry (which for poultry, would also remove the need to shackle birds prior to slaughter) with particular interest being paid to a mix of argon and CO_2 in order to induce anoxia. We welcome research into new gas stunning techniques

and call for the necessary changes in legislation to be made to allow their application in commercial practice. ...

Religious slaughter

50. The legal requirement for stunning does not apply to the slaughter of animals under Halal (Muslim) or Shechita (Jewish) procedures. The failure to stun animals before slaughter constitutes a major welfare problem. Many Moslems now accept that pre-slaughter does not compromise their religious beliefs. We greatly welcome this attitude and strongly urge Jewish and other Muslim authorities to reconsider their positions on pre-slaughter stunning. ...

Pigs

Farrowing cradles

67. It is essential that there is a balanced debate about the role of farrowing cradles in pig rearing since the welfare of both the sow and her new-born piglet is at stake.

68. While the use of close confinement systems for gestating dry sows is to be banned in this country, in order to safeguard the piglets while they are most vulnerable it is still legal to confine the sow for a limited period of farrowing. Research is being carried out into alternative farrowing systems, notably the Freedom Farrowing System, but the results have been disappointing in terms of pre-weaning mortality in piglets born alive and other problems. To date no better alternative to the modern farrowing crate has been developed.

Slats verses straw

69. The popular conception is that pigs kept on solid manure/straw based systems enjoy a higher standard of welfare than those on slats. In practice there are pros and cons to both systems. Straw-based systems may provide more comfortable lying conditions as well as providing a medium with which pigs may display certain behavioural traits such as nesting or playing. However, slat systems separate pigs from their manure and confer health benefits which are of particular importance for young pigs. The use of straw can require more management and labour and give rise to greater disease risks. We see no clear net welfare benefits of one or the other system. ...

Outdoor systems

72. Keeping pigs outdoors enjoys a positive image amongst some of the public. The reality does not, however, always match up to this image and the simple assumption that outdoor is *de facto* better is not a valid one. At times, inevitable adverse weather conditions lead to serious welfare problems, eg health problems or even drowning in wet conditions, sunburn in hot conditions. It should also be borne in mind that outdoor pigs are vulnerable to the same welfare hazards of those kept indoors (aggression and bullying) and additional ones (young piglets from outdoor farrowing sows are vulnerable to predation by foxes and sows may ingest stones which can cause ulcers).

73. Good stockmanship, vital with all production systems, is critical with outdoor pig units. Very high levels of stockmanship are required to ameliorate the impact of external conditions in order to maintain welfare standards and commercial performance. ...

Poultry – laying hens

75. In welfare terms, there is currently no ideal commercial egg production system; all have their pros and cons. Cages provide the best conditions for maintaining bird health by protecting against the introduction of disease and controlling its spread, for providing shelter and security against predators and for minimising aggressive behaviour and cannibalism. Premature mortality – the ultimate welfare threat – is higher in alternative systems. But cages do restrict the ability of birds to display natural behaviour; in this regard, alternative systems overcome some of the disadvantages of cages. However, as leading poultry vet Howard Hellig has noted, the extent to which the restriction of the natural behaviour of laying hens compromises their welfare has yet to be quantified and it will be extremely difficult to do so. To achieve an acceptable level of welfare, alternative systems undoubtedly require extremely high management standards and inadequate management can have disastrous results. Overall, no one egg production system has clear net welfare advantages over the others. ...

77. The relatively confined space of laying cages inhibits exercise leading to weaker bones and, in turn, to breakages, notably at depopulation. Recognising this problem, the NFU and the British Poultry federation have issued a guide to the handling of end-of-lay hens. However, research shows that hens in alternative systems, such as perchery or free range, suffer more breakages as a result of collisions during everyday activity. Measured in 'fracture days' (the number of days a bird is alive with an unhealed fracture) hens in alternative systems suffer more than do hens in cages; figures from Gregory and others show that the total fracture days per 100 birds are 63 in cage systems, 146 in perchery systems and 121 in free range systems. ...

Beak-trimming

79. The optimum cage population is 4–5. In such numbers a stable social order is achieved which reduces aggressive behaviour and so eliminates the need to beak-trim. Alternative systems give rise to feather pecking and cannibalism and, therefore, the need to beak-trim.

Prelaying, nesting and dust bathing behaviour

80. There is considerable debate and disagreement amongst researchers and welfare groups about the behaviour of modern hens kept under commercial conditions. Opinions vary as to the extent to which conditions in a commercial caged situation (eg the absence of a nest, dust or perch) prevent 'natural' behaviour (eg prelaying and nesting behaviour, dust-bathing or perching) and thereby may lead to frustration at a level which constitutes a welfare problem. There are considerable hazards in extrapolating the behaviour of non-commercial birds or birds under

experimental observation to commercial conditions. But, as Howard Hellig has emphasised, unless and until welfare researchers agree on the weighting to be given to the various health and behavioral factors, unproductive acrimony will not serve to advance the welfare interests of the birds themselves.

Disease

81. Disease is a major welfare problem. since the overwhelming evidence is that levels of disease are higher in alternative systems than in cages, we are in no doubt that cages are a better system for maintaining the health of laying hens. ...

Dairy cows

87. Lameness remains a major welfare concern in the dairy sector and has many causes. Around 80% of cases are connected to problems with feet, particularly hind feet, rather than the hind leg. It is vital that farmers take the necessary steps to prevent lameness. These include:
   – increased cow lying time, ensuring sufficient space and the availability of suitable bedding;
   – suitable housing;
   – improved hygiene, in particular suitable cleaning systems;
   – suitable floor surfaces and passageways;
   – proper nutrition;
   – regularly trimmed feet by properly trained staff;
   – use of foot baths. ...

Housing

89. Badly designed or inappropriate housing can lead to serious welfare problems, including lameness and teat or other injuries. Farmers must ensure a sufficient number of cubicles are available (indeed, more cubicles than cows), that plenty of suitable bedding is available and that concrete areas are cleaned regularly.

90. The increasing size and weight of modern cows sometimes means that existing cubicles are too short and/or too narrow to house comfortably. Farmers must be aware of this issue and investigate carefully the best options when planning new housing or making appropriate improvements to existing housing.

Mastitis

Mastitis is a widespread condition in dairy cows and a serious welfare problem. Farmers must take the clear recommended steps in order to identify and treat mastitis.

The Farm Animal Welfare Council has a great deal of influence in the UK regarding any welfare improvements to be made in the keeping of farm animals.[44] At the time of writing (late 1996) they had produced seven reports

---

44   For more detailed information on the FAWC, see later in the chapter, p 199.

covering topics such as transportation of animals (1991), the welfare of broiler chickens (1992), the welfare of sheep (1994) and the welfare of pigs kept outdoors (1996). In making recommendations for action they are mindful of weighing the competing interests involved: 'Interpretation of animal welfare is not so simple. "Animal welfare" means many things to many people ... In reaching decisions we endeavour to take a balanced view which draws not only on the considerable range of experience of all members but also on the evidence submitted by outside organisations and individuals ...'.[45] Some of their findings regarding animal welfare are given below, extracts which also include general observations on the reintroduction of extensive pig-farming techniques. Their recognition of potential pain, suffering and distress in farm animals is apparent throughout the report. Perhaps the most interesting aspect of the report is the light it sheds on the possibilities for more extensive methods of farm animal production and the effect this might have on the 'life experience' of those animals:

Report on the welfare of pigs kept outdoors[46]

6. The welfare of an animal includes its physical and mental state and we believe that good animal welfare implies both fitness and a sense of well-being. Any animal kept by man must, at least, be protected from unnecessary suffering. ...

12. ... At the present time it is estimated that between 18 and 20% of the UK breeding herd is kept outdoors and in some areas of the country this is increasing.

13. The major reason for the recent increase in outdoor production have been commercial. Indoor production has been under severe pressure. Continual low margins have resulted in a lack of investment, which has made many units uncompetitive. The capital that has been invested has often been directed at the need to comply with legislation. This includes welfare legislation, such as the impending ban on stalls and tethers, and also pollution control. These factors have combined to provide circumstances in which many farmers have opted to cease pig production.

14. Businesses wishing to expand and fill the gap left by those indoor producers who have left the industry, have found that outdoor systems offer many opportunities.

    (a) Capital cost is significantly lower. For example, equipment costs for outdoor production are in the order of £250 to £350 per sow. In comparison, an equivalent indoor unit could cost up to £1,500 per sow ...

    (b) Using improved breeds and management techniques, performance and production can be comparable to indoor systems. The results of

---

45 Farm Animal Welfare Council, *Welfare and Some of the Issues Involved* (information leaflet), 1996.

46 Farm Animal Welfare Council, *Report on the Welfare of Pigs Kept Outdoors,* May 1996, London: Ministry of Agriculture, Fisheries and Food.

national recording systems show that indoor herds only average about one pig reared per sow more than outdoor herds. ...

17. (c) Generally, outdoor pigs suffer the same diseases as those kept indoors. However, because of much lower stocking densities, enteric and respiratory diseases tend to be less of a problem. Potentially, parasites can be a problem but these can be adequately controlled by a good preventive programme. ...

22. The outdoor farming of pigs is a method that is close to the ideals of organic farming. Recognised organic standards (eg UKROFS and the Soil Association) require high levels of stockmanship and exacting attention to animal welfare to ensure healthy stock while avoiding routine drug use ...

25. We have considered the welfare of pigs kept in outdoor units against the ideals listed in the five freedoms.[47] We conclude that outdoor pig keeping can achieve the objectives of the five freedoms but it is particularly susceptible to variations in management, stockmanship, climate and site suitability.

26. Pigs can be provided with freedom from hunger and thirst through proper management and stockmanship which ensure that adequate food and water are available daily and are distributed in a manner which minimises competition. Account should be taken of the climatic conditions, for example, the possibility of cold winter weather which could cause water to freeze.

27. Freedom from discomfort can be achieved through the provision of appropriate shelter (eg huts) which should keep the pigs comfortable in all weather conditions. This shelter should include a comfortable, dry resting area, be free from draughts and should be properly maintained.

28. If the pigs are to kept free from pain, injury and disease it is essential that the herd is adequately managed, inspected at least daily and equipment is properly maintained. Action must be taken promptly to respond to any problems discovered. There may be short-term pain caused by management procedures such as tagging but long-term pain should be avoidable.

29. Pigs kept outdoors have a great deal of freedom to express normal behaviour, although those which are nose-ringed are denied the freedom to root. Provision of straw or other suitable bedding material will encourage nesting.

30. Freedom from fear and distress is seldom completely achieved in any farming system and there are times when fear stimulates avoidance action by animals. Stockmen can minimise fear and distress by careful supervision and responding to problems during, for example, feeding, mixing and handling. ...

130. Mutilations can cause considerable pain and therefore constitute a major welfare insult to farm animals. FAWC considers that, on ethical grounds,

---

47   The 'five freedoms' proposed by the Farm Animal Welfare Council are detailed later in the chapter in the section on the UK control of agriculture.

the mutilation of livestock is undesirable in principle. However, there are systems throughout farming where such procedures may be necessary to avoid worse problems, largely due to aggression, as the animals grow. In this study we have considered nose ringing, tooth-clipping, tail-docking, castration and individual identification by ear notching or tagging. We are concerned about the present position regarding nose-ringing, tooth-clipping and tail-docking. We believe that without effective analgesia these will inflict pain on the pig.

The issues of pain, suffering and the expressions of natural behaviour which have been illustrated here together form the focal point of the development of the law in relation to farm animals. Regulation which recognises these concerns is already apparent and may be expanded. The introduction of more organic or extensive systems by encouragement or coercion seems likely but will not end expressions of welfare concern. It is clear from the evidence of those involved in such farming systems that their introduction does not mean an end to welfare problems. Extreme cold, extreme heat, exposure, extreme wet, predation, cannibalism and inadequate stockperson training would remain as inherent problems arising from the use of animals in agriculture.[48]

EUROPEAN CONTROL OF ANIMALS IN AGRICULTURE

In the 1980s the EU became a major source of suggestions and action on the protection of farm animals. Indeed, Richard Ryder noted that:[49]

> [P]rogress often seemed faster than in the UK, although, ironically, the main movers were often British MEPs and the British-sponsored Eurogroup. The attitude of European officials and parliamentarians to the animal protection lobby was certainly more positive and helpful than the dead hand of Whitehall. Belgian and French MEPs sometimes showed a confidence that they could get things done which contrasted with the resigned air of impotence too often encountered in Westminster.

The Treaty of Rome 1957 sets out as one of its basic objectives a common commercial policy to progressively abolish restrictions on international trade. Article 38.1 extends this objective to agriculture and trade in agricultural products. But it is in Article 39 that we find the two objectives which have had the greatest impact on the development of EC law regarding the welfare of animals:

> to increase agricultural productivity by promoting technical progress and by ensuring the rational development of agricultural production and the optimum utilisation of all factors of production, in particular labour;
>
> to ensure supplies to consumers at reasonable prices.

---

48 Parry, M, 'The Animal Welfare Implications of Outdoor Pig Breeding' in UFAW, *Extensive and Organic Livestock Systems*, above n 21, p 63.

49 Ryder, R, *Animal Revolution*, 1989, p 268, Oxford: Blackwell.

Article 36 also has an effect on the moral issues which surround issues of animal welfare:

> The provisions of Articles 30–34 shall not preclude prohibitions or restrictions on imports, exports or goods in transit justified on grounds of public morality, public policy or public security; the protection of health and life of humans, animals or plants; the protection of national treasures possessing artistic, historic or archaeological value; or the protection of industrial and commercial property. Such prohibitions or restrictions shall not, however, constitute a means of arbitrary discrimination or a disguised restriction on trade between Member States.[50]

In light of the objectives of Article 39(1) it is not surprising that farmers in Europe received a very clear message from the EC to farm as intensively as possible which, in turn, led to increasing welfare concerns. Conversely, the EC became a leading player in the creation of specific animal welfare legislation after concerns began to surface in the 1960s and 1970s.

As its original name, the 'European *Economic* Community', suggests, the EC was formed primarily to engender peace in Europe by tying the Member States together through economic means. The principles of animal welfare were included much later as a response to concerns over animal welfare and were not originally included in the Treaty of Rome. As economics, not morality, is the cornerstone of the EU, the issue of animal welfare has always settled a little uncomfortably within the original economic objectives of the Treaty. Richard Bennett has summarised the difficulties created by the relationship between economics and concerns for animal welfare: 'Economics (as a discipline) is human centred and does not take account of the needs and "wants" of other species, except in relation to the welfare of the human population. Thus, if man did not exist as a species, animal welfare would be of no concern.'[51]

Many decisions, directives and regulations have been introduced by the EU regarding farm animals. An up-to-date comprehensive summary is published by the Eurogroup for Animal Welfare.[52] As a general guide, legislation from the EC concerning farm animals has included the following which were still in force at the end of 1996:

- Council Directive (74/577/EEC) of 18 November 1974 on the stunning of animals before slaughter;
- Council Decision (78/923/EEC) concerning the conclusion of the Convention on the protection of animals kept for farming purposes;

---

50 For a recent example of when Article 36 might have been invoked, see Brooman, S and Legge, D, 'Animal Transportation' (1995) 146 *New Law Journal*, No 6706, 1131–33.

51 Bennett, R, 'The Value of Farm Animal Welfare' (1995) 46(1) *Journal of Agricultural Economics* 46 at 47.

52 Eurogroup for Animal Welfare, *Summary of Legislation Relative to Animal Welfare at the Levels of the European Community and the Council of Europe*, revised November 1995, Brussels: EAW.

- Council Decision (88/306/EEC) of 16 May 1988 on the conclusion of the European Convention for the Protection of Animals for Slaughter;
- Council Directive (88/166/EEC) laying down minimum standards for the keeping of hens in battery cages;
- Council Directive (91/628/EEC) on the protection of animals during transport;
- Council Directive (91/629/EEC) of 19 November 1991 laying down minimum standards for the protection of calves; proposals for change at the end of 1995;
- Council Directive (91/630/EEC) of 19 November 1991 laying down minimum standards for the protection of pigs;
- Council Directive (93/119/EEC) of 22 December 1993 on the protection of animals at the time of slaughter or killing;
- Council Directive (95/29/EC) adopted on 29 June 1995 which amends Directive (91/628/EEC) and lays down new guidelines regarding journey times and other requirements during transportation.[53]

A crucial factor in the increased influence of the EU in the debate over animal welfare was the creation of the Eurogroup for Animal Welfare (EAW) in 1980, a federal body set up specifically to lobby in the EU and funded initially, in large part, by the RSPCA. The EAW joined the World Federation for the Protection of Animals (WFPA) which had already achieved notable successes in its European campaigning by being instrumental in the introduction of the European Convention for the Protection of Animals in Transportation which came into force on 20 February 1971. The Eurogroup's activities played a central role in the gradual shift from pronouncements from the Council of Europe to EC directives which compelled Member States to tighten regulation of animal welfare in the production of food. There is no doubt that the formation of this group represented a success for the role of the EU in bringing about change. Unlike many of the areas of criticism levelled at the EU and the doubts over its future which came to the fore in the early 1990s, the EU's involvement in the continuing revision of animal welfare control appears to have attracted relatively widespread support from all over Europe. In 1983 the European Parliament recognised the significance of the animals issue by setting up an 'Intergroup' on animal welfare and they asked the Eurogroup to provide its administrative and policy support by becoming its secretariat.[54]

This is not to say that the EU has always found it easy to pass animal-related legislation. There is a noticeable difference in general attitudes towards animals between southern and northern European countries. The welfare of

---

53 See Brooman and Legge, above n 50.
54 EAW, *Summary of Legislation Relative to Animal Welfare,* above n 52, p X.

animals is not considered to be a priority in southern European countries, a point which was acknowledged by William Waldegrave, Minister of Agriculture, when the transportation of animals outcry erupted in Britain late in 1994 and early 1995. He indicated that he felt that accession of the 'green-minded' Scandinavian countries was going to help the more animal welfare conscious north European countries in passing animal welfare legislation in the EU.[55]

Even though the EU has played an important role in the development of animal welfare protection it has always had to balance the different opinions it represents. In relation to the use of veal crates, some countries such as the UK abandoned this widely criticised practice in 1990, but in 1996 they were still commonly used in France, Italy and the Netherlands. This led Franz Fischler, the farm commissioner, to recommend the phasing out of the use of the crates over a period of 13 years up to 2008, a period of time which was criticised by welfare groups but acceptable to those EU countries using the crates.[56] Differences also emerged in the debate concerning the transportation of live animals from the UK in 1994–95. When EU agriculture ministers met in October 1994 the Netherlands, Germany and the UK requested a maximum journey times of eight hours without water, food and rest, whereas Spain, France, Italy, Portugal and Greece refused to go below 22 hours. This actually represented a U-turn in the UK's position of some months previously when Nicholas Soames, the food minister at the time had said that the UK would accept journey times of up to 22 hours before water, food and rest. At the last moment, Gillian Shepherd, the minister of agriculture at the time, blocked a directive which would have allowed such journey times.[57] The agriculture ministers eventually reached a compromise in the summer of 1995, William Waldegrave meanwhile having replaced Gillian Shepherd, when the EU Council of Ministers agreed that animals could be transported for a maximum of eight hours in ordinary lorries but with increased times on the road possible for younger animals or where lorries are specially equipped.[58] Animal welfare groups were disappointed with the outcome of what had been a heated passage in the development of EC regulation of agriculture, and indicated that they felt dissatisfied with the directive.[59]

The Treaty of Rome itself has also been blamed for the fact that animals have to endure long-distance transportation,[60] but negotiators decided not to include a provision regarding animal welfare in the Maastricht Treaty in 1992.

---

55 Ghazi, P, 'Minister who'd like to say no', *The Observer*, 5 March 1995, p 21.

56 *The Guardian*, 16 December 1995, p 6.

57 *The Guardian*, 21 June 1994, p 3.

58 Council Directive (95/29/EEC) amending Council Directive (91/628/EEC) to be implemented by Member States by 31 December 1996.

59 Brooman and Legge, above n 50.

60 The Compassion in World Farming Trust argued for animals to be given a new status in the Treaty of Rome as 'Sentient Beings' in *The Welfare Argument*, above n 29.

As a result, provision for animal welfare in Europe depends upon isolated directives or EC commitments to enforce treaties such as the Convention on International Trade in Endangered Species 1973 (CITES). A Declaration on the Protection of Animals was, however, appended to the Final Act of the Treaty on European Union agreed in December 1991 and signed at Maastrict by all EC Heads of State on 7 February 1992. This called for the European Parliament, the Council and Commission, as well as Member States: 'when drafting and implementing legislation on the common agricultural policy, transport, the internal market and research, to pay full regard to the welfare requirements of animals'.[61]

In 1976 the Council of Europe, a body set up in 1949 to achieve greater unity between its members, and separate from the EU, adopted the Convention on the Protection of Animals Kept for Farming Purposes, following a recommendation from the World Federation for the Protection of Animals. Compliance by the 25 or so members is dependent on States ratifying the Convention and having legislation in place which complies with the Convention. The following articles represent the general principles of the Convention.[62]

Article 3

Animals shall be housed and provided with food, water and care in a manner which – having regard to their species and to their degree of development, adaptation and domestication – is appropriate to their psychological and ethological needs in accordance with established experience and scientific knowledge.

Article 4

1. The freedom of movement appropriate to an animal, having regard to its species and in accordance with established experience and scientific knowledge, shall not be restricted in such a manner as to cause it unnecessary suffering or injury.

2. Where an animal is continuously or regularly tethered or confined it shall be given the space appropriate to its psychological and ethological needs in accordance with established experience and scientific knowledge.

Article 5

1. The lighting, temperature, humidity, air circulation, ventilation, and other environmental conditions such as gas concentration or noise intensity in the place in which an animal is house, shall – having regard to its species and to its degree of development, adaptation and domestication – conform to its physiological and ethological needs in accordance with established experience and scientific knowledge.

---

61 *Summary of Legislation Relative to Animal Welfare*, above n 52, p 155.

62 See the *Official Journal of the European Communities*, 1978, vol 21, L 323, 17 November 1978, pp 12–17. The other articles in the Convention related mainly to the setting up and administration of a Standing Committee to monitor developments in the area of farm animal welfare and to recommend changes in practice to contracting parties.

Article 6

No animal shall be provided with food or liquid in a manner, nor shall such food or liquid contain any substance, which may cause unnecessary suffering of injury.

Article 7

1. The condition and state of health of animals shall be thoroughly inspected at intervals sufficient to avoid unnecessary suffering and in the case of animals kept in modern intensive stock-farming systems at least once a day.

2. The technical equipment used in modern intensive stock-farming systems shall be thoroughly inspected at least once a day, and any defect discovered shall be remedied with the least possible delay. When a defect cannot be remedied forthwith, all temporary measure necessary to safeguard the welfare of the animals shall be taken immediately.

The EC became a signatory to the Convention, which then proceeded to provide a useful launching pad to the development of specific European Community legislation.[63] The intention of this legislation, based upon the Convention, is not to be proscriptive but to provide general guidance, thereby moving practices forward by consent rather than coercion. The Convention's main characteristic is that, dependent as it is on phrases such as 'established experience and scientific knowledge' (in Article 3), it will always generate debate between welfare and farming lobbies as to where the state of experience and knowledge actually stands at any given time.

UNITED KINGDOM CONTROL OF ANIMALS IN AGRICULTURE

In 1964, a public outcry and intense media coverage followed the publication of a book by Ruth Harrison which was serialised in *The Observer*.[64] Within two months of this, the Brambell Committee, under the chairmanship of Professor Roger Brambell, was set up to look into the conditions under which farm animals were kept and to recommend legislative change.

Amongst the findings of the 1965 Brambell Committee Report,[65] which ran to 85 pages, were the following principal findings and recommendations:

Principal findings

6. It is difficult to define precisely the term 'intensive livestock husbandry'. We have considered the keeping of poultry of all sorts, whether hens,

---

63 Council Decision (78/923/EEC); see list of EC directives in text, above p 190.

64 Harrison, R, *Animal Machines*, 1964, London: Vincent Stuart.

65 *Report of the Technical Committee to Enquire into the Welfare of Animals kept under Intensive Livestock Husbandry Systems*, 1965, above n 2.

turkeys or other birds, entirely within doors on deep litter, slats or wire in battery cages; the keeping of rabbits under comparable conditions; beef, veal calf, sheep and pig production under cover, as falling clearly within our terms of reference. All these methods result in the rapid production of animal products by standardised methods involving economy of land and labour. All are capable of exploitation on a large scale, and units of varying sizes, some very large and some quite small, are in operation. A high degree of mechanisation and automation is a feature of the larger establishments.

7. Intensive husbandry is not new. Some traditional methods still in use fall clearly within this definition. We have frequently heard the expression 'factory farming', which we understand to relate only to those intensive methods which are of large scale and highly automated ...

8. A number of factors have contributed to the development and spread of intensive methods of animal husbandry ... probably the most important have been economic pressure on producers ...

9. Historically the evolution of our society has been marked by increasing concern for the welfare of animals. Many cruel practices, such as badger baiting and cock-fighting, have been proscribed by law. Others, including castration or dehorning of adult cattle, can now be carried out only under anaesthesia. The movement and slaughter of animals for food are controlled in the interest of the animals. Indeed, this Committee was established in response to widespread concern for the welfare of animals under systems of intensive husbandry. It appears to us reasonable to anticipate continuing development of concern for animal welfare and that conditions which appear to us tolerable today may come to be considered intolerable in the future. ...

27. There are sound anatomical and physiological grounds for accepting that domestic mammals and birds experience the same kinds of sensations as we do: the structure of a mammal's nervous system is essentially similar to that of man and the function of the ductless glands is known to be comparable. The sensations certainly differ in degree; for example, the senses of hearing and smell may be much better developed in some animals than in man. It is probable, however, that imaginative anticipation, which plays such a large part in human suffering, is incomparably less well-developed in most animals. They appear to live much more in the present and their suffering appears to be correspondingly more transitory, although many mammals can both remember the past and fear the future to some extent. It is justifiable to assume that the sufferings of animals are not identical with those of human beings; it is equally justifiable to assume that they suffer in similar ways; the valid point where the line should be drawn between these two extremes is very difficult to determine and must be a matter of balanced judgment. It is extremely important to realise this because the whole of our recommendations ultimately must rest on such judgments. ...

37. ... In principle we disapprove of a degree of confinement of an animal which necessarily frustrates most of the major activities which make up its natural behaviour ... An animal should at least have sufficient freedom of

movement to be able without difficulty, to turn round, groom itself, get up, lie down and stretch its limbs. ...

46. Above and beyond all these matters, important and relevant though each is, stands the fact that modern, intensive animal production methods most markedly increase the responsibility of those who use them towards the animals in their charge. If any creature is wholly and continuously under control, we believe that this total human responsibility must be acknowledged, and that there is widespread public concern that it be seen to be acknowledged. Changing patterns of husbandry may mean varying degrees of frustration and discomfort to animals whose normal patterns of behaviour are still imperfectly understood. We are certain that a beginning must be made to safeguard their welfare ...

223. There are many factors affecting the welfare of animals which are difficult or impossible to control by statutory requirements (for example, the quality of stockmanship) but which, individually or cumulatively, may have a profound effect. We are concerned that it could still be possible for animals to be kept in full conformity with the standards we have recommended and yet to suffer 'pain' or 'cruelty' through, for example, neglect, or wilful refusal to accept advice on measures which would remedy their conditions. Again, we do not believe that the 1911 Act provides sufficient cover for this situation and we consider additional legislation to be necessary. One of the problems is to establish a clearer definition of 'suffering' and in this respect we have studied with great interest the report of the Departmental Committee on Animals (*The Littlewood Report*). We endorse the concept of suffering which they provide in paragraph 181 of that report:

(a) discomfort (such as may be characterised by such negative signs as condition, torpor, diminished appetite);

(b) stress (ie a condition of tension or anxiety predictable or readily explicable from environmental causes whether distinct from or including physical causes);

(c) pain (recognisable by more positive signs such as struggling, screaming or squealing, convulsions, severe palpitation).

Principal recommendations

1. ... we have concluded that the use of such [intensive husbandry] methods should not in itself be regarded as objectionable and may often benefit the animals; but certain practices are contrary to animal welfare and need to be controlled ...

4. The existing animal welfare legislation does not adequately safeguard farm animals and a new act is needed incorporating a fuller definition of suffering and enabling Ministers to make regulations requiring conditions for particular animals. ...

8. Cages for laying poultry should not contain more than three birds. The three-bird cage should measure at least 20 inches wide and 17 inches deep and have an average height of 18 inches with the lowest part not less than 16 inches. For two birds the width should be 16 inches and for one bird 12

inches. The floor of the cage should consist of rectangular metal mesh, no finer than 10 gauge. ...

14. The de-beaking of battery hens and broilers should be prohibited.

15. Housed pigs, between 150 lb–210 lb live weight, should have a minimum of eight square feet of floor space per animal. Those above 210 lb should have a minimum of 10 square feet. ...

18. Pregnant sows should not be kept without daily exercise in quarters which do not permit them to turn round and, in any case, should not be tethered indoors. ...

20. The yoking or close tethering of calves, except for short periods and for specific purposes, should be prohibited.

21. Individual pens for calves should be of sufficient size to allow the calf freedom of movement including the ability to turn round ...

26. Housed turkeys should have at least ½ square feet of floor space up to eight weeks; 2½ square feet from 8–12 weeks and 4 square feet above 12 weeks.

The UK government delayed implementing the recommendations of the Brambell Committee for three years, a delay which has been criticised by Ruth Harrison in that:[66]

... no action whatsoever was taken on the Brambell Committees recommendations for immediate action to counter suffering on farms. There is no doubt that if government had been brave enough to make the regulations at the time the face of livestock farming throughout the world would have been vastly different today ...

Some of the recommendations of the Brambell Committee were implemented in the Agriculture (Miscellaneous Provisions) Act 1968.

Section 1. Prevention of unnecessary pain and distress for livestock

(1) Any person who causes unnecessary pain or unnecessary distress to any livestock for the time being situated on agricultural land and under his control or permits any such livestock to suffer any such pain or distress of which he knows or may reasonably be expected to know shall be guilty of an offence under this section.

Section 2. Regulations with respect to the welfare of the livestock

(1) The Ministers may, after consultation with such persons appearing to them to represent any interests concerned as the Ministers consider appropriate, by regulations make provision with respect to the welfare of livestock ... as they think fit. ... the regulations may include provision:

(a) with respect to the dimensions and layout of accommodation for livestock, the materials to be used in constructing any such accommodation and the facilities by way of lighting, heating, cooling, ventilation, drainage, water supply and otherwise to be provided in

66 Harrison, R, 'Case Study: Farm Animals', *Environmental Dilemmas: Ethics and Decisions*, 1993, pp 118–35, London: Chapman & Hall.

connection with any accommodation;

(b) for ensuring that the provision of balanced diets for the livestock and for prohibiting or regulating the use of any substance as food for livestock and the importation and supply of any substance intended for use as food for livestock;

(c) for prohibiting the bleeding of livestock and the mutilation of livestock in any manner specified in the regulation, and for prohibiting or regulating the use of any method of marking or restraining livestock or interfering with the capacity of livestock to smell, see, hear, emit sound or exercise any other faculty.

Section 3. Codes of recommendations for the welfare of livestock

(1) The Ministers may from time to time, after consultation with such persons appearing to them to represent any interests concerned as the Ministers consider appropriate:

(a) prepare codes containing such recommendations with respect to the welfare of livestock for the time being situated on agricultural land as they consider proper for the guidance of persons connected with livestock; and

(b) revise any such code by revoking, varying, amending or adding to the provisions of the codes in such a manner as the Ministers think fit. ...

Section 8. Interpretation

(1) In this part of this Act:

'agricultural land' means land used for agriculture (within the meaning of the Agriculture Act 1947 or, in Scotland, the Agriculture (Scotland) Act 1948) which is so used for the purposes of a trade or business; and

'livestock' means any creature kept for the production of food, wool, skin or fur or for use in farming of land or for such purpose as the Minister may by order specify.

The Act also provides powers for the State Veterinary Service to enter and inspect premises, examine livestock, analyse foodstuffs and to receive a certain measure of cooperation from the occupier or servant of the premises in question (s 6).

Since 1968 the powers granted under ss 2 and 3 have been frequently used to implement EC directives regarding hens, pigs and cattle and to implement the Council of Europe Convention on the protection of animals kept for farming purposes. As of 1996 there were six sets of regulations issued which were still in force: the Welfare of Livestock Regulations 1994 (SI 1994/2126) which, being the largest set of regulations covering several species of animal, consolidate much of the legislation relating to the welfare of livestock on agricultural land. These regulations contain schedules relating to each type of livestock which is protected by setting requirements relating to matters such as prevention of injury, inspection, provision of feed and water, and provision and testing of alarms on automatic ventilation equipment;[67] the Welfare of

Livestock (Deer) Regulations 1980 (SI 1980/593) which extended the definition of livestock in the 1968 Act to cover deer kept for the production of antlers in velvet; the Welfare of Livestock (Prohibited Operations) Regulations 1982 (SI 1982/1884), which prohibit certain procedures such as penis amputation, tongue amputation in calves and hot-branding of cattle. The tooth grinding of sheep was added to this list by the Welfare of Livestock (Prohibited Operations) (Amendment) Regulations (SI 1987/114); The Docking of Pigs (Use of Anaesthetics) Regulations (SI 1974/798) which prohibits the docking of the tail of a pig more than seven days old without anaesthetic; and the Removal of Antlers in Velvet (Anaesthetics) Regulations (SI 1980/685) which prohibits the removal of antlers of deer when they are in velvet without the use of anaesthetics.

As of 1996 there were nine codes of recommendations in existence indicating standards of husbandry regarding cattle, sheep, goats, pigs, domestic fowl, turkeys, ducks, farmed deer and rabbits.[68] The legal status of codes of practice mean that they do not have the direct effect of specific regulatory legislation but are used, as s 3(4) suggests, to indicate whether an offence has been committed under the 1968 Act. Before issuing mandatory guidelines or codes the relevant minister should consult with interested parties (s 2), although there is no absolute requirement to do so.

The Farm Animal Welfare Council (FAWC), formed in 1979 as an independent body consisting of academics, welfare proponents, farmers and vets, is one of these 'interested parties'. It replaced the Farm Animal Welfare Advisory Committee which had been formed as a result of the Brambell Report. The new body has a wider jurisdiction to recommend, investigate and report to the relevant minister on any subject relating to farm animal welfare and the UK government has often placed considerable weight upon its findings.[69] As soon as it was formed it issued a press notice stressing that it would push for the introduction of 'five freedoms' for farm animals:[70]

– freedom from thirst, hunger or malnutrition;

– appropriate comfort and shelter;

– prevention, or rapid diagnosis and treatment, of injury and disease;

– freedom to display most normal patterns of behaviour;

– freedom from fear.

---

67 See the Ministry of Agriculture, Fisheries and Food, *Summary of the Law Relating to Farm Animal Welfare*, 1996, London: MAFF.

68 Codes of Practice can be obtained free of charge from MAFF Publications, London SE99 7TP.

69 Excerpts from one of the reports of the FAWC are shown above in the section on issues of pain and suffering.

70 Universities Federation for Animal Welfare, *Management and Welfare of Farm Animals*, 1994, p 4, London: Universities Federation for Animal Welfare.

Important provisions for the welfare of animals are contained in the Welfare of Animals (Slaughter or Killing) Regulations 1995 (SI 1995/731) which came into force on 1 April 1995 implementing EC Directive (93/119/EC). The regulations provide specific protection for animals immediately before and during slaughter, with detailed requirements for the movement, lairaging, restraint, stunning, and killing or slaughter of animals, and generally provide against unnecessary excitement, pain or suffering. Slaughtermen must be licensed and a person in authority is required to be available to take whatever action is necessary to safeguard the welfare of the animals.

If the 1968 Act is seen as providing for the 'quality of life' of farm animals, the Animals (Scientific Procedures) Act 1986 (ASPA) provides a framework in which farm animals' welfare can sometimes be dispensed with in the cause of scientific advance. Although it is mainly aimed at animals inside the laboratory, ASPA does provide a measure of protection to farm animals used in experimental work.[71] This Act covers those animals which are used, for example, in genetic modification work: s 2(3) brings within the coverage of the Act 'anything done for the purpose of, or liable to result in, the birth or hatching of a protected animal', and s 5(4) requires the Home Secretary to 'weigh the likely adverse effects on the animals concerned against the benefit likely to accrue' in determining whether to grant a project licence.[72]

The Protection of Animals Act 1911 also provides some protection to farm animals in that it regulates the causing or failure to alleviate the unnecessary suffering of any captive or domestic animal (thus excluding wild animals).[73] This Act completes the main legislative coverage of farm animals by providing against unnecessary suffering of farm animals to go alongside the 'lifestyle' provisions of the 1968 Act and the specific lifting of protection afforded by ASPA in relation to animal experimentation.

Other relevant legislation includes the Protection of Animals (Anaesthetics) Acts 1954 and 1964 which together provide that animals should be appropriately anaesthetised during operations. The Royal College of Veterinary Surgeons has some influence in this area as a statutory body charged with regulating the conduct of its members. To this end they also issue guidelines for acceptable practice, investigate complaints and discipline members where breaches occur. The Veterinary Surgeons Act 1966 also protects animals from invasive treatment by unqualified people, by requiring certain qualifications to perform different types of operations.[74]

---

71 For details see Chapter 4 on experimentation.

72 The Committee's specific recommendations regarding the protection of animals afforded by the Animals (Scientific Procedures) Act 1986 are examined in Chapter 4.

73 Extracts from the Protection of Animals Act 1911 are contained in Chapter 2.

74 The three statutes mentioned here have been amended several times. A full list of currently applicable amendments will be found by referring to the current edition of Halsbury's Statutes.

Mention should also be made of the Animals Act 1971 which includes provisions on the detention and sale of trespassing livestock which has a direct effect on the welfare of animals in specific circumstances; the protection of livestock with regard to worrying by dogs; and livestock which trespass onto the highway.[75]

CONTROL OF ANIMALS IN AGRICULTURE IN OTHER COUNTRIES

Switzerland

In 1978 Switzerland introduced new legislation which has come to be considered by pressure groups in other countries as a blueprint for regulation giving greater credence to the physiological and ethological needs of animals. The Animal Protection Act 1978 came into effect in 1981 and amounted to the most animal-centred legislation in Europe at that time. In the following extract, the Swiss Society for the Protection of Animals describes what the provisions of the Act have meant to the farming of poultry:[76]

> The Swiss Animal Protection Act came into force in 1981. This prescribes minimum requirements for the behaviourally appropriate housing of productive livestock and experimental animals and for animals kept in homes. It has become famous for its section on the housing of chickens.
>
> By prescribing sheltered, darkened nest boxes, perches or slatted grids for all hens and a minimum area of 800 sq cm per bird on mesh floors, it effectively prohibited battery housing of laying hens which was hitherto customary. Thus, Switzerland was the first country in the world to put an end to the battery cage.
>
> The new regulations applied to all new buildings and conversions of existing housing. For practical economic reasons, poultry keepers were granted a ten-year transition period to bring their existing housing into line with the new regulations. The Swiss keepers of laying hens completed the changeover punctually by 1 January 1992 – without State subsidies. Today in Switzerland, the keeping of hens in batteries is a thing of the past.
>
> At the same time as prescribing minimum standards for the appropriate housing of livestock, the Swiss Animal Protection Act also established State test centres for livestock housing systems and their equipment.
>
> Before they may be placed on the market, all systems which are to made and sold as series products must be shown to be appropriate to the needs of the animals. This form of consumer protection for farmers and keepers of animals has given a good account of itself.
>
> The Swiss Animal Protection Act empowers the federal government to give financial support to scientific research on animal behaviour and animal

---

75 See also the excerpt from the Animals Act in Chapter 2.

76 *Laying Hens: Twelve Years of Experience with New Husbandry Systems in Switzerland,* 1994, Basel: Swiss Society for the Protection of Animals. By permission of the Swiss Society for the Protection of Animals.

welfare. In addition, private institutions including in particular animal protection organisations have given financial support to the study and development of new housing systems.

Since the 1970s, many alternatives to the battery housing of laying hens have been developed by ethologists and livestock specialists, as well as by animal feed suppliers and firms specialised in the construction of livestock housing. Some systems, such as colony cages or housing with slopping floors, proved unsuccessful and taught an expensive lesson to some poultry keepers.

In the meantime, where housing systems are concerned, the wheat has now been removed from the chaff and there has been a widespread adoption of the aviary system. This system is conceived in accordance with the natural behaviour of fowls and is based upon the idea of providing installations and equipment such as nest boxes, scratching areas or perches which enable the birds to very largely follow the patterns of behaviour specific to their species.

By means of elevated perches and multiple levels, this system also makes use of the birds' ability to fly and to 'populate' a third dimension in the poultry house. This results in a better utilisation of the floor area in the building. Extensive studies in Switzerland over a number of years have shown that production costs in the aviary are 6–10% higher than with the battery system as a result of higher labour, surveillance and investment costs.

Eggs grown in the free-range system are gaining a growing share of the Swiss egg market. Of the 2 million layers in flocks of 500 and more birds, more than 20% are now regularly permitted to range and graze outside.

Producers in Switzerland have succeeded in recouping the increased costs of egg production through the market. This has been possible on the one hand because a corresponding price increase, with an average egg consumption of 200 eggs per person per year, does not place an appreciable burden on the household budget: The changeover to more animal friendly systems costs the egg consumer in Switzerland little more than the price of a cinema ticket each year.

On the other hand, producers and animal protection organisations have conducted education campaigns aimed at increasing consumer awareness of livestock-friendly Swiss egg production and influencing shopping habits in an appropriate manner.

Thirteen years ago the Swiss poultry farmers were presented with a challenge. They face up to this challenge and have now successfully mastered it. There is no logical reason why poultry farmers in other countries should not be at least as successful in the same situation.

To illustrate how the introduction of the 1978 Act affected other animals, and the general reaction to the new law, an extract is included from a conference paper given by Andreas Steiger of the Swiss Federal Veterinary Office:[77]

---

77   Steiger, A, 'Effects of the Swiss Animal Welfare legislation Since 1981', *Environmental and Management Systems for Total Animal Health Care in Agriculture,* Proceedings of the 8th International Congress on Animal Hygiene, 12–16 September 1994, pp 53–54, St Paul, Minnesota: University of Minnesota and Washington State University.

In pig housing the legislation had the following effects:

1) additional provision for occupational material to pigs, such as straw, hay, silage or roughage pellets as well as straw cubes in special cribs;

2) the ban on cages for piglets on different levels and on the neck tethering of sows;

3) the development of group housing systems for sows and of improved perforated floors;

4) the tendency towards new, more natural housing systems such as open front housing of fattening pigs and group housing of sows;

5) difficulties with the implementation of the requirements concerning occupational material for all pigs, concerning regular outside exercise for sows in tethers or in crates and a lack of regard for the minimal measurements of crates for sows in new constructions ...

The regulations for livestock management have led to many improvements, but also some difficulties in application ... In the future, improved training and more modern, professional information for farmers concerning animal welfare will be provided.

Sweden

In 1988 Sweden passed some of the most stringent legislative requirements in the world regarding farm animal welfare.[78] The new law amounted to an abolition of farming techniques which do not recognise the ethological needs of the animals. It has been noted by Bernard Rollin that: 'The law moved through the Swedish Parliament virtually unopposed and was perceived by the Swedish public not as radical but as a return to traditional agricultural values of husbandry'.[79] Rollin has also suggested that the new Swedish laws represent the closest approach to 'animal rights':[80]

> What the law mandates is that farm animals be allowed to live their lives in accordance with their natures, or *telos* as I have called it. Indeed, the entire bill is informed by the notion of rights I discussed. While acknowledging that people will eat animals and animal products, the law reaffirms the ancient idea of husbandry – that cattle have a right to graze; that chickens and pigs have the right to freedom of motion; that animals who would naturally use it have a right to straw; that animals have the right to separate feeding and bedding places; and so forth. Drugs such as antibiotics can only be used to treat disease, not to conceal the untoward effects of confinement. Slaughtering must be as painless as possible.[81]

---

78 Regulations printed in English can be obtained from The National Board of Agriculture, S-551 Jonkoping, Sweden.

79 Rollin, B, *Farm Animal Welfare*, 1995, p 19, Iowa: Iowa State University Press.

80 The definition of, and the specific claims for, 'animal rights', are explained in Chapter 3.

81 Rollin, B, *The Frankenstein Syndrome: Ethical and Social Issues in the Genetic Engineering of Animals*, 1995, p 167, Cambridge: Cambridge University Press.

As with animals used for scientific purposes (discussed in Chapter 4), farm animals are covered by provisions in the Animal Protection Act 1988. The main provisions regarding farm animals are given below:

The Animal Protection Act 1988

Section 3

(1) Animals shall be provided with sufficient food and water and adequate care.

(2) Livestock buildings and other premises where the animals are kept shall provide animals with adequate space and shelter and shall be kept clean.

Section 4

(1) Animals bred or kept for the production of food, wool, skins or furs, or for use in races, shall be kept and handled in an environment that is appropriate for animals and in such a way as to promote their health and permit natural behaviour.

Section 5

(1) Animals must not be overstrained.

(2) They must not be beaten or driven with implements which are liable to cut or otherwise injure them.

Section 6

(1) Animals must not be kept tied in a painful way or in a way that does not allow them necessary freedom of movement or sufficient shelter against wind and bad weather. ...

Section 8

(1) The means of transport used for the treatment of animals shall be suitable for the purpose and provide shelter against heat and cold and protect the animals from shocks and abrasions and the like. To the extent necessary, the animals shall be kept separate from each other.

Section 9

A sick or injured animal shall be given the necessary care without delay, unless the injury is so severe that the animal must be killed immediately.

Section 10

(1) Surgery must not be performed on animals for other reasons than those of veterinary medicine, unless provisions granting derogations from this provision are adopted [by the government or National Board of Agriculture]. ...

Section 13

When animals are taken to slaughter and when they are slaughtered, they shall be spared unnecessary discomfort and suffering.

Section 14

Domestic animals shall be anaesthetised before being bled prior to slaughter. No other measures may be taken in connection with slaughter until the animal is dead.

Further clarification on this Act and specific regulations are given in the Animal Protection Ordinance, which has been amended several times, and the National Board of Agriculture Regulations and General Recommendations concerning Animal Management in Agriculture.[82] Together they lay down specific regulation concerning, for example, care and management of animals, climate control in buildings used for farming animals, lighting provisions and cleaning of facilities. The Animal Protection Ordinance in particular makes provision for specific species:

Animal Protection Ordinance 1988 (as amended)

Section 5

(1) Buildings for horses, cattle, reindeer, pigs, sheep, goats, poultry or furred animals must not be built, extended or rebuilt without prior approval of the building with respect to animal protection and animal health ...

Section 7

(1) New animal management techniques and equipment shall be approved with reference to animal health and protection before use. ...

Section 9

Hens for egg production shall not be housed in cages.[83]

Section 10

Cattle for milk production that are older than six months shall be sent out to pasture in the summer.

Section 11

(1) Cattle, other than cattle kept for milk production, shall be sent out to pasture or otherwise kept outdoors in the summer.

Section 12

Pigs kept for breeding shall be given the opportunity to stay outdoors, where possible.

Section 13

(1) Exemptions from the provisions of ss 10 and 11 may be granted where special climatic conditions make outdoor grazing unsuitable for reasons of animal protection ...

Section 14

Pigs shall be housed in lounging barns.

Taken as a whole, the legislation means that Sweden has committed itself to what amounts to a prohibition of battery systems of farming by 1998, the year

---

82   Issued on 24 May 1989.

83   Section 9 will not be implemented in full until 1998, until which time birds already caged can be so kept. Strict regulations on the size and design of these cages remain in force until that time.

set for final implementation of some of the legislative provisions. This is certainly more than would have been demanded by their entry into the EU in 1995 and is more than is demanded by legislation in the UK. Only Switzerland has a system which approaches the proscriptive nature of the Swedish system.

The US

The fate of farm animals in the US is certainly far worse than for those within the EU. Groups such as the Humane Farming Association (HFA) based in San Francisco have highlighted poor conditions for animals on American farms caused by familiar pressures placed on farmers after the Second World War just as they were in Europe. The first is the pronounced move from small-farm production to the use of large intensive, indoor factory sites. In 1970, for example, there were 900,000 farms raising pigs in the US. By 1990, although the number of pigs being produced had remained relatively static, the number of farms had been reduced to less than 250,000, involving the close confinement of many more animals as farms sought to reduce costs in a drive for profit.[84] The second, far more insidious reason is that powerful lobby groups managed to ensure that farm animals were excluded from the Animal Welfare Act 1966 as amended in 1970, 1976 and 1985. Federal and State regulation of animal welfare contains very little on the subject of farm animals. They are excluded from the 1966 Act and its amendments, leaving the US with most to do to create even the most basic standards of care for farm animals.

This development led the HFA to comment that 'there are virtually no laws which protect farm animals from even the most harsh and brutal treatment as long as it takes place in the name of production and profit.'[85] Bernard Rollin highlights the anomalies that this can create in the treatment of the same species of animal in the US:[86]

Imagine a flock of sheep maintained for research at a university. The researcher in question engages both in biomedical and agricultural research, and utilises his sheep for both sorts of research. Let us further imagine that one of the ewes gives birth to twin lambs. One of the lambs is fated to go into a biomedical research project; one into an agricultural project. Both require castration as part of the protocol. The lamb going into biomedical research will be anaesthetised, have surgery under aseptic conditions, be supervised during recovery, and will receive post-surgical analgesia. The lamb entering the food and fibre protocol, in dramatic contrast, may be castrated with a pocketknife or

---

84 *Bringing Home the Bacon,* 1995, San Francisco: Humane Farming Association.
85 *The Dangers of Factory Farming,* 1985, San Francisco: Humane Farming Association.
86 Rollin, B, 'Agricultural research and the new ethic for animals', in *Farm Animals in Biomedical and Agricultural Research,* 1996, pp 51–58, Australia: Australian and New Zealand Council for the Care of Animals in Research and Teaching.

have a constricting rubber ring applied around the scrotum and above the testes, as often occurs in field conditions.

This illustrates some inconsistency in the framework of US legislation. Animal welfare groups have looked to developments in the EU regarding the care and treatment of farm animals as a model which could be copied in the US. Incidences of cruel practices in the US are too numerous to mention here, save for a few examples: cattle are castrated without anaesthesia or analgesia; the hot-iron branding of cattle, possibly several times during its lifetime as it is bought and sold; sow confinement and the use of farrowing crates; the use of veal crates; and the practice of dragging from trucks by tractor injured, sick or crippled animals – 'downer cattle'– at farms, markets and other places. There is growing unease at the use of such practices, illegal in most of Europe, which may force legislation to be introduced in the near future. The more that the US public finds out about the treatment of farm animals there, the more likely it is that this will occur, unless the industry is ready to radically and openly clean up its act. In the mean time, the fate of US livestock seems bleak indeed: 'It is in the US, the birthplace of "factory farming" that most remains to be done.'[87]

SHOULD UK/EU REGULATION OF THE USE OF ANIMALS IN AGRICULTURE BE CHANGED?

Animals involved in the production of meat and other animal products are the subjects of a controversial trade-off between the demand for cheap produce and a growing recognition that animals have a need for more protection by the law. Some philosophers, as well as farmers, have sought to defend the present use of animals in agriculture. Michael Leahy, while recognising the problems associated with close confinement farming since the war, defends intensive farming methods and the practice of consuming meat and animal products on the following grounds.[88]

–   The catastrophic effects on humans in terms of lost jobs and the partial wipe-out of certain national economies such as New Zealand and Australia. This would far outweigh the suffering endured by animals.

–   Not all animal products are produced intensively and, therefore, following the utilitarianist reasoning of Singer, we would be doing nothing wrong in consuming it.

–   The doubts over whether animals actually do suffer in modern farming practices. He argues that while certain images of 'suffering' may look bad, they do not necessarily involve 'pain' as such.

87 Garner, R, *Animals, Politics and Morality*, 1992, p 109, Manchester: Manchester University Press.

88 Leahy, M, *Against Liberation*, 1991, London: Routledge.

His arguments do seem, taken as a whole, to leave room for improved welfare and do not entirely discount animals from moral consideration.[89] He concludes that:[90]

> [A]ttempts to convince us that eating of meat and fish is an evil invasion of the inalienable rights of animals and that it should cease forthwith are a sham. They can only succeed with the help of opportunistic flights of fancy such as inherent value or theos rights, or by otherwise obscuring the differences between creatures like ourselves, who use language, and those that do not. The result of so doing is the sad and mischievous error of seeing little or no moral difference between the painless killing of chickens and that of unwanted children.

In relation to the gradual improvement in welfare standards which is favoured by most proponents of 'animal rights' at present,[91] the UK farming lobby claims that the regulation of farming in the UK is the tightest in Europe. They argue that the protection provided to farm animals, particularly by the Agriculture (Miscellaneous Provisions) Act 1968 and its commitment to protect against unnecessary pain and suffering, supported by State veterinary services and inspectors, affords animals the best protection that is feasible and practical. It is also pointed out that the Farm Animal Welfare Council's codes of practice which have been issued regarding all major species of farm animal adequately protect the essential five 'basic freedoms' regarding nutrition and food, freedom from discomfort, freedom from disease, pain and injury, freedom from fear and the ability to display most normal behaviour which were first highlighted by the Brambell Committee in 1964 (see above). They also point to progress being made by a gradual improvement in the law which saw veal crates banned in 1990 and which will see other close confinement techniques phased out in the UK by 1999.

One of the most notable fears of the farming lobby in the UK about the tightening up of UK legislation and an enforced move to organic methods of farming is the effect this would have on exports and imports. It is feared that the enforced introduction of expansive farming techniques would raise prices and lead to an influx of cheaper produce from abroad. The UK would certainly have problems in preventing imports from other EU countries, any attempt at which would probably be in contravention of EC regulations regarding the free movement of goods. Unless there were an EU-wide initiative, the UK farming industry might be put at a disadvantage in terms of the relative cost of its produce and meat. The same applies to exports which would become less attractive abroad if production costs forced up the price of UK produce.

---

89   See extract in Chapter 3.
90   Leahy, above n 88, p 220.
91   Francione, G, *Rain Without Thunder: The Ideology of the Animal Rights Movement*, 1996, Chapter 2, Philadelphia: Temple University Press.

To counter these arguments the animal welfare lobby points out that animal welfare is too important to be left to the whim of market forces. They argue that animals' welfare is being sacrificed in the name of competition, which is immoral and unacceptable. There is, they argue, a need for the public to decide what really matters to them: the ability to have cheap products which involve cruelty as their major cost, or more expensive products which take farm animals' welfare more into account.

The critics of the current situation fall into three main groups when it comes to proposing a blueprint for the future. First, there are those who argue the radical position for a complete prohibition on the use of animals for food, and a moral obligation to be vegetarian. Secondly, there are those who see the use of animals as being economically and environmentally damaging, because of the hidden costs of intensive farming. Thirdly, there are those who, for pragmatic and philosophical reasons, fall short of advocating complete prohibition, and instead campaign for changes in farming practice to give better welfare protection to farm animals through the law, as well as advocating radically altered methods of farming.

Merely changing animal farming practices assumes that the use of animals in the production of food is morally acceptable *per se*, a presumption not accepted by all groups. Some writers argue that the use of animals in this way is a waste of valuable resources on a global scale, as animals consume a large slice of limited food resources. The production of animals involves a great cost in terms of the food which the animals consume themselves, whereas the production of grain and other vegetables does not involve such high 'wastage'. Thus, it is argued, hunger across the globe would more easily be alleviated if we were to switch to more cereal production.[92] However, as 90–95% of people consume meat and other animal products, an absolute prohibition on the consumption of meat seems unlikely to represent political reality for some time to come. This leads many campaign groups to abandon end-point arguments and to concentrate on the immediately possible, specifically a move to organic techniques.

Jon Wynne-Tyson sees our attitude towards the acceptance of the production of animals in agricultural intensive husbandry systems and their slaughter as part of a more intrinsic malaise of humankind which has seen most people avoid addressing the issue of animal suffering in favour of accepting the compromise position of merely improving animal welfare:[93]

> No amount of proof or persuasion concerning the mere rights and sufferings of other living beings will alter the majority's behaviour a jot. Schooled early enough in insensitivity, there are all too many of our kind who can spend a

---

92 For an example of an author who uses all these arguments see Gold, M, *Assault and Battery*, 1983, London: Pluto Press.

93 Wynne-Tyson, J, *Food for a Future*, 1988, 4th edn, pp 140–41, Wellingborough: Thorsons. By permission of Jon Wynne-Tyson.

lifetime without experiencing a twinge of pity, although afforded every opportunity to open their minds and hearts to the facts of mankind's pitiless treatment of its own and other species.

This is why it has seemed best to place most emphasis on [vegetarianism], showing why we all stand to benefit from a more humane diet in, first, the short term (through adopting a diet for which we are chemically and physiologically better attuned) and, secondly, the long term (because of the ecological and economical facts of modern life that we can no longer afford to ignore). For most of us these are more powerful arguments than anything so irrelevant to our daily lives as mere unkindness to animals. The poverty of human imagination, the strength of greed, the shortness of memory, the pressure to which we are subjected in business and family life, and our willingness to believe only what we want to believe – these are the barriers that have confronted anyone who has ever taken a clear look at the natural world and has been anguished by the rapacious and pitiless part played by the human race.

Inasmuch as any of us are concerned at all by such matters, most of us are satisfied by what Curtis Freshel called The Legislative Illusion – those measures taken to modify or make acceptable some of our cruelties, rather than to renounce them. it has been said, of course, that if we cared about suffering and injustice; about the facts of politics, poverty and war; about starving nations; about the true extent of child, adult and animal misery that lies below that unsubmerged one millionth of the iceberg that sticks above the sea of newsprint from which most of us make our judgments of the condition of the world we live in – if we really cared about and concentrated on these things 'we should go mad, no doubt, and die that way'. Possibly, in their wisdom, the mind-controllers know, or think they know, that there must be a limit to what we can take.

He continues:[94]

[S]eldom does the mass-circulation media permit a genuine and full examination of whether the basic uses to which animals are put can be justified. After all, it is because of these everyday uses of animals that innumerable cruelties are inevitable. If you make your reader or viewer feel really uncomfortable, you may lose him. It is safer to fool oneself and others that with a little bit of tightening up here and a little more supervision there, everything that we wish to do with animals, and damned well intend to go on doing with them, will soon be within 'permissible' limits of suffering.

We no longer have any excuse for such cowardice and hypocrisy. We are fed with too much information to be able to pretend any longer that we do not know what is done to living, feeling creature in order that we may cling to the interminable meat-and-two-veg routine that with minor variations is still the centrepiece of Western culinary art.

Some may protest: 'Oh, but things have improved so much lately. People are so much more concerned. Cruelty and suffering have been reduced to a

---

94 *Ibid*, pp 149–50.

minimum.' Many of them genuinely gulled by The Legislative Illusion, they point to some Bill passed, usually after repeated readings and blockings in Parliament, to ameliorate one aspect of our fundamentally unchanged insensitivity towards the creatures we wish to eat, chase, torture or wear; and because public concern is still so feeble, such Bills are little more than a sop to minority feeling, their implementation being in the hands of breeders, slaughterers, inspectors and government officials who know all too well the shortness of public memory and the power of commercial interests to override almost any measure that is backed not by the pursuit of profit and power, but by mere abstract whimsy about kindness to animals.

The second argument regarding the wider environmental impact of animal farming and the conclusions it gives rise to are examined in the following extracts from *Counting the Costs*,[95] published by the Soil Association:

It is now widely acknowledged that modern agriculture has become badly misaligned both with the ecosystem within which it operates and the society which it serves. Even amongst the former proponents of industrial agriculture, a consensus is emerging that we cannot afford to wait any longer to act; that we must find a way to establish sustainable systems which can meet our social and economic needs, and yet preserve the integrity of the world's natural resources for future generations.

Prevailing measures to develop and encourage such alternative systems are, however, piecemeal and inadequate. Social and environmental factors still remain a very long from being the central part of the decision-making processes that influence agricultural policy and practice ...

It is increasingly accepted by many sectors of government and industry that the pursuit of sustainability requires account to be taken of the external costs caused by economic activity and development. These costs include:

– the depreciation of natural capital through the use of non-renewable natural resources (eg oil and coal) or the loss of other natural assets (eg biodiversity and landscape);

– declines in personal or collective 'welfare' eg public health;

– the cost of environmental degradation ie the cost of cleaning up environmental damage;

– the cost of defensive expenditure ie the cost of preventive action to prevent environmental damage.

The principal challenge with such 'green accounting' is the assignment of appropriate monetary values to the areas of external cost – whether these are *financial* costs (eg incurred in water treatment) or *economic* costs (eg due to the loss of a landscape feature valued by people).

Valuing agricultural externalities is certainly still in its infancy. Identifying them is not too much of a problem, but much of the basic knowledge and research methodology needed to fully evaluate them remains to be developed. Although some external costs (especially financial) can in principle be

---

95   *Counting the Costs*, 1996, Soil Association.

relatively easily quantified, many others involve non-traded items and depend on the appliance of subjective, potentially controversial, judgements of value.

For example, while there is acceptance that farm animals have an intrinsic moral status, this status continues to be abused within intensive livestock systems in the interest of producing cheap food. The suffering and loss of welfare endured by farm animals in these production systems is therefore a significant externality which, while subsiding the price of food, is also causing a growing number of people considerable concern. Putting a cost on the routine violation of animal welfare must therefore involve some judgement on the part of consumers in weighing up their own interests against those of animals. But this judgement may itself be complicated by other concerns about further externalities associated with the farming system; for example, water and air pollution or the quality and safety of food products (some of these can also be valued in financial terms) ...

Case Study 1: BSE (bovine spongyform encephalopathy)

As the external costs of agriculture are increasingly being discussed, 1996 has witnessed the climax of the BSE crisis. Not only is BSE the most profoundly acute and expensive agricultural crisis in a generation, but it is also the most financially transparent. For the first time it has been possible to observe *and* quantify the public expenditure incurred by the government's attempts to resolve the errors of an agricultural industry that did not think it '... unwise at the time' to routinely feed recycled abattoir waste (meat and bone meal) as a source of protein to high-yielding dairy cows ...

[The Ministry of Agriculture, Fisheries and Food] now estimate that a total of £1,156 million (ie £1.2 billion) of public money will be spent in 1996–97 – over 100 times that originally predicted!

Furthermore, these are only the direct costs incurred directly through additional public expenditure. There remain a number of hidden costs which are equally, if not more, significant. Some of the costs are quite tangible (eg one meat processor reported losses of over £7 million due directly to BSE). Others are far more difficult to quantify, such as the loss of quality of life incurred by farmers and their families, or the accelerated decline of mixed farming in environmentally-sensitive upland areas. And what, ultimately, is the cost that can be placed upon the violated welfare of an already over-worked dairy cow succumbing to the confusion and eventual terror of spongiform encephalopathy induced by a wholly aberrant feeding practice? ...

Case Study: farm wastes

The risk of river pollution from agriculture has increased significantly as farming practices have intensified. The production, storage and disposal of increasing amounts of animal waste and silage effluent especially, presents significant risks to the aquatic life of streams and rivers.

The National Rivers Authority spends approximately £5 million/year in relation to farm pollution incidents. MAFF also spend over £2.2 million/year on its general Environmental Protection research programme for reducing farm pollution (excluding pesticides and nutrients) and nuisance.

The third argument against current farming practices as they relate to animals, the one which tends to dominate current discussion of animal welfare, concentrates on incremental changes to the law or farming practice based on welfare concerns. This is illustrated earlier in this chapter in relation to pain and suffering of farm animals. Criticism of intensive husbandry farming, particularly 'factory farming' which involves the use of large-scale production units, has come not just from animal rights activists or groups such as CIWF or the FAWC. Other objections to intensive farming have been based both on theological grounds and a respect for the 'natural order' of things in stressing that is wrong to treat animals as mere objects for our scientific or agricultural endeavours. This approach was considered to be a significant objection in the Ministry of Agriculture, Fisheries and Food's investigation into the ethical implications of emerging technologies in the breeding of farm animals.[96]

There are many instances of official, political and governmental contributions to the issue of improved animal welfare. One of the most authoritative contributions is that from the following parliamentary committee. The first part of their report returns to the issue of pain and suffering which was examined earlier. It then moves on to recommend action for the future:

The First Report of the Agriculture Committee 1980–81

Guiding principles

13. Much has been written about whether and how far animals suffer; indeed discussion has sometimes reached a degree of philosophical subtlety worthy of medieval schoolmen. We are impressed by the arguments set out by Professor Thorpe in Appendix III to the Brambell Committee Report,[97] and we are content to take as our starting point the Committee's conclusions that:

   – although pain, suffering and stress are certainly not identical in animals and men, there are sound reasons for believing that they are substantial in domestic animals and that there is no justification for disregarding them.[98] ...

   – it is morally incumbent upon us to give the benefit of the doubt and to protect it so far as is possible from conditions which may be reasonably supposed to cause it suffering, though this cannot be proved.[99] ...

   – It is justifiable to assume that the sufferings of animals are not identical with those of human beings; it is equally justifiable to assume that they suffer in similar ways; the valid point where the line should be drawn between these two extremes is very difficult to determine and must be a matter of balanced judgement.'[100]

---

96 Ministry of Agriculture, Fisheries and Food, *Report of the Committee to Consider the Ethical Implications of Emerging Technologies in the Breeding of Farm Animals*, 1995, Chapter 2, London: HMSO.

97 The Brambell Committee Report, above n 2, pp 71–79.

98 *Ibid*, para 28.

99 *Ibid*, para 30.

100 *Ibid*, para 27.

14. More recently, Dr Marian Stamp Dawkins has built on this foundation, arguing, convincingly, that although in the last resort subjective judgment is necessary, it can and should be based on as much knowledge as possible of the behaviour, physiology and external appearance of the animals concerned, their social behaviour, ways of expressing emotion and fear, powers of learning and so on. 'The important thing is that the final assessment is based on all the available evidence ... and not just on well-meaning guesswork'.[101]

15. It follows that we reject the implication in some of the evidence that, because the suffering of animals cannot be measured or scientifically proved, it is impossible to take satisfactory account of it. We have sought the bast evidence we could find on those practices which have claimed our attention, but having done so we have not hesitated to form our own judgements. ...

27. We do not accept the contention, frequently stated or implied, that the public demand for cheap food decrees that the cheapest possible methods of production must be adopted. As we have said above, society has a duty to see that undue suffering is not caused to animals, and we cannot accept that duty should be set aside in order that food may be produced more cheaply. Where unacceptable suffering can be eliminate only at extra cost, that cost should be borne or the product forgone. On the other hand, all methods of domestic livestock rearing entail some loss of freedom, and where an imperfect but not unacceptable system can be improved only at disproportionate cost, it may be unreasonable to insist this be done. Once again a balance has to be struck, and this can only be done in the light of subjective judgement; but our emphatic view is that the welfare of animals must come first. ...

Government's role in animal welfare

35. We heard much criticism to the effect that existing animal welfare legislation is inadequate for its purpose, both because its basic general provisions are not definite enough and because too many undesirable practices, even where discouraged by codes of practice, are nevertheless permitted under the law. Much was made of the fact that present legislation is notably less stringent than was recommended by the Brambell Committee. To assess this question we must first consider how far reliance should be placed on legislation at all and how much should be left to example and persuasion.

37. ... We accept that , so long as it is seen to be effective, persuasion is better than compulsion. But there is a danger that if disregard of the law goes unpunished this may bring the law into disrepute.

38. The authorities should ... be ready to prosecute not only cases of wilful or persistent disregard of the law but also cases of neglect of carelessness in which exemplary consequences would have a deterrent effect ...

39. ... in the case of regulation as opposed to reliance on non-mandatory codes, we have no wish to advocate regulation for the sake of regulation. We

101 Stamp-Dawkins, M, *Animal Suffering,* 1980, p 98, London: Chapman & Hall.

recognise the flexibility and adaptability to new developments which is given by codes, and the difficulties of definition which confront any one who tries to draft regulations clear and precise enough to be readily understood and enforced ... We have much sympathy with those who say that some practices should be forbidden even though it cannot be proved they inflict unnecessary pain or discomfort and we think that a shift of emphasis in this direction is desirable. We agree with the Professor of Animal Husbandry at the Royal Veterinary College that 'it is clear there are occasions under modern intensive husbandry conditions where the bounds of compassion are crossed and we can name these things and these are the things that should be regulated against.'

62. We have gained the impression that within the UK Departments the whole weight and thrust of policy has, until recently at least, been directed towards ever greater productivity and profit, and that the welfare of the animals concerned has played at best a minor part in Ministerial and official thinking. Today, whether owing to more enlightened ideas or in response to public pressure, animal welfare is receiving more attention, but we feel that it is still regarded as a tiresome complication engendered by vocal sentimentalists who need to be placated at minimum cost to producers profits. To the extent that this is true, it is time for a change of attitude.

Some of the Committee's specific recommendations for particular species came to fruition with, for example, the prohibition of veal crates and improved conditions for chickens. But the animal welfare lobby still point to the intrinsic cruelty of specific practices which remain as examples of what the Committee had referred to as evidence of the importance of profit over welfare. As an example of this, the Committee recommended a minimum amount of space for adult laying chickens of 750 sq cm per bird and that the UK should not accept anything less than 550 sq cm per bird. As of the end of 1996, the figure used in practice remained at 450 sq cm per bird. As seen above, Sweden (and Switzerland) have decided that certain methods of rearing or using animals in agriculture raise sufficient welfare concerns to see them banned. In contrast the UK is still committed to the use of codes of practice and has not yet gone as far as those countries.

There have been other specific recommendations for change which amount to an incremental improvement in the regulation of farm animal agriculture. In 1984, the government's Farm Animal Welfare Council (FAWC) recommended that there should be changes in the regulation of the production of poultry and red-meat animals. But, as seen with some of the recommendations of the Brambell Committee, the government decided not to act. In addition, the main findings of the MAFF investigation of emerging breeding technologies in 1995 were that: there is a need to clarify the notion of 'adverse effects' under s 15(1) of the Animals (Scientific Procedures) Act 1986 (see Chapter 4 above) which would have some effect as regards farm animals; there should be a prohibition of the use of non-therapeutic surgical artificial insemination in relation to sheep, goats and deer and in relation to embryo transfer in those same species and in pigs; and that most other breeding techniques do not involve significant welfare concerns and only minor regulatory changes were required.

The two alternative methods of farming which are advocated by some of those suggesting change are extensive farming and organic farming. Both these methods involve farm animals being moved outdoors, but organic farmers generally go further by also advocating the use of mixed farming systems incorporating a rotation of arable and animal use. Specifically in relation to animal welfare and health, the proponents of organic farming advocate providing housing and management systems which conform to animals' full range of behavioural needs, feeding which acknowledges the physiological needs of the animals and a switch to more preventative health controls, rather than a reliance on the use of drugs. Some of these ideas are incorporated into the notion of extensive farming, but not all. Measures describes the approach of organic farming in relation to dairy farming:[102]

> In conventional dairy farming there is emphasis on economies of labour, minimising capital investment and motivating staff by annual yields and short-term margins. Organic dairy husbandry moves that emphasis very firmly on to providing optimum conditions for the cow with particular attention to the farming system, to breeding, rearing, housing, feeding and management. The effect may be to increase costs but most significantly, this management approach reduces stress on the cow and maximises health.

In the following extract, Roger Ewbank, former Director of the Universities Federation for Animal Welfare, sets out his vision of the future. This is less dependant on formal legal frameworks than on change from within the farming industry itself.[103]

> Most welfare criticism is directed against three intensive systems:
>
> 1. traditional (single animal) crate-rearing of veal calves;
> 2. stalling and/or tethering of pregnant sows;
> 3. confinement of laying birds in battery gages.
>
> Legislative action (The Welfare of Calves Regulations (SI 1987/2021)) has been taken by the UK government, which should in effect stop the crate-rearing of calves. It is interesting to speculate that this change in the law could only really be brought about because the farming industry itself had developed and largely changed to the alternative, yarded veal-rearing system.
>
> It is likely that, sooner or later, legislation will be introduced to phase out stalling and/or tethering of pregnant sows. Many pig farmers realise this and, if they are replacing old buildings and worn out equipment, they are tending to put in the well tried 'small-group-of-sows-in-a-straw-yard' systems or the

102 Measures, M, 'Organic Dairy Farming' in UFAW, *Extensive and Organic Livestock Systems*, p 46, Potters Bar, Hertfordshire: Universities Federation for Animal Welfare.

103 Ewbank, above n 16, pp 10–11. By permission of the Universities Fund for Animal Welfare.

newly developed 'large-group-of-sows-on-automatic-feed-dispenser' systems. Both these replacements are more costly to install/run and demand a higher level of stockmanship than stall/tethers, but they have considerable welfare benefits for the animals. One difficulty may be that strains of pigs which are selected because they thrive under confinement systems, may not be behaviourally suited to social life in yards. An appropriate breeding programme should solve this.

The problem of battery cages is less easily resolved. It could be both a welfare and an economic disaster to force the present population of battery birds out into the relatively untried alternative systems. Free range and intermediate systems (percheries, aviaries, straw yards, deep litter, etc) do give the birds considerably more freedom but they are more difficult to run than battery units: they demand a higher level of stockmanship, the outdoor system seems to have a higher level of disease, and the eggs cost more to produce. There is a real need for further research and development work on the intermediate and free range systems, in the hope that problems will be solved and that it will finally be possible to phase out battery cages.

It has been suggested that the regular inspection and possibly the annual licensing of intensive farm units would be one way of improving welfare. This may be so – the manpower and administrative costs could be high but the inspection and licensing might help to allay or remove some of the worst and sometimes unfounded fears of the general public.

Real progress mainly comes through changes in the attitude of those involved in the use of animals. Farmers, stockmen, veterinary surgeons, agriculturalists, etc. are not separate from the rest of the community; they are members of society and influenced by what society wants. If society wants its animals to be treated in a particular way then sooner or later it will happen. And it will largely come about because the animal users themselves will eventually want it to happen, and will acquire the knowledge and skills needed to make a change.

Animal welfare is of increasing relevance to the farming industry ... It is vital both for the health and well-being of the animals involved and for the financial future of the farming industry that an increasing and critical interest should be taken in that mixture of economic, scientific, ethical, aesthetic and practical concepts which make up the complex subject of animal welfare, and that action should be taken on the new knowledge and ideas thus gained.

In 1996, Compassion in World Farming submitted a suggestion to the Intergovernmental Conference on farming arguing for a change to the Treaty of Rome to classify animals as 'sentient animals' in order for their welfare to be properly considered in the formulation of policy and legislation. This would add the requirement to consider animal welfare as a fundamental *moral* consideration in addition to usual human-centred *economic* considerations, and would be a big step forward for the incremental approach:[104]

104 CIWF, *Proposal for Animals to be given a new status in the Treaty of Rome as 'Sentient Beings'*, January 1996, Petersfield, Hampshire: Compassion in World Farming. By permission of Compassion in World Farming.

The status of animals in the Treaty of Rome

In 1991 a massive petition was presented to the European Parliament's President, Enrique Baron Crespo. Filling 36 large boxes, a van was needed to ferry it to Strasbourg. Signed by over one million people from all the Community's Member States, Compassion in World Farming's petition was the largest ever presented to the Parliament.

And the object of all this concern? Animals. In particular their status in the Treaty of Rome, which is the cornerstone of EC law.

The Treaty classifies animals as goods or 'agricultural products'.[105] The petition calls for them to be given a new status in the Treaty as 'sentient animals'.[106] Acknowledging animals as sentient would recognise the fact that they are living creatures capable of feeling pain and fear, but able also, if we let them, to enjoy a state of well-being.

In January 1994, the European Parliament endorsed the petition's requests and called on the Community to make provision after Union for further amendment of the Treaties to enable animals to be treated as sentient beings.[107]

The next, vital step is to secure the inclusion of a new status for animals in the 1996 round of Treaty changes. (Changes to the Treaty will be decided towards the end of 1996 – or in 1997 – at the Inter-governmental Conference.) Already on 20 April 1995, the European Parliament's Environment Committee has called for animals to be included in the 1996 Treaty amendments.

Moreover, in 1995 the European Parliament called for the Treaty to be strengthened to make concern for animal welfare one of the fundamental principles of the European Union.

Why animals should be given a new status

In essence, the Treaty views animals as goods or products. It makes little attempt to distinguish them from inanimate objects. This is illustrated by the classification of farm animals as agricultural products in Annex II to the Treaty.

This Annex contains a detailed list of agricultural products which includes 'live animals' alongside vegetables, cereals, meat and 'guts, bladders and stomachs of animals' – as if the living creature were no different from the dead one.

The low legal status accorded to animals by the Treaty means that their welfare has often been neglected in Directives. For example, the 1991 Calves Directive legitimises the continued use of the narrow veal crate in the European Union (EU). Moreover, the Treaty's classification of animals as goods has led directly to the misery of long distance transport.

---

[105]Treaty establishing The European Community, Rome, 25 March 1957. In particular, see Annex II to the Treaty.

[106]Petition presented to the European Parliament in March 1991. The petition bears 1,034,526 signatures of nationals from all the EU Member States.

[107]On 20 December 1993, the European Parliament's Committee on the Environment, Public Health and Consumer Protection adopted a report which agreed with the requests included in the petition by Compassion in World Farming. The Environment Committee's Report was adopted by the European Parliament in the January 1994 part-session pursuant to r 52 of the Rules of Procedure.

A new treaty status will help give animal protection a higher profile in EU legislation and policy-making. And such a higher profile is urgently needed.

In particular, a new status for animals in the Treaty as sentient beings could lead to an end to the cruel live export trade and to inhumane rearing systems such as the veal crate, the battery cage and sow stalls and tethers.

Just as the European Community has taken on board a variety of issues of human rights and social justice, so now it is time for the Community to treat our animal population in a manner appropriate to our civilisation.

The paper went on to outline proposals to: acknowledge that animals are sentient beings and require that they be treated accordingly in EC legislation, including a respect for the welfare of animals among the fundamental activities of the EC set out in Article 3; and to add 'the welfare of farm animals' to Article 39.2 as one of the factors to be taken into account in working out the common agricultural policy. These suggestions are not just the preserve of animal rights groups:[108]

In March 1991, during the Inter-governmental Conferences on Economic and Political Union, the German government proposed that the protection of farm and laboratory animals should be expressly included among the objectives of the Treaty of Rome. At the same time, a Motion for the Resolution was tabled in the European parliament. Broader in its scope, this suggested the inclusion of two references to animal protection in the Treaty. The first should list as one of its objectives of Community environment policy under Article 130R, and the second, under Article 39.2, as one of the factors to be taken into account during implementation of the objectives of the common agricultural policy.

The National Farmers' Union has a different view on the attempt to include animals in the Treaty of Rome:[109]

One of the most recent policy initiatives of the welfare lobby has been to seek a change in the definition of animals under the Treaty of Rome from agricultural product to sentient beings, a curious initiative which seems to ignore the mechanisms of government. The Treaty of Rome exists in order to lay out the principles and powers which enable the European Union to function. It was never intended to be a detailed charter for the welfare of animals or indeed anything else and it is frankly misleading to suggest that it could act as such. Pigs are referred to as agricultural product because they are kept in order to produce pigmeat which is clearly an agricultural product, hence its relevance to the principles of the Common Agricultural policy as writ in the Treaty of Rome.

The Treaty lays out the powers under which the European Commission can propose legislation governing technical standards and this includes welfare. The European Commission has demonstrated its ability and willingness to

---

108 Eurogroup for Animal Welfare, *Analysis of Major Areas of Concern for Animal Welfare in Europe*, 1994, p 128, Brussels: EAW.

109 From a circular sent to the Pig Chairman's Group of the NFU, 2 October 1996.

propose legislation on welfare issues in a number of areas, including the welfare of pigs on farm and during transport. It is difficult to see what defining pigs as 'sentient beings' would achieve when the Treaty of Rome, as it refers to the Common Agricultural Policy, is actually concerned with pigmeat.

John Webster is unconvinced by the approach of the European legislators to animal welfare legislation and has other suggestions for the way forward:[110]

I suggest that the whole European approach to legislation for quality of life in farm animals is on the wrong track. Instead of agonising at interminable length over trivial pieces of restrictive legislation almost totally confined to space requirements, it would be more constrictive to consider legislating for incentives to improve welfare. Incentives imply cost, which means cost to the consumer. However, when 42% of European farm incomes are currently in the form of subsidy, governments cannot pretend that they cannot legislate for financial incentive to achieve the common good. If they control 42% of the income, they can do anything they like!

At the moment agricultural subsidies, for example, those which encourage farmers not to grow food, are seen by the consumer as achieving only the good of the farming community. There has, as yet, been no attempt to use subsidy as a direct incentive to improved welfare. If politicians were to devise subsidies designed to encourage high welfare systems, (and did not define the rules too precisely), these subsidies would be more popular with all parties, welfare-minded consumers, farmers who wish to farm with pride and the animals themselves. The political party which enforced such legislation might also be rewarded with a few more votes.

It is generally recognised that new biology involving the physiological and genetic manipulation of farm animals will require new legislation to protect man, the environment and, not least, the animals themselves. The welfare implications of new biology must be defined not by the method used to manipulate the animal but by its consequences. Unacceptable 'tinkering' has been defined by the Farm Animal Welfare Council as 'the manipulation of body size, shape or reproductive capacity by breeding, nutrition, hormone therapy or gene insertion in such a way as to reduce mobility, increase the risk of pain, injury, metabolic disease, skeletal or obstetric problems, perinatal mortality or psychological distress'.

It is neither ethical nor practical to legislate to stifle research *a priori* on the grounds that something might just go wrong. FAWC (1987) prefaces its definition of unacceptable tinkering with the words. 'We accept that scientific investigation aims to be impartial and without prejudice so that it is impossible to pronounce *a priori* how any particular piece of new knowledge will affect farm animals'. During the period of scientific investigation of any application of new biology to animal production the animals are protected by the Animals (Scientific Procedures) Act 1986 which applies a cost:benefit analysis to all procedures weighing the cost to the animal in terms of suffering, however slight, against the likely benefit to society (or other animals). I can think of no

---

110 Webster, J, *Animal Welfare: A Cool Eye Towards Eden,* 1994, pp 261–63, Oxford: Blackwell Science Ltd. By permission of Blackwell Science Ltd.

ethical reason why farm animal should not receive the same protection as laboratory animals. If they did, procedures which require a Home Office licence while conducted to advance knowledge would need to be submitted to a cost:benefit analysis at least as rigorous before being pronounced acceptable for commercial application.

A valid objection to the imposition of controls on the application of new science is that it holds up progress. This argument is only valid, of course, if the progress can be shown to be humane ... most welfare problems arising from the application of new biotechnology can be resolved (one way or the other) within two generations, or the length of time required for experimentation under the 1986 Act. Some complex, low incidence conditions like mastitis and lameness in cattle treated with BST, cannot be resolved without allowing the procedure to expand onto a commercial scale. I suggest, therefore, that all new technologies to manipulate animal production and reproduction developed initially under a Home Office licence should be subject to a two-stage review process. If after two or three generations the procedure appeared not to 'reduce mobility, increase the risk of pain, injury, metabolic disease, skeletal or obstetric problems, perinatal mortality or psychological distress', then it should be given a provisional licence for commercial exploitation, subject to properly designed monitoring procedure for untoward effects in practice (such as an increase in the incidence of mastitis) and reviewed after, say, five years, the costs to be met by those promoting the procedure.

In Europe, Sweden and Switzerland have extended the role of the State in terms of agriculture beyond that seen in other countries by including strict control of husbandry practice and equipment used around animals, both of which require approval.[111] They have introduced a similar licensing system to those seen in relation to the Animal (Scientific Procedures) Act 1986 in the UK. This might present a realistic alternative to the broadly advisory stance taken up in the EU, except where specific legislation has been instituted. Such a system might have resource implications but would introduce the possibility of local peer review of animal husbandry systems and practice, and might instill more public confidence that animals were being treated as well as possible.

An argument to change the composition of animal welfare legislation in order to give it teeth has been suggested by Steven Wise. Although he is not an advocate of the 'strong animal rights' position (discussed in Chapter 2), Wise suggests that the main object of anti-cruelty legislation is to protect people from the damage that might be done to them from witnessing or inflicting cruel behaviour, rather than granting rights to the animals concerned. Wise suggests that modern statutory anti-cruelty definitions are insufficient:[112]

---

111 For Sweden, see ss 5 and 7 of the Animal Protection Ordinance 1988, above p 205.

112 Wise, SM, 'A Day in Court – Corporations, towns, estates and ships can have one; farm animals cannot', *The Animals Agenda*, May 1986, pp 14–15 and 36.

These statutes are vague and define cruel acts as those that cause 'unnecessary' suffering or 'unjustifiable' pain and make no differentiation among the needs of different species. They contain nothing that approaches even the often-maligned standards promulgated for the care of laboratory animals. Farm animals sometimes even lose the thin protections of anti cruelty laws when they are excluded from the statutory definition of 'animal', or when factory farming practices are exempted from the scope of the statutes.

The defects in the use of anti-cruelty laws to regulate human conduct towards farm animals become more apparent when one considers their utter lack of similarity to laws that regulate the fundamental needs of just one species, *homo sapiens.* For instance, State sanitary codes do not merely require a landlord to avoid subjecting his tenants to 'unnecessary' suffering or 'unjustifiable' pain, but spell out a landlord's responsibilities in detail and in a way that takes human need into account ...

While farm animals are not rightsholders, they are sentient beings and should not be abandoned to utter helplessness before our courts, where they are even less capable of defending their interests than is the youngest human infant or the most profoundly retarded human adult. Clearly, normal human beings must be given the capacity to speak for farm animals or mankind will remain forever deaf to their plight. But, as children had no legal voice under Roman law, and as slaves had no legal voice in the days of Dred Scott, so farm animals have no voice today ...

Despite the rigors of the factory farm, the animals who exist there live their lives as best they can in accord with their ancient rhythms and needs, created eons before the dawn of factory farming. Meanwhile, their human advocates have begun legal challenges that will lead towards new interpretations of old law, and to new law that will take these needs into consideration and that will inform consumers of the conditions under which farm animals are raised. Both legal and economic pressure must be brought to bear if the institution of factory farming is to be reformed.

Legislation in the UK, indeed in most of the developed countries, reflects competing interests in the animal welfare debate by accepting a compromise between the overriding public demand for cheap animal products and demands for humane treatment. There is a significant difference between the aims of, for example, the Protection of Animals Act 1911 and its prohibition of direct cruelty, which remains as disturbing to most people today as it did in 1911, and the new breed of legislation of recent times which tries to protect the 'basic freedoms' of animals as put forward by the FAWC. These newly recognised welfare requirements of animals involves scientists and farm animal experts in trying to discover what a chicken or a pig actually wants. This is a far more difficult task than recognising the wrong of beating or overworking a horse on the streets of pre-First World War London. We also have the problem of the interests of farmers, transporters and the European Community economic 'level playing field' to consider. It is no wonder, then, that we have apparently 'trivial discussions'[113] about the acceptable size of close-confinement cages or pens which might have negligible effects on the actual life experience of the animals concerned. The law relating to farm animals represents a compromise and, as the evidence of the history of recent change shows, constantly finds itself needing to respond to scientific evidence and public welfare concerns. Whether it responds quickly enough or goes far enough is the most significant question asked of the law relating to farm animals.

113 See extract from Webster, above n 110.

FURTHER READING

Fox, MW, *Farm Animals*, 1984, Maryland; University Park Press. A thorough overview of the welfare problems created by intensive farming and the alternatives.

Ministry of Agriculture, Fisheries and Food, *Summary of the Law Relating to Farm Animal Welfare*, 1996, London: MAFF. (Can be obtained from MAFF publications, London SE99 7TP.) Provides comprehensive detail of all the UK provisions relating to farm animal welfare. MAFF publications (address above) publish a catalogue of their current publications which would be invaluable for anyone wishing to find out about current statutory or other regulations regarding farm animals.

Rollin, B, *Farm Animal Welfare*, 1995, Iowa: Iowa State University Press. Another, more contemporary account of the suffering of farm animals, with particular reference to the US.

Universities Federation for Animal Welfare, *Management and Welfare of Farm Animals*, 1997, Potters Bar, Hertfordshire: UFAW. A comprehensive account of the issues facing different farm animal species.

CHAPTER SIX

DOMESTIC ANIMALS

INTRODUCTION

This chapter will examine the law in relation to domestic and captive animals and the measures in place to protect them from cruelty. Domestic and captive animals have a high degree of protection in the UK. However, cases of cruelty to animals are reported each year. The chapter will consider the measures that have been passed in the UK to protect these animals, assessing whether they are adequate and what, if any, reforms are needed.

HISTORICAL DEVELOPMENT

Animals have been domesticated for centuries. Dogs were first tamed during the Stone Age, and they have a long history of protection.[1] This protection, however, did not arise from any feelings of compassion, but generally as a consequence of animals' status as property. Domestic animals, like other personal and moveable chattels, are the subjects of absolute property. The owner can maintain an action for the detention or conversion, or for trespass to goods in respect of them, and retain his property in them if they are stray or lost.[2]

In the 19th century, organisations such as the Society for the Prevention of Cruelty to Animals (1823) (which later became the RSPCA) and the Battersea Dogs home (1860) were set up. In 1891 the National Canine Defence League was founded. The Cat Protection League was set up later, in 1927. These societies aimed to prevent cruelty to animals and the organisers were often social reformers as well as animal welfare campaigners. The first Protection of Animals Act was passed in 1822, amended in 1835 and 1849 (see Chapter 2). The Protection of Animals Act 1911 amalgamated the 1849 Act with the Wild Animals in Captivity Protection Act 1900.[3]

---

1 Johnson, W, *The Rose Tinted Menagerie*, 1990, London: Harcourt Brace.
2 *Putter v Roster* (1682) 2 Mod Rep 318.
3 See Brown, A, *Who Cares for Animals? 150 years of the RSPCA*, 1974, Chapter 1, London: Heinemann.

WHAT IS A DOMESTIC ANIMAL?

The first question to determine is what is a domestic animal? In law, animals are divided into domestic and captive animals and, on the other hand, wild animals. This is an important distinction, as there are different rights and responsibility in relation to the different categories of animal. While wild animals now have a degree of protection under the Wildlife and Countryside Act 1981 and the Wild Mammals Protection Act 1996, the distinction may still be important in cases of liability for damage. This distinction was examined in the case of *McQuaker v Goddard*,[4] where a camel had bitten a visitor at a zoo. The question the court considered was whether a camel was a wild or domestic animal. If the camel was a wild animal then the owner would not be liable. If the camel was a domestic animal then the owner would be liable. The judge decided that a camel was a domestic animal.

McQuaker v Goddard [1940] 1 All ER 471

Scott LJ: ... On the question of law, it is important to bear in mind that, in the old common law of England, a rule was laid down long ago that domestic animals are regarded in quite a different light from wild animals. Wild animals are assumed to be dangerous to human beings because they have not been domesticated. The law does not assume domestic animals to be dangerous. That is the reason why, in English law, a keeper of a wild animal must keep it in at his peril. If he lets it out and it causes damage to any human being personally, or to the property of another, the keeper or owner of the animal, as the case may be, is liable in damages for the injury so caused.

On the other hand, in the case of domestic animals, the presumption of law is the other way. The plaintiff has to prove that the defendant was aware of the particular propensity of the animal to hurt human beings which was evinced in the case where, *ex hypothesi*, the plaintiff suffered. Unless the plaintiff proves that knowledge, at common law there is no liability upon the defendant. That liability has, in the case of dogs worrying sheep and in the case of certain other animals, been altered by legislation in Parliament. Apart from those exceptional statutory cases, however, there is no liability without proof of knowledge on the part of the defendant, or, as it is called in law, *scienter*.

In the present case, it was argued strongly on behalf of the appellant that the camel stands in a different category from that of ordinary English domestic animals, because it has not become a domestic animal in England. In my view, that argument is fallacious. If an animal does not exist in a wild state in any part of the world, it has ceased altogether to be a wild animal, whether it is in England or in any other country. It is a domestic animal, and an animal which has become trained to the uses of man, and, *ex hypothesi*, become accustomed to association with man. Therefore, in my opinion, that argument falls to the ground altogether. With regard to that argument, it is also well to remember that it is the function of the judge, and not of the jury, to decide whether an

---

4   [1940] 1 All ER 471.

animal belongs to the class of domestic animals or to the class of wild animals. I need say no more for the moment on this head. ... It is enough, for the purposes of my judgement, to say that in this case the judge decided – and, in my view, rightly decided – that the camel must be regarded as a domestic animal.

This distinction was enshrined in statute under s 15 of the Protection of Animals Act 1911:

a) the expression 'animal' means any domestic or captive animal;

b) the expression 'domestic animal' means any horse, ass, mule, bull, sheep, pig, goat, dog, cat, or fowl, or any other animal of whatsoever kind or species, and whether a quadruped or not which is tame or which has been or is being sufficiently tamed to serve some purpose for the use of man;

c) the expression 'captive animal' means any animal (not being a domestic animal) of whatsoever kind or species, and whether a quadruped or not, including any bird, fish, or reptile, which is in captivity, or confinement, or which is aimed, pinioned, or subjected to any appliance or contrivance for the purpose;

d) of hindering or preventing its escape from captivity or confinement.

COMMON LAW CONTROL AND PROTECTION OF DOMESTIC ANIMALS

Under common law there are obligations placed on the ownership of animals. These will be dealt with briefly here but for more information please refer to *Halsbury's Statutes*, vol 2: Animals.

The contract of agistment concerns a contract to take animals onto land for some reward, with an implied term that they will be returned to the owner. It is in the nature of a bailment and therefore confers no right to any interest in the land and the contract does not need to be in writing. The agister has to take reasonable and proper care of the animals and is liable for any injury caused by negligence or the failure to take proper care unless the owner was aware of the dangerous state of the field in which the animal is kept. In the absence of any special agreement, the agister has no lien on the animals, however, the agister will have sufficient possessory property in them so that they can sue in trespass or conversion.

Domestic animals are property within the definition of the Criminal Damages Act 1971 (as are wild animals or their carcasses, but only if they have been reduced into possession which has not been lost or abandoned or are in the course of being reduced into possession). If someone without lawful excuse destroys or damages another animal belonging to someone else and they do so intentionally or recklessly, or they threaten to do so, then it will be an offence. If harm is caused to their own animal then it will be an offence of cruelty under the Protection of Animals Act 1911. The owner can be compensated for any loss or damage to the animal. The shooting of a tame or domestic animal renders the shooter liable to a civil action for its value unless the shooter can show they had no other means of protecting their property. If they do not have this justification then they may be charged under the Protection of Animals Act 1911 (s 1) with an offence of cruelty.

Sale of goods

Domestic animals are goods and chattels and the ordinary law of the sale of goods applies to them (Sale of Goods Act 1979). However, there is no implied guarantee of quality, although there is an implied condition that the seller has a right to sell and if the seller holds out the animal as being fit for a particular purpose, there is an implied term that the animal will be reasonably fit for that purpose. Thus, any buyer should protect themselves through an express term in the contract, Supply of Goods and Services Act 1982. (See also the Sales Description Act 1968/72.)

Theft

Under the common law, domestic or mate animals, or those fit for food, their young and eggs, can be the subject of larceny. Dogs, cats and animals of base exceptions are not. However, under statute all animals which have a value and are the property of any person can be the subject of theft (ss 1–6 of the Theft Act 1968). Domestic animals are to be regarded as belonging to any person who has possession or control over them or having any proprietary right or interest over them, other than an equitable interest arising from an agreement to transfer or to grant an interest (s 5(1) of the Theft Act 1968).

Liability for negligence

In relation to the liability of owners for the action of animals, the owner of a domestic animal may be liable on the grounds of negligence to third parties, eg in the case of a runaway horse. If the animal is of a dangerous species, then the keeper is strictly liable for any harm (s 1 of the Animals Act 1971). The liability of the owner for the damage is set out in s 2:

(1) Where any damage is caused by an animal which belongs to a dangerous species, any person who is a keeper of the animal is liable for the damage, except as otherwise provided by this Act.

(2) Where damage is caused by an animal which does not belong to a dangerous species, a keeper of the animal is liable for the damage, except as otherwise provided by this Act, if:

a) the damage is of a kind which the animal, unless restrained, was likely to cause or which, if caused by the animal, was likely to be severe; and

b) the likelihood of the damage or of its being severe was due to characteristics of the animal which are not normally found in animals of the same species or are not normally so found except at particular times or in particular circumstances; and

c) those characteristics were known to that keeper or were at any time known to a person who at that time had charge of the animal as that keeper's servant or, where that keeper is the head of a household, were known to another keeper of the animal who is a member of that household and under the age of 16.

The question of when an animal became dangerous under s 2 was examined in the following case:

Jaundrill v Gillett **(1996)** *The Times,* **30 January (CA: Russell LJ and Singer J)**

The plaintiff was driving on a highway at night when he saw a number of horses galloping towards his car. They had escaped from a field where they were kept by the defendant and it was common ground that a malicious intruder had opened the gate and driven them out. The plaintiff collided with the horses and brought an action for damages against the defendant on the basis of his liability under the 1971 Act (s 2(2)(b)). The plaintiff relied on the evidence of a veterinary surgeon that a group of horses when moved from their accustomed environment tended to behave abnormally and that horses removed from their field on to a road with other horses in the dark would tend to panic and gallop aimlessly in any direction. The recorder found that the plaintiff satisfied s 2(2)(b) and made an award of damages. On the defendant's appeal, held, there had to be a causal link between the animal's characteristics under s 2(2)(b) and the damage. The court had grave reservations whether a horse which galloped on a highway and panicked was displaying a characteristic under s 2. The real and effective cause of the accident was the release of the animals on to the highway, as it was their presence there which was the cause of the damage sustained. Accordingly, the appeal was allowed.

The owner will not be liable for the damage unless there was fault or the voluntary assumption of risk on behalf of the third party (s 5). If the person was trespassing, then the offence is not one of strict liability (s 5(3)), so long as the animal was not kept at the premises for the protection of any person or property unless it was reasonable in those circumstances to do so (s 11 Animals Act 1971).

Section 5. Exceptions from liability under ss 2–4

(1) A person is not liable under ss 2–4 of this Act for any damage which is due wholly to the fault of the person suffering it.

(2) A person is not liable under s 2 of this Act for any damage suffered by a person who has voluntarily accepted the risk thereof.

(3) A person is not liable under s 2 of this Act for any damage caused by an animal kept on any premises or structure to a person trespassing there, if it is proved either:

(a) that the animal was not kept there for the protection of persons or property; or

(b) (if the animal was kept there for the protection of persons or property) that keeping it there for that purpose was not unreasonable.

(4) A person is not liable under s 3 of this Act if the livestock was killed or injured on land on to which it had strayed and either the dog belonged to the occupier or its presence on the land was authorised by the occupier.

(5) A person is not liable under s 4 of this Act where the livestock strayed from a highway and its presence there was a lawful use of the highway.

(6) In determining whether any liability for damage under s 4 of this Act is excluded by subsection (1) of this section the damage shall not be treated as due to the fault of the person suffering it by reason only that he could have prevented it by fencing; but a person is not liable under that section where it is proved that the straying of the livestock on to the land would not have occurred but for a breach by any other person, being a person having an interest in the land, of a duty to fence.

Section 8 of the Act lays down the extent to which a person has a duty to take care to prevent damage from animals straying on to the highway:

(1) So much of the rules of the common law relating to liability for negligence as excludes or restricts the duty which a person might owe to others to take such care as is reasonable to see that damage is not caused by animals straying on to a highway is hereby abolished.

(2) Where damage is caused by animals straying from unfenced land to a highway a person who placed them on the land shall not be regarded as having committed a breach of the duty to take care by reason only of placing them there if:

(a) the land is common land, or is land situated in an area where fencing is not customary, or is a town or village green; and

(b) he had a right to place the animals on that land.

Negligence may also be claimed against veterinary surgeons and practitioners.[5]

STATUTORY PROTECTION OF DOMESTIC ANIMALS FROM CRUELTY

The more general protection of animals from cruelty more generally is found in the Prevention of Cruelty to Animals Act 1911–64. (See Chapter 2.)

Under the Protection of Animals (Amendment) Act 1954 owners can be disqualified from owning an animal if they are convicted of a case of cruelty.

---

5   Foster, C, 'The Price of Animal Suffering' (1993) 143 *New Law Journal*, No 6585, pp 123–24.

The case of *RSPCA v Isaacs*[6] considered the question of what degree of control would mean that the disqualified owner had retaken custody of the animal, in this case, a dog.

RSPCA v Isaacs [1994] Crim LR 516; The Times, 8 March 1994

Ralph Gibson LJ: Parliament did not enact that a person disqualified, after conviction for an offence of cruelty, should be prohibited from having any contact with the dog or control of a dog. I agree that in many circumstances proof of control of a dog will be evidence for which custody of it will be proved. In this case, the control was clearly nothing more: Mr Miller had the control of the dog under the immediate supervision of the owner and in circumstances in which control could be immediately and effectively resumed by the owner.

ANIMAL BOARDING AND BREEDING ESTABLISHMENTS

Animal boarding and breeding establishments are regulated under the Animal Boarding Establishments Act 1963 through a licensing system (s 1(1)). The licences are granted by local authorities under s 5(1). A licence will not be granted if a person has previously been disqualified from running such an establishment, or from keeping any animal (s 1(2)). The licence is granted at the discretion of the local authority, which may take into account the suitability of the accommodation and whether the animals are well fed, exercised and protected from disease and fire (s 1(3)). These requirements may be provided for in licence conditions. A fee is payable for the licence and a register has to be kept of owners' names and addresses and the dates of the arrival and departure of animals. There is the right of appeal (s 4).

An offence is committed if a person runs such an establishment with no licence or fails to comply with the licence conditions (s 1(8)). The premises can be inspected by local authority officers or veterinary surgeons or practitioners, and it is an offence to wilfully obstruct such persons. There are similar provisions in relation to the breeding of dogs.

THE REGULATION OF PET SHOPS

Pet shops are regulated under the Pet Animals Act 1951. They are subject to licensing controls by the local authority (s 1). Certain requirements have to be met by an owner under s 1(3).

(3) In determining whether to grant a licence for the keeping of a pet shop by any person at any premises, a local authority shall in particular (but

---

6   [1994] Crim LR 516; The Times, 8 March 1994.

without prejudice to their discretion to withhold a licence on other grounds) have regard to the need for securing:

(a) that animals will at all times be kept in accommodation suitable as respects size, temperature, lighting, ventilation and cleanliness;

(b) that animals will be adequately supplied with suitable food and drink and (so far as necessary) visited at suitable intervals;

(c) that animals, being mammals, will not be sold at too early an age;

(d) that all reasonable precautions will be taken to prevent the spread among animals of infectious diseases;

(e) that appropriate steps will be taken in case of fire or other emergency; and shall specify such conditions in the licence, if granted by them, as appear to the local authority necessary or expedient in the particular case for securing all or any of the objects specified in paragraphs (a)–(e) of this subsection.

Under s 2, pets cannot be sold in the street, including on barrows and markets, and under s 3, pets are not to be sold to children under 12 years of age. Pet shops have to be inspected by the local authority. The requirements for the inspection are set down under s 4:

(1) A local authority may authorise in writing any of its officers or any veterinary surgeon or veterinary practitioner to inspect (subject to compliance with such precautions as the authority may specify to prevent the spread among animals of infectious diseases) any premises in their area as respects which a licence granted in accordance with the provisions of this Act is for the time being in force, and any person authorised under this section may, on producing his authority if so required, enter any such premises at all reasonable times and inspect them and any animals found thereon or any thing therein, for the purpose of ascertaining whether an offence has been or is being committed against this Act.

(2) Any person who wilfully obstructs or delays any person in the exercise of his powers of entry or inspection under this section shall be guilty of an offence. There is the right of appeal to the court.

RIDING ESTABLISHMENTS

Riding establishments are licensed under the Riding Establishments Act 1964 by the local authorities, which can impose conditions on the licence (s 1). The local authority cannot grant a licence unless it has been inspected by a veterinary surgeon/practitioner within the past 12 months (s 1(3)). The local authority, in the exercise of its discretion, may take into account the suitability of the applicant/manager, the accommodation and pasture, adequacy of the provisions for the horses' health, welfare and exercise, precautions against fire and disease and the suitability of the horses as regards the reasons for which they are kept. There is the right to an appeal (s 1(5)). Section 1(4) sets down the conditions that have to be fulfilled for a licence to be granted:

(a) whether that person appears to them to be suitable and qualified, either by experience in the management of horses or by being the holder of an approved certificate or by employing in the management of the riding establishment a person so qualified, to be the holder of such a licence; and

(b) the need for securing:

(i) that paramount consideration will be given to the condition of horses and that they will be maintained in good health, and in all respects physically fit and that, in the case of a horse kept for the purpose of its being let out on hire for riding or a horse kept for the purpose of its being used in providing instruction in riding, the horse will be suitable for the purpose for which it is kept;

(ii) that the feet of all animals are properly trimmed and that, if shod, their shoes are properly fitted and in good condition;

(iii) that there will be available at all times, accommodation for horses suitable as respects construction, size, number of occupants, lighting, ventilation, drainage and cleanliness and that these requirements be complied with not only in the case of new buildings but also in the case of buildings converted for use as stabling;

(iv) that in the case of horses maintained at grass there will be available for them at all times during which they are so maintained adequate pasture and shelter and water and that supplementary feeds will be provided as and when required;

(v) that horses will be adequately supplied with suitable food, drink and (except in the case of horses maintained at grass, so long as they are so maintained) bedding material, and will be adequately exercised, groomed and rested and visited at suitable intervals;

(vi) that all reasonable precautions will be taken to prevent and control the spread among horses of infectious or contagious diseases and that veterinary first aid equipment and medicines shall be provided and maintained in the premises;

(vii) that appropriate steps will be taken for the protection and extrication of horses in case of fire and, in particular, that the name, address and telephone number of the licence holder or some other responsible person will be kept displayed in a prominent position on the outside of the premises and that instructions as to action to be taken in the event of fire, with particular regard to the extrication of horses, will be kept displayed in a prominent position on the outside of the premises;

(viii) that adequate accommodation will be provided for forage, bedding, stable equipment and saddlery;

and shall specify such conditions in the licence, if granted by them, as appear to the local authority necessary or expedient in the particular case for securing all the objects specified in sub-paragraphs (i)–(viii) of paragraph (b) of this subsection.

Sections 40–42 of the Animal Health Act 1981, restricts the export of ponies and horses (see also the Export of Horses Protection Order (SI 1969/1784)). The Docking and Nicking of Horses Act 1949 prevents the docking and nicking of horses unless a veterinary surgeon states that it is necessary for the health of the horse to prevent disease, or to prevent injury to the tail.

OTHER MEASURES

While the measures set out below are primarily for the protection of domestic or captive animals, in certain situations the controls and protection will also apply to wild animals.

Abandonment of Animals Act 1960

Under this Act, it is an offence of cruelty to abandon any animal without reasonable excuse in circumstances likely to cause it unnecessary suffering. In *Hunt v Duckering*[7] the meaning of abandonment was stated to imply:

> [Abandonment is] something more than merely 'left or being unattended'. Emphasis should be placed rather upon the character of the 'act of abandonment'. It was not merely a question of measuring time, passed or potential, as distinct from considering the circumstances at the time when the animal was 'left unattended'. There must be a physical leaving unattended of the animal in circumstances where suffering was likely and where there was sufficient evidence to prove that the defendant had relinquished, wholly disregarded or given up his duty to care for the animal. Where he had either made, or attempted to make, arrangements for the animal's welfare during the time that he was unable to attend to them himself, he could not be said to have 'abandoned' the dog.

Protection of Animals (Anaesthetics) Act 1954/64

This Act makes it illegal to carry out an operation on an animal's sensitive tissue unless it has been given enough anaesthetic to prevent it feeling pain.

Section 8 of the Protection of Animals Act 1911

This makes it illegal to:

(a) ... sell, or offer or expose for sale, or give away, or cause or procure any person to sell or offer or expose for sale or give away, or knowingly be a party to the sale or offering or exposing for sale or giving away of any

---

7   QBD [1993] Crim LR 678.

grain or seed which has been rendered poisonous except for *bona fide* use in agriculture; or

(b) ... knowingly put or place, or cause or procure any person to put or place, or knowingly be a party to the putting or placing, in or upon any land or building any poison, or any fluid or edible matter (not being sown seed or grain) which has been rendered poisonous, such person shall, upon summary conviction, be liable to a fine ...

[Provided that, in any proceedings under paragraph (b) of this section, it shall be a defence that the poison was placed by the accused for the purpose of destroying insects and other invertebrates, rats, mice, or other small ground vermin, where such is found to be necessary in the interests of public health, agriculture, or the preservation of other animals, domestic or wild, or for the purpose of manuring the land, and that he took all reasonable precautions to prevent injury thereby to dogs, cats, fowls, or other domestic animals and wild birds.]

See also the Animals (Cruel Poisons) Act 1962, which prohibits the use of certain poisons.

DOGS

General controls and protection of dogs

Dogs have been the subjects of particular attention and controversy in recent times. They are accorded a wide range of legal protection and control.

Cruelty

Owners of dogs can be disqualified from owning a dog if they are convicted of cruelty under the Protection of Animals Act 1911 or under the Badgers Act 1992 if a dog is used in the commission of an offence. Under s 9 of the Protection of Animals Act 1911 the use of dogs for purposes of draught is prohibited.

The regulation of dogs

There is no dog registration scheme in the UK. The previous scheme was abolished under s 38 of the Local Government Act 1988. However, regulations can be drawn up under s 37 of the Act allowing for such a scheme to be set up in the future.

Every dog that is on the highway or in a public place must wear a collar with the name and address of the owner on it; there is an exception for sheep dogs and dogs used for sporting purposes. The Collar and Tags (Control of

Dogs) Order 1991 made under the Animal Health Act 1981, s 13 makes it an offence for a dog to be allowed on a public highway without a collar and tag with the owner's address on it or in a plate ascribed to the collar. Under ss 3 and 4, which were added by s 151 of the Environmental Protection Act 1990, enforcement of this requirement can be undertaken by local authorities. Stray dogs are regulated under the Dogs Act 1906, as amended by s 39 of the Local Government Act 1988. This provides for the seizure and detention of stray dogs. Under the Dogs Act 1906 and the Dogs (Amendment) Act 1928, when a stray dog is found then it must be taken back to its owner or to a police station by the finder of the dog. The collection and detention of stray dogs is provided for under ss 149–50 of the Environment Protection Act 1990. Animal wardens are authorised officers under this Act and undertake work on behalf of the local authority which is their employer. The police also accept stray dogs when they are brought into Police Stations. Section 27 of the Road Traffic Act 1988 requires that dogs be kept on a leash on public roads, and local authorities can make byelaws to require that dogs be kept on a leash in certain parks, public gardens and amenity areas.

The Dogs (Fouling of Land) Act 1996

This makes provision for the control of dog fouling to be regulated by local authorities. Section 1 describes the land to which the Act applies, namely subject to qualifications under s 1(2)–(4), any land which is open to the air (including covered land which is open to the air on at least one side) and to which the public are allowed access, with or without payment. Exceptions to the general rule under s 1 are highways with a speed limit of more than 40 mph; land used for agriculture or woodlands; land which is predominantly marshland, moor or heath; and common land under s 193(1) of the Law of Property Act 1925 (right of access to common land). Section 2 enables local authorities to designate land to which the Act applies. Section 3 defines the offence committed by a person will be guilty of if, when in charge of a dog which defecates on designated land, he fails to remove the faeces from the land. Claiming to be unaware of the defecation or of not having a suitable device for removal is not a reasonable excuse. If convicted, such a person is liable to a fine. Section 4 enables an authorised officer to give a notice to a person whom he has reason to believe has committed an offence under s 3, by offering to discharge liability by payment of a fixed penalty fine, based upon s 88 of the Environmental Protection Act 1990 (litter fixed penalty scheme). Section 5 enables the Secretary of State to make orders and regulations. Section 6 provides that existing byelaws relating to dog fouling made by local authorities cease to have effect with regard to land which is designated under s 2 of the Act. Further, all such byelaws will cease to have effect 10 years after the commencement of the Act.

Liability for the action of dogs

In an action for damages for a dog bite, it has to be proved that the dog was ferocious to mankind. This was set out in the following case which looked at the position of whether a dog was ferocious to mankind. The judge, in this case, decided there was no evidence to suggest the dog was so, just because it had bitten a goat:

Osborne v Chocqeel (1896) 2 QBD 109

In order to support an action for damages for the bite of a dog it is necessary to shew that the dog had to the defendant's knowledge bitten or attempted to bite some person before it bit the plaintiff; it is not sufficient to shew that it had to the defendant's knowledge attacked and bitten a goat.

Lord Russell of Killowen CJ: I am of opinion that this appeal should be allowed. [His Lordship stated the facts.] There was no evidence before the learned county court judge that the dog had on any previous occasion manifested any tendency to bite mankind. It never had bitten or attempted to bite anybody; its record was quite clean except for the unhappy incident of the goat. Was the judge entitled to arrive at the conclusion that the defendant was liable? That leads to the question, was there sufficient evidence of scienter to make the defendant liable? I think there was not. I do not say that the law is in a satisfactory condition; I think it is unsatisfactory. It would, in my opinion, be more in accordance with sound reason and principle to make a man responsible for what his dog did – that he should take the risk of keeping it. We have not, however, to decide whether the law in this respect is satisfactory or unsatisfactory, but only to say what it is as applied to the particular case before us. If a dog bites sheep or cattle the owner is, by Act of Parliament, liable although he had not the least reason to suppose his dog had any tendency to bite sheep or cattle. An attempt was made in the House of Commons some years ago to abolish the doctrine of scienter, but that attempt was unsuccessful. It is impossible, looking at the long series of cases, extending over many years, in which the doctrine of scienter has been applied and acted upon, to arrive at any other conclusion than that, in actions for injury sustained by man through the bite of a dog, the scienter which it is necessary to shew is that the dog had a ferocious disposition towards mankind – that he had bitten or attempted to bite mankind. In the present case the county court judge has not found that the dog, before it bit the plaintiff, had any ferocious disposition towards mankind; he has only found that it was ferocious, and ferocious to the knowledge of the defendant. As I have said, there was no evidence upon which it could be found that the dog had previously bitten or attempted to bite mankind. I am, therefore, of opinion that the judgment was wrong.

Under the Metropolitan Police Act 1839, if an unmuzzled ferocious dog is on the thoroughfare, then if the dog is 'at large' the owner will be liable. The case of *Ross v Evans* looked at when a dog was 'at large' under the Act.

Ross v Evans [1959] 2 QB (Lord Parker CJ, Donovan and Salmon JJ)

The defendant was charged with two offences under s 54(2) of the Metropolitan Police Act 1839 by suffering an unmuzzled ferocious dog to be at large in a public thoroughfare on two occasions. The justices found that the defendant on the occasions in question was exercising a number of greyhounds in a public street. The dogs were on leads but on each occasion one of them, which the defendant made no effort to control, jumped up and bit a passer-by. They held that on each occasion the offending dog, although on a lead, was 'at large' within the meaning of s 54(2) and, accordingly, found both offences proved. On appeal against conviction:

Held, that s 54(2) was aimed at the case where the person in charge of a dog had no physical control over it at all, and no offence was committed under the section where the person in charge had the physical means of controlling the dog, such as a lead, but failed to do so. The offending dog was not 'at large' on either occasion within the meaning of s 54(2), and the appeal must be allowed.

Lord Parker CJ: This is an appeal by way of case stated by justices for the petty sessional division of Gore, sitting at Harrow Magistrates' Court, before whom the defendant was charged with two offences contrary to s 54(2) of the Metropolitan Police Act 1839, in that he suffered to be at large an unmuzzled ferocious dog. The justices found the offences proved and imposed a fine of 40s on each summons and ordered the defendant to pay costs. [His Lordship stated the facts and continued:] The sole question, a short one and a novel one, is whether in each of these cases the dog concerned was at large within the meaning of the Act. The Act concerned, the Metropolitan Police Act 1839, is 'An Act for further improving the police in and near the Metropolis' and by s 54 there are set out a number of acts which are described as 'prohibition of nuisances by persons in the thoroughfares.' Subsection (2) provides: 'Every person who shall turn loose any horse or cattle, or suffer to be at large any unmuzzled ferocious dog, or set on or urge any dog or other animal to attack, worry, or put in fear any person, horse, or other animal,' shall be liable to a penalty.

The justices in this case clearly, I think, came to the conclusion that although a person might have control of a dog by some physical means such as a lead, yet if he did not control the dog, the dog was at large. They say, with regard it is true to only one of the offences charged, but I understand the facts were the same in each case, that the dogs were all on leads, and 'the defendant did not try to control the dog,' that is, the dog that jumped up and bit the passer-by. For my part I am quite satisfied that an offence is not committed under the section where a person has the physical means of controlling the dog but does not do so. I think that the section is aimed at the case where a person has no physical control of the dog at all. The case was put in argument of a person who had a dog on a lead so long that he could not exercise any physical control. That is certainly not this case, and it may well be that in such a case it could be said that the control was so minimal that the dog was to all intents and purposes a dog at large. However, that is not this case. This is a case where a man could exercise control over the dog by means of the lead but did not do so. In my judgment, the justices were wrong in convicting the defendant on these two charges, and the appeal must be allowed.

Donovan J: I should be glad, if I could, to take the same view as the justices did of the meaning of the expression 'suffer to be at large any unmuzzled ferocious dog' where it occurs in s 54(2) of the Metropolitan Police Act 1839. One has little sympathy with anyone exercising six or seven greyhounds on the public highway controlled only by a lead of such a design that the dog cannot, it seems, be effectively prevented from biting passers-by. But the question here is purely one of construction of the section. The prosecutor relies upon the expression 'turn loose any horse or cattle' in the same subsection as contrasted with the words 'suffer to be at large' used in relation to a dog, and he says that this shows that the legislature contemplated that a dog could be at large although not turned loose. The expression 'to turn loose', however, is one commonly used to describe horses or cattle which are set free; but where dogs are concerned the same idea is commonly expressed by the term 'suffer to be at large'. Of more weight, I think, is the inference to be drawn from s 54(4) which reads:

> Every person having the care of any cart or carriage who shall ride on any part thereof, on the shafts, or on any horse or other animal drawing the same, without having and holding the reins, or who shall be at such a distance from such cart or carriage as not to have the complete control over every horse or other animal drawing the same.

If the legislature intended s 54(2) to apply to a dog on a lead giving less than complete control over it, I think similar language would have been used. My Lord has said that it may be that if a dog were on a lead which was so extravagantly long that it was for practical purposes just as free to be a nuisance on the highway as if it were loose, it could be said to be 'at large' within the meaning of the subsection. There is no evidence of that here. All that the court knows is that in the first episode there was a master lead with small leads from it, and in the second that all the dogs were on leads and the defendant did not try to control the offending dog. That implies that he could have controlled it and that the lead was of such a kind that would have enabled him to do so. Accordingly, when the prosecutor urges that this is a question of fact, I think the answer must be that there was no evidence to justify the conclusion that the leads were so extravagantly long or so hopelessly inadequate as to leave the dog for the purposes of being a nuisance practically at large. That being the case, I do not feel it possible to say that a dog on a lead or leads such as are described in the case is 'at large' within the meaning of s 54(2), and I agree, therefore, that the appeal must be allowed. I hope there is some by-law which can be invoked in this district to stop a repetition of these incidents.

The protection of livestock from dogs

Under s 3 of the Animals Act 1971, where a dog causes damage by killing or injuring livestock, any person who is a keeper of the dog is liable for the damage. If a dog trespasses onto another's land then if the owner allowed the dog to trespass wilfully or to search for game, the owner is liable for any damage to the owner's livestock.

Under s 9 of the Animals Act 1971 there is a defence to killing or injuring a dog worrying livestock:[8]

(1) In any civil proceedings against a person (in this section referred to as the defendant) for killing or causing injury to a dog it shall be a defence to prove:

    (a) that the defendant acted for the protection of any livestock and was a person entitled to act for the protection of that livestock; and

    (b) that within 48 hours of the killing or injury notice thereof was given by the defendant to the officer in charge of a police station.

(2) For the purposes of this section a person is entitled to act for the protection of any livestock if, and only if:

    (a) the livestock or the land on which it is belongs to him or to any person under whose express or implied authority he is acting; and

    (b) the circumstances are not such that liability for killing or causing injury to the livestock would be excluded by s 5(4) of this Act.

(3) Subject to subsection (4) of this section, a person killing or causing injury to a dog shall be deemed for the purposes of this section to act for the protection of any livestock if, and only if, either:

    (a) the dog is worrying or is about to worry the livestock and there are no other reasonable means of ending or preventing the worrying; or

    (b) the dog has been worrying livestock, has not left the vicinity and is not under the control of any person and there are no practicable means of ascertaining to whom it belongs.

The breeding of dogs

Under s 1 of the Breeding of Dogs Act 1973/1991 a licence is needed for breeding establishments for dogs. Under s 1(4):

In determining whether to grant a licence for the keeping of a breeding establishment for dogs by any person at any premises, a local authority shall in particular (but without prejudice to their discretion to withhold a licence on other grounds) have regard to the need for securing:

(a) that the dogs will at all times be kept in accommodation suitable as respects construction, size of quarters, number of occupants, exercising facilities, temperature, lighting, ventilation and cleanliness;

(b) that the dogs will be adequately supplied with suitable food, drink and bedding material, adequately exercised, and (so far as necessary) visited at suitable intervals;

(c) that all reasonable precautions will be taken to prevent and control the spread among dogs of infectious or contagious diseases;

(d) that appropriate steps will be taken for the protection of the dogs in case of fire or other emergency;

---

8   See the Dogs (Protection of Livestock) Act 1953, and see Chapter 2.

(e) that all appropriate steps will be taken to secure that the dogs will be provided with suitable food, drink and bedding material and adequately exercised when being transported to or from the breeding establishment.

The adequacy of this Act has been questioned regularly by the RSPCA. An article[9] in their magazine *Animal Life* states that while establishments have to be licensed, once owners have two breeding bitches on their site this requirement is often flouted, if the breeders know that the conditions in which the dogs are kept mean that they will not be granted a licence. There is also no right of entry to unlicensed premises. There is no limit under the Act to the number of litters a bitch should have, nor is there a limit on the number of stud dogs. Often, the conditions in which dogs are kept, even on licensed premises, are unacceptable. The article ends by stating: 'What we'd like to see is legislation which would give RSPCA inspectors the right of entry to places where indiscriminate breeding is even just suspected so that we could check on numbers and conditions. Until we gain this, we are likely to come across more and more breeders that deliberately avoid licensing because they know we have no rights of entry.'

A Private Member's Bill was introduced on 14 January 1996 (The Breeding and Sale of Dogs Bill) to improve conditions and to introduce some of the above reforms. This was rejected at second reading but it will be introduced again in the new parliamentary session.

Guard dogs

Under the Guard Dogs Act 1975 a licence is required to keep a guard dog in certain situations under s 2. Otherwise a warning has to be posted under s 1:

(1) A person shall not use or permit the use of a guard dog at any premises unless a person ('the handler') who is capable of controlling the dog is present on the premises and the dog is under the control of the handler at all times while it is being so used except while it is secured so that it is not at liberty to go freely about the premises.

(2) The handler of a guard dog shall keep the dog under his control at all times while it is being used as a guard dog at any premises except:

(a) while another handler has control over the dog; or

(b) while the dog is secured so that it is not at liberty to go freely about the premises.

(3) A person shall not use or permit the use of a guard dog at any premises unless a notice containing a warning that a guard dog is present is clearly exhibited at each entrance to the premises.

The owner of a guard dog may be liable for any injury to a person under s 2(2) of the Animals Act 1971, unless they come within one of the exceptions in s 5.

---

9   Summer 1991, pp 24–25.

However, the requirements of the Guard Dogs Act 1975 have to be taken into account. The actions of a guard dog and the liability of the owner were considered in the following case:

Cummings v Granger [1977] QB 397

The defendant was the occupier of a breaker's yard in the East End of London. At night the yard was locked up and the defendant's untrained Alsatian dog was turned loose to deter intruders. One night an associate of the defendant, who had access to a key, unlocked the side gate and, accompanied by the plaintiff, who knew about the dog, entered the yard. The dog attacked the plaintiff causing her serious injury. The plaintiff brought an action for damages based on, *inter alia*, breach of the duty contained in s 2(2) of the Animals Act 1971. At the trial, expert evidence was given that the dog's behaviour in the circumstances was normal for an untrained Alsatian with a territory to defend. The judge held that the defendant was liable under s 2(2) of the Act and that he did not come within any of the exceptions in s 5 but that the plaintiff was 50% to blame for her injuries.

On the defendant's appeal:

Held, (1) that if the dog were to bite anyone the damage was likely to be severe;[10] that the likelihood of such damage was due to characteristics not normally found in Alsatians except in the 'particular circumstances', namely an untrained dog roaming a yard which it regarded as its territory;[11] that it could be assumed that those characteristics were known to the defendant;[12] and, accordingly, that the requirements of s 2(2) were satisfied.

But (2), allowing the appeal, that in all the circumstances it was not unreasonable for the defendant to keep the dog in the yard to protect his property;[13] that, accordingly, as the plaintiff was a trespasser, the defendant was excepted from liability under s 2 by s 5(3)(b); and, further, that as the plaintiff entered the yard knowing all about the dog she must be taken to have voluntarily accepted the risk of damage, thereby absolving the defendant of liability as provided by s 5(2).[14]

Lord Denning MR: The Guard Dogs Act 1975 may have the effect in civil proceedings of making it unreasonable for a defendant to let a dog free in a yard at night and may thus deprive him of a defence under s 5(3)(b) of the Animals Act 1971.[15]

The case is of some interest because it is the first we have had under the new Act about a guard dog. This Alsatian seems to have been a typical guard dog. A veterinary surgeon gave evidence as to the behaviour of this Alsatian. Was it

[10] At p 404F–G.
[11] At pp 404G–H, 407F, 409C–F.
[12] Below, pp 407G, 409F).
[13] At pp 405C–D, 408C, 410G.
[14] At pp 405H, 408F–G, 410H–411B.
[15] At p 406C.

exceptionally ferocious? He answered: 'No, I think this is perfectly normal behaviour for a good number of Alsatians or, indeed, many other breeds of dogs.' The judge asked: 'What – to leap up and seize somebody by the face?' The veterinary surgeon answered:

> In these circumstances, yes. The Alsatian is a dog which is a very insecure, very nervous type of animal. This dog has had no formal discipline or training at all. The plaintiff has already said that she was frightened of the dog. The dog would be perfectly well aware of this, instantly. We know perfectly well that even in our profession if a dog comes in and we have a smell of fear about us that from then on we cannot handle it. Equally, we can master a lot of dogs that are already terrorising their owners. If a dog feels threatened, and this dog has a job to do, which is to guard its territory, if it feels threatened, it wants to defend that territory; if it then smells fear, this is the next reaction and it is a very, very common one.

A little later he was asked whether it was not unusual for an ordinary house Alsatian to seize somebody's face because she bends down to pat it. The veterinary surgeon answered: 'No, many house dogs will not accept strangers, and this sort of behaviour where you bend down straight out of the blue, you are likely to get attacked by many dogs – Alsatians and many other sorts of dogs.'

So this Alsatian was just a typical guard dog.

This brings me to the law. At common law, when a dog bit a man, the owner or keeper of the dog was strictly liable if he knew that it had a propensity to bite or attack human beings. Apart from this, however, he was liable for negligence if the circumstances were such as to impose upon him a duty of care towards the injured plaintiff, which he had failed to observe: see *Fardon v Harcourt-Rivington* (1932) 48 TLR 215, 217 by Lord Atkin; and *Draper v Hodder* [1972] 2 QB 556. Now so far as strict liability is concerned, the common law has been replaced by the Animals Act 1971. But the common law as to negligence remains. If the plaintiff's version – that she was on the pavement – had been accepted, we might have had to consider the issue of negligence. But she was not on the pavement. She was a trespasser: and the only duty owed to her was the duty considered by the House of Lords in *Herrington v British Railways Board* [1972] AC 877 and by the Privy Council in *Southern Portland Cement Ltd v Cooper* [1974] AC 623. Those were cases of children trespassing and their presence was to be expected. But this was a case of a grown-up person. The defendant had no reason to expect that anyone would enter unlawfully, especially as he had a large warning notice and a guard dog. It seems to me that he was not under any duty of care towards her. Nor, indeed, was it suggested in argument. The only case put before the judge or before us was that the keeper was strictly liable under the Animals Act 1971.

The statutory liability for a tame animal, like a dog, is defined in s 2(2) of the Act, subject to exceptions contained in s 5. Now it seems to me that this is a case where the keeper of the dog is strictly liable unless he can bring himself within one of the exceptions. I say this because the three requirements for strict liability are satisfied. The section is very cumbrously worded and will give rise to several difficulties in future. But in this case the judge held that the three requirements were satisfied and I agree with him for the following reasons. Section 2(2)(a): this animal was a dog of the Alsatian breed; if it did bite anyone, the damage was 'likely to be severe.' Section 2(2)(b): this animal was a guard dog kept so as to scare intruders and frighten them off. On the defendant's own evidence, it used to bark and run round in circles, especially when coloured people approached. Those characteristics – barking and running around to guard its territory – are not normally found in Alsatian dogs except in circumstances where they are used as guard dogs. Those circumstances are 'particular circumstances' within s 2(2)(b). It was due to those circumstances that the damage was likely to be severe if an intruder did enter on its territory. Section 2(2)(c): those characteristics were known to the defendant. It follows that the defendant is strictly liable unless he can bring himself within one of the exceptions in s 5. Obviously s 5(1) does not avail. The bite was not wholly due to the fault of the plaintiff, but only partly so.

Section 5(3) may, however, avail the keeper. It says that if someone trespasses on property and is bitten or injured by a guard dog, the keeper of the guard dog is exempt from liability if it is proved 'that keeping it there for that purpose was not unreasonable.' The judge held that the defendant was unreasonable in keeping it in this yard. He said:[16]

> It seems to me that it was unreasonable to keep an untrained dog, known to be ferocious and known to be likely to attack at least coloured people, if they came near the place, to protect a lot of old broken-down scrap motor cars in this yard, by night.

I take a different view. This was a yard in the East End of London where persons of the roughest type come and go. It was a scrap-yard, true, but scrap-yards, like building sites, often contain much valuable property. It was deserted at night and at weekends. If there was no protection, thieves would drive up in a lorry and remove the scrap with no one to see them or to stop them. The only reasonable way of protecting the place was to have a guard dog. True it was a fierce dog. But why not? A gentle dog would be no good. The thieves would soon make friends with him. It seems to me that it was very reasonable – or, at any rate, not unreasonable – for the defendant to keep this dog there. Long ago in 1794 Lord Kenyon said in *Brock v Copeland* (1794) 1 Esp 203 that 'every man had a right to keep a dog for the protection of his yard or house.'

Alternatively, there is another defence provided by s 5(2). It says that a person is not liable 'for any damage suffered by a person who has voluntarily accepted the risk thereof.' This seems to me to warrant a reference back to the common law. This very defence was considered in 1820 in *Ilott v Wilkes* (1820) 3 B & Ald 304. It was a case about a spring gun which went off and injured a trespasser, but Bayley J put this very case, at 313:

> if a trespasser enters into the yard of another, over the entrance of which notice is given, that there is a furious dog loose, and that it is dangerous for any person to enter in without one of the servants or the owner. If the wrong-doer, having read that notice, and knowing, therefore, that he is

---

[16] [1975] 1 WLR 1330 at 1336–37.

likely to be injured, in the absence of the owner enters the yard, and is worried by the dog, (which in such a case would be a mere engine without discretion,) it is clear that the party could not maintain any action for the injury sustained by the dog, because the answer would be, as in this case, that he could not have a remedy for an injury which he had voluntarily incurred.

That reasoning applies here. The plaintiff certainly knew the animal was there. She worked next door. She knew all about it. She must have seen this huge notice on the door 'Beware of the Dog.' Nevertheless she went in, following her man friend. In the circumstances she must be taken voluntarily to have incurred this risk. So with any burglar or thief who goes on to premises knowing that there is a guard dog there. If he is bitten or injured, he cannot recover. He voluntarily takes the risk of it. Even if he does not know a guard dog is there, he might be defeated by the plea *ex turpi causa non oritur actio.*

There is only one further point I would mention. This accident took place in November 1971 very shortly after the Animals Act 1971 was passed. In 1975 the Guard Dogs Act 1975 was passed. It does not apply to this case. But it makes it quite clear that in future a person is not allowed to have a guard dog to roam about on his premises unless the dog is under the control of a handler. If he has no handler, the dog must be chained up so that it is not at liberty to roam around. If a person contravenes the Act, he can be brought before a magistrate and fined up to £400. But it is only criminal liability. It does not confer a right of action in any civil proceedings. It may, however, have the effect in civil proceedings of making it unreasonable for the defendant to let a dog free in the yard at night (as this defendant did) and it may thus deprive the defendant of a defence under s 5(3)(b). But he might still be able to rely on the defence under s 5(2) of *volenti non fit injuria.*

Coming back to the present case, I think the defendant is not under any strict liability to the plaintiff because she was a trespasser and also because she voluntarily took the risk. I would therefore allow the appeal and enter judgment for the defendant.

Dangerous dogs

The Dangerous Dogs Act 1991 was passed after a series of highly publicised cases of 'fighting' dogs biting people. The legislation remains controversial and there have been a number of cases which have examined how the legislation should be applied in practice.

Section 1. Dogs bred for fighting

(1) This section applies to:

    (a) any dog of the type known as the pit bull terrier;

    (b) any dog of the type known as the Japanese tosa; and

    (c) any dog of any type designated for the purposes of this section by an order of the Secretary of State, being a type appearing to him to be bred for fighting or to have the characteristics of a type bred for that purpose.

(2) No person shall:

(a) breed, or breed from, a dog to which this section applies;

(b) sell or exchange such a dog or offer, advertise or expose such a dog for sale or exchange;

(c) make or offer to make a gift of such a dog or advertise or expose such a dog as a gift;

(d) allow such a dog of which he is the owner or of which he is for the time being in charge to be in a public place without being muzzled and kept on a lead; or

(e) abandon such a dog of which he is the owner or, being the owner or for the time being in charge of such a dog, allow it to stray.

(3) After such day as the Secretary of State may by order appoint for the purposes of this subsection no person shall have any dog to which this section applies in his possession or custody except:

(a) in pursuance of the power of seizure conferred by the subsequent provisions of this Act; or

(b) in accordance with an order for its destruction made under those provisions;

but the Secretary of State shall by order make a scheme for the payment to the owners of such dogs who arrange for them to be destroyed before that day of sums specified in or determined under the scheme in respect of those dogs and the cost of their destruction.

Section 2. Other specially dangerous dogs

(1) If it appears to the Secretary of State that dogs of any type to which s 1 above does not apply present a serious danger to the public he may by order impose in relation to dogs of that type restrictions corresponding, with such modifications, if any, as he thinks appropriate, to all or any of those in subsection (2)(d) and (e) of that section.

(4) In determining whether to make an order under this section in relation to dogs of any type and, if so, what the provisions of the order should be, the Secretary of State shall consult with such persons or bodies as appear to him to have relevant knowledge or experience, including a body concerned with animal welfare, a body concerned with veterinary science and practice and a body concerned with breeds of dogs.

Section 3. Keeping dogs under proper control

(1) If a dog is dangerously out of control in a public place – then the owner or the person in charge of the dog is guilty of an offence, or, if the dog while so out of control injures any person, an aggravated offence, under this subsection. Under s 2(2), in proceedings for an offence under subsection (1) above, against a person who is the owner of a dog but was not at the material time in charge of it, it shall be a defence for the accused to prove that the dog was at the material time in the charge of a person whom he reasonably believed to be a fit and proper person to be in charge of it.

(3) If the owner or, if different, the person for the time being in charge of a dog allows it to enter a place which is not a public place but where it is not permitted to be and while it is there:

(a) it injures any person; or

(b) there are grounds for reasonable apprehension that it will do so, he is guilty of an offence, or, if the dog injures any person, an aggravated offence, under this subsection.

There are various steps that can be taken whether or not the dog has injured a person, including muzzling the dog (s 7) or keeping it on a lead, and if the dog is male it may be neutered. Under s 4 destruction and disqualification orders can be made, while s 5 provides for the seizure, entry of premises and collection of relevant evidence, this can include the dog. The complexity of establishing an offence under the Act is illustrated by the three cases below:

Greener v DPP (1996) *The Times*, 15 February (QBD: Saville LJ and Blofeld J)

Section 3(3) of the Dangerous Dogs Act 1991 provides that if the owner of a dog allows it to enter a place which is not a public place but where it is not permitted to be and while it is there it injures any person, he is guilty of an offence.

The owner of a Staffordshire bull terrier kept his dog chained in an enclosure in his garden. The dog escaped into a nearby garden where he bit a young child on the face. The justices found the owner guilty of an offence under s 3(3) of the 1991 Act. They fined him and ordered that the dog be destroyed. The owner unsuccessfully appealed to the Crown Court, which found that if a dog was secured with what the owner genuinely believed to be adequate precautions and it escaped and entered a place where it was not permitted to be, the owner had allowed the dog to enter that place. On further appeal by way of case stated the owner submitted that (1) it had to be proved that he had allowed the dog to enter the garden as a positive or permissive step, and (2) on the true construction of s 3(3) there had to be some mental element in the form of intention, desire or foresight of the consequences.

Held, s 3(3) did not require proof of a positive or permissive step; the word 'allows' included taking and omitting to take a positive step. Section 3(3) did not qualify 'allows' with intentionally or negligently or knowing of the consequences that would ensue and it was impossible to conclude that Parliament intended any mental element to be part of s 3(3). An offence under s 3(3) could therefore be committed by omission and, accordingly, the appeal would be dismissed.

R v Walton Street Magistrates' Court, ex p Crothers (1994) 160 JP 427 (QBD: Beldam LJ and Buxton J)

The police brought proceedings against the owner of a dog under s 1(3) of the Dangerous Dogs Act 1991. The prosecution was discontinued but the dog remained in police custody and magistrates ordered the dog's destruction under s 5(4) of the 1991 Act. The owner was not notified of the hearing and was granted judicial review of the order. He then gave the dog to his son, the applicant. The dog was released from police custody to the applicant and was instantly seized again on the basis that proceedings might be brought against the applicant as he was the owner of an unregistered pit bull terrier. No prosecution was brought but the applicant was notified that magistrates were to hear an application for a destruction order under s 5(4). The applicant attended court with a witness and sought an adjournment so he could be legally represented. The magistrates refused that request and refused to hear the witness and a destruction order was made. The applicant sought judicial review of the order on the grounds that (1) s 5(4) could not apply if a person had been prosecuted for an offence under the 1991 Act in relation to the dog, (2) there ought to have been an adjournment, and (3) the witness should have been allowed to give evidence.

Held, (1) It was not the case that once a prosecution had been initiated against someone in respect of a particular dog that the dog was protected from further proceedings of any sort under s 5(4) whoever its owner was. (2) The request for an adjournment was a matter for the discretion of the magistrates and they were right in the present case to refuse it. (3) The magistrates refused to hear the evidence because s 5(5) required an accused to give 14 days' notice in order to do so. The present proceedings, however, were of a civil nature under s 5(4) and the magistrates were not right to think that they were precluded from hearing the evidence. Although the magistrates were wrong, it could not be said that any injustice had been done and, accordingly, the application would be dismissed.

R v Trafford Magistrates' Court, ex p Riley (1995) 160 JP 418 (QBD: Balcombe LJ and French J)

Under s 4(1) of the Dangerous Dogs Act 1991, where a person is convicted of an offence under s 3(1), the court must order the destruction of any dog in respect of which the offence was committed if the dog while out of control injures any person.

The owner of a dog had an argument with a friend. Following the dispute, and without the owner's knowledge, the friend took the dog to a nearby car park. Although the dog was on a leash, the friend was unable to restrain it and it bit a police officer. A summons was subsequently issued against the friend under s 3(1) of the 1991 Act. She pleaded guilty to the offence and the magistrates ordered the destruction of the dog. On the owner's application for judicial review of the magistrates' decision to destroy the dog, she submitted that she ought to have been given notice of the hearing.

Held, although the magistrates had no discretion as to whether to order the destruction of the dog, had the owner been notified she could have attended the hearing and argued before the magistrates that, in all the circumstances, the prosecution was an abuse of the process of the court. Further, she may have argued that the car park was not a public place or that the friend had entered her guilty plea maliciously. Whether or not the magistrates' power was mandatory or discretionary, in any case concerning the destruction of property, the rules of natural justice required a known owner of property at least to be given the opportunity to be heard. As a result, the order for destruction could not stand.

Accordingly, the application would be allowed, the conviction would be quashed and the matter remitted to the magistrates.

In a recent case the High Court ordered the Metropolitan Police to free a pit bull terrier that had been detained by the police under the Dangerous Dogs Act 1991.[17] There is a problem with the law given that there is no appeal from a destruction order unless it is on a point of law. A Private Member's Bill, the Dangerous Dogs (Amendment) Bill was introduced in 1996 to give the courts discretion as to whether a dog should be destroyed. It would also expand the listing of the types of dangerous dogs on the register.

THE REFORM OF THE LAW RELATING TO DOMESTIC ANIMALS

While the UK has the reputation of being a nation of animal lovers, some of the cases of cruelty to animals are horrific and there clearly needs to be some revision of the law to give domestic animals more protection. Under the Police and Criminal Evidence Act 1984 a crime of animal cruelty is not a serious arrestable offence. No national records are kept of cruelty cases in the UK, except by the RSPCA. In 1995 there were 1,812 convictions under the Protection of Animals Act 1911: 1,650 were for neglect, 65 for abandonment, 28 for ill-treatment, eight for beating and kicking and seven for improper killing.[18] A few of the many cruelty cases that happen each year are reproduced below:[19]

> On 31 May 1996, X of Newcastle-upon-Tyne admitted burglary and destroying property, and was sent to a young offenders' institution for three years after what can only be described as a sadistic act of cruelty to a family's pet cat. It was revealed in court that X had waged a hate campaign against a 17-year-old girl who had only been out of prison for 17 days (after serving five months for another offence), broke into the girl's flat last December. He daubed the walls with obscene graffiti then placed the pet cat into the oven. When the girl returned to her flat she found the cat had been roasted alive. The RSPCA said they were sickened by the attack. Inspector T said 'The animal would have gone through excruciating pain before dying. It was burned alive.' The family have now fled the area and are living in Cumbria and Yorkshire. ...

> Y of Manchester was banned from keeping animal for 20 years and ordered to do 140 hours' community service for causing unnecessary suffering to a Staffordshire bull terrier. He was also ordered to pay costs of £160. During the case, in 1996, the court heard how Y walked into a pub in Manchester with the bull terrier. Blood was oozing from a wound on the dog's neck and it had

---

17 *The Guardian*, 18 January 1997.

18 *Wildlife Guardian* (League Against Cruel Sports magazine), London, Issue 34, Summer 1996, p 9. Details of cruelty cases can also be found in *Howl*, the hunt saboteurs' magazine, and *Animal Life*, the magazine of the RSPCA, Horsham, Surrey.

19 *Howl*, no 62, Autumn 1996, pp 16–18, Hunt Saboteurs Association, Brighton.

difficulty in breathing. The landlord of the pub was shocked by what he saw; he rang the RSPCA. Y claimed he had just bought the dog and had not noticed the fresh wounds. ...

Two men, W and Z, of Bolton were banned from keeping animals for life and ordered to pay costs of £250 following their appearance at Bolton Magistrates Court in 1996 on charges of cruelty to three dogs. Inspector V found three lurcher-type dogs being kept in a seven foot by six foot 'shed-like construction'. There was also a strong smell from the shed and the animals were suffering from hair loss and skin complaints,. Since the trial, one of the dogs has been found a new home and the other two are still waiting in kennels. ...

A soccer fan who kicked a puppy to death while he watched *Euro 96* on TV was jailed for 28 days for cruelty to an animal by Oldham Magistrates in 1996. The court was told how T of Oldham had lost his temper when the six-week-old puppy wouldn't stop crying. The dog was then kicked several times and it was left with a broken jaw, four smashed ribs, bruised lungs and a torn liver. The magistrates ordered that T should be banned for life from owning any animal.

Suggested legislative provisions for companion animals[20]

The World Society for the Protection of Animals has suggested a comprehensive reform of the legislation on companion animals:

General

1   Any person who keeps a pet animal or who has agreed to look after it shall be responsible for its health and welfare.

2   Any person who is keeping a pet animal or who is looking after it shall provide accommodation, care and attention which takes account of its physiological and behavioural needs, including appropriate food and water, shelter, exercise and companionship.

3   No non-domesticated animals shall be kept as companion animals. There could be a strict provision against this, or a list of animals which can be kept (in regulations), with the requirement to seek permission (or a licence) for the keeping of any other species. The licence would only be granted in exceptional cases, such as the keeping of wild animals in a sanctuary where release is not possible.

4   Nobody shall cause a companion animal any avoidable suffering, pain or distress.

5   Sick or injured animals shall be provided with care without delay. Where necessary, veterinary advice shall be sought. Where euthanasia is necessary to relieve suffering, this should be done immediately by a

---

20   World Society for the Protection of Animals, *Stray Dog Control*, pp 21–24 London: WSPA. Reproduced with kind permission of the World Society for the Protection of Animals.

qualified or competent person, and with the minimum suffering, pain and distress.

Measures preventing stray animals

6. Nobody shall abandon a companion animal.

7. Dogs and cats (and any other companion animals which cause local stray problems) shall be permanently identified by some appropriate means which causes no enduring pain, suffering or distress, such as tattooing (or microchip). Each shall be given a unique identification number, which will be recorded in a central register together with full contact details of the owner or keeper.

8. It shall be compulsory for dogs to wear collars, clearly indicating their owner or keeper's full contact details, at all times when outside the territory of their home.

9. Dog taxes shall be introduced for the acquisition of any new companion dogs. The tax shall be well-publicised before it is introduced. The tax could be waived for certain groups, such as pensioners. The funds raised from the tax must be reinvested in stray control and associated educational programmes.

10. Neutering shall be provided to reduce the unplanned breeding of cats and dogs. Reduced dog taxes could be applied to neutered animals.

11. Any person finding an injured or suffering stray shall seek the animal's owner, and if not successful, report this to the competent authorities without delay.

12. Where it is considered necessary to remove unaccompanied or unidentifiable animals, they shall be caught with the minimum of physical and mental suffering to the animal.

13. Where stray animals are housed after capture, this shall be in conformity with these provisions.

14. Where it is considered necessary to kill unwanted animals, this shall always be done in conformity with paragraphs 46–48.

Information and education

15. The competent authority shall carry out information and education programmes in 'responsible companion animals ownership'. These would include the discouragement of impulse purchase, stress the duties and responsibilities involved in companion animal ownership and promote neutering.

Restriction on use of companion animals

16. Organising or attending animal fights shall be prohibited.

17. The use of dogs for draught purposes shall be prohibited.

18. The giving of animals for prizes shall be prohibited.

19. Companion animals shall not be bred or used for other commercial purposes, such as the production of food, furs, skins, etc. (A derogation may be needed for purpose-bred animals for licensed scientific procedures.)

20. Unwanted or ownerless companion animals shall not be used for scientific procedures.

21. The use of animals in competitions which test speed, strength or endurance shall be prohibited, unless specific permission is given by the competent authority (which could, for example, give special permission for certain events which were not detrimental to the animal's health and welfare, eg some horse races). Each competition shall be reviewed and no permission granted where the animal's health and welfare is in danger (eg greyhound racing). Where such competitions are granted, this shall be conditional upon compliance with certain rules such as:

    rules on the age and health condition of the animals permitted to take part;

    rules on the frequency with which animals may take part;

    rules on veterinary presence at such competitions;

    rules on the construction of tracks and obstacles;

    prohibitions on the use of certain animals.

22. No animal used for races or competitions shall be subjected to the administration of any substances or treatments which affects the animal's performance or temperament (doping).

23. No companion animals shall be detained in a way that is detrimental to its health and welfare, especially by forcing it to exceed its natural capabilities or strength by employing artificial aids which cause unnecessary suffering, pain or distress.

24. No animals shall be used for shows, advertising or similar purposes where this entails suffering, pain or distress.

Surgical procedures and manipulations

25. No non-therapeutic `mutilations' shall be carried out on companion animals, except neutering which shall be promoted for social and welfare reasons, and ear tipping of feral cats when used as a sign of neutering. Prohibited procedures shall include de-clawing, ear-cropping, tail-docking and destruction of vocal cords.

26. Any surgical operation which may inflict suffering on an animal shall be performed only by a veterinarian, unless the operation is urgent and delay would be detrimental to the animal's welfare. Suffering and pain shall be reduced to the greatest possible extent.

27. The competent authority shall lay down more detailed rules on surgical and similar operations, including permissible methods, use of anaesthetic and any age limitations.

28. There shall be a ban on the patenting of animals.

29. There shall be a moratorium on the use of genetic techniques on companion animals (or a licensing system, with stringent controls and supervision).

Dangerous dogs

30. If deemed necessary, restrictions could be introduced to control, certain breeds of dog which have been proved to be dangerous. Subsequent

regulations could include provisions on compulsory registration and identification, muzzling in public places, compulsory neutering and a ban on imports.

Breeding

31. Any breeder or breeding establishment producing for sale commercially, shall be licensed and controlled by the competent authority. Controls shall include restrictions on the minimum and maximum age of breeding bitches, and on the number and regularity of litters. Licences shall only be granted where conditions of housing and care are acceptable.

32. Licensed breeders shall be required to keep full records of all litters bred, sales and purchases of companion animals. These records shall be available for scrutiny and, if necessary, removal by the competent authority at all reasonable hours.

33 Breeding for certain external features, which may be to the detriment of the animal's health and welfare, shall be prohibited.

34. Any person who selects a companion animal for breeding shall be responsible for having regard to the anatomical, physiological and behavioural characteristics which are likely to put at risk the health and welfare of either the offspring or the female parent.

Selling/dealing

35. Any person selling or dealing in companion animals, shall be licensed and controlled by the competent authority. The licence will stipulate certain welfare requirements to be fulfilled.

36. Licensed dealers shall only be permitted to purchase companion animals from licensed breeders. Licensed breeders shall be encouraged to sell their own litters directly, rather than passing these through a dealer.

37. Licensed dealers shall be required to keep full records of all purchases and sales. These records shall be available for scrutiny and, if necessary, removal by the competent authorities, without prior notice, at all reasonable hours.

38. Companion animals should only be sold in licensed venues. Licenses shall only be granted where there are suitable conditions for the animals, veterinary attention and official control.

39. When companion animals are sold, the full history of the animal, including its former owners and breeder's details, shall be available on request (with the exception of wounded stray animals where this information is not available).

40. No companion animal shall be sold to persons under the age of 16 years.

Boarding

41. Boarding establishments for companion animals shall be licensed and controlled by the competent authority. Boarding establishments with inadequate facilities or care shall be given notice of improvement, whereby if specified conditions are not complied with in a set period of time, they will be banned from trading.

Shelter/refuges

42. Shelters and refuges for companion animals shall also be licensed and controlled by the competent authorities.

Transport

43. Companion animals shall be transported so as to avoid suffering, pain and distress.Transport shall comply with the provisions of live transport welfare legislation.

Import/export

44. No companion animal shall be imported or exported without the approval of the competent authority, and the issue of an import or export licence. Full and detailed import and export statistics shall be kept for companion animals, divided by species and destination/origin. Arrangements for quarantine of imported animals shall be laid down.

Killing/euthanasia

45. Only a veterinarian or another competent person shall kill a pet animal except in an emergency to terminate an animal's suffering when veterinary or other competent assistance cannot be quickly obtained.

46. All killing shall be done with the minimum of physical and mental suffering. The methods chosen shall either:

   a) cause immediate loss of consciousness and death; or

   b) begin with the induction of deep general anaesthetic to be followed by a step which will ultimately and certainly cause death without recovery of consciousness.

47. The person responsible for the killing shall make sure that the animal is dead before the carcass is disposed of in any way.

48. The following killing methods shall be prohibited:

   a) Drowning and other methods of suffocation;

   b) The use of any poisonous substance or drug, the dose and application of which cannot be controlled so as to give the effect mentioned in paragraph 46;

   c) Electrocution unless preceded by immediate induction of loss of consciousness.

Enforcement

49. The competent authority shall be stipulated, and a duty to enforce included. Practice enforcement shall be performed, rather than purely response to complaints. Powers of entry shall be given and penalty provisions included. Penalties shall cover:

   fines;

   prison sentences;

   ban on keeping animals;

   removal of animals.

Ethical Committee

50. An Ethical Committee for Companion Animals shall be established to advise the Minister of the competent authority on all aspects of companion animal welfare, including:

    problems with existing laws/and enforcement;
    new regulations needed;
    new issues of concern regarding companion animals;
    new and relevant research in the field of companion animals.

51. The Ethical Committee shall include representatives of the main interest groups and experts, for example,

    animal protection society representatives;
    veterinarians;
    scientists and academics;
    breeder representative;
    dealer representative;
    consumer representative.

CONCLUSION

There clearly needs to be a reform of the legislation to tighten up the provisions for the protection of domestic animals from cruelty. The various provisions for the control and protection of dogs should be consolidated into one piece of legislation and some form of dog registration scheme is needed, possibly with the animals being micro-chipped. This could be extended to all animals kept as domestic animals.

There is also a need for an educative programme on responsible ownership. This should include education on how the animals are bred, and where many 'domestic' animals and birds actually come from. Three million birds are imported annually into the EC. In 1991, 129,000 exotic birds, such as parrots, were imported into the UK; 19,000 died in the first five weeks.[21] It is important that domestic animals are bred properly, housed in the appropriate manner and treated well in the home. The WSPA draft provisions for companion animals should be used as a basis for reform, so that all companion animals are treated equally by the law. It would also ensure that various pieces of legislation could be consolidated into one statute. The enforcement of the law would need to be strict and the fines or penalties harsh enough to ensure that those convicted of cases of cruelty are adequately dealt with. An ethical committee for domestic animals would be able to advise the government on possible reforms and could stimulate an informed debate about our control and protection of all domestic animals.

---

21 RSPCA leaflet, *Thinking of buying a parrot?*, April 1994, p 13, Horsham: RSPCA.

FURTHER READING

Brown, A, *Who Cares for Animals? 150 years of the RSPCA*, 1974, London: Heinemann.

Cotterell, R, 'Dangerous Dogs – Dangerously Out of Control' 158 *JP* 302.

Foster, C, 'The Price of Animal Suffering' (1993) 143 *New Law Journal* No 6585, pp 123–125.

CHAPTER SEVEN

ANIMALS, SPORT AND ENTERTAINMENT

INTRODUCTION

This chapter will examine some of the most controversial aspects of our treatment and protection of animals: (the use of animals) in circuses, zoos and for hunting. These three areas provide interesting studies as to our use of animals and their welfare.

Circuses are in decline due to the public's changing perception of animal welfare together with the growth of other attractions such as television. One of the greatest reasons for the decline of circuses is that they are seen by their very nature to be cruel. This can be contrasted with the public's attitude towards zoos, which are not necessarily seen as cruel. The debate in relation to zoos is about the standards which make zoos acceptable.[1] The use of animals in zoos, it is argued, is justified on the grounds of conservation. The conservation argument is also used as a justification by the pro-hunting lobby. Animal welfare groups are divided on these issues. The RSPCA does not support circuses or hunting, but will support the concept of zoos. Other groups, such as the World Society for the Protection of Animals, question the role of zoos in relation to conservation and education.

This chapter will explore these issues and suggest some possible areas for reform. It will also look at the controls placed on the use of performing animals in films and on television, the plight of which was highlighted by Keiko, the whale used in the film *Free Willy*. The chapter will also consider the illegality of animal fights and other 'entertainments' such as rodeos and bullfights.

CIRCUSES

History

Circuses have a long history, as outlined in the extract below:[2]

> The circus as we know it today owes its origins to Philip Astley, a one-time Sergeant Major in the 15th Light Dragoons, who gave his exhibitions of

---

1   See Kiley-Worthington, M, *Animals in Circuses and Zoos – Chiron's World?*, 1990, Basildon: Little Eco-Farms Publishing. With knid permission of Little Eco-Farms Publishing.

2   Croft-Cooke, R and Cotes, P, *Circus a World History*, 1976, pp 7–8, London: Elek.

equestrian expertise, and later of performing animals, in London in the 1770s. But these can be traced by the historically-minded to similar shows and performances of wild beasts seen in the Circus Maximus and the Amphitheatres of Ancient Rome. These in turn were derived from the wondrous exhibitions of exotic animals species and perhaps from chariot-racing in Egypt and Greece.

Philip Astley was not a highly educated man and it is doubtful whether he was fully aware of these fascinating precursors of the art of the circus which he founded. Yet the parallel is an interesting one, since in all the centuries between the demise of the Roman circus in the 4th century and the foundation of Astley's Amphitheatre at the end of the 18th century there was nothing in existence which could properly be called a circus-circus, that is defined as an organised sequence of performances within a ring of spectators.

There is a another curious parallel between exhibitions in the civilisations of the Ancient World and those of Victorian England (and ... Soviet Russia and the US). At particular stages of their history, these empires were at their height. The adoption of the circus as a form of popular entertainment seems to have been stimulated in the heart of a thriving empire, and it may be noted that all circuses provide acts involving foreign animals, in addition to the more usual shows of horsemanship, acrobatics, wire-walking and the rest. In the days when he who was not conquered was a potential enemy, the only certain way in which unusual animals might be procured was through imperial colonists and explorers. Rome, like Greece before it, had established links with India and Persia which facilitated the supply of animals from these countries, just as the establishment of British rule in India made it easy for the followers of Astley to obtain elephants to enrich their shows. ...

Finally, the empires of Rome and Great Britain in their heyday were in the process of expansion and innovation. Rich Roman generals and Victorian capitalists encouraged circus entertainment to satisfy the working classes to whom their abundant wealth was in itself a thing of curiosity. Although the Roman prescription of 'bread and circuses' was not consciously employed to keep the masses quiet in early Victorian England, it is possible that without such entertainment to relieve the grim reality of poverty and urban squalor, in the days before the establishment of music-hall, melodrama and those flickering movies that followed the bioscope, they might have been far more ready to pick up revolutionary ideas.

The legal framework regulating circuses

There are between 16 and 20 circuses in the UK which use animals in their performances; 12 of these are members of the Association of Circus Proprietors. The number of animals kept by circuses ranges from 200–300.[3] Circuses are regulated under the Performing Animals (Regulations and Rules) Act 1925/1968.

---

3   International Animal Welfare Alliance (IAWA) factsheet 'Circuses – the Facts'.

A person who exhibits or trains any performing animal must be registered with a local authority; this licence is for life. The definition of exhibiting an animal is laid down in s 5(1): 'to exhibit at any entertainment to which the public are admitted whether for the payment of money or not'. This legislation does not cover invertebrates. Section 2 gives courts the power to prohibit or restrict exhibition and training of performing animals. Section 3 gives powers to the police and the local authority to enter premises at all reasonable times to require a person to show their certificate. The offences are set out in s 4:

1) If any person:

   (a) not being registered under this Act exhibits or trains any performing animal; or

   (b) being registered under this Act exhibits or trains any performing animal with respect to which or in a manner with respect to which he is not registered; or

   (c) being a person against whom an order by a court of summary jurisdiction has been made on complaint under this Act, contravenes or fails to comply with the order in any part of Great Britain, whether within or without the area of jurisdiction of that court; or

   (d) obstructs or wilfully delays any constable or officer of a local authority in the execution of his powers under this Act as to entry or inspection; or

   (e) conceals any animal with a view to avoiding such inspection; or

   (f) being a person registered under this Act, on being duly required in pursuance of this Act to produce his certificate under this Act fails without reasonable excuse so to do; or

   (g) applies to be registered under this Act when prohibited from being so registered;

   he shall be guilty of an offence against this Act and shall be liable on summary conviction upon a complaint made by a constable or an officer of a local authority to a fine ...

(2) Where a person is convicted of an offence against this Act, or against the Protection of Animals Act 1911, as amended by any subsequent enactment, the court before which he is convicted may in addition to or in lieu of imposing any other penalty;

   (a) if such person is registered under this Act order that his name be removed from the register;

   (b) order that such person shall either permanently or for such time as may be specified in the order be disqualified for being registered under this Act;

   and where such an order is made, the provisions of subsections (2), (3) and (4) of s 2 of this Act shall apply to the order as they apply to an order made under that section.

Under s 7 the Act does not apply to the training of animals for *bona fide* military, police, agricultural or sporting purposes, or the exhibition of any animals so trained. The offences are prosecuted by the police or local authorities. They have powers of entry, at all reasonable times, although they cannot go on or behind the stage during a performance. Any conviction under the Act may mean that the circus has its name removed from the register either permanently or for a specified time (s 4 (2)). If there has been cruelty in the training or exhibiting of a performing animal, an order can be made prohibiting the training or exhibition of animals or allowing it only under certain conditions (s 2 (1)). There is the right of appeal.

Liability for the action of circus animals

Circuses are liable for the actions of their animals that are out of control, as illustrated in the following case, which considered whether an elephant was dangerous even if it had been trained:

Behrens and Another v Bertram Mills Circus Ltd [1957] 2 QB 1

Devlin J read the following judgment, 30 January 1957:

The second cause of action, generally known as the *scienter* action, is the one on which Mr Brown chiefly relied. Since one of the defendants' submissions goes to the root of that form of action, I propose to begin by stating just what I take its basis to be. Before doing this I must acknowledge my indebtedness to Professor Glanville Williams, who in his book on *Liability for Animals* (1939) has dealt with the whole subject in such detail and with such clarity as to make it possible for me at least to hope that I can successfully grapple with this antiquated branch of the law and also to omit from this judgment much of the elaboration that would otherwise have to be there.

A person who keeps an animal with knowledge (*scienter retinuit*) of its tendency to do harm is strictly liable for damage it does if it escapes; he is under an absolute duty to confine or control it so that it shall not do injury to others. All animals *ferae naturae*, that is, all animals which are not by nature harmless, such as a rabbit, or have not been tamed by man and domesticated, such as a horse, are conclusively presumed to have such a tendency, so that the *scienter* need not in their case be proved. All animals in the second class *mansuetae naturae* are conclusively presumed to be harmless until they have manifested a savage or vicious propensity; proof of such a manifestation is proof of *scienter* and serves to transfer the animal, so to speak, out of its natural class into the class of *ferae naturae*. Professor Williams has traced at 265 the origin of this 'primitive rule,' as Lord Macmillan described it in *Read v J Lyons & Co Ltd* [1947] AC 156. No doubt in its time it was a great improvement on the still more primitive notion that only the animal was 'liable' for the harm it did. But now this sort of doctrine with all its rigidity – its conclusive presumptions and categorisations – is outmoded and the law favours a flexible and circumstantial approach to problems of this sort. Four years ago a committee appointed by the Lord Chancellor and presided over by Lord Goddard CJ recommended that the *scienter* action should be abolished and that liability for harm done by an animal should be the same as in the case of any other chattel; it should depend on the failure to exercise the appropriate degree of care; which might in the case of very dangerous animals be 'so stringent as to amount practically to a guarantee of safety' *per* Lord Macmillan in *Donoghue v Stevenson* [1940] 1 KB 687. I wish to express the hope that Parliament may find time to consider this recommendation, for this branch of the law is badly in need of simplification.

The particular rigidity in the *scienter* action which is involved in this case – there are many others which are not – is the rule that requires the harmfulness of the offending animal to be judged not by reference to its particular training and habits, but by reference to the general habits of the species to which it belongs. The law ignores the world of difference between the wild elephant in the jungle and the trained elephant in the circus. The elephant 'Bullu' is in fact no more dangerous than a cow; she reacted in the same way as a cow would do to the irritation of a small dog; if perhaps her bulk made her capable of doing more damage, her higher training enabled her to be more swiftly checked. But I am compelled to assess the defendants' liability in this case in just the same way as I would assess it if they had loosed a wild elephant into the funfair. This is a branch of the law, which, as Lord Goddard CJ (quoting Blackburn J *ibid,* 400) said recently in *Wormald v Cole* 25 QBD 258 has been settled by authority rather than by reason. But once the fundamental irrationality is accepted of treating circus elephants as if they were wild, I think it is possible to determine sensibly in the light of the *scienter* rule the other points on liability that arise in this case.

The defendants submit five answers to the *scienter* action. They are: First, that elephants are not *ferae naturae* within the meaning of the rule. Secondly, that the rule does not impose liability for every act that an animal does if it escapes control, but only for those acts which are vicious and savage, which the action of Bullu was not. Thirdly, that the plaintiffs' injuries were caused by their own fault. Fourthly, that the maxim *volenti non fit injuria* – that is that the plaintiffs accepted the risk – applies to them. Fifthly, that it is a good defence to liability under the rule if the action of the animal is caused by the wrongful act of a third party, in this case Whitehead and his dog.

The first submission is, in my judgment, concluded so far as this court is concerned by the decision of the Court of Appeal in *Filburn v People's Palace and Aquarium Co Ltd* (1890) 25 QBD 258; 6 TLR 402 which held that as a matter of law an elephant is an animal *ferae naturae*. Mr Van Oss has sought to distinguish this case on the ground that the elephants belonging to the defendants are Burmese elephants and he submits that it is open to me to hold that while elephants generally are *ferae naturae*, Burmese elephants are not. In my judgment, it is not open to me to consider this submission. It is not stated in *Filburn v People's Palace and Aquarium Co Ltd* (1890) 25 QBD 258; 6 TLR 402 what the nationality of the elephant was with which the court was there dealing, and the case must be regarded as an authority for the legal proposition that all elephants are dangerous. The reason why this is a question of law and not a question of fact is because it is a matter of which judicial notice has to be taken. The doctrine has from its formulation proceeded upon the supposition that the knowledge of what kinds of animals are tame and what are savage is common knowledge. Evidence is receivable, if at all, only on the basis that the judge may wish to inform himself. This was clearly settled by the Court of Appeal in *McQuaker v Goddard* [1907] 2 KB 345; L3 TLR 548 (*sub nom Hadwell v Rightson*) where Clauson LJ [1954] 1 QBD 614; [1954] 1 All ER 687 said: 'The reason why the evidence was given was for the assistance of the judge in forming his view as to what the ordinary course of nature in this regard in fact is, a matter of which he is supposed to have complete knowledge.' Common knowledge about the ordinary course of nature will extend to a knowledge of the propensities of animals according to their different genera, but cannot be supposed to extend to the manner of behaviour of animals of the same genus in different parts of the world. Nor can one begin a process of inquiry which might lead in many directions (for example, I am told that female elephants are more docile than male, and that that is why circus elephants are usually female) and be productive of minute subdivisions which would destroy the generality of the rule.

The defendants' second contention raises a point of doubt and difficulty. It may be approached in this way. The reason for imposing a specially stringent degree of liability upon the keeper of a savage animal is that such an animal has a propensity to attack mankind and, if left unrestrained, would be likely to do so. The keeper has, therefore, in the words of Lord Macmillan in *Read v J Lyons & Co Ltd* [1947] AC 156 'an absolute duty to confine or control it so that it shall not do injury.' But if it escapes from his control, is he liable (subject, of course, to the rules on remoteness of damage) for any injury which it causes, or only for such injury as flows naturally from its vicious or savage propensity?

Mr Van Oss submits that it is the latter part of this question which suggests the correct answer and that the rule of absolute liability applies only when an animal is acting savagely and attacking human beings. On the facts of this case, he submits that Bullu was not acting viciously but out of fright; she was seeking to drive off the small dog rather than to attack it; maybe she or another elephant trampled on the dog (there is no conclusive evidence of that, and it might have been crushed by falling timber) but there is nothing to show that she trampled on it deliberately. Certainly she never attacked Mrs Behrens who was injured only indirectly. In short, if Bullu could be treated as a human being, her conduct would not be described as vicious but as quite excusable.

It does not, to my mind, necessarily follow that the scope of the rule is coextensive with the reason for making it. It may equally well be argued that once the rule is made, the reason for making it is dissolved and all that then matters are the terms of the rule. That would certainly be the right approach in the case of any statutory rule of absolute liability. Is it so in the case of this rule of common law? There appears to be no authority directly in point. Mr Van Oss derives the chief support for his contention from an argument which may be summarised as follows. If an animal *mansuetae naturae* manifests a vicious tendency, the *scienter* rule applies to it as if it were *ferae naturae*. The law has often been put in that way; for example, by Lord Wright in *Knott v London County Council* [1934] 1 KB 126, 139; 50 TLR 65. How is the principle applied?

Suppose a large dog collides with a child and knocks him down, that is an accident and not a manifestation of a vicious propensity and the *scienter* rule does not apply at all; if it bites a child, it becomes *ferae naturae,* and the strict rule thereafter applies. But it would seem to be unreasonable that the strict rule should require it to be kept under complete restraint. Suppose that its keeper muzzles it and that while muzzled it playfully or accidentally knocks a child down, ought the keeper to be liable? There is a good deal of authority, referred to by Professor Williams, to show that the keeper is not liable; and the learned author considers that the damage must have in some way been intended by the animal, that its benevolence or its *mens rea* is relevant and that at least in the case of harmless animals the rule is that the injury must be the result of a vicious propensity.

This is an impressive argument. But it does not seem to me that the logic of the matter necessarily requires that an animal that is savage by disposition should be put on exactly the same footing as one that is savage by nature. Certainly practical considerations would seem to demand that they should be treated differently. It may be unreasonable to hold the owner of a biting dog responsible thereafter for everything it does; but it may also be unreasonable to limit the liability for a tiger. If a person wakes up in the middle of the night and finds an escaping tiger on top of his bed and suffers a heart attack, it would be nothing to the point that the intentions of the tiger were quite amiable. If a tiger is let loose in a funfair, it seems to me to be irrelevant whether a person is injured as the result of a direct attack or because on seeing it he runs away and falls over. The feature of this present case which is constantly arising to blur the reasoning is the fact that this particular elephant Bullu was tame. But that, as I have said, is a fact which must be ignored. She is to be treated as if she were a wild elephant; and if a wild elephant were let loose in the funfair and stampeding around, I do not think there would be much difficulty in holding that a person who was injured by falling timber had a right of redress. It is not, in my judgment, practicable to introduce conceptions of *mens rea* and malevolence in the case of animals.

The distinction between those animals which are *ferae naturae* by virtue of their genus and those which become so by the exhibition of a particular habit seems to me to be this: that in the case of the former it is assumed (and the assumption is true of a really dangerous animal such as a tiger) that whenever they get out of control they are practically bound to do injury, while in the case of the latter the assumption is that they will only do injury to the extent of the propensity which they have peculiarly manifested. It would not be at all irrational if the law were to recognise a limited distinction of this sort while holding that both classes of animals are governed by the same *scienter* rule. In the case of dangerous chattels, for example, the law has recognised, though it is not perhaps now of much importance, the distinction between chattels that are dangerous in themselves and chattels that are dangerous when used for certain purposes; and animals *ferae naturae* have frequently been compared with chattels in the former class: see, for example, *per* Hilbery J in *Parker v Oloxo Ltd* [1937] 3 All ER 524, 528 and *per* Lord Wright in *Glasgow Corporation v Muir* [1943] AC 448,464; 59 TLR 266; [1943] 2 All ER 44.

As I have said, there is really no authority on this point. There are indeed not many cases which have dealt with an animal that is *ferae naturae* by genus as distinct from disposition. In such cases as there are – *Besozzi v Harris* (1858) 1 F&F 92 and *Filburn v People's Palace* (1890) 25 QBD 258 – the rule was stated in the widest terms; but in these cases the court was dealing with an attacking animal, so that the point did not arise. Nevertheless, in my judgment, they laid down the principle that I should follow; and I think that the statement of the law by Lord Macmillan in *Read v J Lyons & Co Ltd* [1947] AC 156, 71 which I have quoted, namely that there is 'an absolute duty to confine or control it so that it shall not do injury', needs no qualification.

This conclusion is supported by *Wormald v Cole* [1954] 1 QB 614. I do not rely on that decision as an authority directly in point because it concerned the rule of absolute liability for cattle trespass, and these rules of absolute liability, while similar in effect, have different origins. But it furnishes strong support by way of analogy. In that case the plaintiff, when she was trying to get straying cattle out of her garden, was injured not because they attacked her but because in blundering about they had knocked her down. It was argued that the plaintiff could not recover because her injuries were not the result of any vicious action on the part of the cattle. This argument was rejected by the Court of Appeal. Lord Goddard CJ *ibid* 625 pointed out that in many cases it would be impossible to say with certainty whether the injuries were caused by vice or playfulness or by mere accident.

It follows that, subject to any special defence, the defendants are liable for any injury done while the elephant was out of control. It does not follow (I say this because of a point that was raised in the argument) that if an elephant slips or stumbles, its keeper is responsible for the consequences. There must be a failure of control. But here there was such a failure, albeit a very temporary one. It follows also that the ordinary rule on remoteness of damage applies. It was not suggested that if an animal which is out of control knocks over a structure and injures a person the other side of it, that is not under the ordinary rule a consequence of the failure of control.

The following case considered whether the owners of a dangerous animal were liable in the situation where a 7-year old girl had left the circus tent to look for a toilet. She entered a 'zoo' enclosure whether she was mauled by a lion. The question was whether the defendants were liable and whether the child was a trespasser. The court held that the defendants were liable as the child was, in fact, a licensee not a trespasser.

Pearson v Coleman Bros (1948) 2 KB 359

Lord Greene MR: This is a most unusual case and it is important, for its correct decision, to scrutinise the facts very carefully, because there is here a combination of facts which, in my opinion, together lead inevitably to a certain legal conclusion.

Before I read further, I want to say something about the notice on the lions' cage, because a good deal of argument was based on it. It is clear that, if the hypothesis as to the line of approach which the learned judge preferred was the right one, the plaintiff would not have read that notice, even if she could read. If, on the other hand, she approached not from the south but from the north and had seen the notice, which would have been high up above her head, and could read and understand it, it is right to say that the notice was clearly intended only as a warning to persons who might be minded to open the doors that they would find lions inside. It is clear that it was not intended as a warning to persons that lions in the cage might get their paws through the bars and injure people. In the circumstances of this case, I myself attach no importance to that notice. To read it as a warning to herself, the plaintiff, assuming that she could read it, must have interpreted it as indicating that anywhere near that cage she would be in danger, whether she opened the doors or not. It would have to indicate to her that there were lions there who could get their paws through what, to a child, I should have thought, would have seemed to be an adequate barrier, and, further, it would have meant that she must form a just estimate of the reach of the lion's paw and the extent to which she would be in danger if she passed near it. The notice was not put up for any such purpose, it was not put up to warn people of any such danger, and, in my opinion, it could not have been so interpreted by the plaintiff, even assuming that she went in by the north and even assuming that she could look up and read it.

It will be observed that I have been careful to consider all the relevant facts of the case as they appear to me – the fact of her need, the fact of her age, the fact that no lavatory was provided, the fact that she made a circuit round the tent and found nothing, and the fact that she did find a very attractive place in the end. The combination of all those facts is what leads me inevitably to the conclusion that the defendants cannot succeed. I say nothing of what the position would have been in the case of an adult who had found himself in a similar need. If he had followed the same route as this girl and had crawled through the fence or under the runway, he might very well have been met with the answer: 'To you, an adult, it was quite indicated that this was a prohibited area.' In the case of adults it can scarcely be necessary to stop up every hole through which they could possibly crawl. Adults are not expected to crawl. That might have been the answer, but I say nothing about it. I merely refer to it as showing the importance of paying due regard to all the facts of the case. Again, I say nothing about what would have happened if this little girl, being bored with the circus performance, had chosen to go out for no particular reason except curiosity and wandered into the 'zoo'. In the circumstances, she being under a compelling need, for the satisfaction of which a convenient and inviting aperture was left in what was intended to be an enclosure of the 'zoo', she is, in my opinion, justified in saying that the invitation must be taken, in her case, to have extended to this point. I think I have said sufficient to explain why, in my opinion, the appeal is entitled to succeed. The conclusion that I have come to is based on what seems to me to be the only possible inference in law on the facts of this case. Accordingly, the plaintiff is entitled to succeed and to have judgment for the amount which the judge found for damages for what she suffered.

Problems with the legal framework

The following concerns about the adequacy of the legal framework have been raised by the RSPCA. Circus proprietors claim that the RSPCA can visit training sessions, but the situation is not as straightforward as it may appear. There is a great distinction between an initial training session and a daily rehearsal, and it is the rehearsal to which the RSPCA is invited. The other problem is in relation to the fact that licences are given for life. The very nature of circuses, in that they are always on the move, also makes the enforcement of licences very difficult.[4]

Animal welfare in circuses

The concerns about animal welfare in relation to circus animals were examined in a report by M Kiley-Worthington, *Animals in Circuses and Zoos – Chirons World?*, part of which is reproduced below.[5] This highly controversial report had been partly funded by the RSPCA; however, the RSPCA criticised it as being subjective, and rejected the conclusion that circuses were no more cruel than other forms of husbandry. The report was also criticised by W Johnson, in *The Rose Tinted Menagerie*.[6] Johnson argued that instead of comparing the animals in circuses with wild animals, they had been compared to other captive animals, thus suggesting that the animals were, in fact, domesticated. Johnson argues that this is clearly not the case as wild animals keep their innate wildness in circuses, and are not domesticated:[7]

> The carnivores, except the dogs, were housed in beast wagons and now have exercise yards when encamped. The space allowance varied from 0.17–4.5 cubic metres for an adult lion in the beast wagon. The beast wagons rarely had any cage furniture although shelves are being introduced in some. The ungulates were housed in stalls, looseboxes or loose yards in tents. Some were tethered outside and some could run free some of the time. The elephants were shackled habitually in tents, although during my study electric-fenced yards were introduced and some elephants spent the majority of the day in them. Half of the elephants were allowed to move around freely with their handler for approximately one hour per day. Because a circus might have only one of a species, some animals were isolated from conspecifics. However, the nature of a moving circus is such that it was not possible for animals or people to be completely isolated. In the zoos and static circuses and winter quarters this was not always the case. The animals were transported in either their living quarters or horse boxes and converted lorries. No evidence of distress or

---

4   *Animals in Circuses* leaflet, Horsham, Surrey: RSPCA.

5   Kiley-Worthington, above n 1.

6   Johnson, W, *The Rose Tinted Menagerie*, 1990, London: Harcourt Brace.

7   *Ibid*, p 323.

trauma as a result of transportation was seen as the animals became very used to this. The animals were adequately fed and they had on the whole good veterinary supervision from the circus and zoo veterinarians. The majority of the animals were in good condition: 90% on tour. However, at the winter quarters, 70% of animals are considered not to be in peak condition. During the past two years 5.4% of the animals had reported sickness. There was a 0.97% mortality reported to me. These figures are low when compared to farms, zoos and stables. Drugs and surgery were not used to maintain the system.

The longevity of the animals compared favourably with zoos and domestic animal husbandry systems. The stockmanship was not always skilled. The stockpeople spent from ½ hour to three hours per animal per day. The handling of the stock varied from adequate to good. The training of the animals was generally professional and of a high standard and skill. There was, however, insufficient training of the animals going on in many of the circuses. Some animals had been performing the same routine for some years with no effort to teach them new things. There was no evidence for cruelty, or prolonged pain and suffering during the training of any of the animals I witnessed. Most of the training was done with the aid of positive reinforcement. Negative reinforcement (a whip or verbal scolding) was used sometimes, but no more than is usual with a good horse or dog trainer. There was some evidence of prolonged or acute behavioural distress in some of the animals in some of the housing conditions. In general, there was not significantly more of this in the circus animals than in zoos or other animal husbandry systems. There was, in the case of the horses, slightly less. However, it can be suggested that if the animal husbandry is appropriate and ethnologically and ethically sound, there should be no evidence of this ... Certain housing conditions (such as being permanently confined to beast wagons, stalls or shackled) severely behaviourally restricted the animals. Such practices are unnecessary and should and can be eliminated ... This study shows that the welfare of the animals in British circuses, as judged by physical and psychological criteria, is not as a rule inferior to that of other animal husbandry systems such as in zoos, private stables and kennels. It also points out that even if this were to be the case, there is no reason why it should be a *necessity* of the circus way of life.

It is therefore irrational to take a stand against circuses on grounds that the animals in circuses necessarily suffer, unless they are to take the same stand against zoos, stables, race horses, kennels, pets and all other animal-keeping systems.[8]

The concern over animal welfare in circuses is recognised by the RSPCA and it has lobbied extensively for local authorities to ban circuses from council-owned land. Over 200 local authorities have done so, although some still allow circuses with only domestic performing animals. This has been criticised by the International Animal Welfare Alliance (IAWA), which state in their factsheet that this leads to circuses making applications on the basis of

8   Kiley-Worthington, above n 1, pp 219–20.

domestic animals and either using their wild animals on other sites or confining them during their stay at the restricted venue. The International Animal Welfare Alliance also questions the use of domestic animals in performances. In Sweden, Denmark and India the display of performing animals in circuses has been banned or severely restricted.[9]

ZOOS

The historical development of zoos

Julius Caesar mentions in his *Commentaries* that even in those days rich English land-owners had parks in which they kept hares, geese and chickens, not for eating but almost as 'pets'. The Norman lords who came over with the Conqueror appropriated parks such as these and stocked them with deer for the chase and sometimes with less common animals also. There is a record of a nobleman receiving a bear from William Rufus, and William of Malmesbury tells us that Henry I had at Woodstock lions, leopards, lynxes, camels and other animals, including a remarkable owl which had been sent to him by William of Montpellier. Henry III, who in 1252 transferred the Woodstock collection to London, had a polar bear for whose maintenance at the Tower of London the City's sheriffs were made responsible; they were also obliged to furnish it with a muzzle and an iron chain, and a stout rope to hold it when, to save expense, it was taken down to the Thames to fish for its supper. In 1254 Henry was sent by his son-in-law, King Louis IX of France, a sensational present: the first elephant ever to be seen in England.[10] Again the unfortunate sheriffs had to bear the substantial cost of feeding it and of constructing a cage, 40 feet by 20, to house it.
...

The animals at the Tower were miserably housed in Stuart times, and Evelyn, when in Florence in 1644, commented that the city's wolves, cats, bears, tigers and lions, kept in a deep-walled court, were 'therefore to be seen with much more pleasure that those at the Tower of London, in their grates'.

In the 18th century the public was admitted to the Tower menagerie on the payment of three-halfpence or, alternatively, the provision of a cat or dog to be fed to the lions. George IV inherited only one elephant, one grizzly bear, and a few wild birds, but by the end of his reign the menagerie was again well stocked. Then came William IV who closed it down and presented the animals to the Zoological Society of London.

While zoos have had a long history, as Blunt argues it was not until the founding of London Zoo that the modern zoos began to develop.

---

9   See Johnson, above n 6 and the IAWA factsheet *Animal Circuses – the Facts*.

[10] The Macedonian historian of the 2nd century AD, Polaenus (*Stategematum*, BK VIII), is the only authority for the suggestion that Caesar used an elephant to effect a crossing of the Thames, near Chertsey. It seems improbable.

The founding of the Zoological Society of London in 1826 was, however, a landmark, and the opening of the Zoological gardens in Regent's Park a year later began the era of the modern zoo as we know it (the diminutive 'zoo' was first used in the mid-1830s).[11]

However, the first zoos were often poorly maintained:

The conditions in which the animals were kept in the typical European or American zoo of the 19th century were, to put it mildly, grim. Cramped and barred cages were the norm, little attention was given to the creatures' needs for exercise (apart from the tricks that those amenable were trained to perform to amuse the public), hygiene was non-existent, and the only minimal research took place into the special problems generated by captivity. The impossibility of keeping chimpanzees alive for more than a few months was an instructive case in point. Being, for obvious reasons, an animal in great demand, numerous healthy samples were delivered from the tropics and then promptly died. It was not discovered until the 1930s that the apes were susceptible to our minor respiratory ailments which for them are lethal. (Capture and delivery, given the rigors of sea passage, was itself barbaric and incredibly wasteful. Normal procedure was, and still is, to shoot the powerful and ferocious adults and take the babies. Even in 1985 Dale Jamieson could write: 'The rule of thumb among trappers is that 10 chimpanzees die for every one that is delivered alive to the US or Europe'. Clearly such profligacy cannot be confined only to the capture of apes.)

Nor, in the 19th and early 20th centuries, was much thought given to the actual purpose of zoos. Davy and Raffles, in London, had the provision of specimens for scientific research in mind but no sense of the need for conservation as the term now tends to be used. (Synthetic captive breeding in something approaching a natural setting was not put into practical effect until the opening of the UK's Whipsnade Zoo in 1931, although the establishment by the US Congress in 1872 of the first National Park at Yellowstone was a significant omen.) There were 19th century critics who were outspoken not only about the conditions in which the animals were kept but also the indignities and baiting to which they were subjected to please an unruly public (circuses were also a prime target in this respect), and the campaigns eventually led to the Cruelty to Wild Animals in Captivity Act of 1900.[12]

The zoo concept really began when a small number of European cities developed zoos in the early part of the 19th century. Paris, Vienna, Dublin and London are generally credited as being the first 'modern' zoos.[13]

The background to the development of London Zoo is examined in the following extract:

11 Blunt, W, *The Ark in the Park – the Zoo in the Nineteenth Century*, 1976, pp 15–17, London: Hamish Hamilton.

12 Leahy, L, Against Liberation: putting animals into perspective, 1991, pp 237–38, London: Routledge. With kind permission of Routledge.

13 World Society for the Protection of Animals/Born Free Foundation, *The Zoo Inquiry*, 1994, p 10, London.

Our modern zoological gardens and zoological parks owe their origins to the enthusiasm and foresight of one man, Sir Stamford Raffles, and a group of collaborators. After his death Lady Raffles revealed that Sir Stamford had for a long time cherished the idea of establishing in London a collection of animals from all parts of the world. Most of his life, however, was spent in the Far East as a distinguished servant of the East India Company, and it was not until he returned home for good in 1824 that he was able to go ahead with the project. He had already been in contact with a number of people in London, and even while he was on the way home a meeting of 'friends of a proposed Zoological Society' met in London and drew up a prospectus. A good deal of correspondence between Raffles as Chairman and the other members of the committee must have preceded this meeting, but unfortunately none has survived.

The earliest record we have from Raffles himself is in a letter he wrote to a cousin, Dr Thomas Raffles, in 1825: 'I am much interested in present in establishing a Grand Zoological Collection in the Metropolis, with a Society for the introduction of living animals bearing the same relations to Zoology as a science that the Horticultural Society does to Botany ... Sir Humphrey Davy and myself are the projectors, and, while he looks to the more practical and immediate utility to the country gentleman, my attention is more directed to the scientific department'. Next to Raffles, Davy, President of the Royal Society from 1820 until 1829, and the acknowledged leader of British Science at that time, played the most important part in the development of the Society. His backing probably had a considerable effect in enlisting the support of other eminent and influential men.

Frequent meetings of the committee over a period of nearly two years led finally to the first General Meeting of the Friends of the proposed Zoological Society. This took place on the 29 April 1826 at the offices of the Horticultural Society. It was at this meeting that the Zoological Society was definitely constituted, and a series of resolutions adopted fixing its principle features. The affairs of the Society were to be conducted by a President, Secretary, Treasurer and Council, and not unnaturally Raffles was elected first President. At this meeting it was also announced that the Commissioners of Woods and Forests had agreed to allocate to the Society a plot of Crown land in Regent's Park extending to about five acres.

Almost at once the Society suffered a serious blow with the death of Sir Stamford Raffles on the 6 July. He had, however, lived long enough to see the main features of his idea incorporated in a plan, and it was left to his associates to convert the plan into a reality. So well had Raffles thought out his idea that none considered any drastic modifications necessary, so the evolution of the Society followed along the lines which he had already laid down.

When we look back we can realise the profound importance of the founding of the Zoological Society, but at the time the new Society did not receive an enthusiastic welcome. The press generally ignored it altogether, and those papers which did mention it had little to say in its favour. The *Literary Gazette*, an influential journal devoted to science and literature, held the whole idea up to ridicule. 'Like too many of our modern associations and companies', it wrote, 'this is extremely sonorous on paper; but, alas for the execution of the design – is it not altogether visionary?' To be fair, such criticism at the time was probably not unreasonable. No one except those actually concerned with the development of the Society could really have been expected to believe that within a few years London would possess the world's first Zoological gardens with a large and varied collection of wild animals obtained from all parts of the world – in fact that the zoo, in the sense in which the word is now understood throughout the world, was about to be invented.

As soon as the grant of land in Regent's Park was confirmed the Council of the Society asked Decimus Burton, a famous contemporary architect who had been responsible for designing the layout of Hyde Park, to submit plans for its utilisation. Subsequently, Burton was appointed official architect to the Society. With the minimum of delay he had his plans ready, and the Council considered that the financial state of the Society justified allocating £5,000 for initial development of the Gardens. By 27 April 1828 they were ready to be opened to the public for the first time. During this first year 98,605 people paid to enter the Gardens, and the Society's income for the year was £11,515. By 1830 the Zoo was definitely established as a major public attraction and the attendance figures rose to 224,750. Plans for assembling a large and varied collection of animals were also progressing very satisfactorily. Already 178 species of mammals and 195 species of birds were on exhibition, making the collection far more representative than any other collection of wild animals which had ever been assembled anywhere before. In 1831 and in 1834 came further grants of Crown land, 10 acres on each occasion, making the total area only about five acres less than its present size.

Royal recognition was soon granted to the new venture. In 1830 William IV became Patron of the Society, and in the same year presented to the Society all the animals belonging to the royal menagerie in Windsor Park. In the following year the collection of animals in the Tower was also presented to the Zoo.

In a remarkably short time London Zoo had established its claim as the world's first zoo, and a reputation which meant that later zoos turned to Regent's Park as their guide and model. Within 10 years three other zoos, all destined to become famous in their turn, were founded in different parts of Britain.[14]

The World Society for the Protection of Animals examines the modern development of zoos and the challenges zoos face in the future:

Since that time the number of zoos has grown in fits and starts, but never more so than in the 1950s and 1960s when municipalities in search of status and businessmen in search of profit, put money into zoos. What had previously been the preserve of nations, cities and the occasionally wealthy individual became *de rigeur* throughout the developed and many parts of the developing world.

During these boom years zoos were no more than recreational facilities which displayed animals to satisfy the curiosity of the general public. Even the long-

---

14 Street, P, *Animals in Captivity*, 1965, pp 17–20, London: Faber & Faber. Reproduced with kind permission of Faber & Faber.

established scientifically-based zoos paid only marginal attention to a more serious agenda. For instance, such research as was conducted centred on efforts to breed and maintain wild animals more successfully in captivity. Hardly any zoos looked beyond their immediate circle towards their responsibilities in the wild.

During the 1970s and 1980s three factors arose which were bound to confront and challenge such an introspective attitude:

– the development of sophisticated television natural history documentaries which conveyed a more accurate interpretation of the natural world;

– expanded opportunities for global travel which made it possible for more people than ever before to see and appreciate wildlife in its natural habitat;

– increased recognition of the welfare implications of captivity as information became available about the causes of stereotyped behaviour in zoo animals.

These developments, linked to the issues of animal welfare, conservation and education, led more and more people to question the acceptability of zoos.[15]

The law relating to zoos

Zoos are licensed under the Zoo Licensing Act 1981. The Act was passed as a result of concern about the number of zoos that had opened in the 1970s and about the conditions under which many of the animals were kept. The problem was that the Protection of Animals Act 1911, while protecting captive animals, often did not cover the type of abuse that was found in the zoos, ie, animals being kept in solitary confinement. This led to lobbying by groups such as the RSPCA for a change in the law.[16]

A zoo is defined under s 1(2) of the Act as 'an establishment where wild animals (as defined by s 21) are kept for exhibition to the public otherwise than for the purpose of a circus (as so defined) and otherwise than in a pet shop; the Act applies to any zoo to which the members of the public have access with or without charge for admission, on more than seven days within any 12 consecutive months'. It is unlawful to operate a zoo without a licence from a local authority; ss 2–4 cover the licence application. Section 4 covers the considerations to be taken into account in the granting or refusal of a licence:

(1) Before granting or refusing to grant a licence for a zoo, the local authority shall:

(a) consider inspectors' reports made in pursuance of inspections of the zoo under this Act; or

---

15 *The Zoo Inquiry*, above n 13, p 10.

16 For the background to the Act and a critique of the Zoo Licensing Act 1981, see *RSPCA Today*, Summer 1988, pp 24–25, Horsham: RSPCA.

(b) if no inspection of the zoo has been made under this Act, consult such persons on the list as the Secretary of State nominates for the purposes of this section.

(2) The local authority shall refuse to grant a licence for a zoo if they are satisfied that the establishment or continuance of the zoo would injuriously affect the health or safety of persons living in the neighbourhood of the zoo, or seriously affect the preservation of law and order.

(3) The local authority may refuse to grant a licence for a zoo if they are not satisfied that the standards of accommodation, staffing or management are adequate for the proper care and well-being of the animals or any of them or otherwise for the proper conduct of the zoo.

(4) The local authority may also refuse to grant a licence if:

(a) the applicant; or

(b) (where the applicant is a body corporate) the body or any director, manager, secretary or other similar officer of the body; or

(c) any person employed as a keeper in the zoo,

has been convicted of an offence under this Act or under any of the enactments mentioned in subsection (5) or of any other offence involving the ill-treatment of animals.

(5) The enactments are:

– the Protection of Animals Acts 1911–64;

– the Protection of Animals (Scotland) Acts 1912–64;

– the Pet Animals Act 1951;

   . . .

– the Animal Boarding Establishments Act 1963;

– the Riding Establishments Acts 1964 and 1970;

– the Breeding of Dogs Act 1973;

   . . .

– the Dangerous Wild Animals Act 1976;

– the Endangered Species (Import and Export) Act 1976;

– [Part I of the Wildlife and Countryside Act 1981.]

(6) If the local authority are not satisfied that any planning permission required under Part III of [the Town and Country Planning Act 1990] or under the Town and Country Planning (Scotland) Act 1972, for the establishment of the zoo or for the continuance of the zoo during the period for which the licence would be in force, has been, or is deemed to be, granted, they shall either refuse to grant the licence or grant the licence but suspend its operation until the local planning authority within the meaning of [the said Act of 1990] or, as the case may be, 1972 have notified the local authority that any such planning permission has been or is deemed to be granted.

(7) Except as provided by this section the local authority shall not refuse to grant a licence pursuant to an application and if they do refuse to grant it they shall send to the applicant by post a written statement of the grounds of their refusal.

(8) When a licence is granted the local authority shall send it to the applicant by post and the licence or a copy of it shall be publicly displayed at each public entrance to the zoo.

The Act also covers small bird collections, butterfly houses and aquaria. Inspectors are nominated by the Secretary of State and local authorities. The Secretary of State under s 9 can set down standards of modern zoo practice. These contain minimum standards for the management of both the zoo and the animals in it in relation to accommodation, food, disease control, veterinary care, insurance, record keeping, the movement of animals and the safety of staff and visitors. The Secretary of State also has to compile a list of veterinary surgeons/practitioners who have experience of zoo animals and persons who are competent to inspect animals and zoos and to advise on the management of zoos and on the welfare of animals. The Secretary of State can consult the National Federation of Zoological Gardens and National Zoological Association and any other person the Secretary of State thinks fit (s 8).

Local authorities can also undertake periodic inspections, but have to give 28 days' notice (s 10). They must inspect a zoo every three years and the inspection must be carried out not later than six months before the end of the fourth year or after the first year or six months before the end of the sixth year if it is renewed in the third year (s 10(1)). The local authority is required to carry out informal inspections once a year (s 12). If there is a complaint, the local authority may instigate a special investigation (s 11). The licence may have conditions attached to it under s 3 in relation to the following areas:

(a) precautions to be taken against the escape of animals, and steps to be taken in the event of any escape or unauthorised release;

(b) records to be kept of the numbers of different animals, of acquisitions, births, deaths, disposals or escapes of animals, of the causes of any such deaths, and of the health of animals;

(c) insurance against liability for damage caused by animals.

(4) In deciding what (if any) conditions to attach to a licence, a local authority shall have regard to any standards specified by the Secretary of State under s 9 and sent by him to the authority.

(5) A local authority shall attach to a licence any condition which the Secretary of State directs them to attach.

(6) The authority shall not attach to a licence any condition inconsistent with one they are so directed to attach.

(7) The authority shall not attach to a licence a condition which relates only or primarily to the health, safety or welfare of persons working in the zoo.

Special procedures are set down in s 13 in relation to local authority zoos. These include the requirement to send the Secretary of State a copy of the licence and the inspector's report. The Secretary of State then decides whether a licence should be revoked.

A zoo licence can be revoked under s 17:

(1) The local authority may, after giving the holder an opportunity to be heard, revoke a licence for a zoo granted by them under this Act–

    (a) if any reasonable requirements relating to the premises or conduct of the zoo notified by them to the holder in consequence of the report of any inspection under this Act are not complied with within such time as is reasonable in the circumstances;

    (b) if they are satisfied that the zoo has been conducted in a disorderly manner or so as to cause a nuisance, or in breach of any conditions of the licence;

    (c) if the holder (or, where the holder is a body corporate, the body or any director, manager, secretary or other similar officer of the body) is convicted of any offence mentioned in s 4 (4);

    (d) if any person who, to the knowledge of the holder, has been so convicted is employed as a keeper in the zoo.

(2) No licence may be revoked under subsection (1)(a) or (b) on grounds involving the care or treatment of animals unless the authority first consults such persons on the list as the Secretary of State may nominate for the purposes of this subsection.

(3) The local authority shall take reasonable steps to secure that the holder of the licence is notified in writing of their decision to revoke the licence.

There is also a code of conduct governing the Health and Safety of Employees issued by the HSE.[17]

Do we need zoos?

Zoos tend to base the rationale for their existence on the grounds of conservation, science and education.[18] These grounds were outlined in the House of Commons Environment Committee's *Fifth Report on London Zoo* published in 1991:

> Zoos are under a lot of pressure these days to justify their existence. In the past, collections of animals were assembled largely to entertain the public or to satisfy the private whim; there was often little understanding of the animals' biological or behavioural needs and even less perception of a responsibility to

---

17 See Slapper, G, (1996) 146 *New Law Journal*, No 6730, p 189.

18 These claims were outlined in the House of Commons Environment Committee 5th Report, *London Zoo*, 1991, Cmnd 427. Parliamentary copyright is reproduced with the permission of the Controller of Her Majesty's Stationery Office.

justify the collection in terms of science, conservation or popular education. For responsible zoos this has changed dramatically.

The process of change really began in the 1950s with a new awareness that the world's wildlife resources were limited. Over the next 20 years, it became more difficult to obtain animals from the wild for a variety of reasons, including protective legislation in the countries of origin, reduced availability of animals, increased expense of obtaining animals and stricter health regulations governing the import of exotic species. Simultaneously, the science of exotic animal care developed veterinary techniques and the management expertise necessary to create captive environments where animals flourished and reproduced successfully. Thus, self-sustaining captive populations were founded for many species.

In the 1970s, increased restrictions on trade in wild species further encouraged zoos to build up their captive breeding programmes. In addition to the new technology and expertise, many zoos established co-operative arrangements amongst themselves to facilitate the exchange of information and of individual animals necessary for the maintenance and growth of such programmes. Today in the UK we have the Joint Management of Species Programme under which threatened and high risk species are managed as a group by a consortium of zoos to maximise reproductive success. Similar programmes also exist in the US and now the European continent.

Zoos are now entering yet another stage, one in which they contribute directly to the conservation of species in the wild and, increasingly where 'the wild' no longer exists, to preserve species from extinction. At the same time, zoos are facing threats to their own survival, threats which stem from criticism of their cost, sensationalist media stories and argument, usually ill-informed, about the role that zoos play in science and society. To respond to the growing debate, zoos must rationalise their existence in relation to three important concepts: conservation, education and research.

Each of these words is much bandied about and means different things to different people. Indeed the word 'zoo' is loosely used to describe a variety of operations, many of which are nothing more than roadside menageries still aimed solely at providing popular entertainment and making a commercial profit for their owners. Such enterprises are often deservedly criticised and some have closed with the coming of the Zoo Licensing Act. Unfortunately there is a tendency to tar all zoos with the same brush, regardless of fundamental differences in their philosophy, the quality of care given to their animals and their contribution to science and conservation.

Ultimately the conservation of animals and plants in the wild depends upon recognition of their financial, scientific or cultural importance. Such recognition takes time to develop. By acting as a reservoir for species, zoos not only act as a safety device in case of or when they become extinct in nature, but can also provide the animals necessary to reintroduce the species into the wild once the threats to their survival have been controlled. Such was the case, for example, with the Arabian oryx, a species which was totally exterminated in the wild but eventually returned to its native habitat using entirely zoo-bred stock.

Another example is the scimitar-horned oryx which is down to dangerously low levels if not extinct in the wild but which has flourished in captivity.

There is already a programme underway for their reintroduction into Tunisia and there are plans to expand the work, involving not only oryx but addax and damn gazelles amongst others in other parts of North Africa. Examples of candidates for future reintroduction projects are the Priewalski horse, the Bali mynah, and the Partula snail, to name but a few of the potential candidates.

A second important function of any good zoo must be the education of the visitor. Regardless of the scientific expertise of the individual, he or she can expect to learn something every time he walks through the zoo gate. Catering to the intellectual demands of a spectrum of educational and age groups so that they learn something and appreciate it is not easy and at ZSL[19] we maintain a large education department and a graphics unit specifically to inform our visitors about the animals, where they come from, what they like to cat, how many babies they have, etc.

For many people, especially those living in towns, this is the closest they will come to seeing wild animals and even with the high quality of the current wildlife films, there is no replacement for seeing the real thing. One must appreciate that for many people an animal simply isn't real if they only see it on a television screen. Of course it is argued that seeing an animal in the zoo is no substitute for seeing it in the wild and that may be true. However for many people it is simply a financial impossibility to go to Africa or South America to see the animal (if they are lucky) in the wild. For these people and many more, zoos provide an opportunity to make the emotional and rational commitment essential to the future of conservation.

Finally, it should be appreciated that zoos provide a unique opportunity for research, the results of which may be crucial to the survival of species. Veterinary information obtained in captivity on the capture, handling and transport of animals has proven vital to the successful relocation of wild animals. Reproductive information, again obtained in captivity, has been extremely useful to field studies. For example, analysis at ZSL of rhino urine makes it possible to pinpoint exactly when the female is in oestrus and when she becomes pregnant – significant information for a project in Kenya on the biology of rhinos. Zoos provide a wealth of information in other ways too. Data on the analysis of elephant milk, for example allows us to provide the correct dietary substitute for orphaned elephants in Kenya. Zoo personnel are involved in field projects all over the world, either by making their specialised knowledge available or by themselves directly participating in the projects. Nobody is arguing that zoos are perfect or that they are a substitute for the wild, but it is important to place them the responsible, good zoos – in the overall context of conservation and to recognise that they perform a valuable function.

---

19   London Zoological Society.

Conservation

A pragmatic argument for the importance of zoos in relation to their work in conservation is examined in the next extract:[20]

> The extent to which zoos can help by captive breeding to save endangered species is of course limited, and most obviously so by the minute selection of species from the animal kingdom as a whole that they are able to keep. But why should that invalidate the contribution that they *can* make to the immensely important cause of animal conservation, especially as it is likely to be possible for them, if necessary, to keep a very large proportion of the larger – and threatened – vertebrates, mammals especially? We could, true, make the real situation clearer by calling zoos 'selected charismatic mega-vertebrate conservation centres', to emphasise their limited role, and perhaps then, just as bird gardens, presumably, need not feel morally inadequate for not even trying to breed endangered mammals, SCMCCs (or zoos) would not be condemned, as Kieran Mulvaney seeks to condemn them, for having saved at the most a dozen species from extinction; 'a mere 0.00012% of all the life forms on earth', perhaps 'less species within the last 150 years than have become extinct over the last couple of days'. What Mulvanely leaves out is that we don't value all species equally, although he clearly differentiates between them as much as the rest of us. The evidence is there in his photograph, in the presence of his English setter. Dogs are special – to humans. We would regret their extinction more than we would regret the extinction of any of the vast number of invertebrate species, mostly beetles, that allow Mulvaney to shrink, as he does, the zoo achievement. I accept that every species – protozoan, alga, bacterium – is of immense scientific interest and sometimes (eg many protozoans) of exquisite beauty too. Every one is the product of thousands of millions of years of evolution. Still more do I accept that to save the rainforest from the appalling way in which it is being destroyed for the shortest of short-term advantages is of the utmost importance, and much more important even than saving any charismatic mega-vertebrate. But what I do not accept is that the need to save natural habitats such as rainforests, and the millions of species contained in them, can in any way mean that it is not right to try to save such exceptional species – in terms of their appeal to humans – as the Arabian oryx or the Californian condor. To save either of these is comparable, as an achievement, to saving the Taj Mahal.
>
> My emphasis on the animals zoos keep as being invariably ones that appeal to humans may seem unduly anthropocentric, and it also fails to recognise the responsibility a zoo like Jersey feels to save species in need of help (such as the many threatened island populations of boas, for example, or the Volcano rabbit, or peccaries) irrespective of their human appeal. The scientific importance of such work should not be underrated, or indeed the way in which Jersey emphasises the importance of conservation in the field and *ex situ* as two sides of one coin. But it is still the case that the saving of a species like

20   Bostock, S St C, *Zoos and Animal Rights*, 1993, pp 151–53, London: Routledge. Reproduced with kind permission of Routledge.

the Arabian oryx can be quite properly compared to the saving of some great work of art and given proper credit as something immensely worth doing – even though it isn't as important as saving the South American rainforest.

Zoos are accused of swallowing up large sums of money which would be better spent protecting actual natural habitats, and it is noted that both Operation Oryx and the attempt to save the Californian condor by captive breeding have been immensely expensive. Both the oryx and the condor are charismatic mega-vertebrates, and their appeal to us is and should be perfectly comparable to that of some great human work of art (like the Taj Mahal). We would spend millions to save that; it is creditable, not profligate, to spend millions trying to save the two species. The second point is that in these two cases captive breeding happens or happened to be the only way to do it, or at least seems the best way. Of course, if we could have saved either of these for the same or less money by protecting their habitats, that would have been the way to do it. But we are right to try to save them, and by the best method available in the particular circumstances.

To say that zoos' money would be better spent on the protection of natural habitats may be correct, but not necessarily more so than the fact that (as Mulvaney reminds us) the claims of disappearing forest are so desperately serious as to dwarf the claims to public money of the Royal Shakespeare Company or the Royal Opera House or any such inessential institution. But in any case it is true of any zoo that much of its money comes form the gate, and, if the zoo did not exist, would in no way be available instead for conservation of wild habitats – just as, indeed, government grants for London Zoo (in as much as they exist) would, if withdrawn, be highly unlikely to be diverted to conservation in the wild instead. On the other hand, if zoos directly or indirectly raise money for conservation in the wild, that is as it were a bonus for the wild; money that would not otherwise have been available.

However, this argument is rejected in an article first published in the *Evening Standard* and later reproduced in *Outrage*, 'Why we Should Get Rid of London Zoo',[21] by Andrew Tyler, which considers whether, in fact, zoos are adequate to further the aims of conservation, science and education:

Conservation

The way to conserve vanishing species is to preserve their habitats not pickle them in zoos, either as specimens or frozen embryos. Captivity induces psychological and physical damage, making most creatures unsuitable for reintroduction into the wild. Repatriating predators is next to impossible, anyhow, since they won't know how to hunt. Not surprisingly, and despite great self-congratulatory fanfares, Western zoos (which, until the mid-70s, were the main consumers of wildlife) have been responsible for repatriating just a few members of the handful of the 5,000 species on the World Conservation Union's threatened list – and at no small cost. Compare the £25 million and years of work needed to save a few Arabian oryx using captive

---

21 Tyler, A, 'Why we Should Get Rid of London Zoo', *Outrage*, Oct/Nov 1991, Tonbrigde, Kent: Animal Aid Society. Reproduced with kind permission of the London Evening Standard.

breeding strategies, with the £500,000 currently required to complete the erection of a protective electric fence around a black rhino sanctuary in Kenya's Aberdere National Park. Wild animals don't need help in breeding, which is what much zoo conservation activity is about. They already know how to do that. They need help in surviving. They need to be conceded actual territory, inside which they will be protected. The £18 million London Zoo wants for its conservation centre would buy lots of protection for, say, the gorillas of Zaire, or the orang-utans of Indonesia. But, apart from the inefficiency, captive breeding comes replete with serious hazards and pitfalls. Zoos breed from too narrow a genetic pool, notwithstanding swaps between different zoological collections.

The result is a high incidence of congenital deformities typical of in-breeding. Equally serious, is the risk of taking novel, potentially devastating diseases into the wild with the repatriated group. Eleven golden lion tamarins from a Washington zoo nearly went 'home' to Brazil in January harbouring a deadly virus believed to have been picked up from mice. Zoos are a hospitable environment for such bugs, being packed with numerous different species and with a plentiful supply of free-running rodents and insects. The wild-born groups with whom the zoo tamarins were to join would have had no immunity against the mouse bug, and could thus have been wiped out.

Science

The Zoological Society of London engages in much experimental work related to animal reproduction and nutrition. Yet, for all of its state-of-the-art brilliance, it couldn't work out that you don't feed meat to herbivores, not even if the meat comes temptingly cheap in pelleted form as fed to farm animals. The penalty paid was an outbreak, early last year, of 'Mad Cow' spongiform encephalopathy (BSE). One of the victims was an Arabian oryx, a member of the very same species that is claimed as a great captive breeding success. Oryx from the Society's stocks are still due for reintroduction to Arabia. Will these returnees be carrying the BSE bug – an agent that incubates without symptoms for up to eight years? If so, the whole Arabian Oryx population could be in danger, given that the latest research indicates that the disease can be passed on from parent to offspring.

Beyond all this, the general public might be somewhat startled to learn of some of the other work going on at the Zoo's research institute: for instance, the decapitation of fully conscious wallabies in an experiment designed to understand reproduction in giant pandas and also to shed light on jet lag and 'winter depression' in human beings: the use of surgical burning and chemical techniques to destroy the sense of smell of a group of marmoset monkeys to see if their breeding rates improved; the force-feeding of rats with chemicals used in dyes and explosives to see how their fertility was affected – this last a collaborative effort with ICI.

Education

What kind of message does such work send out to a public that has been instructed to think of their zoos as animal arks, as places of safety for wild beasts? And what kind of message does the London Zoo itself send out when few of the inhabitants are afforded the space or logistics to do what comes naturally?

It has birds who are not permitted to fly, big cats with no room to run, elephants who live in an arid concrete structure and monkeys trapped behind glass in stone cells. The only educational value of such exhibits is to teach the public that when it comes to animals, human beings can be incomparably stupid.

Far from having the right kind of credentials for running or co-running a theme park dedicated to explaining the stresses suffered by endangered species, the Royal Zoological Society and its principal officers are uniquely unfitted for such a task.

Their insensitivity on these matters was exposed once again this summer with a seven stage music festival right in the heart of the zoo complex. No doubt the electronic ear bashing given the animals, together with the rowdy cries of drunken revellers, came under the heading of behavioural enrichment.

David Attenborough recently spoke out in favour of a rehashed Regents Park 'collection' but he must have been blinded by sentiment and old zoological loyalties. His own TV documentaries are a powerful enough argument that there are more effective ways of witnessing the majesty of nature.

One hundred and sixty years has been too long. It's time for London Zoo or whatever else it might call itself to go and to go now.

Even if the conservation aims of a zoo are accepted, some authors such as N Myers highlight the problem of the adequacy and effectiveness of zoos engaging in captive breeding as a conservation strategy:[22]

Breeding animals in captivity often results in breeding them for captivity. By way of illustration, the Nene goose, frequently cited as a success story, was rescued from its native Hawaii (where it had been reduced from about 25,000 in the year 1700 to only 43 by 1940) and the survivors were bred up at the Wildfowl Trust in England until a sufficient number could be released into the wild to establish a new population. The wild stock of over 3,000 individuals now shows a high level of infertility among males, apparently associated with in-breeding. This population bears out the rule of thumb that a vertebrate breeding stock with fewer than 50 individuals is liable to carry on built-in potential with its own destruction, since in-breeding brings together the harmful genes that larger pools can accommodate. While some species are much better adapted than others to captive breeding, scientists have almost none of the necessary background information for virtually all species that are threatened or rare.

Furthermore, many species seem disinclined to breed in captivity. Cheetah, penguins and humming-birds are notoriously difficult. There has been very limited reproduction on the part of whales in captivity and virtually none of bats. Only about 10% of reptile species in zoos have propagated themselves.

In any case, zoos as a 'last-ditch strategy' for conservation do not always produce the best return per dollar. The cost of maintaining, say, a 100-plus

---

22   Myers, N, *The Sinking Ark*, 1979, pp 219–20, Oxford: Pergamon Press. Reproduced with kind permission of N Myers.

herd of certain herbivores could range from $75,000 to $250,000 per year, much more than is generally the cost of maintaining a similar number in the wild – and even then, the stock could well lose half its genetic viability. Similarly, while it is true that genes may shortly be synthesised on a sizeable scale, opening the way to eventual development of whole new organisms, this procedure would prove far more costly than conserving gene pools already available in natural form.

Welfare of the animals

There is a concern about the welfare of wild animals confined in zoos. Bill Jordan and Stefan Ormrod argue that the issue of confinement is more complex than it would first appear. The concerns centre around the question of the effects of confinement on the well-being and health of the animals in the zoo:[23]

> As for the issue of confinement, this is largely a matter of degree. A Robin redbreast in a cage might understandably put all Heaven in a rage, but before a zoo biologist passed judgment he would want to know the size, shape and quality of that cage. A conventional goldfish bowl or parrot cage, for instance, should make Heaven rage because they can be classed as precise cruelty (even though legal), whereas some of the better aquariums and free-flight aviaries to be seen in zoos might be expected to placate even the severest critics.

> No wild animal is free in the sense understood by the average citizen. Each living creature is confined by a maze of restrictions. These may be environmental, or may involve the presence of other animals or members of its own species, or the availability of food. If these factors are taken into consideration and the animal's normal biological needs are catered for, what does it suffer by being captive? As our scientific knowledge improves so does the lot of the zoo animal. It is infinitely better off than its wild counterpart (and also the average pet hamster), for it has a regular, well-balanced diet, constant shelter, no territorial disputes, plus the benefits of the most up-to-date advances in surgery and medicine. Is it to be wondered at that the zoo specimen can expect a longer life than it would in the wild?

The authors, however, question that while the above maybe 'a credible hypothesis of the functions of the modern zoo ... that it bears little resemblance to the state of affairs in Britain' (p 14). They criticise zoos on the grounds that they fail to provide adequate research, education or conservation facilities.

---

23   Jordan, W and Ormrod, S, *The Last Great Wild Beast Show – a discussion of the failure of British animal collections*, 1978, pp 13–14, London: Constable.

Reform of the zoo concept

Some practical reforms for zoos have been suggested by David Hancocks, executive director of Arizona-Sonara Desert Museum:[24]

> The zoo concept has remained unchanged since 1828. Typically, zoos are still arranged taxanomically. This means that visitors go to one place to see bears, then another to see monkeys, or cats or birds, or reptiles and so on. In addition, almost every zoo duplicates the same collection focusing principally on mammalian, diurnal, African, cute, pretty, social and essentially charismatic large species. Several important problems result.
>
> Because of their self-imposed limitations, zoos cannot present the connections between soils, plants, and animals; are unable to reveal the dynamics of ecological systems; do not tell how the little life forms, with greater biomass and more direct links to ecosystems, are essential to running the world; are incapable of explaining why biological diversity is so vital; have no tools to discuss the interdependencies of all living things. In short they do not exhibit and interpret the complexity of habitats. Most zoos are still characterised merely by lions and tigers and bears.
>
> None of this refutes the fact that many zoos, notably in North America and Australia, have made significant improvements in recent years. Accredited zoos in the US alone have spent over one billion dollars in capital developments in the past three years. Moreover, these same zoos now operate more than 70 co-ordinated Species Survival Programs. The problem is that these changes have not gone far enough, or in the right direction.
>
> Physical improvements have been mostly superficial. Too many new zoo 'habitats' include such things as mud banks made of concrete, and trees of plastic resin, sometimes with metal leaves. Too often, electric fences surround any natural vegetation. Worse, the off-exhibit service areas, where animals commonly spend most of their time, are unchanged from the iron-barred cages of the Victorian era, with clanging metal doors and reverberating screams.
>
> Further, the typically shallow composition of most zoo collections is reflected in the Species Survival programs. Thus 70% of them are for mammals, almost entirely large, exotic charismatic species. The program includes only six reptiles and, despite the cataclysmic decline of frogs, just one amphibian. The planet's millions of invertebrate species are represented in the program by only the parula snail. Zoos are undoubtedly working hard to save several rare and endangered species, but principally only those important to zoos, not necessarily the most vital for nature. In any case, if you set out to create an institution dedicated to breeding and maintaining animals for reintroduction to the wild, you would not design a public zoo. Essentially, zoos are places for exhibition.
>
> Zoos have potential to make very significant contributions to conservation, but not in their present form. Their greatest opportunity lies in public education. Millions visit zoos each year, many with open minds, hungry for contact with

24 Hancocks, D, 'Can Zoos Survive?', *Animals International*, Summer 1995, no 51, p 11, WSPA. Reproduced with the kind permission of the World Society for the Protection of Animals.

the 'other world' of nature. The Victorian zoo-goer wanted to only see what big, wild animals looked like. That was sufficient for then. Today we have different needs. Now, we are engaged in massive destruction of the planet's biological diversity. We've destroyed nature since the dawn of our time on Earth. But we do it now on a terrifying scale and in such awful ignorance.

We therefore need a better informed more sympathetic citizenry that will learn to tread lightly on the Earth. Our present day zoological and botanical gardens, with their narrow focus on exotic species as charismatic curiosities, are insufficient to the task, We should instead develop Gardens of Ecology: places that dedicate equal time to geology, botany, and zoology: give emphasis to the microfauna: interpret natural habitats: so that conservation messages can be brought directly home.

An Ecology Garden, more than any Zoological or Botanical Garden would at least give us the chance to remind ourselves, as John Muir told us, that 'we all live in a house of one room'.

As regards legislation, various proposals have been put forward. At a European level the Community Association of Zoos and Aquaria has suggested this outline for an EU directive on standards for the accommodation and care of animals in zoos:[25]

The Council of the European Communities has decided that the aim of this Directive is to establish minimum acceptable standards in the laws of the Member States for the protection of animals in zoos. National legislation should ensure that animals are suitably cared for and housed with due regard for their specialised physical and behavioural needs, their safety, and the health and safety of the public.

In the context of zoo animals, care is a word which encompasses all aspects of the relationship between the owner/operator, management and curatorial staff of a zoo and the animals exhibited or held by that zoo. Its substance is the sum of all material and non-material resources allocated to the welfare of the animal and the satisfaction of its needs. It should begin from the moment an animal is born or hatched or taken into captivity and continue until that animal dies.

Identification and satisfaction of the specialised needs of the multitude of species kept in zoos is a complex and developing science. It is unrealistic to expect that all establishments falling within the spectrum of the definition of zoos will be able to devote the resources necessary to advance this science. However, there are minimum standards of care and husbandry which it is not only possible but necessary for zoos to implement. Those zoos which cannot meet these standards should be closed and the animals involved either found suitable accommodation elsewhere or, if this proves impossible, humanely destroyed. In short, keeping animals in captivity under conditions which result in poor welfare or suffering is unjustifiable and unacceptable.

Satisfaction of an animal's needs does not require duplication of its natural environment. Indeed, it would be unacceptable under captive conditions to

25   For a discussion of the proposed directive, see Plant, G (1995) 4(7) EECR 204–09.

reproduce certain elements of every animal's existence in the wild, for example, predation and disease, both of which may impose serious, albeit natural suffering, upon the wild individual. Animals respond to the quality of their environment in which the quantity of space available to them is but one factor. Captivity is unnatural but provided the care, environment and husbandry of the animal caters to its needs, it is not cruel. For a growing number of species, zoos represent a last refuge from extinction. Furthermore, the techniques and expertise being developed today in zoos will increasingly be required in the management of fragmented and isolated populations of species in the wild. In addition to this vital role in conservation, zoos can also provide an invaluable opportunity to increase public awareness of the diversity and fragility of animal life provided the animals are exhibited in a way which enhances the onlooker's understanding of the species.

Accepting that zoos have a vital role in the conservation of species and public education, it must also be accepted that the keeping of animals under conditions which impose suffering upon the animal, and/or jeopardise public health and safety is morally unacceptable, and scientifically and educationally without value.

Article 1

The aim of this Directive is to ensure that the provisions laid down by law, regulation or administrative provisions in the Member States for the protection and welfare of animals kept in zoos and the safety of the public visitor are harmonious and to ensure that all zoo animals are subject to minimum standards of care and management.

Article 2

For the purposes of this Directive the following definitions shall apply:

a) *Zoos* shall refer to all establishments open to and administered for the public to provide education, recreation and cultural enjoyment through the exhibition of animals. This definition shall include zoos, animals parks, safari parks, bird gardens, dolphinaria, aquaria and specialist collections such as butterfly houses;

b) *Animals* shall refer to all species of the animal kingdom including species of the classes Mammalia, Aves, Reptilia, Amphibia, Pisces, Arthropoda and Mollusca.

c) *Welfare* shall refer to the physical and social well-being of animals through the provision of appropriate conditions for the species involved including but not necessarily limited to housing, environment, diet, medical care and social contact where applicable.

d) *Authority* means the authority or authorities designated by each Member State as being responsible for ensuring the compliance of zoos with the provisions of this Directive.

Article 3

Within two years of the entry into force of this Directive Member States shall take the requisite measures to ensure that all zoos conform to this Directive.

Article 4

1. Any zoo shall be subject to the harmonised standards of animal husbandry and maintenance contained in Annex 1 of this Directive.

2. Any zoo shall also be required to conform to the standards of public safety specified in Annex 1 of this Directive.

Article 5

Each Member State shall adopt legislation to ensure that every zoo shall be required to do the following:

1. To maintain a high standard of animal husbandry with a developed programme of preventative and curative veterinary care, nutrition and scientifically based breeding.

2. To maintain its animals under conditions which are suited to the behavioural, social and biological requirements of the individual species.

3. To maintain its animals under conditions which ensure their safety and the health and safety of the staff and the public visitor.

4. To ensure that staff responsible for the care of the animals are adequately trained so as to execute their responsibilities properly.

5. To comply with and promote the spirit of international treaty obligations as well as national legislation regarding the acquisition, import, export, transit and transport of animals; and to promote an understanding of nature and the natural world.

6. To display accurate identification of the species exhibited and descriptions of some biological aspects of these species.

7. To keep records to the extent possible of the numbers, species and sex of the animals and of the numbers and conditions of births, the numbers and causes of deaths and the method of disposal of animals in accordance with Annex 1.

8. To provide access to the animals, premises, equipment and records of the establishment at all reasonable times by authorised inspectors designated by the competent authorities of the Member States.

Article 6

1. Each Member State shall designate an authority competent for the inspection of all parts of the zoo premises, their husbandry techniques and equipment to ensure compliance with this Directive, particularly the requirements defined in Article 5.

2. Member States shall adopt the necessary measures in order that the authorities designated under paragraph 1 of this Article may have the advice of experts competent to assess the matters in question.

Article 7

Each zoo shall require a licence to operate. Such licences shall be issued following inspection and at the discretion of the competent authorities of the Member States, who may attach conditions to the licences requiring improvements to be made to ensure compliance with this Directive.

Article 8

Each licence issued by the Member States shall be reviewed by the Member State's designated authority every four years to ensure continued compliance with this Directive.

Article 9

Each Member State shall provide to the Commission of European Communities a list of all licences issued by that State and the conditions imposed upon these licences. This list will be updated every two years.

Article 10

Failure by any zoo to comply with this Directive or to implement the necessary improvements in order to comply within a reasonable period of time to a maximum of 12 months from date of inspection shall result in the removal of that zoo's licence to operate and the closure of that zoo to the public.

Article 11

This Directive shall take effect within two years of adoption.

This Directive has not yet been implemented in the EU and was withdrawn in 1995.

Wider reforms have been called for and are presented by the World Society for the Protection of Animals/Born Free Foundation in The Zoo Inquiry:[26]

2.0 Summary of the Recommendations

2.1 Welfare recommendations

A legislative programme of zoo reform should be undertaken which will:

1   Establish enforceable minimum animal welfare standards, initially on a European basis.

2.   Establish a mandatory licensing system to include as licence to operate, a licence to breed and compulsory accredited staff training programmes.

3.   Introduce a 'passport system' for wild animals in zoos to ensure accountability in the transfer, sale exchange or disposal of stock.

4.   Draw up provisions for a 'Zoo Bond' in the form of a guaranteed closure fund into which all zoos pay. This will underwrite operational and care costs in the event of closure for a limited period thereby ensuring that the closure of zoos does not cause the unnecessary suffering of zoo animals.

5.   Establish a national consultative council to include wildlife professionals, humane society representatives, zoo professionals and animal behaviourists and psychologists charged with drawing up, as a matter of urgency, ethical guidelines, procedures and a Code of Conduct aimed at protecting wild animals in captivity.

---

26   World Society for the Protection of Animals/Born Free Foundation, *The Zoo Inquiry*, 1994, pp 6–7, London. Reproduced with the kind permission of the World Society for the Protection of Animals.

2.2 Conservation recommendations

1. A programme of preventive measures aimed at involving, empowering and supporting local people in conserving and valuing their wildlife heritage *in situ* should be the primary engine of the global conservation strategy.

2. There should be a national and international shift in emphasis and resources towards habitat-based conservation, including, where appropriate, *in situ* captive breeding.

2.3 Educational recommendations

1. Zoo education strategies should not be based around the confinement of wild animals but should focus on the protection of the ecosystems.

2. Zoos should develop educational outreach programmes to link with conservation and environmental initiatives in the field.

3. Zoos' educational strategies for the future should be pro-active, encouraging participation in problem-solving rather that crisis-watching.

3. Philosophy and challenge

3.1 Philosophy

The most appropriate place to undertake wildlife conservation is in the natural habitat. BFF and WSPA campaign to deploy resources away from captivity towards *in situ* conservation.

The majority of animals in zoos have no other purpose than for human recreation. The BFF and WSPA are opposed to the confinement of wild animals for entertainment.

Most zoo animals face a life in captivity in which their welfare is severely compromised. The BFF and WSPA are totally opposed to unnecessary animal suffering.

Present zoo-based conservation strategies have, at best, only a marginal impact on species conservation.

The educational value of zoos merely confirms attitudes towards confinement, domination, entertainment and trivialises the intrinsic worth of wild animals. The BFF and WSPA support the development of non-animal education initiative to focus attention on conservation in the wild and to encourage an understanding of entire ecosystems.

3.2 Challenge to Zoo Directors

Does the keeping of animals in zoos in any way help the survival of ecosystems and their animals in the wild?

1. What proportion of your resources are spent on *in situ* conservation?

2. What justification is there for keeping animals in your zoo?

3. Should any animal be kept in captivity if it cannot be provided with appropriate physical, social and environmental conditions. Are your animals provided for?

4. Should zoos be devoting captive space to species that are not categorised as being under threat and which are not part of recognised captive breeding and reintroduction programmes. How many such species do you have?

5. Does the exhibition of live captive animals at your zoo significantly advance the conservation of species and ecology?

6. Does your zoo promote the importance of individual animal welfare?

If these challenges cannot be adequately answered, what is your zoo achieving?

HUNTING

Historical background to hunting

Hunting has a long history as a means of obtaining food for our ancestors. However, hunting as a pastime or 'sport' in the UK began in the Anglo-Saxon and Norman period. Hunting has always been associated with property rights; its history and the continuation of hunting into our modern society are examined in the following extract.[27]

> One claim of the hunting community is that hunting must be preserved because it is part of the nation's heritage and as such is worthy of preservation on the basis of tradition alone. The evidence suggests that the origins of hunting lie in the Anglo-Saxon and Norman period. It was the conception of the Norman Court that hunting was an exclusive and entertaining sport which required both ritual and etiquette in its practice. It is this conception which has provided the basis for the hunt as it is today. Hunting as a 'sport' is therefore foreign rather than English in origin, although its change from stag hunting to fox hunting is a feature that English conditions made necessary. If the claim is that hunting is traditional and that the length of its survival makes acceptable, even necessary, its preservation in its original and authentic state, then the hunting community can be well satisfied, for the traditions have shown a remarkable consistency over many centuries.
>
> Moreover, the traditions of hunting can be seen to have fitted naturally into society when England was predominantly rural and agricultural. But that being so it must be asked: how did hunting survive when English society became both urban and industrialised? What were the changes that would have been expected to destroy the hunting scene? How has hunting adapted to the changing social environment, the different availability of huntable animals and the changing membership of the hunting community? The historical evidence shows that hunting very quickly became established as the exclusive occupation of the elite who preserved that exclusivity by harsh penalties for other classes indulging in the same activity. During the period between the Conquest and the Industrial Revolution the traditions and rituals of hunting

---

27   Thomas, R, *The Politics of Hunting*, 1983, pp 11–12, Aldershot: Gower Publishing.

were most assiduously observed by those who aspired to elite status, most particularly by the squirearchy which rose to prominence during the late Middle Ages. Its observation of the rules and rituals of hunting was an extension of its desire for power and social status, rather than a necessity of the sport itself. In which case the question arises as to whether the preservation of hunting owes more to its exclusive than to its traditional nature, limited access having enhanced its value.

The legislative framework of hunting

The animals used as chase for hunting, such as foxes and deer, have varying degrees of legal protection. Under s 1(1)(c) of the Protection of Animals Act 1911 there is general prohibition on the fighting or baiting of animals. Section 5(3)(b) provides an exception to the Act in the case of coursing or hunting of any captive animal. The law makes a distinction between the fighting of animals as sport and the hunting of animals as sport. Fighting animals are protected by the Protection of Animals Act 1988, which increased the penalties relating to animal fights and the attendance at fights.

Hunting, like the fighting of animals, has a long history. But unlike the latter, which is largely a working-class preoccupation, hunting has long been tied into the ownership and rights over the land.[28]

The law has dealt harshly with those who sought to abuse or disrupt game, and the amount of legislation relating to game underlies the importance of the property-owning nature of the law. There is no statutory definition of game.[29] If an owner/occupier has game rights then so long as they have a game licence they can take game however and whenever they please, under the Game Act 1931 and Game Licences Act 1860. There are exemptions for the Crown and members of the Royal Family under s 5 of the 1860 Game Licences Act.

The nature of the right to take game is interconnected with a person's property rights; tenants have different rights over game to their landlords. Under the Ground Game Act 1880 a tenant has the right to kill hares, rabbits or any animal over which the owner has not reserved sporting rights (Waters v Phillips [1910] 2 KB 465 D–C). The tenant requires written authorisation of the person authorised to take or kill the game on the land between the first hour after sunset and the last hour before sunrise (s 6 of the Ground Game Act 1880 as amended by s 5(2)(6) of the Prevention of Damage to Rabbits Act 1939). Private rights over game, whatever their origin, are essentially local in character, and the principle upon their security depends is that of the law of trespass.[30]

---

28 Shoard, M, *This Land is our Land*, 1987, Pakadin; Temple and Smith, *The Theft of the Countryside*, 1980.

29 See s 2 of the Game Act 1831 as amended by s 15 (2) of the Protection of Birds Act 1954.

30 Now see the Police and Criminal Justice Act 1995 and ss 4,5 and 39 of the Public Order Act 1986.

There are also criminal offence relating to game rights, eg poaching and trespass, as well as, under s 4(4) of the Theft Act 1968. against the taking of young birds or the eggs of game birds. A poacher who takes or kills game is not, however, guilty of theft. There is a specific offence of poaching at night under the Night Poaching Act 1828 and there are powers of arrest, search and seizure under the Poaching Prevention Act 1862. Under the Offences Against the Persons Act 1861 the use of spring-guns and mantraps is forbidden.

Other exemptions are provided in the interest of the protection of wildlife under the Wildlife and Countryside Act 1981 and the Badgers Act 1991. The National Parks and Access to the Countryside Act 1942 as amended by the Nature Conservancy Council Act 1971 and the Environmental Protection Act 1990 can protect living creatures through byelaws, including prohibiting the shooting of birds. This is enforced by English Nature. Under the Hares Act 1948 the right to kill a hare is confined to owners of land. These are persons in actual occupation or persons authorised by them in writing. They also need a licence (s 5(5) of the Game Act 1860). Closed seasons are set out under the Game Act 1831 and there are restrictions on the purchase and sale of game during these closed seasons. A licence is needed to deal in game under the Game Licences Act 1861.

In relation to dead game, the Wild Game Meat (Hygiene and Inspection) Regulations 1995 SI 1995/2148 address the handling of dead game prior to reaching processing facilities licensed under these regulations. The regulations state that the carcasses have to be transported to the processing site under satisfactory hygiene conditions, within a reasonable time and in such a condition as to allow post mortem health inspection to be carried out. This should be done within 12 hours after killing, or the carcass can be taken to a cold store from which it should be delivered to the processing site within another 12 hours. In the case of venison, if abnormalities such as bovine tuberculosis are found during garrotting or removal of the head, then this is notifiable to the divisional veterinary officer of MAFF. See also the Food Safety (General Food Hygiene) Regulations 1995 SI1995/2200 which apply to game larders. These implement the EU Wild Game Meat Directive 96/137/EC.

The hunt itself must also respect the rights of other property owners. This was established in the following case.[31]

League Against Cruel Sports Ltd v Scott and Others **[1986] QB 240**

Members of a hunt and staghounds entered the LACS's land, over which hunting was prohibited.

Held, giving judgment for the plaintiff, that the master of a hunt was liable for trespass to land in respect of an entry on land by hounds where he either intended to cause hounds to enter the land or by his negligence in controlling the hounds failed to prevent them from doing so, and that he was vicariously

---

31 For a discussion of the area see Grayson, E, *Sports and The Law*, 1994, pp 112–17, London: Butterworths.

liable for the intentional or negligent acts or omissions of any hunt servants, agents or followers over whose conduct he could exercise control; that the question of the master's intention or negligence, or that of anyone for whose conduct he was responsible, was to be inferred from his or their conduct in all the circumstances of the case and that if it was impossible to prevent hounds from entering on certain land, an intention could be inferred from persistence in hunting in that area; and that since, on the facts, the plaintiff had proved a number of trespasses by the defendants it was entitled to the relief sought by way of damages and, in respect of one of the parcels of land, an injunction against further incursions by the defendants.[32]

Park J: The first question to be decided is whether the entry by hounds on the league's land on any, and if so which, of the seven occasions complained of constituted a trespass for which the defendants are liable in law.

On the law of trespass generally I have been referred by both counsel to numerous decisions of the courts over the last 300 years, and to passages in well-known text books and in *Halsbury's Laws of England*. I am grateful to counsel for the learning their industry provided, but having carefully considered all the material put before me I have come to the conclusion that the law relevant to the liability of a master of hounds for trespass to land by hounds when hunting is to be found in judgments in a few cases decided in the 19th century.

It is convenient to begin with a statement of the law relating to hunting about which there is no dispute. In *Paul v Summerhayes* (1878) 4 QBD 9, the appellants, who were fox-hunters, appealed against their conviction for assault on a respondent, committed when attempting to prevent them from entering his field in pursuit of a fox. It was argued on behalf of the appellants that fox hunting as a sport could be carried out over the land of a person without his consent and against his will. In the course of his judgment Lord Coleridge CJ said, at 10–11:

> I am of the opinion that no such right as that claimed exists. The sport of fox-hunting must be carried on in subordination to the ordinary rights of property. Questions such as the present fortunately do not often arise, because those who pursue the sport of fox-hunting do so in a reasonable spirit, and only go upon the lands of those whose consent is expressly, or may be assumed to be tacitly, given. There is no principle of law that justifies trespassing over the lands of others for the purpose of foxhunting. ... If persons pursue the fox for the purpose of sport or diversion, they must do so subject to the ordinary rights of property.

Eight years later *Paul v Summerhayes* was referred to in the course of the argument in *Calvert v Gosling* (1889) 5 TLR 185. The court was concerned with an appeal by the plaintiffs against the refusal by the judge in chambers to grant an interlocutory injunction against the defendant who was master of a private pack of fox-hounds, restraining him from fox hunting in the ensuing season over their lands. In opposition to the injunction, the defendant made an affidavit in which he stated at 185, that he:

---

[32] At pp 251G–252B, F.

had addressed the hunt asking them to keep off the lands of the plaintiffs, and that he had given distinct orders to his huntsman that he was not to permit the hounds to cross the lands of any of the plaintiffs, and that he and his huntsman had carefully refrained from trespassing upon the lands of any of the plaintiffs, and that he had done, and should continue to do, all in his power to prevent any of the followers of his hounds from trespassing upon the lands of any of the plaintiffs.

Thus, the question for the court was whether the discretion of the judge in chambers should be overruled. In the course of the argument counsel for the appellant referred to *Paul v Summerhayes* [1878] 4 QBD 9 and submitted that the law therein applied to the instant case. According to the report, Lord Coleridge CJ then said, 5 TLR 185, at 186:

> No; that was a very different case indeed. There the defendant[s] had wilfully ridden on the land of the plaintiff [*sic*] and insisted on his right to do so. Here, on the other hand, he disclaims any right or intention to do so; and the sole question is now whether it is proper to grant an interim injunction before trial.

Counsel then said: 'It appears that the defendant has trespassed on the plaintiff's lands since the trial,' and Lord Coleridge CJ said: 'It is stated in a very vague and general way – not saying where.' The court decided that the injunction ought not to be granted. In the course of his judgment Lord Coleridge CJ said, at 186:

> [The defendant] had made an affidavit which had left a strong impression on [the judge's] mind, and in which he stated that he had desired the hunt not to trespass upon the lands of the plaintiffs, and had given his huntsman strict orders to refrain from going on their lands. That was an undertaking which it was impossible to keep literally, for no one could keep the fox from going in any direction or the hounds from following it. There was a vague and general affidavit that since then the defendant had trespassed on the lands of some of the plaintiffs, but that was quite consistent with this, that a single hound had gone over the lands of one of them. Under those circumstances, it was not a case for an interim injunction, for no case was shown of an intention to trespass on the lands of the plaintiffs.

Hawkins J agreed, observing that:

> the law was clear that no one had a right to go over the land of another without his consent; but the defendant had disclaimed any intention of so doing, and, on the contrary, had declared his resolution not to go over the lands of the plaintiffs. They were, therefore, in no danger of any trespass on his part, and might safely wait for the trial of the case, when the merits of the case would be tried, and if a wilful trespass was proved no doubt an injunction would be granted; ...

Although the court was concerned only with the question of whether the judge in chambers had properly exercised his discretion when he had refused to grant an interlocutory injunction, I am nevertheless entitled to attach much weight, as I do, to the court's opinion that the master would not be liable for trespass by his hounds in the absence of an intention by him that they should trespass.

In *Read v Edwards* (1864) 17 CBNS 245, the court was concerned with the liability of the owner of certain dogs for damage done by one of them when it entered the plaintiff's wood where it killed and drove away a large number of young pheasants being bred there. The plaintiff alleged that the defendant, knowing that the dogs were accustomed to hunt, chase and drive about pheasants, negligently and carelessly controlled and restrained them. Willes J, delivering the judgment of the court said, at 260:

> The question was much argued, whether the owner of a dog is answerable in trespass for every unauthorised entry of the animal into the land of another, as in the case of an ox. And reasons were offered, which we need not now estimate, for a distinction in this respect between oxen and dogs or cats, on account, – first, of the difficulty or impossibility of keeping the latter under restraint, – secondly, the slightness of the damage which their wandering ordinarily causes, – thirdly, the common usage of mankind to allow them a wider liberty, – and, lastly, their not being considered in law so absolutely the chattels of the owner, so as to be the subject of larceny. It is not, however, necessary in the principal case to answer this question; because it was proved at the trial that the dog which did the damage was of a peculiarly mischievous disposition, being accustomed to chase and destroy game on its own account, that that vice was known to its owner, the defendant, and that he notwithstanding allowed it to be at large in the neighbourhood of the plaintiff's wood, in which there were game; so that the entry of the dog into the wood, and the destruction of the game, was the natural and immediate result of the animal's peculiarly mischievous disposition, which his owner knew of, and did not control.

It is clear, I think, that if the damage complained of by the plaintiff in that case had been done, not by one of his dogs, but by a number of them, each of which had the particular disposition of the dog which actually did the damage, the plaintiff would still have succeeded in his claim. Thus, this decision in my view provides support for the proposition that a person responsible for the control of a pack of stag hounds, when hunting in the neighbourhood of land on which deer were likely to be, is liable in trespass to the owner of such land if, owing to the negligence in his control of the pack, hounds entered or crossed that land.

A modern example of liability for harm done by a pack of dogs is *Draper v Hodder* [1972] 2 QB 556. In that case a pack of Jack Russell terriers belonging to the defendant savaged the infant plaintiff. The defendant was held guilty of negligence in failing to keep them confined.

On the other hand Mr Blom-Cooper submits that intention, willfulness, and indeed any concept of fault liability do not constitute an element in the tort of trespass to land. When hounds enter or cross forbidden land the only question is whether such intrusion is voluntary or involuntary. The only defences recognised by law to an action for trespass are inevitable accident and necessity.

Accordingly he contends that the authorities support the proposition that where the organisers of a hunt take a pack of hounds out, deliberately setting them in pursuit of a stag or hind, and foresee that as a consequence there is a real risk that any of the pack of hounds may enter or cross land on which no permission is given by the landowner, the organisers become liable in trespass.

In support of that proposition he cites *Beckwith v Shordike* (1767) 4 Burr 2092. In that case the defendants entered the plaintiff's close with guns and dogs; a dog killed one of the plaintiff's deer. The plaintiff claimed damages. It would appear from the report that the defendants' case was that the dog escaped from them and killed the deer against their will. But their case was not put by the trial judge to the jury, who found for the plaintiff. The discussion in the Court of Appeal appears to have been on the question of whether the defendants were guilty of an intentional trespass, or whether what happened was an accidental involuntary trespass. The appeal was dismissed because upon the evidence the case could not be considered to be an accidental trespass.

Mr Blom-Cooper also relies on *Reg v Pratt* (1855) 4 E & B 860. The defendant appealed against his conviction under s 30 of the Game Act 1831,[33] for committing a trespass by being in the day time on land occupied by another in search of game. While on a public road he waved his hand to his dog which entered the cover occupied by the owner on the side of the road; a pheasant flew out across the road; the defendant fired at it and missed. The court dismissed the appeal on the grounds that as he was on the road, not for the purpose of exercising a right of way, but in search of game, he was a trespasser. Lord Campbell CJ and Crompton J also held that the sending in of the dog into the cover, though a trespass by the defendant, would not by itself justify a conviction, as the Game Act 1831 required a personal trespass.

Mr Blom-Cooper also quoted the following passages from Locke, *The Game Laws*, 5th edn, 1866, pp 46–47:

'The upshot of these cases seems to be that to pursue a fox or vermin in the way of pleasure, after the fashion of present fox-hunting, over the land of another, is to commit an unjustifiable trespass; and that it is a doubtful matter how far it is justifiable to pursue even *bona fide* for the mere purpose of its destruction for the general good. Where a person goes out sporting with his friends, and purposely leads them on to another's land, he is equally guilty of a trespass although he may remain off the land while his friends go on it; ... and, as we have seen, if he send his dog into the land he will be liable for a trespass; ... but if the dog of his own accord break the close, the master will not be liable. ... And where, in an action of trespass, it appeared that the defendant was a qualified person, and had permission to sport on the right-hand side of a road, but his dog crossed over the road and ranged over a field on the other side, the judge left it to the jury whether the dog had crossed over by the incitement of the defendant or not. If the jury find that the dog escaped against the defendant's will, and that he had no intention of sporting on the other side of the road, they must accordingly find a verdict for the defendant.'

Mr Blom-Cooper also relied on *Read v Edwards*, 17 CBNS 245 to which I have already referred, and *Baker v Berkeley* (1827) 3 C & P 32. This last decision is relevant to the question of the extent of a master of hounds' liability, if any, for the acts and omissions of the hunt's servants or agents or mounted followers.

---

[33] 1 & 2 Will 4, c 32.

Mr Blom-Cooper did not define the persons he included in his proposition in the description of 'organisers of the hunt'. But such persons, he submitted, were liable for any trespass committed by themselves, their hounds, the horse-riders, whippers-in, or persons assisting in the organisation of the hunt, and all those who subscribed or followed as visitors to the hunt, whether mounted, in a vehicle or on foot.

Mr Cazalet, on the other hand, submitted that in relation to a trespass a master is not liable for the acts or omissions of hunt servants, except when acting in the course of their employment, nor for the acts or omissions of mounted followers, unless he in some way authorised or encouraged them to enter forbidden land or, knowing that they were about to enter forbidden land, stood by and took no steps to prevent them from doing so.

Useful guidance on this subject is to be found in *Baker v Berkeley*, 3 C & P 32, where Lord Tenterden CJ said, at 33:

> 'If a gentleman sends out his hounds and his servants, and invites other gentlemen to hunt with him, although he does not himself go on the lands of another, but those other gentlemen do, he is answerable for the trespass that they may commit in so doing, unless he distinctly desires them not to go on those lands; and if (as in the present case) he does not so desire them, I think he is answerable, in point of law, for the damage that they do'.

In addition to mounted followers, the Devon and Somerset staghounds have a large army of other followers, on foot, in cars and on motor cycles. Over a substantial number of those the master can have no control whatsoever. But on the evidence, he can exercise considerable control over the conduct of a mounted subscriber in the chase. I can find no reason why the master should not be held vicariously liable for trespass committed by such a person.

The master's liability for trespass by a hunt servant will largely depend on the facts relating to the particular incident complained of. Suppose his servant was acting in the general course of his duty, but without specific orders from his master. If the servant, when committing the trespass, was doing something he had been put in a position to do by the master, the master would have to accept responsibility for the manner in which he did that thing. A good example of a master's liability for trespass by a servant is the Canadian case, *Turner v Thorne* (1959) 21 DLR (2d) 29, a judgment of McCruer CJ in the Ontario High Court.

I come back to the main dispute on the law. I have given the most careful consideration to the arguments addressed to me. I am, however, unable to spell out from the authorities cited by Mr Blom-Cooper the proposition he has advanced. I have, therefore, come to the conclusion that, before a master of hounds may be held liable for trespass on land by hounds, it has to be shown that he either intended that the hounds should enter the land, or by negligence he failed to prevent them from doing so.

In my judgment the law as I take it to be may be stated thus: where a master of staghounds takes out a pack of hounds and deliberately sets them in pursuit of a stag or hind, knowing that there is a real risk that in the pursuit hounds may enter or cross prohibited land, the master will be liable for trespass if he intended to cause hounds to enter such land, or if by his failure to exercise proper control over them he caused them to enter such land.

In the present case, on each of the occasions on which the League alleges trespass by hounds the master (or on some occasions the masters) had taken out the pack and set hounds in pursuit of a stag or hind. On each occasion the master or masters knew that there was a real risk that one or more hounds might enter league land; on each occasion one or more hounds did, in fact, enter League land. The question is, therefore, whether on any, and if so which, of those occasions the trespass was caused either by the master intending that hounds should enter or by his failure to exercise proper control over them.

This is, in each case, a question of fact. The master's intention, or the intention of those servants or agents or followers of the hunt for whose conduct he is responsible, has to be inferred from his or their conduct in all the circumstances of the case. For example, whether he or they stood by and allowed hounds which were plainly about to enter prohibited land to do so, or allowed hounds which were plainly on the land to remain there; or whether, by making appropriate sounds vocally or on the horn, he encouraged hounds to go on to or to remain on such land.

Further, if it is virtually impossible, whatever precautions are taken, to prevent hounds from entering League land, such as Pitleigh, for example, yet the master knowing that to be the case, nevertheless persists in hunting in its vicinity, with the result that hounds frequently trespass on the land, then the inference might well be drawn that his indifference to the risk of trespass amounted to an intention that hounds should trespass on the land.

The master's negligence, or the negligence of those servants or agents or followers of the hunt for whose conduct he is responsible, has also to be judged in the light of all the circumstances in which the trespass in question occurred.

It involves consideration of such questions as the stage in the chase at which it ought reasonably to have been foreseen that there was a risk that hounds might trespass on League land and what precautions, if any, were taken by the master at that stage to prevent trespass by heading off the hounds.

It is not sufficient merely to take the precautions pleaded in paragraph 7 of the amended defence.[34] Over the period between September 1982 and January 1983 there were too many trespassers on League land to lead me to suppose that the precautions taken at that time were on each and every occasion reasonable for the purpose of preventing trespass. Indeed, I have been much troubled by the prospect of a repetition of such trespass if the permanent injunctions sought were not to be granted.

On the other hand, the League has not alleged and therefore has not sought to prove that there was a conspiracy between members of the hunt to enter upon League land wherever that land happened to be, and whenever it suited them to do so.

The arguments for and against hunting

Fox-hunting is controlled by the Masters of Fox Hounds Association. Each hunt has masters who are responsible for organising hunting and ensuring

---

[34] At 242G–243A.

that the rules and the code of conduct are followed. There is a European hunting organisation called Federation des Associations de Chasseurs de la EEC (FACE). Other pro-hunting groups include the British Association for Shooting and Conservation (BASC) which was founded in 1908 and began as the Wildfowlers Association (this later merged with the Gamekeepers Association, founded in 1900. There is also the British Field Sports Society, the Game Conservancy Trust, the Game Farmers Association and the Country Landowners Association. Anti-hunt groups include the RSPCA, the League Against Cruel Sports, Hunt Saboteurs Association and many of the animal welfare organisations.

Arguments in favour of hunting

In 1949 the Scott Henderson Committee stated in its Report on Cruelty to Wild Animals[35] that:

> sentimental concern about animals is directed mainly towards particular animals such as foxes, deer and rabbits which are beautiful or attractive creatures and are viewed as such by those who are not concerned with the damage they may cause. Few people seem to be in the least concerned about what happens to rats, which are generally regarded as vermin and arouse considerable feelings of revulsion. Yet the rat is an intelligent and highly sensitive creature ... Any field sport which has a reasonable measure of support and is a traditional activity of the countryside, and which has some utilitarian value, should not be interfered with except for some very good reason. Interference on the grounds of cruelty would be justified only if it was shown that the amount of suffering involved was excessive or unreasonable.[36]

The Scott Henderson committee recommended that fox-hunting be allowed to continue.

Briefly the main arguments in favour of hunting are as follows:

– Hunting is a traditional rural activity and should not be disrupted by urban city dwellers who know nothing about the countryside. The British Field Sports Society argues that:

> Illicit cruelty to foxes by baiters, fur trappers and poachers using lurchers, is invariably associated with the urban fringe and other areas where properly organised hunts cannot operate. These atrocities, which the law finds it impossible to control, are not tolerated in the rural communities which support fox-hunting.

– Hunting both protects and controls the fox because success in managing foxes depends upon maintaining an appropriate population level for different parts of the country. Hunting is the best way to control foxes, as shooting by an inexpert shot would lead to foxes dying from lingering

---

35 1951, Cmnd 8266, London: HMSO.
36 From British Field Sports Society, *Hunting – the Facts*, undated, p 1, London: BFSS.

deaths and developing gangrene. Snares and trapping also cause the animals unnecessary stress. Hunting is not cruel, as defined by the Scott Henderson Committee, because a fox that is hunted by hounds is either killed instantly or escapes entirely uninjured. The Scott Henderson Report stated:

> We are not satisfied that wild animals suffer from apprehension or the after effects of fear to the same extent as human beings. Wild animals must live very largely in the present and although a hunted fox, for example, may be aware that it is being hunted and that if the hounds catch it something to be avoided will happen, we think that it would be going beyond the evidence to say that a fox realises that it is going to be killed.[37]

- Over 3,000 people's jobs depend upon fox-hunting, either directly or indirectly. There are 12,000 fox-hounds and 196 registered packs of fox-hounds in the UK, supported by more than 41,000 riders and over 160,000 foot or car followers. Fox predation can cause 0.5%–5.2% of lamb losses. Even at 2%, the cost to a typical hill farmer with 1,500 ewes is over £1,000 per year. Nearly one million people participate in stalking and shooting game, clay pigeons and wildfowl. £313 million is spent directly on these sports and 27,500 full-time jobs are generated by them. Angling generates expenditure of £958 million and 20,000 full time jobs.[38]

- Hunting is of benefit to farmers and hunters, in other words, the utilitarian value of the interests of the farmer and the hunter outweigh the cost to the fox.

- Hunting helps conservation as it encourages the sustainable maintenance of species.

- Regulated hunting protects the fox from inexperienced shooters.

- The preservation of hunting areas helps to protect the animals from the urban fringe.

- Foxes often escape or are uninjured.

- The animals will be killed anyway as they are pests.

- It is hypocritical of protesters to campaign against hunting as many people do not condemn the killing of other animals, eg for food.

Hunting and conservation

The British Association for Shooting and Conservation bases its arguments on the benefit of hunting in relation to conservation:

> The British Association for Shooting and Conservation is a representative body for sporting shooting in the UK which advises and assists its members on all aspects of conservation and land management promoting an integrated approach aimed at ensuring viable and healthy wildlife populations that might be shared and enjoyed by a wide range of interests. Hunting is justified on the

---

37 *Ibid*, p 7.
38 Facts from BFSS and BASC factsheets.

grounds that all the animals hunted are agricultural pests. The question is, they say, not whether the animals should be protected, but how they should be managed. The organisation argues that without the traditional rural environments certain birds such as red grouse, grey partridge and wildfowl would disappear and that without country shooting there would be fewer hedgerows, less broad leafed woodland and much less moorland in Britain. They argue that as the International Union for the Conservation of Nature and Natural Resources defined conservation as the sustainable use of a resource. Just as farmers of livestock do not deplete breeding stock, so shooters try to ensure that their quarry are safeguarded. In pursuing species that depend upon a wide range of threatened habitats, shooters must be committed to conservation matters. For example, many wetland sites under the control of BASC members are managed as reserves and refuges. These are un-shot areas where wildfowl are safeguarded. This is not only to the advantage of the quarry species but also to many other species which are not hunted.

English Nature in a survey showed that of 250,000 acres of land under BASC-affiliated club influence over 70% was designated as a SSSI. Conservation is also helped by the control of pest species such as magpies. The group has contacts with EN, RSPB and the farming and wildlife advisory group. They have a wildlife habitat trust.[39]

The British Field Sports Society also defends the hunting of animals on the grounds of conservation:

Many landowners, backed by five million country sports participants, practise conservation in the interest of their sports; were it not for them, millions of acres of countryside would be managed much more expensively, at the expense of natural beauty and wildlife.

Most of the countryside in the UK today is man-made. The woods, fields, ditches, hedges and even open moorland were all developed from the original forest that covered these islands.

Up to the 1940s, the countryside had remained largely unaltered for 150 years. A patchwork of woodlands, hedgerows and fields provided a perfect haven for wildlife. Then came the Second World War and, as a result of food shortages, farmers were encouraged to intensify production and increase efficiency. Over the next four decades thousands of miles of hedgerow were removed to create larger fields, marginal land was cleared and ploughed up, and marshes were drained for crop production. Although current agricultural practices are taking on a more environmentally friendly nature, our landscape is still deteriorating due to economic pressures. Conservation costs time and money.

Farmers and landowners with country sports interests are loath to make changes detrimental to their sport. It is important for the welfare of the quarry species – whether fox, grouse, fish or wildfowl – that a rich and diverse habitat is provided. Country sportsmen have been practising voluntary conservation for centuries. Due to their efforts, hedges are maintained, headlands left unsprayed, small copses planted, ponds dug, and cover for animals and birds provided.

---

39 A news briefing document prepared by the British Association for Shooting and Conservation, Wrexham, Wales.

Hedges

Since 1945, the UK has lost over 150,000 miles of hedgerow, equivalent to a distance of 6 times around the world. Other than shelter for farm stock, hedges are of little use in purely agricultural terms. Wire fences are cheaper and easier to maintain. Bigger hedgeless field are easier to use with large farm machinery. For the sporting farmer, however, hedges are vital for the conservation of game since they provide perfect habitat. But it is not only game which benefits – hedgerows are the home to many species of birds, mammals, plants, butterflies and insects.

Coverts, spinneys and woodland

The management of a pheasant shoot requires woodland to be carefully tended and predators controlled, both of which benefit wild birds and animals as well as the pheasants. The plantation will include hardwoods, amenity trees and a well developed shrub layer, whereas commercial softwood plantations generally support less diverse flora and fauna.

Moorland

The red grouse is unique to Britain and Ireland and depends upon heather moorland for food, nesting sites and general cover. The grouse, along with a myriad of other plants and wildlife, are ecologically suited to no other habitat. Heather moorland needs year-round management which is an expensive undertaking. An interest in shooting gives the landowner the incentive to keep the moor properly burned and drained for grouse. The income from shoots helps to pay for this management. Without a shooting interest, it would be financially more viable to use the moor for grazing or conifer plantations.

Wetlands

Most of the UK's wetlands have been lost to urban development, but those which have survived are home to hundreds of thousands of wildfowl and wading birds. Since wildfowlers have a vested interest in keeping wildfowl habitats, they are a major force in wildlife conservation. They manage over 105,000 hectares of marsh and wetlands on which the wildfowlers warden sites, clear litter, plant trees, create and maintain access routes, control predators and manage vegetation and water levels.

Rivers and streams

Anglers want fish to catch, and fish need clean water and suitable aquatic habitat. The anglers' constant fight against industrial pollution and their efforts in clearing silt, mud and blanket weed from choked waterways are of vital importance not only to fish stocks but to other waterside life, such as voles, frogs, birds, plants and insects.

Less than 20% of rural land in the UK is subject to conservation controls – the rest is controlled by private landowners and farmers. Voluntary conservation by those with country sports interest is vital to the environment.[40]

---

40 BFSS, *This is Country Sports and Conservation Briefing*, undated, London: BFSS. Reproduced with the kind permission of the British Field Sports Society.

The field sports lobby argue that the ethical basis of all field sports is the same – in each case the quarry will either be edible or a pest, with the result that animals involved will be killed whether the pursuit is a field sport or not. It is of no relevance to the hunted deer or the migrating salmon how their pursuers are motivated; but is this really a secure moral footing?

The arguments against hunting[41]

Many opponents of hunting question whether foxes are really a pest. A 1974 NOP survey found that 70% of farmers did not consider foxes to be significantly harmful to their interests; indeed, 36% of farmers questioned considered foxes to be useful in controlling rabbits and rodents. Some 64% of farmers questioned suffered no financial loss from fox damage. Only 1% of lambs in the Highlands of Scotland were lost to foxes.

MAFF also found that fox predation on lambs is 'insignificant'. The fox tends to be a scavenger, carrying off already dead or weak creatures. The fox, like all predators in nature, has its numbers governed by the availability of food and the establishment and defence of territories. Man kills many tens of thousands of foxes annually, but vixens produce enough cubs to bring the numbers back to the density appropriate to the availability of food and territory. Fox killing merely produces an unnaturally young fox population; the actual population remains the same.

A survey carried out by Dr Stephen Harris of Bristol University in 1987 revealed that fox-hunts kill between 12,000 and 13,000 foxes a year. Dr Harris points out that this may represent only 2.5% of the fox population, whereas fox populations can survive an annual mortality rate of up to 70% and still recover. Dr Harris concluded that, 'It is clear that fox-hunts play no significant role in the control of fox populations.' In other words, 12,000 foxes die annually for no other reason than 'sport'. Left alone by man, fox populations will be higher in areas of abundance of food and lower where food is scarce. This can be seen in towns and cities, where large numbers of foxes survive on refuse and high rodent populations. A three-year study by Aberdeen University showed that in the absence of any form of fox control, there was neither an increase in fox numbers nor in the number of lambs lost. Foxes form stable family groups which defend their own territory against intruding foxes, and which will reproduce at a similar rate to their fatalities. The fox population would therefore not explode if all methods of fox killing were suspended. Surplus fox cubs, usually dog foxes, leave the home range when mature and seek to form or join new family groups in vacant territories. Most will be quickly accepted into groups depleted by, for example, road accidents

---

41 The League Against Cruel Sports fact sheets provided the material for much of this section: London.

or human predation, while others may spend a considerable period as 'itinerants' before finding a new territory.[42]

In relation to deer hunting, the LACS accepts that many of the natural predators of deer have become extinct, and so there is no natural culling of the deer; this can lead to lingering deaths from parasites and starvation. Deer hunts kill around 200 animals per year, which is not enough to affect the population.[43] The League Against Cruel Sports reluctantly accepts there should be some culling in the interests of the deer and to reduce damage to agriculture and forestry.

The League feels that such culling should be controlled through legislation to prohibit the infliction of unnecessary suffering. The legislation relating to deer at the moment prohibits poaching, dictates the seasons when the deer can be killed and the types of weapon which may be used. It also prohibits the use of snares and the shooting of deer at night. Some deer are exempted from even this limited protection. Deer have no legal protection from cruelty or hunting with dogs, unless this takes place on land without the landowner's permission.

The LACS also questions the hunts' tactics. High-stamina slow-running dogs are used to deliberately prolong the chase and run the quarry to exhaustion before it is killed. It is questionable whether the hounds kill their prey instantly. The League is also concerned with the length of time of the chase and that often more than one shot is needed to kill the deer. Sometimes the deer are killed by the dogs. Often deer that have escaped die from the stress or from hypothermia. The hunters claim that without hunting there would be no deer; however, they also claim that hunters are conservationists, so surely they would not go out and kill deer if there was no money to be made from the killing of deer as sport:[44]

> In the past, wild predators such as wolves would have selected the old, weak or lame deer, the object being a short chase and a quick kill. Conversely, the object of deer hunting with hounds is to provide a long chase for the hunt followers. Exhausting the victim over a seven hour, 25 mile chase is clearly inefficient, expensive and obviously cruel. The West Country deer hunts kill approximately 150 deer a year, yet the Exmoor and Quantocks herds of 7–8,000 would require an annual cull in excess of 1,000 to maintain a stable population. Nationally each year at least 8,000 deer are killed by shooting. This is the method usually employed and accounts for 99% of the annual cull. Careful controlled shooting will remove the old and sick deer and is necessary to maintain the correct sex ratio to avoid overpopulation. A skilled professional marksman using a high-powered rifle fitted with telescopic sights will kill a grazing deer instantly, humanely and efficiently.

42 LACS Fact Sheet on Foxes and Foxhunting, London.
43 IFAW Briefing for the Labour Party Conference, Blackpool, 1996.
44 LACS Fact Sheet on Deer and Staghunting.

Popular opinion is against hunting – 80% of people questioned in a November 1991 poll disapproved of fox-hunting, a parliamentary ban on fox-hunting would meet the approval of 79% of those questioned, while 67% of Conservative voters disapproved of fox-hunting. By 1992 more than 130 local authorities had voted to ban hunting on council-owned land.

Hunting can result in pollution offences:

Two leading officials of the West Norfolk Foxhounds were fined at Swaffham Magistrates on 11 January 1996, after the National Rivers Authority (NRA) prosecuted them for polluting a tributary of the River Wissey near the hunt's kennels at Necton. They were fined £5,000 each and ordered to pay costs of £449.29 each after admitting that they knowingly permitted the river to be polluted on 18 April 1995. The hunt has also had to find £25,000 to pay for new equipment to ensure that there is no repeat of the incident. Anne Brosnan, prosecuting for the NRA said the river, ' ... was blood red in colour, the colour was so intense that the river bed could not be seen'. An NRA officer found blood and animal waste running down gullies into the river. Samples taken found that ammonia levels were 727 mg per litre (NRA normally allows 5 mg per litre); the material took twice as much oxygen from the river as raw domestic sewage and suspended solids were 166 mg per litre (limit is 30 mg).[45]

As regards the issue of protecting rare animals and species, and preserving habitats, the claims of the pro-hunting lobby have been questioned by the LACS:

The unscrupulous antics of 'sportsmen' continue to cause the death of many rare birds. Recently around a dozen dead whooper swans were found in Forvie Nature Reserve in Grampian, Scotland. Autopsies confirmed that the birds had died after swallowing lead shot left by shooters. Reserve Warden Bob Davis explained that the discarded pellets cause a lingering death. 'The lead paralyses the birds' nervous systems and damages their ability to digest. The result is gradual deterioration and a slow starvation over possibly two to three weeks.' 'One cartridge could literally kill 40 or 50 swans', he added. Whilst shooters maintain that they are actually helping to conserve rare birds habitats, the number of whooper swans continues to fall.[46]

While it is true that the abolition of grouse shooting would probably lead to the loss of this type of habitat, it is not true to say that this would be disastrous for our wildlife and environment. First, the management of the heather on grouse moors being so unnatural has serious consequences for the moors themselves. Heather burning is a policy deliberately adopted to maintain heather at the expense of flora which is less resistant to fire and therefore depletes the moors of the floral variety that would naturally occur. If moor burning were to cease and sheep were removed (from for what is for them a harsh environment) the moors would gradually revert back to forest as has

---

45   LACS *Wildlife Guardian*, no 33, Spring 1996, p 3, London.
46   *Howl*, Summer 1993, no 2, p 6. Reproduced with the kind permission of the Hunt Saboteurs Association, Brighton.

happened on hundreds of acres of grouse moor in the Dee and Spey valleys in Scotland. These areas, once homes for grouse, grouse and yet more grouse, now consist of mainly birch and scots pine woodland and are populated by a vast variety of flora and fauna, including many mammals which were previously indiscriminately slaughtered by gamekeepers. Furthermore, since heather needs a fairly dry soil in which to flourish, many moors in wetter regions which would never have supported natural heather are artificially drained.

Draining these regions leads to wholesale destruction of the 'sphagnum bogs' and the unique wildlife that normally covers such areas. Both draining and heather burning lead to an increase in the erosion of these moors, the effects of which are manifested downstream by the silting up of rivers and on the moors by deep scars or gullies in the surface. Burning is also partly responsible for the gradual loss of fertility in moorland soils which may one day make the moors incapable of supporting any plant or animal life at all. All those animals, birds and plants that now live on the grouse moors would lose a large proportion of their habitat if grouse shooting were to cease, but would not face extinction as a result. All are found on those landscapes from which they originated; the upland regions above the tree line in the mountainous districts of Scotland and Wales. The red grouse would once more revert to its rightful status of a rare upland territorial bird. Indeed it still exists on these regions although not in shootable numbers. The birds of prey which have colonised the grouse moors (despite some illegal killing for grouse protection regions) also inhabitant these more natural environs. As for the grouse moors, one of these fates could await them, depending upon the strength of opinion and legislation.

First, if they were left to nature they would as described above, revert to natural forest. Regeneration of forest would lead to the revival of fortunes for many of our rarer animals and birds. Pine martins, pole cats, and wildcats would benefit immediately. Many of our woodland birds, currently suffering declines because of the erosion of their habitats in farming regions would also see a revival. The moors would return to their natural origins, trees would regulate drainage and prevent erosion while their deaths and leaf mould would refertilise and regenerate the soil.

Secondly, but more probably they would be used for sheep pasture. The chances are, however, that to be profitable, the sheep would have to be kept at near over-stocking numbers and the heather would be wiped out. Where this has happened sheep farming has become unprofitable and the land put up for sale. In our upland regions ex-grouse moors and over-stocked degenerate sheep pastures are usually brought up by forestry interests (the biggest being the Forestry Commission). Whilst it is true that coniferous plantations are unsightly when compared to grouse moors in summer, they do have advantages; if the forest is cut and planted in rotation, the younger trees provide a rich habitat for small mammals and their predators as well as for deer. The timber they provide when mature would reduce our reliance on polluting fossil fuels and imported timber, often from natural forests. This is the third and the most likely result of a cessation of grouse shooting. Ideally it would be preferable if some areas, those covered by our national parks in particular, were left to regenerate naturally. The spectacular sight of the wine-red grouse moors which ramblers are so attracted to, would then be replaced by an even more spectacular and varied landscape, the upland natural forest, a feature of which Britain has little but Europe has plenty. Since conservation is about preserving nature, few of us should worry about the loss of the grouse moor. As one correspondent to *The Field* wrote concerning grouse and nature, 'It is not a matter of balance of nature. Balance is not what is sought, but a massive temporary imbalance in favour of the grouse.[47]

While there may be an argument in favour of culling some animals where they face no natural predator, this culling should be based upon the interest of the animal rather than on that of the hunters. The arguments for and against hunting need to be separated from the issues of conservation.

The other area of concern for animal welfare groups is terrier work. This can be illegal in three ways: through the choice of quarry, ie the badger, the choice of site, ie digging without the permission of the landowner, or through the infliction of unnecessary suffering on the dogs themselves. In September 1991 the LACS successfully prosecuted a terrier man of the New Forest Fox-hounds for cruelty to his terrier. He had entered the dog into a fox earth during a hunt and it had emerged with blood streaming from its muzzle. Despite these injuries the dog was encouraged to re-enter the hole, instead of being sent for veterinary treatment. Magistrates considered this to be an offence under the 1911 Protection of Animals Act inasmuch as it causes the dog unnecessary suffering.[48]

Finally, as regards the social impact of a ban, those employed in hunting would not need to be made unemployed if drag hunting was adopted.

The parliamentary response to the issue of hunting

Parliament has yet to decide directly on the issue of hunting, although the Labour Party has stated that it would allow a free vote.[49] It seems unlikely that a Private Member's Bill would succeed (in the absence of a government Bill on the issue) as witnessed by the failure of the Protection of Wildlife Bill until hunting was excluded.

Many organisations prohibit hunting on their land, such as the Wildfowl and Wetlands Trust and 37 County Wildlife Trusts. Local councils have also banned hunting from land which they own. The question of whether councils can ban hunts on council-owned land was examined in the following case:

R v Somerset CC, ex p Fewings **[1995] 3 All ER 20; [1995] 1 WLR 1037; 93 LGR 515**

In 1921 the respondent local authority acquired certain common land which it later appropriated in 1974 for amenity purposes. In 1993 the local authority's

---

47 Cooke, R, *Turning Point,* no 11, July–September 1988, pp 20–21.
48 LACS Fact Sheet on Terrier Work; London.
49 IFAW briefing 1996.

environment committee met to consider the issue of deer hunting on the land and, after considering various reports prepared for the meeting, resolved to recommend that it be allowed to continue, since a ban would result in the reduction of the deer herd by indiscriminate shooting and an increase in poaching. However, when the matter went to a full local authority meeting a resolution was passed to ban hunting on the land. The majority of the councillors who voted for the ban did so on the basis of the cruelty argument, namely that hunting involved unacceptable and unnecessary cruelty to deer which were the victims of the chase. The applicants, who regularly hunted on the common, applied for judicial review of the local authority's decision and sought a review of the legality of the ban, which they contended had been made on purely moral grounds and without regard to the statutory purpose of the local authority's power to acquire and manage land under s 120(1)(b)1 of the Local Government Act 1972, namely for the 'benefit, improvement or development of their area'.

Held:

(1) A local authority's power under s 120(1)(b) of the 1972 Act to manage land which it had acquired had to be exercised in accordance with the statutory purposes for which that power had been conferred, in that any decision as to the use of the land had to relate to the 'benefit, improvement or development' of its area as a whole. On the facts (Simon Brown LJ dissenting), it was clear that the local authority, in deciding to ban deer hunting over its land, had not exercised its power in order to promote the benefit of its area, since (i) at no point before or during the debate had its attention been directed to s 120(1)(b), which governed the exercise of that power, and (ii) it had failed to appreciate the overriding statutory constraint to which it was subject as a local authority landowner, as distinct from a private landowner, and therefore it had not been entitled to make its decision on the ground relied on.

(2) Moreover (Simon Brown LJ concurring), the local authority's decision was not open to challenge on the judge's alternative ground, since the question of management and conservation of the deer herd did not require an immediate solution and it would have been open to the council to explore alternative measures later and if necessary to revoke the ban.

Per Sir Thomas Bingham MR and Simon Brown LJ; Swinton Thomas LJ dissenting:

In view of the broad language of s 120(1)(b) of the 1972 Act, it cannot be said that the cruelty argument (or the contrary argument that hunting is a less cruel means of controlling a deer herd than available alternatives) is necessarily irrelevant to a consideration of what is for the benefit of the area.

Sir Thomas Bingham MR:

The judge concentrated on whether the use of the powers was reasonable or a misuse of their powers. The judge was at pains to emphasise what these proceedings are not about (see [1995] 1 All ER 513 at 515–16). This is so important that I must repeat it.

The point is often made that unelected unrepresentative judges have no business to be deciding questions of potentially far-reaching social concern which are more properly the preserve of elected representatives at national or local level. In some cases the making of such decisions may be inescapable, but in general the point is well made. In the present case it certainly is. The court has no role whatever as an arbiter between those who condemn hunting as barbaric and cruel and those who support it as a traditional country sport more humane in its treatment of deer or foxes (as the case may be) than other methods of destruction such as shooting, snaring, poisoning or trapping. This is of course a question on which most people hold views one way or the other.

But our personal views are wholly irrelevant to the drier and more technical question which the court is obliged to answer. That is whether the council acted lawfully in making the decision it did on the grounds it did. In other words, were members entitled in reaching their decision to give effect to their acceptance of the cruelty argument?

In seeking to answer that question it is, as the judge very clearly explained, critical to distinguish between the legal position of the private landowner and that of a land-owning local authority (see [1995] 1 All ER 513 at 523–25). To the famous question asked by the owner of the vineyard: 'Is it not lawful for me to do what I will with mine own?' (*St Matthew* 20.15) the modern answer would be clear: 'Yes, subject to such regulatory and other constraints as the law imposes.' But if the same question were posed by a local authority the answer would be different. It would be: 'No, it is not lawful for you to do anything save what the law expressly or impliedly authorises. You enjoy no unfettered discretions. There are legal limits to every power you have.' As Laws J put it, the rule for local authorities is that any action to be taken must be justified by positive law (see [1995] 1 All ER 513 at 524).

The positive law in issue in this case is agreed by the parties to be s 120(1)(b) of the Local Government Act 1972, which provides:

> For the purposes of ... the benefit, improvement or development of their area, a principal council may acquire by agreement any land, whether situated inside or outside their area.

At first sight this section has little to do with the present case, since we are not dealing with the acquisition of land but with the management or use of land which the council acquired over 70 years ago. But the council is a principal council within the statutory definition; we have been referred to no statutory provision or rule of law more closely in point; any other provision, unless more specific, would be bound to require powers to be exercised for the public good; and it seems perhaps reasonable to accept that the purposes for which land may be acquired are or may often be those to which the land should be applied after acquisition. I would therefore agree with Laws J, adapting his language a little, that the primary question in this case is whether the councillors' acceptance of the cruelty argument is capable of justifying the ban as a measure which conduces to 'the benefit, improvement or development of their area' within s 120(1)(b) of the Act:

Did they reach a decision on grounds which transgressed the fetter or limit which Parliament had imposed upon them, so that there was no positive legal justification for what they did? (See [1995] 1 All ER 513 at 525.)

It is noteworthy that s 120(1) does not provide that principal councils may acquire land for the purposes of the benefit, improvement or development of that land. The reference is to the benefit, improvement or development of their area. That indicates that the draftsman was concerned not merely with improved husbandry of particular land but with wider questions of public benefit. The power to acquire land outside the council's area reflects the same intention. So a principal council would, it would seem, be authorised, in the absence of more specific provisions, to acquire land outside its area to be used as an adventure training or fieldcraft centre, or perhaps as a home for the elderly, if to do so would benefit its area.

The researches of counsel have unearthed only one authority in which s 120(1)(b) has been applied. In *Costello v Dacorum DC* (1982) 81 LGR 1 a council, having tried but failed to prevent the use of a site by gypsies and other caravan-dwellers by means of an enforcement notice, itself took a lease of the land and then started proceedings to evict the occupiers. Lawton LJ (with whom Brightman and Oliver LJJ agreed) said (at 10):

> The real problem in this case is whether they had any statutory rights to take leases of land for the purposes for which they said they were taking them, as set out in the council's resolution of 21 June 1978. In my judgment, on the face of that resolution, they were acting well within the powers conferred upon them by s 120(1)(b) of the Local Government Act 1972. That section provides: 'For the purposes of ... (b) the benefit, improvement or development of their area, a principal council may acquire by agreement any land, whether situated inside or outside their area.' The object of the council in acquiring this land under the leases was, in my judgment, clearly for the benefit and improvement of their area. The site had long been, as I have already said, an eyesore. It gave offence, because of what was done on it, to large numbers of people living in the neighbourhood. The council were under pressure from the ratepayers to do something about the site. It follows, in my judgment, that what they did was for the benefit and improvement of the area. They were intending to get rid of the caravan dwellers. They were intending to get the site cleaned up and the rubbish disposed of and the site returned to its proper use as common land. I find it difficult to think of a clearer case of acquisition of land by a local authority coming within the provisions of s 120(1)(b). The fact that the consequence was that they could get rid of the caravan dwellers, even though the Secretary of State had given them temporary planning permission to be there, in my judgment, in no way was a misuse of their powers under s 120.

This case is perhaps too obvious to give much help. The council acquired the land to remedy a nuisance. Had the council acquired the land for another purpose beneficial to its area, and had the nuisance then arisen, it could no doubt have taken appropriate steps to mitigate the nuisance, but it would scarcely have needed to rely on s 120 for that purpose.

Laws J held the council's resolution to be an unlawful exercise of power for reasons which he succinctly summarised as follows ([1995] 1 All ER 513 at 529–30):

> What then is the true scope of the words in s 120(1)(b) 'the benefit, improvement or development of their area'? In my judgment, this language is not wide enough to permit the council to take a decision about activities carried out on its land which is based upon free-standing moral perceptions as opposed to an objective judgment about what will conduce to the better management of the estate. Section 120(1)(b) is not within the class of provisions which require the decision-maker to have regard to moral considerations as such. A prohibition on hunting, which manifestly interferes with the lawful freedom of those who take part in the sport, could only be justified under the subsection if the council reasonably concluded that the prohibition was objectively necessary as the best means of managing the deer herd, or was otherwise required, on objective grounds, for the preservation or enhancement of the amenity of their area. The view that hunting is morally repulsive, however pressing its merits, has nothing whatever to do with such questions. Section 120(1)(b) confers no entitlement on a local authority to impose its opinions about the morals of hunting on the neighbourhood. In the present state of the law those opinions, however sincerely felt, have their proper place only in the private conscience of those who entertain them. The council has been given no authority by Parliament to translate such views into public action; there is nothing in the section to indicate that is has.

The judge did not base his decision on, but found support for it in, *Calder and Hebble Navigation Co v Pilling* (1845) 14 M & W 76, 153 ER 396. In that case the proprietors of a canal were empowered by a local Act to make byelaws 'for the good and orderly using the said navigation'. The proprietors made a byelaw that the canal be closed on Sundays. It was held to be bad, because the power conferred on the proprietors was solely for the orderly use of the navigation and:

> The rules which they are empowered to make have nothing to do with the regulation of moral or religious conduct, which are left to the general law of the land, and to the laws of God. (See 14 M & W 76 at 88; 153 ER 396 at 401 *per* Alderson B.)

It was not open to the proprietors to give effect to their view that use of the canal on Sundays was indecorous. I agree with the judge that this is an interesting case, but I also agree that it does not advance the present case very much. It turned on the construction of a particular statutory provision in terms much more specific than those in issue here and it does not seem to me that acceptance of the cruelty argument imports, otherwise than indirectly, any attempt to regulate the morals or religious conduct of those who hunt deer on the common.

Mr Supperstone QC, for the council, submitted that the judge had construed s 120(1)(b) too narrowly. It was, he reminded us, common ground that 'the benefit ... of their area' included wildlife benefit (see [1995] 1 All ER 513 at 523).Those who accepted the cruelty argument were, he said, entitled to give effect to their view that the use of the council's land for hunting was not for the benefit of the area, and the judge was wrong to treat that expression as applying to the management of the herd alone. He argued that on an issue of this kind councillors were bound, and if not bound entitled, to have regard to the ethical arguments for and against hunting and the judge had been wrong to treat such considerations as irrelevant. Where power had been entrusted to a popular assembly, the court should be slow to interfere with the exercise of that power.

For the hunt, Mr Beloff QC supported the judge's reasoning. The issue was a short point of statutory construction and the judge had construed the section correctly. Acceptance of the cruelty argument had nothing to do with the benefit of the area. The resolution was an impermissible attempt by those who accepted the cruelty argument to outlaw an activity very recently regulated by Parliament in the Deer Act 1991. In resolving as it did the council acted as if it enjoyed the free discretion of a private landowner and without regard to the constraints which bound a local authority.

I accept the council's basic contention that the judge put too narrow a construction on the words 'the benefit ... of their area'. The draftsman would have been pressed to find broader or less specific language. I would not accept the judge's view that the cruelty argument, or the contrary argument that hunting is a less cruel means of controlling the herd than available alternatives (also, in the judge's terms, a moral argument), is necessarily irrelevant to consideration of what is for the benefit of the area. That is in my opinion to place an unwarranted restriction on the broad language the draftsman has used.

There is, however, as I think, a categorical difference between saying 'I strongly disapprove of X' and saying 'It is for the benefit of the area that X should be prohibited'. The first is the expression of a purely personal opinion which may (but need not) take account of any wider, countervailing argument. There are, for example, those so deeply opposed to the capital penalty on moral grounds that no counter-argument (however cogent) could shake their conviction. The second statement is also the expression of a personal opinion, but involves a judgment on wider, community-based grounds of what is for the benefit of the area. Both statements may of course lead to the same conclusion, but they need not. There is nothing illogical in saying 'I strongly disapprove of X, but I am not persuaded that it is for the benefit of the area that X should be prohibited'. Thus a person might be deeply opposed to the capital penalty but conclude that it would not be for the benefit of the community to prohibit it so long as its availability appeared to deter the commission of murder.

The question therefore arises whether, in resolving as it did on 4 August 1993, the council exercised its power to further the object prescribed by the statute, the benefit of the council area. I conclude that it did not, for these reasons.

(1) At no point, before or during the debate, was the attention of the council drawn to what is now agreed to be the governing statutory provision. The minds of councillors were never drawn to the question they should have been addressing. As the judge observed ([1995] 1 All ER 513 at 523): 'It follows that if the ban was lawful, it was so more by good luck than judgment.'

(2) A paper circulated to councillors with the agenda concluded:

In the final analysis people go hunting primarily because they find it a sport they enjoy. The County Council must come to a decision, as the National Trust report said, 'largely on the grounds of ethics, animal welfare and social considerations ...' which are matters for members to decide. I accept that animal welfare and social considerations were relevant matters to take into account, and I have accepted that ethical considerations could be. But this statement does not express or exhaust the statutory test, and could well be read as an invitation to councillors to give free rein to their personal views.

(3) The reference in the resolution to the council 'as landowners', and the statement in the letter (quoted above) written after the resolution that it was for every landowner to decide what activities he wished to allow on his land, appear to equate the positions of private and local authority landowners. This in my view reflected a failure to appreciate the overriding statutory constraint.

(4) The lack of reference to the governing statutory test was not in my view a purely formal omission, for if councillors had been referred to it they would have had to attempt to define what benefit a ban would confer on the area and conversely what detriment the absence of a ban would cause. It may be that they could have done so, but as it was they did not need to try. The note certainly suggests that the debate ranged widely, and reference was made to 'economic grounds' and 'social damage' as well as to the cruelty argument and the contrary moral argument. But the note also suggests that expressions of purely personal opinion loomed large: 'rituals ... unwholesome instincts', 'systematically torture', 'barbaric ... amusement', 'uniquely abhorrent', 'pleasure torturing animals'. In the absence of legal guidance, it was not, I think, appreciated that personal views, however strongly held, had to be related to the benefit of the area.

I accordingly agree, although on much narrower grounds, that the council was not entitled to make the decision it did on the grounds it relied on. I leave open, but express no view on, the possibility that the same decision could have been reached on proper grounds. In reaching this conclusion I gain no assistance from authorities such as *Slattery v Naylor* (1888) 13 App Cas 446 and *Kruse v Johnson* [1898] 2 QB 91; [1895–99] All ER Rep 105 on judicial review of byelaws made by popular assemblies. The present case involves no issue of reasonableness. The question is whether a statutory power was exercised to promote the purpose for which the power was conferred. I conclude that it was not.

Simon Brown LJ:[50] The crucial question therefore becomes: is the cruelty argument relevant to determining what will benefit the council's area or, as I think no different, relevant to their determination of what will advance the public good?

Despite Mr Beloff QC's strenuous arguments to the contrary, I find it impossible to say that the councillors must shut their minds to the cruelty

---

50   The judgement by Simon Brown looked at the issue of the cruelty to deer of hunting.

argument, still less that they must do so as a matter of the strict construction of s 120(1)(b).

I readily accept that the concepts of benefit to the area, and public interest and good, invite consideration first of the council's human community, rather than its wildlife. But the two considerations are not discrete: human well-being for many will depend upon their satisfaction as to animal welfare. That explains much animal legislation and why such activities as bear-baiting and cock-fighting have long since been abolished. It explains too why a spacious zoo provides enjoyment when a cramped one may not, and why bull-fighting is unlikely to catch on here. The examples could be multiplied.

Why then should it be thought illogical and thus impermissible for councillors to have regard to their sentiments as representatives of the local community in deciding whether that community's land – the common – should be hunted? As the judge himself recognised ([1995] 1 All ER 513 at 523):

> ... individual councillors ... may readily suppose that as representatives, not delegates, of their electors they ought to give effect to their opinions about any issue of principle which they perceive as touching a question before them for decision.

He, of course, concluded that the councillors should have been warned to the contrary. I disagree.

I am not convinced that it has assisted the argument hitherto to have qualified the council's statutory duty by the concession that it was bound 'to manage the estate for maximum landscape, wildlife and public recreation benefit' (see [1995] 1 All ER 513 at 523). But even if the focus is properly upon wildlife benefit, that surely encompasses the cruelty argument – what Mr Supperstone QC called 'the deer's quality of life and manner of death'. The cruelty argument is, indeed, only one aspect of the overall ethical debate. There are powerful arguments both ways on the issue of hunting and each side invokes ethical considerations in support. By no means all those in favour of hunting themselves enjoy the sport: rather many believe that it represents the kindest as well as the most effective method of managing the herd. The anti-hunt faction enjoys no moral monopoly. Is it to be said that those opposing the ban must put aside their moral views too? Surely not, and yet I have difficulty in reconciling the judgment below with councillors giving proper consideration to such suffering as would result from uncontrolled shooting and poaching.

It follows that I agree with Sir Thomas Bingham MR that the judge construed too narrowly the statutory power here in question and erred in regarding the cruelty argument as necessarily irrelevant to the council's decision. I, for my part, indeed, would go further than Sir Thomas Bingham MR and conclude that the cruelty argument, as well indeed as the countervailing ethical considerations, were necessarily relevant to the decision. Had they been ignored I believe that the council would have been open to criticism.

There is a passage in the judgment below in which the judge speaks of 'a decision-maker who fails to take account of all and only those considerations material to his task' (see [1995] 1 All ER 513 at 525). It is important to bearing in mind, however, as Mr Supperstone contended and Mr Beloff accepted, that there are in fact three categories of consideration. First, those clearly (whether expressly or impliedly) identified by the statute as considerations to which regard must be had. Second, those clearly identified by the statute as considerations to which regard must not be had. Third, those to which the decision-maker may have regard if in his judgment and discretion he thinks it right to do so. There is, in short, a margin of appreciation within which the decision-maker may decide just what considerations should play a part in his reasoning process. On *Wednesbury* challenges (see *Associated Provincial Picture Houses Ltd v Wednesbury Corp* [1947] 2 All ER 680; [1948] 1 KB 223) it is often salutary to bear in mind this short passage from Cooke J's judgment in *CREEDNZ Inc v Governor General* [1981] 1 NZLR 172 at 183:

> What has to be emphasised is that it is only when the statute expressly or impliedly identifies considerations required to be taken into account by the authority as a matter of legal obligation that the court holds a decision invalid on the ground now invoked. It is not enough that a consideration is one that may properly be taken into account, nor even that it is one which many people, including the court itself, would have taken into account if they had to make the decision.

Even had I not thought the cruelty argument a category one consideration, I should certainly have regarded it as falling into category three. But in either event, of course, it does not follow that those councillors espousing the cruelty argument were bound to regard it as decisive. They could have concluded that it was preferable to allow hunting to continue until Parliament addressed the issue on a national level. Or they might have felt that their own personal views did not properly represent those of the majority of their community so that it would be wrong to give effect to them.

Provided only and always, however, that those councillors espousing the cruelty argument had regard to such other considerations as were necessarily in play, they were clearly entitled to regard it as decisive: its weight in the overall balance was exclusively a matter for them.

I pass, therefore, to the second question: can the council's decision be impugned on the conventional *Wednesbury* basis that those voting for the ban failed to have regard to certain matters that they were bound to consider? The judge found the decision flawed on this ground too; he criticised the council for failing to have regard to the future management of the deer in the event of a ban. In common with Sir Thomas Bingham MR and for the reasons he gives – essentially that it was not necessary for the council to fix upon a contemporaneous solution to whatever problem might result from the ban – I disagree.

What then of other relevant considerations? On this question I reluctantly find myself in respectful disagreement with Sir Thomas Bingham MR. I would not for my part conclude that the council failed to have regard to the true nature of the question before it. I recognise, of course, that the councillors had not been advised as to the actual terms of their statutory power. But, as I have indicated, that power I believe merely to mirror the common law constraints that must in any event invariably rule council decision-making.

I recognise too that both in its resolution, and in Mr Temperley's (the chairman of the council's environment committee) subsequent letter, the council was emphasising the significance of its ownership of the common. But I would not think it right to infer from this that the councillors lost sight of their duty to act in the public interest and for the benefit of their area. The fact of ownership surely was of some significance. Given, as Mr Temperley's letter postulated (although as the respondents reserve the right to contest), that there exists no right to hunt under the provisions of s 193(1) of the Law of Property Act 1925, the council's licence is required (see [1995] 1 All ER 513 at 522). The fact that it could not ban hunting on other land in its area (and may well not have been entitled under s 120(1)(b) to acquire other land in its area with a view to banning hunting over it, or for that matter with a view to allowing hunting over it – questions I think it unnecessary to decide) does not mean that it must allow hunting on its own land, and it seems to me harsh to construe the letter as a bald assertion that the councillors felt entitled merely to indulge their personal wishes in the matter. Given, moreover, that the hunt required the council's continuing licence, it seems to me inappropriate to speak of the prohibition as 'manifestly (interfering) with the lawful freedom of those who take part in the sport' (see [1995] 1 All ER 513 at 529). It would be otherwise if s 193(1) of the 1925 Act conferred the right to hunt; then I accept it would be inappropriate for the council to attach weight to their status as owners of the common and I would be inclined to concur in quashing the ban and dismissing the appeal on that basis.

As it is, however, I find no sufficient reason for holding that those councillors in favour of the ban gave effect to unlawful considerations or failed to address what ultimately was the true question before them: what to do in the public interest and for the benefit of their area. Of course, combing through the notes of the debate, one can always find arguments recorded in terms suggesting an improper approach to the question at issue. That, however, is not a sound basis for impeaching a decision of this nature (see *R v London CC, ex p London and Provincial Electric Theatres Ltd* [1915] 2 KB 466 at 490–91).

In short, I conclude that the majority of the council here genuinely regarded hunting over the common as a cruel and socially undesirable activity inimical to the best interests of their area. It is not, of course, for me to say whether I think that a sound and sensible view. But that being a view which I believe the council was entitled to reach and reached, it follows that I for my part would have found the decision lawful and would accordingly have allowed this appeal.

Hunt policing

In the absence of further restrictions on hunting by Parliament, groups have increasingly resorted to extra-parliamentary tactics. This has led to confrontation between the protestors and the police. Increasingly the clashes between pro- and anti-hunt supporters have become more violent: (See Chapter 10 for a discussion of such tactics.)

A late season venture into Cheshire for one group of saboteurs seemed more like a venture back in time, when the all too familiar 'round 'em up and lock 'em up' tactics were resurrected from previous seasons. All six sab vans present were detained in a police blockade, despite the fact that all sabs (apart from the drivers and map-readers) had disembarked into fields in pursuit of the hunt, as vans travelled down the A49 near Northwich towards the meet of the Cheshire Forest. The police managed to hold the vans for only 25 minutes until all six vehicles escaped and went in search of the hunt. With the help of an enormously expensive spotter plane which circled overhead for several hours, the police later called in reinforcements to track down the vans. Once this had been achieved all drivers and navigators were arrested ('to prevent a breach of the peace') and each vehicle impounded, leaving around 50 sabs stranded in the middle of one of the country's most notorious blackspots for hunt violence. The 11 arrested were then held at Northwich police station for over three hours until the hunt finished, and then released without charge – effectively an admission that they had committed no offence, but were being held to prevent any opposition to the hugely influential Cheshire hunting community. The police later claimed that they had not in fact been arrested, merely detained – a legal nonsense.

This is far from the first time that Cheshire police have used mass arrests to unlawfully detain sabs without any charges being brought. Last season 126 sabs were arrested in Cheshire, with many in batches of up to 30 at a time – of these 126 only two were ever charged with an offence. Until Cheshire police can provide a convincing alternative, one can only assume they are in the habit of arresting large numbers of people who quite manifestly have committed no more criminal act than being opposed to hunting. This is a habit that they will soon have to change, once the many civil cases against their inexplicable policing practices come to fruition and pay dividends to the sabs concerned.[51]

More sab arrests ...

At the Fitzwilliam Hunt 11 sabs were blocked in by hunt supporters and were astonished when the police arrived to be told 'there's nothing we can do'. In fact, such behaviour encompasses about half a dozen public order and road traffic offences. A police sergeant then announced he had been told that sabs had been trespassing so that he could 'probably arrest you all under s 69 of the Criminal Justice Act'. When it was pointed out to him that he was just making this up, he replied 'Right, that's it. I'm arresting you all to prevent a breach of the peace', presumably conceding the point that he had in fact been making it up. It is difficult to see how such arrests can be justified when the 11 sabs in question were sat in a van on a public road. All 11 were held until the hunt had finished and then released without charge. This amounts to an unofficial (and unlawful) 'internment' policy. It is a tactic we have seen before elsewhere in the country, most notably Cheshire (see above), where 11 arrests were made under similar circumstances the weekend before. Similar unlawful arrests in the late 1980s cost various police forces over £250,000 in damages after sabs sued. Unfortunately for the taxpayers of Kettering, their local police haven't

---

51 '11 sabs arrested at Cheshire Forest – no charges', *Howl*, Spring/Summer 1996, no 61, pp 6–7. Reproduced by the kind permission of Hunt Saboteurs Association, Brighton.

got enough sense to be biased properly – six sabs already in the field on foot continued to sab the hunt successfully, ensuring no kills were to be had.

Meanwhile, at the Essex Hunt taxpayers' money was being thrown about with wild abandon as 50 officers and the force helicopter were called in to deal with about 40 sabs. Again the police were not quite so interested in dealing with offences committed by hunt members as with harassing sabs – the officers took no action against a hunt rider who deliberately rode his horse over a woman protester while busying themselves with illegal searches of sab vehicles and confiscation of equipment. One van alone was searched four times, an obvious abuse of power as a delaying of tactic. Staves and baseball bats were found in the hunt stewards' vehicle and these were confiscated, but despite the obviously violent intention of anyone carrying such items, none of the stewards were so much as cautioned. In contrast, the highlight of the day for the police came when sabs entered a field some distance away from the hunt. Despite the fact that they were doing nothing more criminal than walking across a field, a task force of police Land Rovers skidded across the field from all sides and officers leapt on anyone they could grab, making 10 arrests for 'aggravated trespass'.

Cornish sabs attacked ... and then arrested!

During a meet of the Western Hunt where the Cornwall sabs were in attendance, one supporter allegedly grabbed one sab and began pushing him around. Despite the complete absence of any aggressive moves on behalf of the sabs, three protesters were arrested – but later released without charge. One sab, who the police seemed intent on arresting, had to seek sanctuary in the home of some local sympathisers and, thanks to their kindness, successfully evaded the long arm of the law. At a meet of the same hunt three days after, a sab was knocked to the ground after allegedly being hit on the head by a rider, who used the bone handle of his whip for the attack. Despite the sab concerned collapsing and sustaining a severe laceration to the top of his head, the police chose not to target their efforts on his attacker, but instead arrested another sab for an alleged breach of the peace, and only agreed to take the injured sab to hospital after other sabs present pleaded with them. Reports from the group indicate that it is only the persistence of the injured sabs' colleagues that has eventually led to the police taking statements, and at last appearing to take the matter seriously.

And, finally, a case from Sussex. The Sussex police have agreed to pay a West Sussex hunt sab £200 as an out-of-court settlement, following an incident at the Crawley and Horsham Foxhounds during cubbing in October. A member of West Sussex Wildlife Protection, was held for around an hour following his arrest at the meet, and was later released without charge.

He stated 'This is the fourth out-of-court settlement made to me by Sussex Police since 1992. Previously they have paid me a total of £1,100 in settlement plus full legal costs. Given that the police like the courts to fine the public who act unlawfully, it seems appropriate that I should fine the police when they act unlawfully.'

Angling

The concerns over hunting have spread to angling, which opponents claim is as cruel as other forms of hunting and should be made illegal. In order to fish, a licence is needed from the Environment Agency valid for the species concerned. It is a criminal offence to fish without a valid licence. A fishing permit is also needed; these are obtained locally from the fishery proprietor. For the general controls over angling refer to the Salmon and Freshwater Fisheries Act 1975 and the Water Regulation Act 1991 Pt V. The following extract examines the arguments in favour of making angling illegal:[52]

> Many animal rights campaigners seem to shy away from angling, whether sabbing or whatever, because they are not conversant with the necessary facts, especially on the pain issue. The following sections explain why angling is as much a blood sport as any other.
>
> There are three types of angling: coarse, sea and game fishing. Coarse fishing is by far the most popular and also the cruellest form of angling. It is carried out throughout the year except during the close season (in most cases) between the 15 March and the 15 June, when the fish spawn. Coarse fish are mostly inedible and include all freshwater species except salmon, trout and grayling.
>
> When caught, these fish are not killed instantly upon leaving the water, but exposed to an environment they are not designed to cope with. Primarily, they can't breath. Other factors include stress imposed due to the sudden change in temperature, noise, vibration, oxygen concentration, light intensity and damage to a protective mucous layer. If fish survive this ordeal, they are often put into a keepnet. These nets are designed to keep fish underwater, before being released at the end of the fishing session. However, many fish will receive injuries from the net mesh or from being squashed together with other fish and many will die due to depletion of oxygen over a period in these devices. keepnets are most popular at fishing matches, enabling each angler to weigh his complete catch at the end of the match. Many pleasure anglers use keepnets simply as a personal ego boost.
>
> Sea angling is practised from piers, beaches, rocks, harbour walls and boats. One fundamental difference between coarse and sea fishing is at a competitive level; sea fish are weighed at dead-weight. As most fish caught are edible, it is rare for them to be released. Fish targeted include shark, cod, conger eel, turbot, plaice and dog fish, to name but a few. The most brutal form of sea fishing is probably shark fishing. Exhausted and in agony from hooks and gaffs (metal hooks on poles used in landing big fish) through their flesh, the sharks are dragged aboard and beaten upon the nose until dead.
>
> Game fishing quarry include salmon, sea trout, brown trout, rainbow trout and grayling. These fish usually end up eaten and the usual method of killing is with a club called a priest, although sticks and stones are also used.

---

52 'What's wrong with angling?', *Howl*, Summer 1992, pp 9–10. Reproduced with the kind permission of the Hunt Saboteurs Association, Brighton.

Hatchery-reared trout are used to re-stock game fisheries and a substantial degree of 'vermin' control is undertaken at both fish farm fishery, including the extermination of predatory fish and fish-eating birds. Game fishing tends to be the most expensive type and is considered rather elitist by its participants.

The Medway report, published in 1980 and sponsored by the RSPCA, proved that all vertebrates, warm or cold blooded, are capable of experiencing pain. The scientist involved in compiling the report exposed the farcical idea that fishing is humane, to be utter rubbish. In fact Dr McWilliams, fish biologist and member of the National Association of Specialist Anglers, even admitted: 'avoiding subjecting fish to some degree of stress when fishing is impossible'.

The pure barbarity of angling becomes clear on examining the process of hooking, playing and landing a fish. A fish is deceived into impaling itself on a (usually) barbed hook, resulting in the infliction of an injury. The angler may then 'play' the fish in order to tire it and allow it to be landed. On leaving the water, a fish is unable to extract oxygen from the air and is subjected to extreme stress. During the handling process, a protective mucous covering which provides the creature's waterproofing and protects it from infections, is damaged. If a fish has swallowed the hook, the hook's retrieval is very difficult, the suffering is prolonged and is likely to result in damage to the fish's gut and subsequently death.

The moment the fish leaves the water, it enters an alien environment in which it is ill-equipped to cope. The gills collapse and breathing is virtually impossible. After oxygen is exhausted from the bloodstream, bleeding may occur from the gills. Combined with the trauma of capture and handling, considerable stress is inflicted. Following return to the water, an exhausted fish may remain motionless for a long period, during which it is at risk from predators and environmental damage.

People who say that it cannot be proven beyond doubt that fish can feel pain, must also admit that the same can be said of any animal other than humans. Only the latter can report in words the sensations experienced. However, society at large does not accept that the reactions and squeals of warm-blooded animals are purely mechanical. Based on our knowledge of fish biology, there is no logical reason why this widely-held belief should not be extended to fish.

It has been convenient for anglers that fish have been considered in the past not to feel pain. The Medway report noted that the methods used in angling 'if performed in a laboratory on unanaesthetised fish, without licence would very probably be in contravention of the (1876) Cruelty to Animals Act'. (See 1986 Act.)

Angling is justified on the grounds of conservation. Anglers, it is argued, are wild-life guardians, being in a good position to report pollution offences and to put pressure on water companies to clean up or maintain river quality for angling.

OTHER CONTROLS OVER ANIMALS USED FOR 'ENTERTAINMENT'

Animals used in films on television, etc

Section 1 of the Cinematograph Films (Animals) Act 1937 states that:

(1) No person shall exhibit to the public or to supply to any person for public exhibition (whether by him or another person) any Cinematograph film (whether produced in the UK or elsewhere) if in connection with the publication of the film any scene required in the film was organised or directed such a way as to involved the cruel infliction of pain or terror on any animal or the cruel goading of any animal to fury.

(2) In any proceedings brought under this Act in respect of any film, the court may (without prejudice to any other mode of proof) infer from the film as exhibited to the public or supplied for public exhibition, as the case may be, that a scene represented in the film as so exhibited or supplied was organised or directed in such a way as to involve the cruel infliction of pain or terror on an animal or the cruel goading of an animal to fury, but (whether the court draws such an inference or not) it shall be a defence for the defendant to prove that he believed, and had reasonable cause to believe, that no scene so represented was so organised or directed.

This provision comes in addition to the protection afforded to animals under s 1 of the Animals Act 1911. The RSPCA and British Film and Television Producers Association have produced a Guide on Basic Procedure as to the use of animals in filming. This recommends that the RSPCA should be notified when animals are used on set, so that a qualified representative can be present to advise and assist production. The guide states that the Royal College of Veterinary Surgeons has advised its members not to cooperate in sedating or anaesthetising animals if it will be cruel or frightening to the animal or potentially dangerous to its health and well-being, or if it is unnecessary. There are guidelines in relation to the keeping of animals while not on set as well as the use of animals in the actual filming.

Fighting and illegal contests

Under s 1 of the Protection of Animals Act 1934 there is a prohibition of certain public contests, performances, and exhibitions with animals including bullfights and rodeos:

(1) No person shall promote, or cause or knowingly permit to take place any public performance which includes any episode consisting of or involving:

(a) throwing or casting, with ropes or other appliances, any unbroken horse or untrained bull; or

(b) wrestling, fighting, or struggling with any untrained bull; or

(c) riding, or attempting to ride, any horse or bull which by the use of any appliance or treatment involving cruelty is, or has been, stimulated with the intention of making it buck during the performance; and no person shall in any public performance take part in any such episode as aforesaid.

(2) For the purposes of proceedings under paragraph (a) or paragraph (b) of the preceding subsection, if an animal appears or is represented to spectators to be unbroken or untrained it shall lie on the defendant to prove that the animal is in fact broken or trained. In proceedings under paragraph (c) of the said subsection in respect of the use of any such appliance or treatment as is therein mentioned upon a horse before or during a performance, it shall be a defence for the defendant to prove that he did not know, and could not reasonably be expected to know, that the appliance or treatment was to be used.

Cockfighting and other animal fights

Cockfighting was made illegal under s 5A of the Animal Health Act 1911 and attendance at animal fights in general is illegal:

A person who, without reasonable excuse, is present when animals are placed together for the purpose of their fighting each other shall be liable on summary conviction to a fine ...

Section 5B makes the advertising of animal fights illegal:

If a person who publishes or causes to be published an advertisement for a fight between animals knows that it is such an advertisement he shall be liable on summary conviction to a fine ...

Cockfighting seems to happen quite regularly. The following case was highlighted in *Howl*:[53]

Cockfighting reared its ugly head again, but this time in the North East. S of Durham admitted causing cocks to fight in the wooden hut he owned on allotments; using the premises for cockfighting and possessing spurs and other equipment for cockfighting, was sentenced to four months. P of Newark, who was accompanied by an eight year old boy to the fight, was sentenced to 10 weeks, and R of Murton was sentenced to eight weeks. They both admitted assisting at a cockfight. The magistrate also included an order banning them from owning live cockerels for the rest of their lives. A of Annfield Plain was fined £200 with £150 costs; B of Bishop Auckland was fined £800 with £750 costs and C of County Durham was fined £200 with £150 costs. They all admitted being present at a cockfight. Two cocks fitted with spurs were attacking each other in a ring – the 19th bout of 24 listed on a notice calling the event 'The Durham Derby' – when the raid took place on an allotment shed near Durham City. Police also recovered the carcasses of 14 dead birds from

---

53 *Howl*, Autumn/Winter, 1996, no 62, pp 16–18. Reproduced with the kind permission of the Hun Saboteurs Association, Brighton.

earlier fights. They also found 34 live birds, of which nine were injured. Also found in the shed was equipment ranging from spurs to spur sharpeners and plasters used to fit spurs to the legs of the birds and scales for weighing them. Counsel for the defence claimed all six men had gathered for an auction but this developed into a cockfighting session.

CONCLUSION

The use of animals for various forms of 'entertainment' is highly controversial. If circuses are to be allowed, it is argued, they should be subject to the same welfare requirements as zoos. In Australia (NSW), zoos and circuses are regulated under the Exhibited Animals Protection Act 1986 No 123 (NSW). The Act is supervised by the Exhibited Animals Advisory Committee, which includes scientists, environmentalists, agriculturists, animal welfare groups, administrators and vets. There is also an Exhibited Animals Protection Unit. This would be a useful addition to the regulation of animals in circuses and zoos in the UK. In NSW, the Committee's membership has to include a Minister from agriculture, wildlife concerns, prevention of cruelty organisations and representatives of exhibitors and animal welfare organisations. This could be adopted in the UK and so provide an independent body to oversee the policy and administration of the importation, control and welfare of the animals exhibited. The recommendations of the WSPA on zoos should be extended to circuses, if they are to continue. Reforms should be undertaken in the UK to ensure that where animals are kept in captivity, their welfare is a priority.

Many animal welfare organisations would like to see circuses banned, and some question the need for zoos. An advisory or ethical committee could ensure that a public debate takes place and that any necessary reforms are made. The issue of hunting should be re-examined by an independent committee, and the Labour Party's proposal for a free vote on the issue in Parliament should be carried out, whichever party is in power. This would also ensure that the legality of the decision of 160 local councils to ban hunting on their land could be settled.

The areas examined in the chapter base their rationale, in many cases, on conservation and education. If the proponents are to argue successfully for continuing to undertake these activities, then these rationales have to outweigh the importance of preserving animals in their natural ecosystems and the need for all animals to be killed using humane slaughter methods.

FURTHER READING

Cherfas, J, Zoo 2000, *A Look Behind the Bars,*1984, London: BBC.

Freeman, E, 'The Controversy of Field Sports', *Fortnightly Review,* 1870, vol XIV, December, pp 674–91; also 'the Morality of Field Sports', *Fortnightly Review,* 1869, vol XII, October, pp 375–85.

Grayson, E, *Sports and the Law,*1994, London: Butterworths.

Gripps, J, *Beyond Captive Breeding – Re-introducing Endangered Mamals into the Wild,* proceedings of a symposium held at the Zoological Society of London on 24 and 25 November 1989, 1991, Oxford: Clarendon Press.

Heidiger, H, *Wild Animals in Captivity,* 1977, New York: Dover Publications Inc.

Linzey, A, 'Blood Sports and Public Law' (1995) 145 *New Law Journal* No 6688, pp 412 and 430.

Nordell, G, 'The Quantock Hounds and the Trojan Horse' (1995) PL Spring 27–33.

Plant, G, 'Conservation and Welfare–a new era in Europe' (1995) 4(7) *European Environmental Law Review* 204–09.

Strutt, J, *The Sports and Pastimes of the People of England,* 1830, London: William Reeves.

Travers, J and Wray, J (eds) *Beyond the Bars,* 1987, Wellingborough: Thorsons.

Tudge, C, 'A Wild Time at the Zoo', *New Scientist,* 5 January 1991, pp 26–30.

CHAPTER EIGHT

WILDLIFE PROTECTION

INTRODUCTION

This chapter will examine the protection of wild animals and birds, and also the protection of their habitat. Wildlife in the UK faces many pressures: not only from deliberate acts of cruelty, baiting and hunting, but also from developments such as roads and airports, habitat loss and the problem of pollution. Wild animals have for centuries been open to direct and indirect destruction; unless they were scarce or were protected as game, or became captive (when they were then protected, under the Wild Animals in Captivity Protection Act 1900, later to be incorporated into the Protection of Animals Act 1911) or the property of humans, wild animals had no protection under the law.

Domestic animals have received a degree of protection from cruelty since 1832 under the Martin's Act (see Chapter 2), but wild animals have had to wait a lot longer, until the Wild Mammals Protection Act 1996. The distinction between domestic and wild animals continues to this day, as while the fighting and hunting of domestic animals is illegal, wild animals are still not protected. This reflects the inherent anthropocentrism of our response to animals.

This chapter will examine the adequacy of our protection of wild animals in the UK through national and international controls and will examine some of the possible reforms that could be made to ensure that we maintain a diverse and rich number of animals, as well as the habitat to support them.

HISTORY

It is only recently that the law has sought to protect animals in their own right, rather than because they are either a pest or of some economic value. Colin Reid, in *Nature Conservation Law*,[1] outlines the background to wild animal protection and control. Legislation was passed to control animals as pests, for example, foxes, as food and as quarry. In Victorian times concerns arose regarding the conservation of birds and a number of statutes were passed to protect them. The Sea Birds Preservation Act 1869 protected various types of sea birds and this was followed by the Wild Birds Protection Act 1872 and the 1876 Wild Fowl Preservation Act, the legislation finally being consolidated in

---

1   Reid, C, *Nature Conservation Law*, 1994, London: Sweet & Maxwell.

the 1880 Wild Birds Protection Act. After that Act many similar statutes were passed (that dealt with the protection of birds), including the Wild Birds Protection Acts of 1881, 1894, 1896, 1902, 1904 and 1908, the Sand Grouse Protection Act 1888, the Wild Birds (St Kilda) Act 1904, the Captive Birds Shooting (Prohibition) Act 1921, the Protection of Birds Acts 1925, 1933, 1954 and 1967, the Protection of Lapwings Act 1928, the Quail Protection Act 1937 and the Wild Birds (Ducks and Geese) Protection Act 1939. Other animals did not receive the same degree of protection until the Wild Creatures and Wild Plants Act 1975, which was replaced by the Wildlife and Countryside Act 1981. Specific animals have received further protection; for example, seals were covered by the Grey Seals (Protection) Act 1914, replaced by the Conservation of Seals Act 1970.

INSTITUTIONS

The main government department concerned with wild animals and bird conservation is the Department of the Environment (DOE). The DOE's main policies and objectives are: to safeguard and enhance the English landscape; to conserve and protect the English coastline; to promote access to the countryside for informal recreation; to conserve and enhance the diversity and abundance of British wildlife, especially endangered and rare species and their habitats; to promote the planting, management, protection and replacement of trees; to ensure that forestry and agricultural policies take into account the need to conserve and enhance the rural environment; and to stimulate economic and social development in rural areas.

Some statutory control is also enforced by English Nature (formerly the Nature Conservancy Council), the Countryside Commission, National Parks Committee, Sports Council, Forestry Commission, Environment Agency and local authorities. A large number of interest groups influence policy-making, either through lobbying or through their participation on informal governmental and other bodies. These groups include the National Farmers Union, the Country Landowners Association, the Council for the Protection of Rural England, Friends of the Earth, the Royal Society for the Protection of Birds, the Royal Society for the Prevention of Cruelty to Animals, ramblers, various sporting bodies, anglers, local conservation groups such as the British Trust for Conservation Volunteers and the Civic Trust, the Confederation of British Industry, together with residents and business interests.

COMMON LAW CONTROLS

Under common law the term 'wild animals' *(ferae naturae)* is applied to animals that are not domesticated or in captivity (see Chapter 2). This includes not only those animals which are savage by nature but also those of a more mild or timid nature but which cannot be classed as domestic or tame animals: 'there is no absolute property in wild animals while living, and they are not goods or chattels'.[2] Qualified property may be acquired over a wild animal *per industrium*; this arises by lawfully taking, taming or reclaiming them[3] or until they regain their natural liberty.[4]

Bees are *ferae naturae* and no property passes in them until they are hived, when they become the property of the hiver; if they leave the hive, they will remain the hiver's property so long as they can be seen or followed.[5]

Qualified property can also be claimed under *ratione impotentiae et loci* in the young of animals *ferae naturae* if they are born on the land until they can run or fly away.[6]

The final rights of qualified property are *ratione soli and ratione privalegii*, where the owner of the land can take, kill and hunt wild animals, unless he or she grants a licence or grants shooting or sporting rights to another, when the grantee obtains a qualified privilege above the rights of the landowner.[7]

Absolute property can vest in an owner if the animal is dead. If the animal is killed by a trespasser, however, then the trespasser will not obtain ownership of the animal. In an action the tort of conversion will lie against them.[8] If the animal moves onto another person's property then the killer will obtain ownership; however, they will still be liable for trespass. Under common law the property of a wild animal will vest in the owner or occupier of the land if it has been tamed or ordinarily kept in captivity, or has been reduced into possession by a person other than the taker.

STATUTORY CONTROLS

Many of the common law controls over animals have been superseded by statutory controls. Section 4(4) of the Theft Act 1968 and ss 10(1) and (5)(3) of the Criminal Damage Act 1971 provide that wild animals can be the subject of theft or other offences. The Wild Creatures and Forest Laws Act 1971 abolished prerogative rights of landowners over animals and birds and these rights are now limited to fish and swans.

---

2   *Case of Swans* (1592) 7 Co Rep.
3   *Ibid.*
4   See *Blades v Higgs* (1865) 11 HL Cas 621.
5   *Kearry v Pallinston* [1939] 1KB 471.
6   *Case of Swans*, above n 2.
7   See *Blades v Higgs*, above n 4.
8   See s 4(4) of the Theft Act 1968.

The protection of wild birds

Wild Birds are given a degree of protection under the Wildlife and Countryside Act 1981. Wild birds are defined in s 27(10) of the 1981 Act as 'any bird of a kind which is ordinarily resident in or is a visitor to Great Britain in a wild state, not including any birds that have been bred in captivity or poultry or game birds'. Poultry include domestic fowl, geese, ducks, guinea fowl, pigeons, quail and turkeys, while game birds comprise pheasant, partridge, etc.

Except for offences involving the illegal use of weapons and other articles, the Wildlife and Countryside Act 1981 does not cover the following game birds: pheasant, partridge, black grouse, red grouse and ptarmigan. These species are covered by the game acts. Birds are protected in a number of schedules of the Wildlife and Countryside Act 1981:

– Schedule 1 birds are specially protected species which are the subject of increased penalties and cannot intentionally be disturbed while nesting.

– Schedule 2 Part I birds are sporting or quasi-sporting birds which may be shot for a limited period in the winter.

– Schedule 3 Part I birds are species which may be sold alive at all times if ringed with an approved ring and bred in captivity (the sale of all other live wild birds is illegal unless permitted by licence).

– Schedule 3 Part II birds are those that can be sold dead at all times.

– Schedule 3 Part III birds can be sold dead from 1 September to 28 February.

– Schedule 4 birds must be registered and ringed if kept in captivity.[9]

– Schedule 9 birds are introduced birds which are established in the wild in Britain and which cannot be released from captivity.

There are over 500 species of wild birds in Britain, but the schedules only deal with a small number of these. All birds except those listed in Schedule 2, Part I and game birds are fully protected throughout the year.[10]

Section 16(2) of the Wildlife and Countryside Act 1981 allows the collection of certain eggs (gannets' eggs on the island of Sula Sgier, and gulls' eggs); and lapwings' eggs before 15 April each year, as long as they are taken under licence from the Secretary of State. There are also exemptions for agricultural pest control under s 98 of the Agricultural Act 1947, s 16 of the Wildlife and Countryside Act 1981, and under the Animal Health Act 1981.

There are a certain number of wild birds that can be kept, listed in Schedule 4 to the Act. These are covered by a number of regulations: Wildlife

---

9   Wildlife and Countryside Act 1981 (variation of Schedule 4) Order 1994 (SI 1994/1151).

10   RSPB, *Guide to the Law*, undated, London: RSPB.

and Countryside (Registration and Ringing of Certain Captive Birds) Regulations (SI 1982/1221) (amended by Wildlife and Countryside (Registration and Ringing of Certain Captive Birds (Amendment)) Regulations 1982 (SI 1991/478 and SI 1994/1152)). There are a certain number of regulations set out in the Wildlife and Countryside (Registration to sell Etc, Certain Dead Wild Birds) Regulations 1982 (SI 1982/1219) amended by the Wild life and Countryside (Registration to sell, etc Certain Dead Wild Birds) (Amendment) Regulations 1991 (SI 1991/479).

The main offence under the Wildlife and Countryside Act 1981 is found in s 1:

(1) Subject to the provisions of this Part, if any person intentionally:

    (a) kills, injures or takes any wild bird;

    (b) takes, damages or destroys the nest of any wild bird while that nest is in use or being built; or

    (c) takes or destroys an egg of any wild bird,

    he shall be guilty of an offence.

(2) To take, damage or destroy the nest of any wild bird while that nest is in use or being built or;

(3) To take or destroy an egg of any wild bird, the term destroy includes doing anything calculated to protect an egg from hatching (s 1(1)).

An offence is also committed under s 1 of the Wildlife and Countryside Act 1981 if a person has in their possession or control:

(1) any live or dead wild bird, or any part of or anything derived from such a bird, or

(2) an egg of a wild bird, or any part of such an egg.

There are two defences; if the defendant can show, firstly, that the bird or egg was sold to them otherwise than in contravention of the legislation, and secondly, that the bird or egg had not been taken in contravention of the Act (s 1(3)).

Under s 7 of the Wildlife and Countryside Act 1981 it is a further offence:

(3) To have in one's possession or control any live wild bird of prey of any species in the world (with the exception of owls and vultures) unless it is registered and ringed in accordance with the Secretary of State's regulations.

(4) To have in one's possession or control any bird of a species which must be registered and ringed if kept in captivity unless it is so registered.

Some species receive more protection than this; if a person is convicted of an offence under Schedule 1 of the Act then there is a higher penalty under ss 1(4) and 21(1).

There is also an additional offence under s 1(5) of the Wildlife and Countryside Act 1981 of intentionally:

(1) Disturbing any bird included in Schedule 1 whilst it is building a nest or is in or near a nest containing eggs or young, or

(2) To disturb dependent young of such a birds.

The case of *Kirkland v Robinson*[11] established that the possession of birds is a strict liability offence under s 1(2) of the Wildlife and Countryside Act 1981 and that criminal culpability occurs when a person chooses to take possession of such items:

Kirkland v Robinson (1987) 1 JP 377

Stephen Brown LJ: We have been assisted by careful arguments. For my part, I would have no doubt that the offence created by s 1(2) is an offence of strict liability. In my judgment, Parliament intended it to be such and this is evident first, from the fact that the word 'intentionally' does not appear in subsection (2) whereas it does appear in subsection (1); secondly, that subsection (3) provides a specific statutory defence to an offence alleged under subsection (2); and, thirdly, that other provisions in the statute, for example, s 4(2) and the licensing provisions in s 16 provide circumstances in which a person will not be guilty of an offence under s 1(2). ... In this day and age, there are areas of national life which are regarded as being of such importance that there must be an absolute prohibition against the doing of certain acts which undermine the welfare of society. The Wildlife and Countryside Act 1981 is designed to protect the environment. That is an objective of outstanding social importance. In my judgment, the provisions to which I have referred are intended by Parliament to be of strict application. Thus, those who choose to possess *(inter alia)* wild birds are to be at risk to ensure that their possession is a lawful possession within the provisions of the Act.

Under s 3 of the Act areas of special protection can be designated, this requires the owner of the land's consent. Once an area is designated then additional offences can be created. There is an offence of disturbing a bird building a nest or which is in on or near a nest containing eggs or young and of disturbing dependent young. This can be made to apply to any wild birds to which the designation order applies rather than to those listed in Schedule 1. The designation is at the discretion of the Secretary of State. It can also be made an offence for any person to enter into the area, or any specified part of it at any time or during any specified period. It is not, however, an offence to enter if this is done in accordance with provisions for the order. However, only 37 areas have been designated. The aim of the act seems to be to subject to criminal penalties those who trespass onto the land without the approval of the owner or occupier; however, it does not seem to restrict the activities of the owner, the occupier or those they invite onto their land. There are also exceptions to these offences in relation to preventing and controlling animal disease, or if a bird has been severely disabled, or if the offence was the incidental result of a lawful operation and could not have reasonably been avoided.

---

11   (1987) 1 JP.

Under s 4 unless a person is appropriately licensed it is an offence to sell, offer, possess or transport for sale or hire any dead wild bird (or skin or part of such a bird) other than a bird on Schedule 3, Part II or III unless the vendor has been registered and the bird has been marked in accordance with the regulations. It should be noted that game birds may only be sold dead during the open season and for a period of 10 days immediately after the end of the season.

It is an offence to show at any competition, or in premises in which a competition is being held, any live bird unless listed on Schedule 3, Part I and ringed in accordance with the regulations.

The following methods of killing, injuring or taking wild birds are normally prohibited, except under licence (s 5): any springs, traps, gins [note: normally in the form of a pole trap], snares, hook and line, electrical devices, poisonous or stupefying substances, nets (including mist nets and those projected or propelled other than by hand), gas or smoke, baited birds, bird lime or similar substances, and chemical wetting agents. The use of any sound recording or live birds as decoys if tethered, blinded or maimed is illegal as is the use of bows, crossbows, explosives (other than ammunition for firearms), automatic or semi-automatic weapons, guns with an internal muzzle diameter greater than $1^3/_4$ inches, artificial light or dazzling devices and sights for night-shooting ... It is also illegal to use any mechanically propelled vehicle in immediate pursuit of a wild bird for the purpose of killing or capture. It is illegal to have any part in any activity involving the release of birds as immediate targets for shooting. It is also now an offence to 'cause' or 'permit' any such action. This applies where a person directs another to commit an offence or knowingly allows it to happen.

It is illegal to keep any bird (excluding poultry, see Chapter 5) in a cage or other receptacle which is not of sufficient size to permit the bird to stretch its wings freely in all directions. Exceptions to this arise if the bird is undergoing veterinary treatment; is in the course of conveyance or is being exhibited; in the case of exhibition the time the bird is so confined should not exceed an aggregate of 72 hours.

It is an offence to release or to allow to escape into the wild any bird which (a) is not ordinarily resident in, or a regular visitor to, Great Britain in a wild state, or (b) is listed in Schedule 9, Part I.

There are exceptions to the offences provided for in s 1 of the Wildlife and Countryside Act 1981.

- Birds listed on Schedule 3, Part I may be sold or exhibited competitively provided they have been bred in captivity and ringed in accordance with the regulations.

- Any person may take, kill or injure in attempting to kill a bird listed on Schedule 2, Part I (or on Schedule 1, Part II) provided this is done outside the close season and not in an area of special protection or on any Sunday or Christmas day in Scotland or in a prescribed area on any Sunday.

- An authorised person may kill or injure any protected bird (except one on Schedule 1, Part II) if they can show that their action was necessary for the purposes of preserving public health or air safety, preventing the spread of disease or preventing serious damage to livestock, foodstuffs for livestock, crops, vegetables, fruit, growing timber or fisheries.

- A person may take a wild bird if they can satisfy the court that the bird has been injured other than by their own hand and that their sole purpose was to tend it and then release it when no longer disabled; or he may kill it if he can prove it was so seriously disabled as to be beyond recovery. Sick and injured birds on Schedule 4 must be registered with the Department of the Environment or passed to a licensed Rehabilitation Keeper.

- It is not illegal to destroy a bird's nests or egg if it can be shown that such an action was the incidental result of a lawful operation and could not have reasonably been avoided.

- An authorised person may use a cage trap or net for taking Schedule 2, Part II birds; a net may be used for taking wild duck at certain decoys. A cage trap or net may be used for taking game birds for the purpose of breeding.

The main aim of the registration system under the Wildlife and Countryside Act 1981 is to end the unlawful taking of birds from the wild. All species listed in Schedule 4 of the Act, which includes all birds of prey but not owls, must be registered if kept in captivity; birds of prey and some other species in the schedule must also be ringed with a uniquely numbered band supplied by the Department of the Environment. Provision is made in the act for inspection of premises and birds registered.

If a constable suspects with reasonable cause that any person is committing or has committed an offence involving a wild bird, the constable may without warrant under the Wildlife and Countryside Act 1981:

- stop and search that person if the constable suspects with reasonable cause that evidence of the commission of the offence is to be found on that person;

- search or examine anything which that person may then be using or have in their possession if the constable suspects with reasonable cause the evidence of the commissioning of the offence is to be found on that thing;

- seize and detain for the purpose of proceedings anything which may be evidence of the commission of the offence or may be liable to forfeiture.

If the constable suspects with reasonable cause that any person is committing an offence relating to a wild bird they may, for the purpose of exercising the powers listed above, enter any land other than a dwelling house (s 51). These are not arrestable offences; however, general powers of arrest under the Police and Criminal Evidence Act 1984 apply. A justice of the peace may grant a warrant to any constable to search any premises if they are given reasonable grounds to suspect that evidence may be found on the property, in relation to the commission of any offence incurring a special penalty, notably offences involving a Schedule 1 bird, the use of a prohibited method, or the sale of any protected bird.

Anyone found guilty of an offence punishable by a special penalty (s 21), notably offences involving a Schedule 1 bird or the use of poison to kill a bird, is liable to fines. Fines may be imposed in respect of each bird, nest, egg or skin. If more than one such item is involved then the total fine is determined as if the person committed each offence separately – fines accumulate. The police may order the confiscation of any vehicle, animal or weapon or other thing which was used to commit the offence.

Under ss 2 and 4 of the Wildlife and Countryside Act 1981, licences can be granted to allow the following:

–   The killing or taking in cage traps of bullfinches by an authorised person for the purpose of preventing serious damage to the buds of fruit trees in certain areas.

–   The killing or taking of certain birds, including the taking, damaging or destruction of their nests, or the taking or destruction of their eggs by an authorised person for the purpose of preventing serious damage to livestock, crops, vegetables, fruit, growing timber or fisheries. Control is permitted by either shooting, the use of a cage trap or nets.

–   The killing or taking of certain birds, including the taking, damaging, or destruction of their nests or the taking or destruction of their eggs by an authorised person for the purpose of preserving public health or air safety.

–   The killing or taking of certain birds, including the taking, damaging, or destruction of their nests or the taking or destruction of their eggs by an authorised person for the purpose of preserving public health or safety, preventing the spread of disease or preventing serious damage to livestock etc. However, there must be no other satisfactory solution (s 4(4)).

European controls for the protection of birds

The law of the European Union also provides for the protection of birds. The EC Directive on the Conservation of Wild Birds (79/409/EEC), emphasises the need to protect not just the birds but also their habitat. There are measures to protect vulnerable birds and all migratory birds through a network of Special Protection Areas, of which 218 have been proposed:

Despite tough law protecting migratory bird species in Europe under the EC Directive of Conservation of Wild Birds (1979), enforcement is virtually non-existent in some regions. This is due to the political strength of the hunting lobby in many of these Mediterranean countries ... Shooting and netting are the most common methods of hunting birds around the Mediterranean. Also accounting for millions of birds annually is the illegal practice of 'liming' – the application of glue to branches and twigs trapping birds as they land and causing a slow and lingering death by starvation. Italy has a million bird hunters who shoot an estimated 100–250 million birds annually. The straits of Messina is a particular hot spot where the birds cross from Africa to Europe and many species are indiscriminately shot including endangered species such as the honey buzzard ... In France, many species including birds of prey are shot by the estimated 1.7 million active hunters. The main species at risk include finches, turtle doves and some of the raptor species such as goshawk. Experts say that the population of the common songbird in central Europe has dwindled by 1.7% annually since 1974; this implies that we could lose a third of our common birds over a single human generation.[12]

The following case related to whether economic considerations should be taken into account when designating special protection areas.

R v Secretary of State for the Environment, ex p Royal Society for the Protection of Birds (Port of Sheerness Ltd intervening) (1996) The Times, 2 August (ECJ: Full Court)

Council Directive (EC) 79/409, Article 2 provides that Member States must take the requisite measures to maintain the population of species of naturally occurring birds in the wild state in the European territory of the Member States at a level which corresponds in particular to ecological, scientific and cultural requirements, while taking account of economic and recreational requirements. Those species are to be the subject of special conservation measures concerning their habitat in order to ensure their survival and reproduction in their area of distribution and, in this connection, Member States must classify, in particular, the most suitable territories as special protection areas: Article 4(1). In addition, Member States must take similar measures for regularly occurring migratory species not listed in the directive and must, in particular, pay attention to the protection of wetlands of international importance: Article 4(2).

Under Council Directive (EC) 92/43, Article 6(4) if, in spite of a negative assessment of the implications for the site and in the absence of alternative solutions, a plan or project must nevertheless be carried out for imperative reasons of overriding public interest, including those of a social or economic nature, the Member State must take compensatory measures.

An estuary and marsh area, which was wetland of international importance, was used by wild birds as a breeding and wintering area and by migratory birds as a staging post. A nearby port, which was a significant employer in an area of serious unemployment, sought to extend its facilities to better compete with continental ports. The only area into which the port could expand was a mudflat which formed part of the wetland area. The Secretary of State decided to designate the wetland area as a special protection area pursuant to Council

---

12   Birds International X 35, 1990, p 7: London, WSPA.

Directive (EC) 79/409, but he excluded the mudflat from that area on the ground that the contribution that expansion by the port in the area would make to the local and national economy outweighed its nature conservation value. A conservation body sought to quash the Secretary of State's decision on the basis that he was not entitled to have regard to economic considerations when classifying a special protection area and the House of Lords referred questions relating to the interpretation of Article 4(1), (2) to the European Court of Justice. Held, Article 4(1), (2) was to be interpreted as meaning that, when designating a special protection area and defining its boundaries, a Member State (1) was not authorised to take account of the economic requirements mentioned in Article 2, (2) could not take account of economic requirements as constituting a general interest superior to that represented by the ecological objective of the directive, and (3) could not take account of economic requirements which could constitute imperative reasons of overriding public interest of the kind referred to in Council Directive 92/43/EC, Article 6(4).

The protection of wild animals

The provisions covering wild animals parallel those of birds. Section 9 gives protection to certain wild animals:

(1) Subject to the provisions of this Part, if any person intentionally kills, injures or takes any wild animal included in Schedule 5, he shall be guilty of an offence.

(2) Subject to the provisions of this Part, if any person has in his possession or control any live or dead wild animal included in Schedule 5 or any part of, or anything derived from, such an animal, he shall be guilty of an offence.

(3) A person shall not be guilty of an offence under subsection (2) if he shows that:

(a) the animal had not been killed or taken, or had been killed or taken otherwise than in contravention of the relevant provisions; or

(b) the animal or other thing in his possession or control had been sold (whether to him or any other person) otherwise than in contravention of those provisions; and in this subsection 'the relevant provisions' means the provisions of this Part and of the Conservation of Wild Creatures and Wild Plants Act 1975.

(4) Subject to the provisions of this Part, if any person intentionally:

(a) damages or destroys, or obstructs access to, any structure or place which any wild animal included in Schedule 5 uses for shelter or protection; or

(b) disturbs any such animal while it is occupying a structure or place which it uses for that purpose,

he shall be guilty of an offence.

(5) Subject to the provisions of this Part, if any person:

   (a) sells, offers or exposes for sale, or has in his possession or transport for the purpose of sale, any live or dead wild animal included in Schedule 5, or any part of, or anything derived from, such an animal; or

   (b) publishes or causes to be published any advertisement likely to be understood as conveying that he buys or sells, or intends to buy or sell, any of those things he shall be guilty of an offence.

(6) In any proceedings for an offence under subsection (1), (2) or (5)(a), the animal in question shall be presumed to have been a wild animal unless the contrary is shown.

Section 10 sets out the exceptions to s 9:

(1) Nothing in s 9 shall make unlawful:

   (a) anything done in pursuance of a requirement by the Minister of Agriculture, Fisheries and Food or the Secretary of State under s 98 of the Agriculture Act 1947, or by the Secretary of State under s 39 of the Agriculture (Scotland) Act 1948; or

   (b) anything done under, or in pursuance of an order made under, the Animal Health Act 1981.

(2) Nothing in subsection (4) of s 9 shall make unlawful anything done within a dwelling-house.

(3) Notwithstanding anything in s 9, a person shall not be guilty of an offence by reason of:

   (a) the taking of any such animal if he shows that the animal had been disabled otherwise than by his unlawful act and was taken solely for the purpose of tending it and releasing it when no longer disabled;

   (b) the killing of any such animal if he shows that the animal had been so seriously disabled otherwise than by his unlawful act that there was no reasonable chance of its recovering; or

   (c) any act made unlawful by that section if he shows that the act was the incidental result of a lawful operation and could not reasonably have been avoided.

(4) Notwithstanding anything in s 9, an authorised person shall not be guilty of an offence by reason of the killing or injuring of a wild animal included in Schedule 5 if he shows that his action was necessary for the purpose of preventing serious damage to livestock, foodstuffs for livestock, crops, vegetables, fruit, growing timber or any other form of property or to fisheries.

(5) A person shall not be entitled to rely on the defence provided by subsection (2) or (3)(c) as respects anything done in relation to a bat otherwise than in the living area of a dwelling house unless he had notified the Nature Conservancy Council [authors' note: now English Nature] [for the area in which the house is situated or, as the case may be, the act is to take place] of the proposed action or operation and allowed them a reasonable time to advise him as to whether it should be carried out and, if so, the method to be used.

(6) An authorised person shall not be entitled to rely on the defence provided by subsection (4) as respects any action taken at any time if it had become apparent, before that time, that that action would prove necessary for the purpose mentioned in that subsection and either:

(a) a licence under s 16 authorising that action had not been applied for as soon as reasonably practicable after that fact had become apparent; or

(b) an application for such a licence had been determined.

Section 11 prohibits certain methods of killing or taking wild animals:

(1) Subject to the provisions of this Part, if any person:

(a) sets in position any self-locking snare which is of such a nature and so placed as to be calculated to cause bodily injury to any wild animal coming into contact therewith;

(b) uses for the purpose of killing or taking any wild animal any self-locking snare, whether or not of such a nature or so placed as aforesaid, any bow or crossbow or any explosive other than ammunition for a firearm; ...

(c) uses as a decoy, for the purpose of killing or taking any wild animal, any live mammal or bird whatever [; or

(d) knowingly causes or permits to be done an act which is mentioned in the foregoing provisions of this section],

he shall be guilty of an offence.

(2) Subject to the provisions of this Part, if any person:

(a) sets in position any of the following articles, being an article which is of such a nature and so placed as to be calculated to cause bodily injury to any wild animal included in Schedule 6 which comes into contact therewith, that is to say, any trap or snare, any electrical device for killing or stunning or any poisonous, poisoned or stupefying substance;

(b) uses for the purpose of killing or taking any such wild animal any such article as aforesaid, whether or not of such a nature and so placed as aforesaid, or any net (c) uses for the purpose of killing or taking any such wild animal:

(i) any automatic or semi-automatic weapon;

(ii) any device for illuminating a target or sighting device for night shooting;

(iii) any form of artificial light or any mirror or other dazzling device; or

(iv) any gas or smoke not falling within paragraphs (a) and (b);

(d) uses as a decoy, for the purpose of killing or taking any such wild animal, any sound recording; ...

(e) uses any mechanically propelled vehicle in immediate pursuit of any such wild animal for the purpose of driving, killing or taking that animal [; or

(f) knowingly causes or permits to be done an act which is mentioned in the foregoing provisions of this subsection],

he shall be guilty of an offence.

(3) Subject to the provisions of this Part, if any person:

(a) sets in position [or knowingly causes or permits to be set in position] any snare which is of such a nature and so placed as to be calculated to cause bodily injury to any wild animal coming into contact therewith; and

(b) while the snare remains in position fails, without reasonable excuse, to inspect it, or cause it to be inspected, at least once every day, he shall be guilty of an offence.

(4) The Secretary of State may, for the purpose of complying with an international obligation, by order, either generally or in relation to any kind of wild animal specified in the order, amend subsection (1) or (2) by adding any method of killing or taking wild animals or by omitting any such method as is mentioned in that subsection.

(5) In any proceedings for an offence under subsection (1)(b) or (c) or (2)(b), (c), (d) or (e) [and in any proceedings for an offence under subsection (1)(d) or (2)(f) relating to an act which is mentioned in any of those paragraphs], the animal in question shall be presumed to have been a wild animal unless the contrary is shown.

(6) In any proceedings for an offence under subsection (2)(a) it shall be a defence to show that the article was set in position by the accused for the purpose of killing or taking, in the interests of public health, agriculture, forestry, fisheries or nature conservation, any wild animals which could be lawfully killed or taken by those means and that he took all reasonable precautions to prevent injury thereby to any wild animals included in Schedule 6.

[(7) In any proceedings for an offence under subsection (2)(f) relating to an act which is mentioned in subsection (2)(a) it shall be a defence to show that the article was set in position for the purpose of killing or taking, in the interests of public health, agriculture, forestry, fisheries or nature conservation, any wild animals which could be lawfully killed or taken by those means and that he took or caused to be taken all reasonable precautions to prevent injury thereby to any wild animals included in Schedule 6.]

Therefore, in relation to the methods of killing or taking wild animals, certain methods are prohibited in relation to all wild animals, eg the use of any live animal or bird as a decoy and the use of any self-locking snare which is of such a nature and is so placed to be calculated to cause bodily injury to any wild animal. Other methods are prohibited when their use kills, takes or endangers certain species, eg the use of traps or snares to kill or cause bodily injury to any animal listed within Schedule 6. The animals in Schedule 6 also have protection from unsporting methods, sound decoys, automatic or semi-automatic weapons and dazzling lights. In relation to species not on Schedule 6 the use of non-self-locking snares are permitted so long as they are checked once a day.

Individual species protection

Special protection under the law is given to some animals, such as badgers and deer.

Badgers Acts of 1973, 1991 and 1992

Badger baiting was first made illegal in 1835 (see Chapter 2). However, badgers were still hunted with dogs. Badgers were protected under the 1973 Badgers Act, which made it a criminal offence to 'cruelly ill treat' a badger or use badger tongs in the course of killing, taking a badger or to dig for any badger. However, due to pressure from hunters, the Badgers Act emerged from Parliament with a serious flaw, in that landowners and their agents were exempted from the prohibitions on badger persecution on their own land. In 1981 the law was tightened up in the Wildlife and Countryside Act; Parliament removed the 'landowner's loophole' and made it an offence to be in possession of a badger or any part of a badger. Further attempts to tighten the law by protecting badger setts, in addition to the badger, failed due to objections from the hunting fraternity. This loophole was exploited – hunters could claim they were looking for foxes when digging, and it was difficult to prove their intentions. When the Wildlife and Countryside Amendment Act was passed in 1985 the government reversed the onus of proof in cases brought against those suspected of digging for badgers.

Although the number of convictions rose initially, diggers became more adept at arguing that they were, in fact, digging for foxes. There have been attempts to strengthen the legislation protecting setts through the use of Private Members' Bills. In 1991 two Badger Bills were passed to create a new criminal offence of interfering with a badger sett without a government licence. The 1973 and 1991 Badgers Acts has now been consolidated into the Badgers Act 1992. The introduction of dogs into setts was also made illegal and if dogs were used they could be removed and disposed of. However, the National Federation of Badger Groups estimates that 9,000–10,000 badgers die each year as a result of baiting.[13]

Section 1 Taking, injuring or killing badgers

(1) A person is guilty of an offence if, except as permitted by or under this Act, he wilfully kills, injures or takes, or attempts to kill, injure or take, a badger.

(2) If, in any proceedings for an offence under subsection (1) above consisting of attempting to kill, injure or take a badger, there is evidence from which it could reasonably be concluded that at the material time the accused was attempting to kill, injure or take a badger, he shall be presumed to have

---

13 *The Observer*, 2 May 1993.

been attempting to kill, injure or take a badger unless the contrary is shown.

(3) A person is guilty of an offence if, except as permitted by or under this Act, he has in his possession or under his control any dead badger or any part of, or anything derived from, a dead badger.

(4) A person is not guilty of an offence under subsection (3) above if he shows that:

(a) the badger had not been killed, or had been killed otherwise than in contravention of the provisions of this Act or of the Badgers Act 1973; or

(b) the badger or other thing in his possession or control had been sold (whether to him or any other person) and, at the time of the purchase, the purchaser had had no reason to believe that the badger had been killed in contravention of any of those provisions.

(5) If a person is found committing an offence under this section on any land it shall be lawful for the owner or occupier of the land, or any servant of the owner or occupier, or any constable, to require that person forthwith to quit the land and also to give his name and address and if that person on being so required wilfully remains on the land or refuses to give his full name or address he is guilty of an offence.

Under s 2 an offence of cruelty is committed if:

(1) ...

(a) he cruelly ill-treats a badger;

(b) he uses any badger tongs in the course of killing or taking, or attempting to kill or take, a badger;

(c) except as permitted by or under this Act, he digs for a badger; or

(d) he uses for the purpose of killing or taking a badger any firearm other than a smooth bore weapon of not less than 20 bore or a rifle using ammunition having a muzzle energy not less than 160 footpounds and a bullet weighing not less than 38 grains.

(2) If in any proceedings for an offence under subsection (1)(c) above there is evidence from which it could reasonably be concluded that at the material time the accused was digging for a badger he shall be presumed to have been digging for a badger unless the contrary is shown.

Section 3 Interfering with badger setts

A person is guilty of an offence if, except as permitted by or under this Act, he interferes with a badger sett by doing any of the following things:

(a) damaging a badger sett or any part of it;

(b) destroying a badger sett;

(c) obstructing access to, or any entrance of, a badger sett;

(d) causing a dog to enter a badger sett; or

(e) disturbing a badger when it is occupying a badger sett, intending to do any of those things or being reckless as to whether his actions would have any of those consequences.

Section 4 makes it illegal to sell or possess live badgers and s 6 provides the general exceptions under the Act:

A person is not guilty of an offence under this Act by reason only of:

(a) taking or attempting to take a badger which has been disabled otherwise than by his act and is taken or to be taken solely for the purpose of tending it;

(b) killing or attempting to kill a badger which appears to be so seriously injured or in such a condition that to kill it would be an act of mercy;

(c) unavoidably killing or injuring a badger as an incidental result of a lawful action;

(d) doing anything which is authorised under the Animals (Scientific Procedures) Act 1986.

Section 8 provides for the exceptions under s 3;

(1) Subject to subsection (2) below, a person is not guilty of an offence under s 3 above if he shows that his action was necessary for the purpose of preventing serious damage to land, crops, poultry or any other form of property.

(2) Subsection (2) of s 7 above applies to the defence in subsection (1) above as it applies to the defence in subsection (1) of that section.

(3) A person is not guilty of an offence under s 3 (a), (c) or (e) above if he shows that his action was the incidental result of a lawful operation and could not reasonably have been avoided.

(4) A person is not guilty of an offence under section 3 (a), (c) or (e) above by reason of obstructing any entrance of a badger sett for the purpose of hunting foxes with hounds if he:

(a) takes no action other than obstructing such entrances;

(b) does not dig into the tops or sides of the entrances;

(c) complies with subsection (5) below as to the materials used for obstructing the entrances and with subsection (6) below as to how and when they are to be placed and removed; and

(d) is acting with the authority of the owner or occupier of the land and the authority of a recognised Hunt.

(5) The materials used shall be only:

(a) untainted straw or hay, or leaf-litter, bracken or loose soil; or

(b) a bundle of sticks or faggots, or paper sacks either empty or filled with hunt tainted straw or hay or leaf-litter, bracken or loose soil.

(6) The materials shall not be packed hard into the entrances and:

(a) if they are of the kind mentioned in paragraph (a) of subsection (5) above, they shall not be placed in the entrances except on the day of the hunt or after midday on the preceding day;

(b) if they are of the kind mentioned in paragraph (b) of that subsection, they shall not be placed in the entrances except on the day of the hunt and shall be removed on the same day.

(7) A person is not guilty of an offence under s 3(a), (c) or (e) above by reason of his hounds marking at a badger sett provided they are withdrawn as soon as reasonably practicable.

(8) Each recognised Hunt shall keep a register of the persons authorised to act under subsection (4) above.

(9) In this section 'recognised Hunt' means a Hunt recognised by the Masters of Fox Hounds Association, the Association of Masters of Harriers and Beagles or the Central Committee of Fell Packs.

Section 9 sets down the exceptions to s 4:

A person is not guilty of an offence under s 4 above by reason of having a live badger in his possession or under his control if:

(a) it is in his possession or under his control, as the case may be, in the course of his business as a carrier; or

(b) it has been disabled otherwise than by his act and taken by him solely for the purpose of tending it and it is necessary for that purpose for it to remain in his possession or under his control, as the case may be.

Section 10 provides the licencing details:

(1) A licence may be granted to any person by the appropriate Conservancy Council authorising him, notwithstanding anything in the foregoing provisions of this Act, but subject to compliance with any conditions specified in the licence:

(a) for scientific or educational purposes or for the conservation of badgers:

(i) to kill or take, within an area specified in the licence by any means so specified, or to sell, or to have in his possession, any number of badgers so specified; or

(ii) to interfere with any badger sett within an area specified in the licence by any means so specified;

(b) for the purpose of any zoological gardens or collection specified in the licence, to take within an area specified in the licence by any means so specified, or to sell, or to have in his possession, any number of badgers so specified;

(c) for the purpose of ringing and marking, to take badgers within an area specified in the licence, to mark such badgers or to attach to them any ring, tag or other marking device as specified in the licence;

(d) for the purpose of any development as defined in s 55(1) of the Town and Country Planning Act 1990 or, as respects Scotland, s 19(1) of the Town and Country Planning (Scotland) Act 1972, to interfere with a badger sett within an area specified in the licence by any means so specified;

(e) for the purpose of the preservation, or archaeological investigation, of a monument scheduled under s 1 of the Ancient Monuments and Archaeological Areas Act 1979, to interfere with a badger sett within an area specified in the licence by any means so specified;

(f) for the purpose of investigating whether any offence has been committed or gathering evidence in connection with proceedings before any court, to interfere with a badger sett within an area specified in the licence by any means so specified.

(2) A licence may be granted to any person by the appropriate Minister authorising him, notwithstanding anything in the foregoing provisions of this Act, but subject to compliance with any conditions specified in the licence:

(a) for the purpose of preventing the spread of disease, to kill or take badgers, or to interfere with a badger sett, within an area specified in the licence by any means so specified;

(b) for the purpose of preventing serious damage to land, crops, poultry or any other form of property, to kill or take badgers or to interfere with a badger sett, within an area specified in the licence by any means so specified;

(c) for the purpose of any agricultural or forestry operation, to interfere with a badger sett within an area specified in the licence by any means so specified;

(d) for the purpose of any operation (whether by virtue of the Land Drainage Act 1991 or otherwise) to maintain or improve any existing watercourse or drainage works, or to construct new works required for the drainage of any land, including works for the purpose of defence against sea water or tidal water, to interfere with a badger sett within an area specified in the licence by any means so specified.

The legal protection of foxes

Foxes are protected under the Wildlife and Countryside Act 1981. The use of self-locking snares is illegal, and snares set to catch foxes must be inspected at least once every 24 hours. It is an offence to set snares for, or to otherwise try to kill foxes, without taking all precautions to prevent the capture of other more protected species, such as badgers. In addition, s 8 of the Protection of Animals Act 1911, prohibits the use of poisonous substances. The use of gin-traps is also prohibited under s 8 of the Pests Act 1954. The Control of Pesticide Regulations 1997, SI 1997/188, control the use of chemical repellents and only approved products may be used. Under Pt II, s 19, of the Animal Health Act 1981, in the event of the outbreak of rabies, foxes can be destroyed by the authorities in designated areas.[14] The Spring Traps Approval Order 1995 (SI 1995/2427) revokes and replaces SI 1975/1647 and the Animals (Cruel Poisons) Act 1962.

Deer

Under s 2 of the Deer Act 1991 it is an offence to take deer in the closed season. There are also prohibitions on the type of weapons that can be used to

---

14 RSPCA information leaflet, *Foxes in your Neighbourhood*, 1992, p 65.

kill deer under s 4. These include traps, snares, spears, missiles or poisoned bait. Certain exceptions to the Act are provided for in s 6, including any act done by any person to prevent the suffering of any injured or diseased deer. There is also a defence under s 7 for occupiers of land if the person had reasonable grounds to believe that the deer were damaging crops.

See also the Removal of Antlers in Velvet (Anaethesics) Order 1980, SI 1980/685.

The Wild Mammals Protection Act 1996

Background

The problem of protecting wild animals under the Protection of Animals Act 1911 is examined in the following cases.

Rowley v Murphy [1964] 2 QB 43; [1964] 1 All ER 50, [1963] 3 WLR 1061, 128 JP 88

A wild stag, which was being hunted, jumped over the hedge of a field on to a main road, slipped on the tarmac surface and went under a stationary furniture van between its front and rear wheels. The stag was dragged from beneath the van by two or three men, partly dragged and partly carried some few yards through a nearby gate into an enclosure, where it was killed with a knife. The carrying of the animal to the enclosure took some five to ten minutes, the killing of it took, so it was said, a matter of seconds. An information was laid against M, as master of the hunt, charging him with cruelly terrifying an animal by cutting its throat with a knife, contrary to s 1(1) (a) of the Protection of Animals Act 1911.

Held: a mere temporary inability to get away was not a state of captivity, and as the words 'captive animal' mean by definition an animal in captivity or confinement, the stag was not a captive animal within s 15(a) of the Protection of Animals Act 1911, and was not within the protection of that Act.

Judgment–1:

Lord Parker CJ: The facts as they emerge in the prosecution evidence can be shortly stated. At 3.30 pm on 30 August 1962, in the village of Timberscombe a wild stag which was being hunted, jumped over a hedge on to the main road and its feet slipped on the tarmac, it went under a furniture van which was at that time stationary on the road. The stag was thereupon dragged from beneath the van by two or three men and thereafter dragged and partly carried through a gate inside an enclosure belonging to the Village Hall where it was killed with a knife. The suggestion of the prosecution was that the method of killing was such as to terrify cruelly the stag. Let me say at once, because feelings sometimes run high on these matters, that this court is in no way concerned whether what was done was cruel or not. The sole question here is whether this stag in all the circumstances came within the protection of the Protection of Animals Act 1911. That Act s 1 provides that if any person (a) shall 'cruelly ... terrify any animal ... such person shall be guilty of an offence'. 'Animal' as defined by s 15 (a) of the Act of 1911, 'means any domestic or captive animal'. There is no question here but that this wild stag was not a domestic animal and the sole question is whether it was a captive animal. The definition section [s 15] goes on to define a captive animal as meaning:

> (c) ... any animal (not being a domestic animal) of whatsoever kind or species, and whether a quadruped or not, including any bird, fish or reptile which is in captivity or confinement ...

The sole question therefore is whether in the circumstances of this case once the stag had fallen and was being dragged into and kept in the enclosure, it was in captivity or confinement.

For myself I have found this by no means an easy question. What the difference is between captivity and confinement no one has been able to say. Confinement no doubt contemplates some outside barrier confining the animal. Captivity may or may not mean much the same. It is argued by counsel for the appellant that an animal is in captivity the moment it is captured. I confess that at first blush there is a good deal to be said for that argument. It at any rate has the virtue of simplicity, that you just look and see; were hands laid on this animal and was it kept from escaping for however short a time, if so it was in captivity. On the other side it is maintained by counsel for the respondent that 'in captivity' denotes a state of affairs in which domination is exercised over an animal beyond mere capture. In favour of counsel for the appellant's argument I personally would attach importance to two matters: the first is this, that in the further definition of 'captive animal' [in s 15 (c) of the Act of 1911] which I have not read, these words occur:

> Any animal ... which is maimed, pinioned, or subjected to any appliance or contrivance for the purpose of hindering or preventing its escape from captivity or confinement.

It seems to me that that is capable of dealing with the position of a wild animal which is captured and is then maimed or pinioned, etc to prevent if from escaping from the capture, in other words 'captivity' there looks as if it is referring to mere capture. Again, even if an animal is a captive animal, there is an exception in regard to coursing or hunting; that is to be found in subsection (3) of s 1, which provides, so far as material, that:

> Nothing in this section ... shall apply ... (b) to the ... hunting of any captive animal, unless such animal is liberated in an injured, mutilated, or exhausted condition; but a captive animal shall not, for the purposes of this section, be deemed to be coursed or hunted before it is liberated for the purpose of being coursed or hunted, or after it has been recaptured, or if it is under control.

It is to be noted there that the exception ceases to apply in the case of a captive animal when it is recaptured; in other words Parliament is using 'recapture' as signifying the state when it again becomes in captivity. Those as it seems to me are powerful arguments in favour of counsel for the appellant's submission.

So far as the cases are concerned, there is really no case to which this court has been referred which is of any real assistance. *Steele v Rogers*,[15] the case of the stranded whales, was referred to and concerned whales which were stranded on the foreshore and were surrounded by a crowd of people. They exercised

---

[15] (1912) 106 LT 79.

no acts of dominion over the whales and their inability to get away was in no sense due to the crowd but due to the fact that they were stranded above the waterline. In that case Pickford, J said:[16]

> I think 'in captivity or close confinement' means something more than merely temporarily being unable to get away from the spot on which they are ...

The question here, however, is whether something more than capture, in other words some further acts of dominion, are necessary before it can be said that the animal is in captivity. Counsel for the respondent on the other hand invokes the history of the matter, and in particular the Wild Animals in Captivity Protection Act 1900. By the earlier [Cruelty to Animals] Acts of 1849 and 1854 [repealed], domestic animals came under protection, and this Act of 1900 for the first time dealt with wild animals, whether they were birds, beasts, fishes or reptiles.

Section 2 of that Act provided that:

Any person shall be guilty of an offence who, whilst an animal is in captivity or close confinement, or is maimed, pinioned, or subjected to any appliance or contrivance for the purpose of hindering or preventing its escape from such captivity or confinement, shall, by wantonly or unreasonably doing or omitting any act, cause, or permit to be caused any unnecessary suffering to such animal; or cruelly abuse, infuriate, tease or terrify it, or permit it to be so treated.' It seems to me that certainly when one looks at the title of that Act, an 'Act for the prevention of cruelty to wild animals in captivity', the natural meaning is that it applies to animals who are reduced to a state of captivity in the ordinary state of the word, something more than mere captivity.

It is to be observed that s 15 of the Act of 1911 follows exactly the words of that section in regard to its definition of 'captive animal' save only that the words 'close confinement' in the Act of 1900 have become 'confinement'. To that extent there has been a change in the meaning. If, however, I am right in thinking that the Act of 1900 clearly is referring to something more than mere capture and to an animal reduced to a state of captivity in consequence of some further act or acts of domination, then it would seem that there is no reason to give the words in s 15 of the Act of 1911 any different meaning. As I have said, I think it is a matter of difficulty. I think that looking at s 15 alone I should uphold counsel for the appellant's submission, but bearing in mind the history of this matter, and in particular the Act of 1900, I think that on the whole, just as in *Steele v Rogers*[17] a mere temporary inability to get away was not a state of captivity, so that something more than mere captivity, some period of time during which acts of dominion are exercised over the animal, is necessary before it can be said to be in a state of captivity. I would only add that if the true view here be that the words are ambiguous, then this being a penal section must be strictly construed in favour of this respondent. On the whole, though not without some difficulty, I have come to the conclusion that the justices were right and this appeal should be dismissed.

---

[16] (1912) 106 LT, at 80.
[17] Above n 13.

Hudnott v Campbell, **The Times, 27 June 1986**

Judgment–1:

Otton J: This matter comes before this court by way of case stated by the justices for the Petty Sessional Division of Canterbury and St Augustine sitting at Canterbury.

On 10 October 1985, an information was laid by the appellant, on behalf of the Royal Society for the Prevention of Cruelty to Animals, against the respondent, Ian Charles Campbell. It alleged that he on 1 July, at Herne Bay, did cruelly beat a certain captive animal, namely, a hedgehog, contrary to s 1(1)(a) of the Protection of Animals Act 1911.

On 18 December, the day of the hearing, a second information was laid by the appellant against the respondent, which was subsequently amended, alleging that the respondent between 30 June and 3 July did cause unnecessary suffering to a certain animal, namely, a hedgehog, by unreasonably omitting proper and necessary care and attention while the animal was in a state of suffering, again contrary to s 1(1)(a)of the same Act.

Section 1(1)(a) of the Protection of Animals Act 1911, provides, for the material purposes of this matter, as follows: 'If any person shall cruelly beat, kick, ill-treat ... any animal ... or shall, by wantonly or unreasonably doing ... any act, cause any unnecessary suffering ... to any animal he shall be guilty of an offence of cruelty within the meaning of this Act.' The word 'animal' is defined in s 15(a) of the Act as follows: 'The expression "animal" means any domestic or captive animal.' Subparagraph (b) defines domestic animal, which the hedgehog clearly is not. Subparagraph (c) provides as follows: 'The expression "captive animal" means any animal (not being a domestic animal) of whatsoever kind or species, and whether a quadruped or not, including any bird, fish, or reptile, which is in captivity, or confinement, or which is maimed, pinioned, or subjected to any appliance or contrivance for the purpose of hindering or preventing its escape from captivity or confinement.' The question therefore arises as to whether the hedgehog was a captive animal, as opposed to a domestic animal within s 15, or was still a wild animal with the ordinary meaning of those words.

Mr Allardyce, on behalf of the respondent, submits that the Protection of Animals Act 1911 affords protection only to domestic animals and captive animals and that in the circumstances of this case the hedgehog was neither a domestic animal nor a captive animal. He further submits that a proper construction of s 15(c) of the Act is, that the word 'maimed' in the section cannot be read in isolation and that an animal which is maimed is not thereby to be treated as a captive animal for the purpose of the Act unless it is maimed for the purpose of hindering or preventing its escape from captivity or confinement.

On behalf of the appellant, Mr Critchlow contends that the hedgehog was at all times a captive animal within the meaning of s 15(c) and was therefore within the protection afforded by s 1. He further submits that when a hedgehog is in the circumstances that this particular hedgehog found itself it is in captivity in that when attacked a hedgehog rolls itself up into a ball and thus would have been a captive animal for the purpose of s 15(c) of the Act from the commencement of the beating.

This matter first came before the court in the case of *Steele v Rogers*.[18] Stated briefly, a whale was stranded on the foreshore above the waterline and was surrounded by a crowd of people. The whale was cut by a knife held by a member of the crowd. The question therefore arose as to whether an offence had been committed, contrary to s 2 of the Wild Animals in Captivity Protection Act 1900. This was a forerunner of the Act which this court has to consider. The later Act is a consolidating Act, but apart from the omission of the word 'close' before the word 'confinement' there is no material difference in the consolidating Act. In a short judgment, Mr Justice Pickford held as follows: 'that the appeal must be dismissed. This result was very much to be regretted, because the respondent fully deserved to be punished. Unless it was proved that the whale was in captivity or close confinement no offence was committed. Here the whale was only temporarily confined because it could not walk. When the tide came in it could have got away, and many of the other whales on the beach did so escape.

In his opinion the words in the statute meant something more than 'being temporarily unable to get away from the place where you are.' In dismissing the appeal, however, he wished to say that the case was decided on its own peculiar facts, and he must not be taken to have decided any of the numerous illustrative cases raised.'

In 1964, a similar case came before the Divisional Court and is reported in *Rowley v Murphy*.[19] Here, 'A wild stag, which was being hunted, jumped over a hedge into a main road and ... fell under a stationary van. It was dragged out from under the van by several men and then partly dragged and partly carried into a nearby enclosure where it was killed with a knife.' The court on that occasion held, 'That, on its true construction, an animal was not a "captive animal ... in captivity, or confinement" within the definition in s 15(c) of the Act of 1911 unless there was some period of time when there was more than mere capture and when acts of dominion were exercised over the animal; that, on the facts, no acts of dominion had been exercised, therefore, the stag was not "in captivity" and, accordingly, being neither a domestic nor a "captive animal" was not protected by the Act of 1911. Accordingly, the justices' decision was right and the appeal was to be dismissed.' At p 50, the then Lord Chief Justice, Lord Parker, having considered the earlier authority of *Steele v Rogers*[20] said as follows:

> The question here, however, is whether something more than capture, in other words, some further acts of dominion, are necessary before it can be said that the animal is in captivity.

> Mr McCreery, for the defendant, invokes the history of the matter, and, in particular, the Wild Animals in Captivity Protection Act, 1900. By the earlier Acts of 1849, and 1854, domestic animals came under protection, and the Act of 1900 for the first time dealt with animals, whether they were birds, beasts, fishes or reptiles.

The Lord Chief Justice then quoted s 2 of the 1900 Act. He went on:

---

[18] (1912) 106 LT 79.
[19] [1964] 2 QB 43, [1964] 1 All ER 50.
[20] Above n 16.

It seems to me that certainly when one looks at the title to that Act, namely, an Act for the Prevention of Cruelty to Wild Animals in Captivity, the natural meaning is that the Act applies to animals who are reduced to a state of captivity in the ordinary sense of the word or to a state where there is something more than mere capture.

It is to be observed that s 15 of the Act of 1911 follows exactly the words of s 2 of the Act of 1900 in regard to its definition of 'captive animal' save only that the words 'close confinement' in the Act of 1900 have become merely 'confinement'.

Later he said:

As I have said, I think it is a matter of difficulty. I think that, looking at s 15 of the Act of 1911 alone, I should uphold Mr Wrightson's submission; but bearing in mind the history of this matter, and in particular the Act of 1900, I think that on the whole, just as in *Steele v Rogers*,[21] a mere temporary inability to get away did not amount to a state of captivity, so here something more than mere captivity, some period of time during which acts of dominion are exercised over the animal, is necessary before the animal can be said to be in a state of captivity.'

I would only add that, if the true view be that the words are ambiguous, then this section being a penal one must be strictly construed in favour of the defendant. On the whole, though not without some difficulty, I have come to the conclusion that the justices were right and this appeal should be dismissed.

Mr Critchlow rightly points out that doubt permeated the court and they found it a difficult matter to decide. In particular Mr Justice Fenton Atkinson said as follows: 'During the course of the argument it seemed to me that there was very much to be said for the view that once a wild animal had been captured it was in captivity on the plain meaning of the word and did not cease to be in captivity at that stage because the captor did not intend to keep it in captivity for any length of time but, in fact, intended to kill it.' In the event, however, Mr Justice Atkinson did agree with the result and with the reasons given by the then Lord Chief Justice.

Mr Justice Winn, as he then was, stated as follows:

I agree with the conclusion that Lord Parker CJ has proposed and, in particular, I agree with the reason that he has given that mere captivity is not to be equated with the expression 'in captivity'. The mere fact that an animal has been captured does not by itself make that animal one which is in captivity. I would add that I myself think that the words 'which is in captivity', in s 15 of the Act of 1911 and the words which occur after the intermediate phrase 'or confinement' point to a state of captivity not necessarily still continuing. When I look at the provision in s 1(3)(b) of the Act, it seems to me that it is impossible to say that 'any captive animal' in that context has the same meaning as 'an animal which is in captivity' in the ordinary sense of those words. *Ex hypothesi*, an animal which is being hunted is not then a captive; at that moment no one has hands upon it or ropes upon it or is in a position physically to restrain its movement. If then

[21] *Ibid.*

it is impossible to read the words 'any captive animal' in s (1)(3)(b) as meaning an animal which is then captive or in a state of restraint arising from captivity, it seems to me that, construing the Act as a whole and having regard to the history of the legislation and, in particular, to the title and scope of the Act of 1900 ... a clear distinction is drawn between 'in captivity' meaning a state of captivity and the fact of being a captive, ie, subject temporarily to restraint by human beings.

In my judgment, the meaning of the words 'any captive animal' ... is any animal which has been subjected to but subsequently released from a state of captivity. I agree with what Lord Parker CJ has said about the meaning of 'state of captivity' for the purpose of this Act. I would dismiss this appeal.

Mr Critchlow has, during a careful and succinct argument, sought to distinguish the two authorities, in particular the latter. He has submitted that the fact that the hedgehog was reduced to a maimed state brings it within the word 'captive' and it is thus entitled to the protection of the Act. He also submitted that beating the hedgehog in this savage and ruthless manner reduced it to a state where the respondent, in so behaving in a barbarous way, had exercised an act of dominion over the unfortunate hedgehog. He further submitted that the omission of 'or' within s 15(c) between the words 'maimed' and 'pinioned' is not fatal. Therefore he submitted that the word 'maimed' can be construed on its own and once that state is established the protection of the Act bites. He submitted that it was not necessary, to give effect to the section, to construe it as: 'Maimed or subjected to any appliance or contrivance for the purpose of injuring or preventing its escape from captivity or confinement.'

Finally, he submitted that this court should hold that the decision of the Divisional Court in the case of *Rowley v Murphy* was wrong and that we should say so and come to a contrary conclusion.

For my part I have come to the conclusion that the case of *Rowley v Murphy*[22] was correctly decided. I can see no ground for holding otherwise. The Act must be construed in the way that it was construed by the Divisional Court on that occasion. It does not permit the construction adumbrated by Mr Critchlow. I cannot find that the fact that the animal was maimed in that way renders it a captive animal within s 15(c). I am also not persuaded that beating a hedgehog to the extent that this one was amounts to an act of dominion over it. The interpretation claimed by Mr Critchlow would, in my judgment, require the specific word 'or' between the words 'maimed and pinioned' and the omission of that word means that the word 'maimed' must be construed with the rest of the paragraph as contended by Mr Allardyce. I further consider that the purpose of the Act is such that it was not meant to cover the maiming of wild animals when they are still in that state. Maiming can only become an offence when they are in a state of captivity.

For those reasons I have come to the conclusion that the justices were correct in coming to the conclusion that they did and in dismissing both of these summonses. For those reasons I would dismiss this appeal.

---

[22] [1964] 2 QB 43; [1964] 1 All ER 50.

These cases now have to be read in the light of the Wild Mammals Protection Act 1996 which was passed after many years of lobbying of the government by various pressure groups and the introduction of a number of Private Member's Bills. In 1995, MPs voted by 253 to 0 in favour of John McFall's Wild Mammal Protection Bill. This Bill would have made hunting with hounds and snaring illegal, as well as protecting wild animals, but was watered down as it went through the parliamentary process. The Bill was later reintroduced by Alan Meale without the provisions on hunting, and was passed:[23]

The Wild Mammals Protection Act 1996

Section 1

If, save as permitted by this Act, any person mutilates, kicks, beats, nails or otherwise impales, stabs, burns, stones, crushes, drowns, drags or asphyxiates any wild mammal with intent to inflict unnecessary suffering he shall be guilty of an offence.

Section 2

A person shall not be guilty of an offence under this Act by reason of:

(a) the attempted killing of any such wild mammal as an act of mercy if he shows that the mammal had been so seriously disabled otherwise than by his unlawful act that there was no reasonable chance of its recovering;

(b) the killing is in a reasonably swift and humane manner of any such wild mammal if he shows that the wild mammal had been injured or taken in the course of either lawful shooting, hunting, coursing or pest control activity;

(c) doing anything which is authorised under any enactment;

(d) any act made unlawful under s 1 if the act was done by means of any snare, trap, dog or bird lawfully used for the purpose of killing or taking any wild mammal; or

(e) the lawful use of any poisonous or noxious substance on any wild mammal.

Section 3

In this Act 'wild mammal' means any mammal which is not a domestic or captive animal within the meaning of the Protection of Animals Act 1911 or the Protection of Animals (Scotland) Act 1912.

Section 4

Where a constable has reasonable grounds for suspecting that a person has committed an offence under the provisions of this Act and that evidence of the commission of the offence may be found on that person or in or on any vehicle he may have with him, the constable may:

(a) without warrant stop and search that person and any vehicle or article he may have with him; and

---

23   See *Wildlife Guardians*, LACS, Issues 33–34, 1996: LACS, London.

(b) seize and detain for the purposes of proceedings under any of those provisions anything which may be evidence of the commission of the offence or may be liable to be confiscated under s 6 of this Act.

Section 5

(1) A person guilty of an offence under this Act shall be liable on summary conviction to a fine not exceeding level five on the standard scale, or a term of imprisonment not exceeding six months, or both.

(2) Provided that where the offence was committed in respect of more than one wild mammal, the maximum fine that can be imposed shall be determined as if the person had been convicted of a separate offence in respect of each such wild mammal.

Section 6

(1) The court before whom any person is convicted under this Act may, in addition to any other punishment, order the confiscation of any vehicle or equipment used in the commission of the offence.

(2) The Secretary of State may, by regulations made by statutory instrument and subject to annulment in pursuance of a resolution of either House of Parliament, make provision for the disposal or destruction in prescribed circumstances of any vehicle or equipment confiscated under this section.

ENFORCEMENT

While wild animals now have a greater degree of protection, there are still concerns about how adequately the legislation is being enforced. Strict enforcement is needed if wild animals are to be protected from acts of cruelty. In the UK, the Department of the Environment Global Wildlife Enforcement Division provided the following number of successful prosecutions under the Wildlife and Countryside Act 1981 and Control of Trade in Endangered Species Enforcement Regulations (SI 1985/1155).

Date	WCA 1981	CITES 1985
1987	106	13
1988	145	10
1989	152	25
1990	114	29
1991	89	9

The first prosecution after the Badgers Act 1991 became effective to protect setts was brought by the League Against Cruel Sports (LACS) after the Crown Prosecution Service did not bring an action. A terrier man attached to a hunt pleaded guilty to damaging a badger sett; he was given a 12-month conditional discharge and was ordered to pay £75 prosecution costs to the LACS.[24] In the 1994 Annual Report of the National Federation of Badger Groups stated that there had been 12 prosecutions of badger-related cases. Nine of these resulted in convictions, seven being for interference with a sett. The average fine was £500, but there was a striking variation in punishments, ranging from custodial sentences to community service for exactly the same type of offence. There was only one recorded conviction for attempting to take, kill or injure a badger and one conviction for possession of a dead badger. However, there were many cases of illegal badger persecution which did not result in prosecution, including snaring, badgers being battered to death or killed by dogs.[25]

Howl, the magazine of the Hunt Saboteurs Association, lists some of the recent cases in relation to the treatment of wild animals:[26]

An update from *Howl* no 61, three men from Tyne and Wear all pleaded guilty to digging for a badger and two charges of causing unnecessary suffering to dogs.

In 1996, Durham Magistrates heard how the three were spotted by a motorist at a wood on the outskirts of Durham in May 1995, who then tipped off the police. The police then watched as the three dug up a sett with a pick and shovel. Their three dogs were later examined by the RSPCA and a vet, and were found to have suffered injuries. Part of the bottom lip of one of them had been torn away. After all the evidence was read out the Magistrate said 'Civilised society will not countenance such violent behaviour which you would no doubt regard as sport'. The magistrate then sentenced all three to five months in jail, banned them from keeping dogs for 10 years, and ordered the forfeiture of all their equipment.

In 1996, three men from Manchester appeared before Macclesfield Magistrates. They all pleaded guilty to interfering with a badger sett . A charge of cruelty to a dog was dropped previously by the prosecution. They were caught by the police who saw them standing by a known badger sett with a terrier down the hole; they later told the police they were after foxes (there goes that old story again). They were sentenced to 150 hours' community service and ordered to pay costs of £100 each. They were also banned from keeping dogs for three years and the court ordered the confiscation of their equipment.

Three men from the Midlands were convicted by Oswestry Magistrates in July 1996 for interfering with a badger sett after being caught in August 1995. They had claimed in court they were digging for foxes when a local resident heard dogs barking and went to investigate. On arrival, he was told that it was a rabbit warren and they were digging for foxes. The local resident then began to take pictures of the men digging, One of the men then proceeded to chase him across the field and at one point hit him across the back with a spade. The

---

24 *Wildlife Guardian*, LACS, Autumn 1992, no 22: London
25 *Wildlife Guardian*, LACS, Summer 1995, p 5: London
26 *Howl*, Autumn 1996, no 62, pp 16–18. Reproduced with the kind permission of Hunt Saboteurs Association, Brighton.

same defendant also admitted stealing a camera and assaulting the local resident. During a search of the defendant's house by the RSPCA they found three wildlife traps and a stuffed badger on top of the TV.

The magistrates sentenced one defendant to four months for assaulting the local resident, one month for stealing the camera and two months for interfering with a badger sett, all to run concurrently. The other two defendants were sentenced to 150 hours' community service each and ordered to pay £150 costs each for interfering with a badger sett; they were all banned from keeping dogs for 10 years.

D of North Yorkshire who was an amateur terrierman with the York and Ainsty South Fox Hounds was fined £750 with £60 costs by magistrates, after admitting interfering with a badger sett. The incident happened during a meet of the York and Ainsty South earlier this year. A local landowner who had fenced off an area of his land which contained a badger sett, felt the fewer people who knew about the it the better. However, later that day the landowner noticed the fence had been broken down and somebody was digging up the sett. D who has 20 years' experience as an amateur terrierman did not believe it was a sett; he thought it was a rabbit warren, and was told there was a fox down it and it was his job to get the fox out. Counsel, in mitigation, said: 'It wasn't his intention to harm the badger or the sett and he has expressed his remorse'.

G of County Durham admitted three offences of digging a badger sett in September 1995. Durham Magistrates heard that G was spotted by a local gamekeeper who then phoned for the police. The gamekeeper then made three return trips to the sett after G had disappeared; a puppy could still be heard yapping from inside the sett. The following day G returned with the puppy's mother, who had been fitted with a tracking device and was put into the sett to find it. The police then swooped after being tipped off, G told them he knew it was a badger sett but was trying to retrieve his puppy.

In 1996 Penrith Magistrates found E of Carlisle, who is the terrier man for the Cumberland Farmers FH guilty of interfering with a badger sett by causing a dog to enter it, and P, guilty of aiding and abetting E in interfering with a badger sett by causing a dog to enter the sett. The magistrates heard that the Cumberland Farmers were out hunting near Penrith when P found that a fox had gone down a hole, he then called over E. The holes were then blocked and some nets were put over other entrances, a terrier was then entered into the holes. Both men admitted in interviews that they had put a terrier down but said the contentious issue was whether there were signs of the sett being an active one. After a trial lasting nearly three days, the magistrates found the pair guilty and they were fined £150 each with £250 costs.

Three men from West Cumbria have been fined after admitting taking rabbits from an estate. In 1996 Penrith Magistrates were told the three men all took rabbits at night from farmland. The three were kept under observation by police and a gamekeeper; they had in their possession lamps and batteries. They were all fined £60 plus costs of £40 and the court ordered the seizure of their equipment.

Gamekeeper W of Ellesmere Port, Cheshire was found guilty in June 1996 by Wrexham Magistrates of four charges of setting traps and two charges of possessing them and was fined £400 and £100 costs. The traps were found by RSPB investigators on an estate where W worked. During a search of 13 pheasant pens on the estate evidence was found of illegal pole-traps in all but two, and in four of the pens the steel spring traps were set. On a search of the defendant's house five identical traps were found and restraining wires hanging from a hook. W claimed a trespasser with a grievance had placed them there while he was on holiday.

Four men from the Lake District were caught poaching fish near Grasmere when they were confronted by Environment Agency bailiffs in 1995. Windermere Magistrates heard how two of the men were armed with rifles, often used by poachers to shoot fish, and they were also shining bright lamps into the river. When the men were challenged by the bailiffs they said they were after rabbits and foxes, one of the men tried to run away but slipped and fell . All four were fined £60 for possessing a light intending to use it to take or kill fish, they were also ordered to pay £250 costs between them to the Environment Agency.

The Department of the Environment Wildlife Enforcement Working Group has examined at some of the problems of enforcing wildlife legislation. Under s 19(2) Wildlife and Countryside Act 1981 the police are given powers of entry onto land. However, this power is not available to the police in relation to the badgers legislation. If this was amended it would bring the Badgers Act 1992 into line with the EC Habitat Directive. Under s 69 of the Wildlife and Countryside Act 1981 corporate liability is established, but there is no comparable provision under the Badgers Act 1992 – the police can only prosecute individuals. The Working Group suggest that there should be a statutory requirement to make registers available for those persons authorised to 'stop' badger sets on a hunts behalf under s 8 of the Badgers Act 1992. At the moment there is no requirement that these be made available to the police.

The Working Group has also identified problems with the sentencing regime. There are inconsistencies between the penalties imposed by various statutes. For example, the report notes that primary offences such as nest-robbing or killing animals do not attract prison sentences, whereas secondary offences, eg selling the birds, do. Many sentences are reduced because of the offender's inability to pay and for other reasons, which reduces the deterrent effect of the original penalty. There is little deterrence for habitual offenders. The RSPCA has calculated that of the 442 convictions the Society obtained in 1994 under the Wildlife and Countryside Act 1981, the average fine was £16.25, or £42.41 including costs. It is a fact that this is often a fraction of the value of the wildlife specimens involved.

In relation to enforcement, the key conclusions of the DOE working group were that:

– a permanent committee should be established 'to take a strategic overview and to improve co-ordination of wildlife enforcement activity';

- the network of Police Wildlife Liaison Officers should be retained and properly resourced, strengthened and formalised;

- all offences, such as illegal taking, killing, keeping or offering for sale of wildlife should be made notifiable offences;

- the inconsistencies between the penalties imposed for different offences should be removed;

- custody, probation and community service should be an option that the courts can consider; and

- better information and the use of DNA profiling of the animals should also be expanded.

The importance of DNA testing can be seen from the following extract:[27]

> Police taking part in Operation Dutch Lady have found 36 rare peregrine falcons in raids on addresses all across Britain. The discoveries came during the biggest ever operation against the illegal trade in birds of prey with officers raiding properties in Essex, Wales, Thames Valley, Wiltshire, Derbyshire, Northumbria, Bedfordshire and West Yorkshire. The birds, which are valued at £1,000 each, were allowed to stay with their 'owners' while each bird was being genetically 'fingerprinted' by DNA experts to establish whether the birds were bred in captivity or stolen from the wild. Essex proved to be a productive hunting ground with around 23 birds found in the county.

Each police force has a Wildlife Liaison Officer or some identified person responsible for the enforcement of wildlife legislation. The police are the main enforcers of wildlife legislation, along with the RSPB/RSPCA and other wildlife groups. The main problem in terms of enforcement is detection. The Police Wildlife Liaison Officer Conference suggests that a nature watch scheme would help to alleviate this problem.[28] The court process is also problematic as there is often a lack of specialised knowledge in this area amongst solicitors, magistrates and judges. In the US and Australia there are wildlife enforcement agencies with designated police officers who can enforce any statute protecting wildlife. Such a system would be an important step forward in the fight against wildlife crime in the UK, if it was adopted.[29]

THE PROTECTION OF BIODIVERSITY

> Biodiversity is defined as all hereditary based variation at all levels of organisation, from the genes within a single local population or species, to the species composing all or part of a local community, and finally to the

---

27 *Wildlife Guardian*, Spring/Summer 1994, p 8.

28 These issues were raised by the Police Wildlife Liaison Officers Conference, Ryton-on-Dunsmore Police Training Centre 21–22 June 1989 organised by the RSPB/RSNC and supported by the Nature Conservancy Council and the World Wildlife Fund for Nature, p 3.

29 *Ibid*, p 4.

communities themselves that compose the living parts of the multifarious ecosystems of the world.[30]

The importance of biodiversity and the threats to animals and birds that the loss of biodiversity raises are examined below:[31]

[A] great variety of unique wildlife inhabits a very small part of the world. Some 20% of all bird species are confined to just 2% of the earth's land surface. The same places also accommodate 70% of the world's threatened birds and are of great importance for mammals, reptiles, amphibians, plants, molluscs and insects ... In order to use birds as indicators, locality records have been gathered for all bird species with breeding ranges below 50,000 km2, which is about the size of Sri Lanka, Costa Rica or Denmark. Remarkably there are 2,609 species or 27% of the world's birds with such small ranges ... An analysis of the patterns of bird distribution shows that species of restricted range tend to occur in places which are often islands or isolated patches of a particular habitat, especially montane and other tropical forests.

The above report goes on to state that there are 221 of these areas and they have 2,484 species within them, comprising 95% of all restricted range birds. Some 76% of these areas are in the Tropics, and Indonesia is the most important country as it contains 24 of these areas with 441 restricted range species. The report states that while the maintenance of biodiversity is important for ethical and economic reasons:[32]

Beyond this, however, lies a non-material valuation of biodiversity ... often expounded and still less often grasped, but in many ways more powerful still. Scientists, conservationists and the planet's liberal public do not seek to defend biodiversity (any more than they do whales) because of the potential material gains of our or future generations. They do so rather in tacit recognition of the values of intellectual inquiry, spiritual fulfilment and recreational satisfaction that the mere existence of biodiversity bestows. While in an economic sense biodiversity represents unimaginable wealth, in this ethical sense it is simply priceless.

The article reproduced below highlights the loss of bird species and the impact of this on biodiversity:[33]

Of almost 10,000 bird species, more than 1,000 are in danger of extinction and 6,000 are noticeably declining in numbers ... Extinctions are not uncommon in nature says Dr Nigel Collar, a researcher. But to be on the point of losing a tenth of the world's biodiversity is decidedly unnatural. It's unprecedented in scale and is linked directly to the global intensification of development in the last 25 years. Natural extinctions occur where a species fails to respond to

30 Reaka-Kudla, M, Wilson, D and Wilson, E (eds), *Biodiversity II Understanding and Protecting our Biological Resources,* 1996, p 1, Washington: Joseph Henry Press.

31 *Putting Biodiversity on the map – priority areas for global conservation,* 1992, Cambridge: International Council for Bird Preservation.

32 *Ibid,* p 3.

33 Vidal, J and Moss, J, *The Guardian,* 4 February 1994, pp 14–15, London. Reproduced with the kind permission of Guardian Newspapers.

changing circumstances or when one evolves into something else. But man's hand is behind almost every one of the 1,000 threats ... birds are now recognised as past of the ecological web. Essential to the vitality of plants, they help prevent insect plagues, suppress explosions of rodents, scatter seeds and generally protect. Farmers, foresters, botanists and agronomists are concerned too. The Corollary is obvious: lose the birds and the economic problems will multiply ... Most of the threatened extinctions are tropical forest species, whose habitats are falling to the chainsaws, whose range is limited and whose numbers are small. The Philippines ... is a disaster zone with 126 species immediately threatened with extinction, Brazil has 97, China 81, Peru and Colombia more than 50. But extinctions are only the tip of the problem. Birdlife research being collated now ... from 45 European countries will show that 280 out of 530 species are vulnerable. More than a third of European species have declined in numbers in the last 20 years, some rapidly.

The article goes on to cite the main reasons for the loss of birds as:

– overgrazing and ploughing causing loss of grassland;

– drainage of wetlands – in the US this has cut fowl numbers by one third;

– desertification – whitethroat warblers that breed in Britain but winter in Africa have declined by 75% in 25 years;

– the logging of over 20% of the world's forest in 40 years;

– fragmentation leading to parasitic birds driving others out;

– irrigation causing to widespread loss of habitats;

– pesticides, ie DDT, carbofuran and other sprays which kill millions of birds each year in many countries;

– death from lead shot, which the birds eat;

– hunting is responsible for the death of more than 50 million birds in Italy;

– urbanisation, which is devastating for vulnerable species.

In June 1992, at the United Nations Conference on Environment and Development, the Biodiversity Convention was signed by 150 countries.

Article 2 of the Biodiversity Convention describes biodiversity as:

The variability among living organisms from all sources including, *inter alia*, terrestrial, marine and other aquatic ecosystems and the ecological complexes of which they are part; this includes diversity within species, between species and of ecosystems.

Article 6a of the Convention on Biological Diversity states that each contracting party should 'develop national strategies, plans or programmes for the conservation and sustainable use of biodiversity'.

The UK government's biodiversity strategy was laid down in *Biodiversity – the UK Action Plan*, 1994.[34] Its goals are to conserve and where practicable to enhance:

---

34 Cmnd 2428, HMSO.

- the overall population and ranges of native species and the quality and range of wildlife habitats and ecosystems;
- internationally important and threatened habitats, ecosystems and species;
- species, habitats and natural and managed ecosystems that are characteristic of local areas;
- the biodiversity of natural and seemingly natural habitats where this has been diminished over recent past decades;
- public awareness and involvement in conserving biodiversity; and
- the conservation of biodiversity on a European and global scale.

Survival plans are being drawn up for a range of animals. One example of these plans is reproduced here:[35]

1.Introduction

There are six amphibian and reptile species in the UK and five marine turtle species. The following rationale sets the context for action.

Amphibians and reptiles are important and integral parts of the UK's natural and cultural heritage, and are valuable indicators of environmental change. Their future should be safeguarded. This will require a co-ordinated approach to integrate active conservation programmes at various levels, improve and disseminate knowledge of the species and develop effective protection mechanisms.

Partnerships should be developed to further the conservation of these species and to achieve heightened awareness and concern among a wide audience. Through these partnerships, understanding of the ecology and distribution of the species should develop, thereby ensuring that viable populations are conserved throughout their traditional ranges.

2. Overall aims

The overall aims are, through the most effective use of resources, to:

(i) prevent further declines in the range, distribution, and viability of amphibians and reptiles;

and

(ii) where feasible, enhance the distribution and abundance of amphibians and reptiles.

3. Specific objectives

Objectives for the conservation of amphibians and reptiles in the UK are:

(i) to ascertain the existing status (distribution, abundance, trends and threats) of amphibian and reptile species and to set objectives for the desired status of each species;

(ii) to develop survey methods, monitoring systems and data storage systems which allow efficient access to, exchange of, and use of information;

---

35 *A Framework for the Conservation of Amphibians and Reptiles in the UK: 1994–1999*, 1994, pp 5–6, London: Joint Nature Conservancy Council.

(iii) to refine knowledge of the ecology of all species and determine the value of conservation measures, so that future conservation action can be implemented more effectively;

(iv) to define priority measures needed to conserve amphibians and reptiles and to clarify roles and responsibilities between relevant organisations for their implementation;

(v) to promote the development and implementation of amphibian and reptile conservation policies within statutory nature conservation authorities and other governmental bodies;

(vi) to increase the involvement of non-governmental bodies, local authorities and individuals in the development and implementation of amphibian and reptile conservation; and

(vii) to promote a wider and more sympathetic understanding of amphibians and reptiles.

The report goes on to highlight further action areas: science and monitoring, including recording species distribution, the development of conservation targets at all levels of decision-making in relation both to the species and to the protection and sustainable management of their habitats. Conservation requires guidance and dissemination of information; conservation projects need to be included in habitat protection initiatives and other wider countryside initiatives, and captive-rearing and release projects should be developed. In relation to legislation, doubts have been expressed as to the effectiveness of Part I of the Wildlife and Countryside Act 1981 concerning the designation of SSSIs and National Nature Reserves in reptile and amphibian conservation.

THE CONSERVATION OF ANIMAL AND PLANT HABITATS

To put the use of rural land into its historical context, it is important to realise that such use has always been tied into property rights. Much of the English landscape has been changed over the centuries. Deforestation occurred as wood was required for building and other purposes. During the Middle Ages land ownership was seen as a reward for loyalty and as a way of acquiring wealth. Many of the restrictions on the commoners' use of land, as well as the types of activities permitted, were fixed after the Norman Conquest and are still evident today. William the Conqueror put England under the heel of a landowning class of knights and claimed all the land for the Crown. After this, land would be owned by permission of the King. William the Conqueror therefore created the legacy that this group of landowners would enjoy a privileged status and an associated passion for hunting. Forests had some legal protection from this time until the 14th century, as the Crown saw them as a way of raising revenue. Originally, the Royal Forests had covered a quarter of England. By 1330 the area of Royal Forest had shrunk to two-thirds of what it had been in 1250. This led to restrictions being placed on the use of this land by commoners who had previously enjoyed many rights over it.[36]

Who owns the land now?

At the present time, 76% of land in the UK is used for agriculture and 10% is covered by forest. Land in urban use is projected to increase from 10% of the total land area in 1981 to just under 12% by 2016.[37] In 1985 the Ministry of Defence owned 561,710 acres; in 1986 the Forestry Commission owned five times this amount, 2,878,785 acres. During the 1980s a lot of land was sold off – the Forestry Commission sold off 10% of its estate. More than 87% of land is in private hands

The loss of the countryside

Changes in the countryside since 1947 include the following:
–   109,000 miles of hedgerows have been destroyed – enough to go round the world four times;
–   95% of hay meadows have been destroyed;
–   half of the remaining 5% have been damaged;
–   99% of lowland heaths have vanished;
–   80% of chalk downlands have been lost;
–   80% of limestone grassland has been destroyed;
–   half of the fens/mires have been destroyed;
–   90% of ponds have been filled in;
–   half of annual lowland woods have been cleared for farmland/forestry.[38]

Habitat protection

The Ramsar Convention

Wetlands are particularly vital for many types of birds. The need to take a global view and co-operate internationally to encourage wetland conservation was recognised at Ramsar, Iran, in 1971 by the Convention on Wetlands of International Importance especially as Waterfowl Habitat. By 1990 a total of 52 countries ranging from Australia to Venezuela had signed the Convention. Between them 445 sites had been listed as internationally important wetlands

---

36   Shoard, M, *This Land is Our Land*, 1987, London: Pakadin.
37   Figures from the open government site on the Internet.
38   Nature Conservancy Council, *Conservation of Nature in England and Wales*, Cmnd 7122.

across the world, covering nearly 30 million hectares. Some countries have protected vast areas of land under the Convention. For example, Canada has notified about 13 million hectares, whilst even the much smaller Denmark has protected nearly two million hectares. In Britain the total so far is about 130,000 hectares. Such a network is of key importance to the continued survival of many wetland plants and animals.[39]

Under the Convention the contracting parties have to ensure that wetland conservation is considered in the development of national land use planning. They should formulate the appropriate use of wetlands as far as possible. Each contracting party has to specify at least one wetland site which is of international importance based on ecology, botany, liminology or hydrology. This is then included in the international 'List of Wetlands of International Importance'. The conservation of the wetlands is to be promoted by means of nature reserves as specified in the Convention. There have been 154 proposed Ramsar sites identified by EN in the UK.

The Bonn Convention

The Convention on the Conservation of Migratory Species of Wild Animals (the Bonn Convention) arose from a recommendation of the 1972 United Nations Conference on the Human Environment which recognised the need for countries to co-operate in the conservation of species that migrate across national boundaries or between areas of national jurisdiction and the high seas.

There are a number of factors that can threaten migrating species, including hunting, loss of habitat and degradation of feeding sites. Conferences of the Parties to the Convention are held every three years. In 1985 a Standing Committee was established to provide guidance on the implementation of the Convention. It comprises one elected party from each of the five major geographic areas (Africa, America, Asia, Europe and Oceania). There are two appendices to the Convention: Appendix I lists species in danger of extinction throughout all, or a significant proportion of, their range, and these are given full protection from hunting, fishing, capturing, harassing and deliberate killing. Conservation measures also have to be taken by range States (countries that exercise jurisdiction over any part of a species' distribution). The range States have to protect habitat and counter factors that might endanger them or impede their migration. Appendix II sets out two forms of agreement: an agreement intended to benefit migratory species, especially those with an unfavourable conservation status over their entire range, and an agreement for populations of species that periodically cross national jurisdictional boundaries but are not necessarily migratory under the definition provided by the Convention.

---

39   English Nature information leaflet, *Internationally important bird sites: Special Protection Areas and Ramsar sites*, 1990, Peterborough: English Nature.

A number of accords have been arrived at under the Convention. The Agreement on the Conservation of Bats in Europe, which came into force on 16 January 1994, encourages co-operation within Europe to conserve all its species of bats. It restricts the killing or capture of bats, protects their habitat, co-ordinates research and increases public awareness of bat conservation. The Agreement on the Conservation of Small Cetaceans of the Baltic and North Sea entered into force on 29 March 1994 and sets out measures to conserve over 30 species of small cetaceans. The African-Eurasian Waterbird Agreement aims to create a legal basis for the conservation policy of 116 range States for all migratory waterbird species and populations, individuals of which migrate in the Western Palearic and Africa. It covers 170 species, with 417 separate population sites and would span an area of 60 million km^2 (almost 40% of the earth's surface).[40]

The Habitats Directive

The EC Habitats Directive may provide a another way of protecting animals through the protection of their habitat (92/43/EC). It was adopted in May 1992. Under the Directive each member State must compile a list of areas containing the habitat types and species listed in the Directive. The Directive sets out the scientific criteria for doing this. Special Areas of Conservation (SACs) have to be designated by 2004. SACs will be those 'which make a significant contribution to the conservation of the habitats and species identified by the Directive. They will be the best area to represent the range and variety of those habitats and species'. The Habitats Directive lists, 1686 natural habitat sites in Europe; they are all rare and becoming rarer, they are given priority status if they are at greater risk of disappearing altogether. SACs in UK will cover the best examples of 75 of these habitat types including 22 priority habitat sites. The Directive lists 632 animal and plant species whose conservation requires the designation of SACs. Some species are given priority status. Forty of the 632 species are listed in the UK one as a priority. These flora and fauna are given strict protection to prohibit their deliberate capture, killing, destruction, disturbance or sale. Other less threatened species may be managed or taken from the wild provided this can be done sustainably, that is without threat to the conservation of the species. The Habitats Directive has been implemented in the UK by the Conservation (Natural Habitats &c.) Regulations 1994. This requires all statutory bodies to act in accordance with the Directive. Management plans also have to be established, these are already in place, ... The damage to the site has to be assessed to decide whether it would damage the nature conservation interest of the site ... If it would, the plan or project can only go ahead where there is no alternative solution and where it must be carried out for imperative reasons of overriding public interest. ... The management of sites through voluntary agreements, between owners, occupiers, managers and users on the one hand and the statutory nature conservation agencies on the other, is better than a coercive approach.

---

40   From the open government site on the Internet.

SACs are required for all species listed on Annex H of the Habitats Directive. There are 52 species on Annex 19 that are found in Britain, or that have been recorded as British species (and may now be extinct) or as vagrants to Britain. Of these, five species are listed as priority species. These are loggerhead turtle *Caretta caretta* (vagrant in GB waters); sturgeon *Acipenser sturio,* houting *Coregonus oxyrinchus* (now possibly extinct), the Jersey tiger moth *Callinorpha quadripunciata* and a liverwort *Marsupelia profunda.* However, *M profunda* is the only one of the priority species for which an SAC is considered appropriate in the UK. Listing as a priority species means that the process of notification as SAC is likely to be faster and that reasons for allowing loss or damage to a designated site are fewer (eg economic arguments will not be considered appropriate). All species listed on the Annexes to the European Directive are included in the appendix to *Species Conservation Handbook* advice note 'International obligations for the protection of British species other than birds'.[41]

The Habitats Directive will provide an important impetus to the development of protection areas. This can only benefit the birds and animals that need the habitat for their survival. The importance of these areas is examined in the extract below.

> The natural areas approach provides a framework for an integrated approach to nature conservation, taking into account both local needs and national priorities. ... Natural areas will also be used as the framework to deliver those objectives and targets which are being concurrently developed in other areas at both a national level (eg the UK Biodiversity Action Plan) and locally (eg local authority Nature Conservation Strategies). Local biological action plans will be developed at a County or District level and may include parts of several Natural Areas or may only represent part of one. However, in all cases the Natural area profiles will inform the development of local BAP (Biodiversity Action Plans), not only in relation to key species and habitats, but also those features that are characteristic of the local area or to which local people attach particular significance. They will pick up on the appropriate elements on the Natural Areas profiles for their areas and adopt them as specific local targets. These will work alongside Nature Conservation strategies.[42]

Other forms of wildlife protection

There are a number of wildlife designations which are important in the protection of wildlife habitat, which is essential to ensure the survival of animal and plant species. The legislation is based on the Wildlife and Countryside Act 1981 (WCA 1981).

---

41 *English Nature Species Conservation Handbook,* Gen 3, March 1995, pp 1–2, Peterborough: English Nature. Reproduced with kind permission of English Nature.

42 Cooke, R, (Manager of English Nature's Natural Areas Project), *Nature's Place,* Issue 11, March 1996, p 21, Peterborough: English Nature.

The founding legislation on which many of the site protection measures are based is the National Parks and Access to the Countryside Act 1947. This allowed the introduction of specific management measures for nature and landscape conservation at designated sites and has since been updated and superseded by the Wildlife and Countryside Act 1981, (amended in 1985) and other conservation related legislation. The provisions of these Acts and, for Northern Ireland, related Orders, has led to the establishment of a network of designated sites for nature and landscape conservation. Site designation has been complemented by the efforts of private organisations who manage many of the reserves as well as promoting conservation based management at other properties. The National Trust is most significant in this respect as the largest conservation society and private landowner in Britain. The Trust owns 353 miles of the coastline of Great Britain which it protects for the nation. On a smaller scale the County Wildlife Trusts and the Royal Society for the Protection of Birds own and manage both coastal and inland properties, many of which are designated protected areas. ...

Areas of Outstanding Natural Beauty (AONB) – s 28 of the WCA 1981

This designation applies to England, Wales and Northern Ireland. AONBs are considered to be areas of fine landscape quality. They are principally established to conserve natural beauty however recreation is also recognised as an objective of designation where it is consistent with the conservation measures. In pursuing these objectives account should be taken of the need to safeguard agriculture, forestry and other rural industry and the economic and social needs of the local communities. Designation is intended to assist sound planning and development by giving clear official recognition to the importance of preserving the attractiveness of the areas. ...

National Parks – ss 42–46 of the WCA 1981

National Parks cover exceptionally fine stretches of relatively wild countryside. They have been established in England, Wales and Northern Ireland and are managed to maintain the natural beauty of these areas for the benefit and enjoyment of the public as well as to protect wildlife and places of architectural and historic interest. Established farming use is maintained and development plans are required. Mineral extraction and civil engineering projects are permissible but only if they are clearly in the public interest. Farmers need to consult the park authority on the design of farm buildings, farm and forest roads.

Heritage Coasts

The Heritage Coast programme applies to England and Wales. It covers coastlines considered to be of exceptionally fine scenic quality, which are substantially undeveloped and containing features of special significant interest. Although these areas do not have any statutory protection, they have management plans developed with local authorities and they are indicated on planning documents. The management is supported by Heritage Coast officers and much of the land is in private ownership.

National Nature Reserves (NNR) – s 35 of the WCA 1981

NNRs, together with Sites of Special Interest (see below), have been established to protect key areas representative of the major natural and semi-natural habitats in the UK. The sites are managed by the statutory nature conservation agencies, or through agreement with them to provide opportunities for study and research and/or to preserve flora, fauna or geological or physiographical features of special interest.[43]

Sites of Special Scientific Interest[44] – ss 28–33 of the WCA 1981

When land is thought to be of potential SSSI quality, English Nature follows strict procedures to evaluate it, and if it is up to standard, notify it. The task of formally surveying land with possible SSSI value is undertaken by English Nature conservation staff, who will often seek to confirm the findings of experts from other partner organisations like the County Wildlife Trusts.

English Nature staff weigh the information against local and national guidelines and statistics and will in most cases discuss with the landowners and occupiers before deciding to notify the site under the Wildlife and Countryside Act 1981. The case goes to English Nature's Council at one of its regular meetings. If approved, staff send formal notice to those with a legal interest in the land. After notification, the English Nature Council looks at any representations and/ or objections and will only confirm, modify or withdraw an SSI after careful deliberation. The Council, chaired by the Earl of Cranbrook, comprises people appointed by the Environment Secretary for their knowledge of, and involvement with the English countryside, wildlife, agriculture and woodlands.

When land is designated as an SSSI, English Nature notifies the owners and occupiers, the local planning authority and the Secretary of State. Site owners and occupiers receive: a site map; a description of the site's special interest; a letter detailing their legal obligations; a list of operations likely to damage the site's conservation interest. While modifications are legal documents, English Nature is busy talking to SSSI owners and occupiers to agree more plainly-worded Site Management statements with them. The statements are designed to ensure that everyone concerned is clear on what action is expected to maintain the nature conservation interest- and what actions are harmful. Owners and occupiers are required by law to consult English Nature in writing if they want to undertake any operations listed as being damaging to the site. If English Nature and the owners or manager cannot agree a mutually satisfactory course through informal discussion, a formal four-month negotiating period comes into play. If there is still stalemate, English Nature can apply to the Environment Secretary for an order to further protect the site. In practice, it's rare for matters to go that far. Only 26 orders have been made in England in the past 15 years. Even less common is for English Nature to acquire the land through compulsory purchase. It's happened just twice in 46 years.

---

43 Gubbay, S, *Marine Protected Areas in European Waters, The British Isles*, September 1993, pp 3–5, London: Marine Conservation Society/World Wide Fund for Nature.

44 *English Nature* No 24, March 1996, p 8, Peterborough: English Nature.

SSSI agreements are now based on English Nature's Wildlife Enhancement Scheme. This offers a simple agreement on the management tasks necessary to maintain and enhance a particular SSSI for nature conservation. It reimburses owners and managers for carrying out positive management. 'Standard payments have been devised for dealing with many different types of habitat. These make future nature conservation agreements much more straight-forward than the old-style arrangements which compensated signatories for loss of potential agricultural benefits.'[45]

English Nature provide figures on the damage to SSSIs and the reasons for the damage. In 1991–92 there were 183 reported cases; by 1994–95 this had fallen to 111. Between these dates only one site had been totally destroyed. In 1991–92, 27,000 ha had suffered some damage; in 1994–95, 2,000 ha had been damaged. Around 80% of the damage is caused by overgrazing. Damage by planning permissions and forestry has fallen and damage from recreation remains constant.

English Nature's *4th Report* provides the most recent information relating to SSSIs, the extent of SSIs and the damage done to them:[46]

SSSIs contain the best of England's wildlife and natural features. At 31 March 1995, there were 3,825 SSSIs covering 893,335 ha – an increase of 31 sites and 22,269 ha on last year. Of the new SSSI notifications, four were river SSSIs which bring river listings to 15 and which build towards a national series with a planned total of 27 (3% of England's river length). Together, our SSSIs comprise the core of our natural heritage. They are looked after by 23,000 owners and managers. [In 1994/95 the Report states that English Nature carried out over 3,000 site unit visits.] ...

... In percentage terms, damage affected 2.9% of sites by number or 0.3% by area. The largest category is again agriculture which accounts for 51 reported cases (80% of the total area). Excessive grazing levels, particularly on upland grasses and mires, were responsible for 40% of the damage by farming activities. Insufficient management was considered damaging in 21 cases, nearly all on lowland calcareous grassland. Development-related activities caused partial loss at three sites – all by statutory undertakers.

Other reserves

Local nature reserves are set up by local authorities. They may be of scientific importance but are primarily for the enjoyment of the general public. In addition there are reserves owned by private charities such as the National Trust which complement the statutory protected areas network and indeed many of these sites have some sort of designated status.[47]

---

45   *English Nature*, No 24, March, 1996, p 6, Peterborough: English Nature.

46   *English Nature 4th Report*, 1994/95, 1996, pp 17, 53, Peterborough: English Nature.

47   From English Nature species conservation handbook, *Species Protection and the Habitats Regulations*, 1994, Peterborough: English Nature.

The protection of other habitats

There are many different types of habitat which need to be protected. Limestone pavements, for example, are covered by the Limestone Pavement Orders, s 34 of the WCA 1981, which prohibit the removal or disturbance of the limestone. Another vulnerable habitat is caves:[48]

> [Caves] are an often forgotten part of our natural heritage ... Current estimates give the total length of mapped cave passage in the British Isles at a figure of around 800 kilometres ... Caves also provide an important habitat for wildlife, including protected species such as bats. Bats are protected by the Wildlife and Countryside Act 1981, and it is illegal intentionally to kill, injure or take any bat, or to disturb them whilst roosting. It is also an offence to damage, destroy or obstruct access to any place used by bats for roosting ... Very few bats now breed in caves, but many rely on the underground environment for hibernation and for shelter during inclement weather. Cave dwelling bats, such as the two horseshoe bats, are threatened by loss of underground sites and by excessive disturbance. Although it is not uncommon for bats to wake and move their roost during the hibernation period, it can be very damaging for them to wake at unscheduled times. A conservation code has been produced for those wishing to use caves where bats may be present, and this stresses the importance of leaving hibernating bats undisturbed.

The adequacy of nature conservation in the UK

The Nature Conservancy Council (now English Nature) has examined the adequacy of nature conservation in the UK. The problem of judging how well the legislation has worked in protecting our countryside is examined in the extract below:

> 10.1 Objectives for nature conservation have been rather loosely and qualitatively set in the past, so that measures of attainment or shortfall are not easily made. While the 1949 NC Charter did not set any quantitative targets for the three main functions, Cmnd 7122 nevertheless made quite specific recommendations, with its lists of proposed nature reserves and other protected area categories. For the wider countryside no targets for conservation achievement were even discussed. It was generally assumed that the NC would do what was feasible and should be satisfied if species' populations could be maintained somewhere between the extremes of explosion and extinction and if habitat loss could be contained within reasonable limits. Although the SPNR had its own list of prospective nature reserves, the voluntary movement as a whole had imprecise targets.

> 10.2 The most obvious yardstick of attainments would be to assess how much of the resource of nature is left, and how much of the resource of nature is left, and how much has been lost, since conservation programmes began. This is no easy task since earlier base-line measurements of the resource are so sketchy. The setting of a base-line is arbitrary also, though 1950 would seem an

---

48   NCC, *Bats underground – a conservation code*, 1990, Peterborough: NCC.

appropriate date. In general, too, conservation successes amount to no more than maintaining the *status quo*. There are few opportunities for actually increasing or enhancing the resource of nature and the victories are usually the prevention of further loss. In this sense, conservation is a largely defensive process, reducing the scale of human impact and contrasting with other land land-use activities such as agriculture, which are positive through continuous development and expansion of their products. The positive avenues for nature conservation are largely through management activity, notably the recreation or restoration of lost or damaged habitats and the reintroduction or re-stocking of vanished or declining species. Only a few modern man-made habitats incidentally provide important wildlife opportunities, for example reservoirs for wintering birds and flooded gravel pits for aquatic life generally.

10.3 Even when conservation gains and losses are measurable, or at least identifiable, their significance as successes or failures must inevitably be a matter for subjective judgment. Views on some issues also vary widely according to standpoint. And it is seldom that any particular issue can be regarded wholly as a success or a failure, so that qualifications of such judgments are usually necessary.[49]

OTHER FORMS OF PROTECTION FOR ANIMALS

Planning

Planning law has an important role to play in relation to rural areas.[50] *Planning Policy Guidance on Nature Conservation* (PPG 9) advises on how government policies for the conservation of our natural heritage are to be reflected in land use planning, and contains the commitment to sustainability and to conserving the diversity of our environment.[51] The main objectives of the policy note are: to ensure that government policies contribute to the conservation of the abundance and diversity of British Wildlife and its habitats; to minimise the adverse effects on wildlife where conflicts of interest are unavoidable; and to meet the State's international responsibilities and obligations for nature conservation.

Local plans

These plans ensure that environmental protection is considered at the level of policy-making; they set down the basic ground rules for development, but

---

49 *Nature Conservation in Great Britain,* 1984, p 41, Peterborough: Nature Conservancy Committee.

50 The problem with planning controls as an adequate method of protecting our countryside is that agricultural/forestry operations are exempt under s 55(c) of the Town and Country Planning Act 1990.

51 *Nature's Place,* Issue 8, 1995, Peterborough: English Nature.

they are increasingly being overtaken by central government circulars and policy guidance notes.

There are three types of plan:

– Structure plans – these are a statement of general strategic policies, usually for an entire county.

– Local plans – these are more detailed, consisting of written policies and specific land use allocations.

– Unitary development plans – these cover the metropolitan areas.

The plans often allocate set-aside land and can include environmental measures such as limiting traffic pollution by means of a general commitment not to build more roads, etc. Under the Planning and Compensation Act 1991 development plans should include policies for the conservation of the natural beauty and amenity of the land and for the improvement of the physical environment.

The Town and Land Planning (Development Plan) Regulations 1991 expressly require local authorities to take into account environmental considerations when preparing their development plans.

PPG 12 *Regional Planning Guidance* underlines the need for environmental concerns to be incorporated in development plan preparation. PPG12 *Good Practice Guide* also requires local planning authorities to conduct an environmental appraisal of plans, policies and proposals during their elaboration and examines the importance of development plans to protect nature:[52]

> Some species protected by law are largely confined to sites notified as Sites of Special Scientific Interest. Most protected species, however, are not restricted to sites with designations. They may occur almost anywhere, including areas of otherwise limited nature conservation value (eg stone curlews breeding on arable fields or bats roosting in buildings). Their occurrence may be unpredictable (eg migratory or rare breeding birds) both in terms of their location and their population. Animal breeding, roosting or feeding locations often change and even the occurrence or distribution of rarer plants can be surprisingly variable. These characteristics of protected species mean that the conservation of particular sites is only a part of nature conservation. Designating SSSI, or non-statutory sites of importance for nature conservation cannot achieve the adequate protection of species on its own.

The planning process can make a further significant contribution to species protection by including species protection policies in development plans and by being alert to the needs of protected species in development control. This should be at the stage of development plans and the importance of protected species is acknowledged as they are a planning consideration.the author states; there are two policies which can help. The above author continues:

---

52 Tyldesley, D, 'Nature's Place', in *English Nature,* issue 9, April 1995, Peterborough: English Nature.

Firstly, a policy restricting the grant of planning permission (either by refusal or by the imposition of conditions) where protected species occur. Secondly, where a large area – more than one particular site or series of sites – is the general location of particular protected species but where the exact location of the species, within that area, at any particular time, or season, or year cannot be predicted. In these cases a policy referring to 'Areas' of importance for nature conservation may be more appropriate than polices for 'Sites' of importance of nature conservation. These area polices can also be valuable where a species, such as a bird of prey, may need an extensive area or territory over which to roam.

Environmental impact assessment

The procedure for carrying out an environmental impact assessment under the Environmental Impact Assessment Directive 85/337 is set out below.

–   The developer must submit an environmental statement to the 'competent authority' – this will be the Local Planning Authority if planning permission is also required, while in other cases it will be the public body with responsibility for that particular area, eg the Forestry Commission. The statement should identify the potential environmental effects and the steps it is envisaged will avoid, reduce or remedy them.

–   The competent body then consults with others, eg English Nature.

–   The competent body must prepare an environmental assessment of the proposal before deciding whether it may go ahead. This should take into account the views of the public and consultees.

The adequacy of the procedure was looked at in *R v Poole ex p BeeBee and others*[53] and in *Twyford Parish Council and others v SOSE*.[54]

Tree preservation orders

The use of other planning controls is limited: s 55(2) of the Town and Country Planning Act 1990 exempts the use of land for agriculture/forestry from planning controls, while planning permission is not necessarily required for the development of buildings on such land or for bringing land into agricultural use or changing from one agricultural use to another.

The control of pesticides

These are mainly controlled through the Food and Environmental Protection Act 1985. This protects human and plant health and the environment. It aims

---

53   (1991) JPL 643.
54   (1992) JEL.

to secure a safe and efficient means of controlling pests as well as making information about pesticides publicly available. The Act states that no pesticide can be made, imported, sold, supplied, stored, used or advertised without approval. Enforcement powers include powers of seizure, disposal or remedial action by MAFF. (See Control of Pesticides Regulations 1997, SI 1997/188.)

Nitrates

These are controlled in relation to water pollution by means of designated nitrate sensitive areas (Schedule 12, Water Resources Act 1991). Nitrate Sensitive Areas areas are defined by the Department of the Environment and farmers receive compensation for not using nitrates within their bounds.

Codes of good agricultural practice

These set down good practice for farmers to follow in relation to water pollution. They were set up under s 93 of the Water Resources Act 1991. Farmers will not be prosecuted if they breach these codes, but such non-compliance can be used as evidence of bad practice if they are being prosecuted for another offence.

A CASE STUDY – THE IMPACT OF ROADS ON WILDLIFE

Road building has become a controversial issue in recent years, with the protests at Twyford Down, the A34 and Newbury. The building of roads causes a number of problems, as the following extracts highlight:

Habitat fragmentation is a major threat to wildlife not just in Britain but throughout Europe and a 1995 conference in the Netherlands looked at the particular problems created by roads, railways and canals. During the first part of the meeting in Maastrict, research workers showed how breeding bird populations in wetland and woodland were reduced close to roads, probably because of the increased noise. Others found that populations of moor frogs were less likely to occur in ponds close to busy roads ... The conference then went on a tour of the countryside to see how the Dutch were trying to deal with these problems in practice. As well as road underpasses for toads (and frogs and newts) badger tunnels and specially designed culverts that provided a dry pathway for small mammals, stoats and martens alongside streams were seen. The most substantial (and expensive) works were 'green bridges' up to 80 m wide which were covered in grass and had shrubs planted along their edges. These had been conceived originally in France to help deer and other game animals cross roads at critical points. The Dutch ones, usually built to connect patches of woodland, were used by red and roe deer and by wild boar, but also by hares, hedgehogs, badgers and various other small animals. Even bats were seen to use them as flyways across the road and one had an artificial hibernaculum built into one end of it ... Habitat fragmentation is not just about the effects of roads and railways however. For some species blocks of housing, industrial sites, arable fields and intensively managed grassland may be almost as much as a barrier as a strip of tarmac. Nor is there much point making links across roads if the habitat patches on either side are too small to support the populations in the long term ... The challenge for the next decade is not just to protect what we have left but to reverse past fragmentation.[55]

In fact, roads are often a problem for the protection of species, not only through the loss of their habitat, but also from the effects of pollution as well as the loss of wildlife on our roads. The law in this area is contained in various acts. The Highways Act 1980 which covers the main provisions on road building; the Road Traffic Act 1991 and the Road Traffic Regulation Act 1984 which allows for the development of priority routes.[56] The environmental assessment of roads is covered by Directive 85/337. Inquiries are held under the Highways (Inquiries Procedure) Rules (SI 1994/3263). PPG13 and s 54A of Town and Country Planning Act 1990 cover traffic reduction policies. Traffic reduction policies have been improved by the passing of the Road Traffic Reduction Act 1997.

The aims of the government's nature conservation policies, while laudable, have been seriously thrown into doubt at Newbury by the destruction of ancient woodlands, SSSIs and the blatant ignoring of the Birds Directive. There are three sites that are local nature reserves, AONB, ancient woods, rare heaths and meadows, and two of the last unspoilt lowland rivers, with badgers, kingfishers, dormice and bats. No proper Environmental Impact Assessment was ever carried out and the Public Inquiry was held in 1988 at a time before many of the environmental impacts were known.[57]

CONCLUSION

This chapter has examined a range of controls and protection for wild animals. The Wild Mammals Protection Act 1996 has strengthened the law in this area and it should provide a foundation for further protection in the future. Wild animal conservation and habitat protection should be in the hands of one agency. There are a range of threats facing both the animals and their habitats, and a strong enforcement agency is needed. The Environment Agency set up under the Environment Act 1995 does not include nature conservation; this would have been an ideal time to amalgamate the pollution control and nature conservation functions to provide a holistic view of nature conservation, the workings of ecosystems and pollution control.

---

55   *Urban Wildlife News* ,Vol 13, no 1, February 1996, Peterborough: English Nature.
56   See also the National Audit Office Report, Department of Transport, *Environmental Factors in Road Planning and Design*, 1994, London: HMSO.
57   Friends of the Earth leaflet.

FURTHER READING

Ball, S and Bell, S, *Environmental Law*, 1995, London: Blackstone Press.

Hughes, N, *Environmental Law*, 1996, London: Butterworths. A general discussion on environmental law.

Reid, C, *Nature Conservation Law*, 1994, Edinburgh: Sweet & Maxwell. Looks at nature conservation law more specifically.

For a general discussion on the issues of wild animal welfare, see

Clark, S, 'The Rights of Wild Things' (1979) 22 *Inquiry* 171–88.

Garner, R, *Wildlife Conservation and the Moral Status of Animals Environmental Politics*, 1995, vol 3, Pt 1, pp 114–29.

Kirkwood, J, in Ryder, R and Singer, P (eds), *Animal Welfare and the Environment*, 1992, pp 139–54, Melksham: RSPCA; also Broom, D, on Welfare and Conservation, Chapter 10, pp 90–101.

Rodman, J, 'The Liberation of Nature' (1977) 20 *Inquiry* 83–145.

On the Wild Mammals Protection Act 1996, see:

Radford, M, 'Protecting Wild Animals' (1991) 146 *New Law Journal* 458.

Conservation:

See also English Nature, Kirby, K 'Rebuilding the English Countryside: habitat fragmentation and wildlife corridors as issues in practical conservation', *Science*, no 10, 1995. English Nature, Peterborough.

Conserving Britain's Biodiversity – a report of the statutory nature conservation agencies' contribution under the UK Biodiversity Action Plan, 1995, JNCC.

Symposium on the United Nations Conference on the Environment and Development (UNCED), the Convention on Biological Diversity and the Bern Convention: the next steps Monaco 26–28 September 1994, *Environmental Encounters* 22.

De Klem, C and Shine, C, *Biological Diversity Conservation and the Law – legal means for conserving species and ecosystems*, IUCN Environmental Protection and Law Paper, no 29, 1993.

CHAPTER NINE

INTERNATIONAL CONTROL OF ENDANGERED SPECIES

INTRODUCTION

This chapter will focus on how we protect the most vulnerable animals: those that are in danger of extinction. The chapter will examine the control of trade in endangered species, which is regulated under the Convention on International Trade in Endangered Species (CITES). The chapter will then focus on a case study of the measures in place to protect whales and dolphins. The legislative framework and the success of the legislation in protecting these animals will be examined. Habitat protection is as important in this area as the individual protection given to the various animals. The international protection of habitat and of biodiversity was the subject of Chapter 8. This chapter will, however, look briefly at the protection of the marine environment, as this affects the survival or otherwise of whales and dolphins, which has not been covered elsewhere. The loss of species through slaughter, war, pollution and habitat destruction does not have to be an inevitable consequence of our existence on earth. The chapter explores some of the choices that we have to make if we are to save some of the most vulnerable species.

We may not have much time, as the following extract highlights:[1]

A completely new bird to science has been discovered in Parana State, southern Brazil. Marcos Bornschien, Bianca Reinert and Dante Teixxeira discovered this previously undocumented species on the Parana coast only 60 m from the road connecting two of the region's busiest resorts.

Incredibly, it is not just a new species but also a new genus. *Stymphalornis acitirostris*, as the bird has been named, showed affinities with the Antbird genus *Formicivora*. However, differences prompted internal examinations, and on the structure of the bird's vocal apparatus it was felt that this bird represented a new genus within the Antbirds. The bird has a long tail and a long narrow beak, weighs about 10g and is 14cm long.

Sadly, there are fears that the birds could already be on the endangered species list. The taboa swamp where the bird was found is being steadily encroached on by human activities.

---

1   *World Bird Watch*, June 1996, vol 18, no 2, p 2, Cambridge: Birdlife International.

THE PROBLEM OF EXTINCTION

History

The phenomenon of extinction has been in existence for many years. The following extract puts the problem into perspective:[2]

> Over the past two million years there have been seven so-called Ice Ages or glacial periods, which have been interrupted by warmer interglacial periods. These fluctuations have resulted in numerous extinctions. However, when our ancestors entered the scene between one and four million years ago the loss of species accelerated dramatically. Primitive Stone Age hunters caused extinctions of large mammals. Humans continually developed more sophisticated hunting techniques., ensuring ever greater levels of extinction. But now, in the 20th century, the wave of extinction is reaching levels quite unprecedented in the history of our planet. One great mass extinction observed in recent times has been the loss of the bulk of the amazing cichlid fish diversity in Africa's Lake Victoria, which resulted directly from interference by humans. The most troubling cause of extinction is the combination of factors that result from the activities of people, primarily overpopulation and habitat destruction.
>
> In many instances the rate of habitat destruction and degradation has reached the point where the damages and losses are probably irreversible, even if blocks – greatly diminished – of natural habitat remain. Particularly worrisome is whether declared conservation areas are in fact viable in the long term, given that they are, or certainly will be, marooned in oceans of degradation and agricultural land, and have to resist an inexhaustible demand for natural resources. Will they be able to maintain their original diversity in the long run?

In relation to bears:[3]

– the giant panda (China) is highly endangered, with only 1,100 left in the wild, and is vulnerable to inbreeding;

– the sun bear (SE Asia) is the last known bear and is captured for the pet trade – there has also been serious destruction of its habitat;

– the sloth bear (India/Nepal) is captured for use as a dancing bear and is poached for its gall bladder (bears' gall bladders are used, along with those of many other animals, for traditional Chinese medicine) – there are maybe less than 10,000 in the wild;

– the spectacled bear (S America) is shot as a pest and suffers from loss of habitat – there may be less than 10,000 left;

– the American black bear (population 500,000) is hunted for sport and its gall bladder; while the brown bear is hunted and used as a dancing bear – its numbers have decreased by 50% in the last 150 years; and

---

2   Stuart, C and T, *Africa's Vanishing Wildlife*, 1996, pp 3–4, Shrewsbury: Sawn Hill Press.

3   From Libearty, Bears in the Wild, the World Campaign for Bears, WSPA: London.

– the Asiatic black bear (SE Asia) is captured for the pet trade and for its gall bladder – there are a maximum of 50,000 left in the wild (all threatened), while the polar bear is a vulnerable species – although its numbers are now stable at 25,000, its habitat is under threat from oil spillage/exploration.

Extinction faces many bird and animal species; for instance, only 60 Javan rhino exist, 300 Siberian tigers and 24 south China tigers. Seventy-seven parrot species are in danger of extinction, the Caspian tiger became extinct in the 1970s, and in the 1980s it was the turn of the Javan tiger.[4] Some 1,111 bird species are threatened with global extinction.

The solution to the problem of extinction

Organisational structure

One of the most important NGOs operating at the international level, merits special mention, is the International Union for the Conservation of Nature (IUCN), also known as the World Conservation Union. This is a federative membership organisation, founded in 1948, consisting primarily of governments or their agencies but also including scientific, professional and conservation bodies such as the World Wide Fund for Nature (WWF) with which it has close association. In this respect it is unique among environmental bodies. By its 40th anniversary in 1988 it included 61 States and 128 government agencies, 383 national and international NGOs, and a few affiliated members. The diversity of its membership is remarkable.

IUCN has a small secretariat located in Gland, Switzerland, and an Environmental Law Centre in Bonn, in the Federal Republic of Germany. It convenes a triennial General Assembly of its members, as a deliberative forum and for the passing of resolutions which members present to government and relevant bodies, but it operates mainly through numerous standing commissions and committees. The former include Ecology, National Parks, and Protected Areas; Environmental Policy, Law and Administration; Species Survival and Environmental Planning. IUCN lacks real powers, however, its resolutions do not bind and it has no enforcement mechanisms.

Nevertheless, it has played a catalytic role in initiating new legal developments. (It early perceived the need to link environment and development and prepared the IUCN/WWF/UNEP World Conservation Strategy published in 1980, in which FAO and Unesco collaborated. This lays down principles for conservation of living resources and for legal developments which will enable their sustainable utilisation.) A revised strategy for the 1990s has now been prepared. It identifies the need for sustainable development, identifies the main issues, sets targets within a framework of a mutually supportive efforts but at the time of writing omits to

---

4   Figure from Birdlife International – a global conservation alliance, Cambridge: Birdlife International.

identify the rule of law in securing its goals; it is to be hoped that this will be remedied in the final version. Although IUCN's mission is now primarily to provide knowledge and leadership for sustainable development by publishing studies, issuing its *Bulletin* and organising meetings, it helps governments develop international declarations and conventions, sometimes providing first drafts through its Law Centre. It has worked on a Convention on Preservation of Biological diversity and an Earth Charter or Declaration for adoption by the UNCED, and has previously contributed to the 1972 World Heritage Convention, the 1973 Convention on Trade in Endangered Species, the 1971 Convention on Wetlands of International Importance, and the 1979 Convention on Conservation of Migratory Species of Wild Animals. It seeks, as far as possible, to fill gaps in legal developments, or to co-operate with other organisations in preparing drafts, or in commenting on them.[5]

The Convention on International Trade in Endangered Species of Wild Flora and Fauna (CITES) (the Washington Convention)

The main legislation that protects endangered species is CITES, which covers some 34,000 plants and animals[6] and also regional agreements in relation either to particular areas or to a particular species. The first global agreement to conserve endangered species and their habitat was the Biodiversity Convention (which has already been discussed in relation to the UK's protection of wildlife, in Chapter 8).

CITES was signed in 1973. It regulates international trade in wild animals and prohibits trade in those which are threatened with extinction. It allows some controlled trade in species which are not yet endangered but may become so. There is also a mechanism which allows each country to introduce domestic legislation regulating the export of species not in either of the above categories; the country can then seek the support of other countries in enforcing its domestic legislation. CITES operates a permit system which has to be overseen on a domestic level by a management and scientific authority; there is an international body to oversee the workings of the permit system.

CITES aims to prevent the hunting of endangered species by prohibiting the trade in animals or artefacts. The control is implemented according to three appendices.

Appendix I prohibits the trade in animals threatened with extinction; it requires those persons wishing to export animals to obtain both an import and export permit. Export permits are only granted where a specimen has been lawfully obtained, the granting of a licence will not be detrimental to the species and there are appropriate transport facilities. An import licence can only be granted if it is not detrimental to the species, they have the

---

5   Birnie, P and Boyle, A, *International Law and the Environment*, 1992, pp 77–78, Oxford: Oxford University Press. Reproduced by kind permission of Oxford University Press.

6   From *EIA News*, 1984–1994, London.

appropriate housing, and the trade should not be primarily for commercial purposes. Around 600 animal species and 180 plant species are listed.

Appendix II controls the trade in those animals which are threatened with becoming extinct. For these animals only an export licence is needed. There are 2,500 animal species and 35,000 plant species listed.

Appendix III lists those animals which individual parties to the convention choose to make subject to the regulations and for which the co-operation of other parties is required in controlling trade.

CITES came into force on 1 July 1975 and currently has 124 signatories. The Swiss government is the official depository of the Convention and the Secretariat, based in Geneva, co-ordinates the activities of the Convention. The States meet every two years in a Conference of the Parties. The Conference looks at the procedures to control trade, in order to adapt them where necessary. The Secretariat is supervised and guided by a standing committee. The Secretariat gathers up-to-date information and provides the Parties with permanent technical support. In 1993 the Secretariat issued 57 notifications on enforcement, regulations, scientific organisations, security stamps, captive breeding operations, transmission of documents, meetings and decisions of the standing committee, transport of live specimens, and criteria for the classification of species in the appendices and identification manuals. The Secretariat also provides regular information on the Convention, its implementation and the accession of new parties, as well as publishing technical documents such as identification manuals, training personnel responsible for implementation of the Convention, and supplying technical back-up through advice, expertise and participation in meetings organised by local authorities. It also publishes technical books on the evolution of the convention, and maintains two data bases, one on trade in species and the other on national legislation. It also works to provide information and raise public awareness and carries out enforcement operations and surveillance of trade in Appendix II-listed endangered species.

Each Party must designate one or more Management Authorities to issue permits/certificates. Before these are granted, one or more scientific authorities should be consulted. The permit lasts for six months and covers any international trade – this means any export, re-export, import and introduction from the sea of animals or plants, any part or derivative of specimens of species. The parties frequently use security paper and stamps, as measures to avoid abuse and counterfeits. The management authority must have proof that live specimens will be transported and handled in accordance with IATA regulations on the transportation of wild animals, in order to avoid any risk of injury, damage to health or cruel treatment. There are a certain number of trial derogations from these rules. They can only be used under strictly limited conditions with pre-Convention specimens, those in transit or customs trans-shipment, those bred in captivity or artificially propagated, those intended for non-commercial exchanges between scientists and scientific institutions, those included in travelling exhibitions, and personal objects and household effects.[7]

The UK's Implementation of CITES

In the UK, CITES is administered by the Department of the Environment through its Wildlife Trade licensing branch. Two scientific authorities are designated in the UK in relation to applications for CITES permits and for advice on the conservation status of the species; these are the Joint Nature Conservation Committee for animals and the Royal Botanic Gardens at Kew for plants. The import and export controls are enforced by Customs and Excise. In the UK the legislation that originally implemented CITES was the Endangered Species (Import and Export) Act 1976; this has largely been superseded by the EC CITES Regulations. European Commission Regulations 3626/82 and 3418/83 give the provisions of CITES legal force throughout the EC and set out the rules for importing species into and exporting species from the EC. For some species, they also impose stricter trade controls and restrictions on sale and display.

An Open General Licence (OGL) has been issued allowing the import of non-CITES species covered by the Act without the need to apply for individual licences. However, individual import licences under the Act are required for the import of furskin of any whitecoat pup of the harp seal (*Phoca (Pagophilus) groenlandica*) or the hooded seal (*Cystophora cristata*), or any articles made from them. The Endangered Species (Enforcement) Regulations SI 1985/1155 and the Control of Endangered Species (Designated Ports of Entry) Regulations 1985 SI 1985/1154 reiterate the need for an import and export licence. It is an offence to sell unlawfully obtained animals or any product which contains them. It is also a breach of customs and excise legislation. The list under the UK legislation covers a wider number and range of animals than that found under CITES. If an offence is committed then the animal, etc can be confiscated and the person fined or imprisoned.[8]

There are a number of cases arising under CITES each year. Two such cases are reproduced below:[9]

A taxidermist who encouraged people to kill some of the world's rarest creatures was jailed for two years after pleading guilty to six charges of illegal trafficking in wildlife that were protected under the CITES convention on endangered species, he also had to pay costs of £8,500. S of mid-Wales, who is Dutch, was found to have freezers, an attic and two barns stuffed with more than 500 animals from all over the world when his house was raided. During the trial in May 1996 the court heard among the specimens in his possession were a Siberian tiger, a ring-tailed lemur and a Philippine eagle, which is one

---

7   Information fact sheets from CITES.

8   From The DOE Wildlife Trade Licensing Branch, 1995, London: DOE.

9   *Howl*, Autumn 1996, no 62, p 18. Reproduced by kind permission of Hunt Saboteurs Association, Brighton.

of the most endangered species in the world with only 50 pairs surviving. Some of the specimens were pickled and some frozen ready for preparation for sale to the black market. S already had convictions in France and Germany; after the trial his counsel said 'His business will suffer irreparable damage after today's outcome.'

An egg collector was fined £750 after police found hundreds of eggs from rare and endangered birds in his home. Police noticed that E of Sunderland, was looking very nervous as they searched his garage. After a closer look it was found to have a false ceiling and an oven and cooker had false bottoms. One thousand, two hundred and seventy five eggs were found. E had eggs belonging to species such as the Ruff, Peregrine Falcon, the Avocet and the Red-backed Shrike. The court was told there were only 10 pairs of breeding Ruffs left in the country.

The US's Implementation of CITES[10]

The US has a long history of protecting endangered species. The Lacey Act, passed in 1900, prohibits the import, export, sale, receipt, acquisition or purchase of fish, wildlife or plants that are taken, possessed, transported or sold in violation of federal, State, tribal or foreign law. The Act was amended in 1981. As for wild animals, they must be transported into the US under humane and healthy conditions. The Interior Secretary can also designate certain species as being injurious to humans and prohibit their importation into the US.

US Endangered Species Act 1973

Under s 4 of the Act, animals are listed either as in danger of extinction or as likely to become extinct and thus as endangered or threatened species. The animals are listed by the Secretary of State for the Interior and the US Fish and Wildlife Agency. There is a provision under which a petition can be made to have an animal defined as endangered. However, at the moment there is a moratorium on such listings (at present more than 1,000 species are listed).

Section 7 of the US Endangered Species Act 1973 allows federal agencies to authorise, and/or carry out development projects so long as this does not jeopardise the continued existence of threatened or endangered species. Section 10, as amended, allows for the creation of Habitat Conservation Plans. These plans are designed to protect a species whilst allowing for development. An HCP allows the US Fish and Wildlife Service to permit the taking of endangered species incidental to otherwise lawful activities, when the taking is mitigated by conservation measures. This is meant to encourage creative partnerships between the private sector and government agencies. A typical HCP will outline measures for the maintenance, enhancement and

---

10 Information from US open government site on the Internet.

protection of a habitat area. Some 35 plans are in place, with 130 more under development. There are also voluntary conservation agreements which take the form of management plans. These cover those species listed as endangered or threatened, as well as those proposed for listing or candidates for listing, and the aim is to remove the threats to a listing candidate and so, if this is accomplished in time, avert the need to list the species as endangered.The other provision is for the Fish and Wildlife Service to identify areas that are essential to an endangered or threatened species' survival and conservation. These are designated as Critical Habitat. This is a legally described list of those areas designated. It does not create a wildlife refuge or wilderness area and it does not preclude human activity in an area. The designation only covers the activities of federal agencies which may have an adverse impact on an area. The designation has two effects; first, federal agencies have to consult with the Fish and Wildlife Service on any activities which may adversely affect the habitat; and secondly, it has an educational role, stressing that an area is important. Endangered and threatened species are also covered by recovery programmes. These delineate, justify and schedule the research and management plans necessary to ensure the recovery of a species. Thus there are species-specific recovery goals which are drawn up by identifying and ranking species information and management needs in terms of relative importance and timing for recovery. It will also identify all known recovery actions for a species, estimated associated costs and co-operating agencies. To date, eight species have been recovered and removed from the endangered species list but more than 25 are approaching recovery goals. Some 38% of species on the list are either stable or improving.

The definition of harm to endangered species under the Endangered Species Act 1973 was considered in the following case:

Babitt v Sweet Home Chapter of Communities for a Great Oregon US Supreme Court 1995[11]

This case concerned the definition of harm under the ESA 1973. Section 9(a)(1)(B) makes it unlawful for anyone to 'take' endangered species; this is further defined in s 3(18) as 'to harass, harm, pursue, hunt, shoot, wound, kill, trap, capture or collect, or attempt to engage in any such conduct'. Regulation 50 CFR 17.3 further defines harm as 'an act which actually kills or injured wildlife. Such an act may include significant habitat modification or degradation where it actually kills or injures wildlife by significantly impairing essential behavioural patters, including breeding, feeding, or sheltering.' This regulation was challenged by a coalition of timber groups which filed a suit in the US District Court in Washington, challenging the regulation. Timber industry lawyers argued that the Interior Department which issued the regulation had exceeded its statutory authority under the ESA by defining harm in the regulation to include significant habitat modification or destruction.

---

11   Irvin, WR, *Endangered Species Update*, vol 12, no 7, 1995.

The timber industry's challenge was rejected in 1992 by the US District Court for the District of Columbia. On appeal, the District Court's decision was initially upheld by the US Court of Appeal for the District of Columbia Circuit in 1993. On rehearing in 1994, the Court reversed the decision, stating that Congress had intended that harm should be narrowly construed involving the application of direct force to an individual or endangered species.

The DC's ruling contradicted an earlier ruling by the US Court of Appeals for the Ninth Circuit, *Palila v Hawaii Dept of Land and Natural Resources*, 852 F 2d 1106 (1988). In this case the Ninth Circuit ruled that the State of Hawaii's maintenance of an exotic mouflon sheep herd for sport hunting was destroying the forest habitat of the Palila, an endangered bird, harming the species and constituting a prohibited take under the ESA. The Supreme Court heard the *Sweet Home* case to reconcile the conflict between the circuit's decision. By a vote of six to three the Supreme Court held that the Interior Department's regulation should be upheld on the grounds that; the regulation was consistent with the plain meaning of harm, which is to cause hurt or damage or to injure. This included habitat destruction which results in an actual injury or death to members of an endangered species.

The court also found that the regulation is supported by the broad purposes set forth in s 2(b) of the ESA to protect endangered species and the ecosystem on which they depend. See *Tennessee Valley Authority v Hill* 437 US 153 (1978).

The Court also found support in the reauthorisations of Congress, in particular the 1982 amendment of s 10(a)(1)(B) authorising incidental take permits which indicated that Congress understood the ESA to prohibit indirect as well as deliberate take of endangered species in accordance with the challenged regulation. Within the US, individual States have the responsibility for regulating the use of resident wildlife.

In the US, the legislators have passed the African Elephant Conservation Act as well as the general federal laws restricting the importing and exporting of animals and birds, etc under CITES. The Act was passed in 1988 and forbids the import of raw African ivory from any country other than an ivory-producing country (any African country that contains any part of the population range of African elephant), as well as the US export of African raw ivory. Also forbidden are: the import of African raw or worked ivory that was exported from an ivory-producing country in violation of that country's laws or CITES; imports of worked ivory from any country unless that country has certified that such ivory was derived from legal sources; and the import of raw or worked ivory from a country in which a moratorium is in effect. From 9 June 1989 the US established a moratorium on ivory imports from all countries except for ivory trophies from certain approved countries, and ivory antiques.

Wild Bird Conservation Act 1992

This Act prohibits the import of all CITES-listed birds except for those on an approved list, either by country of origin or wild-caught birds for specific captive breeding facilities. For wild-caught approved birds a management plan provides for the conservation of the species and its habitat; there is a moratorium on trade in any non-CITES species. Exemptions include game birds and indigenous bird species. The Act also establishes an Exotic Bird Conservation Fund that is funded through fines, penalties and donations and which is used for conservation projects in their native countries, under the Act.

The problem of enforcement

CITES is seen as an example of a successful international treaty:[12]

> [The] Convention is attractive to the 'producer' nations who see controls at the place of imports as well as the place of export as essential weapons in their fight to protect their valuable wildlife resources from poachers and illegal traders. The 'consumer' nations support it because without controls their legitimate dealers might have no raw material in which to trade in the generations to come.

However, while the Treaty is well supported there are problems in relation to its enforcement. One of the greatest problems is in combating the illegal trade in wildlife.

For example, in relation to the wild bird trade, the US Fish and Wildlife Service is underfunded and the EU has no enforcement agency. Some of the techniques used by the illegal traders include the falsification/related mis-use of documents, the under-declaration of numbers and the mis-declaration of species. Many employees identifying species of birds are not properly trained.

Australia is also a signatory to CITES. The legislation which covers CITES in Australia is the Wildlife Protection (Regulation of Exports and Imports) Act 1982. The body that administers the Act is the Australian Nature Conservation Agency (ANCA). The Australian Customs Agency, as in many countries, is at the forefront of the fight against the illegal importation of endangered species.[13]

As in many countries, problems arise when a person has an endangered species at some distance from the customs barrier, as this creates difficulties of proof. In the US this has been resolved through the Lacey Act; however, Australia has no such corresponding legislation. The problem is aggravated by differences in legislation and enforcement practices in the various States.

Halstead has identified some basic provisions that have been enshrined in legislation in one or more States. Halstead argues that these measures should all apply in every State. These include, for intrastate transactions:

---

12 Lyster, S, *International Wildlife Law*, 1994, p 241, Cambridge: CUP. Reproduced by kind permission of Cambridge University Press.
13 Halstead, B, *Wildlife Legislation in Australia*, 1994, Canberra: Australian Institute of Criminology.

– maintenance by licence-holders of up-to-date records of all transactions and changes in stock;

– submission by all licence-holders of regular returns to the licensing authority;

– notification of names and number of both parties required;

– application of strong penalties to taking from the wild;

– where the wildlife is consigned, clear indication of the licence number of the sender and receiver;

– strong penalties for being in possession of wildlife illegally acquired from any jurisdiction;

– penalties for engaging in transactions with unauthorised persons to apply to all licence-holders;

– strong penalties for failure to comply with record-keeping requirements and submission of returns;

– strong penalties for false or misleading information;

– restriction of licences to individuals in order to locate responsibility;

– limitation of all transactions and licences to licensed premises;

– some assessment of the licence applicant's suitability, ie verification of any records for wildlife offences.

For interstate transactions:

– authorisation from the outside State prior to the import/export transaction;

– notification and approval of exports and imports;

– proof of their legality to be demonstrated prior to the transaction;

– mutual recognition between the States of origin and destination of classification of species concerned.

Other difficulties identified by Halstead include the problems that arise because the burden of proof of illegality is on the prosecutor. In many Australian States, however, there is a different onus of proof. There are also differences in relation to the range of species that can be held. The use of record-keeping as an enforcement tool varies across States and Halstead argues that up-to-date information is needed which is well maintained and comprehensive, and the retrieval system should be sophisticated enough to allow searching and cross-referencing of data.

Obviously it is important for those countries with endangered species to be able to control the movement of animals within their own States and also to other countries. It is important that CITES is enforced uniformly around the world in order to ensure that endangered species can survive.

Obstacles to successful protection under CITES

The main factor hindering the reform of trade is economic. Many countries rely on wild birds and animals for valuable export cash. Military regimes and corrupt rulers may rely on animals and birds to finance military expenditure.

The other problem is that legal trading often covers up illegal trading, as it may be difficult to establish the origins of a wild bird or animal. It is important to ensure that animals are not removed from the protection of Appendix I, as this puts commercial pressure on governments from dealers. Many governments do not have the resources to protect animals from illegal poaching, let alone to police a legal trade:[14]

> As species become rarer and their trade value increases, some dealers are stockpiling products like rhino horn and are actively speculating on the extinction of the species to send their profits soaring. Asian rhino horn has already reached a high of $60,000 per kilo – five times the price of gold. The legal wildlife trade amounts to billions of dollars. However, this does not take into account the massive illegal traffic in wildlife, estimated as the third largest illegal trade after drugs and weapons. In 1992, this brutal and destructive business was estimated to be worth around $3 billion – and it is growing, often using the legal commerce to mask its cynical operation.

Because of the problems of illegal trading there have been calls to legalise various aspects of trade in endangered species:[15]

> Several arguments are made in favour of a legalised horn trade. The first and most important is that rhinos do not have to be killed to produce a harvest of horn, even though poachers certainly kill rhinos. Horns continue to grow throughout life to counteract wear on their tips, although growth areas are slower in older animals ... Horns that have been lost in fights or removed regrow, but in a slightly deformed shape ... Rhino horns can be cut off without discomfort as they comprise compressed hair and are not enervated ... though it will usually be necessary to restrain the rhino by immobilisation. The second argument is that considerable quantities of confiscated and found horn are now building up in warehouses, and future de-horning operations of rhinos will produce increasing quantities of horn that would otherwise be added to these stockpiles. Dehorning as means of protecting rhinos has been discussed since the 1950s, but was first attempted in 1989 in Namibia ... It is now being carried out as a routine measure on all translocated rhinos in Zimbabwe. The third main argument is the economic consideration that selling such a valuable product legally would produce a much greater income per unit area of wildlife land for re-investment in rhino conservation than many alternatives available to State and private land-owners ...

> Many of these arguments will founder on the philosophy, whether rational or not, of individual conservationists, range States and other parties to CITES. In

---

14 *EIA News,* June 1994, London.

15 Leader-Williams, N, *The World Trade in Rhino Horn: a Review,* A Traffic Network Report, 1992, pp 34–36, Cambridge. Reproduced by kind permission of Traffic International.

the recent debate on whether African elephants should be transferred to Appendix I of CITES, the African continent became polarised between a group of southern African countries that favoured sustainable trade in ivory versus the rest of Africa that saw rampant and illegal over-exploitation and wished for a total ban on trade. Most parties to CITES sided with the majority of the range States and the majority of Africa's elephant populations, and voted for a ban and its continuance in 1989 and 1992. In one sense, therefore, a discussion on the possible opening of a legal rhino horn trade could not be started at a more inopportune time, given that the majority of world opinion is in favour of international trade bans as the method for saving Africa's endangered pachyderms. However, the situation with respect to rhinos differs markedly from that of elephants for two reasons. First, the southern countries now possess most of Africa's rhinos ... and therefore the countries' views on how they see best to conserve their rhinos merit wider attention than they were granted in the ivory debate. Second, if the ivory trade ban is indeed working, this is most probably because of a voluntary reduction in demand by users of a luxury commodity in response to the publicity surrounding the plight of the elephants and the 'ivory ban', rather than the ban *per se*. In contrast, Chinese users of traditional medicines appear unwilling to cease including rhino horn in their portions ... even though substitutes like water buffalo horn are as effective pharmacologically ... Therefore, the much longer-standing trade bans for rhino horn have been ineffective because they appear not to have caused a voluntary reduction in demand.

Aside from the philosophical arguments, what evidence is there to suggest that a legalised trade could benefit rhino conservation? Theoretical economic models suggest that the sales of confiscated and harvested horn will alter the supply curve and depress the equilibrium price ... Assuming that the number of animals killed by poachers is an increasing function of the price of horn ... then legal sales should be a preferred option to destroying or stockpiling confiscated material, or not harvesting horn ... Clearly more empirical work is needed on the relationship between commodity prices and demand under legal and illegal trade regimes, but these theoretical models on the economics of crime and confiscation point the way forward. More empirical models show that it would be profitable to dehorn secure populations of rhinos on private land, but suggest it would be necessary to dehorn rhinos for their protection very regularly to make poaching unprofitable on State land ... Further work is also necessary here, but these models again point the way forward. Whatever, the economic arguments, however, any proposals to re-open a legal trade in rhino horn must be translated into successful policies.

The South African proposal for transferring its white rhino population to Appendix II notes that the transfer of one species to a different appendix should not lead to a reduction in controls for other species. It is for that reason that proposals to open up trade in African rhino horn need further consideration. At this stage it would appear that there is insufficient knowledge of the following:

a) the dynamics of the trade in African and Asian rhino horn and the extent to which the trades may differ. To date it is known that 'Fire' (Asian) horn is more effective than 'Water' (African) horn and that Asian horn is considerably more expensive ...

However, until we know more about the differences and similarities in the trade in the two types of horn, it cannot be said with certainty that a southern African trade would not have serious repercussions for the highly endangered Javan and Sumatran rhinos. The situation with Indian rhino horn also merits investigation, for it is building up into stockpiles while rhinos in Assam are being poached by such new methods as electrocution ...

b) the volumes of horn traded and demanded by world markets. There are educated guesses of the approximate volumes of horn traded over the past two decades which have been justified on various grounds and disputed on others ... This parameter needs better estimation in order to assess the potential supply available from aspiring producers and its effect upon present price structures and demand for illegal horn. The recent study in Taiwan breaks new ground in having counted the total number of pharmacy shops and estimated the number of medicinal outlets in a particular country ... With a large sample of shops having been surveyed also for stocking horn, this has enabled an estimate to be made of the total stocks of horn held in the country. Further unpublished work by Nowell and her colleagues has shown that a sample of pharmacists and doctors prescribe and sell on average around 45g of rhino horn annually.[16] When multiplied by the total number of pharmacies and clinics selling horn ... this suggests the consumption of a total of 486kg annually. Hopefully Nowell's approach can be extended to provide an estimate of annual demand in other consuming nations.

c) the likelihood that the trade will continue in its present form in the foreseeable future. The argument has been made that the trade in horn is traditional and will continue. However, there are no published data on the age structure on users of traditional medicines, and whether younger people, now more subjected to Western ideas ands conservation appeals, are coming on stream as consumers of traditional medicines or turning to aspirins.

d) the role of stockpiling in influencing illegal demand for rhinos in the wild, and the role that legalising a trade in rhino horn might have on reducing speculation and demand for rhino horn. Investigations of demand have centred mainly on quantifying trends in consumption. Economic studies of the role of stockpiling on influencing volumes demand, using case studies for other commodities, would seem a good starting point for examining whether or not a legalised trade in rhino horn would reduce the demand side that is driven by speculators.

In summary, the question of whether or not a legalised trade in rhino horn should be re-opened is a complex issue, and this review has not produced the answer, one way or another. However, it is hoped that the review will provide the basis for a rational debate on the issue before the next conference of the Parties to CITES, and that it highlights areas where further research is needed.

---

16 See Nowell, K, Chiu, W and Pei, K, *The Horns of a Dilemma: the Market for Rhino-horn in Taiwan*, 1992, Cambridge: Traffic International.

Habitat protection

Even if the trade in endangered species can be stopped or curtailed, the animals still face a range of other threats to their survival. One of the greatest threats is the loss of their habitat. The international protection of habitat has been considered in Chapter 8, but it is important to realise the severe impact that habitat loss is having on the efforts to conserve and save endangered species.

The importance of preserving habitat is examined in a report for the World Society for the Protection of Animals, *Slaughter of the Apes.*[17] The report states that the tropical rainforests in Africa were originally extensive but are now confined to the Central African countries of Zaire, Congo, Cameroon and Gabon. These forests are rich in terms of biodiversity and yet only 7% of them are protected, and in many areas law enforcement is weak if not non-existent. Africa is the third-largest producer of tropical timber at 11 million cubic metres of wood a year, compared with 92 million in Asia and 28 million in Latin America. Forestry operations are rarely, if ever, carried out in a planned or sustainable manner. Eighty-seven per cent of the timber goes to the EU; the UK is the biggest importer by value. Much of the development is undertaken by foreign companies – of 150 logging licences issued un 1987/88, only 23 were operated by Cameroonian concerns in. Sixty-seven foreign companies operated there and controlled 81% of the exploitable forest. Approximately 40% of these companies were EU subsidiaries of multinational companies, 20 of which had been awarded logging concessions. Development aid is also used to help the logging trade. Often this pays for new roads used by the European logging companies. The roads built provide the impetus behind the bush meat trade and are often used to transport the meat from the forests to towns. The development of the forests by the logging companies has also dramatically increased the populations of the regions. For example, the report states that in an area around Mbang in the heart of Cameroon's South Eastern logging district, the population increased from 14,000 to 23,000 in four years. This provides a widely expanded market for bush meat. The hunting of fruit-eating mammals and birds poses a long-term threat to the survival of the habitat as they play a key role in seed dispersal. The report focuses on the plight of apes, giving the numbers of apes left in Africa as up to 200,000 chimpanzees, 3,000–5,000 eastern lowland gorillas, and 50,000–100,000 western lowland gorillas. The 1,500 bonobo gorillas are listed as threatened, and there are only 650 mountain gorillas left. These are listed by the IUCN as endangered.

The report estimates that, in one area of Cameroon alone, up to 800 gorillas a year and maybe 400 chimps are being killed. The International Primate Protection League has estimated 400–600 gorillas being killed in Northern Congo.

---

17   Pearce, J, *Slaughter of the Apes* , 1995, London: WSPA.

The report concludes that:[18]

The hunting of protected species in Africa's tropical forests is escalating out of control. Logging companies, as developers of the forests, are the prime cause of this increase. By transporting hunters, distributing bush meat and allowing the sale of meat to their workers they are promoting and assisting in poaching. They are therefore actively breaking national laws. Until now most of the debate concerning the impact of logging has concentrated on the amount of forest which is cleared. This report shows that although some regulations on selective logging are being implemented, nothing is being done to prevent hunters from stripping the forests of wildlife. Even schemes which have been set up to certify sustainable logging operations appear to take little account of the effects of hunting. In African forests, where clear cutting is rarely practised, this eradication of wildlife may be the most significant threat to the region's biodiversity, damaging not only the animal species but the entire future of the ecosystem.

The report makes eight recommendations:

– an international convention should be introduced to govern logging practices throughout the world;

– the charter should cover not just tree loss but also the effects of hunting;

– any companies operating logging concessions should adhere to strict guidelines controlling hunting and should respect national laws;

– governments should reaffirm and properly enforce existing hunting laws;

– any tropical timber sold and labelled as sustainable should be subject to an evaluation of the impact of its extraction on wildlife;

– a review of all European companies should be undertaken to establish their policies on hunting;

– sales of the gun cartridge should be banned.

Until these provisions are in place, the logging companies should prohibit the transportation of bush meat on their vehicles, prohibit commercial hunters from operating within their concessions and prohibit employees from purchasing or eating bush meat and provide them with other food sources.

Reforming CITES

A report by the Environmental Investigations Agency highlights the importance of CITES:[19]

---

18 *Ibid*, p 15.

19 Environmental Investigations Agency, *News*, 1994, p 5, London: EIA Reproduced by kind permission of the Environmental Investigations Agency.

Prior to 1989, between 70,000 and 100,00 elephants were being poached every year to supply the international ivory trade. Africa's elephant population was halved from 1.3 million elephants in 1979 to just 624,000 in 1988.

Highly organised poaching gangs swept down from the north to east, west, central and southern Africa throughout the 1970s and 1980s. High-level corruption, wars, murder and escalating prices for ivory caused poaching to intensify. The CITES ban caused ivory prices and elephant poaching to drop dramatically virtually overnight. As the major consumers of Europe, Japan and America closed their markets to ivory imports, the impact was profound. Tanzania had been losing up to 10,000 elephants a year to poaching. Since the ban, fewer than 100 elephants a year have been killed there. Wildlife enforcement officers from all regions of Africa have told EIA that the CITES ban has made it much easier to crack down on illegal trade. The psychological impact of the ban throughout Africa has often been dismissed but EIA investigations reveal that it has in fact been profound. Even in countries such as those in Central Africa, where there is minimal risk involved in poaching, the ban has reduced all profit and discouraged poachers. It has also served to make countries more aware of their elephants as tourist attractions and therefore a previously untapped source of revenue which should be protected.

Whilst there have been successes with some species, many animals still become extinct each day and the implementation of various Endangered Species Acts needs to be improved. The adequacy of the US ESA is examined in *Endangered Species Recovery – finding the lessons, improving the process.*[20] The book begins by putting the problem into perspective: we are set to lose 20% of the earth's biological diversity; 100 or more species are becoming extinct each day; extinctions in the rain forest are 10,000 times greater than background extinction rates; in the US one-third of freshwater fish are seriously harmed by environmental problems; about 3,000 plants and animals are in danger of becoming extinct and by the year 2,000, 675 US plant species may be extinct. The book's authors argue that 'poor implementation of the ESA is itself a major cause of the continuing decline of species, and professionals and organisations are significantly responsible for the quality of implementation'.[21]

In the US, 650 species are listed under the ESA and approximately 600 other species are on the waiting list for classification as category 1 species. For category 2 species there may be more than 3,000 species where the current data to list them as endangered is not conclusive. The service is slow listing – 16 years on average just to list each category 1 species, and so on average only 44 species are listed each year. Since the passing of the ESA, 16 species have been removed from the endangered species list – seven because they became extinct, four because the populations were higher than at first thought or the species had become disqualified due to hybridisation with non-listed species, and five because their levels recovered.

20   Clark, T, Reading, R, and Clarke, A, *Endangered Species Recovery – finding the lessons, improving the process*, 1994, Washington: Island Press.

21   *Ibid*, p4.

This has led to criticism of the ESA for various reasons, including: imprecise standards for delineating species standards; inappropriate units of protection; undue attention to high-profile species; insufficient protection of habitat; inadequacy of the recovery plan process; inadequacy of interagency consultation; inappropriate discounting of uncertainty; insufficient consideration of economic factors; and lack of funding.

Some possible reforms to CITES include:

– Adoption of the precautionary principle. This would require evidence to be provided that populations would not be adversely affected by trade. At the moment there is often no basic information on the species, eg in relation to the numbers in the general populations.

– A change in emphasis in relation to those animals protected under Appendix I to those animals that *can* be traded rather than *not* traded. This would make life much easier for enforcement officers, and would avoid an ever-lengthening list, as well as reflecting the precautionary principle rather than being reactive. This is important as, in 1991, a new species of the bishop (a type of) bird was discovered. Unfortunately the birds were found at the premises of a bird exporter in Tanzania; two out of the four were already dead and two died later.

– Development of a sustainable trade. This would include: population surveys for each species; monitoring the populations to assess effects of trade; biological studies of reproduction, natural mortality, behaviour and nutrition; studies of population dynamics and trends; habitat and ecological studies; trade studies to estimate the expected level of illegal trade and other use of birds and animals; trade mortality studies to ascertain the number of birds and animals dying prior to export. For each exporting country: vet checks at point of export and vet checks at all trade premises; management staff to administer the trade, issue permits, collect levies and liaise with importing countries and the CITES Secretariat; scientific staff to advise of changes in species status and oversee scientific studies; enforcement officers to inspect all facilities and shipments; intelligence officers to infiltrate illegal trade. These controls should be repeated for importing countries which should also appoint enforcement officers to inspect all quarantines, holding premises and pet shops, as well as points of import.

A POSSIBLE SOLUTION TO THE PROBLEM OF PROTECTING ENDANGERED SPECIES

One recent development with a part to play in saving endangered species is ecotourism. However, this industry/activity will also have to be regulated to prevent abuses and the destruction of animals and their habitat if it is to be part of a sustainable survival strategy for endangered species. 'The first stirrings of eco-tourism started when holiday-makers returned from popular tourist sites complaining of environmental destruction caused by the growth of tourist villages.'[22] The RSPCA article lists some problem areas:

–   Africa, where wildlife safaris disturb wild animals and elephant poaching takes place for ivory souvenirs;

–   Australia, where souvenirs made from kangaroos' testicles are on sale;

–   Belize, where sewage from tourist villages is killing the coral reef;

–   Greece, where tourists are disturbing the nesting grounds of turtles on beaches;

–   Kenya, where chimpanzee skulls are sold as souvenirs;

–   Malaysia, where railway development is destroying the forests;

–   Nepal, where trekkers are polluting the Himalayan trail, home of the rare snow leopard;

–   Peru, where trekkers are polluting the Inca trail in the Andes;

–   Rwanda, where gorillas have caught dysentery after contact with tourists;

–   Singapore, where the building of ports is destroying fish breeding grounds;

–   Spain, where photographers use chimps and lion cubs as props;

–   West Indies, where tree-felling has taken place for golf courses;

–   the Alps, where acid rain caused by tourist traffic and skiing destroys alpine pasture.

Other tourism-related threats include:

–   animals' natural routines being disturbed in the Kenyan Amboesi National Park, where a cheetah nearly starved to death because demands from tourists never gave it the peace to hunt;

–   road deaths caused by increased traffic from fly drive holidays;

–   unregulated sewage and garbage disposal around lodges and campsites which harms animals and disrupts their normal feeding patterns as well as destroying their habitat;

–   hunting safaris, still permitted in some East African countries;

–   demand for wildlife souvenirs.

The following report looks at the general issues surrounding tourism and the development of ecotourism. It also provides practical guidelines for those with involvement in the tourist industry:[23]

---

22   RSPCA, *Animal Life*, Summer 1995, Horsham: RSPCA.

23   Ceballos-Lascurain, H, *Tourism, eco tourism and protected areas*, 1996, IV World Congress on National Parks and Protected Areas Gland, Switzerland: International Union for the Conservation of Nature. Reproduced by kind permission of the International Union for the Conservation of Nature.

In recent years a specific category of nature-based tourism has developed along these lines. 'Ecological tourism', or 'Ecotourism' as defined by IUCN's Ecotourism Programme is 'environmentally responsible travel and visitation to relatively undisturbed natural areas, in order to enjoy and appreciate nature (and any accompanying cultural features – both past and present) that promotes conservation, has low visitor impact, and provides for beneficially active socio-economic involvement of local populations' ... The Ecotourism Society's definition is similar: 'ecotourism is responsible travel to natural areas that conserves the environment and sustains the well-being of local people' ... In both definitions, ecotoursim denoted tourism with a normative element. A response to the desire to permit access to areas of natural beauty, ecotourism's underlying premise is that the enjoyment of future generations should not be affected negatively by that of today's visitors ... it provides its greatest benefits (especially if applied at a local level) through pursuit of a widespread but controlled 'small is beautiful' philosophy.

The report states that while tourism is important in protected areas to experience the natural world, this also poses serious problems such as over-visitation, the opening of national parks without appropriate management plans, misuse of natural resources, the construction of buildings and infrastructure, increased pollution, soil erosion and impact on rocks, the impact on water resources and vegetation. The report examines the impact of tourism in general on wildlife and ecosystems:[24]

The most extreme effects of tourism on wildlife arise from hunting, shooting and fishing, all of which may severely deplete local populations of certain species. But it is also well established that the mere presence of people can be sufficient to disrupt the activities of wild animals (particularly birds and large mammals) whatever the recreational activity or number of people involved. A survey of the breeding status of the little tern *(Sterna albifrons)* in Britain provides a number of instances of breeding failure of the species, apparently caused simply by the presence of fishermen and bathers on nesting beaches.

In some instances, disturbances may be caused more by the equipment people use in association with recreational activities, than by the people themselves. Noise, for example, produced by portable radios and the engines of motorboats and motor vehicles can be extremely alarming for animals. And various forms of pleasure craft can affect bird life merely by their presence. Motorboats and sailing craft can also disturb waterfowl in deeper water, especially during those periods when some of these birds are flightless. Bird species that build floating nests on inland waters, such as the great crested grebe *(Podiceps cristatus)*, are likewise easily affected by motor boats and water-skiers.

Some waterfowl – particularly nesting waterfowl – are agitated by punts, canoes and rowing boats. This is because the latter have shallow draught and can approach close to the water's edge. Disturbance of water fowl may even cause these birds to desert water-bodies that they used to frequent. Tourists taking boat rides in the Celestun area of the Yucatan Peninsula in Mexico cause much disturbance to the enormous concentrations of flamingos *(Phoenicopterus ruber)* that winter here. (Boat operators should maintain a minimum distance of 200 meters between their boats and the flocks). Boating activities may affect fish populations too, particularly as a result of oil spillage or due to noise.

Some bird species are of course much less sensitive to human presence. For example, evidence suggests that breeding success among the red grouse *(Lagopus lagopus)* and ptarmigan *(Lagopus mutus)* on ski slopes, is not affected by people using the cable cars or walking through the area. Similarly, on the Galapagos Islands, tourists walk amidst nesting sea birds to no (apparent) ill effect. However, the blundering of uninformed walkers, picnickers, or fishermen, will disrupt the breeding activities of many bird species and also, for example, of turtles. Such situations may be aggravated if people wear brightly coloured clothing.

Many mammal and bird species will alter their behaviour patterns if disturbance becomes severe. For instance, deer and chamois may avoid areas frequented by people during the day. In general, animals of open habitats are those that are most susceptible to human presence. There are indications that, for some species at least, it is frequency of human presence rather than the number of people present at any one time, that is the most important factor.

Consumption of wildlife by tourists can be harmful to local populations if that wildlife is not controlled. For instance, demand for sea food by tourists can have a severe impact on local fisheries and threaten wildlife populations within protected areas. Spiny lobster and conch populations are now much reduced in the Caribbean, and consequently luxury foods in many places, consumed in hotels rather than as a staple by local people. Tourism has also been largely responsible for the enormous increase in the marine curio trade. Corals and shells are sold in resorts throughout the world, and often poached from marine parks. Tortoiseshell is still popular, although its sale is illegal in most countries.

Other species benefit from tourism activities, but often to the detriment of rarer species. Organic litter left at campsites and picnic areas is 'collected' by scavenging species. There are many examples of this, especially in temperate countries. Observed long-term effects of tourist litter include:

– immigration and build-up in rat populations;

– local increases in house sparrow populations;

– increase in local populations of black-backed, herring and common gulls, jackdaws and foxes in the UK;

– habitat changes and population localisation of the brown and grizzly bears attracted by picnic rubbish in US national parks, and migrations of wild boar during the winter into areas of Belgium where they had not previously been seen, due to increased availability of camp-site rubbish have also been observed.

But although many animal species are directly affected by outdoor recreational activities, many more are affected indirectly by alterations in their habitat. For instance, if a ground flora is eradicated by trampling, insects dependant upon that ground flora will also disappear. Likewise, if a flooded gravel pit is planted with marsh vegetation for the benefit of wild-fowling interests, not only wildfowl but also a host of other vertebrate and invertebrate species will colonise the habitats that develop, possibly displacing species that formerly inhabited the area.

Some ecosystems and habitats are particularly vulnerable to development pressures. This applies especially to marine ecosystems and habitats since these are often the foci of tourism activity. For instance, less visually attractive habitats such as mangroves and marshes, are often drained and used for resort construction. And since visitors generally want a view of the sea and easy access to the beach, hotels tend to be sited close to the tide line. This can result in changes in natural sand movement, and accretion, and lead to serious erosion. Other activities that are often associated with tourism development, such as coast stabilisation, causeway construction and mariculture development, can also have severe negative impacts.

The report goes on to suggest practical tips for developing ecotourism, including the creation of an ecotourism strategy providing environmental impact assessments of tourism and guidelines for tourists, operators and those providing tourist facilities.[25]

CASE STUDY – THE PROTECTION OF WHALES

The historical background to the protection of whales

The report below gives an interesting account of the history of whales, beginning with Aristotle, who was the first person to write about whales, and then considering the celebration of whales in Maori culture, and the shrines to dead whales in Vietnam and Japan. The Basques began whaling in the 11th century, followed by the Dutch and English, and whaling then spread to the US. In the 19th century whaling was revolutionised by steam-powered whaling boats and the exploding grenade that was attached to a harpoon. These factory ships killed more whales in four decades than had been killed in the previous four centuries. In 1925 the League of Nations recommended that the whaling industry should be regulated, to stop overhunting, and in 1930 the Bureau of International Whaling Statistics was set up by the International Council for the Exploration of the Sea. The first treaty on whales, the Convention for the Regulation of Whaling, was signed in 1931 by 22 nations; unfortunately the largest whaling nations were not parties to the agreement and in that year 43,000 whales were hunted.

---

25 This report is based on papers given at the World Parks Congress. The Congress passed a recommendation – the Caracas Declaration which was adopted in 1992 at the United Nations Conference on Environment and Development.

The chair of WWF was also the Chair of IUCN's Species Survival Commission which had a cetacean specialist group. The 1964 List of rare mammals and birds (the precursor to the IUCN red data book) listed six species of great whales. Until 1972 the IWC did not set catch limits by individual species of whales, but grouped the commercially important species of Baleen whale together, and only in the Antarctic. Quotas were given in Blue Whale Units. The report gives an interesting account of how the WWF lobbied the various agencies for a moratorium on commercial whaling:[26]

Even though the true extent of the killing was not known at the time, public concern and anger at what was happening to the great whales was building up rapidly in many countries around the world, especially among WWF supporters. 'Saving the whales' came to symbolise the fast-growing concern for saving the whole planet from overexploitation by humans. As Sir Peter Scott said in 1972: 'If we cannot save the whales from extinction we have little chance of saving mankind and the life-supplying biosphere'.

WWF helped channel this public concern into action at the 1972 United Nations Conference on the Human Environment at Stockholm. A symbolic whale-sized balloon led a procession through the streets of Stockholm, and whales were the focus of much discussion. With the help of vigorous lobbying of the delegates, a recommendation calling for a 10-year moratorium on commercial whaling was adopted – including Norway, the only nation conducting commercial whaling 23 years later. One abstention was Japan, the most important whaling country. Japan recorded its technical reasons for abstaining, but also declared that 'it was favourable to a moratorium on commercial whaling'.

Although this landmark recommendation was endorsed by the UN General Assembly, and was later reaffirmed several times by the UNEP Governing Council, the IWC rejected it. At the IWC meeting only two weeks after the Stockholm Conference, Peter Scott again appealed in vain to the delegates and heed world opinion and to stop defying 'the collective conscience of mankind'. Only four members (US, UK, Argentina and Mexico) out of the 14 members of the Commission present at the meeting voted for a moratorium.

During the next few months international support for a 10-year moratorium on commercial whaling reached an all time high: On the opening day of the 1973 meeting of the IWC in London, conservationists published in the form of an advertisement in *The Times* of London an open letter to the Commission under the headline, ' One is killed every 20 minutes: Is this carnage necessary?'

Signatories of this open letter to the IWC – which urged the IWC to uphold the Stockholm recommendation – were WWF president and Chairmen, HRH Prince Bernhard of the Netherlands, Sir Peter Scott, WWF National Organisations in the UK and the US, and the IUCN President and Director General.

---

26 Kempf, E and Phillips, C, *Whales in the Wild,* World Wildlife Fund Special Species Report 1995, pp 6–8, London: World Wildlife Fund. Reproduced with kind permission of World Wildlife Fund.

As of 1973, the USSR and Japan were hunting around 80% of the world's whales. Dr Sidney Holt, then the advisor on Marine Affairs with the Food and Agriculture Organisation (FAO) of the United Nation's Department of Fisheries, and other scientists questioned the principles and methods used by the IWC to regulate whaling and set catch quotas. A proposal for the 10-year moratorium was put forward by the US at the meeting and was defeated. WWF kept the pressure on the world's whalers to stop the unregulated slaughter and in October of that year renewed the call for a moratorium on the hunting of whales at its 3rd International Congress in Bonn, Germany.

In order to alleviate the growing global concern over the fate of the world's whales, a compromise was struck. In 1974, a new management procedure (NMP) for whales was adopted by the IWC. This strategy was an attempt – for the first time ever – to manage whales on a 'sustainable basis'. Catch quotas were set on a stock by stock and species by species basis. The NMP also aimed at fully protecting severely depleted whale populations in order to maximise their chances of recovery. The responsibility for developing the NMP was placed on the IWC's Scientific Committee.

Within a few years it became obvious that the NMP had failed. Whale populations were continuing to decline. The whalers were not providing the data to the IWC which the Scientific Committee could use to access more realistically the status of whale stocks. Under the NMP, whalers could kill the same number of whales as they had previously done, until evidence showed that these whale stocks were declining. This did not motivate whaling nations to provide information or data to the IWC which would lower the number of whales they could hunt ... By 1978 the atmosphere of the IWC had undergone a sea change. It had acquired new members, many of then conservation-minded. people around the globe were listening to 'whale songs', first recorded by scientists Dr Roger Payne and Katy Payne, and television viewers were spell bound by underwater images of *Survival* Anglia's *Gentle Giants of the Pacific*, filmed by world renowned underwater cameraman, Al Giddings. Whale enthusiast flocked to Hawaii, Mexico's Gulf of California, and Cape Cod to witness firsthand the mystery of the world's whales. They swam with them, photographed them leaping from the water, and listened to their voices vibrate the boats from which they beheld these wonders of nature.

Scientists and environmentalist joined forces. Massive demonstrations were held protesting against the whaling nations. In London, in 1979, just before the opening of the annual IWC meeting, thousands of people rallied at Trafalgar Square where Sir Peter Scott announced that a million signatures had been presented to prime minister Margaret Thatcher by WWF's junior unit, the Wildlife Youth Service. The petition pressed all Members of Parliament to support a ban on whaling.

During the 1979 meeting, a moratorium on all deep sea whaling using factory ships for whales other than minkes was carried by a vote of 18 to two, with Japan and the USSR the only nations to vote against it. At the same meeting, the IWC accepted evidence that Japan's Taiyo fisheries Company, the largest privately-owned fisheries company in the world, had been involved in setting up and dealing with illegal pirate operations.

Also in 1979, a news item in the London *Sunday Times* reported that a prominent British scientist had received a letter from a Soviet scientific worker aboard a factory ship alleging that the USSR was breaking the laws of the whaling industry. His fleet alone had taken 1,916 whales more than its quota. In 1993 the world learnt that this letter was not a hoax: Soviet fleets had been killing massive numbers of the world's most endangered whales right throughout the 1960s and 1970s and selling the meat to Japan. In 1973, a letter sent to WWF from a leading Russian scientist, Dr A V Yablovokov, revealed the 'enormous scale of the Soviet falsifications of the official data for IWC'. Between 1949 and 1980, the USSR killed over 3,200 right whales (protected since 1953) and over 48,450 humpback whales (protected by the IWC in 1963). The new data also shows that 1,433 highly endangered blue whales (protected by the IWC in 1965) were also slaughtered. The Soviet fleet reported that they had killed only 156. Further depletions involved large catches of Bryde's whales and sei whales in the Indian Ocean in 1962, and of sperm whales north of Hawaii up to 1975 when that population was wiped out. All of this happened despite the presence of national observers on the ships, and continued even after an international observer scheme was in force, with Japanese observers.

However, some hope for the whales was on the horizon. In 1979, the IWC declared the entire Indian Ocean – from the coast of Africa west to Australia, and from the Red and Arabian seas and the Gulf of Oman south of 55° latitude – as a whale sanctuary. Development for the proposal grew out of discussions during a joint IUCN/WWF/UNEP workshop on Cetacean Sanctuaries in Mexico in 1978.

At the 1979 meeting of the IWC, the government of the Seychelles successfully approved the proposal for the Indian Ocean sanctuary (IOS), ensuring that commercial whaling would be prohibited there for at least 10 years. In 1989 the IOS was extended for a further three years, and then in 1992 the IWC agreed by consensus that it should remain a sanctuary for an indefinite period. As soon as the sanctuary was declared, WWF-Netherlands began to raise funds to help finance research. In 1980, HRH Prince Bernhard, President of the WWF Netherlands launched an appeal which raised 400,000 guilders (US$250,000) dedicated to the study of living whales in the new sanctuary.

Public outcry over IWC-sanctioned whale hunting and pirate whaling reached a crescendo in 1980: the IWC set quotas for the killing of some 14,000 whales, rejected a moratorium on commercial whaling, ignored the Scientific Committee's recommendation for a zero quota for the sperm whales in the Western North Pacific, and slated Japan for involvement in pirate whaling activity. Japan promised to tighten whale import controls, after admitting that in 1979–80, more than 850 tonnes of whale meat had been imported from Taiwan *via* South Korea. In 1979, its total import of whale meat was 27,000 tonnes.

Conservation-minded delegates went to the 1981 meeting of the IWC in the UK armed with new ammunition to halt the whales' steady plunge to extinction. Many IWC member nations cited and actively supported the 1980 World Conservation Strategy (WCS), prepared by IUCN with the support of

UNEP, WWF, FAO and Unesco. The WCS, recognised globally as a benchmark for conservation, calls for a moratorium on all commercial whaling to last until certain conditions can be fulfilled.

At the July 1981 meeting of the IWC, three separate proposals for a global moratorium were made – and defeated. The IWC declared a zero quota on sperm whale hunting in all sectors except the Western North Pacific – a stock exploited by Japan's coastal stations. The majority of members of the Scientific Committee had recommended protection for that stock as well. The Commission agreed to hold a special meeting of the IWC and the Scientific Committee in March 1982. The IWC also set quotas for 13,356 whales, down slightly from the previous year's quota. The special meeting convened by the IWC in March to set a quota on sperm whales in the Western Pacific ended in confusing and deadlock. The commission deferred its decision until its annual general meeting in July. Astonished NGOs and many other conservation-minded IWC Commissioners strengthened their resolve to bring about a moratorium on commercial whaling at the July meeting.

The commercial moratorium was announced at the IWC meeting in July 1982. In 1994 the Southern Ocean Whale Sanctuary was declared around Antarctica; 23 nations voted to set up the sanctuary, with Japan being the only nation opposed to it. While Japan lodged an objection in relation to minke whales, in practice, it cannot take minke whales from the sanctuary or elsewhere as it has signed the moratorium on commercial hunting.

The IWC and the regulatory structure protecting whales

The main duty of the IWC is to keep under review and revise the schedule to the Convention. Aspects covered include the complete protection of certain species, limits on the number and size of whales that can be killed, designating whale sanctuaries, prescribing open and closed seasons, and the prohibition of the capture of suckling calves and female whales. The IWC also compiles catch reports and other statistical and biological records. Each member country is represented by a Commissioner with input from experts and advisers.

The IWC has a full-time Secretariat, and a Commission meeting is held each year. There are various committees, including a scientific committee which looks at levels of whale stocks: the information and advice which it provides forms the basis of the regulation of whaling. Any changes are implemented 90 days later, unless a Member State lodges an objection on the grounds of national interest or sovereignty. If an objection is lodged, then the regulation is not binding on that Member State. The regulations are implemented in the Member States which appoint inspectors. International inspectors can also be appointed by the IWC.[27]

---

27 Fact sheet of the Global Wildlife Division, London: DOE.

The protection of whales in the UK

The UK ceased whaling in 1963 and whaling is prohibited within the UK's 200-mile fisheries limit; cetaceans are protected within territorial waters under the WCA 1981. Policy development is in the hands of MAFF (see the Fisheries Act 1981).[28]

Protection of whales in the US[29]

The Marine Mammal Protection Act 1972 establishes a moratorium on taking or importing marine mammals, their parts and products. The Act provides protection for polar bears, sea otters, walruses, dugongs, manatees, whales, porpoises, seals and sea lions. It is unlawful to take any mammal on the high seas or in waters or lands under US jurisdiction; this applies to persons, vessels or other conveyances.

It is also unlawful to import any marine mammal or marine product into the US or to use any port or harbour under US jurisdiction for any purpose connected with unlawful taking or importation of any marine mammal. It is unlawful to possess any unlawfully taken marine mammal, including parts and products, or to transport, purchase, sell or offer to purchase or sell any marine mammal, including parts and products. There is an exception for the Alaskan Aleuts, Indians and Eskimos who reside in Alaska, who are allowed to take marine mammals for subsistence purposes or to use them for the manufacture and sale of native handcrafts. The Secretaries of Interior and Commerce may grant permits for importation of marine mammals for scientific research or public display purposes.

In the US the National Marine Fisheries Service (NMFS) protects, conserves, and restores populations of marine mammals and other endangered marine species; it is a component of the Commerce Department's National Oceanic and Atmospheric Administration and operates under the Endangered Species Act 1973. It must first determine whether a species needs protection, whether it should be listed as threatened or in danger of extinction, the extent of critical habitat necessary to sustain the survival of the species and provide for its recovery. If a species is listed, the NMFS co-ordinates the development and implementation of a survival plan to recover the species to sustainable levels; it also has to review federal activities to ensure they do not have an adverse impact on the species or the habitat. Sea turtles are protected by the NMFS and the US Fish and Wildlife Service while the NMFS protects marine mammals under the Marine Mammal Protection Act 1972. Currently 11 species of marine mammals in the US are listed as threatened or endangered.

---

28   *Ibid.*
29   Information from US open government site on the Internet.

Areas of controversy under the Convention

Commercial hunting quotas[30]

Current IWC rules adopted by the commission in 1975, and agreed to by Norway, require that stocks that have been reduced to below 54% of their original pristine (before hunting) level should be protected from commercial hunting. In 1985 analysis of scientific evidence by members of the IWC Scientific Committee showed that the north east Atlantic minke whales may have been reduced to as little as 30% of their original numbers, and the stock was defined as 'protected' by the IWC that year. But Norway objected to that management decision, in the same way that it had earlier objected to the commercial moratorium. Norway adamantly claimed for a number of years that there are somewhere in the region of 86,700 minke whales in the Northeast Atlantic. However, Commissioners cannot have failed to note that the Norwegian Fisheries Ministry has admitted that the 1995 commercial quota is to be reduced to 232 from 301 because it had 'misjudged stocks due to a computer programme error'. However, the Norwegian Whalers Association has stated that it will kill the full 301 quota unless the authorities give 'full compensation for the reduction'.

The IWC has been trying to devise a way to resume whaling. They have devised formulae under a Revised Management Plan (RMP). The RMP is based on the concept of Maximum Sustainable Yield. Because of the problems of information on a range of factors the limit was set at zero in 1986. However, revisions of these mathematical formulae will set kill quotas for commercial whale hunts. Devised by pro-whaling scientists it protects populations only when they are reduced to 54% of their pre-hunt levels; the surveys are only required every six years. However, for the time being the whale catches will stay at zero because of the unresolved concerns about safeguards including; adequate inspection, international observation, data reporting and monitoring, and the problems of humane killing.[31]

Aboriginal whaling

Whaling is only recognised by the IWC in relation to aboriginal whaling, ie where communities need to kill whales for food as an essential part of their diet, eg the Innuit population of Greenland. While this exception is seen as legitimate by many States, it caused controversy at the 1996 IWC annual meeting. The controversy arose over an application by the Makah Indian Tribe of Washington State to obtain a quota of five grey whales. Aboriginal whaling is calculated on the basis of nutritional and cultural needs and the Makah's application was based on the fact that they had hunted whales 70 years ago and thus they had a whaling tradition. However, there was concern

---

30 IWC, *Whale and Dolphin Conservation Report*, 1995, p 4, Bath: WDCS. Reproduced by kind permission of the Whale and Dolphine Conservation Society.

31 *Ibid.*

among groups such as the Whale and Dolphin Conservation Society (WDCS) that in fact some of the tribe wanted to commercialise the hunt. The WDCS brought tribal elders to the meeting who opposed the resumption of hunting. Concern arose that the US was willing to change the definition of aboriginal whaling from subsistence use to one of cultural tradition, to allow the application through. As there are another 18 tribes in the US and Canada which wish to start whaling and there are concerns that to change the definition in this way would put many whales at risk.[32]

Small-scale whaling

There is also a concern about the whaling of smaller species of whales due to the size of the boats used:[33]

> Catching smaller species of whales using powered vessels with bow-mounted harpoon cannons is termed (by the IWC) 'small type whaling'. It defines the target species as either minke, bottlenose whale, orca or pilot whale. The term does *not* apply to the size of boats being used. In 1993, the largest vessels of the Norwegian fleet were 310 tons, 213 tons, 156 tons and 124 tons. The rest ranged in size from 90 tons down to 27 tons. These are the same types and ranges of sizes of boats that ravaged and decimated the other baleen stocks of the North Atlantic.

The scientific whaling exception

One of the most controversial areas is the use of the scientific whaling exception, which many believe has been used by countries to carry on their whaling operations:

> Whilst many nations have used scientific permits to keep their struggling whaling industries alive, scientific permits really came into their own during the 1970s. For example, the Faroese used scientific permits to maintain their commercial fin whale hunt despite official IWC protection for the north Atlantic fin whale from 1976. The hypocrisy of the scientific permit kills was clearly shown in an April 1985 statement by the Japanese Minister for Fisheries, Moriyoshi Sato, who said, 'The government [of Japan] will do its utmost to find ways to maintain the nation's whaling in the form of research or other forms'. Japan began its scientific whaling programme in 1987, and continues to take some 300 minke whales every year. In 1986 Iceland was one of the first countries to launch into scientific whaling after the moratorium was put into place. However, the Icelandic human population was only able to consume 7% of all the whale meat their whalers brought home.

> Some conservationists believe that the scientific whaling programme has allowed Japan to keep its whaling fleet afloat and make profits. However, even

---

32 See *Sonar*, the magazine of the WDCS, no 15, September 1996, pp 6–7. Bath: WDCS.

33 IWC, *Whale and Dolphin Conservation Report*, 1995, p 4, Bath: WDCS. Reproduced by kind permission of the Whale and Dolphin Conservation Society.

if the trips are not commercially profitable, the continued pelagic whaling has kept the issue of whaling alive within Japan on a political level. If whaling was to have ceased in 1987 many whalers would have disappeared to seek other work. The capital expense of re-equipping a new fleet and staffing it with skilled men would have been prohibitive. However, more importantly, it is politically easier for the whaling interests in Japan to fight for something tangible that still exists than to fight to reinstate something they had already forgone.[34]

The problem of how the whales are killed

Even if whaling were to be resumed, there are still concerns about how whales are killed and many groups are concerned that whales are not killed through humane methods of killing:

Since the IWC was established it has recognised that the harpooning of whales and killing them with explosive charges is a cruel method of hunting. Some parties to the IWC have taken a stance on humane killing issues. In 1982, the Chairman of the IWC Technical Committee stated that: 'The UK supported the substance of the Seychelles proposal [for a moratorium] because of its concern over the humaneness of whaling'. The 1980 Workshop on Humane Killing Techniques for Whales chose as a working definition: 'humane killing of an animal means causing its death without pain, stress or distress perceptible to the animal'. Despite all the advances in science there is still a fundamental problems in trying to kill a moving target, such as a whale, from a moving platform. In the 1993 Norwegian hunt, one whale was recorded as taking over 55 minutes to die.

Sir Sydney Frost (1978) concluded in his report to the Australian government on humane killing and whaling that '... there is a significant difference in the methods used for the killing of whales and the humane practices required by law for the slaughter of cattle, sheep and pigs. In abattoirs and most slaughter houses the animal is stunned instantaneously and then immediately killed, dying whilst unconscious ...'

The whalers have noted that other hunted terrestrial mammals suffer just as long, if not longer, times to death. However, Jordan has pointed out that whales did not evolve as prey species such as deer. They are not physiologically equipped to cope with being chased and so could be said to suffer 'pathological stress' ...

Unlike deer and other mammals, whales are conscious breathers – which means that their breathing is a voluntary action. Therefore, an injured whale which continues to breathe is awake, and potentially suffering high levels of pain and stress. This is extremely important when one considers that Japanese whalers still use electric harpoons (or lances) to finish off harpooned whales. Unfortunately, these instruments do not kill the whale outright because the current earths into surrounding sea water. The electric charge is believed to

---

34 *Ibid*, pp 6–7.

cause further suffering to the animal by causing muscle contraction whilst the whale dies from shock, respiratory arrest or cardiac fibrilation.[35]

The RSPCA gave evidence to the IWC's Workshop on whale killing methods:[36]

If commercial whaling were to restart tomorrow most whalers would use a grenade-headed harpoon fired from a canon ... The head of the harpoon has two or four claws screwed to an explosive grenade and the grenade is timed to go off as the harpoon enters the whale's body. But the harpoon has to hit the whale's thoracic region or central nervous system for an animal to stand a chance of dying immediately. This would be very difficult to achieve in the choppy seas of the Antarctic where the minke whale would be hunted. An added complication is that the grenade does not always explode in the whale's body, leaving the hapless whale with excruciating internal injuries from the harpoon. The whale would then suffer for several minutes before the second harpoon could be loaded. Even then it may take several more shots before the whale actually dies. In a Japanese survey of 35 minke whale 'death-times' using the most up-to-date harpoon – the penthrite – the average time a whale took to die was more than five minutes. One whale took 13 minutes before it died ... The Society also wants to point out the inconsistent way in which many pro-whaling nations treat animal slaughter. While most of these nations have strict pre-stunning regulations for the slaughter of land mammals, they do not consider the plight of the equally sentient whale.

The IWC has recognised that if it is ever to allow a commercial resumption of whaling it must have a very strict system of inspection, observation and enforcement. This is because of the problems with UN-monitored and unknown whaling, and is important as both Norway and Japan have tried to smuggle out whale meat:

In conjunction with the Endangered Species Project (ESP) and the Hawaii-based organisation Earthtrust, WDCS presented an in-depth report, *Tracking the Pirates*, on the illegal trading of whale meat. The report mapped out whale meat smuggling channels that link Japan, South Korea and Taiwan. Japan has admitted that since 1988, roughly 500,000 kgs of illegal whale meat have been seized by its customs official; frighteningly, they believe this to represent only 15% of the total meat smuggled into Japan illegally. The hunts currently operated by Japan and Norway have helped to serve as a cover for pirate whaling, thus allowing for the sale of illegal whale meat. In the Society's opening statement to the IWC meeting, WDCS called on the Commission to initiate a series of controls on the trade in whale meat. By a strong vote of 21–4, a resolution, on 'Improving Mechanisms to Prevent Illegal Trade in Whale Meat' was passed, which calls upon any country with stock-piles of whale meat to provide annual reports to the IWC on the volume of stocks and enforcement actions taken against traders in illegal meat. The resolution also asks nations to use genetic testing techniques to identify sources of meat, and to dispose of their meat stockpiles in the near future.

---

35 *Ibid*, pp 8–9.
36 *Animal Life*, Spring 1992, pp12–13, Horsham: RSPCA. Reproduced by kind permission of the RSPCA.

There is a real problem in relation to the black market in whale meat. One of the mechanisms for tackling this problem is through DNA analysis of where whale meat comes from. Earthtrust is undertaking such a project. This can find out whether whale meat on the market is legitimate or not. It combines scientists and research organisations to a professionally conducted programme of unannounced international intelligence gathering which is conducted by skilled investigators. The scientists go 'on site' in the country where the samples were obtained. They use state of the art miniaturised DNA cloning equipment to do polymerase chain reaction duplicates of the DNA. The results are analysed using double-blind checking techniques which establish species identity using two different advanced mathematical models on separate parts of the DNA molecule.

Though there exists a growing body of international treaties, laws and conventions that ostensibly protect wildlife, there is also huge and growing 'hidden economy' of organised crime (with tacit government and industry collusion) that directly hinders the effectiveness of these laws. Traditional conservation strategies have focused on visible laws, conventions and treaties due to their accessibility, and great strides have been made in these forums. However, the hidden economy – the real world – has made these gains irrelevant in many cases. As anyone who has travelled internationally knows, wildlife laws and treaties which do exist usually lack effective intelligence-gathering and enforcement provisions and are often simply ignored.

Thus, we have a world with many types of protection 'on the books' for wild species while the poaching and destruction of species goes on unabated. Unfortunately, this is becoming the rule rather than the exception.

Japan's ongoing consumption of endangered whales is one of the best examples. Through illegal trade, Japan has aided the decimation of populations of humpbacks and other whales while publicly remaining a member of the International Whaling Commission (IWC), which has pledged to protect these whales. A number of other nations have been implicated as suppliers: whaling has now become a de-centralised illicit activity much like drug smuggling, driven by 'caviar level' market prices which can reach hundreds of dollars per pound.

This means that the 'whaling moratorium' and the 'whale sanctuaries' may only be as good as our ability to police them in retail markets. Until recently, Japan's policy has been to flatly deny any large-scale trade in illegal whalemeat. All meat looks alike, and Japan's government has each year dumped 'research whaling' meat on the market to help explain the ongoing widespread availability of whale meat.

The IWC has no enforcement power of its own, nor does it have the authority or funding to poke around inside member nations. Rather, the policies set at the IWC must be backed up by the governments of the member nations.

In order to ensure that the samples purchased are truly representative, they must be purchased 'undercover', which is to say without 'tipping off' the seller that an investigation is underway. Several US agencies currently have, in the case of whaling, both the technical capability and the legal mandate to enforce whaling regulations. However, due to considerations of national sovereignty, it would be considered 'spying' if a nation unilaterally sent in a DNA research team to do market testing in another nation.

As for independent DNA scientists, few have the funding, inclination, contacts or training to engage in 'undercover work' on behalf of conservation conventions like the IWC or CITES (Convention on International Trade in Endangered Species). Notably, no one conducted such an investigation before Earthtrust.

Thus, a gap has developed: there is a need for independent DNA reality-checking of the trade in endangered and restricted wildlife products (such as whales and dolphins), and the technology is now available to collect this information. But who is to do it? Until an international monitoring scheme is developed and incorporated into IWC regulations, the answer must be Non-Governmental Organisations (NGOs). Practically speaking, at this point this means Earthtrust and its affiliates, funded by forward looking individuals, foundations and corporations.

Using the techniques demonstrated by Earthtrust in 1993–94, notably 'in situ DNA amplification', it is now possible to gather accurate field data anywhere in the world, and compare genetic sequences to find out just which animals are being killed. As catalogs of DNA 'type sequences' are built up, it becomes increasingly possible to trace back wildlife products to their species, area of origin, subspecies, sex and even lineage. This is the single most powerful tool available to bring illegal trade to light and under control: even after an animal is killed and cut into tiny pieces, each piece can still tell the story of that animal's existence.

This action plan is an outgrowth of Earthtrust's 1993–95 DNA initiatives. Anecdotal evidence of the widespread availability of 'protected species' whalemeat, and dolphin sold as whalemeat, in the Japanese market place had been known for many years. Earthtrust program strategist Don White had since the mid-1980s sought to utilise DNA testing for market-testing whalemeat. Working with Project Director Sue White and other Earthtrust staff, he designed an initial two-phase project which began in 1993 with the undercover collection of meat samples in Japan.

The second phase of this effort involved sending leading whale biologist C Scott Baker to Japan to clone the DNA of the samples for export and analysis. The results were reported to the Scientific Committee of the IWC in May of 1994, and published in the journal *Science* in September 1994. The data indicated the widespread availability of meat form many types of 'protected' whale, including humpback and fin whales, as well as many samples of dolphin meat falsely sold as 'whale'. To a large extent, it was this study which has ignited the current high-level international enthusiasm for whale DNA as a tool for enforcement.

The cells of every animal each contain a minimum library of information, encoded in the base-pairs of nucleotides in molecules of DNA. There is enough information in each DNA molecule to build a complete picture from scratch. These information sequences are unique, and can potentially, provide us with vast amounts of information. In fact DNA identification has become the pre-eminent tool of forensic criminology, since it can establish the identity of an individual form hairs or bodily fluids. It is a much simpler task to use DNA to identify species or subspecies of animals, since the genetic variation between different species and breeding populations is quite notable and unambiguous.

There are two types of DNA in a cell, 'nuclear' and 'mitochondria'. Due to the fact that it mutates less rapidly and passes only from the mother's side of the family, mitochondria DNA (mtDNA) analysis is very useful in establishing species and lineage. It is also reasonably quick and cheap. In the Earthtrust studies different 'control regions' of the mtDNA are compared with a catalog of 'type' sequences known to come from specific whale species and populations. In this way, unambiguous determination can be made of the species, sex, and gross geographical origin of the unlucky whale or dolphin in the sample. As the catalog of 'type' samples grows, increasingly exact localisations of the whale's breeding group and place of origin are possible.

However, there are practical difficulties which have prevent the use of this tool to gather intelligence within 'whale consuming' nations prior to the Earthtrust initiative. Chief among the is the wording of current cites regulations, which gives the 'office of management' authority of each CITES member nation the ability to delay – indefinitely – the export of tissue samples. Even non-controversial tissue samples exported from Japan can take more than three years to receive permits. Thus, CITES, which was designed to prevent the trade in endangered species, has in this case been used as an effective barrier to prevent international inspection of the whalemeat market.

This is where 'in situ PCR' comes in. PCR stands for Polymerase Chain Reaction, which is necessary for all quantitative DNA studies. Simply put, PCR takes a few original DNA molecules and creates millions of exact copies by providing the proper chemical and temperature conditions for DNA to replicate itself. This many-million-fold amplification may be done by a person of the proper training with only a small suitcase of equipment: a PCR thermal 'MiniCycler' and the necessary chemical reagents. The resulting 'cloned' DNA may then be separated chemically from the original tissue sample. Since it is not whalemeat or a whale product but only a 'chemical snapshot' of whale DNA, it is not subject to CITES restrictions. The amplified DNA may be shipped anywhere necessary for analysis. This makes it possible to conduct investigations and get results with a reasonable lag time. In the case of Japan, it is providing the first definitive look at a 'whalemeat' market that has for decades been out of control.

Reform of CITES regulations is needed, to allow direct export of tiny DNA samples for analysis by international conservation conventions. Unless and until that happens, though, 'in situ PCR' using the Earthtrust project protocols will be the main tool of those who wish to stop the illegal whale trade ... The fact that dolphins are increasingly being sold as whalemeat in Japan is noteworthy for both conservation and strategic reasons. based on the prices recently paid by Earthtrust investigators for dolphin-sold-as-whale, the going retail rate for a dolphin sold on such a market is about £2,800. This is enough to create problems for dolphins not only in Japan, but potentially around the world.

While all dolphins have been added to CITES Appendix 2, small cetaceans are not actively protected or otherwise managed by the IWC or any other body.

There are many places around the world where dolphins may be caught easily *en masse*. If it remains easy to substitute dolphin for whale on Japan's market, there is no reason to think that market forces will not create a flow of dolphin meat into Japan from other areas of the world. This may already be occurring. In the 1970s Japan set up numerous 'local' operations in other countries to obtain whalemeat, and they are now doing similar deals in a number of fisheries. A system which swallowed up 48,000 Soviet humpbacks without detection will not blanch at importing dolphins if there is a market. For this reason, Earthtrust scientists will continue to develop and improve techniques for the identification of small cetacean tissue; and when possible we will send a small cetacean DNA specialist along with the primary whale researcher.

It is significant that dolphin-sold-as-whale constitutes mislabelling, and there are a number of reasons – including risks of heavy metal poisoning – that Japanese citizens may be expected to want to see this practice cease. It is important not just to identify products as coming from small cetaceans, but to identify *which* small cetaceans, from which oceans, are being sold as whale meat. This practice is a significant danger to dolphins and must be addressed. DNA identification of these dolphins in the market place and provides an effective way of halting or greatly curtailing their practice ... and may be in time to prevent significant international trade from developing.[37]

The problem of pollution

The other problem with the RMP is that, as well as relying on the whalers to provide catch data and population estimates, it fails to accommodate the effects of environmental pollution on whales. Because of these problems the IWC has also been asked by Mexico to adopt the precautionary principle in relation to its activities. This is because it is felt that there is a conflict between other international initiatives like Rio with its emphasis on sustainability and the development of an orderly whaling industry. The report below states that despite 30 years of protection for whales, seven out of the 11 great whale species are presently endangered or vulnerable. At least three small cetaceans are on the edge of extinction – the Indus and Yangtze river dolphins, the little Mexican porpoise and the vaquita. Shipping constitutes a hazard to many marine mammals through collisions, noise pollution, habitat degradation and toxic contamination:

The Beluga is so contaminated by DDT and PCBs that dead carcasses have to be disposed of as toxic waste ... Latest research also shows that baleen whales, including grey whales and humpbacks, are also affected by chemical pollution. Until recently, it was thought that only toothed cetaceans such as belugas, sperm whales, and dolphins, were affected. The chemicals accumulate in the whales' blubber and are then released into their milk when they migrate to winter calving grounds.

37   Earthtrust Information from the WWW.

What will happen to the next generation is unknown. But evidence is growing that the effects of industrial chemicals and pesticide run-offs on whales and dolphins are potentially the gravest threats to their survival. Even low levels of contaminants could increase susceptibility to disease and decrease fertility. If this continues, it is possible that some apparently stable populations of long-lived animals, including whales and dolphins, could crash suddenly with little warning.[38]

International controls over marine pollution

The main protection is provided under the 1982 Convention on the Law of the Sea and the International Maritime Organisation. The International Convention for the Prevention of Pollution from Ships and the 1978 Protocol MARPOL 73/78 deal with all forms of ship-generated marine pollutants:

– Annex I Oil;

– Annex II Noxious liquid substances;

– Annex III Harmful substances carried in packaged form;

– Annex IV Sewage;

– Annex V Refuse.

The disposal overboard of plastics is totally prohibited. There are also proposals to extend MARPOL 73/78 to cover noxious solid substances and air pollution from ships. The other accords are the International Convention on Civil Liability for Oil Pollution Damage, the Convention Relating to Intervention on the High Seas in Cases of Oil Pollution, the International Convention on Oil Pollution Preparedness, Response and Co-operation, the International Convention on the Establishment of an International Fund for Compensation for Oil Pollution Damage and the International Convention on Oil Pollution Preparedness, Response and Co-operation 1991.

There are a number of risks from the oil and gas industry: the most publicised are the oil spills from tankers such as *Torrey Canyon, Amoco Cadiz, Sea Empress* or *Exxon Valdez*, but there are also smaller accidental spillages, operational discharges of oil and chemicals. The report states that licences for exploration and production are awarded by the DTI, and while the licences can have conditions attached to them to protect the environment these are often vague, do not take into account the local conditions or wildlife and are less rigorous than those applied in a number of other countries:

The UK government has been issuing licences to search for oil and gas in UK waters since 1964. In total, 2,668 exploration and appraisal wells have been drilled, together with a further 2,321 development and production wells. The amount of related seismic survey has not been documented. By the end of 1993, 193 production installations of various types, had been installed, including deep water and floating production systems, shallow water oil and

---

38 Kempf, E and Phillips, C, *Whales in the Wild*, WWF Special Species Report, 1995, Gland, Switzerland: WWF.

gas platforms, production ships and subset production installations. To bring the oil and gas ashore, some 4,000 miles of seabed pipeline had been constructed either direct to the shore or to offshore loading installations for transport by tanker.[39]

The report concludes:

Without adequate regulation and control there is considerable potential for adverse impacts on marine habitats and wildlife to arise from the normal operating procedures of the oil industry. Regulations, to control oil and gas exploration and production are currently inadequate, in part because there is insufficient information on impacts of discharges and on scale of discharges, but also because insufficient attention is given to cumulative impacts, disturbance impacts and to comprehensive assessment of the habitats and wildlife in or adjacent to a licensed area. This leads to an inadequate assessment, if it happens at all, of the impact of activity and therefore little or no consideration of any mitigation including the no activity option. In addition, the monitoring and enforcement of regulations is largely undertaken by the industry and the government department responsible for the interests of the industry. Furthermore, models being developed to control chemical pollution are flawed and considered to be unlikely to form reliable regulatory tools.

If the government is to meet the targets for biodiversity conservation agreed at the Earth Summit in 1992 and is to comply with EU directives, in particular the Habitats and Species Directive, then a better system of regulatory control of the offshore oil and gas industry is required. Some of what is needed is already standard practice in other parts of the world – it needs to become common practice in UK waters as a matter of urgency. The recent moves to license areas in inshore and highly sensitive environments adds to this urgency.[40]

The effects of oil spills on whales were seen after the 1989 *Exxon Valdez* oil spill when the Chevron tanker released 11 million gallons of oil into Prince William Sound. The pod of orca whales in the area at that time numbered 36; today the pod has dwindled to 22, the death of females and juveniles has destroyed the pod's complex social structure and the whales swim alone. Since the spill the number of harbour seals has fallen 6% each year; the seals are the orcas' prey species.[41]

The threat to marine mammals from fishing

Approximately one quarter of the World's tuna catch is in the Eastern Tropical Pacific, and in that area Yellow Fin Tuna are found in association with various species of dolphins which include the Spotted, Spinner and Common varieties.

---

39   The Joint Link Oil and Gas Consortium – Polluting the offshore environment, April 1996, p 4, Wildlife Countryside Link, Wales.

40   *Ibid*, pp 9–10.

41   From *Marine Connection*, Issue 7, Ross-on-Wye, Herefordshire: Marine Conservation Society.

The ETP is more that five million square miles of ocean, stretching from Southern California to Chile and Westward to Hawaii. Increasingly since the late 1940s, tuna fishermen have taken advantage of this association and have caught tuna by setting nets around the herds of dolphins which, being mammals must surface to breathe. The type of net used to catch the tuna, called a *Seine Net*, is approximately one mile long and 600 feet deep – through this method alone thousands of dolphin are being killed each year.

There are in fact three major methods of Purse-Seine fishing – the first being School Fishing in which schools of tuna are fund new the surface and the purse-seine is set around them, secondly is Log Fishing whereby the fishermen look for floating objects on the surface of the Ocean eg driftwood, etc, which usually attracts tuna to swim underneath it and the third method is Dolphin Fishing; the main focus of this fact-sheet is the method whereby catching dolphins means a sure catch of tuna also. Although as mentioned there are three ways of purse-seine fishing, the first two methods, School and Log fishing, catch mostly small, immature tuna thereby making the Dolphin fishing methods more attractive to fishermen.

Since 1960 the fleets of nations other than the US have increased whereas the United Sates have decreased – especially in recent years with their catch decreasing from 90% in 1960 to 11% in 1991. In the 1960s two tuna canneries operated in Southern California, others were located on both coasts of America, today only two canneries (both still in southern California) remain in operation in the US.

The country with the most dramatic increase in canned tuna production is Thailand; it is one of the largest producers and began canning tuna in the early 1980s. Other nations that have increased their tuna canning production during the 1980s include: Mexico, France, Italy and the Philippines. More recently there has been a considerable growth in Indonesia's tuna canning industry.

On 12 April 1990 the three largest US tuna canneries announced they would no longer purchase tuna caught in association with dolphins, which obviously has seen a further decline in the US purse-seine vessels fishing in the ETP. During 1992 only seven US vessels fished for tuna in that area – five fished for tuna by setting on dolphins. The International Dolphin Conservation Act 1992 also places new restrictions on the sale of tuna in the US. From 1 June 1994 it was unlawful to sell, purchase, offer for sale, transport or ship any tuna products in the US that were not 'dolphin safe'.[42]

Habitat protection

This is provided for at an international and national level through the development of Marine Protected Areas:

> The need to devise methods to manage and protect marine environments and resources became apparent during the course of the 1950s and early 1960s. Thus, the First World Conference on National Parks (1962) considered the need for protection of coastal and marine areas.

---

42   *Marine Connection* fact sheet. Ross-on-Wye, Herefordshire: Marine Conservation Society.

The development of practical responses to this need required development of a legal framework for addressing the sovereignty and jurisdictional rights of nations to the seabed beyond the customary three mile territorial sea. In 1958 four conventions, known as the Geneva Conventions on the Law of the Sea were adopted. These were, the Convention on the Continental Shelf, the Convention on the High Seas, the Convention on Fishing and the Convention on Conservation of the Living Resources of the High Seas.

The High Seas Conventions formed the basis for the establishment of the Intergovernmental Maritime Consultative Organisation (IMCO) in 1959 – later to become the International Maritime Organisation (IMO). These organisations have been engaged in developing and implementing measures for the control and prevention of pollution from ships.

Increasing technical capability to exploit mineral resources on or beneath the sea bed and to exploit fishery resources in deep waters led to the long-running Third United Nations Conference of the Law of the Sea between 1973 and 1977. The outcome of this was to enable nations to take a number of measures, including those related to regulation of fishing and the protection of living resources of the continental shelf, to a distance of 200 nautical miles from their national jurisdictional baseline. This provided a legal basis upon which measures for the establishment of marine protected areas and the conservation of marine resources could be developed for areas beyond territorial seas.

During the 1970s there was increasing recognition and mounting concern regarding the regional nature of the environmental problems of the marine living resources of the world. In 1971, the Convention on Wetlands of International Importance Especially as Waterfowl Habitat (known as the Ramsar Convention) was developed. In 1972, the Convention for the Protection of the World Cultural and Natural Heritage (known as the World Heritage Convention) was developed. Also in 1972, the Governing Council of the United Nations Environment Programme (UNEP) was given the task of reviewing the international situation in order to ensure that emerging environmental problems of wide international significance receive appropriate and adequate consideration by governments. UNEP established the Regional Seas Programme to address problems on a regional basis, by the establishment of Action Plans with a particular emphasis on protection of marine living resources from pollution and over-exploitation. The first such Action Plan was adopted for the Mediterranean in 1975. There are now 14 Regional Seas Projects covering all of the world's marine environment regions.

There are many documents, protocols, international treaties and arrangements that address aspects of marine conservation in the contexts of fisheries, shipping, pollution and research.

Marine and coastal protected areas are important and interactive aspects of marine conservation which have been addressed in the IUCN 'Orange Book'.[43] There is, however, no short document which helps decision-makers, policy advisors, non-government organisations and scientists to appreciate the legislation, co-ordination and organisation needed to establish effective marine

---

[43] Salm and Clark, *Marine and Coastal Protected Areas: A Guide for Planners and Managers*, 1984.

protected areas. This document is intended to perform that function. Ideally, this should have a companion paper or papers covering the other elements required for a comprehensive approach to conservation of marine environments and resources, including a comprehensive policy statement, an IUCN Marine Programme and linkages between coastal and marine protective regimes.

Also in 1975, IUCN conducted a conference on Marine Protected Areas in Tokyo. The report of that conference noted increasing pressures upon marine environments and called for the establishment of a well-monitored system of Marine Protected Areas representative of the world's marine ecosystems.

In 1980 IUCN, with World Wildlife Fund (WWF) and UNEP, published the *World Conservation Strategy* which emphasised the importance of marine environments and ecosystems in the goal of providing for conservation for sustainable development.

In 1983 UNESCO organised the First World Biosphere Reserve Congress in Minsk, USSR. At that meeting it was recognised that the Biosphere Reserve concept is potentially applicable to the marine environment and that an integrated, multiple use Marine Protected Areas can conform to all of the scientific, administrative and social principles that define a Biosphere Reserve under the UNESCO Man and the Biosphere (MAB) Programme.

There has been considerable progress. In 1970 there were 118 Marine Protected Areas in some 27 nations. By 1985, 430 MPAs had been proclaimed by 69 nations with another 298 proposals under consideration. In all 85 nations have proclaimed or are considering proclaiming MPAS. In 1981, a workshop was organised as part of the UNESCO Division of Marine Science – COMAR (Coastal and Marine) Programme to consider research and training priorities for coral reef management. An outcome of this workshop, which was held in conjunction with the 4th International Coral Reef Symposium was the publication of the UNESCO *Coral Reef Management Handbook*.[44]

In 1982, the IUCN Commission on National Parks and Protected Areas (CNPPA) organised a series of workshops on the creation and management of marine and coastal protected areas. These were held as part of the 3rd World Congress on National Parks In Bali, Indonesia. An important outcome of these workshops was the publication by IUCN of *Marine and Coastal Protected Areas: A Guide for Planners and Managers*. That guide has been of great use in the development of marine and coastal protected areas around the world.

In 1986, the Australian Committee for IUCN (ACIUCN) published *Australia's Marine and Estuarine Areas – A Policy for Protection*. Also in 1986, the Canadian government published A National Marine Parks Policy which had many similarities in approach to the ACIUCN publication. Major elements in these two policy documents appeared to us to be potentially applicable to many countries.

In 1987 the World Commission on Environment and Development (WCED) published its report *From One Earth to One World – Our Common Future*. In

---

[44] Kenchington and Hudson, 1984.

November 1987, the General Assembly of the United Nations welcomed the WCED report. At the same time, it adopted the *Environmental Perspective to the Year 2000 and Beyond,* which was prepared by the Intersessional Intergovernmental Preparatory Committee of UNEP's Governing Council and developed in tandem with the WCED report. These and other publications have highlighted the serious threats which confront marine areas around the world. However, conservation efforts for the marine environment have lagged far behind those for the terrestrial environment, and an integrated approach to the management of the global marine ecosystem is yet to be implemented. As a result, many marine areas now face serious problems, including stress from pollution degradation and depletion of resources, including species conflicting uses of resources; and damage and destruction of habitat.

Recognising these problems, the 4th World Wilderness Congress in 1987 passed a resolution at our instigation, which established a policy framework for marine conservation. (Appendix 1). A similar resolution was passed by the 17th General Assembly of IUCN in February 1988. (Appendix 2.) These resolutions adopted a statement of a primary goal, defined 'marine protected area', identified a series of specific objectives to be met in attaining the primary goal and summarised the conditions necessary for that attainment. They form the framework for the IUCN policy statement on Marine Protected Areas.[45]

Marine Protected Areas in the UK

In the UK the idea of protecting areas of sea to help conserve marine wildlife and habitats gathered momentum in the late seventies. Concern over threats to sites of marine biological importance, and the absence of statutory measures to protect sites, led to proposals for 'voluntary marine conservation areas'. Within government one of the first signs that this situation might change was a Nature Conservancy Council/Natural Environment Council working party report on advancing nature conservation in the marine environment which included recommendations for protecting marine sites (NCC/NERC, 1979). In 1981 the idea was embodied into the Wildlife and Countryside Act which allowed for the establishment of Marine Nature Reserves and since then two such reserves have been designated. A major research programme, the Marine Nature Conservation Review, got underway in 1986. The work, started by the Nature Conservation Council and now run by the Joint Nature Conservation Committee, will help identify sites of marine nature conservation importance and therefore play a central role in any future marine protected areas programme in Great Britain. A similar research undertaking for marine habitats and species in Northern Ireland was completed in 1986 by the Ulster Museum and has been used to identify potential Marine Protected Areas around the coast of Northern Ireland (Erwin *et al*, 1986).

Marine Nature Reserves (MNRS)

The 1981 Wildlife and Countryside Act. and the 1985 Northern Ireland Amenity Lands Order (SI 1985/170) make provisions for the establishment of

---

45 Kelleher, G and Kenchington, R, *Guidelines for Establishing Marine Protected Areas,* 1991, pp 3–5, Gland, Switzerland: Internation Union for the Conservation of Nature. Reproduced with kind permission of the International Union for the Conservation of Nature.

Marine Nature Reserves. The aim of MNRs is to conserve marine flora and fauna or geological or physiographical features of special interest as well as providing opportunities for study and research. Protection is provided through by-laws which the statutory conservation agencies agree with various authorities, such as Sea Fisheries Committees and Local Authorities where it impinges on their interests. In other cases voluntary codes have been used. Management plans may be drawn up and committees of interested organisations to provide advice on site management.

Voluntary Marine Conservation Areas

In the absence of statutory measures to protect sites of marine nature conservation interest, various organisations and individuals promoted the idea of voluntary reserves. These are generally promoted and managed by local committees and need not be at sites of major marine biological importance. There is a strong educational component at these sites and their aim is usually to promote harmonious use whilst preventing the deterioration of the site. Sites have wardens and codes of conduct for visitors.

Future plans for Marine Protected Areas

The Marine Protected Areas programme in the UK is at an important stage. Legislation to protect sites for their nature conservation importance has been on the statute books for more than 10 years and the voluntary approach to site protection has been running for around 20 years. The record of achievement has nevertheless been poor and very few Marine Protected Areas have been established.

The Marine Nature Reserves programme has come to a virtual halt as statutory measures for protecting sites have been difficult to implement. There have been suggestions on how this might be improved, through a linked system of protected areas for nature conservation, fisheries and other interest groups, for example, but this has not received the widespread support it needs to be put into practice. Instead the government has been promoting a voluntary approach to site protection and more general marine management measures in which marine protected areas are likely to be a much smaller part (HMSO, 1992). This approach is particularly clear in English Nature's proposals for Sensitive Marine Areas and it is also likely to be reflected in the governments proposals for the implementation of the EC Habitats Directive.

The EC Habitats Directive is a major opportunity to rationalise the various approaches to marine site protection which are either being proposed or which are running in the UK. The continuing work of the Marine Nature Conservation Review is helping to develop a system of marine habitat classification and will identify sites for protection. This remains to be complimented by a comprehensive programme for the establishment of Marine Protected Areas.[46]

---

46 Gubbay, S, *Marine Protected Areas in European Waters: The British Isles*, A report for AIDE Environment from the Marine Conservation Society, September 1993, pp 5–8, London: WWF. Reproduced by kind permission of the World Wildlife Fund.

Whale watching

Many organisations are supporting the growth of whale watching as a means of raising revenue for whales and other marine mammals. However, this activity needs to be carefully controlled and codes of good practice must be drawn up.

The future of the IWC

The future of whales is linked inevitably to the success of the IWC. It is important for countries to be encouraged to stay in the IWC and thereby be bound, even with the exceptions of Norway and Japan, to its decisions. The IWC relies on diplomacy and a certain degree of compromise and clearly a lot of work is needed to ensure that the Convention is enforced adequately and that its provisions are not flouted. It is also important for the habitat of the whales to be protected. If countries continue to flout the Convention or leave it, then it is important for the full weight of international opinion to be placed upon them to rejoin or comply with the requirements of the Convention through trade sanctions. The fragility of the co-operation at IWC is examined in the following article:[47]

> Norway began its annual whale cull last month and is now only a few minke whales short of its target of 425. It is the fourth year in succession that the country has defied the international moratorium on whale hunting. As usual, its 35 or so whale boats moved out into the Arctic waters of the North Atlantic to a chorus of disapproval from environmentalists and anti-whaling nations around the world.
>
> Norway insists it is entirely justified in hunting a small number of whales. It points out that the original purpose of the moratorium has been fulfilled: whale stocks seem to be recovering and science has come up with a safe way of setting catch limits. Only moral objections and politics, says Norway, stand in the way of a legitimate commercial hunt.
>
> But these moral objections may well be the straw that breaks the back of the International Whaling Commission – the body which regulates whaling and imposed the moratorium. Britain and other nations are now admitting that they are not prepared to agree to a resumption of whaling in any form, sustainable or otherwise, a view guaranteed to undermine the IWC's *raison d'être*. Equally if the whaling nations are not allowed to resume regulated, commercial hunts, they could decide to leave the IWC. This would lead to a return of the reckless, uncontrolled hunting that whaling and antiwhaling nations alike want desperately to avoid.
>
> Many IWC member nations are now coming to accept that limited commercial whaling would not threaten the survival of the more abundant whales. 'We are approaching a situation,' admits Ivor Llewelyn, head of the British delegation

---

47   Motluk, A, 'Blood on the Water', *New Scientist*, 22 June 1996, pp 12–13. Reproduced with kind permission of the New Scientist.

to the IWC, 'where it will be possible to exploit certain whale stocks on a sustainable basis'. However, Britain wishes to oppose the resumption of commercial whaling whether it is sustainable or not on moral grounds.

One important measure that could be taken to protect whales is under the US's Pelly Amendment to the Fisheries Act which allows the US to impose economic sanctions against nations whose actions interfere with the effectiveness of international conservation agreements. Norway is certified under this Act but so far no economic sanctions have been set.

Reform of the legislative framework protecting whales

Whales face a number of threats, as outlined above; seven out of the 11 great whale species are considered endangered or vulnerable; three of the small cetaceans are on the edge of extinction: the Indus and Yangtze river dolphins, and the little Mexican coastal porpoise, the vaquita, while the status of almost all the rest of the world's 79 species of whales, dolphins, and porpoises is under threat:

In order to secure the future of the world's whales, WWF believes the following actions must be undertaken:

Give whales strong legal protection through laws and treaties

One of the essential tools for conserving cetaceans is the use of national, regional, and international laws and conventions.

Control whaling through the IWC

The IWC, established under the 1946 International Convention for the Regulation of Whaling, is the only international organisation with the authority to regulate for whale conservation worldwide. Without the IWC there would be no international control of the whaling industry, no moratorium on commercial whaling, and no high seas sanctuaries. The moratorium must remain in place, and Norway and Russia's objections to it should be withdrawn. Given the complete failure throughout history of the whaling industry to operate sustainably, and its deplorable record of flouting of controls, extreme doubt will always remain as to whether the regulations could ever be fully enforced if whaling re-opened. Further, WWF sees no benefit to the conservation of whales from commercial whaling, and no justification for its resumption.

The IWC is continuing its work on the Revised Management Scheme (RMS), which includes the Revised Management Procedure (RMP) to replace the discredited 1974 'new management procedure'. Any future RMS would have to include amongst other elements: (a) rigorous provisions for conducting the whale populations surveys producing data for the RMP, with the surveys conducted under IWC auspices and with international inspection; (b) rigorous standards for catch data accuracy and analysis; (c) a stringent observation ad international inspection scheme, with, for example, more than one inspector on each whaling vessel if it is at sea for longer than 12 hours; and (d) provisions to ensure that any scientific whaling catches are included in the total of RMP catch limits. An RMS which included at least all these elements would provide a framework for considering an RMS for aboriginal/subsistence whaling, which needs to be developed by the IWC. In addition, it would serve as a useful insurance to underpin the moratorium.

Strengthen the Southern Ocean Whale Sanctuary

The IWC's 50 million km2 Southern Ocean Whale Sanctuary was established primarily to protect the southern hemisphere whales on their summer feeding grounds. It also provides an important opportunity for non-lethal scientific research and monitoring on undisturbed and recovering whale populations and the ecosystems of which they are part. Large-scale scientific whaling should not be conducted inside the sanctuary.

Control international trade in whale products

CITES' control on international trade are a crucial weapon in the effective enforcement of the moratorium. All whale species whose catching is regulated by the IWC have been listed in CITES' Appendix I since 1986, so international trade in all whale products is prohibited for States that are parties to CITES. 'Importation from the sea', which covers killing whales beyond the 200-mile EEZ and bringing them into the country, is also prohibited when it is for commercial purposes. However, Japan and Russia both have six reservations and Norway four, to the Appendix I listings. These reservations should be withdrawn.

In spite of the efforts of CITES, there have been recent examples of smuggling and illegal trade in whalemeat involving Norway, Russia, Taiwan, Republic of Korea, and Japan, some of them brought to light by Traffic investigations. The IWC has urged its members to clamp down on the trade, but further measures are necessary. In the meantime, NGO monitoring will continue.

Conserve smaller cetaceans through regional agreements

There is a long-standing disagreement as to whether the IWC has the legal authority to regulate the conservation of the smaller whales, dolphins, and porpoises as well as the larger whales. At present, the IWC can collect information about the status and threats to small cetaceans and request range States to take appropriate action. The necessary follow-up to these request needs to be monitored and encouraged by other bodies, including NGOs. In addition, there are a number of regional agreements which provide a framework for addressing the threats to the smaller cetaceans, but more are needed and effective implementation and enforcement of the existing agreements are priorities.

Create more sanctuaries and marine protected areas

Giving special legal protection to certain marine areas is an important tool in achieving the conservation of marine biodiversity, including the reduction of threats to whales and dolphins. As top predators, healthy populations of cetaceans will indicate healthy populations of their prey species, so that their conservation is important for people living and working in coastal areas. Many Marine Protected Areas will protect cetaceans that happen to be resident in them or migrate through them, but some reserves and sanctuaries have been established specifically to protect cetaceans, and many more need to be.

Encourage well-managed whale-watching

Whale- and dolphin-watching is growing dramatically in many parts of the world, with over four million people taking part each year. The total annual revenue generated was estimated at over US $300 million in 1992. Providing it is well regulated so that there are no harmful effects on whale populations, its development should be encouraged both as a valuable non-consumptive sustainable replacement for whaling, and as a means of raising public interest and knowledge of whales and dolphins.

Reduce bycatches in wasteful fisheries

Reduction of fisheries bycatch is essential not only for cetaceans and other non-target species, but also for the conservation of fish stocks and the human communities that depend in them. The use of long driftnets on the high seas is already the subject of a UN moratorium, but this need to be strictly enforced, as does the European Union ban on driftnets.

Codes of practice, technical management measures, selective fishing gear, and practices that will minimise the bycatch of non-target species are all necessary. In some cases, relatively minor changes in fishing techniques can bring about a large reduction in cetacean bycatch, as has happened in the eastern tropical Pacific tuna fishery. Such changes need rigorous observation and effective sanctions if they are to work. In other cases, the only solution will be closing fisheries in certain areas or certain seasons, or a return to less intensive fishing methods. If these measures are used, fishing communities will need government or aid agency help in making the necessary adjustments.

Reduce marine pollution

More research is needed into recent human-induced changes in the marine environment and their effects on the health and population dynamics of whales. Chemical pollution may well be one of the most serious long-term threats to cetaceans, and strict measures to limit contaminants such as DDT and PCBs entering the sea are necessary for their survival. Such measures are essential for conserving all marine life as well as ensuring the health of fish-eating human communities.

Control and reduction of high-intensity undersea noises is also necessary, including precautionary guidelines on conducting seismic surveys in areas of importance to cetaceans.[48]

CONCLUSION

The choices which must be made to save endangered species and their habitats are difficult. Some of the problems facing any conservation programme are set out in the following extract:[49]

---

48 Kempf, E and Phillips, C, *Whales in the Wild*, World Wildlife Fund Species Status Report, 1995, pp 22–24, Gland, Switzerland. Reproduced by kind permission of World Wildlife Fund.

49 Tudge, C, *Last Animals at the Zoo*, 1991, pp 41–42, London: Hutchinson Radius. Reproduced by kind permission of Colin Tudge.

First, the whole cause of conservation is chronically starved of money. The safest way to protect a habitat is to buy it (or declare it as a national park, which is effectively the same thing, but employs public money); but conservationists cannot afford to buy all that they would want to. Neither is money the only issue. Conservationists must compete with a hundred other lobbies. In rich countries, in general, conservationists tend to lose out against farmers. In poor countries they lose out in a hundred ways; but in general, Third World governments have tended to feel (and still do) that they have too many other things on their mind to spend too much time on conservation. On land, the pristine wilderness is fast diminishing, and what remains is largely spoken for and earmarked for some human purpose. The best option nowadays, generally, is the national park; but national parks are created by governments, and governments tumble; and people continue to press their claims. Farmers graze their cattle within every national park in India and many of those in Africa (where else can they go?) and the Aborigines of Kakadu in the Northern Territory would like to begin mining. The national parks of Britain are mostly on the uplands (most of the lowlands long since became agricultural) and they are also farmed, forested and managed for grouse. Even if the best possible efforts were made, then, it would still not be possible to protect more than a fraction of what we would theoretically like to protect; or, in most cases, to devote even the most protected areas to wildlife unstintingly.

Secondly, wild habitats are even more precariously placed than is generally realised. The sheer persuasiveness of environmental pollution is not widely appreciated; for example the fact that wild plants (and animals that feed upon them) suffer at least as much from excess fertility as from frank toxicity (which is probably much rarer) ... There are no absolutes, either, in this untidy world. We may create a national park; protect it with a dozen treaties; monitor and exclude the pollutants as best we can; replant the missing trees; and yet for a dozen reasons of biology, which have to do with area, and populations, and genetics, we may still find (and on continents generally will find) that the species continue to go extinct.

The author argues that while habitat protection is difficult, it must remain as a priority, but that captive breeding may be able to save some animals that will be lost in the wild. Should we therefore accept that some animals can only survive in zoos?

There is not enough money available to provide special assistance to every endangered species. The other problem is to decide, if resources are scarce, which animals should be saved?

Our ark has limited accommodation ... I would argue that priority for the limited number of places in the ark should be based on the degree of biological uniqueness of a species and that the aim of the rescue operation should be to preserve the most representative possible sample of the Animal Kingdom. On this criterion, a species (however unfamiliar or unattractive) qualifies for a first calls ticket table if it is the only member of its family and, if it is the only member of an order, it dines at the captain's table. A species that is one of many in a family that is one of many families in an order either travels steerage or is left on the wharf. I think that most zoologists would agree that some such ranking is desirable, but to my knowledge, nobody has yet undertaken the exercise.[50]

The author goes on to describe a scoring system to decide which endangered species should be saved, with high scoring species representing isolated individuals and low scoring species representing a 'tight cluster of short twigs'. The extinction of a low scoring species involves no great loss, for it has many similar relatives. The loss of a high-scoring species is disastrous:

A species-orientated conservation project is seldom embarked upon until the last minute, when it could well be too late to be effective. The chance of success is highest where the decline of the species is due to human predation and all that is required is that killing cease or be reduced. This has been the case, for example, with the Indian Tiger, the Arabian Oryx, whales, the Polar Bear, crocodiles, and the Cape Barren Goose. Rhinoceroses, dugongs and turtles have become endangered due to human predation but we have not yet managed to stop the killing. Most endangered species have become so because of destruction or alteration of their habitat. Unless their environment can be changed so as to restore the conditions that they need, very little can be done for such species except as very major exercises. The idea that an endangered species can be bred in captivity and then released back into the environment is fallacious, for that environment has already been proved to be unsatisfactory. While particular species-orientated projects may be popular and may even in a few cases, reflect real priorities, they usually tackle symptoms rather than diseases. Except where predation is the major cause of endangerment, the decline of one (popular, visible) species reflects the deterioration or destruction of an ecosystem and the unnoticed disappearance of a great number of species. If a major effort on behalf of a token species leads to regeneration of its habitat, it is likely that many other species in that environment will also benefit. It is, however, much more direct and effective to save and expand our samples of natural environments, with a view to simultaneously ensuring survival of communities of species.

These choices are hard ones to make and it would, of course, be better if we could save all the species left on the earth. How to protect and safeguard our global heritage: this is one of the most pressing problems we face today. However, it is a challenge which we should not be afraid to tackle, as N Myers in *The Sinking Ark* states:[51]

To end on a brighter note, a whole-hearted decision to accept the challenge of a disappearing species could have an important spin-off benefit. The effort could help to articulate the common interest of nations. After all, conservation of species can be presented as a less likely source of political friction than many

---

50 Strahan, R, in Burgin, S, *Endangered Species – Social, Scientific, Economic, and Legal Aspects in Australia and the South Pacific Australia*, 1986, pp 9–10, Sydney, Australia: Total Environment Centre.

51 Myers, N, *The Sinking Ark*, 1979, p 284, Oxford: Pergammon Press. Reproduced with kind permission of N Myers.

other international problems. A strategy to conserve species might even encourage governments to adopt a more collective approach to other collective issues that confront their global community.

In sum, efforts to conserve species could, by promoting a consciousness of humankind's unity, prove a solid step toward a new world order.

FURTHER READING

Burgess, J, *The Environmental Effects of Wildlife Trade on Endangered Species,* 1991, London: Environmental Centre.

Environmental Investigation Agency, *Under Fire Elephants in the Front Line and Flight to Extinction,* 1992, London: Environmental Investigation Agency.

Grove, N, 'Wild Cargo: the Business of Smuggling Animals', *National Geographic,* March, 1991.

McCormick, *The Global Wildlife Movement,* 1995, Chichester: Wiley.

Sands, P, *Greening Environmental Law,* 1993, London: Earthscan.

Simmonds, E and Hutchinson, J, *The Conservation of Whales and Dolphins – Science and Practice,* 1996, Chichester: Wiley.

Wells, D, *Environmental Policy a global perspective for the twenty-first century,* 1996, London: Prentice Hall.

Wilson, E, *The Diversity of Life,* 1992, London: Penguin.

CHAPTER TEN

INCREASING HUMAN CONSCIOUSNESS

> What is crucial to recognise is that the capacity for empathy and identification is not static; the very process of recognising *rights* in those higher vertebrates with whom we can already empathise could well pave the way for still further extension as we move upward along the spiral of moral evolution. It is not only the human liberation movements – involving first blacks, then women, and now children – that advance in waves of increased consciousness. The inner dynamic of every assault on domination is an ever broadening realisation of reciprocity and identity.[1]

As this quote indicates, humankind is on a learning curve when it comes to the treatment of animals. How should we go about increasing human consciousness regarding animals? Throughout this book we have examined specific suggested reforms regarding the treatment of animals in various practices and the various defences of the *status quo*. This chapter aims to address some of the wider issues regarding our treatment of animals which don't fit neatly into those pigeon-holed areas of concern, although they are unquestionably relevant to them.

First, many people are now committed to the cause of animal welfare but they differ in their approaches to increasing human consciousness of animal welfare in order to influence change. How should they exert their influence – what form should any campaign take? Secondly, there is the ever-constant issue of education. Should more legislation/regulation be the ultimate goal of the proponents of improved animal welfare? Animals are only abused because individuals abuse them. Legislation may sometimes fail to reach these people who might better respond to early and continuing education as to how to treat animals. Thirdly, why and how should governments be involved? Do governments have a valid role to play in the development of better treatment of animals. Is there a need for an all-encompassing government ministry to oversee our interactions with animals?

HOW SHOULD PROTEST BE CONDUCTED?
– THE FORMS OF CIVIL PROTEST

The animal rights movement has used a variety of techniques in order to make its case heard. There are tactics involving direct action, such as demonstrations targeted against institutions and people associated with what

---

1   Tribe, LH, 'Ways not to think about plastic trees: new foundations for environmental law', (1974) 83 YLJ 1345.

the animal rights movement considers to be dubious practices such as animal experimentation. There are also the highly controversial tactics of groups such as the Animal Liberation Front involving bombs, letter-bombs and crimes against property, such as sabotage. And there are the more political tactics of groups such as the RSPCA which use the mechanisms of pressure group politics to influence government. Robert Garner examines the effectiveness of direct action in creating change:[2]

> [A]lthough damage to property is a common direct action strategy, unpremeditated violence, or the threat of it, has played a relatively small role. In assessing direct action, a distinction [can be] made between its usefulness as a strategy and the extent to which it is morally and politically justified. In moral terms, the granting of rights to animals leads to the conclusion that direct action in their defence is not only permissable but also a moral duty, although whether this justifies some of the more extreme actions involving violence is an open question. In political terms it [can be] argued that a system of decision making which allows for what Singer calls a 'fair compromise' between competing interests does place constraints on disobeying the law. In reality, however, modern industrial societies can only provide mechanisms which approximate to this ideal of political equality. In the system of pressure group politics, powerful economic interests who benefit from using animals have considerable resources which seriously disadvantage the campaign for change. Although further research into the role of key exploiters is needed, a preliminary examination would suggest that the animal protection movement can make considerable progress through the mobilisation of public opinion.

There is evidence that both direct action and political protest can have an effect. The Animal Liberation Front formed in the US in 1982 has conducted numerous raids on premises, sent letter-bombs and which has never shunned tactics involving arson and theft. For example, it burnt down a diagnostic laboratory at the Davies University of California, stole 1,000 animals from the University of Arizona and set two buildings on fire, illustrating a passionate care for animals and a blatant disregard for property. Their actions have had a significant effect on research projects by either destroying findings or causing considerable delays. But less militant groups have complained that their activities have made it more difficult for moderate proposals for reform to be heard at all.[3]

Richard Ryder, one of the founders of the 'new animal rights' movement in the 1970s, is of the view that both political and militant action of the animal rights movement have had an impact on the issue. He suggests that 'governments move only when pressed' and cites one particular example where both political and direct action played their part in changing practices:[4]

---

2 Garner, R, *Animals, Politics and Morality*, 1993, p 239, Manchester: Manchester University Press.

3 Blum, D, *Monkey Wars*, 1994, pp 115–16, Oxford: Oxford University Press.

4 Ryder, R, 'Speciesism in the Laboratory', in Singer, P (ed), *In Defence of Animals*, 1985, pp 87–88, Oxford: Basil Blackwell.

The classical example of this in animal politics was the stopping of the slaughter of grey and common seals in Scotland in 1978. First, Greenpeace boats confronted the sealers and thus caught the attention of the media. The International Fund for Animal Welfare made the next major move by placing whole-page advertisements in the British press telling members of the public to 'Write to the Prime Minister'. (This caused Mr Callaghan to receive some 17,000 letters on this topic in one week – the most ever received on one subject by the Prime Minister in such a short period.) Finally, I led an RSPCA deputation to the Secretary of State bearing some scientific research findings which cast an element of doubt upon the scientific research of the government; this duly helped to provide the government with the excuse it needed to call off the seal slaughter.

The history of the successes of other radical proponents of social change such as the Suffragettes indicates that a cause can benefit from direct action which brings it into the public eye. However, it is another thing entirely to attack individuals or their families. Groups using direct action, such as the IRA in Northern Ireland, have, in general, had a history of being left out of negotiations for change. The same is true of violent direct action in relation to changes in the law regarding animal welfare. Direct, predominantly non-violent protest such as that which occurred in the UK as a response to animal transportation to the continent of Europe in 1995–96 and involving a whole 'new class' of middle-class protestors along with the continual political pressure of leading welfare groups has, arguably, led to more direct changes in the treatment of animals.

There are continuing questions raised as to whether animal rights advocates should adopt an 'all or nothing approach'. The history of 'green' politics in general is littered with instances of disagreements over what they should be campaigning for and what they should accept as a compromise. For example, in the UK, the Green Party experienced considerable upheaval as competing groups within it tried to steer the Party's political direction in the 1980s and 1990s. An inability to compromise led several well-known figures, such as Jonathan Porrit, to leave the Party and considerably influenced its effectiveness thereafter. This appears to be a repeated pattern as political and pressure groups will always attract a mixture of hard-liners and moderates.

If the inevitability of internal conflict is accepted then the next question for those within a pressure group is whether they are prepared to accept a compromise of their demands at a political level. In relation to animal welfare there are those, usually the same people who adopt hard-line direct action, who find the prospect of compromise difficult to accept. There were those in the animal rights movement who refused to take part in negotiations with David Mellor as he formulated the Animals (Scientific Procedures) Bill in 1985–86. They would not accept a compromise and, as a result, were absent from discussions. Were they right to maintain an immoveable stance, or were those who decided to accept the possibility of achieving less than they might originally have hoped more realistic and helpful to the animal rights cause? In the following extract, Mary Midgley advocates the moderate approach:[5]

There are two quite distinct objections to a moderate approach, and it is essential to take them both seriously and to keep them separate. One is wholly practical and strategic. It is the Marxist objection that piecemeal reform is useless – indeed, it's worse than useless, because it blocks the way to something more radical. 'Reformism', as such, is then an error. Half-a-loaf, said Marx, cannot help your cause and will actually harm it. The half-loaf is offered as a trap by those who know that, if you accept it, your support will fade away and you will never be able to raise the steam to get anything more.

The other quite different objection is a purely moral one. It says that piecemeal reform is wrong in itself, regardless of consequences simply because it involves the acceptance of those evils which it does not immediately remedy. It commits us to condoning those evils. This objection says that we should never accept such mixed packages of good and evil, even temporarily. We must hold out until we can get the good alone. Anything else is a betrayal.

Both these discussions have been strongly expressed during discussions about the recent Animals (Scientific Procedures) Act, as the are during all discussions of measures which reach that stage of being translated into action at all – particularly action on a national scale. Anything that gets this far is inevitably a compromise.

But the two sorts of objection against compromise need quite different treatment. Let us think first about the practical, pragmatic one. What this one requires is a factual enquiry. Whenever a measure is proposed, we have to ask; is it actually true that this will be counter-productive, that it will only stave off the deeper changes that are our long term aim?

Now sometimes this is indeed true. Sometimes the measures proposed are weaker than they need to be. There is a danger that they will be treated as final. More can be secured, and the extremists serve an essential purpose in pointing this out. But this is not always true. There is no general natural law proving that the Marxist approach is always suitable, that all partial reforms block the way to wider changes. To the contrary, in fact, the history of effective reforms brought about by piecemeal means is long and impressive. One interesting case is votes for women. These were eventually achieved in two stages. They were granted first to women over 30, and extended later to younger ones as well. Now it would have been extremely tempting (I should suppose) for the campaigners to have rejected this ludicrous compromise with the disgust that it deserved. They might easily have thought that, if they once settled for votes confined to the over 30s, they would never be able to muster enough public interest to enfranchise the rest.

What in fact happened, however, was a different and quite common process by which the public found that the world had not come to an end as a result of

5   Midgley, M, *Conflicts and Inconsistencies Over Animal Welfare*, The Hume Memorial Lecture, 26 November 1986, pp 4–9, London: Universities Federation for Animal Welfare. By permission of the Universities Federation for Animal Welfare.

the first concession. It then saw that its position was inconsistent, and made no difficulty about straightening out the anomaly.

This interesting mechanism has quite often worked even in far more alarming cases – cases where the first concession has been quite slight, but has served as a reassuring precedent on which far large ones could follow. This happened both with the Factory Acts and with the series of parliamentary Reform Bills in the 19th century. In each of these cases, the first measure in the series was fiercely opposed and treated as alarmingly momentous. In both these cases, the changes introduced were actually quite small. (The Twelve Hours Act only limited daily working hours to 12. The Great Reform Bill enfranchised very few people). But in each case, once it found that the skies had not fallen, more of the same was allowed to follow. People got used to the idea, public feeling did not lie down. Instead it gained strength when measure of this kind were seen to be possible.

Now obviously, for any particular reform that one is attempting, there can be special facts which suggest which of these patterns public opinion is likely to follow. But the wide experience of reforms we have gathered since Marx's day does not seem to give any grounds for a general, fatalistic certainty that half-measures cannot be followed up by whole ones. The fear that public enthusiasm will die down in the wake of any successful measure does have point. But it seems best met by treating it as a challenge – by working to keep the issues from being forgotten. It certainly does not call for the fatalistic response that accepts such weakening as an irresistible natural law ...

Is there anything more in the moral objection than this? There certainly is something more – a point about mood and attitude. It says that we must not delude ourselves – that things, as they are, are horrible and we are making far too little headway in causing them to be any less so. We ought never to lose this sense of outrage. When we accept a compromise, we ought to know that it is only a compromise and that we must always look beyond it. This is right, and it is the essential contribution of extreme positions to the whole debate. But if it is blown up into something wider – into a moral veto on ever accepting compromise – then it seems to grow meaningless. The Walls of Jericho never do fall at a single blast. We have to start somewhere, accepting a limited aim. To refuse all limited aims is not to set one's sights higher. It is to set them lower, refusing to take action at all.

Also associated with this discussion about whether or not to accept compromise are those who argue that the animal rights movement, even though it has achieved some legislative successes, has failed to maximise the potential for reform because it lacked the correct philosophical basis for challenging current uses of animals. The animal rights movement really started to attract a lot of members in the 1980s as a result of a surge in the philosophical contribution to the debate and the enhanced media coverage of the animals issue but, as we have noted earlier in Chapters 1 and 2, the history of the animal rights lobby goes back a great deal further, to the 18th century in the UK. We might assume for a moment that this has resulted in improved conditions for animals and that animals are treated far better than they were before these enlightened groups began to campaign effectively for better treatment of them. It is true that some practices such as bear-baiting, bull-baiting, using dogs as draught animals and the generally barbaric treatment of horses, cattle and other animals have been removed in most of the advanced industrialised nations of the world. But any claim that animals are now accorded greater respect and are 'better off' than they were two centuries ago is questionable. In the UK, for example, the number of animals involved in experimentation can be counted in millions whereas 100 years ago they could be counted in hundreds.[6] In farming the number of animals raised using 'intensive farming' techniques in Western nations reaches into the thousands of millions.[7]

As mentioned earlier, the different organisations representing the animals' cause fall into different camps when it comes to how to go about changing the law in relation to animals. There are those groups which are moderate in their claims regarding animals and look to achieve incremental reform of the law by gradually improving welfare. Some groups campaign in this limited way because they agree with the underlying premise that the use of animals, in agriculture or experiments, for example, should continue as the alleged potential benefits for humans are too great to be lost – they contend that it is right to look for beneficial scientific advance using animals or that it is right to eat meat – as long as there is sufficient welfare protection of those animals.

On the other hand, there are other groups who are parties to the development of new law in relation to animals which do not accord with this underlying premise that the use of animals is correct *per se*. In reality though, these groups often find themselves cooperating with the advocates of the present uses of animals as tools or instruments for human beings or as a means to provide them with the pleasure of eating meat in order to secure welfare advances for animals. To groups which claim to represent a more 'radical' view of animals in terms of granting them enhanced legal status by recognising that they are the holders of intrinsic moral rights, such a situation represents a philosophical dilemma. The criticism of those who follow short-term gain in spite of desires for much more in the long-term is illustrated by the work of the Committee for the Reform of Experimentation (CRAE). The members of CRAE were accused of something akin to a 'sellout' by more radical opponents of experimentation because of their close involvement in the preparation of the Animals (Scientific Procedures) Act 1986 which had the fundamental underlying principle that the continued use of animals as the subjects of experiments is acceptable. The members of CRAE defended their position in a way which is common to groups campaigning for welfare reforms *within the system* – that incremental reform is a necessary and acceptable way of heading towards the eventual aim of total abolition of

6   See Chapter 4 for more detail.
7   See Chapter 5 for more detail.

practices they see as unacceptable and immoral. They pointed to advances in the welfare protection of animals as an immediate gain which might have been lost if they had not been at the negotiating table. In relation to CRAE's involvement in the preparation of the 1986 Act, they were at pains to stress that there were 20 provisions which resulted from their involvement in the passage of the legislation through the House of Commons and that their co-operative role had been beneficial:[8]

> In 1978, after the successful Animal Welfare Year Campaign, which marked the centenary of the Act, it was agreed that a new impetus was needed if the government were to take animal welfare seriously. Plans were drawn up for a novel approach to put animals into politics – a campaign directed at the 1979 general election campaign with a slogan 'Put it in the manifesto'. For the first time in British parliamentary history all the major parties included undertakings on animal welfare in their manifestoes.

> The Committee for the Reform of Animal Experimentation (CRAE), established during Animal Welfare Year to seek the reform of the law governing animal experimentation under the chairmanship of Lord Houghton of Sowerby, realised the need to enlist allies if the government was to be influenced. Thus was born the triple alliance between the British Veterinary Association (BVA), CRAE, and the Fund for the Replacement of Animals in Medical Experiments (FRAME) – a union which had major impact on government thinking. A comparison of the first white paper, 'Scientific Procedures on Living Animals' (Cmnd 8883) 1983, with the supplementary whit paper (Cmnd 9521) published in May 1985, reflects the many changes in the government's approach.

> The alliance continued to play a vital part in the passage of the Animals (Scientific Procedures) Act Bill through both Houses of Parliament. In all, over 80 amendments were tabled in the Lords and a further 100 or so during the committee and report stages in the Commons, out of which 28 were accepted by the government; of these, 20 originated from the BVA/CRAE/FRAME initiatives ...

> The [alliance] may not have achieved the politically impossible but we accepted that, as a government measure, the Animals (Scientific Procedures) Bill would become law and it was therefore important to be in the arena to fight for and negotiate the best legislation possible, in view of the current state of public and parliamentary opinion, to lessen the suffering of laboratory animals – and this we have done.

What are the best political tactics to use? Are pressure groups such as those within the 'alliance' right to co-operate? There are some who suspect that cooperative tactics may not have always used the best philosophical approaches, based as they are upon compromise, to obtain the best for the

---

8   Hollands, C, *Animal Experimentation*, Leaflet published by BVA/CRAE/FRAME, originally published in *The Lancet*, 5 July 1986, London.

long-term future of animal welfare. Gary Francione,[9] for example, although respecting the work which is performed by those in the animal rights lobby, sees their tactics as being too co-operative and without a coherent set of fundamental 'rights-based' objectives.[10] Francione sees this type of involvement as putting groups which claim to be campaigning for total abolitionist principles far too close in practice, to those involved in the process as a means of securing merely welfare benefits for animals whilst upholding the continued acceptance of animals as undeserving of being defined as 'rights-holders'. He terms those who follow short-term welfare gains in spite of more fundamental beliefs as the 'new welfarists' and proposes that they have 'taken a particular position about the *relationship* between animal rights as a long-term goal and welfarist reform as a short-term strategy.'[11] Francione's 'rights-based' proposals follow the same theoretical line as Tom Regan and attempts to define a new theoretical philosophical backdrop to move the animal rights lobby forward. In short, he believes that the willingness of the supposed proponents of 'strong animal rights'[12] positions and their willingness to treat every potential benefit as worthy of their continued involvement to achieve the possible, as being fundamentally flawed.

Francione's blueprint for a new strategy for the animals lobby involves a different approach to securing change which would question every proposed advance in the treatment of animals from how that improvement stands in relation to ensuring that animals are no longer treated as property to do with as the owner pleases, but as intrinsically valuable individuals with 'rights' to certain treatment. He suggests that the lobby should concentrate on achieving legislation which is much more prohibition-centred and which bans practices rather than modifying them to make them more welfare conscious. New legislation would have as its backdrop, not human interests but animal interests and should not mean replacing one morally questionable activity for a less morally questionable one. It would be morally wrong to replace experiments on chimpanzees with experiments on sheep. Above all, there would be a shift in campaigning for improvements which are welfare oriented to improvements involving a respect for intrinsic rights which is the new, distinctive element of arguments put forward by those supporting the animals' cause:[13]

> In sum, the new welfarist prescription for incremental change – that 'any' measure that 'minimises' or 'reduces' suffering should be supported by animal advocates (or at least not opposed) is simply not sensible if new welfarists

---

9   Professor of Law at Rutgers University School, Newark, and Co–director of the Rutgers Animal Rights Law Centre, US.

10 Francione, G, *Rain Without Thunder: The Ideology of the Animal Rights Movement*, 1996, Philadelphia: Temple University Press.

11 *Ibid*, p 45.

12 This position is described in detail in Chapter 3.

13 Francione, above n 10, p 177.

desire to distinguish their position from that of the institutional exploiters of animals who agree that if we ought to treat animals 'humanely' and that they should not be subjected to 'unnecessary' pain or suffering. It is precisely the failure of new welfarists to focus on this serious flaw in their approach that has led to a movement that seeks to distinguish itself from 19th century welfarism paradoxically by using the very methods and reasoning that characterised those earlier efforts.

Sometimes the results would be the same as has already been achieved in the modern era of animal welfare reform which has seen the banning of various practices in certain countries. The UK, for example, has banned veal-crates and Switzerland has gone further in relation to regulating the treatment of other animals. This type of advance can be regarded as a success for each of the underlying philosophies of the movement: for the proponents merely of improved welfare this amounts to a continuance of meat production but with better welfare for the calves; for the utilitarian this amounts to a limited success in that it takes the animals sentience into greater account than the human interest in producing calves cheaply and; it also amounts to a success under the proposed 'rights-based' approach because the rights of an owner to dispose of and use his or her property as he or she feels fit is subsumed by the intrinsic right of the animal not to be treated in this way.

THE PLACE OF EDUCATION

Some would argue that more legislation has many retrograde aspects in that it creates a need for enforcement which usually means a commitment of increased resources and that legislation fails to tackle the underlying causes of the mistreatment of animals which can only be tackled by education: 'To understand why a law is passed may be halfway to compliance but if the law appears meaningless, and there is no appreciation of its purpose, failure of education in the law may be halfway to promoting non-compliance.'[14]

Education regarding animals is important at various times through the life of an individual who has a lot of contact with animals: as a part of initial schooling: as part of education/training for a specific career such as a vet, animal technician or agriculture employee and; as a part of continuing education throughout that career. It is being increasingly recognised that education regarding the requirements of animals is important during all three stages of the education process: 'Since the welfare of animals within our dominion will be determined by the extent to which we both value and understand their welfare, it follows that we can best serve the animals'

---

14   Brown, L, *Cruelty to Animals*, 1988, pp 169–70, London: Macmillan Press.

interests by educating man towards a perception of welfare that is as close as possible to the animals themselves.'[15] Education to promote the necessity to treat animals with respect has importance in the initial schooling of *all* individuals and particularly important relevance to the initial training of those who are to work with animals. It is not possible, in the space available here, to fully discuss the success or otherwise of the ability of society to engender a respect for animals in children and adults. Schools already play the leading role in this – but do they do enough? At the risk of adding yet another responsibility to teachers, might respect for animals be more fully and formally incorporated in the national curriculum for example? Do parents do enough? If not, how could we encourage them to do so? In the proceedings of the Australia and New Zealand Council for the Care of Animals in Research and Teaching (ANZCCART) 1994, Pauline Cowans suggested how important this kind of initial training is and how it might be implemented:[16]

> There is an opportunity now to develop along with networking systems the information that we would like our young people to have.
>
> A six week unit of learning could be developed and registered on the framework. It would earn credits towards [a] National Certificate and could be made available to schools. The degree of usage of such a unit would be determined by student interest in such issues or because it is a prerequisite for tertiary course ...
>
> There is a need for students to appreciate the right of all animals to quality of life, whatever the purpose of that life may be to us, so that students appreciate the need for animals in research, balanced with care for them.
>
> There is also a need to ensure that appropriate and accessible resources are available to schools at all levels and that development of those resources allows for input from the students themselves.

The importance of education for those embarking on a career involving animals by joining courses in higher education was noted in the same conference by Kevin Stafford of the Department of Veterinary Sciences, Massey University, Palmerston North in New Zealand:[17]

> Until recently, veterinary schools and animal science faculties have seldom taught bioethics or animal welfare in a structured manner. Individual teachers and some student groups may have discussed the issues relating to these two subjects, but generally it was considered that such subjects were unworthy of a scientific education, morals being the realm of philosophers, theologians and the individual. Such ethics as were taught related to acceptable and

---

15 Webster, J, *Animal Welfare: A Cool Eye Towards Eden*, 1994, p 263, Oxford: Blackwell Science.

16 Cowans, P, 'Animals in schools – rights, resources, and responding to needs', in *Animal Welfare in the Twenty–First Century: Ethical, Educational and Scientific Challenges*, 1994, p 15, Glen Osmond, South Australia: Australia and New Zealand Council for the Care of Animals in Research and Training.

17 Stafford, K, 'Training animal welfare professionals – animal–based scientists and veterinarians', in *Animal Welfare in the Twenty–First Century: Ethical, Educational and Scientific Challenges*, above n 16, pp 28–29.

unacceptable professional behaviour. In addition, with regard to animal welfare, it was generally accepted that productivity indicated a satisfactory state of well-being and all animal scientists and veterinarians strove towards productivity in food and companion animals ...

It is the opinion of the author that anyone who works with animals has a requirement to consider the ethical aspects of animal utilisation and to consider the well-being of animals in their charge. Thus, farmers, laboratory technicians, veterinary nurses and researchers using animals should have some education with regard to animal as their position and responsibility dictates that be considered animal welfare professionals ...

The behaviour of teaching and support staff in the humane treatment of animals is important, as these provide role models for student behaviour. Lectures relating to relevant legislation are given during the traditional jurisprudence course. Emphasis should be upon discussion and not dogma. Teaching with emphasis upon ideas, discussion and development of thought should be encouraged. Training is inappropriate.

Although law can play a leading role in the implementation of new thinking towards animals, there is no doubt that people also need to be educated about the reasoning behind any specific changes in legislation as it affects them. In the UK and the EU, the fact that we might well have legislated recently in favour of wild animals, badgers and farm animals being transported long distances but without an appreciation of *why* we have done so leaves the possibility of further animal suffering because of non-compliance or ignorance of the law. 'Education' means not only a process which engenders the morals of society in the young or encouraging responsible behaviour in those entering employment areas involving the use of animals, but involves a continuing process of reinforcement and reminder.[18]

As regards *continuing* education we are primarily concerned with those who have the day to day responsibility to look after animals be it in farming, transportation, scientific experimentation or, indeed, in the home. Is there an adequate system to inform people about the needs of animals? Do we need to look at the training and qualifications of those involved as a continuing process as part of the process of reinforcement and refinement? Responsibility here must lie with the government and learned societies. Some countries have already recognised this in relation to specific areas of concern. Both the UK and the Netherlands, for example, require those involved in experimentation to complete a form of training of differing complexions.[19] Why should this be restricted to just those areas when animals are also kept in very large numbers in the home?

The law does seem to be able to play a role in educating people towards

---

18   This was very much the view of the RSPCA in its submission to the Animal Procedures Committee's 1996 review of the Animals (Scientific Procedures) Act 1986. See recommendation 27 of their submission in Chapter 4.

19   See Chapter 4.

change. In the US, Bernard Rollin was part of the team which wrote the 1985 changes to the Animal Welfare Act 1966. He has since noted the educative role which they were attempting to introduce in the changes which require scientists to take the pain of suffering of animals into account: 'This approach assured that concern for animal pain would enter into scientific deliberations. We believed that, eventually, such considerations would become second nature to scientists and thus that the law was essentially a vehicle for introducing an educational vector into the insular scientific community'.[20]

WHY AND HOW GOVERNMENTS CAN PLAY A ROLE

Is it right that society should legislate further in the cause of animals? Henry Salt, whilst recognising the invaluable part that could be played by improved education also recognised the importance of legislation to protect animals:[21]

Legislation, where the protection of harmless animals is concerned, is the fit supplement and sequel to education, and the objections urged against it are for the most part unreasonable. It must inevitably fail in its purpose, say some; for how can the mere passing of a penal statute prevent the innumerable unwitnessed acts of cruelty and oppression which make up the great total of animal suffering? But the purpose of legislation is not merely thus preventive. Legislation is the record, the register, of the moral sense of the community; it follows, not precedes, the development of that moral sense, but nevertheless in its turn reacts on it, strengthens it, and secures it against the danger of retrocession. It is well that society should proclaim, formally and decisively, its abhorrence of certain practices; and I do not think it can be doubted, by those who have studied the history of the movement, that the general treatment of domestic animals in this country, bad as it still is, would be infinitely worse at this day but for the progressive legislation that dates from the passing of 'Martin's Act' in 1822.

The further argument, so commonly advanced, that 'force is no remedy', and that it is better to trust to the good feeling of mankind than to impose a legal restriction, is an amiable criticism which might doubtless be applied with great effect to a large majority of our existing penal enactments, but it is not very applicable to the case under discussion. For if force is ever allowable, surely it is so when it is applied for a strictly defensive purpose, such as to safeguard the weak and helpless from violence and aggression. The protection of animals by statute marks but another step onward in that course of humanitarian legislation which, among numerous triumphs, has abolished slavery and passed the Factory Acts – always in the teeth of this same time-honoured but

20 Rollin, B, *The Frankenstein Syndrome: Ethical and Social Issues in the Genetic Engineering of Animals*, 1995, p 106, Cambridge: Cambridge University Press.
21 Salt, H, *Animals' Rights: Considered in Relation to Social Progress*, 1980, pp 124–25, Pennsylvania: Society for Animal Rights. By permission of the International Society for Animal Rights.

irrelevant objection that 'force is no remedy'.

The same theme, the effectiveness of legislation in relation to animal welfare, is the subject of the following extract from Catherine Roberts who is more doubtful as to whether the final answer lies in legislation:[22]

Today many persons outside the scientific profession feel that the best solution to the problem of painful animal experimentation is to restrict its practice by law. Such a view has long persisted. In a lengthy article on vivisection written more than 50 years ago for the *Encyclopedia Britannica*, this statement appears: 'It would be possible for cruelty of an unnecessary kind to result if the practice of vivisection were unrestricted.' The author, himself a staunch supporter of vivisection, nevertheless felt that scientists needed external restriction of its practice. A more direct admission of the human feelings of scientist and the inadequacy of their objective humaneness could hardly be expressed.

Personally, I do not believe that external restriction, however much it has contributed to the prevention of animal cruelty in the past, will ever solve the present problem satisfactorily, nor that such legislation as is pending or contemplated today is worthy of wholehearted support. It is a superficial attack that fails to go to the heart of the matter. *For further legislation would only prevent many scientists from doing what they now earnestly desire to do.* In other words, it can prevent animal suffering, but it can never make anyone more human. That must come from within. And when it comes, scientific humaneness will be superfluous. It is not external restriction that is needed, it is self-restriction.

If legislation is created it is obviously important that it is enforced effectively. In the UK the number of statutes and governmental bodies dealing with the welfare of animals is considerable. The confusion and consistency of the application of welfare concerns across these bodies is doubtful and has been criticised.[23] Some of the various organisations and systems which are part of the creation and enforcement of animal welfare legislation include the following: the Ministry of Agriculture, Fisheries and Food deals with the welfare of animals used in farming; the courts which have responsibility for enforcing, for example, the Cruelty to Animals Act 1911 which imposes penalties for inflicting unnecessary suffering on 'domestic' animals; the task of bringing offenders to court is officially in the hands of the police but in practice this function has been carried out using the private resources of the RSPCA as the police have found it difficult to direct finite resources into the prosecution of crimes against animals; the regulation of persons and establishments dealing with experimentation upon animals is dealt with by the Home Office.

It may have become evident from the preceding chapters in this book that

---

22   Roberts, C, *The Scientific Conscience: Reflections on the Modern Biologist and Humanism*, 1974, pp 45–46, Fontwell, Sussex: Centaur Press.

23   Jenkins, S, *Animal Rights and Human Wrongs*, 1992, pp 93–94, Hertfordshire: Lennard Publishing.

considerable criticism, rightly or wrongly, is aimed at just about every aspect of the legislative control of the welfare of animals. It is alleged, for example, animals are sometimes treated inconsistently by the law with domestic animals receiving better protection than wild animals as seen in Chapter 2. There are suggestions that laws such as the Animals (Scientific Procedures) Act 1986 are not properly enforced as seen in Chapter 4. As a final example of this criticism it is often suggested that legislation is slow to emerge and that there is a duplication of investigative functions when it comes to ensuring compliance.

In light of these criticisms and the weight of evidence showing the inconsistencies of moral justification and practical application of the law there are strong arguments that a review, in its entirety, of the law relating to animals is necessary. One writer at least has set out the blue-print for an entirely new approach to how the regulation and enforcement of the law relating to animals would be reviewed and monitored:[24]

Wanted: A Minister for Animals

Imagine this. The ruling government appoints a Minister for Animals. After he has been in office for some weeks, Opposition MPs begin to ask questions in the House:

'Does the Minister realise that 90,000 dogs have to be put down every year, and that the cost to the nation of dealing with stray dogs is now running at £77 million per year? How does he propose to deal with these urgent matters?' And:

'Does the Minister realise that dog-fighting and badger-baiting are more widespread now than they have been for the last 50 years? How does he propose to clamp down on these repellent so-called sports?'

I can think of at least a dozen equally embarrassing questions for the new Minister, arising from problems which already exist, here and now, in our homes and on our roads, on our farms and in open countryside throughout the land. It is a scandal that we have no appropriate minister to deal with these pressing questions. If we did, one thing is certain. He would not be able to sweep them aside, as our present, fragmented bunch of administrators do. The press, and public opinion, would not allow that to happen.

A New deal for Animals

Those of us who care for animals have a duty to prevent cruelty to *all* animals. We can, and should campaign to change unjust laws. We must be careful, though, to do this in a civilised, moderate way.

My proposal is that we should work towards setting up a single government department – A Ministry for Animals. It would be completely separate from the Ministry of Agriculture, Fisheries and Food, and would take over that ministry's power in relation to farm animals. The new Ministry would be responsible for all branches of animal welfare. It would have wide powers of

---

24   *Ibid*, pp 95–97. By permission of Lennard Associates.

inspection, from pet shops to farms, from performing animals to zoos. It would monitor the import and export of animals, the registration of all boarding, breeding and riding establishments. It would set up and administer a national dog registration scheme.

Once all these duties were under the control of a single department, millions of pounds would be saved compared with the sums we spend on the present fragmented system. In due course all the laws in relation to animals would be rationalised, brought up to date and made more understandable. The benefits would be tremendous. At last we would have a cohesive means to safeguard the rights and welfare of all animals.

We should also be better equipped to deal with that body of dangerous extremists who have given such a bad name to the cause of animals rights, such as the Animal Liberation Front and similar groups. In recent years they have caused enormous damage and a loss of public sympathy, not only for themselves but for the important work of mainstream, moderate groups who seek reforms through peaceful means.

Below are just some of the duties which Ministry Inspectors would be required to carry out:

– Experiments on Animals. Regular checks on experimental laboratories, questioning not only the way they are run but also whether their work is necessary.

– Transit of Animals. Regular road checks on vehicles transporting animals, chiefly to slaughterhouses and dealers. Compulsory inspection of all animals in transit at railway stations and haulage depots.

– Boarding and Breeding Establishments. Regular monitoring of zoos, pet shops, and all breeding establishments, to enforce the current standards and then raise them to higher levels.

– Cattle markets and Horse Sales. Regular attendance to monitor how farmers and breeders bring their animals to market.

– Dog Registration Scheme. The setting up and running of a national scheme which will deal with any stray dogs and negligent owners.

– Anti-Rabies Patrol. This would be a special squad to guard against the illegal importation of animals which would operate at ports and airports. Monitoring of the Channel Tunnel would be a permanent top priority.

– Education Programme. The presentation of a multi-media programme, combined with regular visits to schools, hospitals, and so on, to teach the proper care of all animals, especially domestic pets.

There is nothing particularly new or radical about any of those schemes. Many of them have been around for years. Now is the time – for the first time – to implement them properly, backed by a single, professional, government-funded organisation. I am convinced that this is the only way forward.

Although not everyone within the animal rights lobby would agree with all the suggestions Jenkins makes or the underlying acceptance of continuing practices which some find entirely abhorrent, the basic concept of a specific ministry might have certain advantages to commend it. A single responsible

Minister would increase the accountability for practices which, at present, are controlled by departments with many competing roles. It would also allow improvements in practice to spread quickly through all aspects of animal welfare covered by the new department – from farming to zoos to domestic animals. A single welfare discovery in relation to farming, for example, might be transferred more quickly to use in scientific experimentation using animals. At present this would be reliant on close co-operation between the Ministry of Agriculture, Fisheries and Food (MAFF) and the Home Office.

A new department might also initiate advances and be proactive in creating change. For example, at the 'cutting edge' of the investigation into the differences between animals and humans are the studies into the intelligence of the primates and dolphins. Not only would a specific department be quick to implement new findings by changing the law but it might also play a valuable role in seeking out such information either by sponsoring studies where necessary or acting as a focal point for the collection of emerging findings. The creation of such a department might also reduce financial wastage in some areas by allowing, for example, inspectors to take on a variety of the roles indicated by Jenkins above thereby reducing duplication.

Perhaps more importantly, the creation of a department with a mission aimed very much at improving the lot of animals would be less willing to compromise its position due to external pressure upon it. There is always the suspicion with ministries such as MAFF that the interests of the groups they respond to, from farmers to farm animals, cannot be reconciled without the sacrifice of principles. A Ministry for Animals might have a clearer identity and function.

In the Hume Memorial Lecture of 1991 Roy Moss, who had wide experience of the workings of national and international agencies dealing with the welfare of farm animals, suggested that there is the need for a body with similar functions to those suggested by Jenkins at an *international* level:[25]

> I suggest there is now a need for one further body within Europe or indeed internationally, since we ought to be thinking in a worldwide dimension, to take on the task of collecting facts and providing advice, perhaps with terms of reference as follows:
>
> – To coordinate and develop the activities relating to the welfare of animals, specifically the activities of scientists and technologists.
>
> – To liaise with and offer advice to the regulatory and legislative authorities.
>
> – To act as a focal point for these scientists, technologists and authorities for the collection, dissemination and exchange of information and views relating to animal welfare and the humane treatment and use of animals.
>
> Then on an international basis as well as within Europe, work relating to the

---

25 Moss, R, *Europe Animal Welfare Concern and Chaos?*, 1991, pp 31–32, Potters Bar: Universities Federation for Animal Welfare.

well-being of animals kept for whatever purposes would have the opportunity to be coordinated and scarce resources used to the best advantage. It would also enable those who wish to resolve problems, to ask questions of an authoritative body, which would have available comprehensive information on which definitive answers can be given.

As an alternative or addition to the kind of structural arrangements suggested by Jenkins and Moss lies the possibility of changing attitudes within substantive law by giving animals more rights. As shown in Chapter 3, there are many who argue that animals should have rights to varying degrees either to allow them to live out a natural life and/or to recognise their sentience. On a practical level, Joyce Tischler proposes a new legal blueprint for the treatment of cats and dogs which enjoy a special status as companion animals in the minds of many people and, indeed, the law of many countries. She suggests that the best way to protect the rights of cats and dogs would be to employ a system of *guardianship* whereby the guardian would have the responsibilities of providing care and custody and of taking or defending any legal actions with any recovery going to the ward:[26]

> The Guardianship model is analogous to the ideas of Justice Douglas as expressed in *Sierra Club v Morton*.[27] In that case the Sierra Club, an organisation devoted to protecting the environment, sought to challenge federal approval of a massive development project in Mineral King Valley, a scenic area in California. The majority held that the organisation itself, without alleging injury to its members, lacked standing to sue. In a creative dissent, Justice Douglas argued that environmental objects should themselves be accorded legal rights.[28] Recognised environmental organisations could then sue on behalf of the natural object.

> To support his position, Justice Douglas analogised to other areas of the law in which inanimate objects are recognised as parties in litigation.[29] This legal fiction has been widely applied to ships and to corporations in order to protect their interests.[30] It should apply as well to valleys, rivers, and mountains and endangered technology. In the same way, animal rights groups should be allowed to represent the interests of dogs and cats when the need arises, so that these beings will have the chance to be heard.

> The guardianship system offers a viable method of extending legal rights to dogs and cats. It gives more effective protection than present anti-cruelty statutes. Although no law can succeed completely in preventing the abuse which makes it illegal, the guardianship model would accomplish at least two things. First, it would supply an additional deterrent to the abuse of cats and dogs, for through their guardians, dogs and cats would be able to sue for their

---

26 Tischler, J, 'Rights for Nonhuman Animals: A Guardianship Model For Dogs and Cats' (1977) 14 *San Diego Law Review* 484–506.

[27] 405 US 727, 741 (1972) (dissenting judgment).

[28] *Ibid*, at 752.

[29] *Ibid*, at 742.

[30] *Ibid*, at 742–43.

own injuries. Thus a potential wrongdoer would be faced not only with stiffer criminal penalties but also with civil liability, including medical expenses and damages for pain and suffering. Second, the guardianship model would have the psychological effect of making humans understand that dogs and cats are members of society who deserve and will receive real protection under the law.

Based on Tischler's reasoning behind the introduction of this model, such as animals' intelligence and their ability to communicate showing attributes deserving of protection, there is no reason why Tischler's reasoning should not be extended to other animals. There is, arguably, no morally consistent reason for not extending the ambit of this blueprint to similarly intelligent *wild* animals if the existence of significant intelligence is our reason for doing so.

FURTHER READING

Osmond, G, *Animal welfare in the twenty-first century: ethical, educational and scientific challenges*, 1994, South Australia: Australian and New Zealand Council for the Care of Animals in research and Teaching (ANZCCART). One of the few publications around which contains more than a mere mention of the importance of education in the realm of animal welfare. Copies can be obtained in the UK from the Universities Federation for Animal Welfare, Hertfordshire.

Garner, R, *Animals, Politics and Morality*, 1993, Chapters 7 and 8, Manchester: Manchester University Press. An excellent examination of the constitutional and direct action routes to secure change.

Paterson, P and Palmer M, *The Status of Animals: Ethics, Education and Welfare*, 1991 edn, Part Two, Oxon: CAB International. An analysis of the use of education in the development of animal rights.

STOP PRESS

SELECTED UPDATES – DECEMBER 1998

Chapter 1 – Philosophy, Science and Animals

Further evidence emerged regarding the sentient abilities of animals. Two American psychologists said that they had taught two rhesus monkeys to count to nine. This is considered to be a challenge to the view started by Descartes that animals cannot comprehend abstract concepts because they cannot use language. See *The Times*, 23 October 1998.

Chapter 2 – Historical and Contemporary Legal Attitudes to Animals

A new book has been produced tracing the development of the animal rights/welfare movement in the UK from 1800 onwards – Kean and Hilda, *Animal Rights*, 1998, London: Reaktion Books.

Chapter 3 – How Should the Law Treat Animals

Concerns continued to be voiced over the ethics of using animals in biotechnology and xenotransplantation. See Fox, M and McHale, J, 'Regulating Xenotransplantation', 147 NLJ 139, pp 139–40; *The Guardian*, 18 April 1998. Despite this, progress in this area continues at a pace. See *The Sunday Times*, 12 April 1998.

Chapter 4 – The Legal Control of Experimentation

Institutions using animal experimentation will have to have a local ethics review process in place by 1 April 1999. The Barry Horne, an animal rights activist, went on hunger strike during October–December 1998 on the ground that the Labour Government was refusing to implement its manifesto promise to set up a Royal Commission on the use of animals in scientific experimentation. He gave up his protest on Sunday 13 December 1998. For discussion surrounding his action, see *The Observer*, 6 December 1998; *The Guardian*, 10 December 1998 and 14 December 1998.

A voluntary ban has come into force on the testing on animals of finished cosmetic products or their ingredients, tobacco or alcoholic products. See *The Times*, 7 November 1997; *The Guardian*, 17 November 1998. Animal rights campaigners appear to have won the right to check academic's proposals for experiments involving animals. See *The Times Higher*, 30 October 1998. The Animal Procedures Committee has a new chairman, Michael Banner. The Report of the Animal Procedures Committee 1997 (November 1998, London: HMSO) says that the APC will be taking a 'long, hard look' at the issues of household product testing and testing involving primates.

Chapter 5 – Animals in Agriculture

The Welfare of Animals (Transport) Order 1997, SI 1997/1480 implemented Council Directive 95/29 on the welfare of animals during transport abroad. In *R v Minister of Agriculture, Fisheries and Food, ex p* Protesters Animal Information Network Ltd, CO 1150/96, PAIN were refused leave to seek judicial review of whether MAFF was properly exercising its authority in relation to the export of live animals. Council Regulation (EC) No 411/98 of 16 February 1998 requires improved standards for road vehicles carrying livestock for more than eight hours: [1998] OJ L52/8. In *R v Minister of Agriculture, Fisheries and Food, ex p* Compassion in World Farming (C1 /96) [1998] All ER (EC) 302, CIWF sought judicial review of the Minister's refusal to prohibit the export of veal calves to countries still using the veal crate system. The application was refused. Pressure continues to be applied by groups such as the Soil Association to encourage more organic farming which uses little or no growth enhancing drugs or antibiotics on animals. See *The Guardian*, 5 December 1998.

Chapter 6 – Domestic Animals

The Dangerous Dogs (Amendment) Act 1997 confers on the court a discretion in the manner of dealing with dogs and owners where an offence is committed under the 1991 Act. See, also, the Dangerous Dogs (Fees) order 1997 SI 1997/1152. There have been a number of cases involving dogs including: *R v Liverpool Magistrates Court, ex p Slade* (1997) *Independent*, 13 June; *Rafiq v DPP* (1997) 161 JP 412; *R v Haringey Magistrates' Court, ex p Cragg* (1997) 161 JP 61; *Briscoe v Shattock* (1998)*The Times*, 12 October; *Isted v CPS* (1997) *The Times*, 11 December. A case has been brought under the Occupiers Liability Act 1957 and s 2 of the Animals Act 1971, *Chauhan v Paul Trans ref: CCRTF* 97/0003/C 19 February 1998. See, also, *Hopson v DPP* CO/2293/96 11 March 1997 on the interpretation of s 1 of the Protection of Animals Act 1911. The Horse Passports (Amendment) Order 1998 SI 1998/2367 has also been passed. See Clayson, C, 'Dangerous Dogs (Amendment) Act 1997', 141 SJ 593.

Chapter 7 – Animals, Sport and Entertainment

In June 1998, a Zoos Directive was agreed by the Council of Ministers requiring all Member States to set up national systems for the licensing and inspection of zoos. In the UK, the Zoos Forum will be set up and the Secretary of State's standards of modern zoo practice and the government's circular containing advice to zoo operators and local authorities will be updated. The Wild Mammals (Hunting with Dogs) Bill introduced in 1997 was defeated on 29 November 1997; however, the government has suggested that local councils will be able to hold referendums in their areas on the issue.

Chapter 8 – Wildlife Protection

Review of the Hedgerow Regulations 1997 (SI 1997/1160) on revising the regulation on hedgerow protection. A Consultation Paper has been published on Better Protection and Management of SSSIs in September 1998: see www.jncc.gov.uk/ukbg. The Birds (Registration Charges) Act 1997 makes provision for the imposition of charges for registration under the Wildlife and Countryside Act 1981. The Partnership for Action Against Wildlife Crime (PAW) has published *Wildlife Crime: A Guide to Wildlife Law Enforcement in the UK*, 1998, London: HMSO. The Wildlife and Countryside Act has been amended, in particular, it adds 11 species to Sched 5. Schedule 9 was also amended by SI 1997/226. The Report 'The Management of Problems involving Badgers' was published by MAFF in 1998. A case under ss 3 and 8 of the Protection of Badgers Act 1992 has been heard: *Lovett v Bussey* (1998) *The Times*, 24 April. The Conservation of Seals (England) Order 1996 SI 1996/2905 has been passed. See Harrop, S, 'The dynamics of animal welfare law' (1997) 9(2) JEL 287, pp 287–302.

Chapter 9 – International Control of Endangered Species

Regulation (EC 894/97OJL 109, 8 April 1998, p 7) has been passed banning the use of drift nets from 1 January 2002. Regulation EC 767/98 has been adopted amending Regulation 939/97 on the protection of species of wild fauna and flora and trade. The 1997 CITES Conference transferred the elephant populations of Botswana, Namibia and Zimbabwe to Appendix II of the CITES Convention to enable limited trade in elephant products to resume. In relation to whaling, the Irish Government introduced a proposal to the IWC in 1997 to allow commercial whaling of Minke whales with various conditions attached. In the UK, a government forum on whaling has been established with other conservation and protection agencies.

INDEX